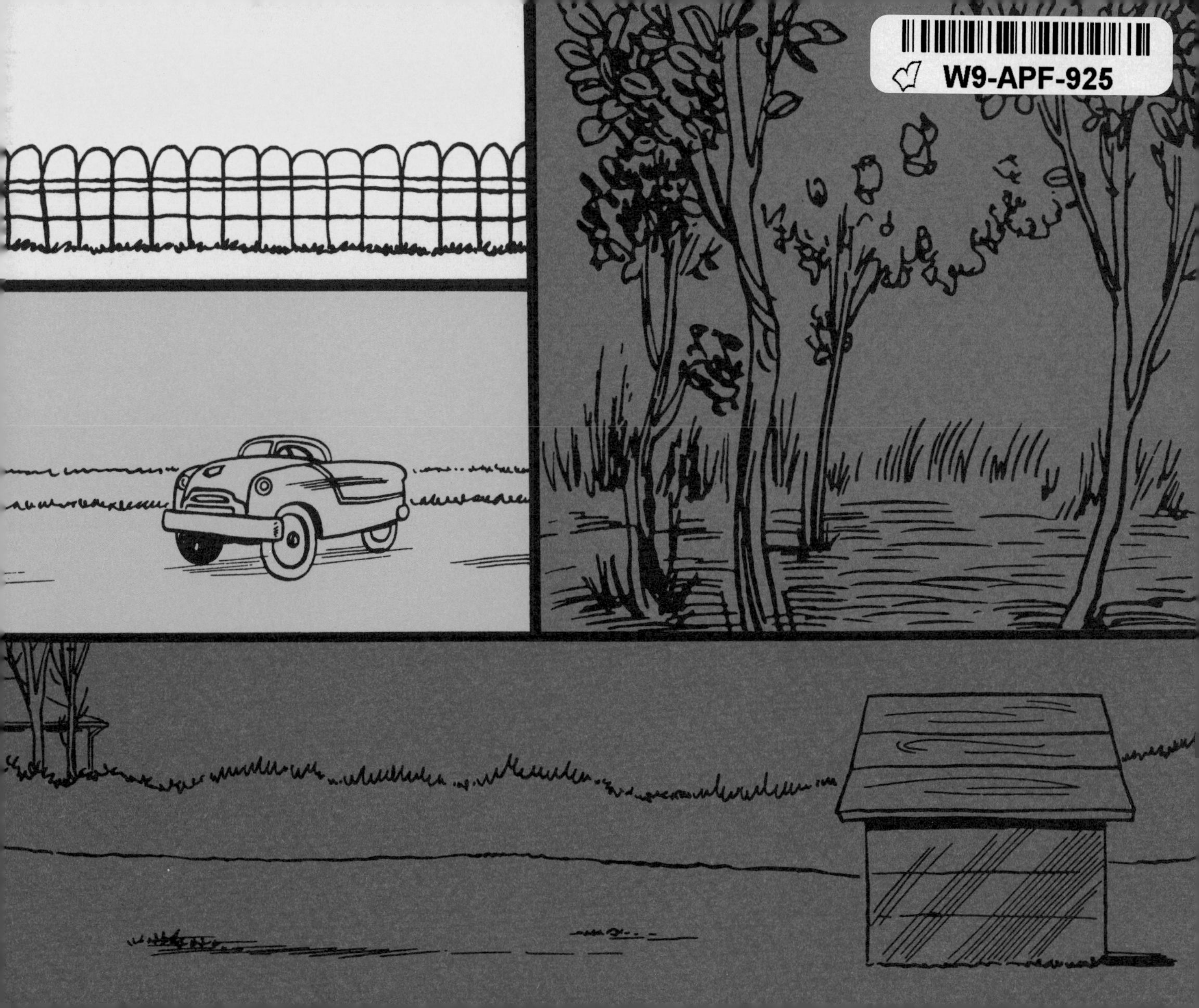

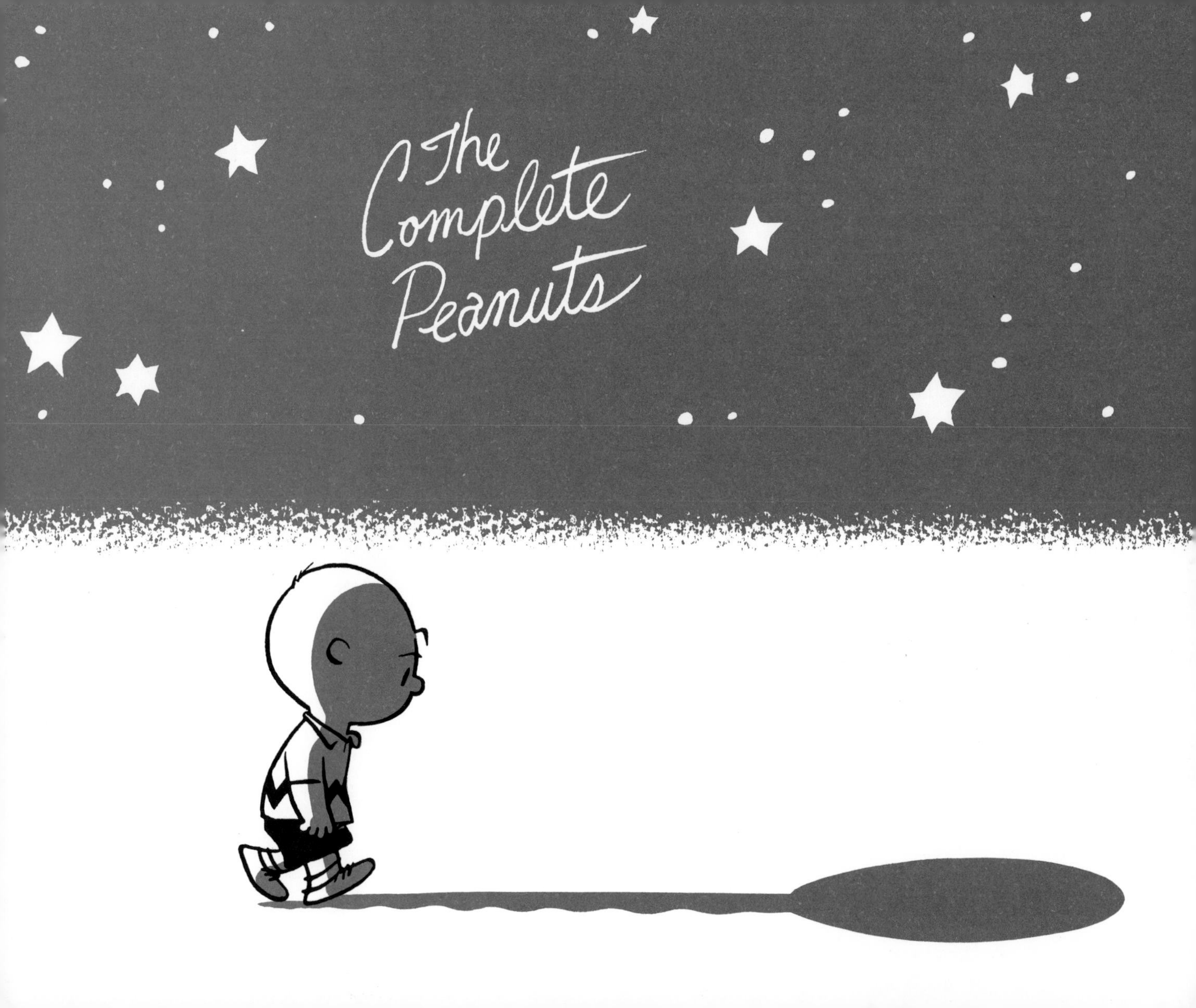
The Complete Peanuts

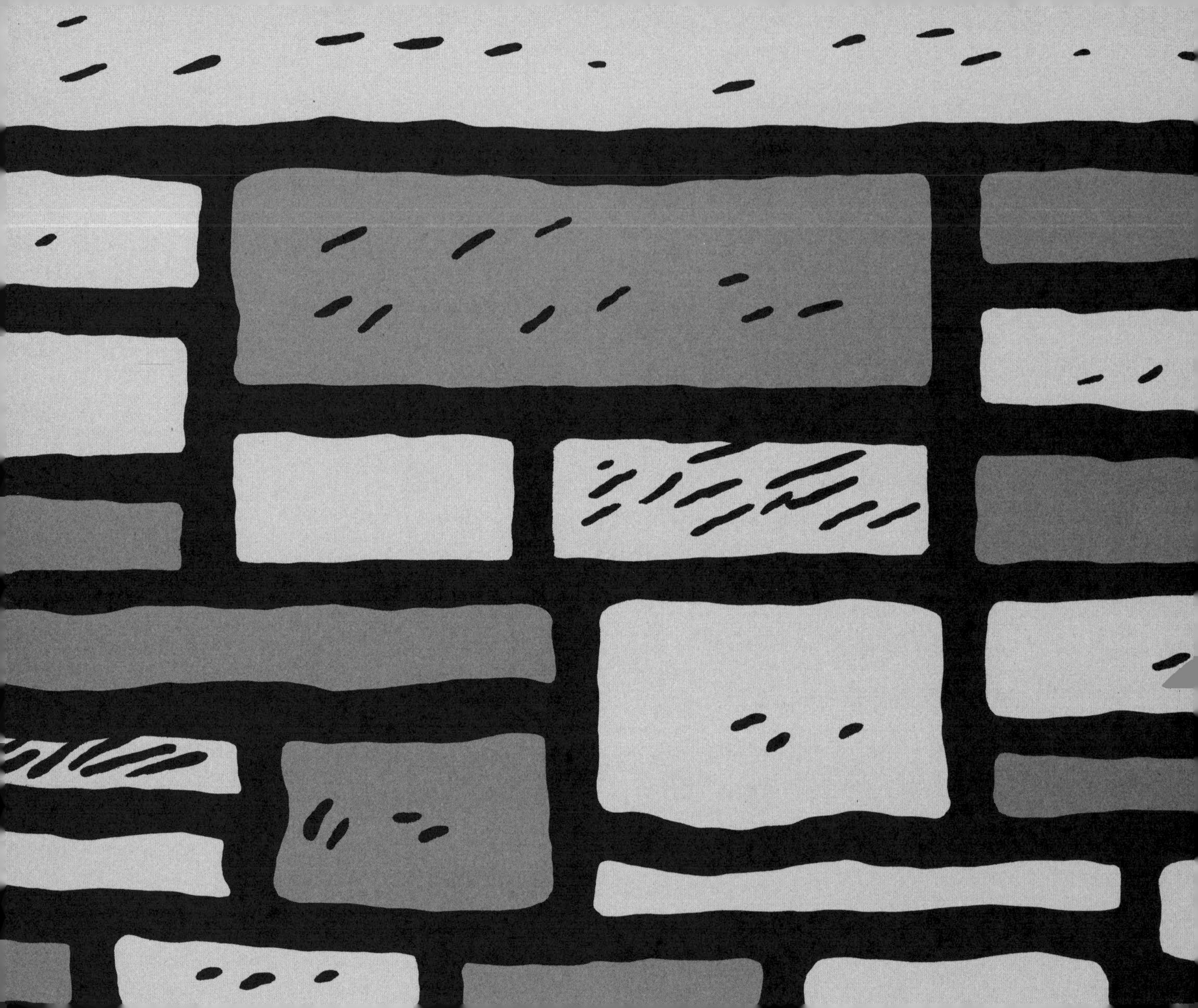

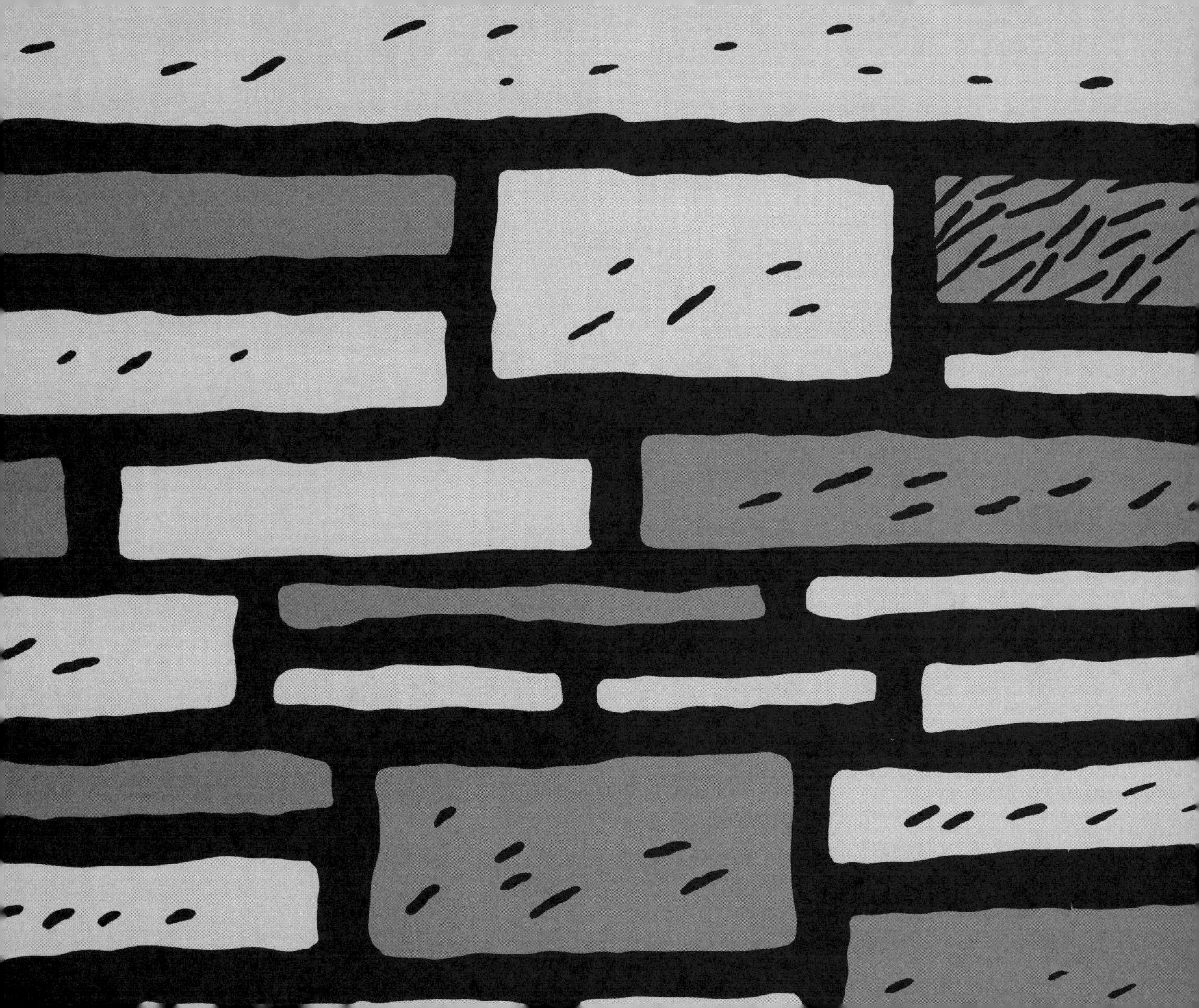

THE COMPLETE PEANUTS
by Charles M. Schulz
published by
Fantagraphics Books

Editor: Gary Groth
Designer: Seth
Production Manager: Kim Thompson
Production, assembly, and restoration: Paul Baresh
Archival and production assistance: Ilse Driggs,
Nat Gertler, Marcie Lee, and Linda McCurdy
Associate Publisher: Eric Reynolds
Publishers: Gary Groth & Kim Thompson

Special thanks to Jeannie Schulz, without whom
this project would not have come to fruition.
Thanks to Charles M. Schulz Creative Associates,
especially Paige Braddock and Kim Towner.
Thanks for special support from United Media.

Fantagraphics Books, 7563 Lake City Way, Seattle, WA 98115, USA. For a free full-color catalogue of
comics, call 1-800-657-1100. Our books may be viewed on our web site at www.fantagraphics.com.

Distributed to the book trade by:
USA specialty stores: Diamond Comics Distributors
800-452-6642 (ex. 215)
USA bookstores: W.W. Norton and Company, Inc.
212-233-4830
CANADA: Canadian Manda Group
800-452-6642 (ex. 862)

ISBN 978-1-56097-614-1
Fourth printing: February, 2012   Printed in China

CHARLES M. SCHULZ

THE COMPLETE PEANUTS

1953 TO 1954

"WE JUST TOOK A VOTE..
YOU'VE BEEN REJECTED!"

▪ FANTAGRAPHICS BOOKS ▪

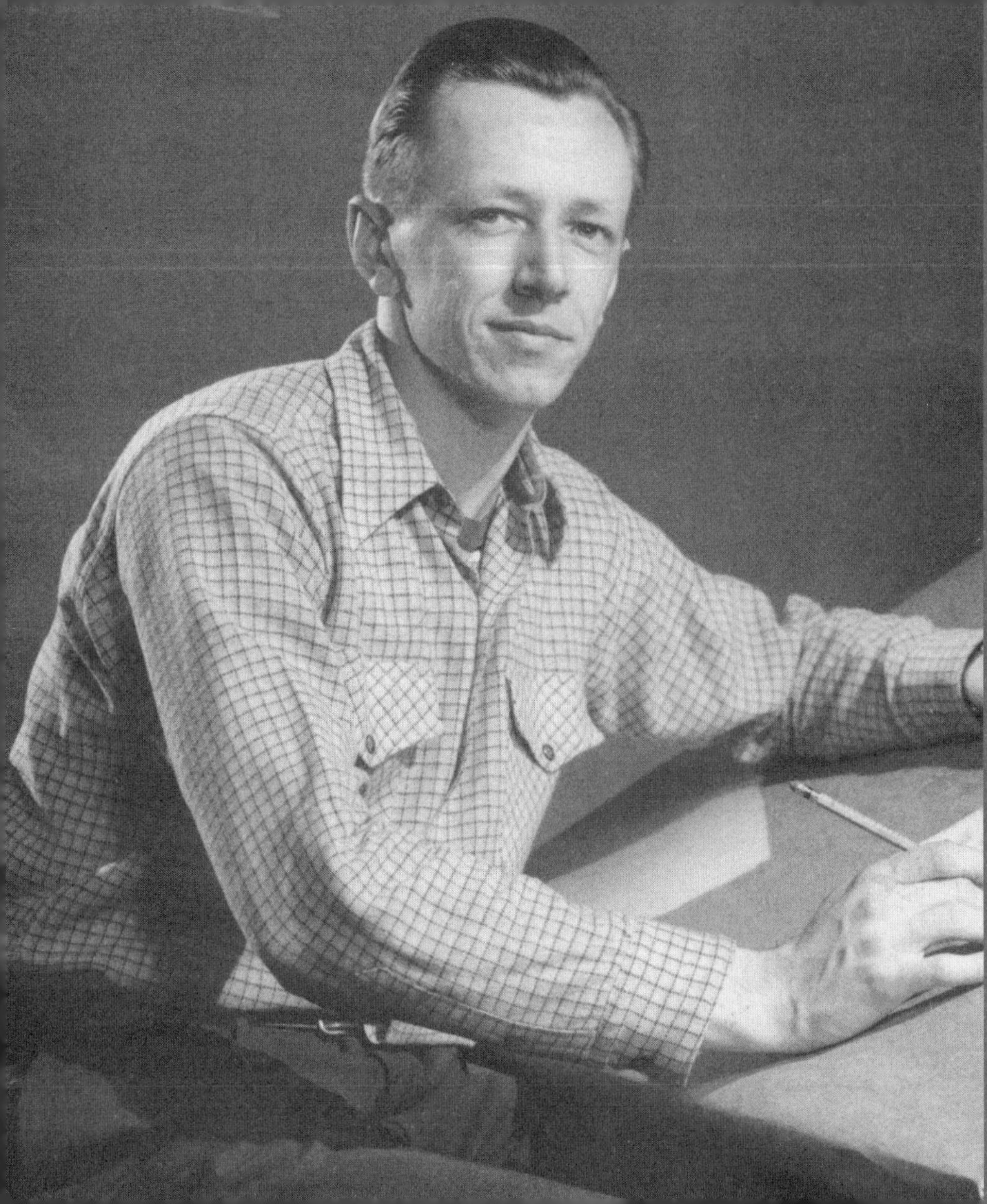

Charles Schulz
circa 1950.

FOREWORD by WALTER CRONKITE

Peanuts has caused me almost as much anguish as has been suffered, through vast disappointment or the dastardly doings of fate, by so many of Charles Schulz's wondrous characters.

The first of my tales of woe concerns a planned visit with Mr. Schulz in his Santa Rosa home, as arranged by a good friend of his, the noted California newspaper editor and columnist, Neil Morgan. A day in July was set.

My anticipation began to grow, like that of a teenager about to meet a rock star. At almost the last moment, a news assignment took me to another corner of the globe. An understanding Schulz agreed to postpone the meeting to another date when I would be back in the States.

And then, tragedy struck — he suffered the cancer attack from which he would not recover. That huge part of the world's population that adored him grieved and I, deprived of the opportunity to at least briefly share his company, was a particularly stricken mourner.

As did others who were luckier and got to know Schulz personally, perhaps I would have assumed the privilege of calling him by his almost onomatopoeic nickname, Sparky.

Back there in 1922, just a few days after he was born to the wife of a barber in St. Paul, Minnesota, an uncle was so enchanted by his infant nephew he started calling him Sparky — after a horse, Spark Plug, featured in a then-popular comic strip called *Barney Google*. The nickname stuck, and Charles Schulz was called Sparky the rest of his life.

Now here you have a confluence of coincidences that would never be accepted even by the producers of a Hollywood pot-boiler: A baby nicknamed after a cartoon character growing up to be one of the greatest and most popular cartoonists of all time!

And second of our coincidences, that name "Sparky" would have been just right for a Peanuts character — a self-promotion Sparky Schulz managed to resist for his entire career.

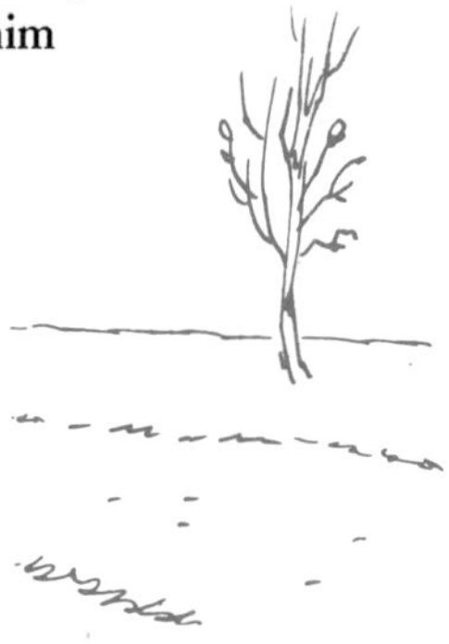

I recount this now because I find it difficult to think (or write) of the great man by any name other than that perfect pseudonym of "Sparky." I would like to think that my talk with him would have been sprinkled with Sparkys and Walters, and would have been as lengthy and fascinating as the one he granted Rick Marschall and Gary Groth for the interview that appeared in the first volume of this series. It was enthralling stuff, and among its interesting revelations was the fact that Schulz in conversation was verbose and rambling, leaving sentences dangling and unfinished. Now that is not unusual when an individual is under interrogation (and that includes this newsman when on the other side of the microphone). However, it deserves notice because of its sharp contrast to the tight discipline he exhibited in his work.

His few words of dialogue — a sentence or two a panel at most — were complemented by an economy of line in his illustrations. His drawings were but scribbles, a few lines scarcely more elaborated than children's stick figures, but his genius was such that with those short few lines he created a panorama of life's experiences as are suffered, or enjoyed, or tolerated by the inhabitants of a cartoon village.

A member of that community, one who experiences all the emotional pangs of his human friends, is the dog Snoopy. I'm a dog lover, as was Schulz, and he is my favorite Peanut. It was in fact Snoopy who, indirectly, caused me the anguish which I mentioned at the top of this essay. (Schulz called his first childhood dog Spike — an inspired play on his own nickname. A sculpture of Spike is on display at the Peanuts Museum in Santa Rosa.)

On a Father's Day many years ago, one of my children bestowed upon me one of those Peanut souvenirs which we are told made millions of dollars for Schulz. It was a little miniature doghouse on which perched Snoopy in his aviator's goggles and helmet as he imagined himself a World War I fighter ace.

The tiny music box it held failed almost immediately, but Snoopy went on to grace my dressing table for several decades. I would greet him every morning and he would put a smile on my face and a little song in my heart as I faced the day, and each night before retiring I would bid him goodnight and wish him well as he

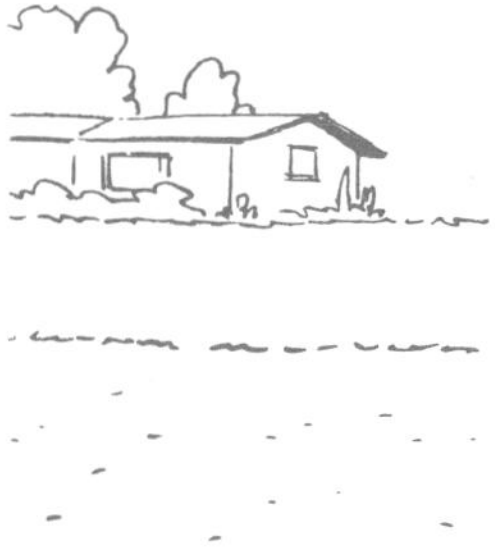

searched the skies for his adversary, The Red Baron.

Then, several decades after our meeting, Snoopy disappeared. It wasn't his fault. He hadn't run away. He was lost as we moved to another house. I was as devastated as anyone losing a pet animal. Oh, of course I might have found another souvenir Snoopy in a Broadway shop, but that would have been disloyal to my Snoopy. And it was a good thing I didn't try to acquire a replacement: He turned up in some misplaced furniture almost a year after his disappearance, and it would have been terrible if he had thought I ever tried to replace him. He is sitting right now on my desk and I think he's throwing a salute to all his loyal fans.

I suppose there are out there some people who will think I'm a foolish old romantic, possibly even a little nuts, to have such an association with, even to the point of talking to, an inanimate object. You *Peanuts* fans know better. You know that the greatest of Charles Schulz's magic tricks was bringing life to all those wonderful folks with which he people our world and brightened our days.

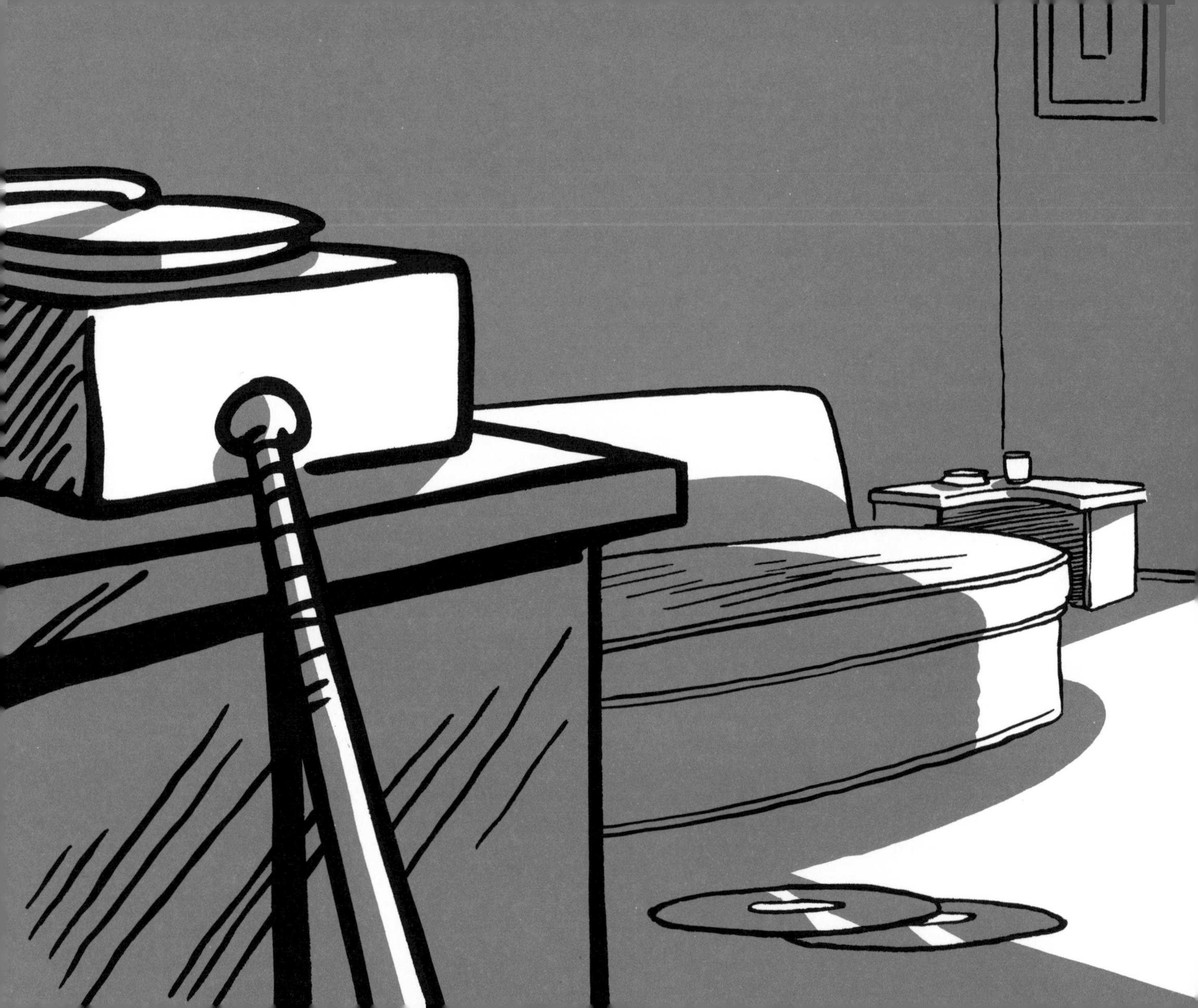

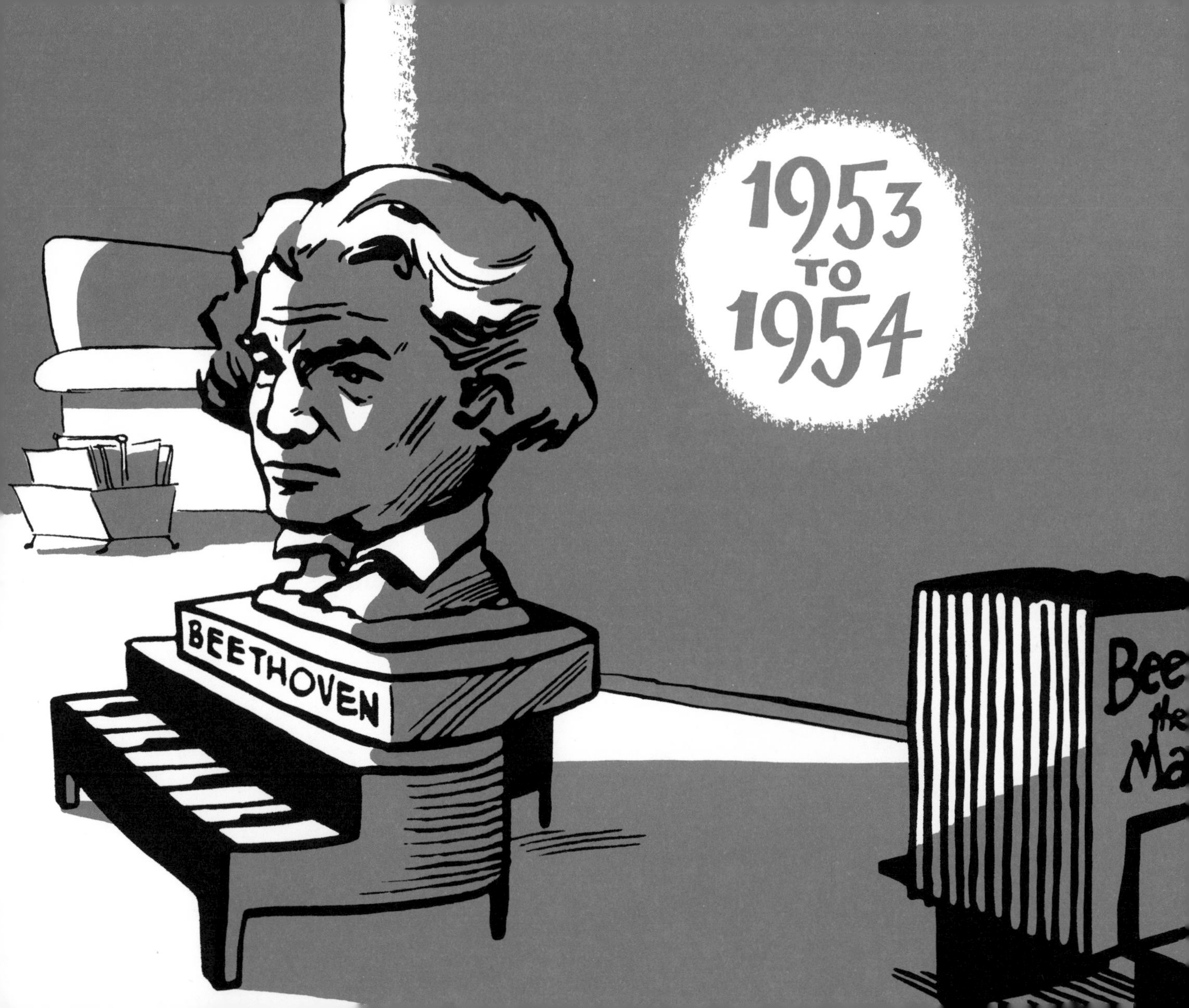
1953 TO 1954
BEETHOVEN

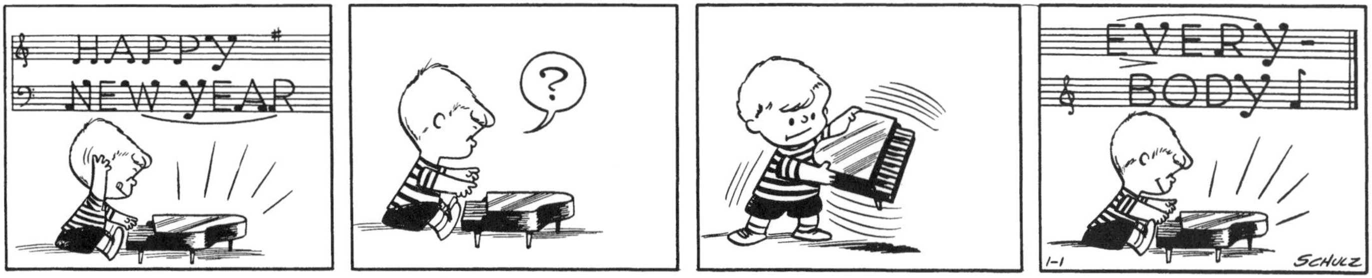
HAPPY
NEW YEAR
?
EVERY-
BODY!
1-1
SCHULZ

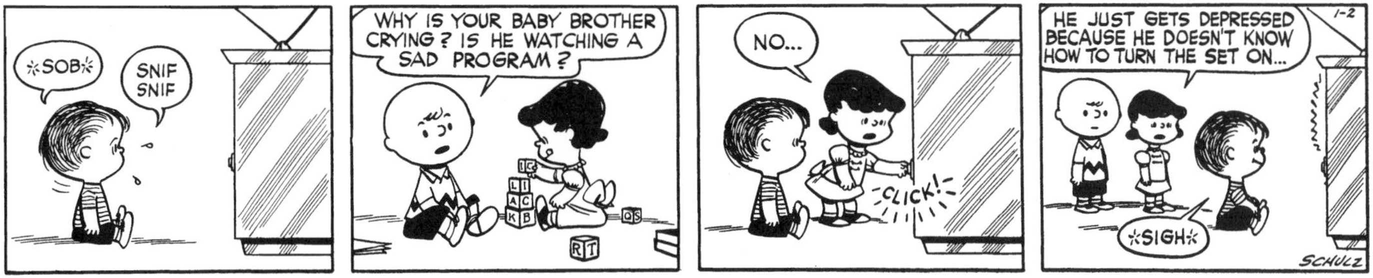
SOB
SNIF SNIF
WHY IS YOUR BABY BROTHER CRYING? IS HE WATCHING A SAD PROGRAM?
NO...
CLICK!
HE JUST GETS DEPRESSED BECAUSE HE DOESN'T KNOW HOW TO TURN THE SET ON...
SIGH
1-2
SCHULZ

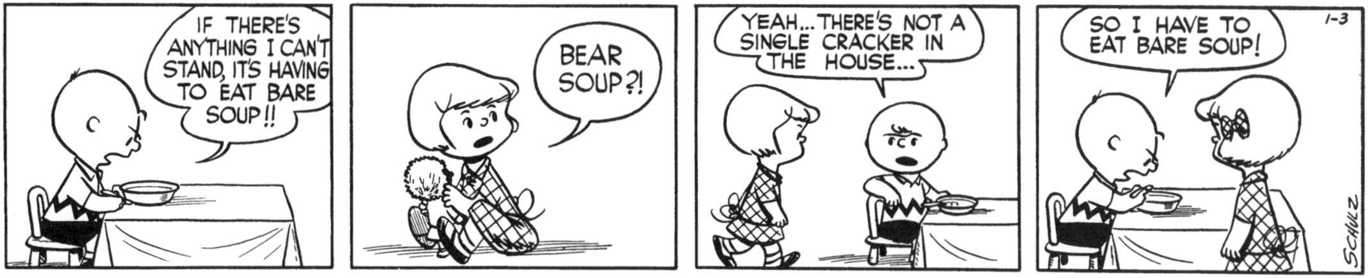
IF THERE'S ANYTHING I CAN'T STAND, IT'S HAVING TO EAT BARE SOUP!!
BEAR SOUP?!
YEAH... THERE'S NOT A SINGLE CRACKER IN THE HOUSE...
SO I HAVE TO EAT BARE SOUP!
1-3
SCHULZ

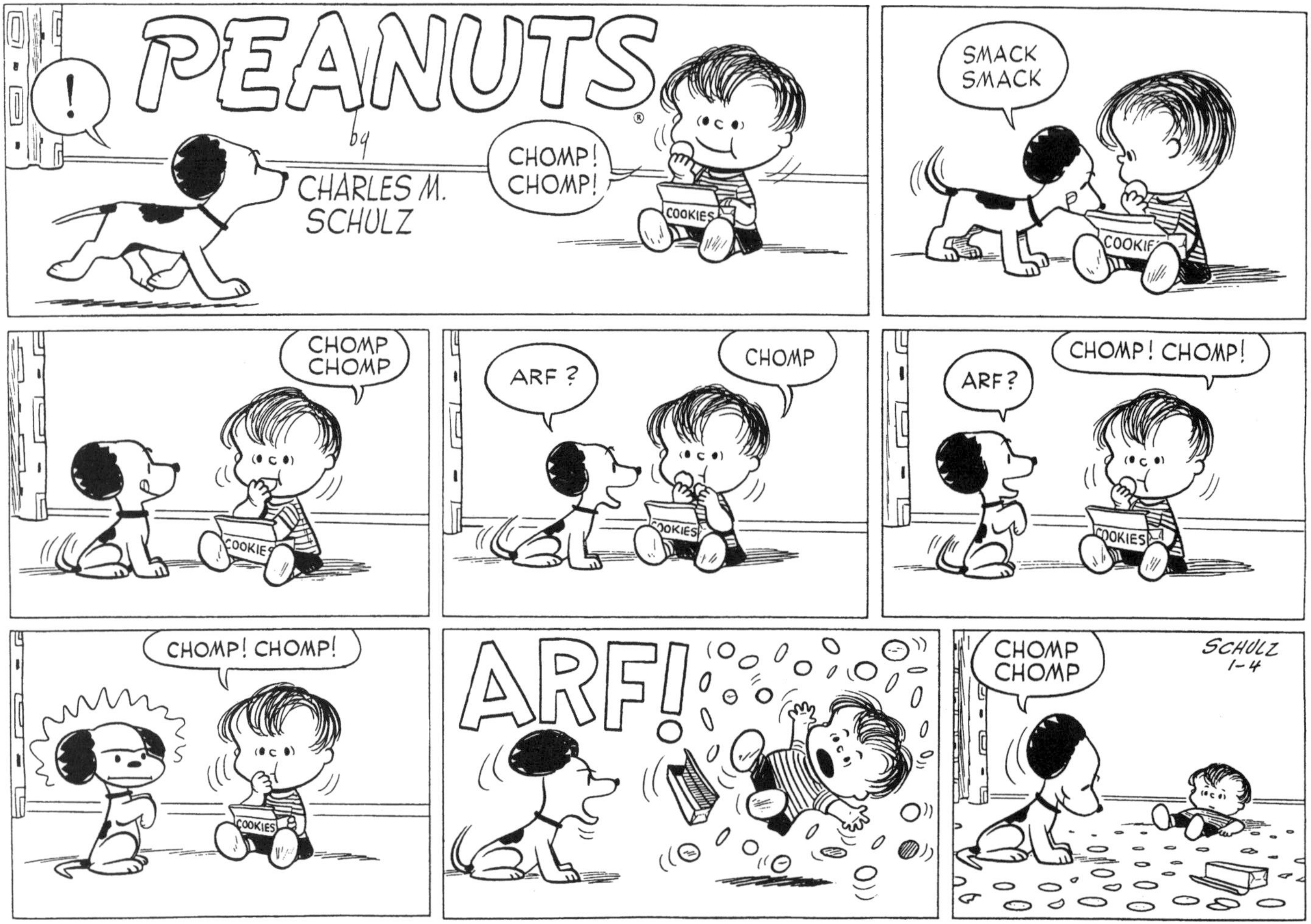
PEANUTS
by
CHARLES M. SCHULZ
!
CHOMP! CHOMP!
COOKIES
SMACK SMACK
COOKIES
CHOMP CHOMP
COOKIES
ARF ?
CHOMP
COOKIES
ARF?
CHOMP! CHOMP!
COOKIES
CHOMP! CHOMP!
COOKIES
ARF!
CHOMP CHOMP
SCHULZ 1-4

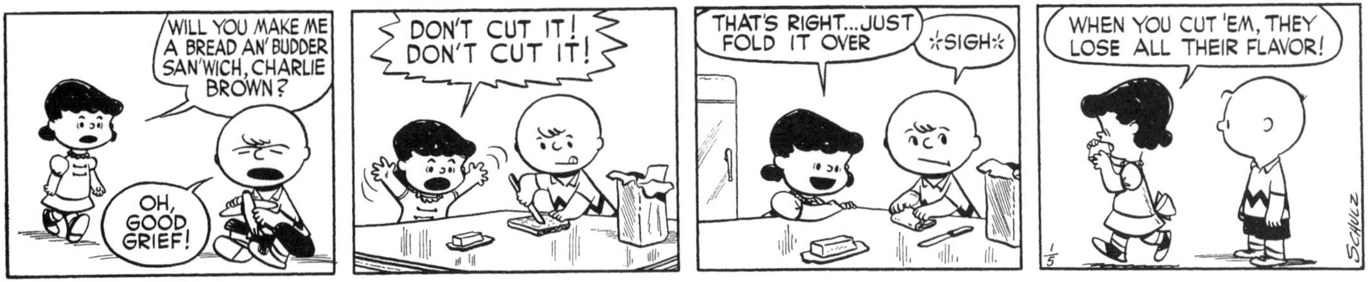
WILL YOU MAKE ME A BREAD AN' BUDDER SAN'WICH, CHARLIE BROWN?
OH, GOOD GRIEF!
DON'T CUT IT! DON'T CUT IT!
THAT'S RIGHT...JUST FOLD IT OVER
SIGH
WHEN YOU CUT 'EM, THEY LOSE ALL THEIR FLAVOR!
1/5
SCHULZ

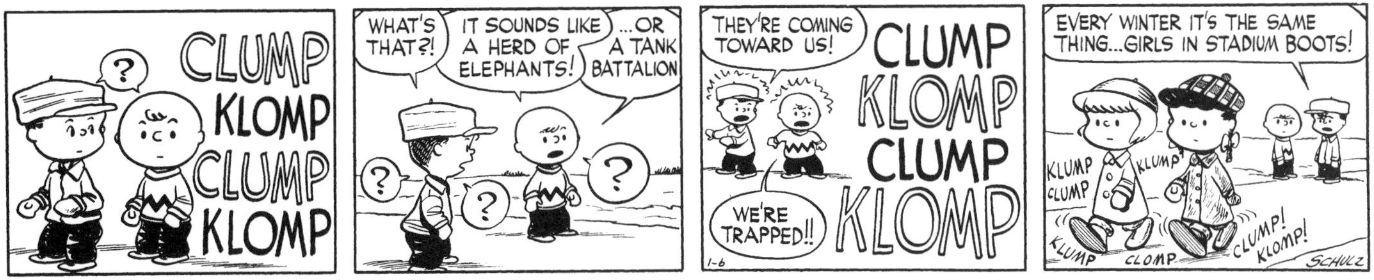
?
CLUMP
KLOMP
CLUMP
KLOMP
WHAT'S THAT?!
IT SOUNDS LIKE A HERD OF ELEPHANTS!
...OR A TANK BATTALION
?
?
?
THEY'RE COMING TOWARD US!
CLUMP
KLOMP
CLUMP
KLOMP
WE'RE TRAPPED!!
1-6
EVERY WINTER IT'S THE SAME THING...GIRLS IN STADIUM BOOTS!
KLUMP
CLUMP
KLUMP
KLUMP
CLOMP
CLUMP!
KLOMP!
SCHULZ

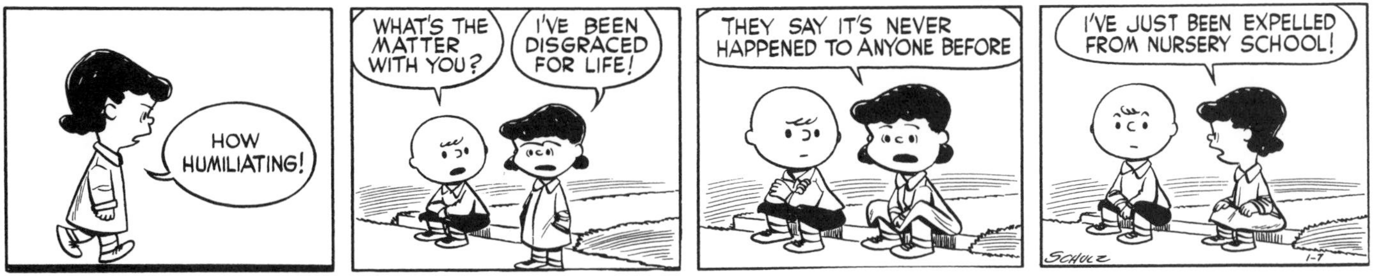
HOW HUMILIATING!
WHAT'S THE MATTER WITH YOU?
I'VE BEEN DISGRACED FOR LIFE!
THEY SAY IT'S NEVER HAPPENED TO ANYONE BEFORE
I'VE JUST BEEN EXPELLED FROM NURSERY SCHOOL!
SCHULZ
1-7

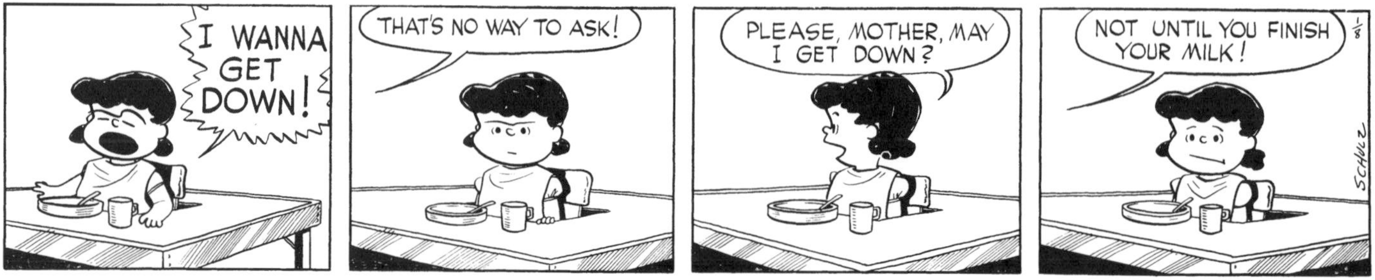
I WANNA GET DOWN!
THAT'S NO WAY TO ASK!
PLEASE, MOTHER, MAY I GET DOWN?
NOT UNTIL YOU FINISH YOUR MILK!
1/8
SCHULZ

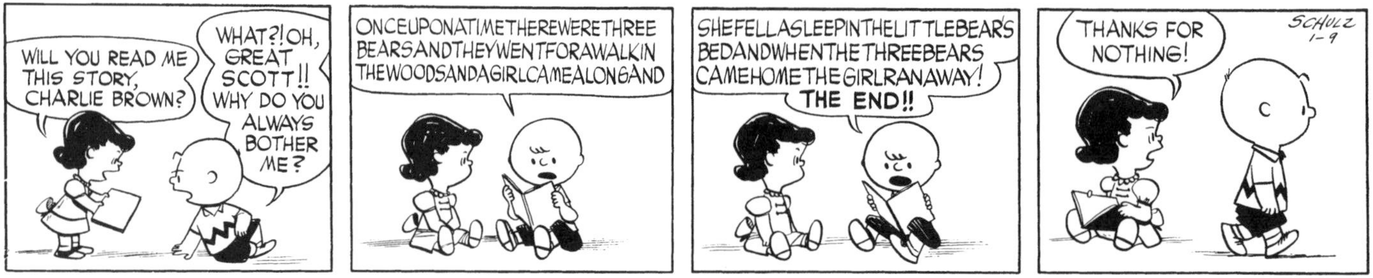
WILL YOU READ ME THIS STORY, CHARLIE BROWN?
WHAT?! OH, GREAT SCOTT!! WHY DO YOU ALWAYS BOTHER ME?
ONCEUPONATIMETHEREWERETHREE BEARSANDTHEYWENTFORAWALKIN THEWOODSANDAGIRLCAMEALONGAND
SHEFELLASLEEPINTHELITTLEBEAR'S BEDANDWHENTHETHREEBEARS CAMEHOMETHEGIRLRANAWAY! THE END!!
THANKS FOR NOTHING!
SCHULZ 1-9

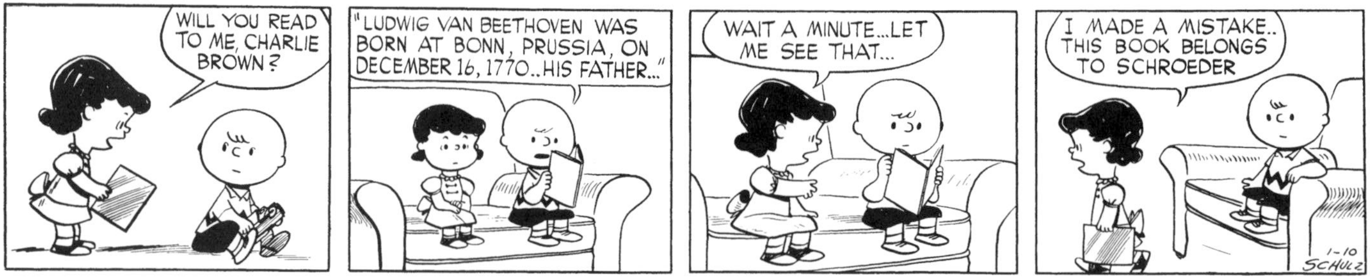
WILL YOU READ TO ME, CHARLIE BROWN?
"LUDWIG VAN BEETHOVEN WAS BORN AT BONN, PRUSSIA, ON DECEMBER 16, 1770.. HIS FATHER..."
WAIT A MINUTE...LET ME SEE THAT...
I MADE A MISTAKE.. THIS BOOK BELONGS TO SCHROEDER
1-10 SCHULZ

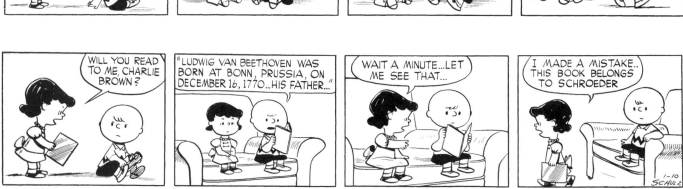

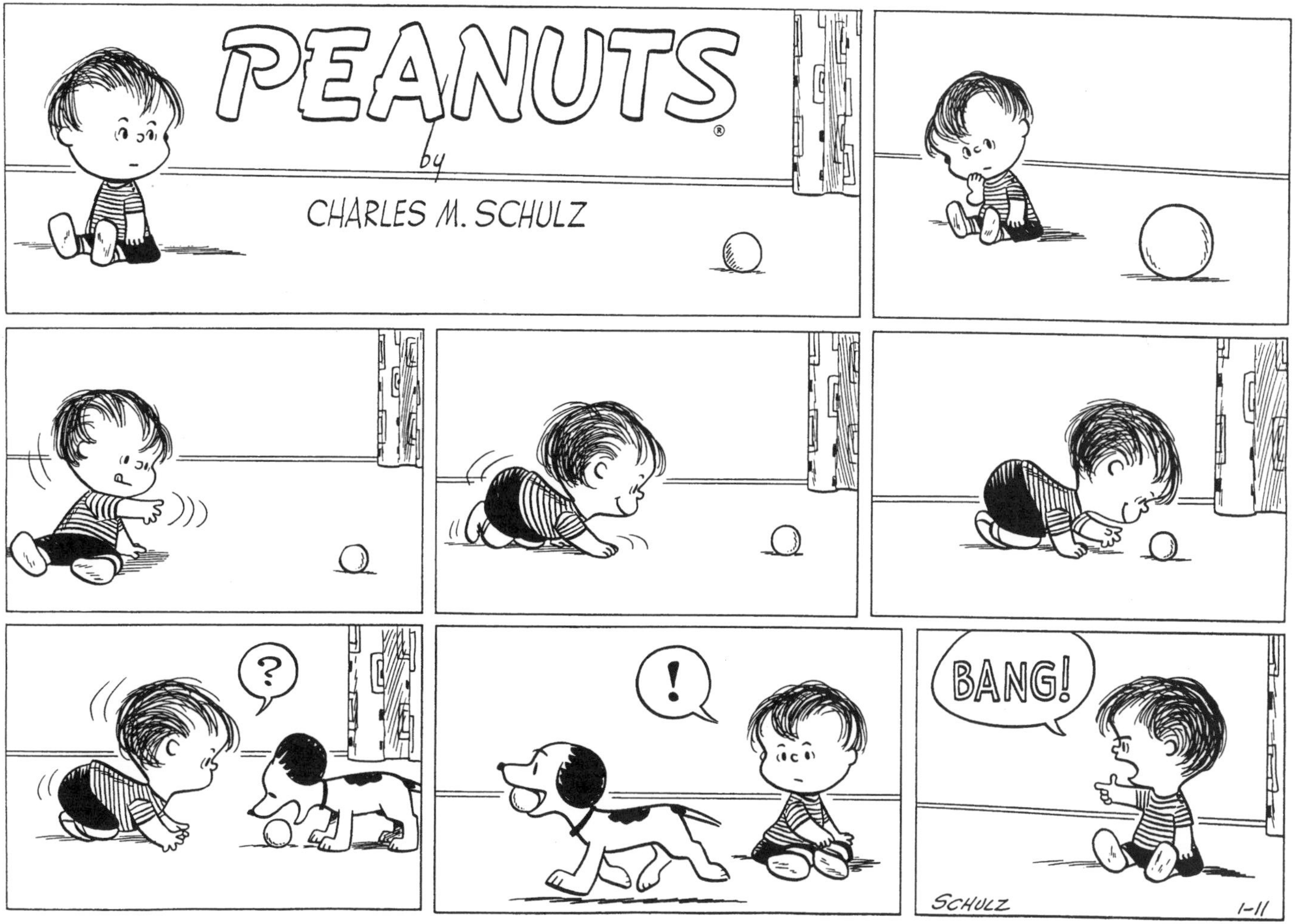
PEANUTS
by
CHARLES M. SCHULZ
?
!
BANG!
SCHULZ
1-11

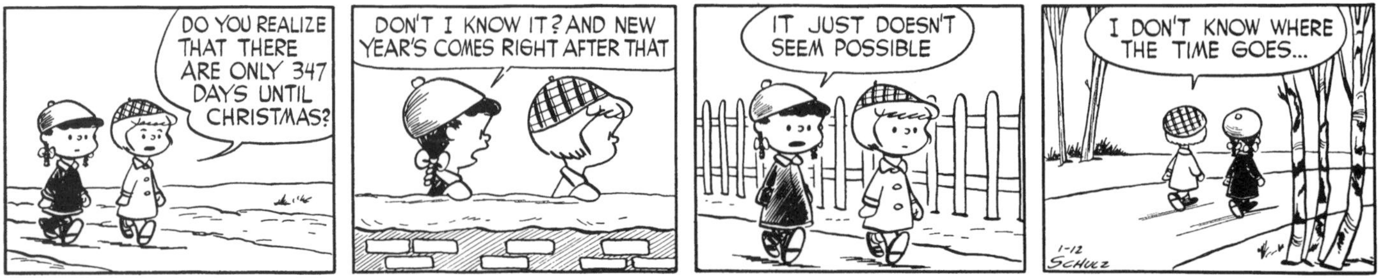
DO YOU REALIZE THAT THERE ARE ONLY 347 DAYS UNTIL CHRISTMAS?
DON'T I KNOW IT? AND NEW YEAR'S COMES RIGHT AFTER THAT
IT JUST DOESN'T SEEM POSSIBLE
I DON'T KNOW WHERE THE TIME GOES...
1-12
SCHULZ

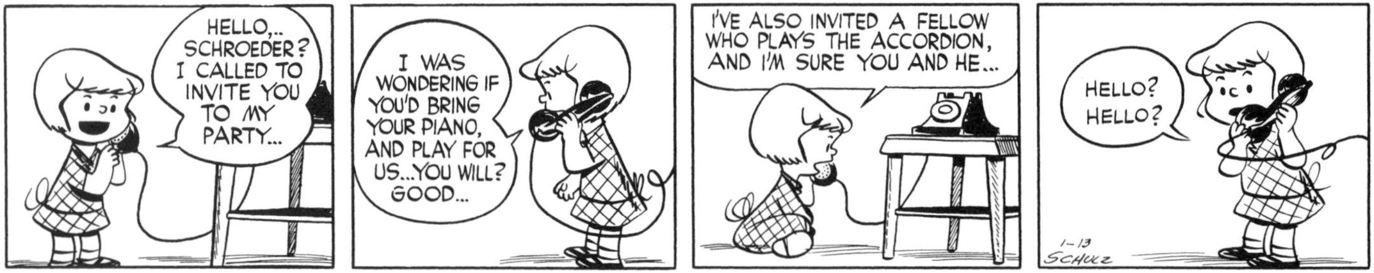
HELLO,.. SCHROEDER? I CALLED TO INVITE YOU TO MY PARTY...
I WAS WONDERING IF YOU'D BRING YOUR PIANO, AND PLAY FOR US...YOU WILL? GOOD...
I'VE ALSO INVITED A FELLOW WHO PLAYS THE ACCORDION, AND I'M SURE YOU AND HE...
HELLO? HELLO?
1-13
SCHULZ

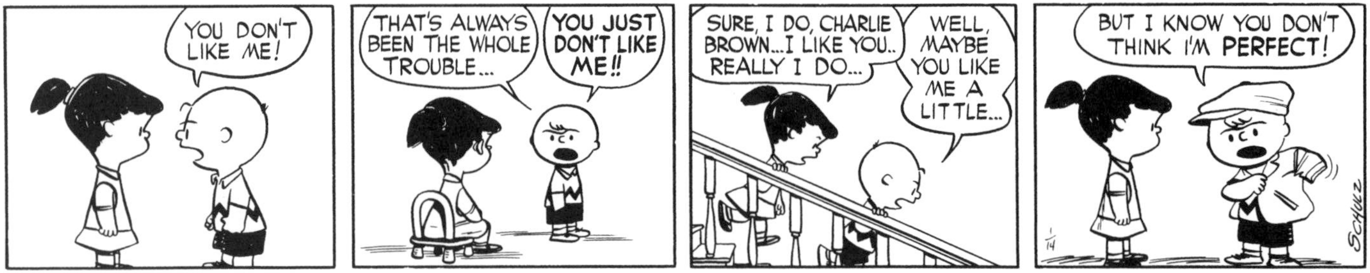
YOU DON'T LIKE ME!
THAT'S ALWAYS BEEN THE WHOLE TROUBLE...
YOU JUST DON'T LIKE ME!!
SURE, I DO, CHARLIE BROWN...I LIKE YOU.. REALLY I DO...
WELL, MAYBE YOU LIKE ME A LITTLE...
BUT I KNOW YOU DON'T THINK I'M PERFECT!
1/14
SCHULZ

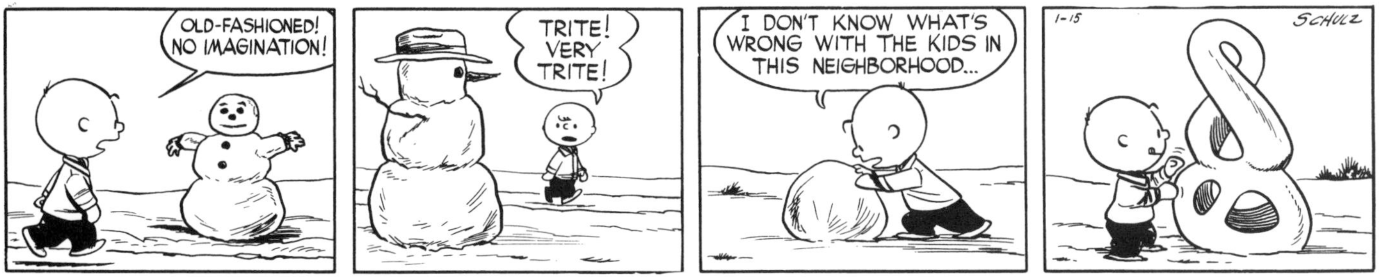
OLD-FASHIONED! NO IMAGINATION!
TRITE! VERY TRITE!
I DON'T KNOW WHAT'S WRONG WITH THE KIDS IN THIS NEIGHBORHOOD...
1-15
SCHULZ

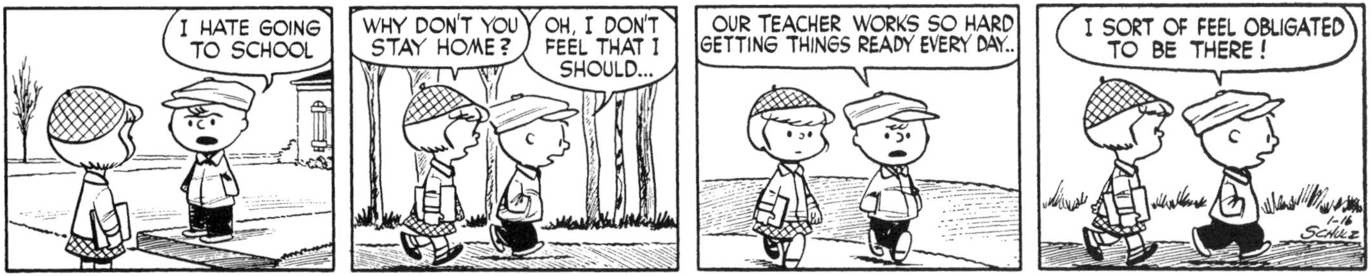
I HATE GOING TO SCHOOL
WHY DON'T YOU STAY HOME?
OH, I DON'T FEEL THAT I SHOULD...
OUR TEACHER WORKS SO HARD GETTING THINGS READY EVERY DAY..
I SORT OF FEEL OBLIGATED TO BE THERE!
1-16
SCHULZ

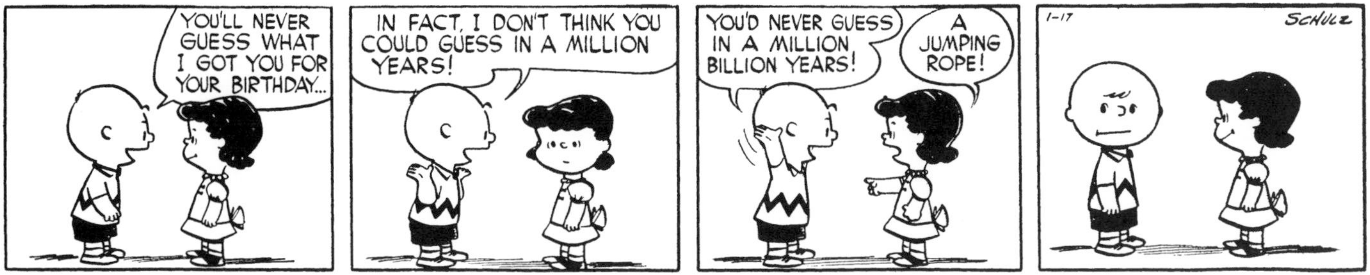
YOU'LL NEVER GUESS WHAT I GOT YOU FOR YOUR BIRTHDAY...
IN FACT, I DON'T THINK YOU COULD GUESS IN A MILLION YEARS!
YOU'D NEVER GUESS IN A MILLION BILLION YEARS!
A JUMPING ROPE!
1-17
SCHULZ

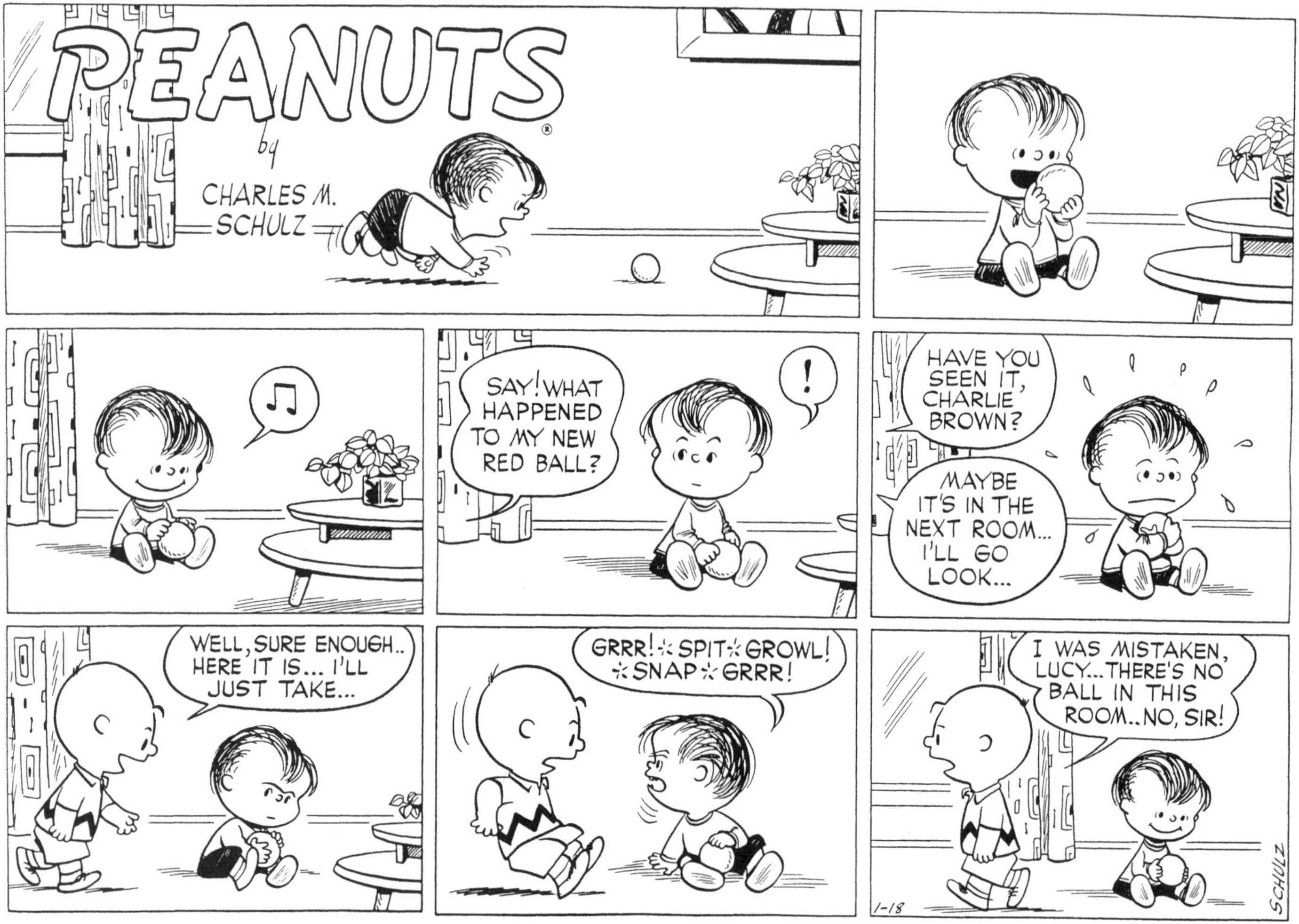
PEANUTS
by
CHARLES M.
SCHULZ
♫
SAY! WHAT HAPPENED TO MY NEW RED BALL?
!
HAVE YOU SEEN IT, CHARLIE BROWN?
MAYBE IT'S IN THE NEXT ROOM... I'LL GO LOOK...
WELL, SURE ENOUGH.. HERE IT IS... I'LL JUST TAKE...
GRRR! ✲ SPIT ✲ GROWL! ✲ SNAP ✲ GRRR!
I WAS MISTAKEN, LUCY... THERE'S NO BALL IN THIS ROOM.. NO, SIR!
1-18
SCHULZ

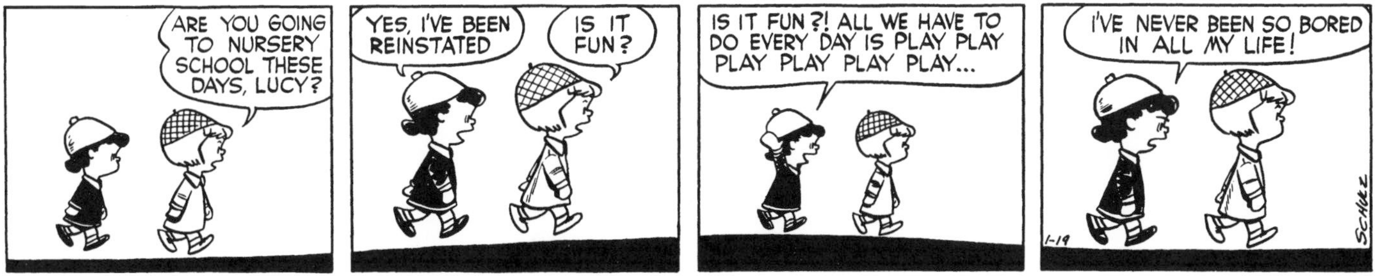
ARE YOU GOING TO NURSERY SCHOOL THESE DAYS, LUCY?
YES, I'VE BEEN REINSTATED
IS IT FUN?
IS IT FUN?! ALL WE HAVE TO DO EVERY DAY IS PLAY PLAY PLAY PLAY PLAY PLAY...
I'VE NEVER BEEN SO BORED IN ALL MY LIFE!
1-19
SCHULZ

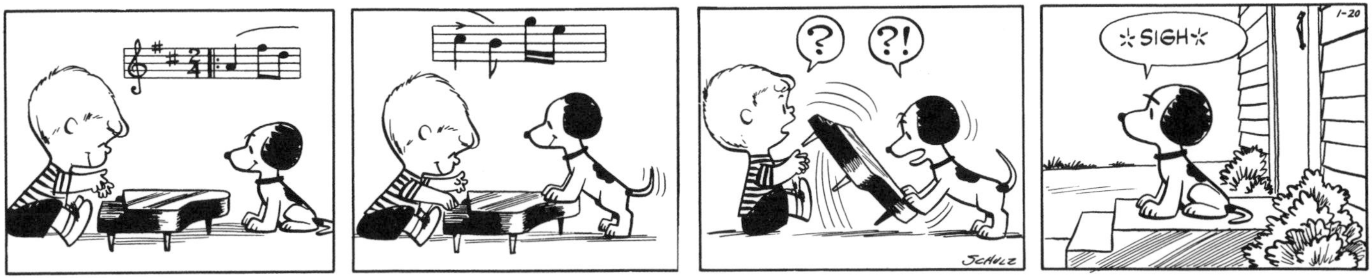
?
?!
SCHULZ
1-20
SIGH

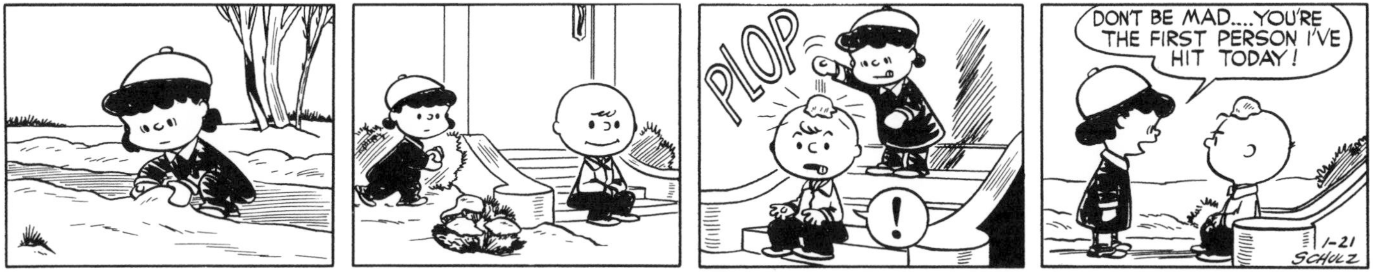
PLOP
!
DON'T BE MAD....YOU'RE THE FIRST PERSON I'VE HIT TODAY!
1-21
SCHULZ

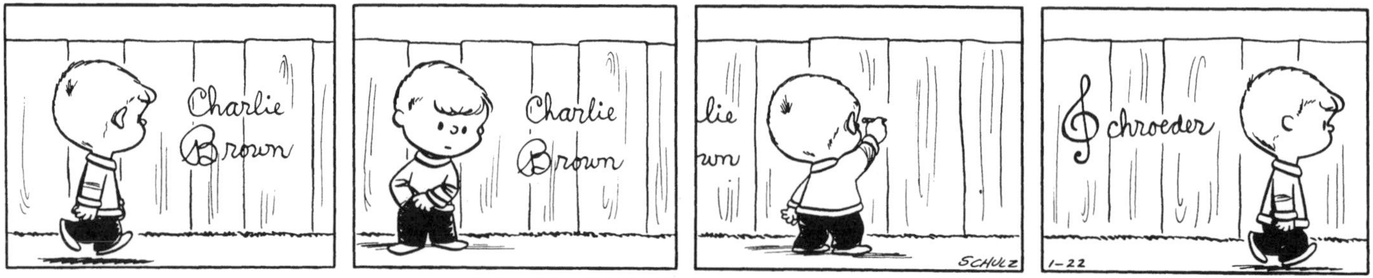
Charlie Brown
Charlie Brown
lie
wn
SCHULZ
Schroeder
1-22

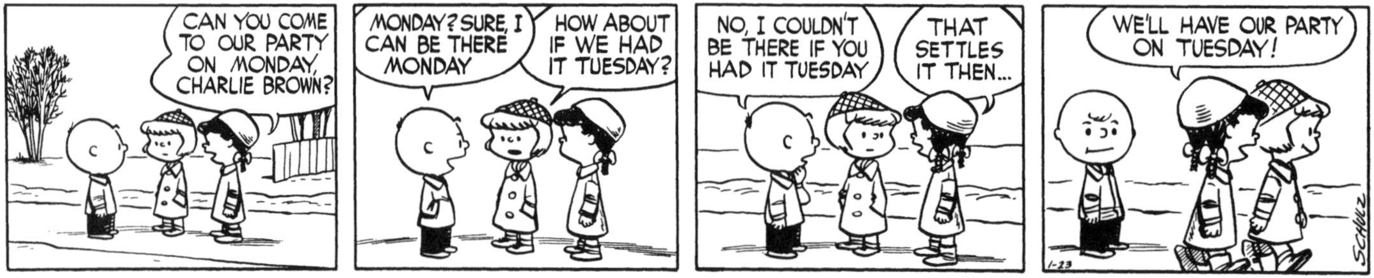
CAN YOU COME TO OUR PARTY ON MONDAY, CHARLIE BROWN?
MONDAY? SURE, I CAN BE THERE MONDAY
HOW ABOUT IF WE HAD IT TUESDAY?
NO, I COULDN'T BE THERE IF YOU HAD IT TUESDAY
THAT SETTLES IT THEN...
WE'LL HAVE OUR PARTY ON TUESDAY!
SCHULZ
1-23

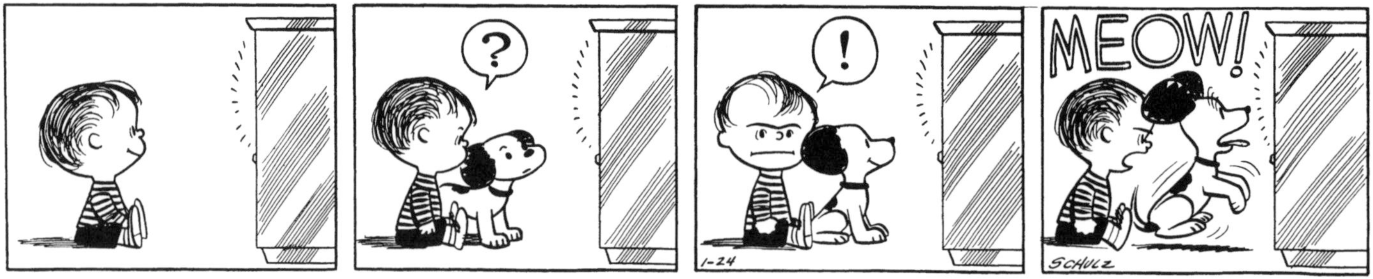
?
!
1-24
MEOW!
SCHULZ

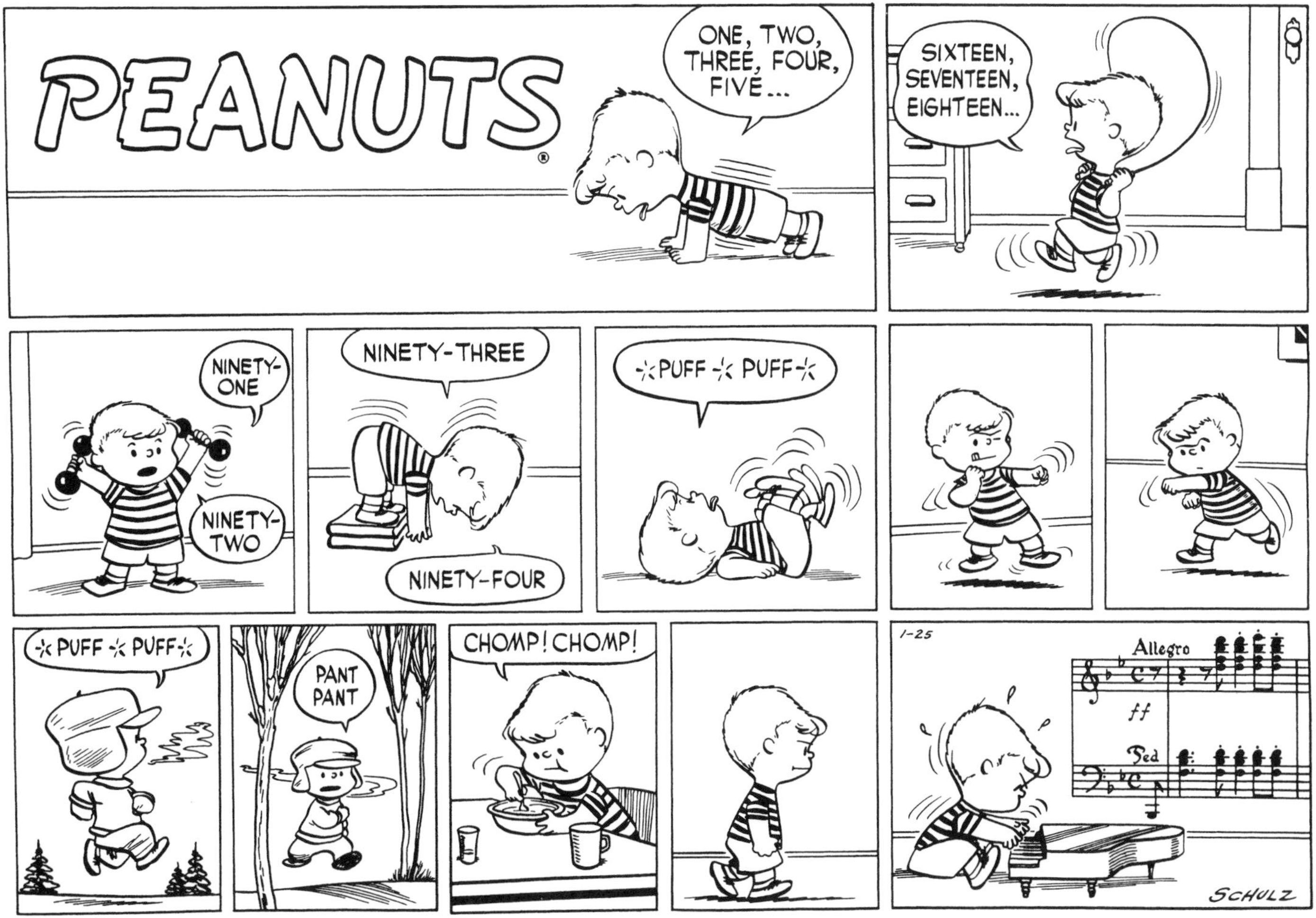
PEANUTS®
ONE, TWO, THREE, FOUR, FIVE...
SIXTEEN, SEVENTEEN, EIGHTEEN...
NINETY-ONE
NINETY-TWO
NINETY-THREE
NINETY-FOUR
PUFF PUFF
PUFF PUFF
PANT PANT
CHOMP! CHOMP!
1-25
Allegro
ff
Ped
SCHULZ

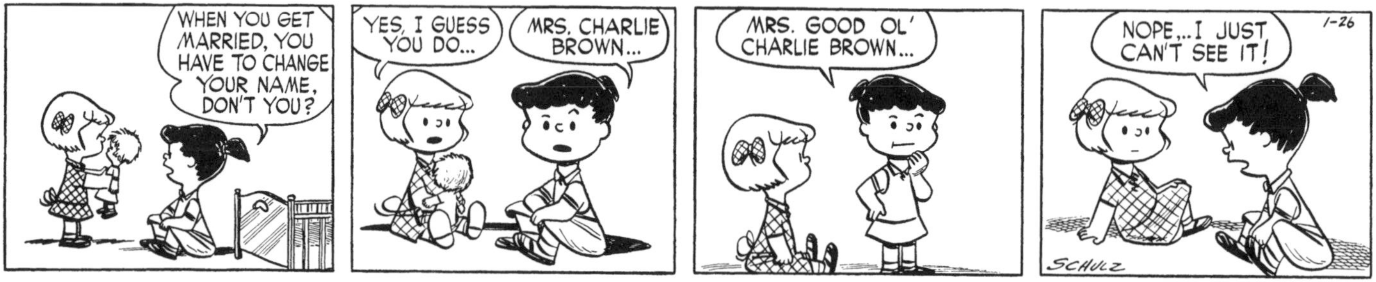
WHEN YOU GET MARRIED, YOU HAVE TO CHANGE YOUR NAME, DON'T YOU?
YES, I GUESS YOU DO...
MRS. CHARLIE BROWN...
MRS. GOOD OL' CHARLIE BROWN...
NOPE,..I JUST CAN'T SEE IT!
1-26
SCHULZ

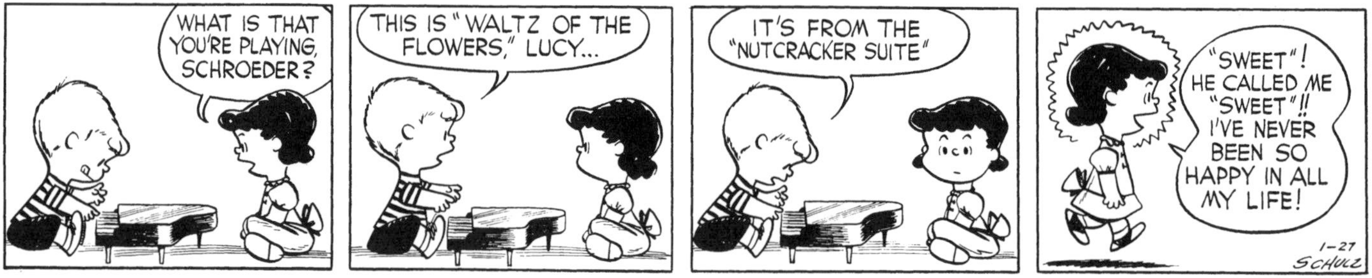
WHAT IS THAT YOU'RE PLAYING, SCHROEDER?
THIS IS "WALTZ OF THE FLOWERS," LUCY...
IT'S FROM THE "NUTCRACKER SUITE"
"SWEET"! HE CALLED ME "SWEET"!! I'VE NEVER BEEN SO HAPPY IN ALL MY LIFE!
1-27
SCHULZ

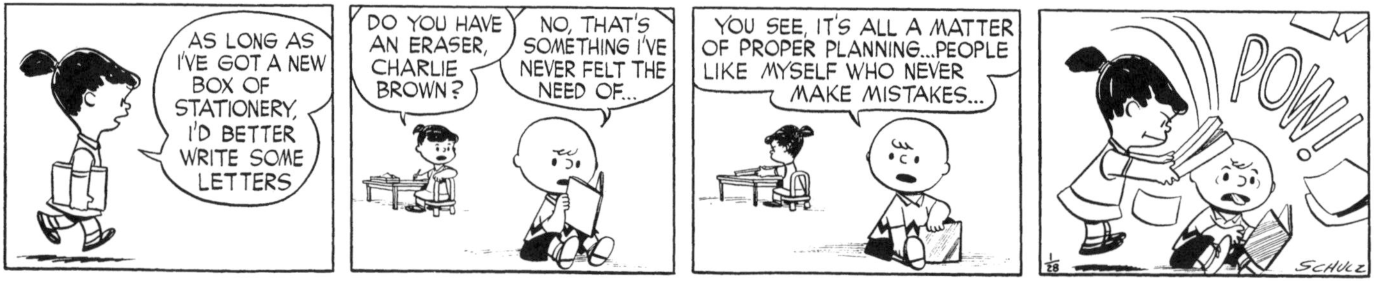
AS LONG AS I'VE GOT A NEW BOX OF STATIONERY, I'D BETTER WRITE SOME LETTERS
DO YOU HAVE AN ERASER, CHARLIE BROWN?
NO, THAT'S SOMETHING I'VE NEVER FELT THE NEED OF...
YOU SEE, IT'S ALL A MATTER OF PROPER PLANNING...PEOPLE LIKE MYSELF WHO NEVER MAKE MISTAKES...
POW!!
1 28
SCHULZ

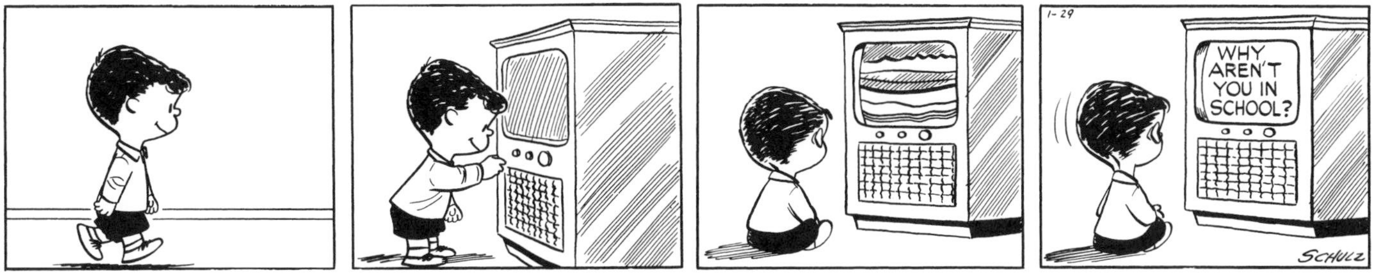
1-29
WHY AREN'T YOU IN SCHOOL?
SCHULZ

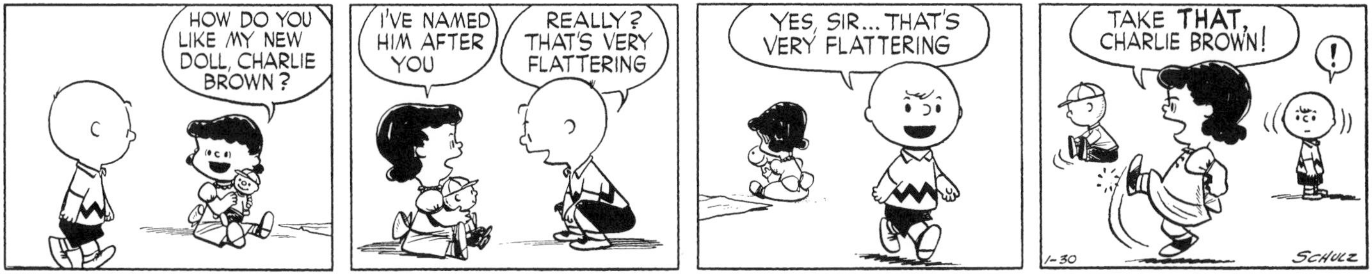
HOW DO YOU LIKE MY NEW DOLL, CHARLIE BROWN?
I'VE NAMED HIM AFTER YOU
REALLY? THAT'S VERY FLATTERING
YES, SIR... THAT'S VERY FLATTERING
TAKE THAT, CHARLIE BROWN!
!
1-30
SCHULZ

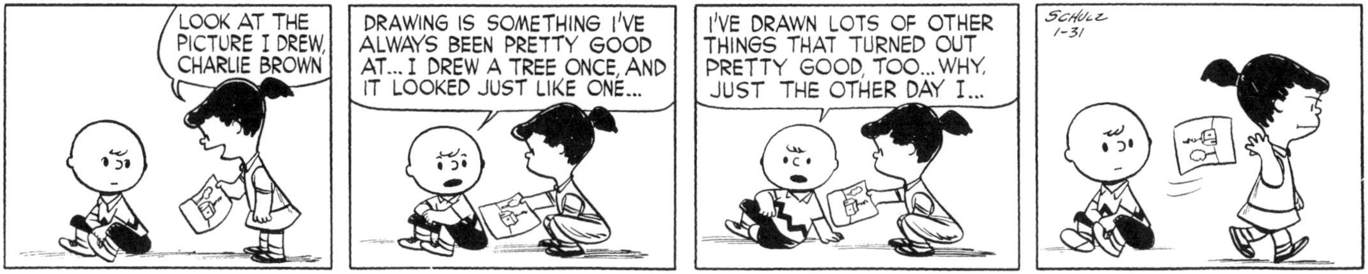
LOOK AT THE PICTURE I DREW, CHARLIE BROWN
DRAWING IS SOMETHING I'VE ALWAYS BEEN PRETTY GOOD AT... I DREW A TREE ONCE, AND IT LOOKED JUST LIKE ONE...
I'VE DRAWN LOTS OF OTHER THINGS THAT TURNED OUT PRETTY GOOD, TOO... WHY, JUST THE OTHER DAY I...
SCHULZ
1-31

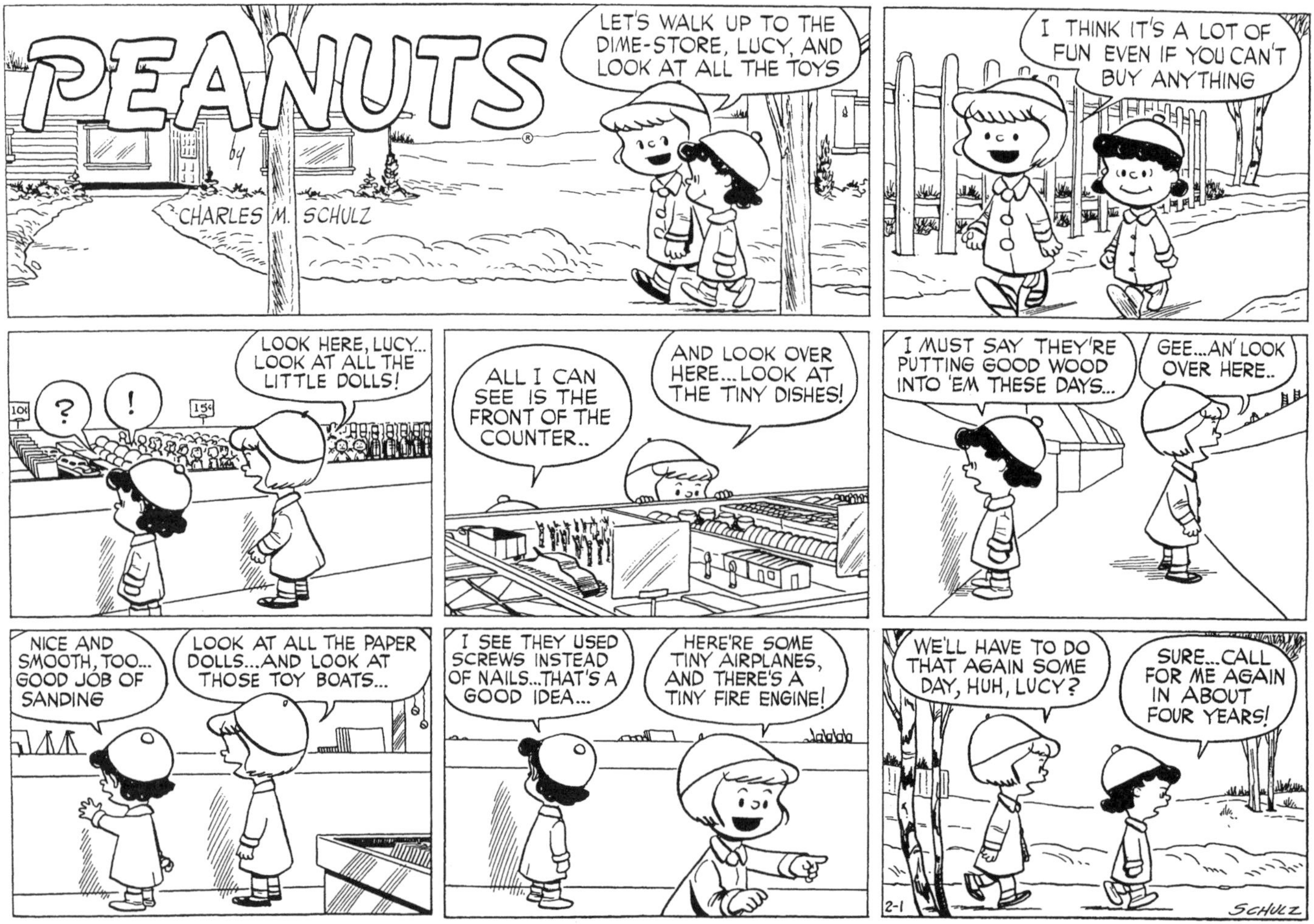
PEANUTS
by
CHARLES M. SCHULZ
LET'S WALK UP TO THE DIME-STORE, LUCY, AND LOOK AT ALL THE TOYS
I THINK IT'S A LOT OF FUN EVEN IF YOU CAN'T BUY ANYTHING
LOOK HERE, LUCY... LOOK AT ALL THE LITTLE DOLLS!
10¢
?
!
15¢
ALL I CAN SEE IS THE FRONT OF THE COUNTER..
AND LOOK OVER HERE... LOOK AT THE TINY DISHES!
I MUST SAY THEY'RE PUTTING GOOD WOOD INTO 'EM THESE DAYS...
GEE...AN' LOOK OVER HERE..
NICE AND SMOOTH, TOO... GOOD JOB OF SANDING
LOOK AT ALL THE PAPER DOLLS...AND LOOK AT THOSE TOY BOATS...
I SEE THEY USED SCREWS INSTEAD OF NAILS...THAT'S A GOOD IDEA...
HERE'RE SOME TINY AIRPLANES, AND THERE'S A TINY FIRE ENGINE!
WE'LL HAVE TO DO THAT AGAIN SOME DAY, HUH, LUCY?
SURE...CALL FOR ME AGAIN IN ABOUT FOUR YEARS!
2-1
SCHULZ

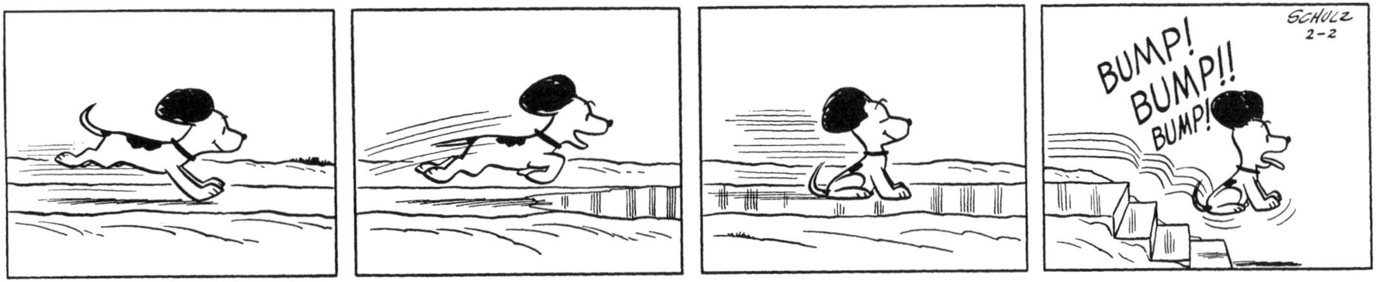
BUMP!
BUMP!!
BUMP!
SCHULZ 2-2

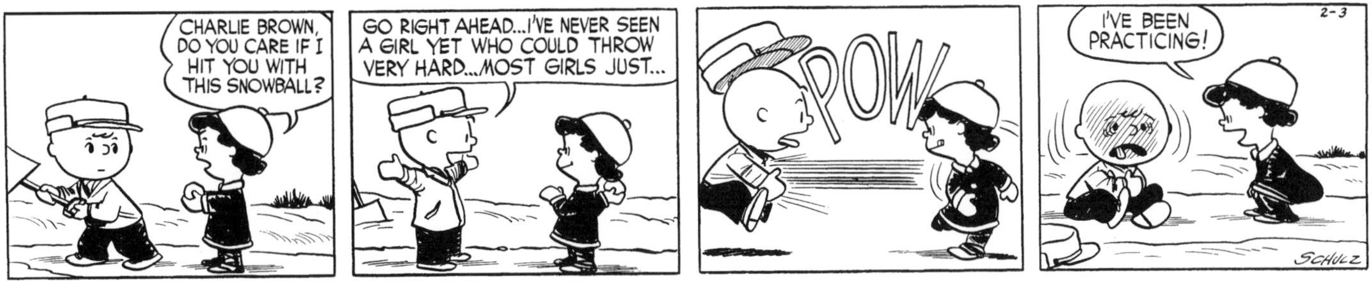
CHARLIE BROWN, DO YOU CARE IF I HIT YOU WITH THIS SNOWBALL?
GO RIGHT AHEAD...I'VE NEVER SEEN A GIRL YET WHO COULD THROW VERY HARD...MOST GIRLS JUST...
POW
I'VE BEEN PRACTICING!
2-3
SCHULZ

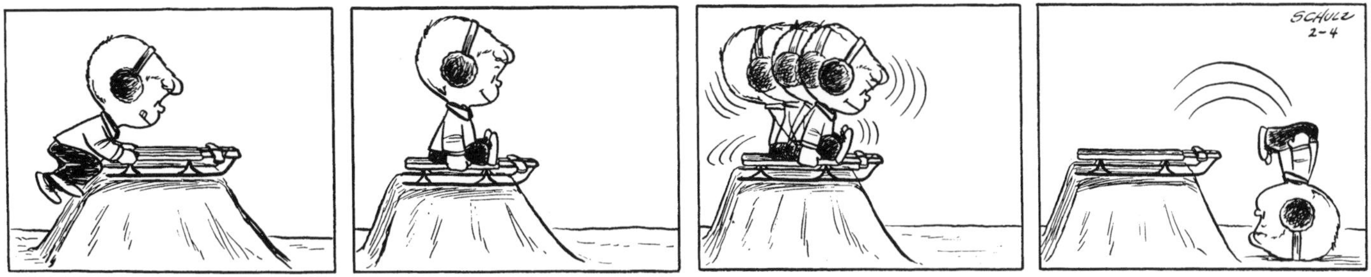
SCHULZ 2-4

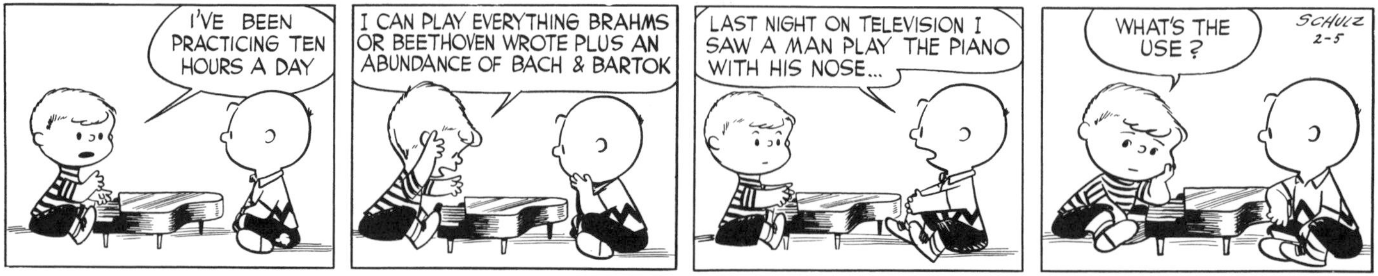
I'VE BEEN PRACTICING TEN HOURS A DAY
I CAN PLAY EVERYTHING BRAHMS OR BEETHOVEN WROTE PLUS AN ABUNDANCE OF BACH & BARTOK
LAST NIGHT ON TELEVISION I SAW A MAN PLAY THE PIANO WITH HIS NOSE...
WHAT'S THE USE?
SCHULZ 2-5

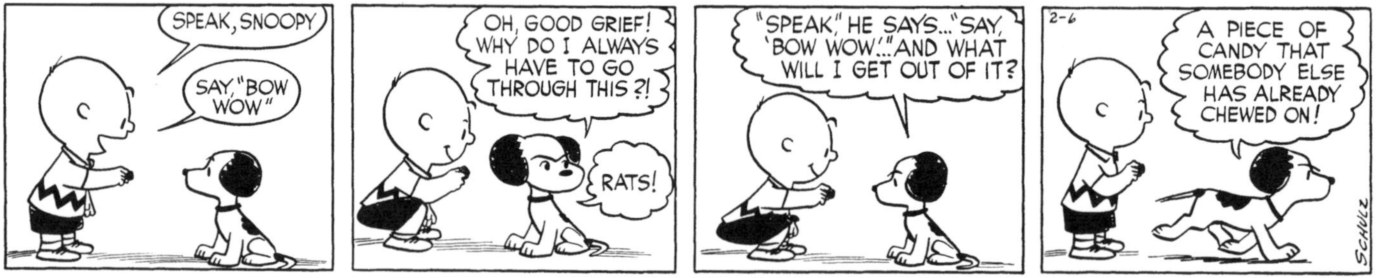
SPEAK, SNOOPY
SAY, "BOW WOW"
OH, GOOD GRIEF! WHY DO I ALWAYS HAVE TO GO THROUGH THIS?!
RATS!
"SPEAK," HE SAYS... "SAY, 'BOW WOW!'" AND WHAT WILL I GET OUT OF IT?
2-6
A PIECE OF CANDY THAT SOMEBODY ELSE HAS ALREADY CHEWED ON!
SCHULZ

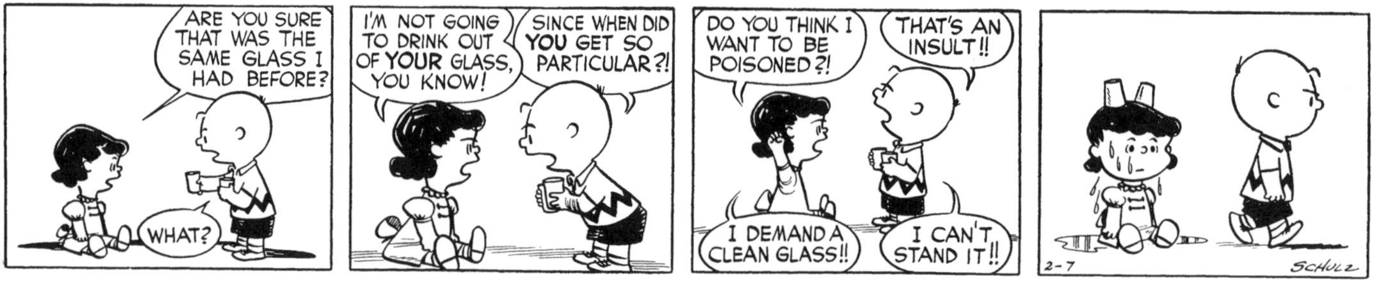
ARE YOU SURE THAT WAS THE SAME GLASS I HAD BEFORE?
WHAT?
I'M NOT GOING TO DRINK OUT OF YOUR GLASS, YOU KNOW!
SINCE WHEN DID YOU GET SO PARTICULAR?!
DO YOU THINK I WANT TO BE POISONED?!
THAT'S AN INSULT!!
I DEMAND A CLEAN GLASS!!
I CAN'T STAND IT!!
2-7
SCHULZ

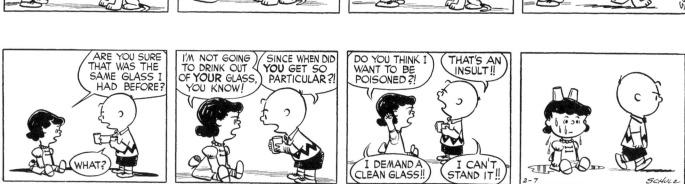

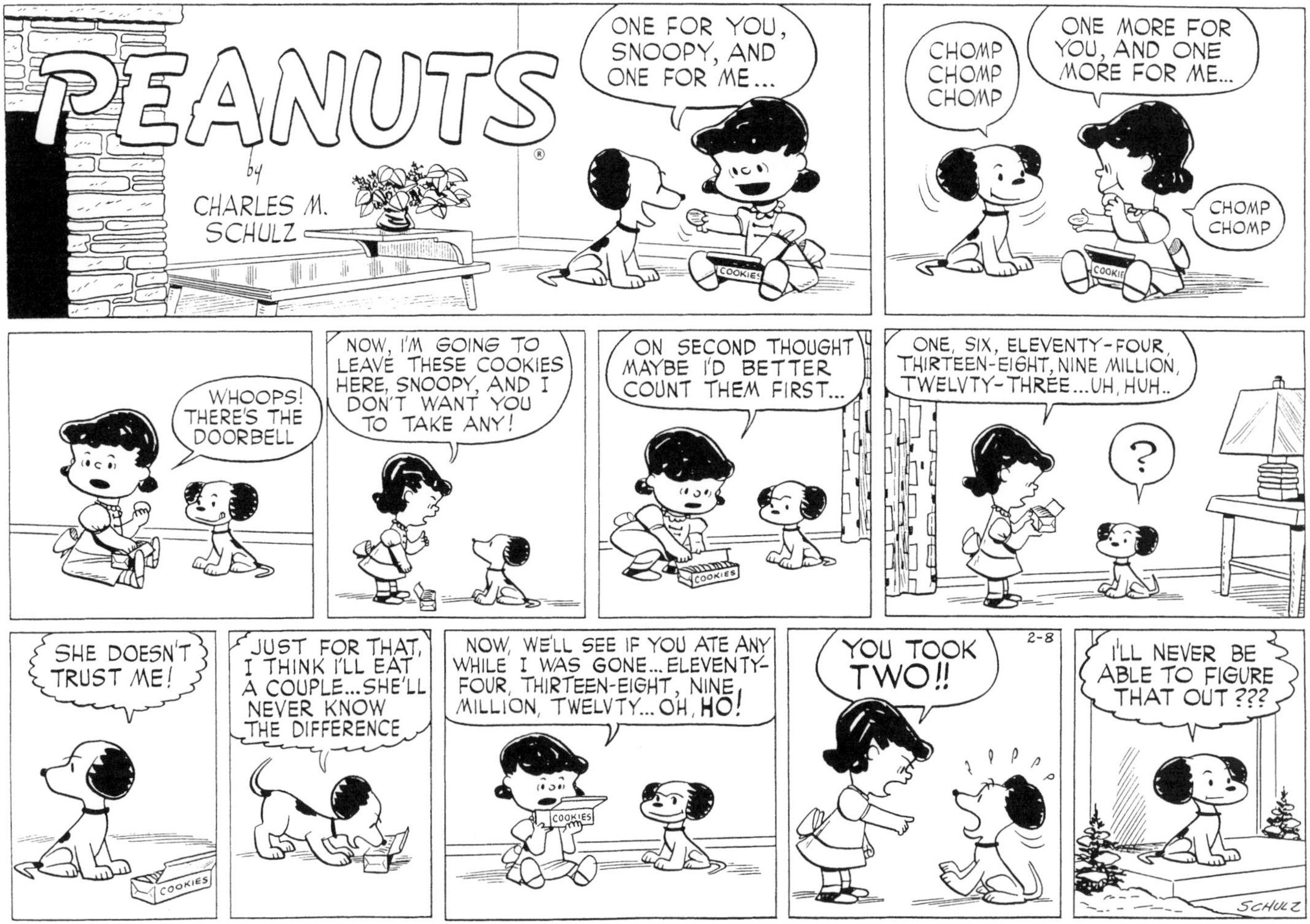
PEANUTS
by CHARLES M. SCHULZ
ONE FOR YOU, SNOOPY, AND ONE FOR ME...
COOKIES
CHOMP CHOMP CHOMP
ONE MORE FOR YOU, AND ONE MORE FOR ME...
CHOMP CHOMP
COOKIES
WHOOPS! THERE'S THE DOORBELL
NOW, I'M GOING TO LEAVE THESE COOKIES HERE, SNOOPY, AND I DON'T WANT YOU TO TAKE ANY!
ON SECOND THOUGHT MAYBE I'D BETTER COUNT THEM FIRST...
COOKIES
ONE, SIX, ELEVENTY-FOUR, THIRTEEN-EIGHT, NINE MILLION, TWELVTY-THREE...UH, HUH..
?
SHE DOESN'T TRUST ME!
COOKIES
JUST FOR THAT, I THINK I'LL EAT A COUPLE...SHE'LL NEVER KNOW THE DIFFERENCE
NOW, WE'LL SEE IF YOU ATE ANY WHILE I WAS GONE...ELEVENTY-FOUR, THIRTEEN-EIGHT, NINE MILLION, TWELVTY...OH, HO!
COOKIES
2-8
YOU TOOK TWO!!
I'LL NEVER BE ABLE TO FIGURE THAT OUT???
SCHULZ

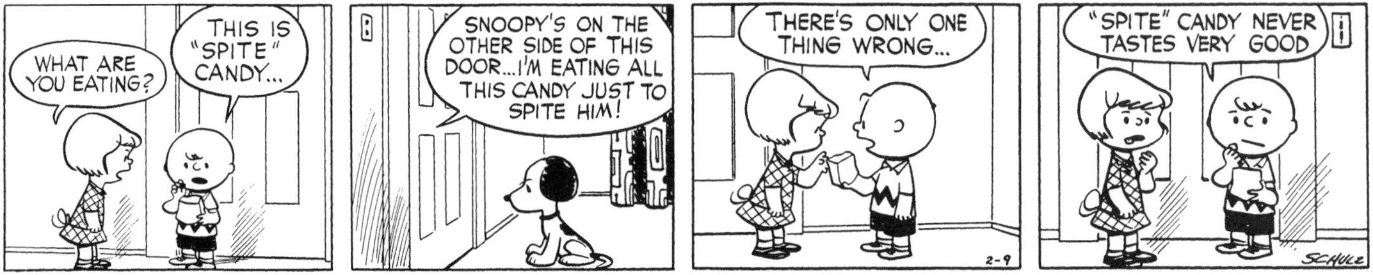
WHAT ARE YOU EATING?
THIS IS "SPITE" CANDY...
SNOOPY'S ON THE OTHER SIDE OF THIS DOOR...I'M EATING ALL THIS CANDY JUST TO SPITE HIM!
THERE'S ONLY ONE THING WRONG...
2-9
"SPITE" CANDY NEVER TASTES VERY GOOD
SCHULZ

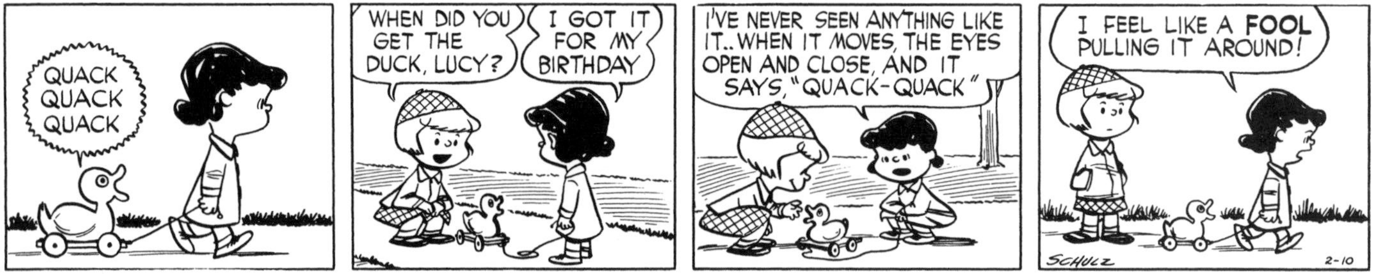
QUACK QUACK QUACK
WHEN DID YOU GET THE DUCK, LUCY?
I GOT IT FOR MY BIRTHDAY
I'VE NEVER SEEN ANYTHING LIKE IT..WHEN IT MOVES, THE EYES OPEN AND CLOSE, AND IT SAYS, "QUACK-QUACK"
I FEEL LIKE A **FOOL** PULLING IT AROUND!
SCHULZ
2-10

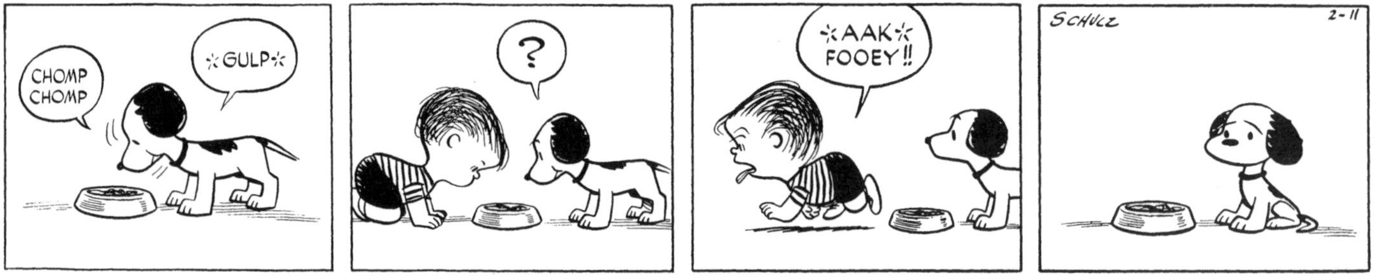
CHOMP CHOMP
GULP
?
AAK FOOEY!!
SCHULZ
2-11

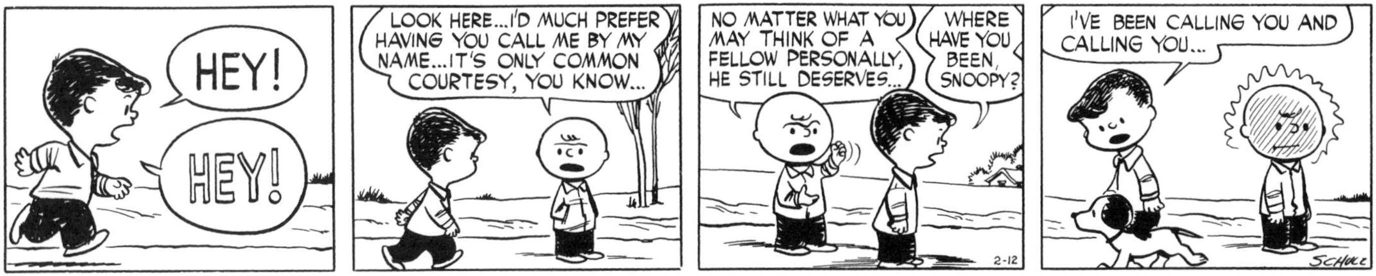
HEY!
HEY!
LOOK HERE...I'D MUCH PREFER HAVING YOU CALL ME BY MY NAME...IT'S ONLY COMMON COURTESY, YOU KNOW...
NO MATTER WHAT YOU MAY THINK OF A FELLOW PERSONALLY, HE STILL DESERVES...
WHERE HAVE YOU BEEN, SNOOPY?
I'VE BEEN CALLING YOU AND CALLING YOU...
2-12
SCHULZ

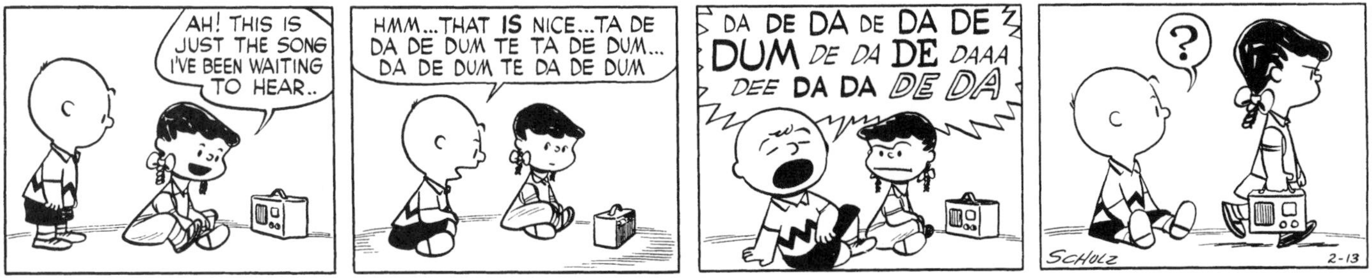
AH! THIS IS JUST THE SONG I'VE BEEN WAITING TO HEAR..
HMM...THAT IS NICE...TA DE DA DE DUM TE TA DE DUM... DA DE DUM TE DA DE DUM
DA DE DA DE DA DE DUM DE DA DE DAAA DEE DA DA DE DA
?
SCHULZ
2-13

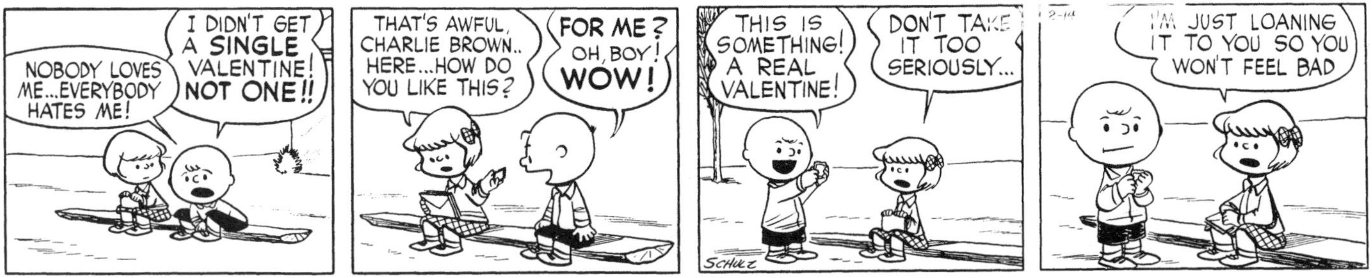
NOBODY LOVES ME...EVERYBODY HATES ME!
I DIDN'T GET A SINGLE VALENTINE! NOT ONE!!
THAT'S AWFUL, CHARLIE BROWN.. HERE...HOW DO YOU LIKE THIS?
FOR ME? OH, BOY! WOW!
THIS IS SOMETHING! A REAL VALENTINE!
DON'T TAKE IT TOO SERIOUSLY...
SCHULZ
I'M JUST LOANING IT TO YOU SO YOU WON'T FEEL BAD

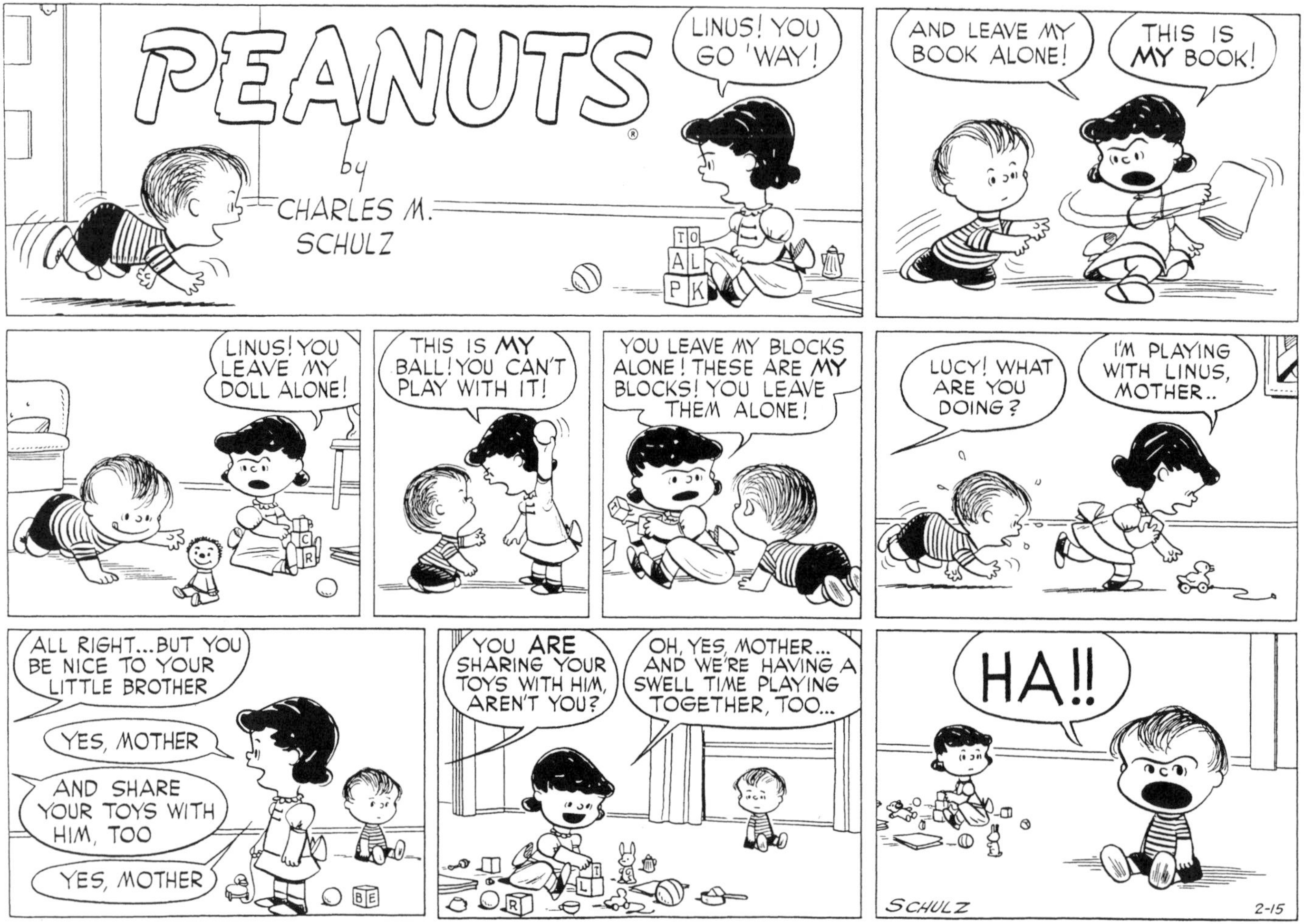
PEANUTS
by
CHARLES M. SCHULZ
LINUS! YOU GO 'WAY!
AND LEAVE MY BOOK ALONE!
THIS IS MY BOOK!
LINUS! YOU LEAVE MY DOLL ALONE!
THIS IS MY BALL! YOU CAN'T PLAY WITH IT!
YOU LEAVE MY BLOCKS ALONE! THESE ARE MY BLOCKS! YOU LEAVE THEM ALONE!
LUCY! WHAT ARE YOU DOING?
I'M PLAYING WITH LINUS, MOTHER..
ALL RIGHT...BUT YOU BE NICE TO YOUR LITTLE BROTHER
YES, MOTHER
AND SHARE YOUR TOYS WITH HIM, TOO
YES, MOTHER
YOU ARE SHARING YOUR TOYS WITH HIM, AREN'T YOU?
OH, YES, MOTHER... AND WE'RE HAVING A SWELL TIME PLAYING TOGETHER, TOO...
HA!!
SCHULZ
2-15

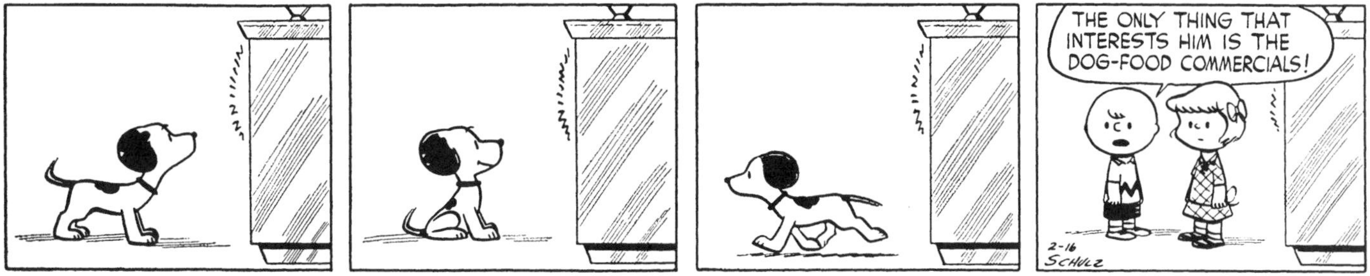
THE ONLY THING THAT INTERESTS HIM IS THE DOG-FOOD COMMERCIALS!
2-16
SCHULZ

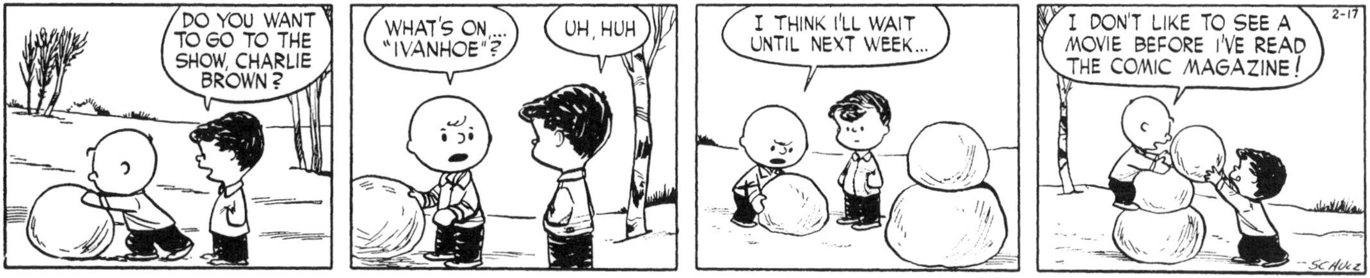
DO YOU WANT TO GO TO THE SHOW, CHARLIE BROWN?
WHAT'S ON.... "IVANHOE"?
UH, HUH
I THINK I'LL WAIT UNTIL NEXT WEEK...
2-17
I DON'T LIKE TO SEE A MOVIE BEFORE I'VE READ THE COMIC MAGAZINE!
SCHULZ

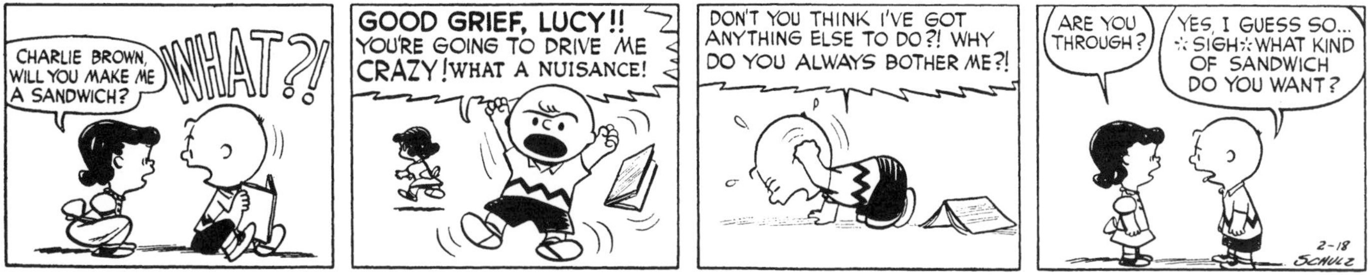
CHARLIE BROWN, WILL YOU MAKE ME A SANDWICH?
WHAT?!
GOOD GRIEF, LUCY!! YOU'RE GOING TO DRIVE ME CRAZY! WHAT A NUISANCE!
DON'T YOU THINK I'VE GOT ANYTHING ELSE TO DO?! WHY DO YOU ALWAYS BOTHER ME?!
ARE YOU THROUGH?
YES, I GUESS SO... *SIGH* WHAT KIND OF SANDWICH DO YOU WANT?
2-18
SCHULZ

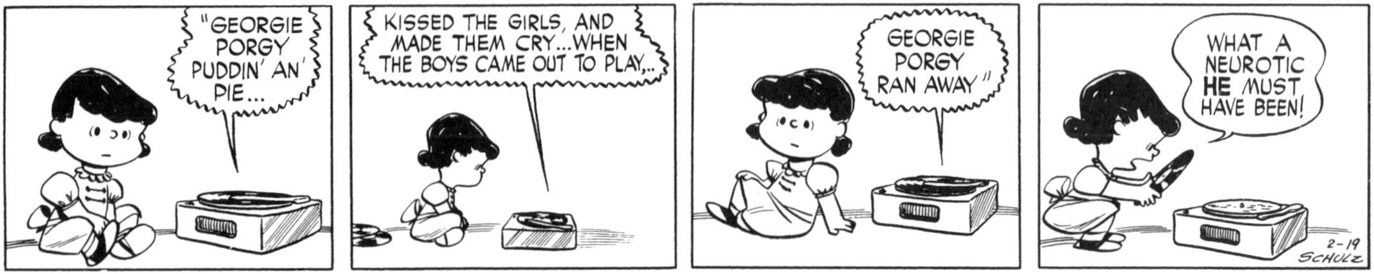
"GEORGIE PORGY PUDDIN' AN' PIE...
KISSED THE GIRLS, AND MADE THEM CRY...WHEN THE BOYS CAME OUT TO PLAY,..
GEORGIE PORGY RAN AWAY"
WHAT A NEUROTIC HE MUST HAVE BEEN!
2-19
SCHULZ

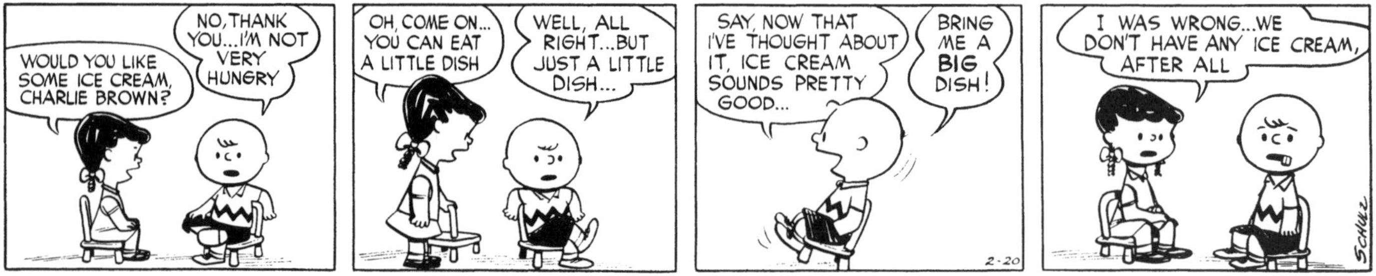
WOULD YOU LIKE SOME ICE CREAM, CHARLIE BROWN?
NO, THANK YOU...I'M NOT VERY HUNGRY
OH, COME ON... YOU CAN EAT A LITTLE DISH
WELL, ALL RIGHT...BUT JUST A LITTLE DISH...
SAY, NOW THAT I'VE THOUGHT ABOUT IT, ICE CREAM SOUNDS PRETTY GOOD...
BRING ME A BIG DISH!
2-20
I WAS WRONG...WE DON'T HAVE ANY ICE CREAM, AFTER ALL
SCHULZ

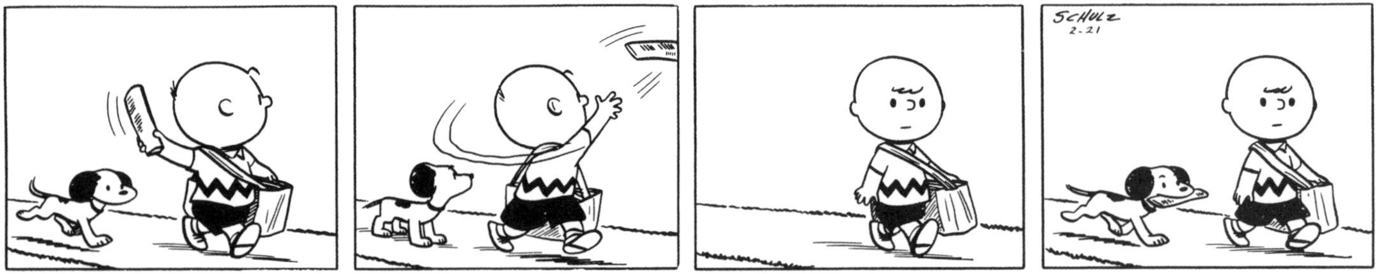
SCHULZ
2-21

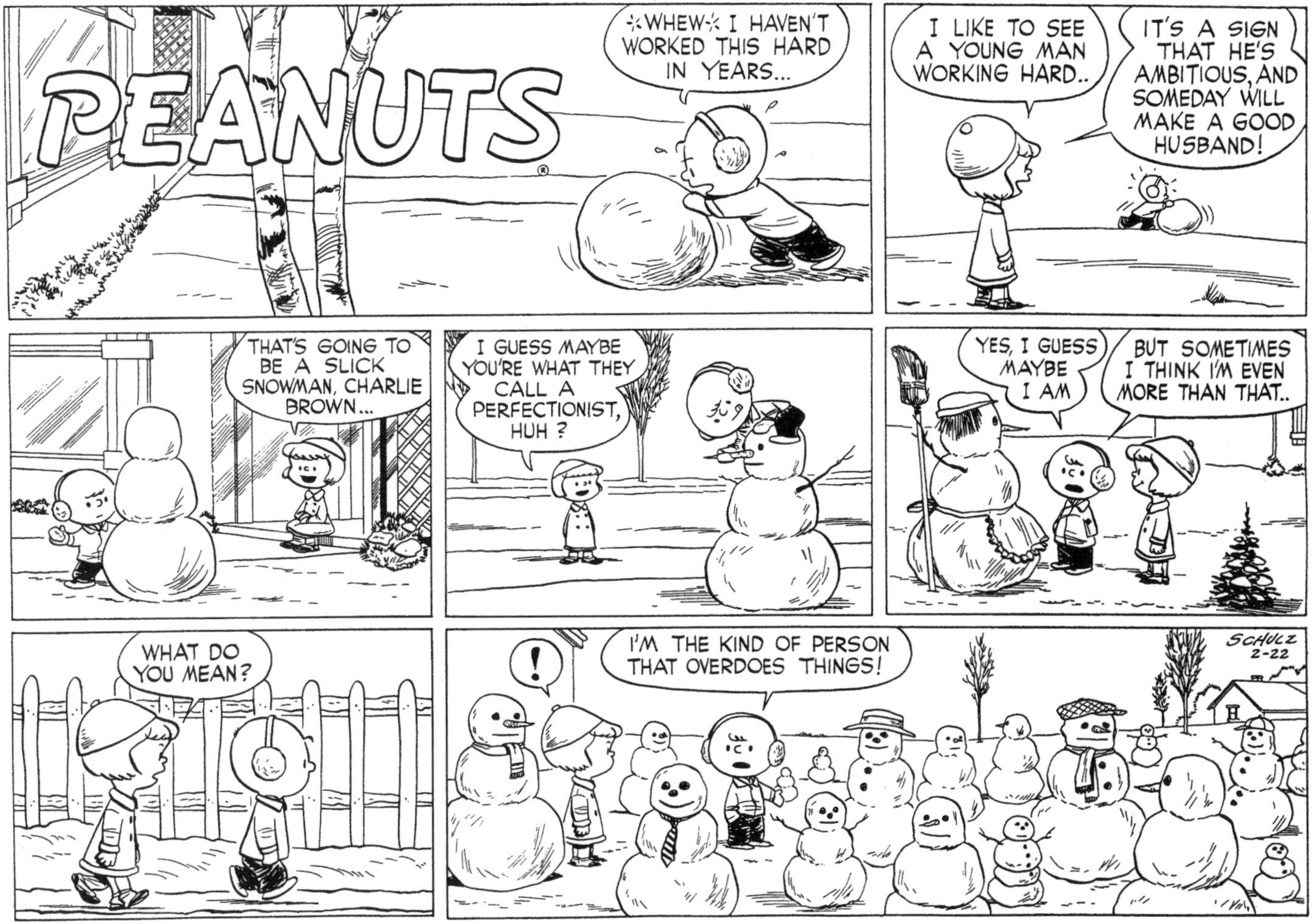
PEANUTS
WHEW I HAVEN'T WORKED THIS HARD IN YEARS...
I LIKE TO SEE A YOUNG MAN WORKING HARD..
IT'S A SIGN THAT HE'S AMBITIOUS, AND SOMEDAY WILL MAKE A GOOD HUSBAND!
THAT'S GOING TO BE A SLICK SNOWMAN, CHARLIE BROWN...
I GUESS MAYBE YOU'RE WHAT THEY CALL A PERFECTIONIST, HUH ?
YES, I GUESS MAYBE I AM
BUT SOMETIMES I THINK I'M EVEN MORE THAN THAT..
WHAT DO YOU MEAN?
!
I'M THE KIND OF PERSON THAT OVERDOES THINGS!
SCHULZ 2-22

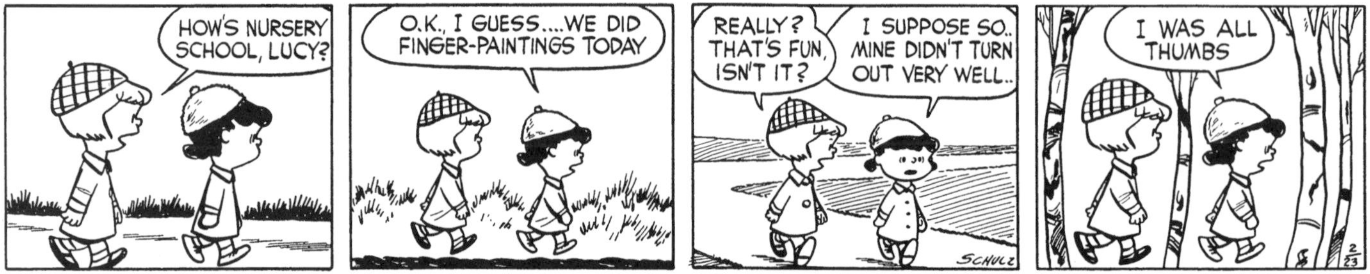
HOW'S NURSERY SCHOOL, LUCY?
O.K., I GUESS....WE DID FINGER-PAINTINGS TODAY
REALLY? THAT'S FUN, ISN'T IT?
I SUPPOSE SO.. MINE DIDN'T TURN OUT VERY WELL..
SCHULZ
I WAS ALL THUMBS
2/23

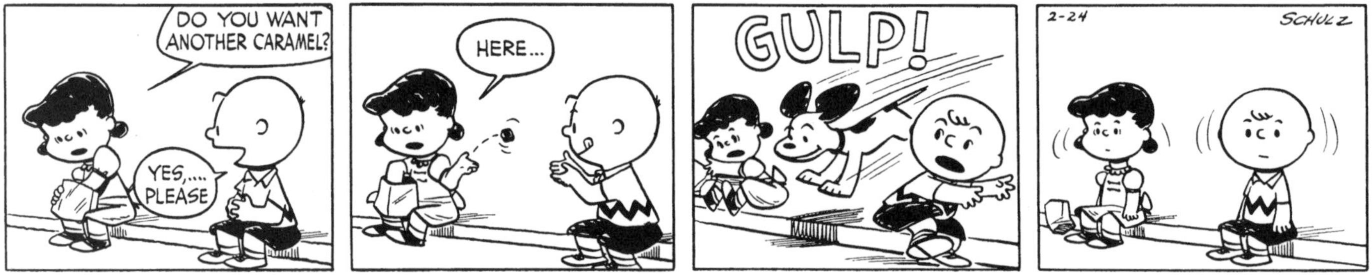
DO YOU WANT ANOTHER CARAMEL?
YES,.... PLEASE
HERE...
GULP!
2-24
SCHULZ

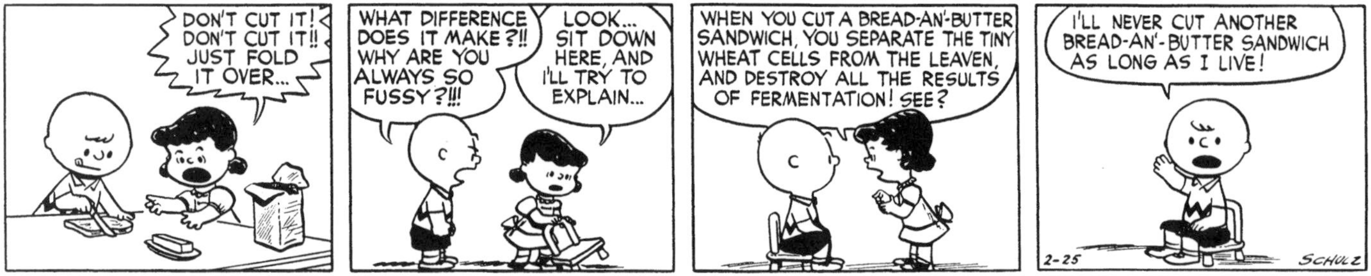
DON'T CUT IT! DON'T CUT IT!! JUST FOLD IT OVER...
WHAT DIFFERENCE DOES IT MAKE?!! WHY ARE YOU ALWAYS SO FUSSY?!!!
LOOK... SIT DOWN HERE, AND I'LL TRY TO EXPLAIN...
WHEN YOU CUT A BREAD-AN'-BUTTER SANDWICH, YOU SEPARATE THE TINY WHEAT CELLS FROM THE LEAVEN, AND DESTROY ALL THE RESULTS OF FERMENTATION! SEE?
I'LL NEVER CUT ANOTHER BREAD-AN'-BUTTER SANDWICH AS LONG AS I LIVE!
2-25
SCHULZ

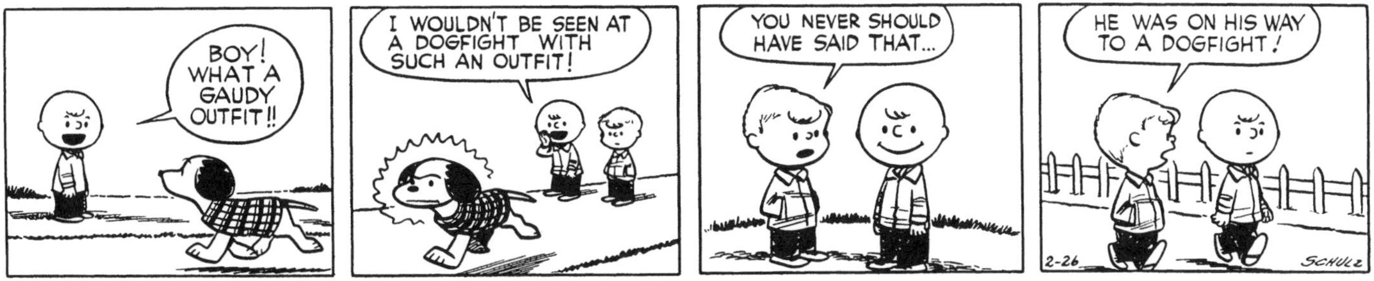
BOY! WHAT A GAUDY OUTFIT!!
I WOULDN'T BE SEEN AT A DOGFIGHT WITH SUCH AN OUTFIT!
YOU NEVER SHOULD HAVE SAID THAT...
HE WAS ON HIS WAY TO A DOGFIGHT!
2-26
SCHULZ

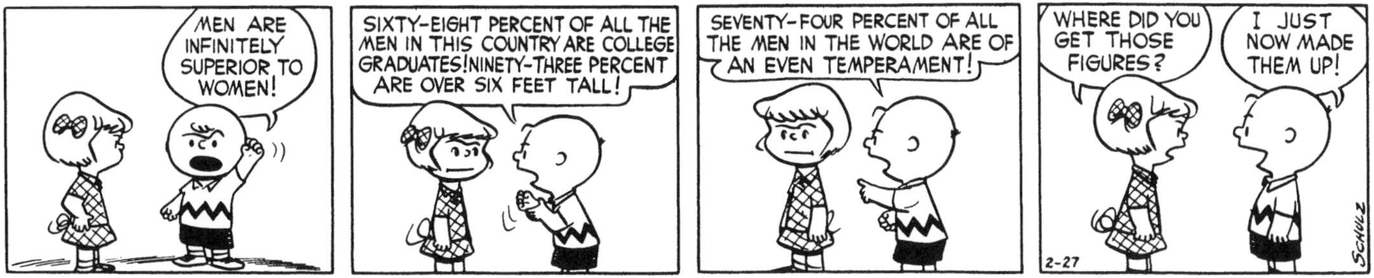
MEN ARE INFINITELY SUPERIOR TO WOMEN!
SIXTY-EIGHT PERCENT OF ALL THE MEN IN THIS COUNTRY ARE COLLEGE GRADUATES! NINETY-THREE PERCENT ARE OVER SIX FEET TALL!
SEVENTY-FOUR PERCENT OF ALL THE MEN IN THE WORLD ARE OF AN EVEN TEMPERAMENT!
WHERE DID YOU GET THOSE FIGURES?
I JUST NOW MADE THEM UP!
2-27
SCHULZ

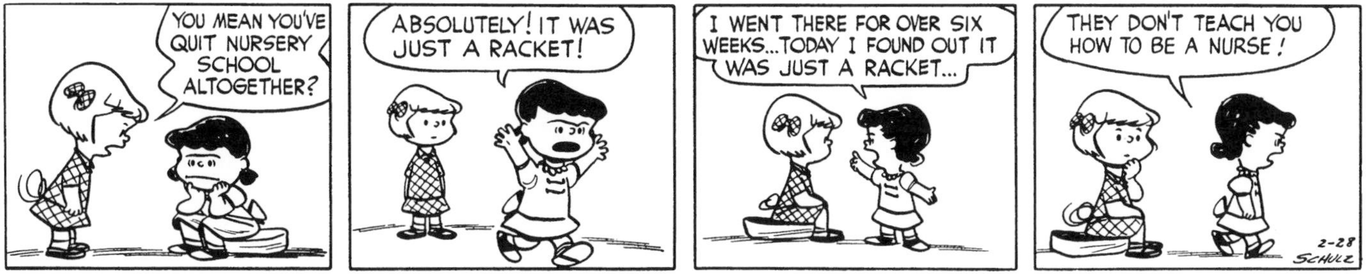
YOU MEAN YOU'VE QUIT NURSERY SCHOOL ALTOGETHER?
ABSOLUTELY! IT WAS JUST A RACKET!
I WENT THERE FOR OVER SIX WEEKS...TODAY I FOUND OUT IT WAS JUST A RACKET...
THEY DON'T TEACH YOU HOW TO BE A NURSE!
2-28
SCHULZ

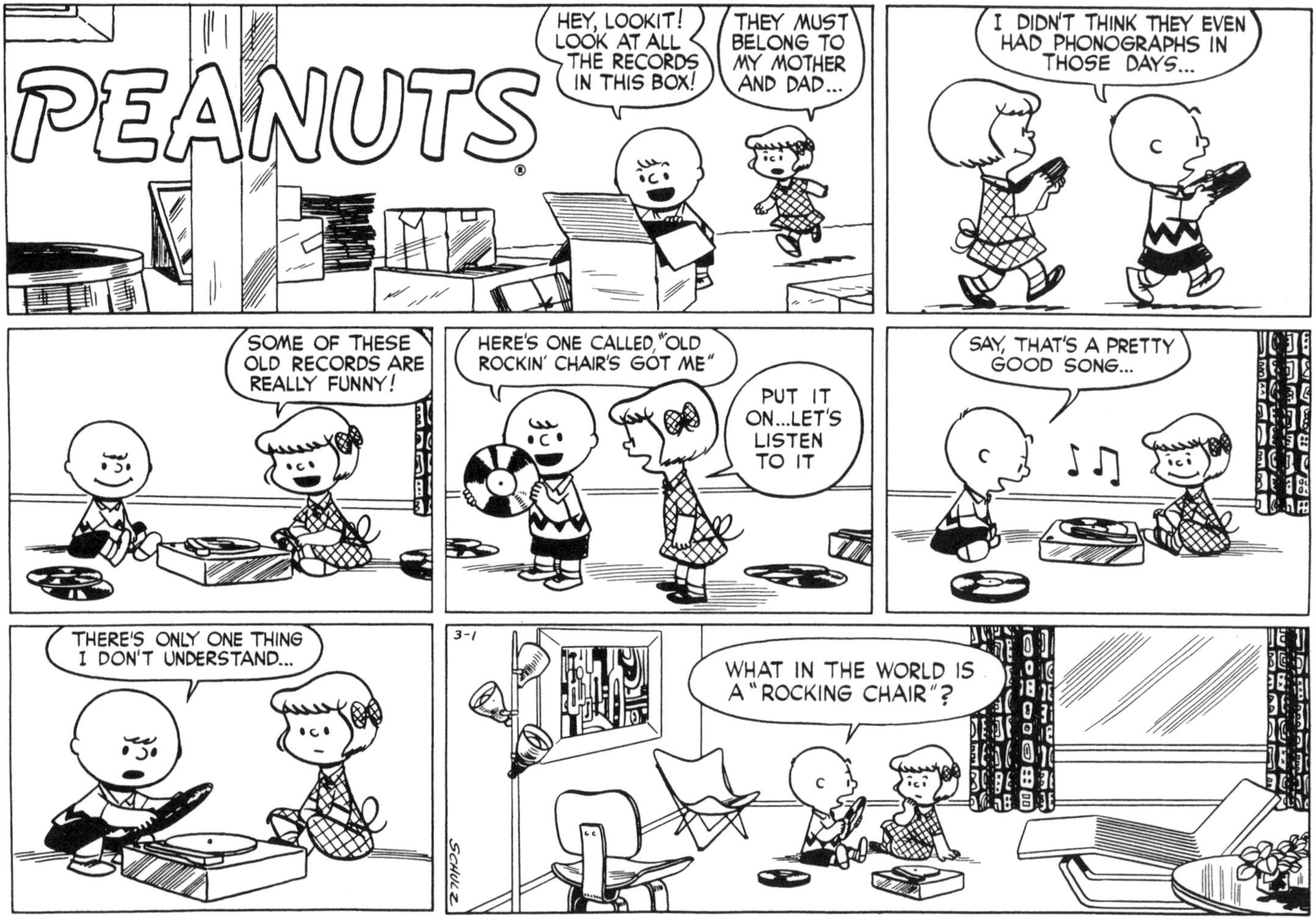
PEANUTS
HEY, LOOKIT! LOOK AT ALL THE RECORDS IN THIS BOX!
THEY MUST BELONG TO MY MOTHER AND DAD...
I DIDN'T THINK THEY EVEN HAD PHONOGRAPHS IN THOSE DAYS...
SOME OF THESE OLD RECORDS ARE REALLY FUNNY!
HERE'S ONE CALLED, "OLD ROCKIN' CHAIR'S GOT ME"
PUT IT ON...LET'S LISTEN TO IT
SAY, THAT'S A PRETTY GOOD SONG...
THERE'S ONLY ONE THING I DON'T UNDERSTAND...
3-1
WHAT IN THE WORLD IS A "ROCKING CHAIR"?
SCHULZ

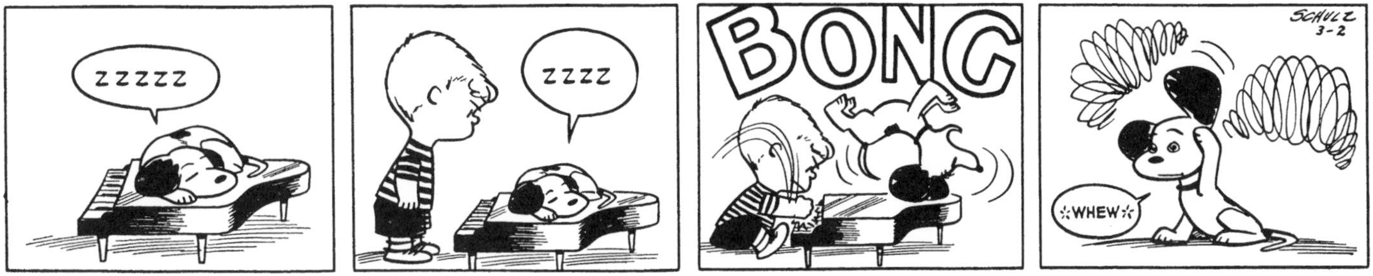

ZZZZZ
ZZZZ
BONG
SCHULZ 3-2
WHEW

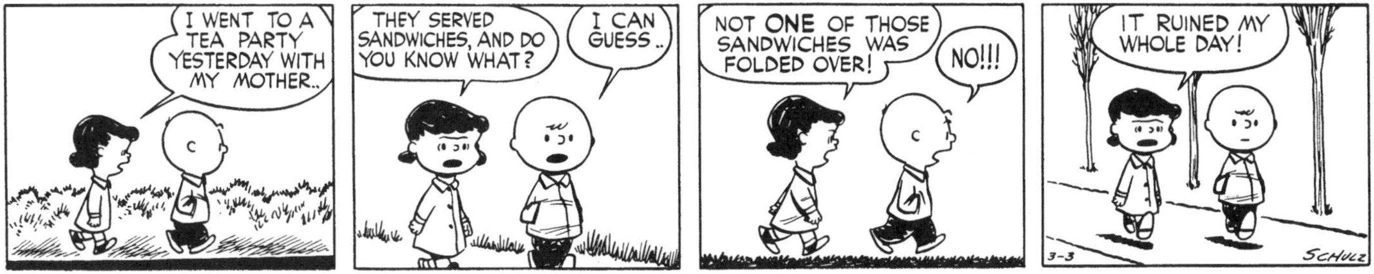

I WENT TO A TEA PARTY YESTERDAY WITH MY MOTHER..
THEY SERVED SANDWICHES, AND DO YOU KNOW WHAT?
I CAN GUESS..
NOT ONE OF THOSE SANDWICHES WAS FOLDED OVER!
NO!!!
IT RUINED MY WHOLE DAY!
3-3
SCHULZ

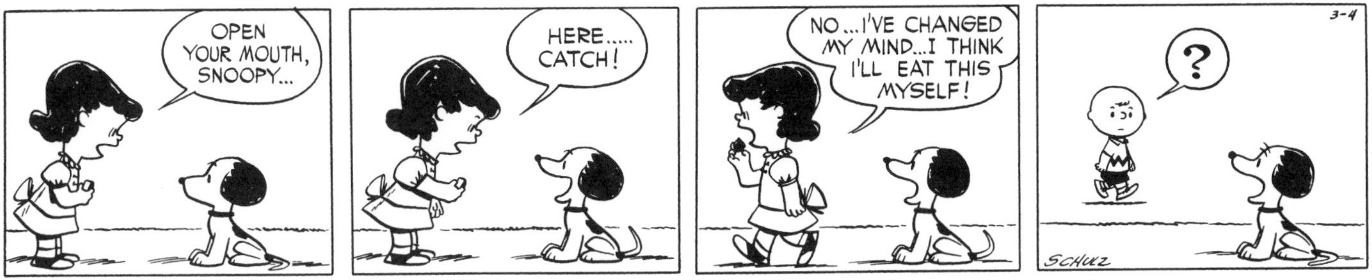

OPEN YOUR MOUTH, SNOOPY...
HERE..... CATCH!
NO...I'VE CHANGED MY MIND...I THINK I'LL EAT THIS MYSELF!
3-4
?
SCHULZ

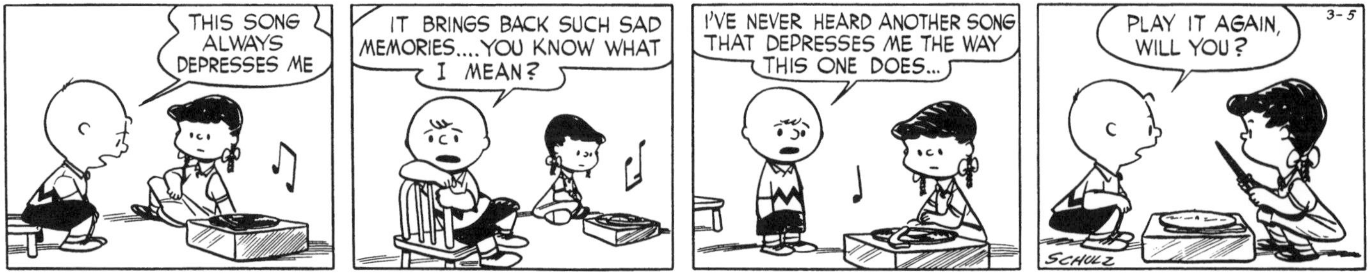
THIS SONG ALWAYS DEPRESSES ME
IT BRINGS BACK SUCH SAD MEMORIES....YOU KNOW WHAT I MEAN?
I'VE NEVER HEARD ANOTHER SONG THAT DEPRESSES ME THE WAY THIS ONE DOES...
PLAY IT AGAIN, WILL YOU?
3-5
SCHULZ

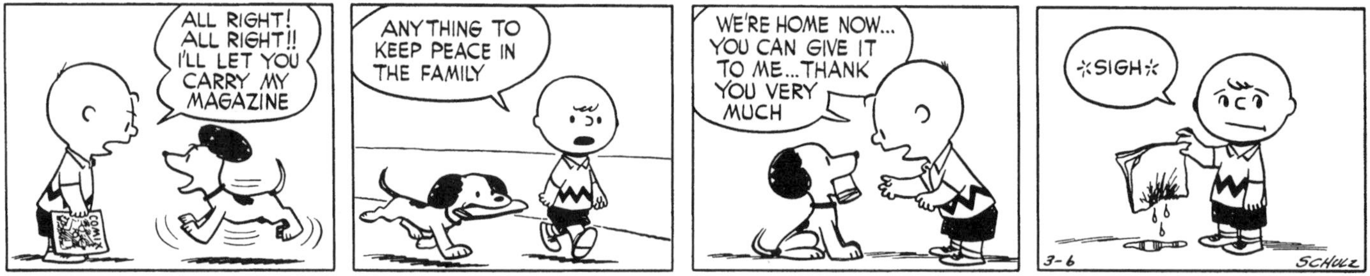
ALL RIGHT! ALL RIGHT!! I'LL LET YOU CARRY MY MAGAZINE
COMIX
ANYTHING TO KEEP PEACE IN THE FAMILY
WE'RE HOME NOW... YOU CAN GIVE IT TO ME...THANK YOU VERY MUCH
SIGH
3-6
SCHULZ

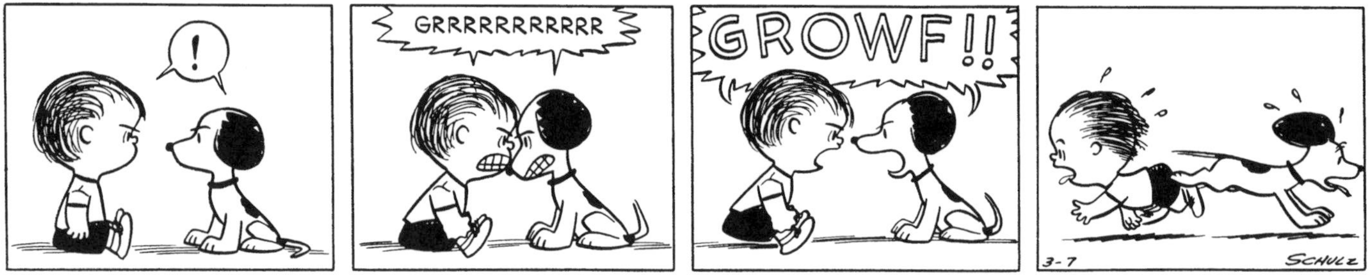
!
GRRRRRRRRRRR
GROWF!!
3-7
SCHULZ

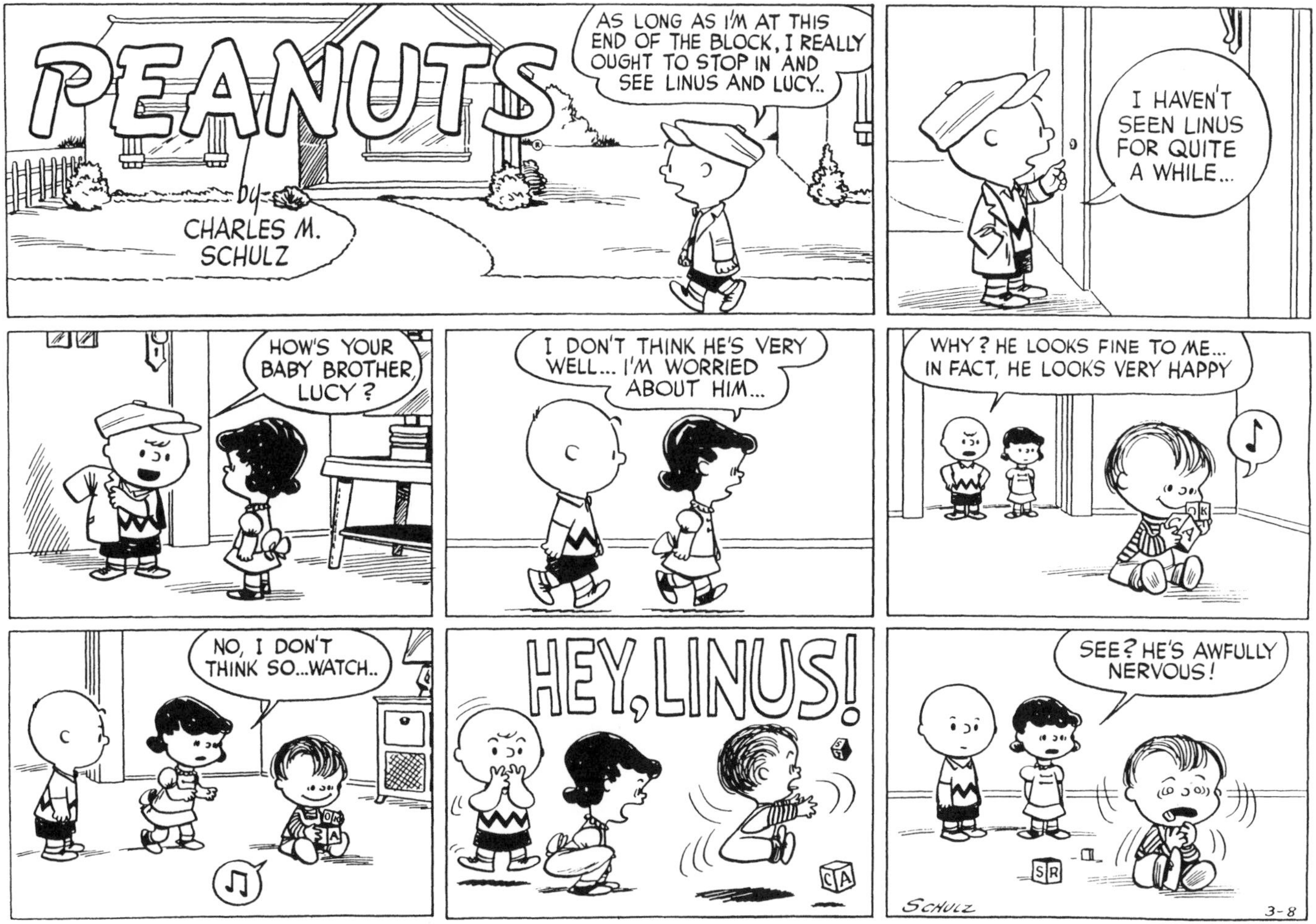
PEANUTS
by CHARLES M. SCHULZ
AS LONG AS I'M AT THIS END OF THE BLOCK, I REALLY OUGHT TO STOP IN AND SEE LINUS AND LUCY..
I HAVEN'T SEEN LINUS FOR QUITE A WHILE...
HOW'S YOUR BABY BROTHER, LUCY ?
I DON'T THINK HE'S VERY WELL... I'M WORRIED ABOUT HIM...
WHY ? HE LOOKS FINE TO ME... IN FACT, HE LOOKS VERY HAPPY
NO, I DON'T THINK SO...WATCH..
HEY, LINUS!
SEE? HE'S AWFULLY NERVOUS!
SCHULZ
3-8

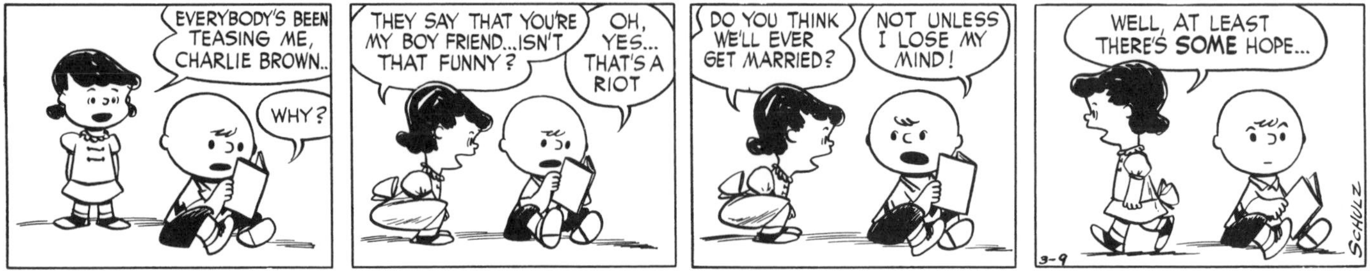
EVERYBODY'S BEEN TEASING ME, CHARLIE BROWN..
WHY?
THEY SAY THAT YOU'RE MY BOY FRIEND...ISN'T THAT FUNNY?
OH, YES... THAT'S A RIOT
DO YOU THINK WE'LL EVER GET MARRIED?
NOT UNLESS I LOSE MY MIND!
WELL, AT LEAST THERE'S SOME HOPE...
3-9
SCHULZ

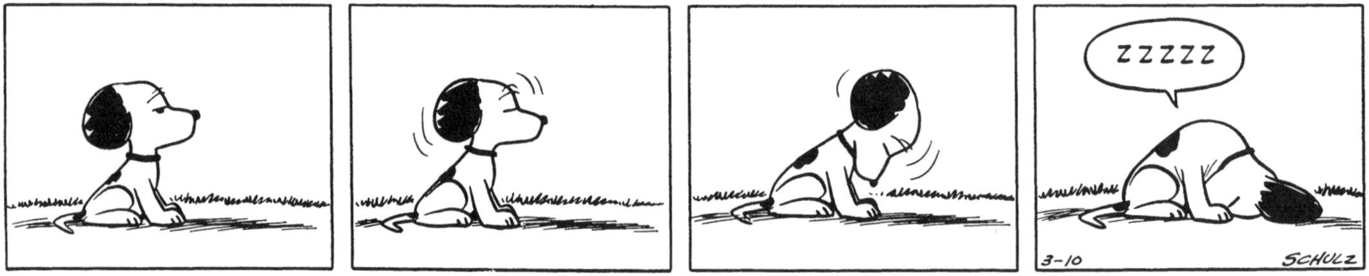
ZZZZZ
3-10
SCHULZ

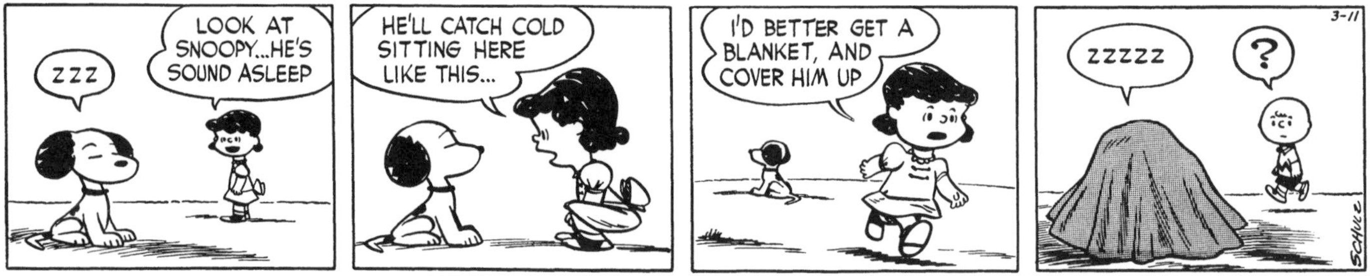
ZZZ
LOOK AT SNOOPY...HE'S SOUND ASLEEP
HE'LL CATCH COLD SITTING HERE LIKE THIS...
I'D BETTER GET A BLANKET, AND COVER HIM UP
3-11
ZZZZZ
?
SCHULZ

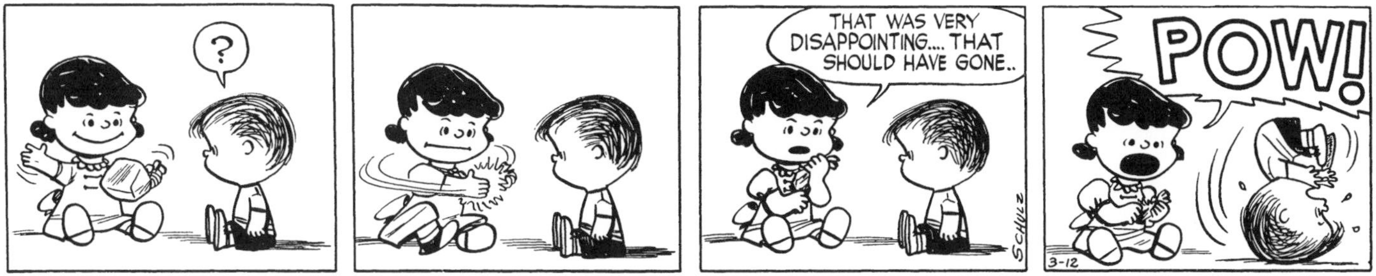
?
THAT WAS VERY DISAPPOINTING.... THAT SHOULD HAVE GONE..
POW!
SCHULZ
3-12

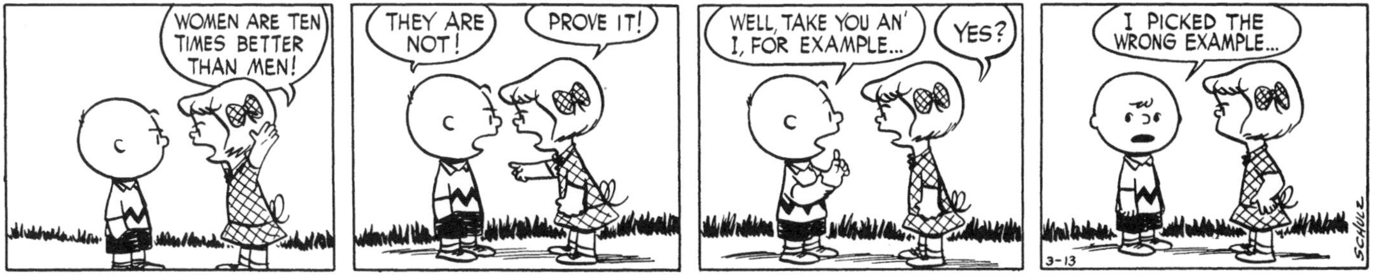
WOMEN ARE TEN TIMES BETTER THAN MEN!
THEY ARE NOT!
PROVE IT!
WELL, TAKE YOU AN' I, FOR EXAMPLE...
YES?
I PICKED THE WRONG EXAMPLE...
3-13
SCHULZ

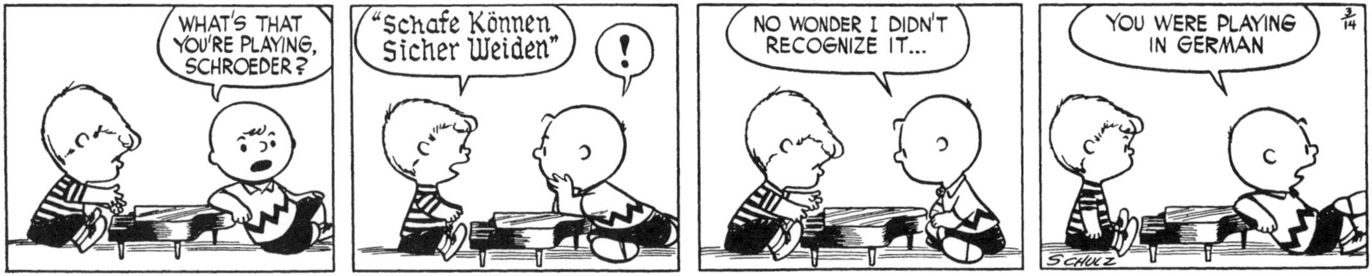
WHAT'S THAT YOU'RE PLAYING, SCHROEDER?
"Schafe Können Sicher Weiden"
!
NO WONDER I DIDN'T RECOGNIZE IT...
YOU WERE PLAYING IN GERMAN
3/14
SCHULZ

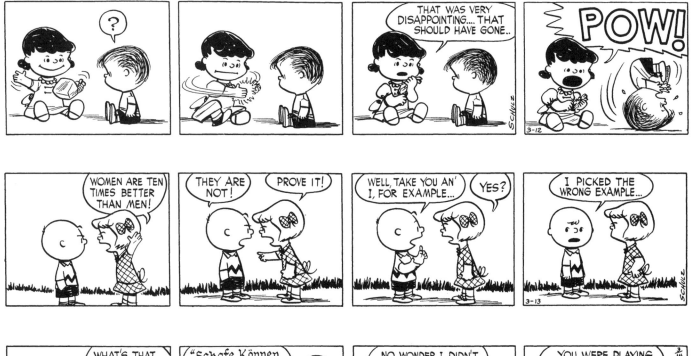

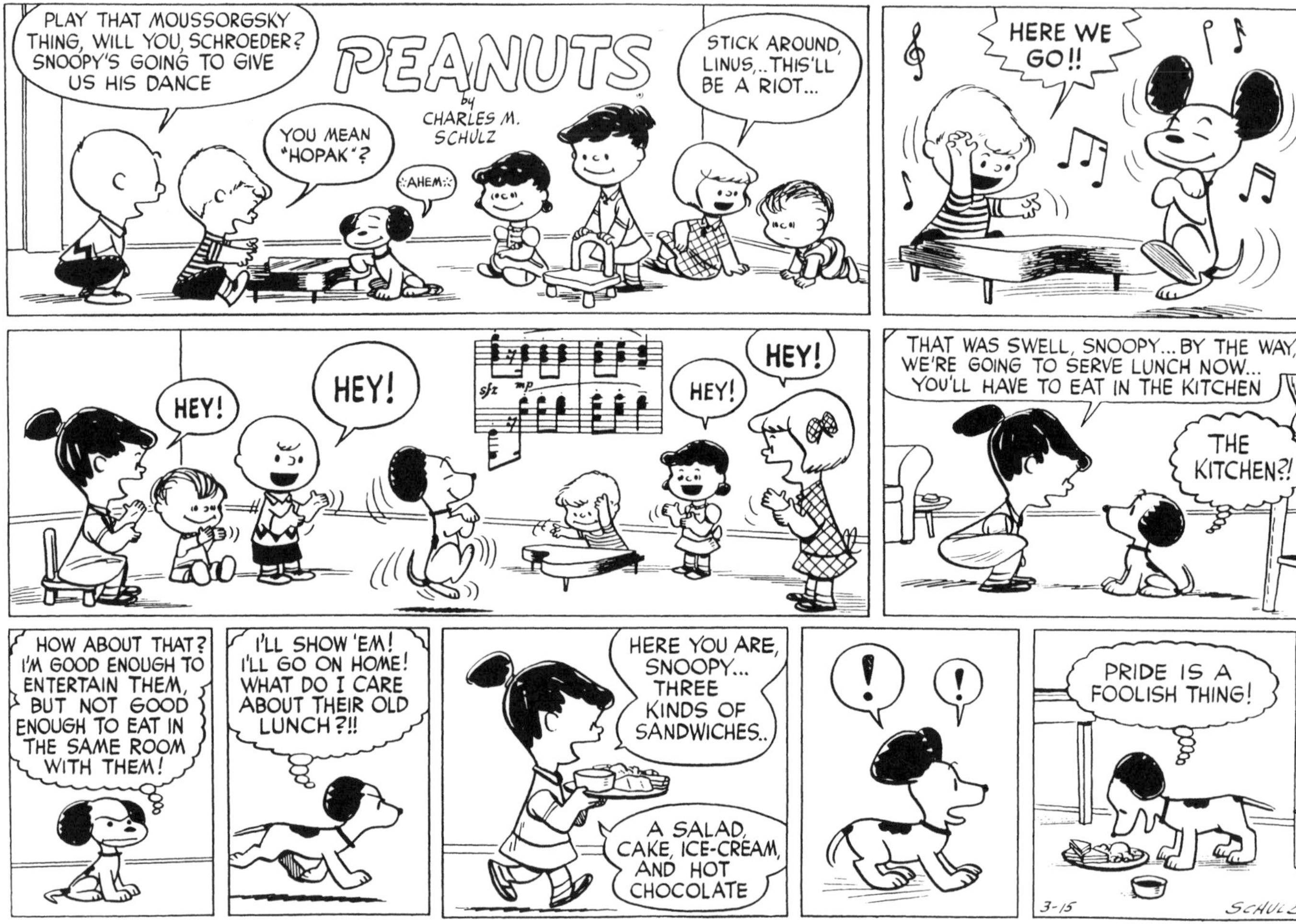
PLAY THAT MOUSSORGSKY THING, WILL YOU, SCHROEDER? SNOOPY'S GOING TO GIVE US HIS DANCE
PEANUTS
by CHARLES M. SCHULZ
YOU MEAN "HOPAK"?
AHEM
STICK AROUND, LINUS,..THIS'LL BE A RIOT...
HERE WE GO!!
HEY!
HEY!
HEY!
HEY!
THAT WAS SWELL, SNOOPY... BY THE WAY, WE'RE GOING TO SERVE LUNCH NOW... YOU'LL HAVE TO EAT IN THE KITCHEN
THE KITCHEN?!
HOW ABOUT THAT? I'M GOOD ENOUGH TO ENTERTAIN THEM, BUT NOT GOOD ENOUGH TO EAT IN THE SAME ROOM WITH THEM!
I'LL SHOW 'EM! I'LL GO ON HOME! WHAT DO I CARE ABOUT THEIR OLD LUNCH?!!
HERE YOU ARE, SNOOPY... THREE KINDS OF SANDWICHES..
A SALAD, CAKE, ICE-CREAM, AND HOT CHOCOLATE
!
!
PRIDE IS A FOOLISH THING!
3-15
SCHULZ

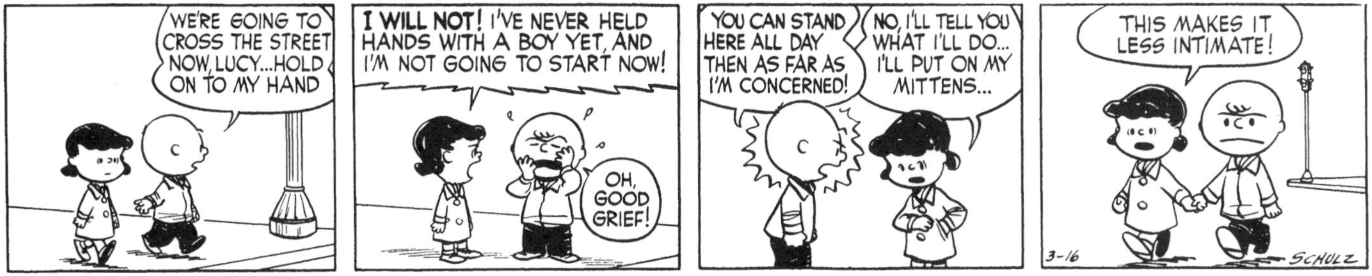
WE'RE GOING TO CROSS THE STREET NOW, LUCY...HOLD ON TO MY HAND
I WILL NOT! I'VE NEVER HELD HANDS WITH A BOY YET, AND I'M NOT GOING TO START NOW!
OH, GOOD GRIEF!
YOU CAN STAND HERE ALL DAY THEN AS FAR AS I'M CONCERNED!
NO, I'LL TELL YOU WHAT I'LL DO... I'LL PUT ON MY MITTENS...
THIS MAKES IT LESS INTIMATE!
3-16
SCHULZ

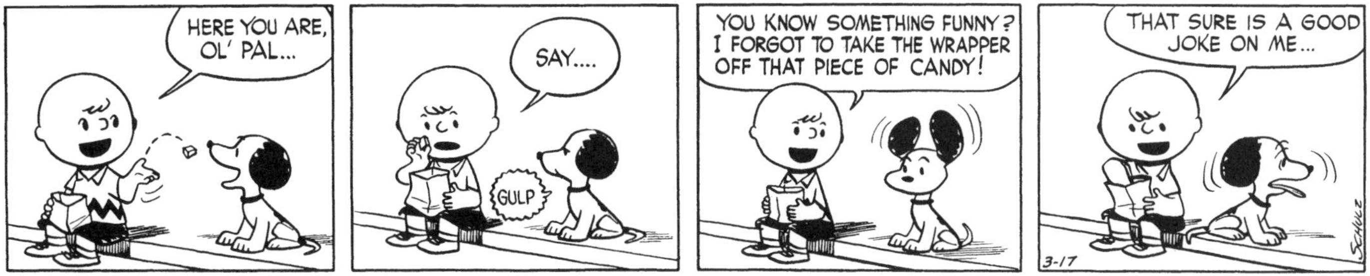
HERE YOU ARE, OL' PAL...
SAY....
GULP
YOU KNOW SOMETHING FUNNY? I FORGOT TO TAKE THE WRAPPER OFF THAT PIECE OF CANDY!
THAT SURE IS A GOOD JOKE ON ME...
3-17
SCHULZ

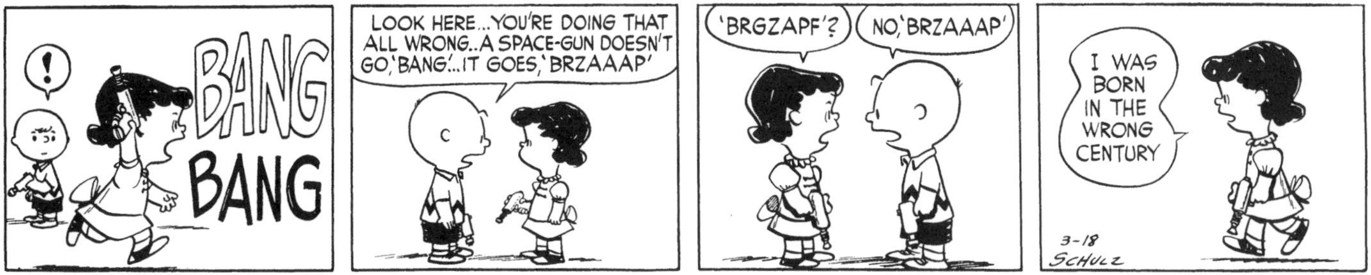
!
BANG
BANG
LOOK HERE...YOU'RE DOING THAT ALL WRONG..A SPACE-GUN DOESN'T GO,'BANG'...IT GOES,'BRZAAAP'
'BRGZAPF'?
NO,'BRZAAAP'
I WAS BORN IN THE WRONG CENTURY
3-18
SCHULZ

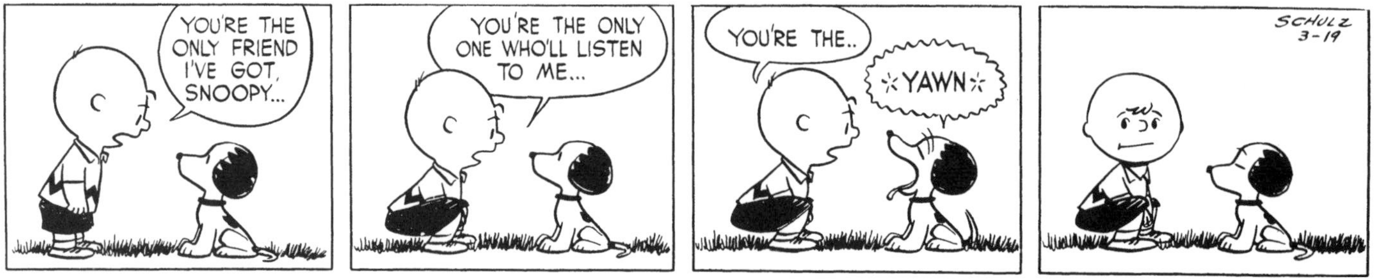
YOU'RE THE ONLY FRIEND I'VE GOT, SNOOPY...
YOU'RE THE ONLY ONE WHO'LL LISTEN TO ME...
YOU'RE THE..
YAWN
SCHULZ 3-19

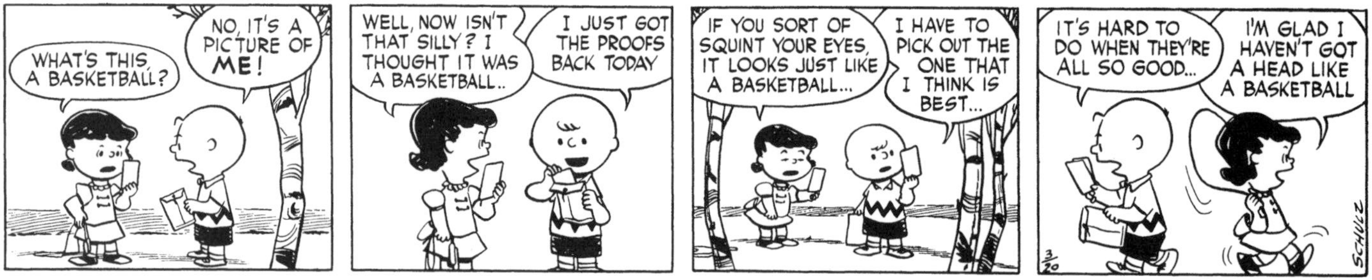
WHAT'S THIS, A BASKETBALL?
NO, IT'S A PICTURE OF ME!
WELL, NOW ISN'T THAT SILLY? I THOUGHT IT WAS A BASKETBALL..
I JUST GOT THE PROOFS BACK TODAY
IF YOU SORT OF SQUINT YOUR EYES, IT LOOKS JUST LIKE A BASKETBALL...
I HAVE TO PICK OUT THE ONE THAT I THINK IS BEST...
IT'S HARD TO DO WHEN THEY'RE ALL SO GOOD...
I'M GLAD I HAVEN'T GOT A HEAD LIKE A BASKETBALL
3/20
SCHULZ

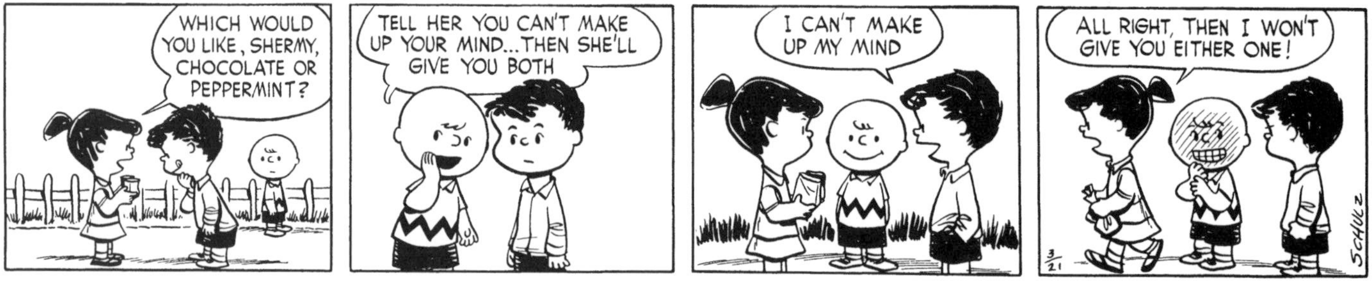
WHICH WOULD YOU LIKE, SHERMY, CHOCOLATE OR PEPPERMINT?
TELL HER YOU CAN'T MAKE UP YOUR MIND...THEN SHE'LL GIVE YOU BOTH
I CAN'T MAKE UP MY MIND
ALL RIGHT, THEN I WON'T GIVE YOU EITHER ONE!
3/21
SCHULZ

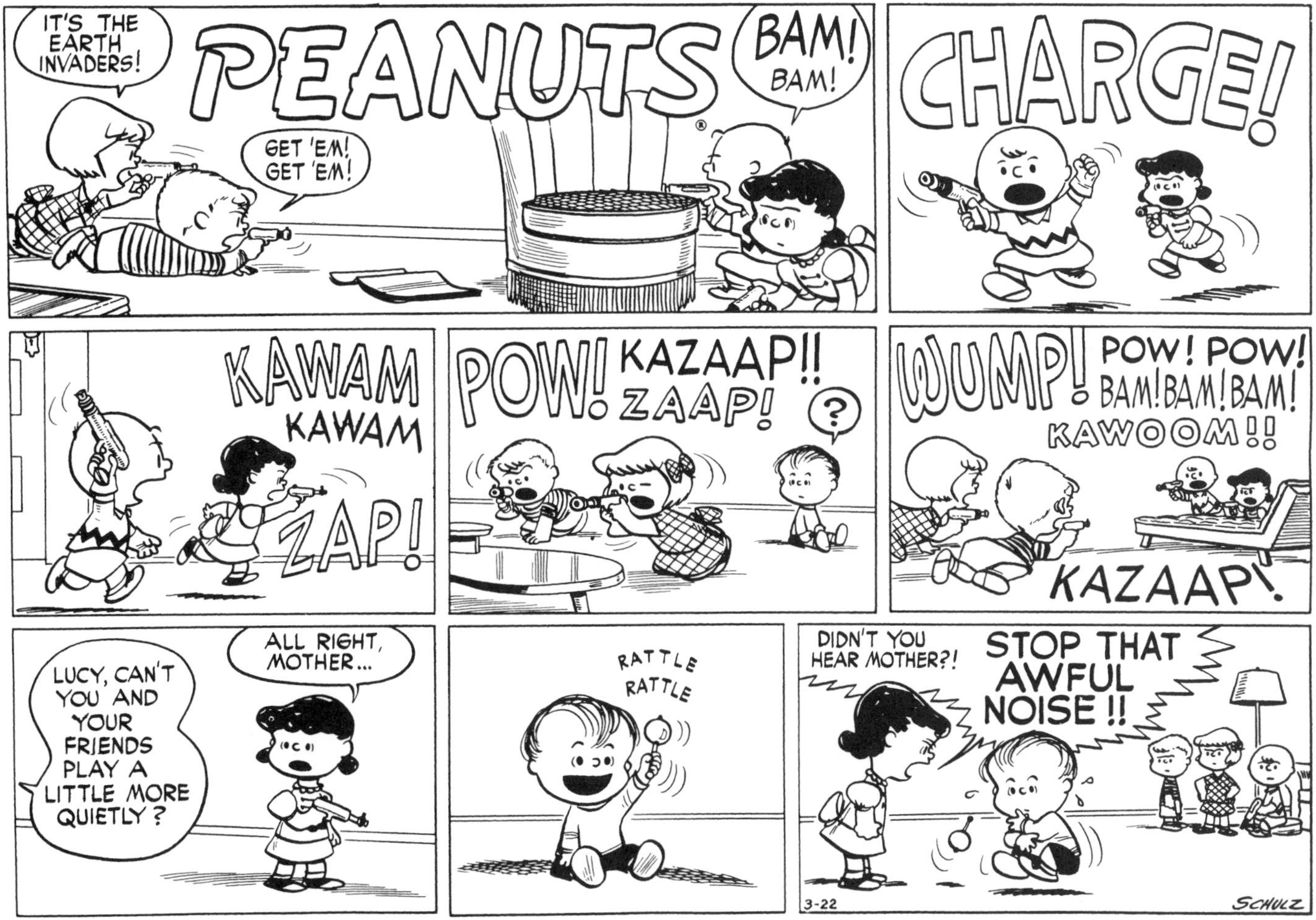
IT'S THE EARTH INVADERS!
PEANUTS
GET 'EM! GET 'EM!
BAM! BAM!
CHARGE!
KAWAM
KAWAM
ZAP!
POW!
KAZAAP!!
ZAAP!
?
WUMP!
POW! POW!
BAM! BAM! BAM!
KAWOOM!!
KAZAAP!
LUCY, CAN'T YOU AND YOUR FRIENDS PLAY A LITTLE MORE QUIETLY?
ALL RIGHT, MOTHER...
RATTLE
RATTLE
DIDN'T YOU HEAR MOTHER?!
STOP THAT AWFUL NOISE!!
3-22
SCHULZ

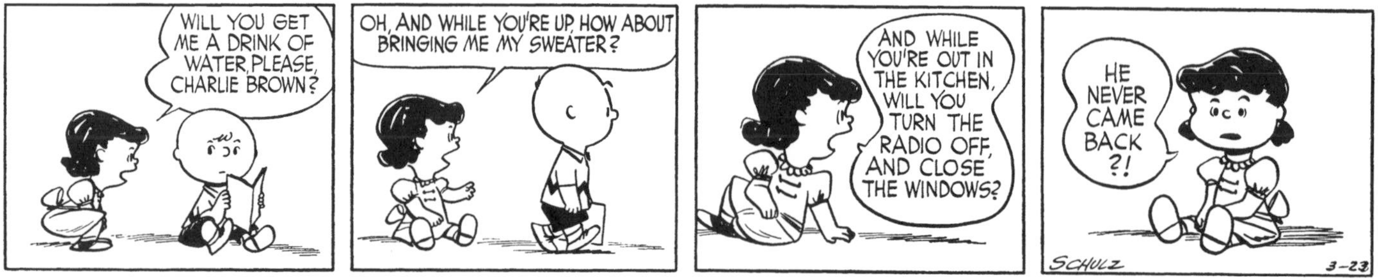
WILL YOU GET ME A DRINK OF WATER, PLEASE, CHARLIE BROWN?
OH, AND WHILE YOU'RE UP, HOW ABOUT BRINGING ME MY SWEATER?
AND WHILE YOU'RE OUT IN THE KITCHEN, WILL YOU TURN THE RADIO OFF, AND CLOSE THE WINDOWS?
HE NEVER CAME BACK ?!
SCHULZ
3-23

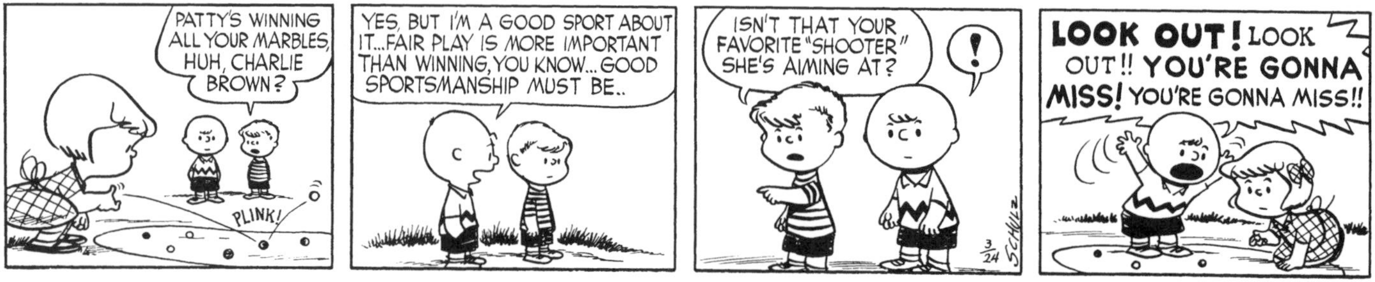
PATTY'S WINNING ALL YOUR MARBLES, HUH, CHARLIE BROWN?
PLINK!
YES, BUT I'M A GOOD SPORT ABOUT IT...FAIR PLAY IS MORE IMPORTANT THAN WINNING, YOU KNOW... GOOD SPORTSMANSHIP MUST BE..
ISN'T THAT YOUR FAVORITE "SHOOTER" SHE'S AIMING AT?
!
3/24
SCHULZ
LOOK OUT! LOOK OUT!! YOU'RE GONNA MISS! YOU'RE GONNA MISS!!

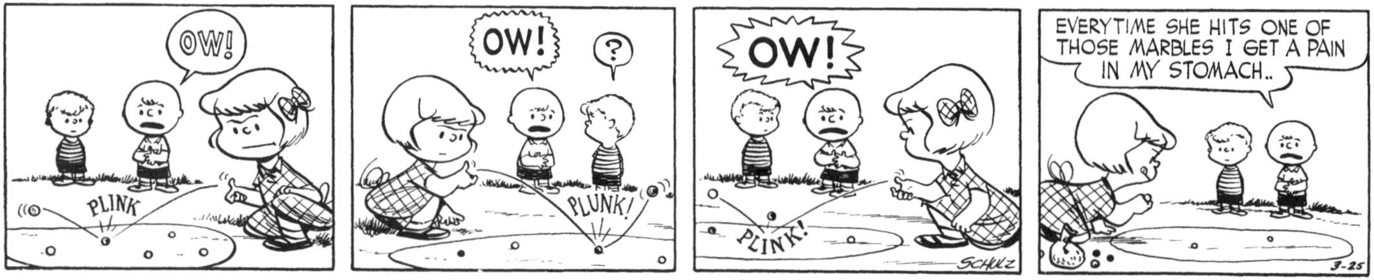
OW!
PLINK
OW!
?
PLUNK!
OW!
PLINK!
SCHULZ
EVERYTIME SHE HITS ONE OF THOSE MARBLES I GET A PAIN IN MY STOMACH..
3-25

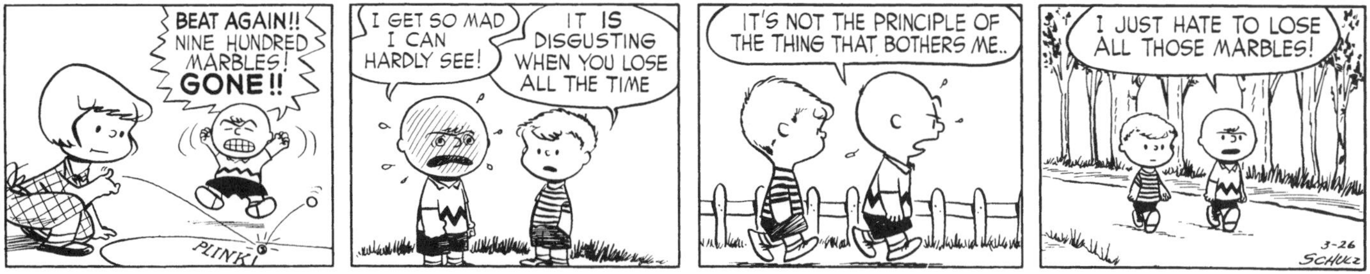
BEAT AGAIN!! NINE HUNDRED MARBLES! GONE!!
PLINK!
I GET SO MAD I CAN HARDLY SEE!
IT IS DISGUSTING WHEN YOU LOSE ALL THE TIME
IT'S NOT THE PRINCIPLE OF THE THING THAT BOTHERS ME..
I JUST HATE TO LOSE ALL THOSE MARBLES!
3-26
SCHULZ

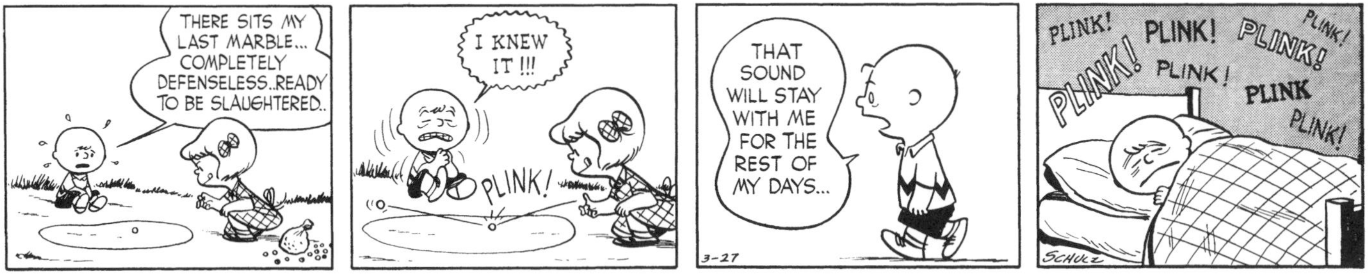
THERE SITS MY LAST MARBLE... COMPLETELY DEFENSELESS..READY TO BE SLAUGHTERED..
I KNEW IT !!!
PLINK!
THAT SOUND WILL STAY WITH ME FOR THE REST OF MY DAYS...
3-27
PLINK! PLINK! PLINK! PLINK! PLINK! PLINK! PLINK PLINK!
SCHULZ

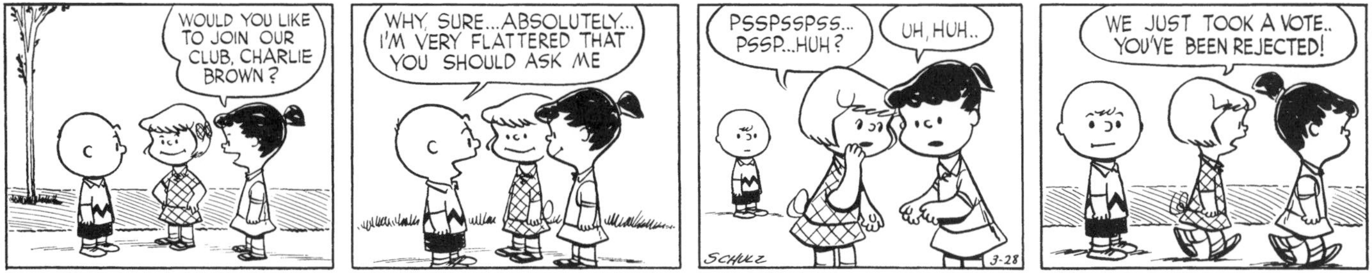
WOULD YOU LIKE TO JOIN OUR CLUB, CHARLIE BROWN?
WHY, SURE...ABSOLUTELY... I'M VERY FLATTERED THAT YOU SHOULD ASK ME
PSSPSSPSS... PSSP...HUH?
UH, HUH..
SCHULZ
3-28
WE JUST TOOK A VOTE.. YOU'VE BEEN REJECTED!

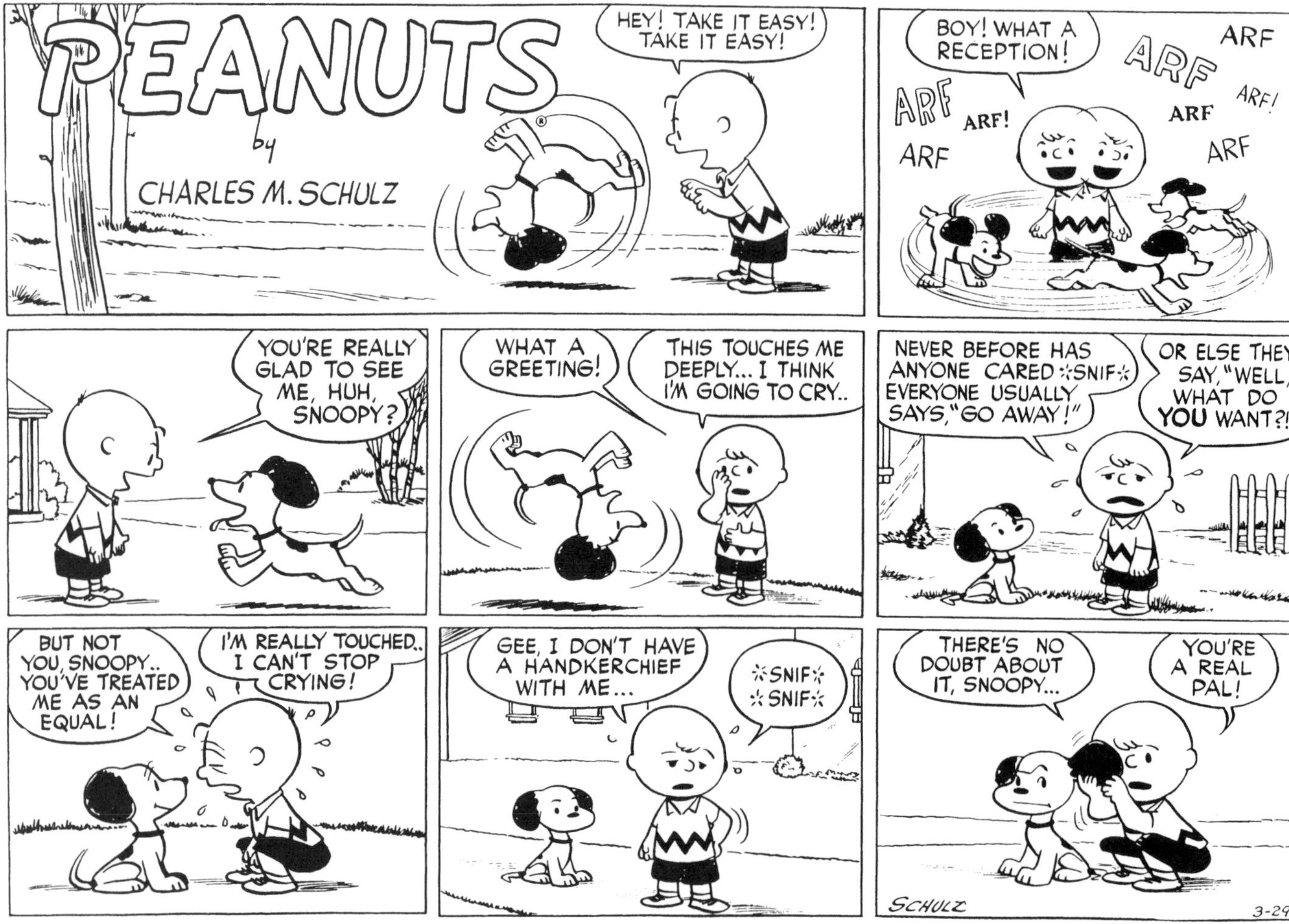
PEANUTS
by
CHARLES M. SCHULZ
HEY! TAKE IT EASY! TAKE IT EASY!
BOY! WHAT A RECEPTION!
ARF ARF ARF ARF! ARF! ARF ARF ARF
YOU'RE REALLY GLAD TO SEE ME, HUH, SNOOPY?
WHAT A GREETING!
THIS TOUCHES ME DEEPLY... I THINK I'M GOING TO CRY..
NEVER BEFORE HAS ANYONE CARED *SNIF* EVERYONE USUALLY SAYS, "GO AWAY!"
OR ELSE THEY SAY, "WELL, WHAT DO **YOU** WANT?!"
BUT NOT YOU, SNOOPY.. YOU'VE TREATED ME AS AN EQUAL!
I'M REALLY TOUCHED.. I CAN'T STOP CRYING!
GEE, I DON'T HAVE A HANDKERCHIEF WITH ME...
SNIF *SNIF*
THERE'S NO DOUBT ABOUT IT, SNOOPY...
YOU'RE A REAL PAL!
SCHULZ
3-29

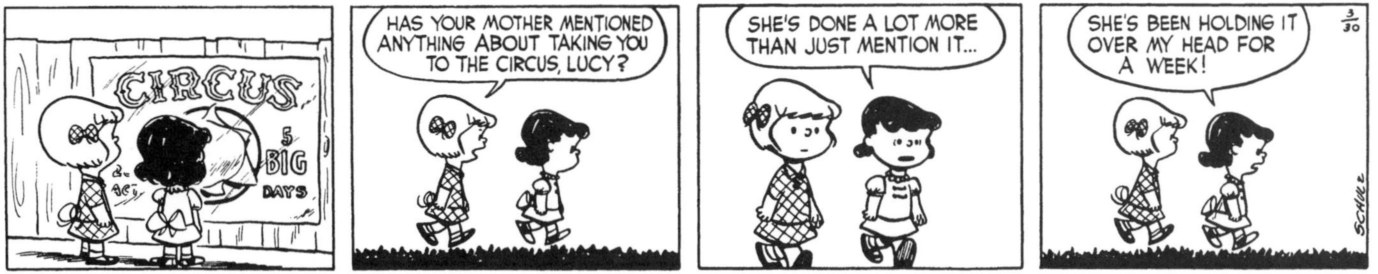
CIRCUS
5 BIG DAYS
HAS YOUR MOTHER MENTIONED ANYTHING ABOUT TAKING YOU TO THE CIRCUS, LUCY?
SHE'S DONE A LOT MORE THAN JUST MENTION IT...
SHE'S BEEN HOLDING IT OVER MY HEAD FOR A WEEK!
3/30
SCHULZ

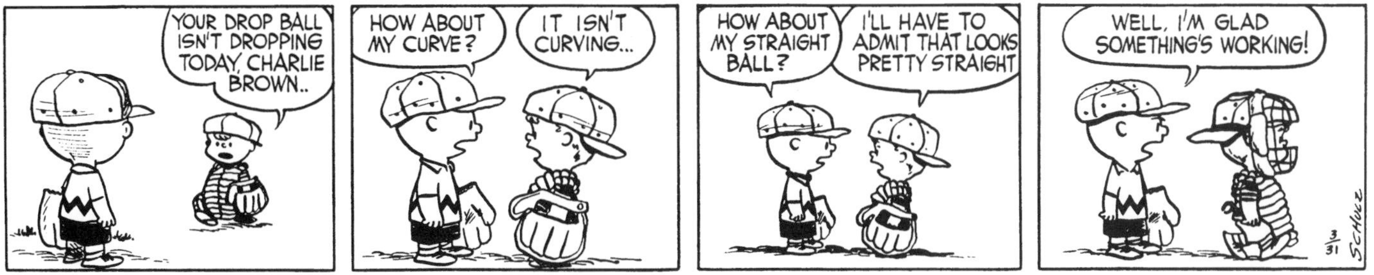
YOUR DROP BALL ISN'T DROPPING TODAY, CHARLIE BROWN..
HOW ABOUT MY CURVE?
IT ISN'T CURVING...
HOW ABOUT MY STRAIGHT BALL?
I'LL HAVE TO ADMIT THAT LOOKS PRETTY STRAIGHT
WELL, I'M GLAD SOMETHING'S WORKING!
3/31
SCHULZ

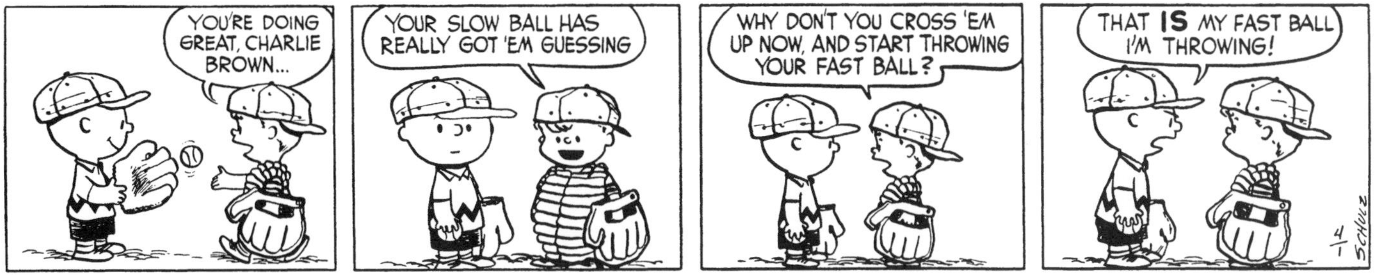
YOU'RE DOING GREAT, CHARLIE BROWN...
YOUR SLOW BALL HAS REALLY GOT 'EM GUESSING
WHY DON'T YOU CROSS 'EM UP NOW, AND START THROWING YOUR FAST BALL?
THAT IS MY FAST BALL I'M THROWING!
4/1
SCHULZ

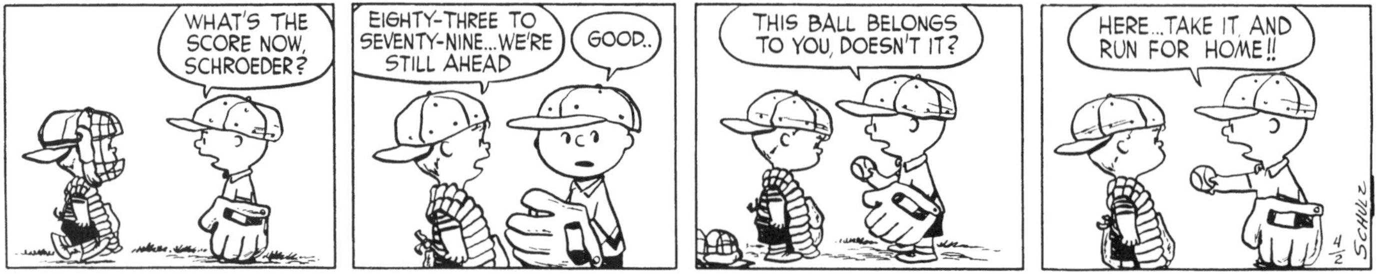
WHAT'S THE SCORE NOW, SCHROEDER?
EIGHTY-THREE TO SEVENTY-NINE...WE'RE STILL AHEAD
GOOD..
THIS BALL BELONGS TO YOU, DOESN'T IT?
HERE...TAKE IT, AND RUN FOR HOME!!
4/2
SCHULZ

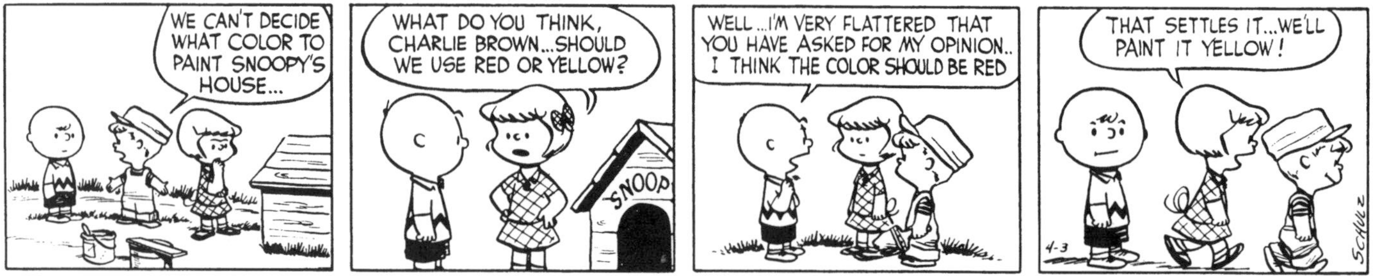
WE CAN'T DECIDE WHAT COLOR TO PAINT SNOOPY'S HOUSE...
WHAT DO YOU THINK, CHARLIE BROWN...SHOULD WE USE RED OR YELLOW?
SNOOP
WELL...I'M VERY FLATTERED THAT YOU HAVE ASKED FOR MY OPINION.. I THINK THE COLOR SHOULD BE RED
THAT SETTLES IT...WE'LL PAINT IT YELLOW!
4-3
SCHULZ

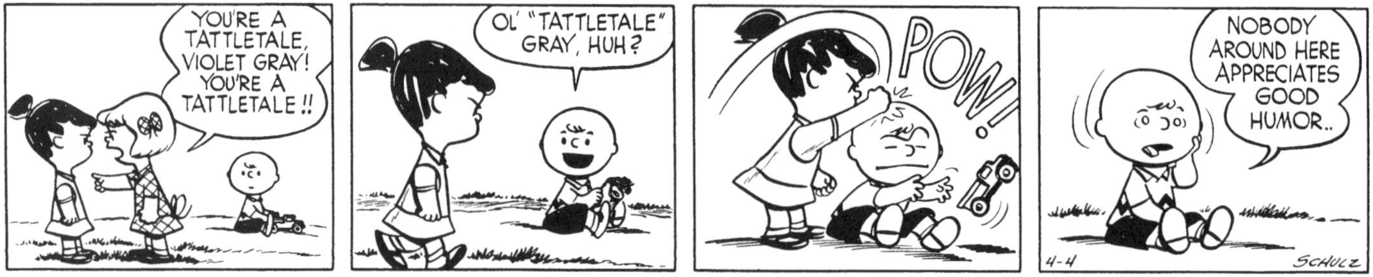
YOU'RE A TATTLETALE, VIOLET GRAY! YOU'RE A TATTLETALE!!
OL' "TATTLETALE" GRAY, HUH?
POW!
NOBODY AROUND HERE APPRECIATES GOOD HUMOR..
4-4
SCHULZ

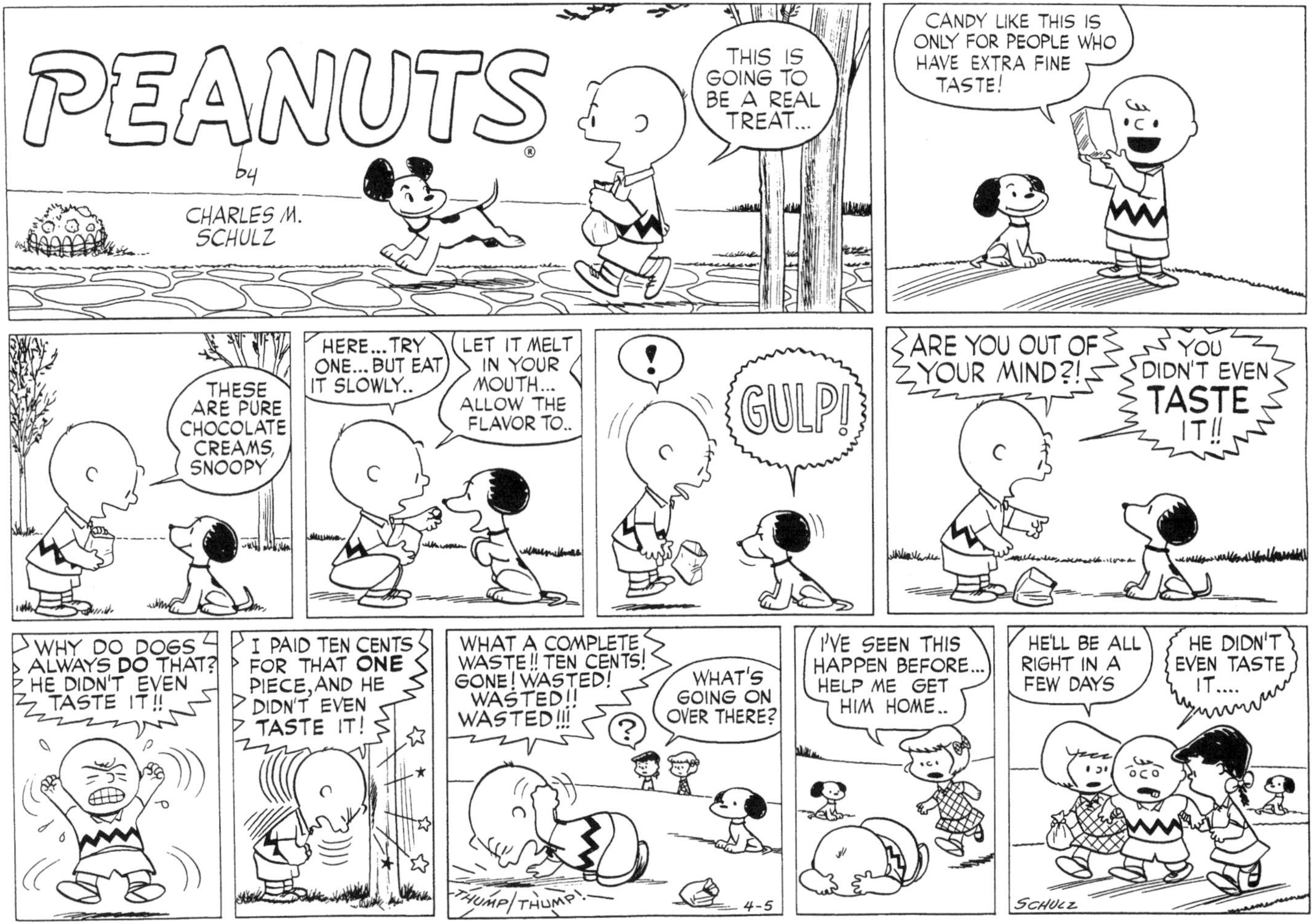
PEANUTS
by CHARLES M. SCHULZ
THIS IS GOING TO BE A REAL TREAT...
CANDY LIKE THIS IS ONLY FOR PEOPLE WHO HAVE EXTRA FINE TASTE!
THESE ARE PURE CHOCOLATE CREAMS, SNOOPY
HERE...TRY ONE...BUT EAT IT SLOWLY..
LET IT MELT IN YOUR MOUTH... ALLOW THE FLAVOR TO..
!
GULP!
ARE YOU OUT OF YOUR MIND?!
YOU DIDN'T EVEN TASTE IT!!
WHY DO DOGS ALWAYS DO THAT? HE DIDN'T EVEN TASTE IT!!
I PAID TEN CENTS FOR THAT ONE PIECE, AND HE DIDN'T EVEN TASTE IT!
WHAT A COMPLETE WASTE!! TEN CENTS! GONE! WASTED! WASTED!! WASTED!!!
?
WHAT'S GOING ON OVER THERE?
THUMP! THUMP!
4-5
I'VE SEEN THIS HAPPEN BEFORE... HELP ME GET HIM HOME..
HE'LL BE ALL RIGHT IN A FEW DAYS
HE DIDN'T EVEN TASTE IT....
SCHULZ

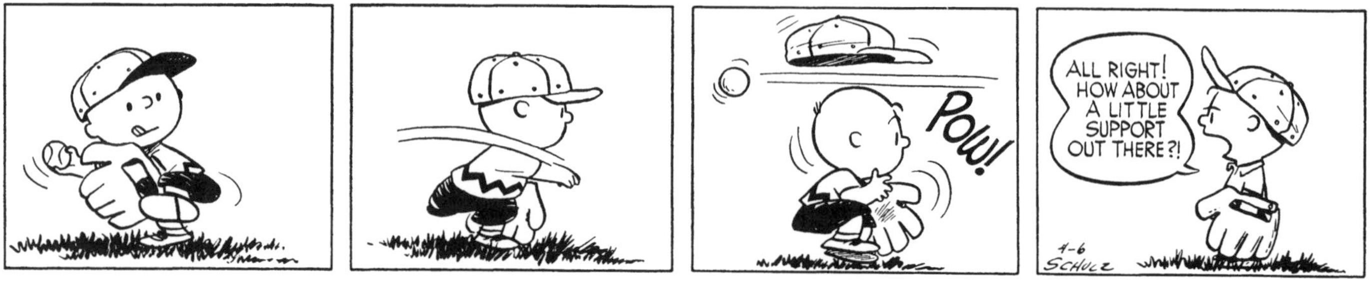
POW!
ALL RIGHT! HOW ABOUT A LITTLE SUPPORT OUT THERE?!
4-6
SCHULZ

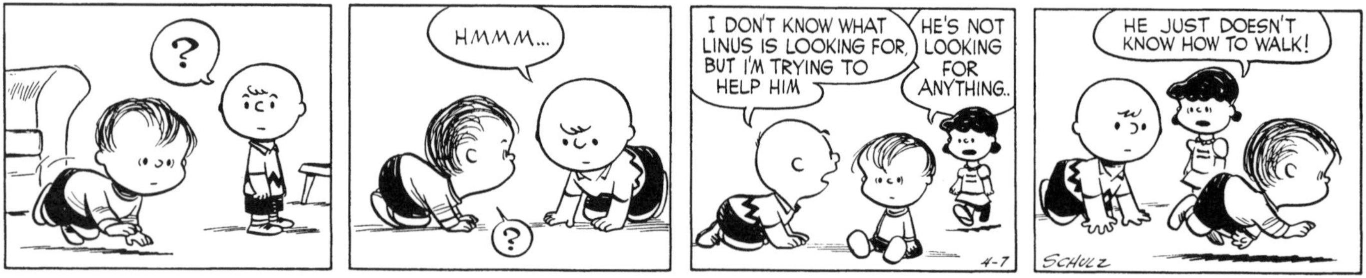
?
HMMM...
?
I DON'T KNOW WHAT LINUS IS LOOKING FOR, BUT I'M TRYING TO HELP HIM
HE'S NOT LOOKING FOR ANYTHING..
4-7
HE JUST DOESN'T KNOW HOW TO WALK!
SCHULZ

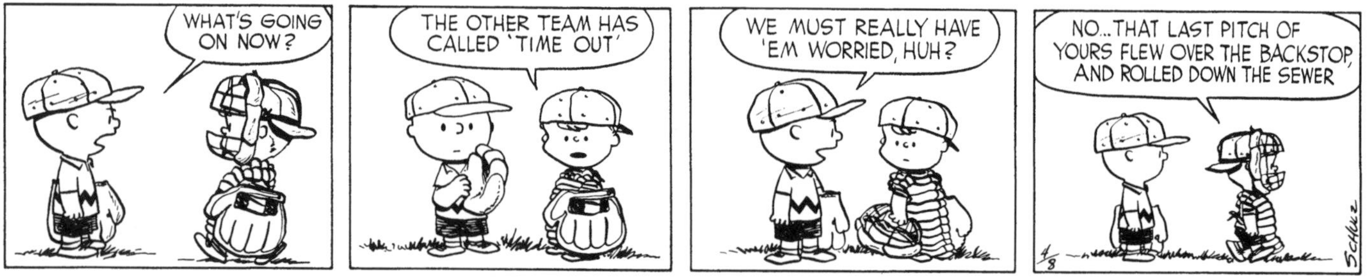
WHAT'S GOING ON NOW?
THE OTHER TEAM HAS CALLED 'TIME OUT'
WE MUST REALLY HAVE 'EM WORRIED, HUH?
NO...THAT LAST PITCH OF YOURS FLEW OVER THE BACKSTOP, AND ROLLED DOWN THE SEWER
4/8
SCHULZ

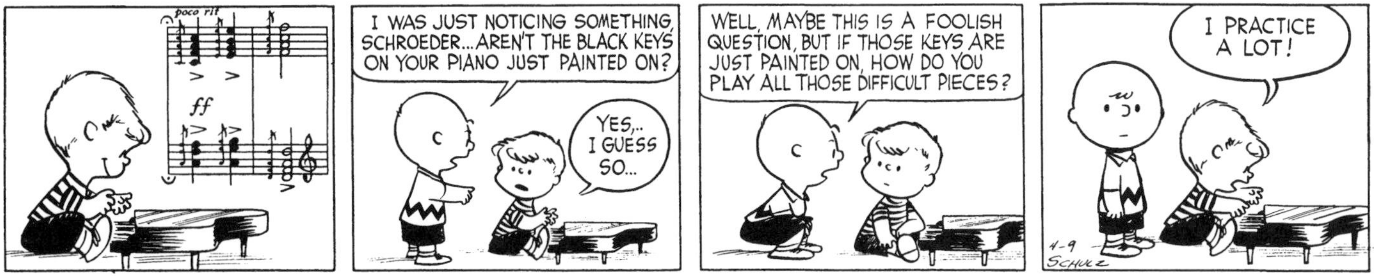
poco rit
ff
I WAS JUST NOTICING SOMETHING, SCHROEDER...AREN'T THE BLACK KEYS ON YOUR PIANO JUST PAINTED ON?
YES,.. I GUESS SO...
WELL, MAYBE THIS IS A FOOLISH QUESTION, BUT IF THOSE KEYS ARE JUST PAINTED ON, HOW DO YOU PLAY ALL THOSE DIFFICULT PIECES?
I PRACTICE A LOT!
4-9
SCHULZ

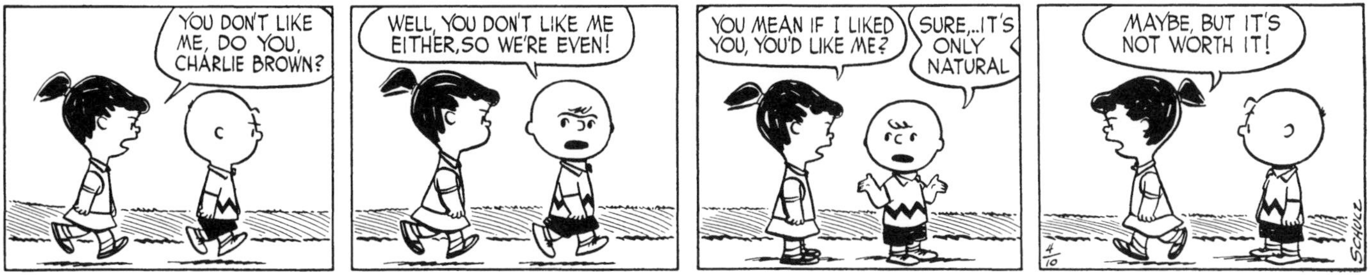
YOU DON'T LIKE ME, DO YOU, CHARLIE BROWN?
WELL, YOU DON'T LIKE ME EITHER, SO WE'RE EVEN!
YOU MEAN IF I LIKED YOU, YOU'D LIKE ME?
SURE,..IT'S ONLY NATURAL
MAYBE, BUT IT'S NOT WORTH IT!
4/10
SCHULZ

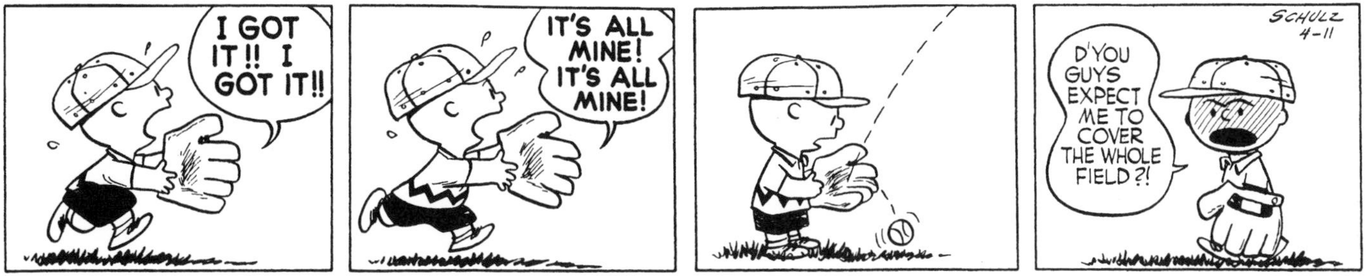
I GOT IT!! I GOT IT!!
IT'S ALL MINE! IT'S ALL MINE!
SCHULZ
4-11
D'YOU GUYS EXPECT ME TO COVER THE WHOLE FIELD?!

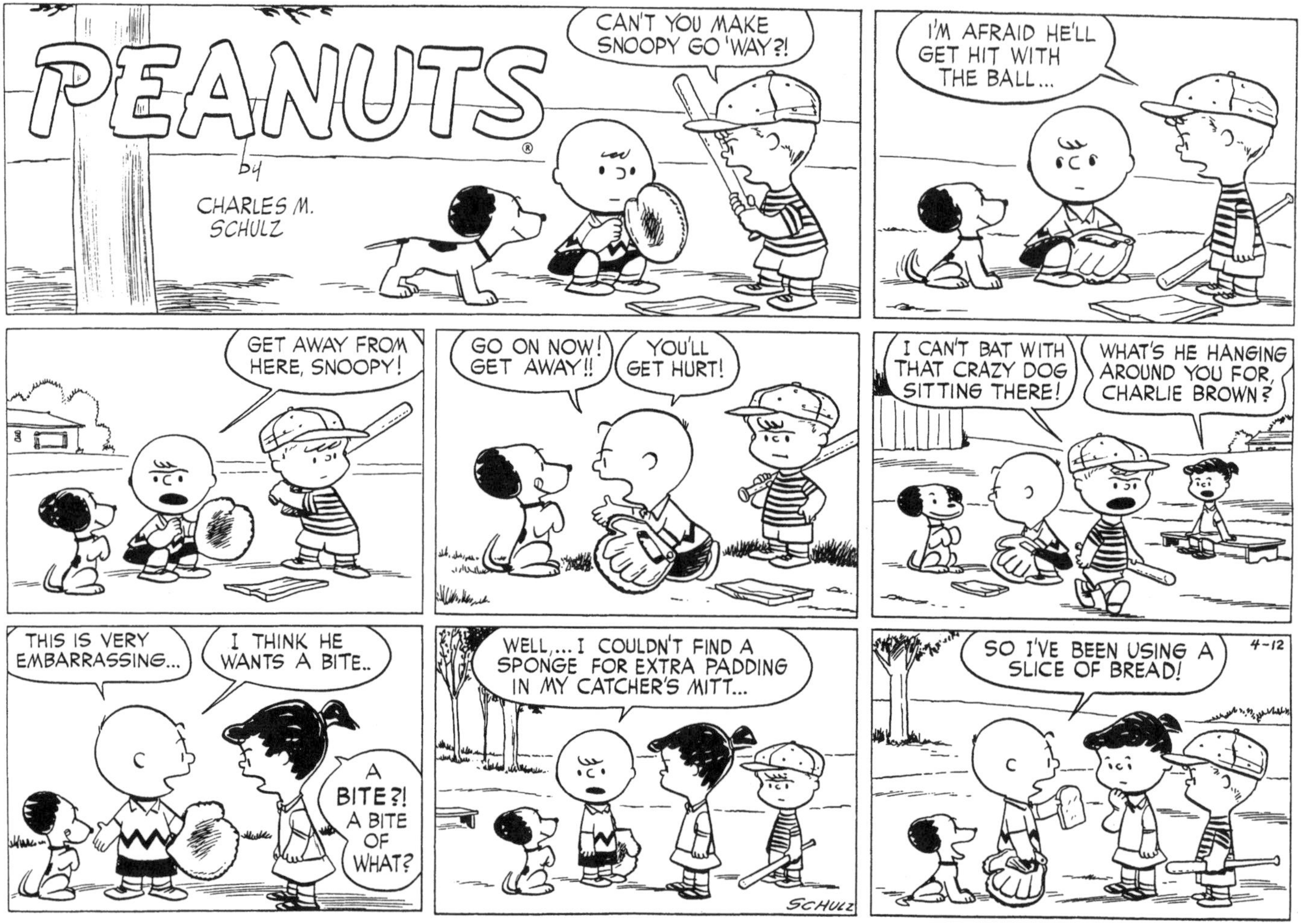
PEANUTS
by CHARLES M. SCHULZ
CAN'T YOU MAKE SNOOPY GO 'WAY?!
I'M AFRAID HE'LL GET HIT WITH THE BALL...
GET AWAY FROM HERE, SNOOPY!
GO ON NOW! GET AWAY!!
YOU'LL GET HURT!
I CAN'T BAT WITH THAT CRAZY DOG SITTING THERE!
WHAT'S HE HANGING AROUND YOU FOR, CHARLIE BROWN?
THIS IS VERY EMBARRASSING...
I THINK HE WANTS A BITE..
A BITE?! A BITE OF WHAT?
WELL,... I COULDN'T FIND A SPONGE FOR EXTRA PADDING IN MY CATCHER'S MITT...
SO I'VE BEEN USING A SLICE OF BREAD!
4-12
SCHULZ

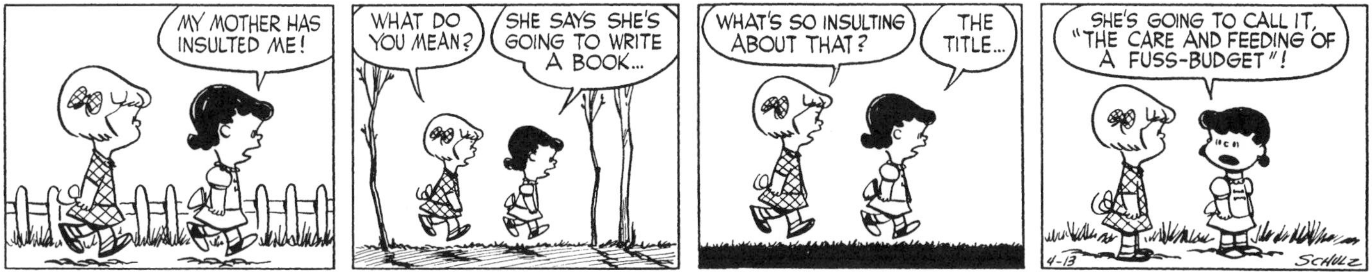
MY MOTHER HAS INSULTED ME!
WHAT DO YOU MEAN?
SHE SAYS SHE'S GOING TO WRITE A BOOK...
WHAT'S SO INSULTING ABOUT THAT?
THE TITLE...
SHE'S GOING TO CALL IT, "THE CARE AND FEEDING OF A FUSS-BUDGET"!
4-13
SCHULZ

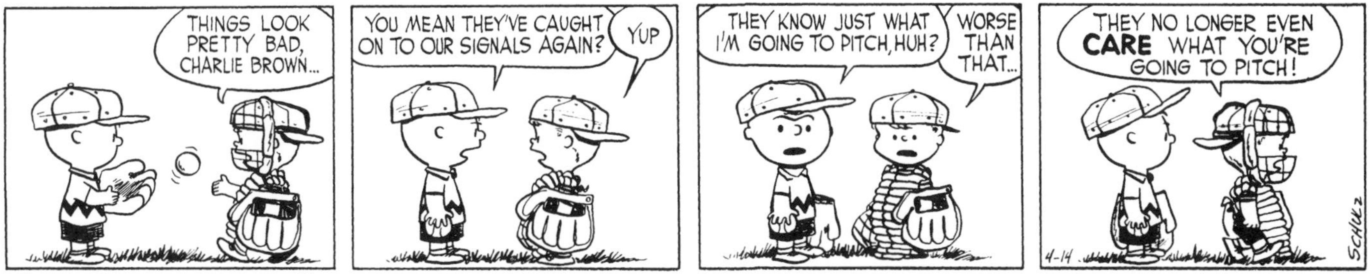
THINGS LOOK PRETTY BAD, CHARLIE BROWN...
YOU MEAN THEY'VE CAUGHT ON TO OUR SIGNALS AGAIN?
YUP
THEY KNOW JUST WHAT I'M GOING TO PITCH, HUH?
WORSE THAN THAT...
THEY NO LONGER EVEN **CARE** WHAT YOU'RE GOING TO PITCH!
4-14
SCHULZ

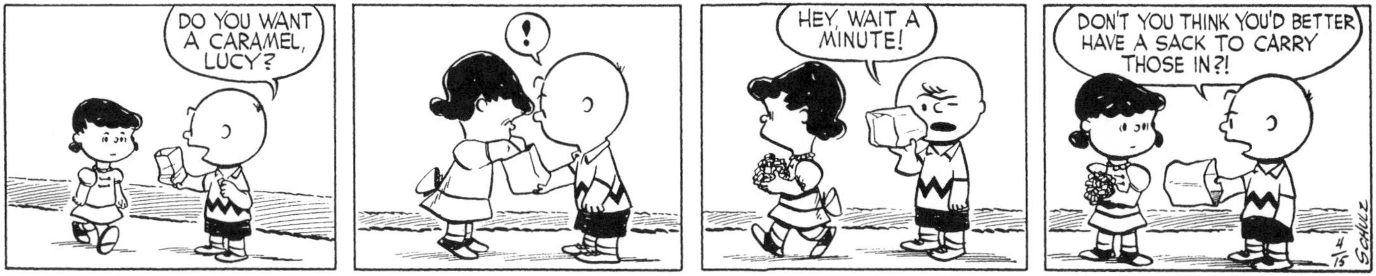
DO YOU WANT A CARAMEL, LUCY?
!
HEY, WAIT A MINUTE!
DON'T YOU THINK YOU'D BETTER HAVE A SACK TO CARRY THOSE IN?!
4/15
SCHULZ

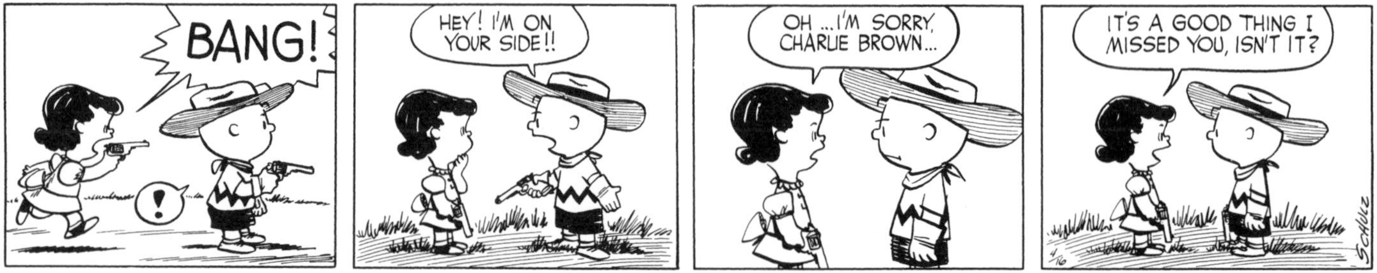
BANG!
HEY! I'M ON YOUR SIDE!!
OH ...I'M SORRY, CHARLIE BROWN...
IT'S A GOOD THING I MISSED YOU, ISN'T IT?
4/16
SCHULZ

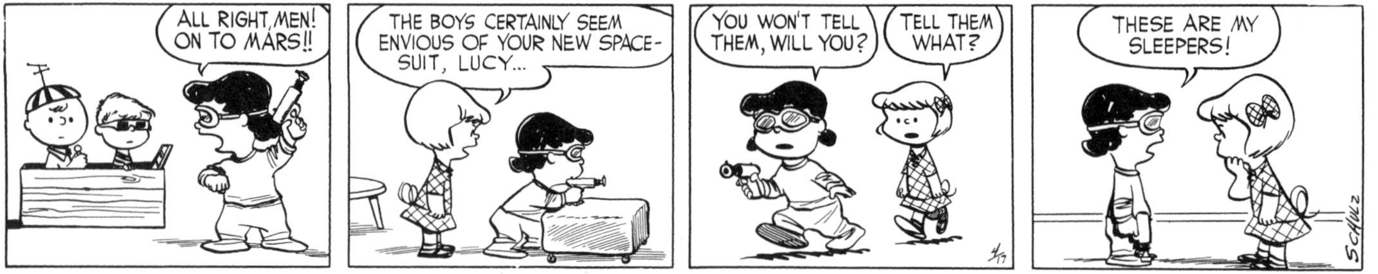
ALL RIGHT, MEN! ON TO MARS!!
THE BOYS CERTAINLY SEEM ENVIOUS OF YOUR NEW SPACE-SUIT, LUCY...
YOU WON'T TELL THEM, WILL YOU?
TELL THEM WHAT?
4/17
THESE ARE MY SLEEPERS!
SCHULZ

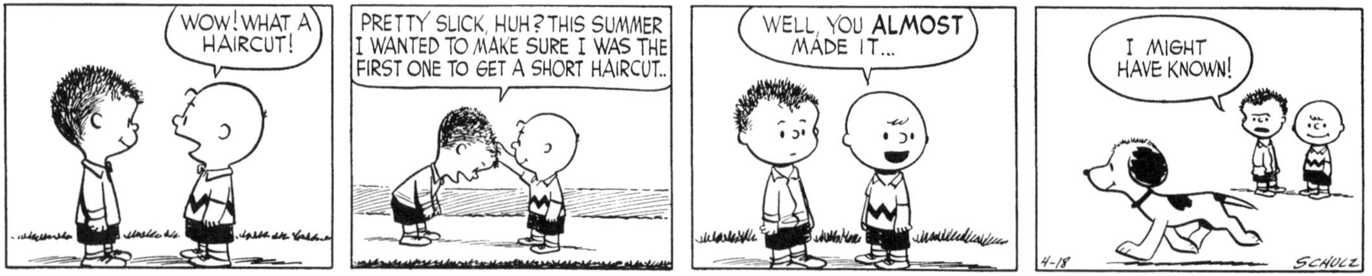
WOW! WHAT A HAIRCUT!
PRETTY SLICK, HUH? THIS SUMMER I WANTED TO MAKE SURE I WAS THE FIRST ONE TO GET A SHORT HAIRCUT..
WELL, YOU **ALMOST** MADE IT...
I MIGHT HAVE KNOWN!
4-18
SCHULZ

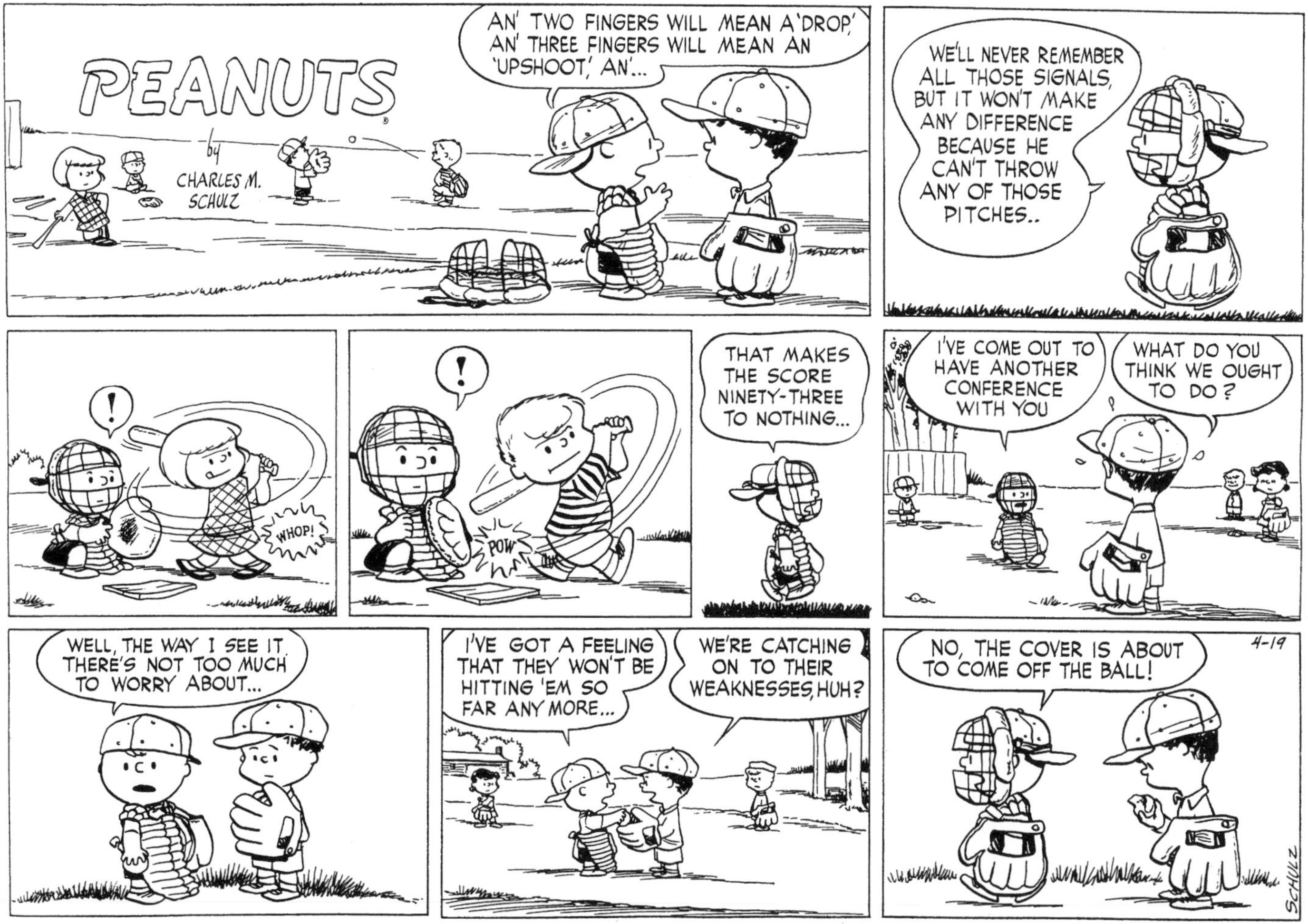

PEANUTS
by CHARLES M. SCHULZ
AN' TWO FINGERS WILL MEAN A 'DROP,' AN' THREE FINGERS WILL MEAN AN 'UPSHOOT,' AN'...
WE'LL NEVER REMEMBER ALL THOSE SIGNALS, BUT IT WON'T MAKE ANY DIFFERENCE BECAUSE HE CAN'T THROW ANY OF THOSE PITCHES..
!
WHOP!
!
POW
THAT MAKES THE SCORE NINETY-THREE TO NOTHING...
I'VE COME OUT TO HAVE ANOTHER CONFERENCE WITH YOU
WHAT DO YOU THINK WE OUGHT TO DO?
WELL, THE WAY I SEE IT THERE'S NOT TOO MUCH TO WORRY ABOUT...
I'VE GOT A FEELING THAT THEY WON'T BE HITTING 'EM SO FAR ANY MORE...
WE'RE CATCHING ON TO THEIR WEAKNESSES, HUH?
NO, THE COVER IS ABOUT TO COME OFF THE BALL!
4-19
SCHULZ

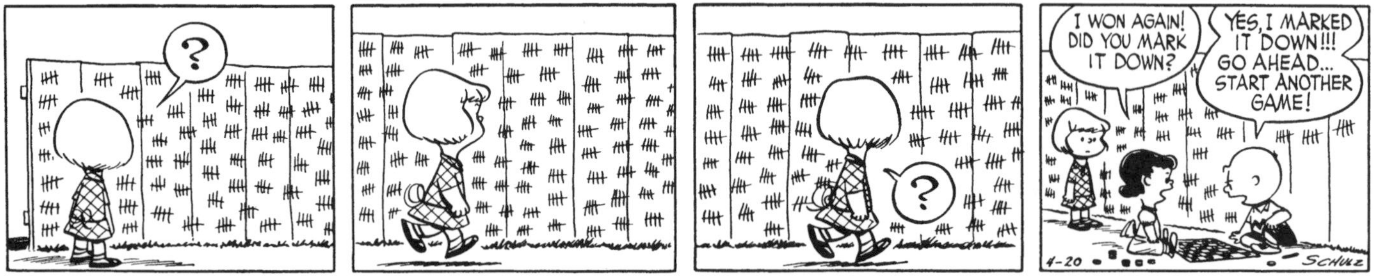
SCHULZ
?
?
I WON AGAIN! DID YOU MARK IT DOWN?
YES, I MARKED IT DOWN!!! GO AHEAD... START ANOTHER GAME!
4-20
SCHULZ

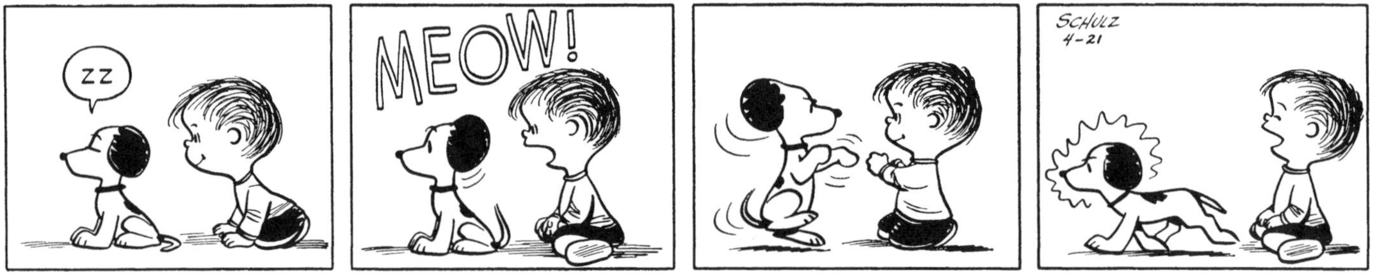
ZZ
MEOW!
SCHULZ
4-21

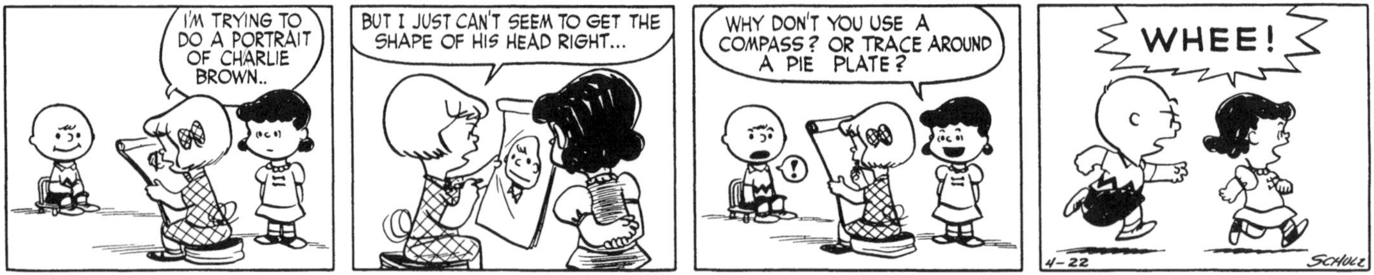
I'M TRYING TO DO A PORTRAIT OF CHARLIE BROWN..
BUT I JUST CAN'T SEEM TO GET THE SHAPE OF HIS HEAD RIGHT...
WHY DON'T YOU USE A COMPASS? OR TRACE AROUND A PIE PLATE?
!
WHEE!
4-22
SCHULZ

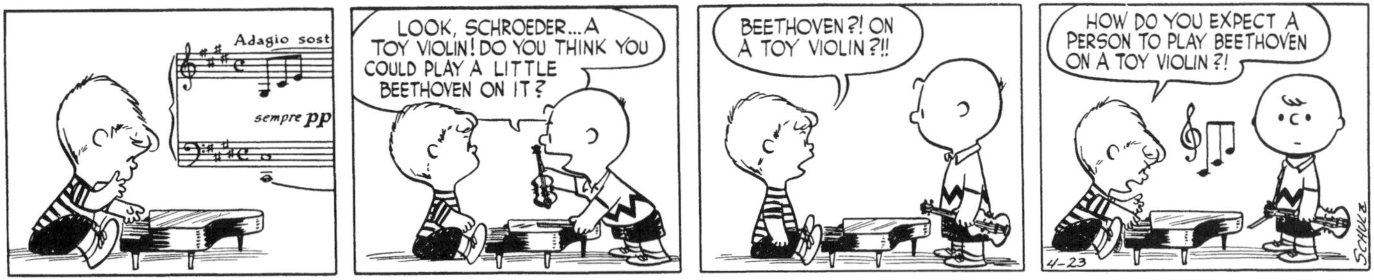
Adagio sost
sempre pp
LOOK, SCHROEDER...A TOY VIOLIN! DO YOU THINK YOU COULD PLAY A LITTLE BEETHOVEN ON IT?
BEETHOVEN?! ON A TOY VIOLIN?!!
HOW DO YOU EXPECT A PERSON TO PLAY BEETHOVEN ON A TOY VIOLIN?!
4-23
SCHULZ

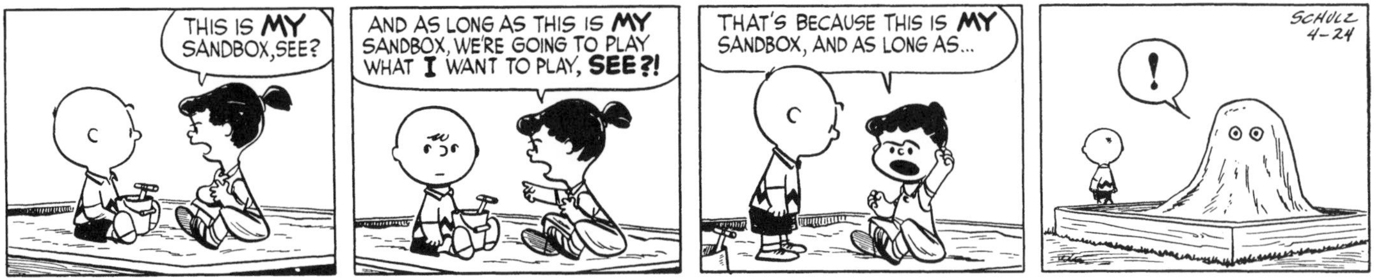
THIS IS MY SANDBOX, SEE?
AND AS LONG AS THIS IS MY SANDBOX, WE'RE GOING TO PLAY WHAT I WANT TO PLAY, SEE?!
THAT'S BECAUSE THIS IS MY SANDBOX, AND AS LONG AS...
SCHULZ 4-24
!

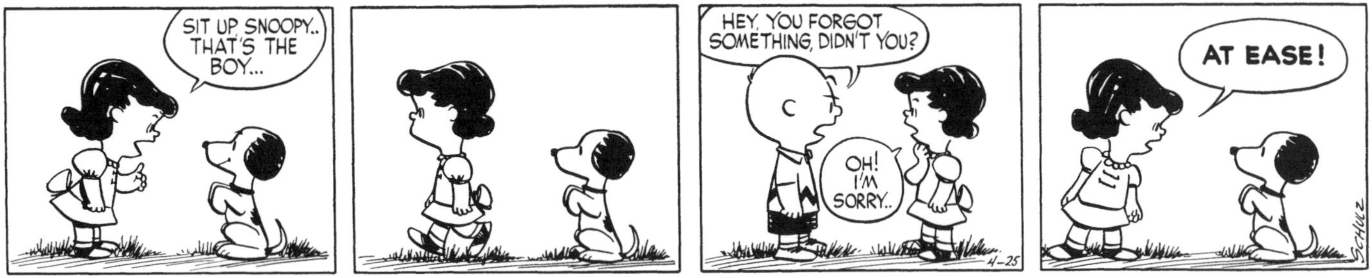
SIT UP SNOOPY.. THAT'S THE BOY...
HEY, YOU FORGOT SOMETHING, DIDN'T YOU?
OH! I'M SORRY..
4-25
AT EASE!
SCHULZ

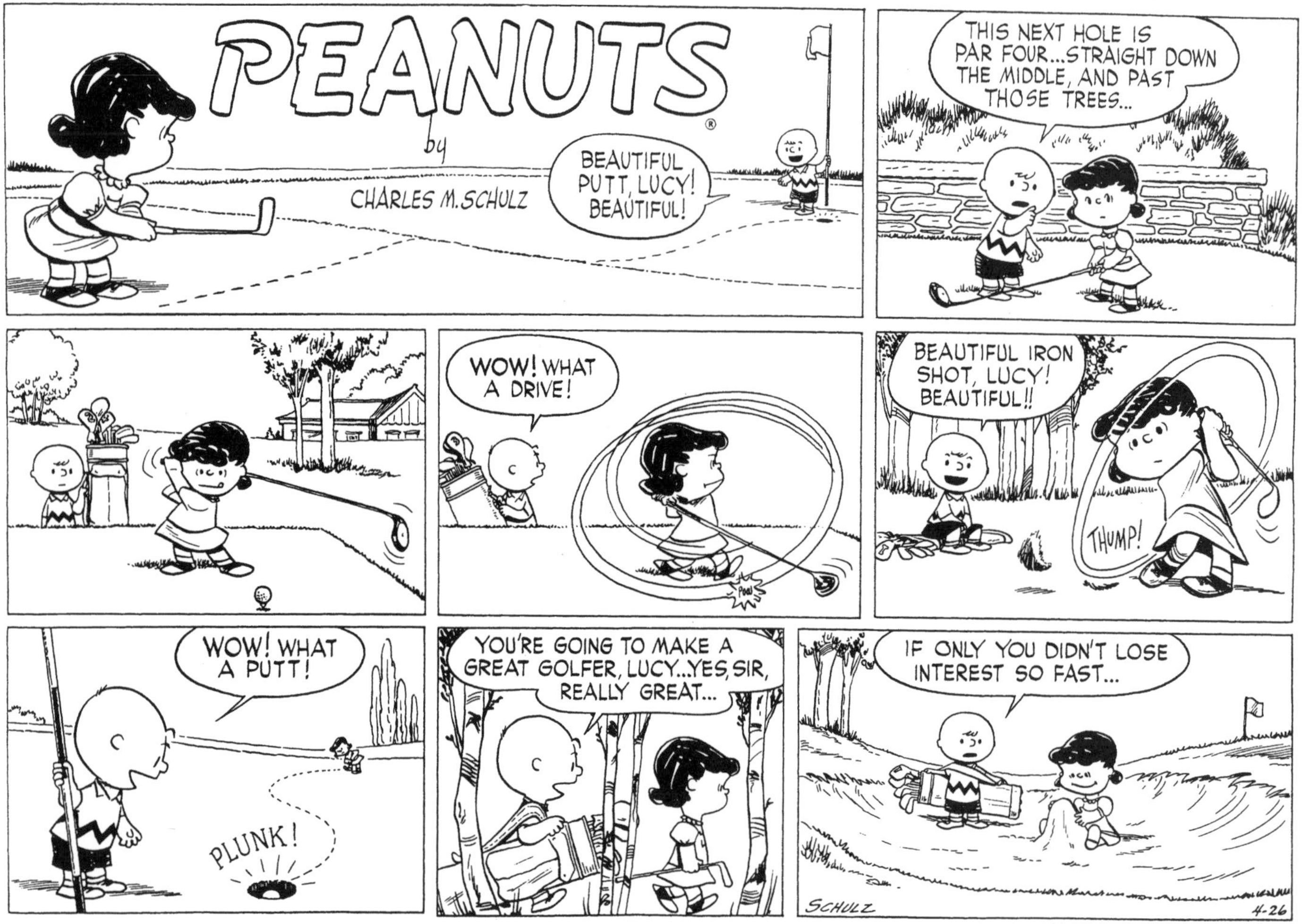
PEANUTS
by
CHARLES M. SCHULZ
BEAUTIFUL PUTT, LUCY! BEAUTIFUL!
THIS NEXT HOLE IS PAR FOUR...STRAIGHT DOWN THE MIDDLE, AND PAST THOSE TREES...
WOW! WHAT A DRIVE!
BEAUTIFUL IRON SHOT, LUCY! BEAUTIFUL!!
THUMP!
WOW! WHAT A PUTT!
PLUNK!
YOU'RE GOING TO MAKE A GREAT GOLFER, LUCY...YES, SIR, REALLY GREAT...
IF ONLY YOU DIDN'T LOSE INTEREST SO FAST...
SCHULZ
4-26

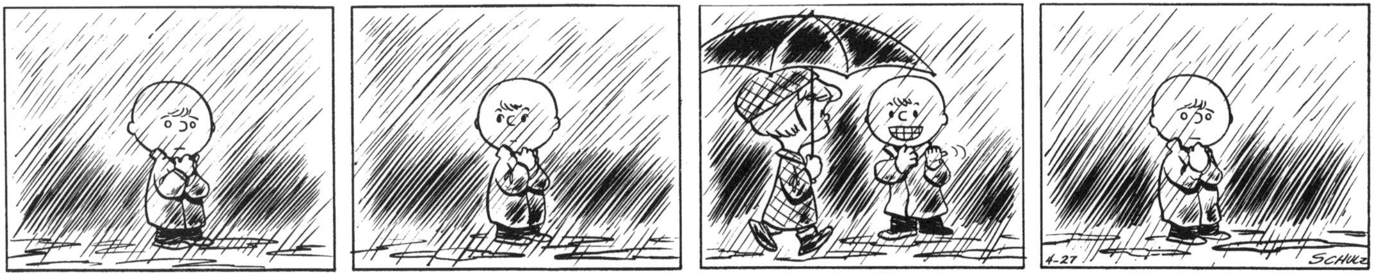

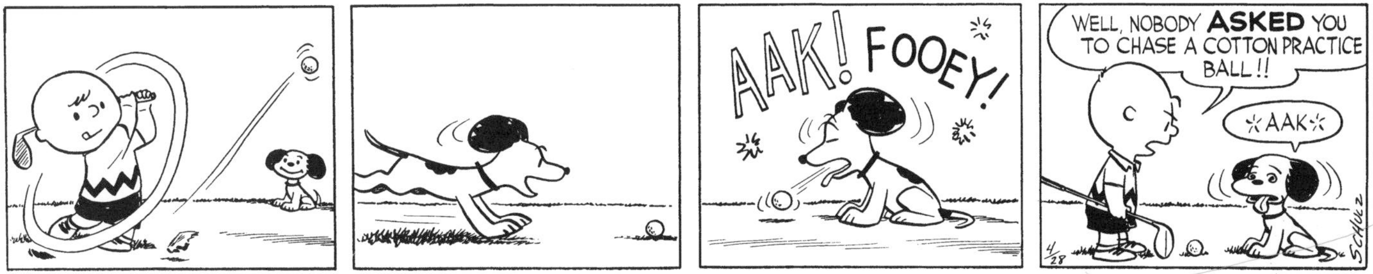
AAK! FOOEY!
WELL, NOBODY **ASKED** YOU TO CHASE A COTTON PRACTICE BALL!!
AAK

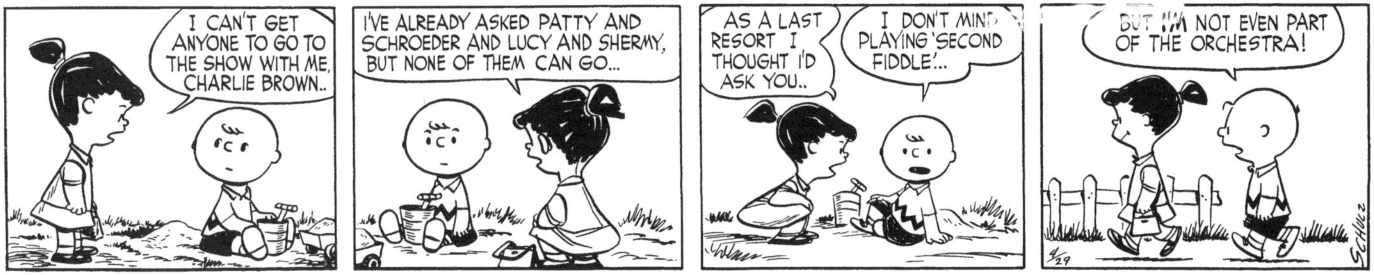
I CAN'T GET ANYONE TO GO TO THE SHOW WITH ME, CHARLIE BROWN..
I'VE ALREADY ASKED PATTY AND SCHROEDER AND LUCY AND SHERMY, BUT NONE OF THEM CAN GO...
AS A LAST RESORT I THOUGHT I'D ASK YOU..
I DON'T MIND PLAYING 'SECOND FIDDLE'...
BUT I'M NOT EVEN PART OF THE ORCHESTRA!

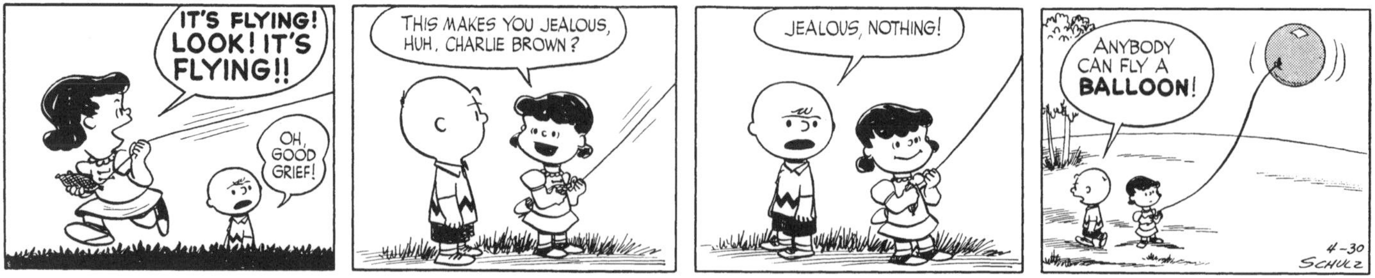
IT'S FLYING! LOOK! IT'S FLYING!!
OH, GOOD GRIEF!
THIS MAKES YOU JEALOUS, HUH, CHARLIE BROWN?
JEALOUS, NOTHING!
ANYBODY CAN FLY A BALLOON!
4-30
SCHULZ

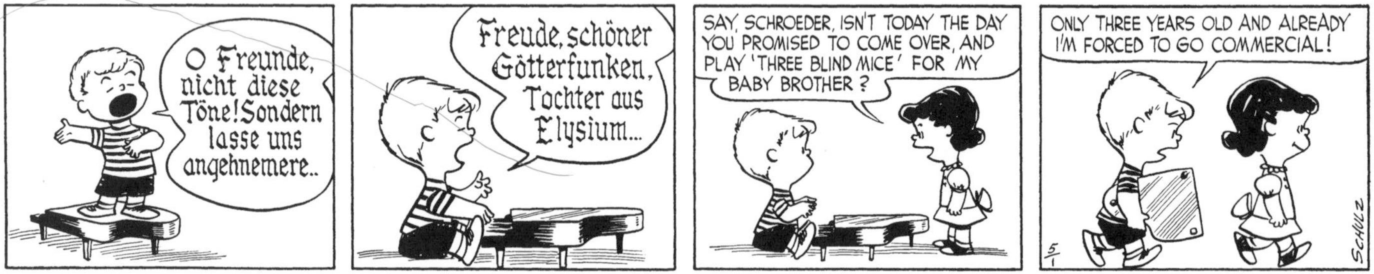
O Freunde, nicht diese Töne! Sondern lasse uns angehnemere..
Freude, schöner Götterfunken, Tochter aus Elysium...
SAY, SCHROEDER, ISN'T TODAY THE DAY YOU PROMISED TO COME OVER, AND PLAY 'THREE BLIND MICE' FOR MY BABY BROTHER?
ONLY THREE YEARS OLD AND ALREADY I'M FORCED TO GO COMMERCIAL!
5/1
SCHULZ

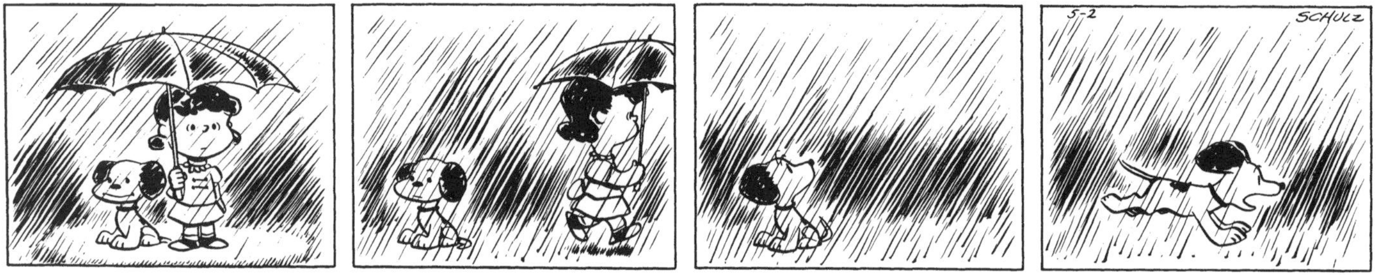
5-2
SCHULZ

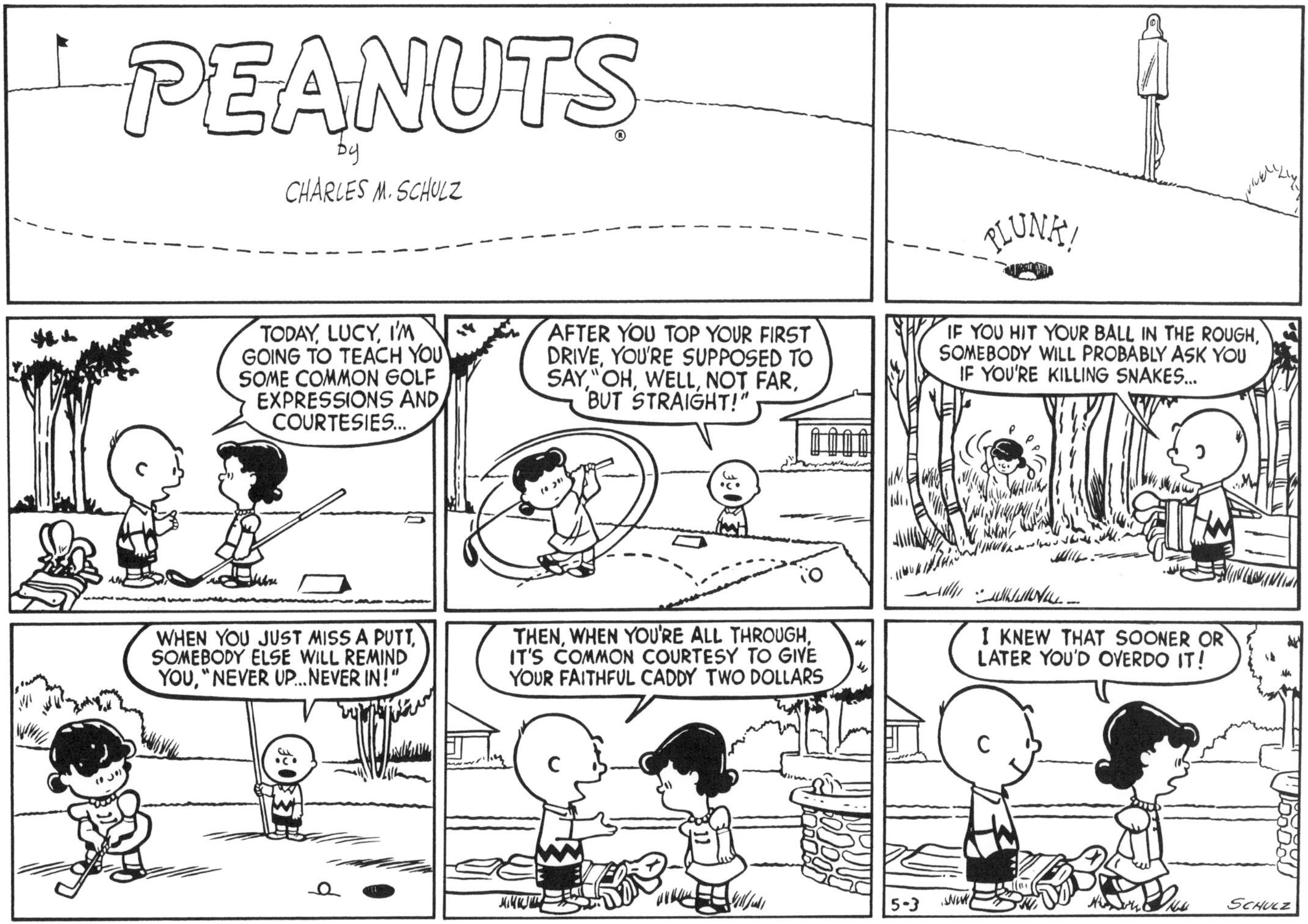
PEANUTS
by
CHARLES M. SCHULZ
PLUNK!
TODAY, LUCY, I'M GOING TO TEACH YOU SOME COMMON GOLF EXPRESSIONS AND COURTESIES...
AFTER YOU TOP YOUR FIRST DRIVE, YOU'RE SUPPOSED TO SAY, "OH, WELL, NOT FAR, BUT STRAIGHT!"
IF YOU HIT YOUR BALL IN THE ROUGH, SOMEBODY WILL PROBABLY ASK YOU IF YOU'RE KILLING SNAKES...
WHEN YOU JUST MISS A PUTT, SOMEBODY ELSE WILL REMIND YOU, "NEVER UP...NEVER IN!"
THEN, WHEN YOU'RE ALL THROUGH, IT'S COMMON COURTESY TO GIVE YOUR FAITHFUL CADDY TWO DOLLARS
I KNEW THAT SOONER OR LATER YOU'D OVERDO IT!
5-3
SCHULZ

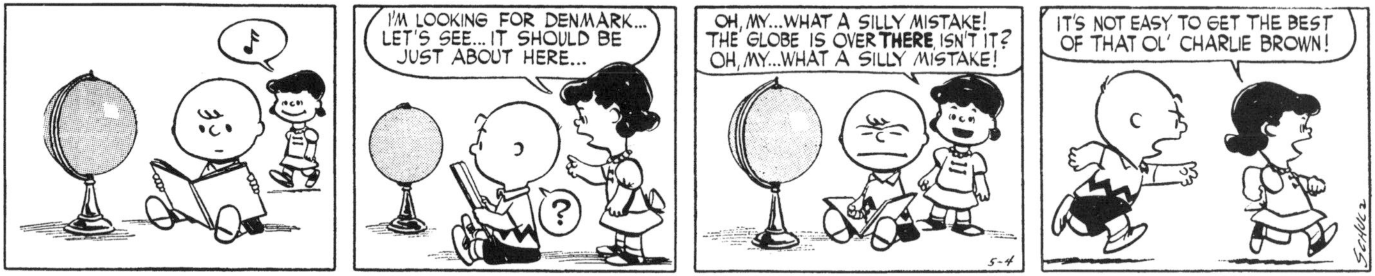
I'M LOOKING FOR DENMARK... LET'S SEE... IT SHOULD BE JUST ABOUT HERE...
?
OH, MY...WHAT A SILLY MISTAKE! THE GLOBE IS OVER **THERE**, ISN'T IT? OH, MY...WHAT A SILLY MISTAKE!
5-4
IT'S NOT EASY TO GET THE BEST OF THAT OL' CHARLIE BROWN!
SCHULZ

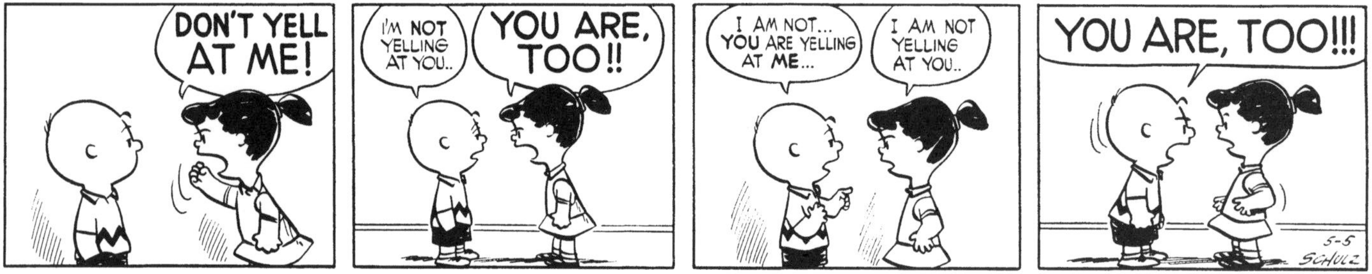
DON'T YELL AT ME!
I'M **NOT** YELLING AT YOU..
YOU ARE, TOO!!
I AM NOT... **YOU** ARE YELLING AT **ME**...
I AM NOT YELLING AT YOU..
YOU ARE, TOO!!!
5-5
SCHULZ

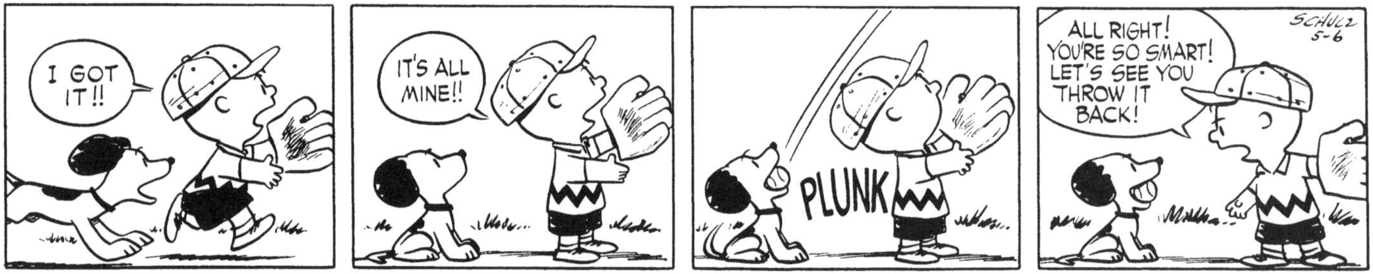
I GOT IT!!
IT'S ALL MINE!!
PLUNK
SCHULZ
5-6
ALL RIGHT! YOU'RE SO SMART! LET'S SEE YOU THROW IT BACK!

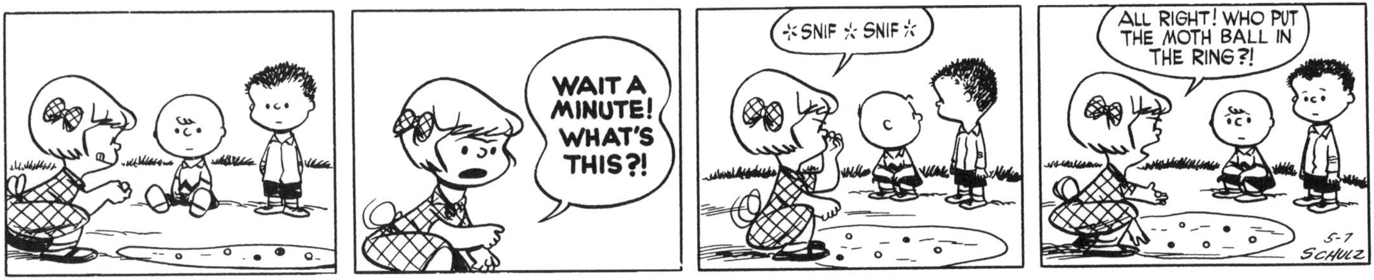
WAIT A MINUTE! WHAT'S THIS?!
SNIF SNIF*
ALL RIGHT! WHO PUT THE MOTH BALL IN THE RING?!
5-7
SCHULZ

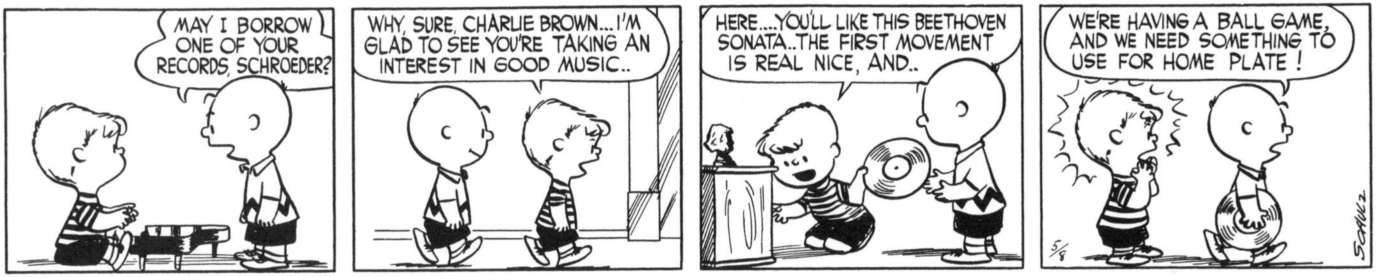
MAY I BORROW ONE OF YOUR RECORDS, SCHROEDER?
WHY, SURE, CHARLIE BROWN...I'M GLAD TO SEE YOU'RE TAKING AN INTEREST IN GOOD MUSIC..
HERE....YOU'LL LIKE THIS BEETHOVEN SONATA..THE FIRST MOVEMENT IS REAL NICE, AND..
WE'RE HAVING A BALL GAME, AND WE NEED SOMETHING TO USE FOR HOME PLATE!
5/8
SCHULZ

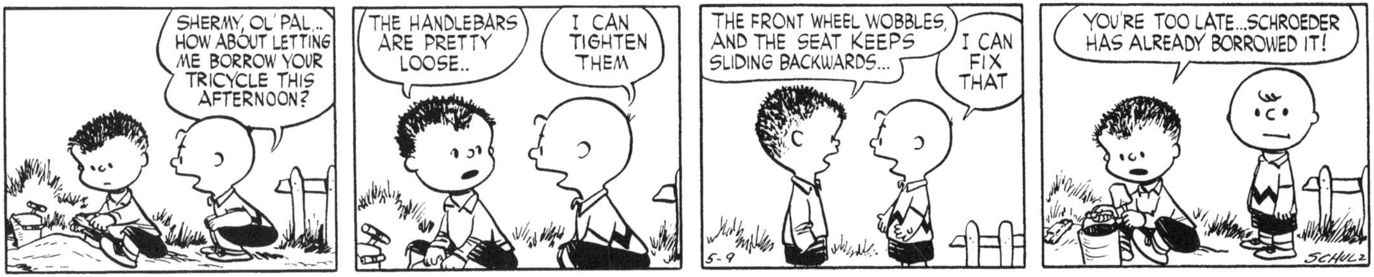
SHERMY, OL' PAL.. HOW ABOUT LETTING ME BORROW YOUR TRICYCLE THIS AFTERNOON?
THE HANDLEBARS ARE PRETTY LOOSE..
I CAN TIGHTEN THEM
THE FRONT WHEEL WOBBLES, AND THE SEAT KEEPS SLIDING BACKWARDS...
I CAN FIX THAT
5-9
YOU'RE TOO LATE...SCHROEDER HAS ALREADY BORROWED IT!
SCHULZ

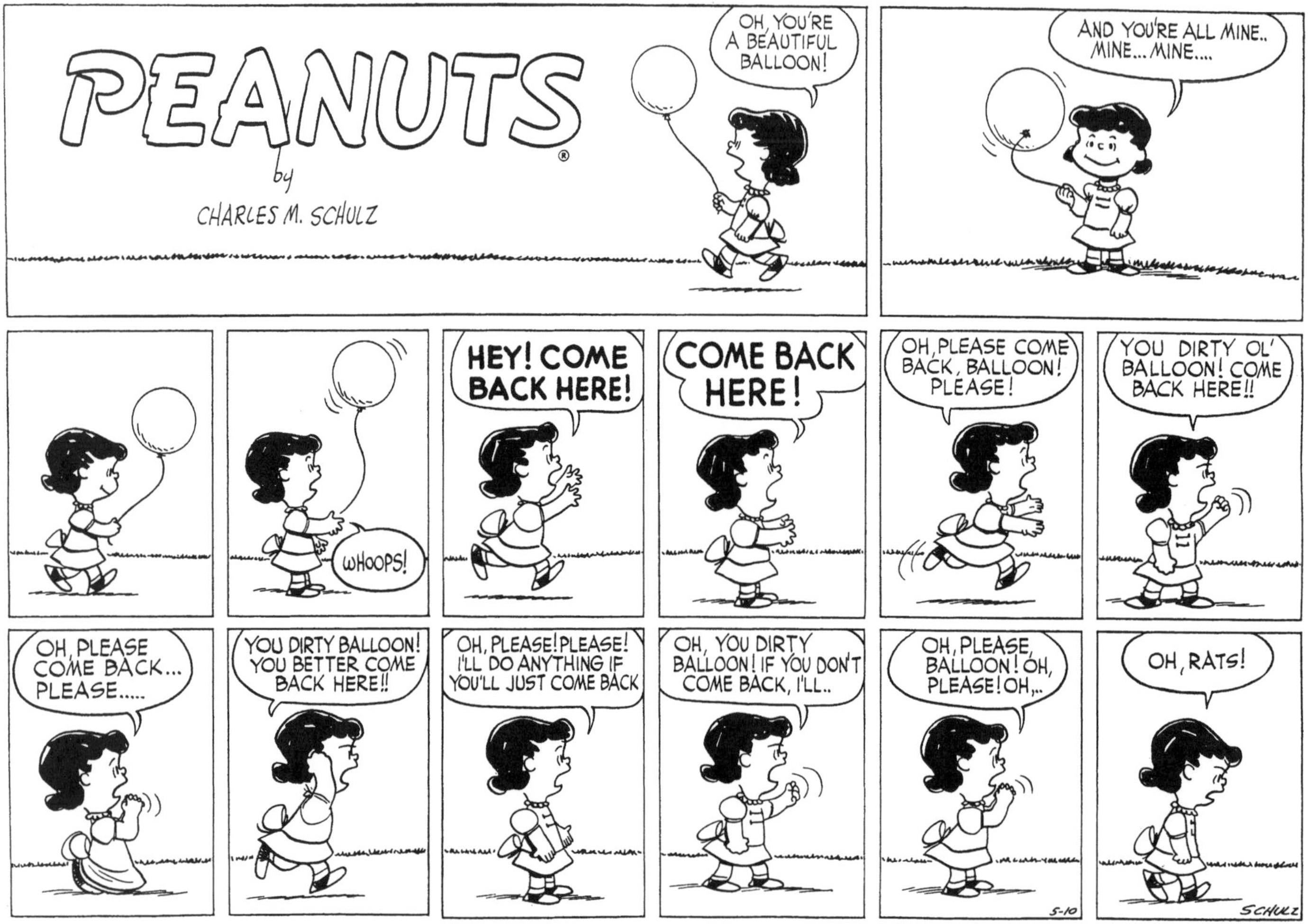
PEANUTS
by CHARLES M. SCHULZ
OH, YOU'RE A BEAUTIFUL BALLOON!
AND YOU'RE ALL MINE.. MINE... MINE....
WHOOPS!
HEY! COME BACK HERE!
COME BACK HERE!
OH, PLEASE COME BACK, BALLOON! PLEASE!
YOU DIRTY OL' BALLOON! COME BACK HERE!!
OH, PLEASE COME BACK... PLEASE.....
YOU DIRTY BALLOON! YOU BETTER COME BACK HERE!!
OH, PLEASE! PLEASE! I'LL DO ANYTHING IF YOU'LL JUST COME BACK
OH, YOU DIRTY BALLOON! IF YOU DON'T COME BACK, I'LL..
OH, PLEASE, BALLOON! OH, PLEASE! OH,..
5-10
OH, RATS!
SCHULZ

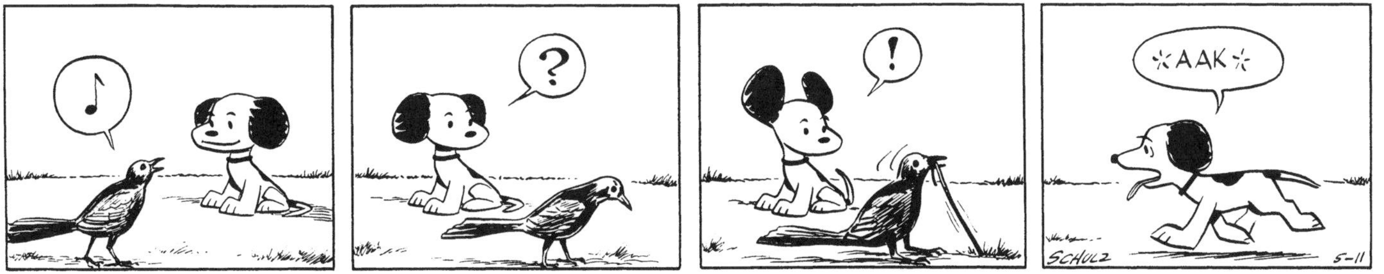
♪
?
!
AAK
SCHULZ 5-11

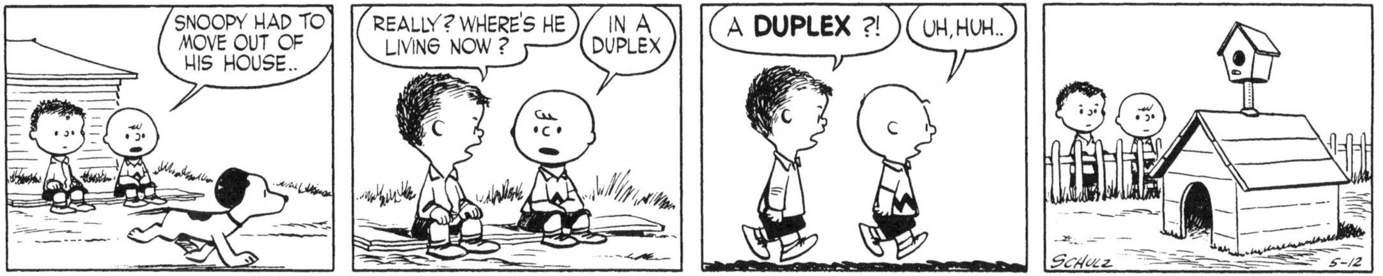
SNOOPY HAD TO MOVE OUT OF HIS HOUSE..
REALLY? WHERE'S HE LIVING NOW?
IN A DUPLEX
A **DUPLEX** ?!
UH, HUH..
SCHULZ 5-12

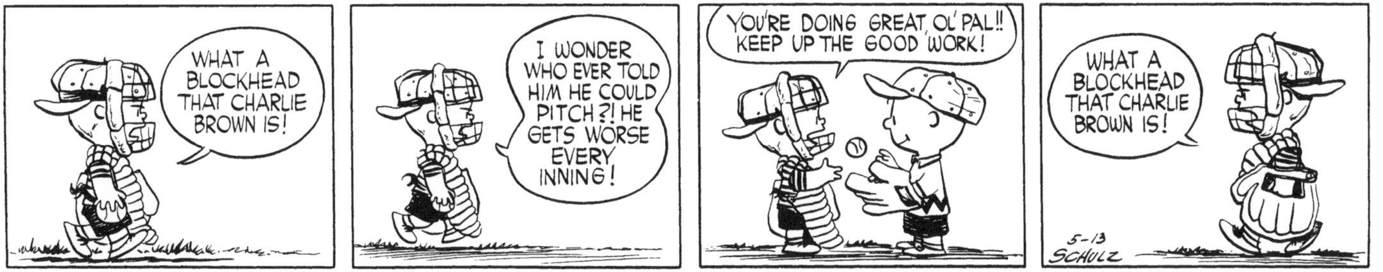
WHAT A BLOCKHEAD THAT CHARLIE BROWN IS!
I WONDER WHO EVER TOLD HIM HE COULD PITCH?! HE GETS WORSE EVERY INNING!
YOU'RE DOING GREAT, OL' PAL!! KEEP UP THE GOOD WORK!
WHAT A BLOCKHEAD THAT CHARLIE BROWN IS!
5-13 SCHULZ

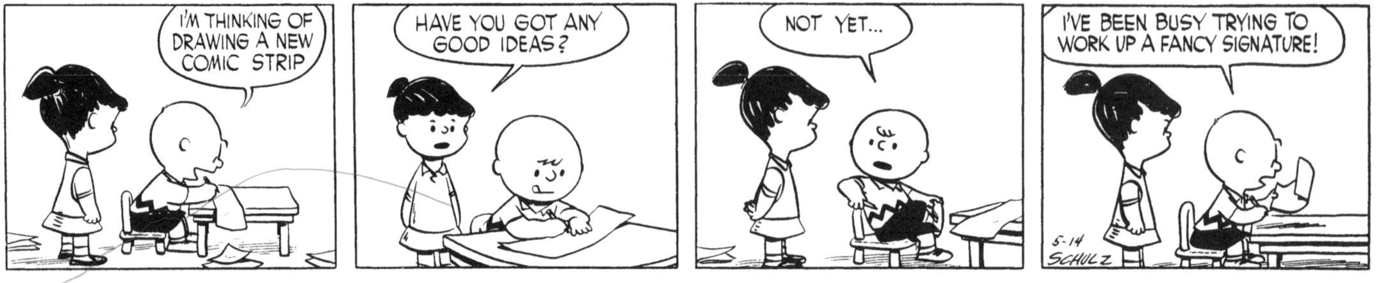
I'M THINKING OF DRAWING A NEW COMIC STRIP
HAVE YOU GOT ANY GOOD IDEAS?
NOT YET...
I'VE BEEN BUSY TRYING TO WORK UP A FANCY SIGNATURE!
5-14
SCHULZ

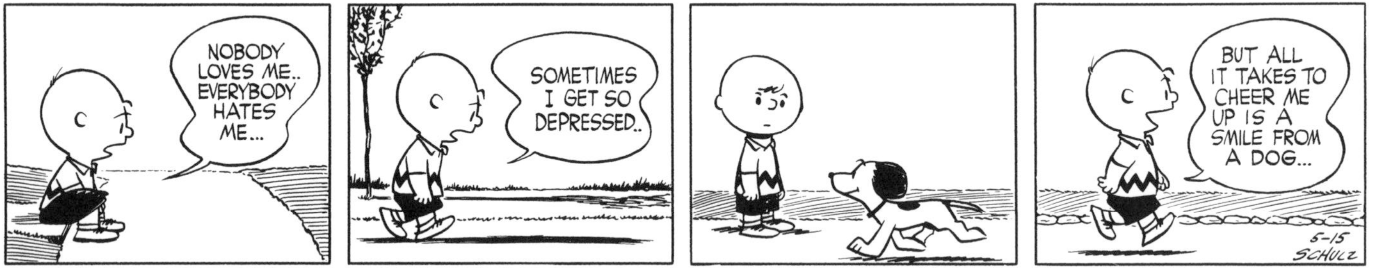
NOBODY LOVES ME.. EVERYBODY HATES ME...
SOMETIMES I GET SO DEPRESSED..
BUT ALL IT TAKES TO CHEER ME UP IS A SMILE FROM A DOG...
5-15
SCHULZ

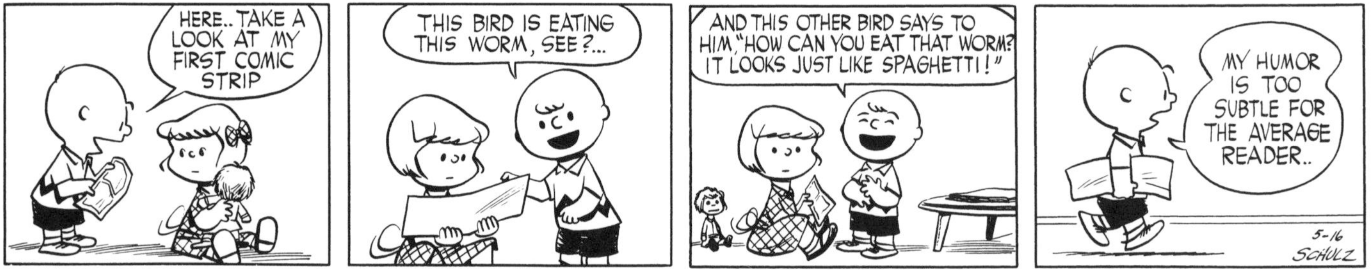
HERE.. TAKE A LOOK AT MY FIRST COMIC STRIP
THIS BIRD IS EATING THIS WORM, SEE?...
AND THIS OTHER BIRD SAYS TO HIM, "HOW CAN YOU EAT THAT WORM? IT LOOKS JUST LIKE SPAGHETTI!"
MY HUMOR IS TOO SUBTLE FOR THE AVERAGE READER..
5-16
SCHULZ

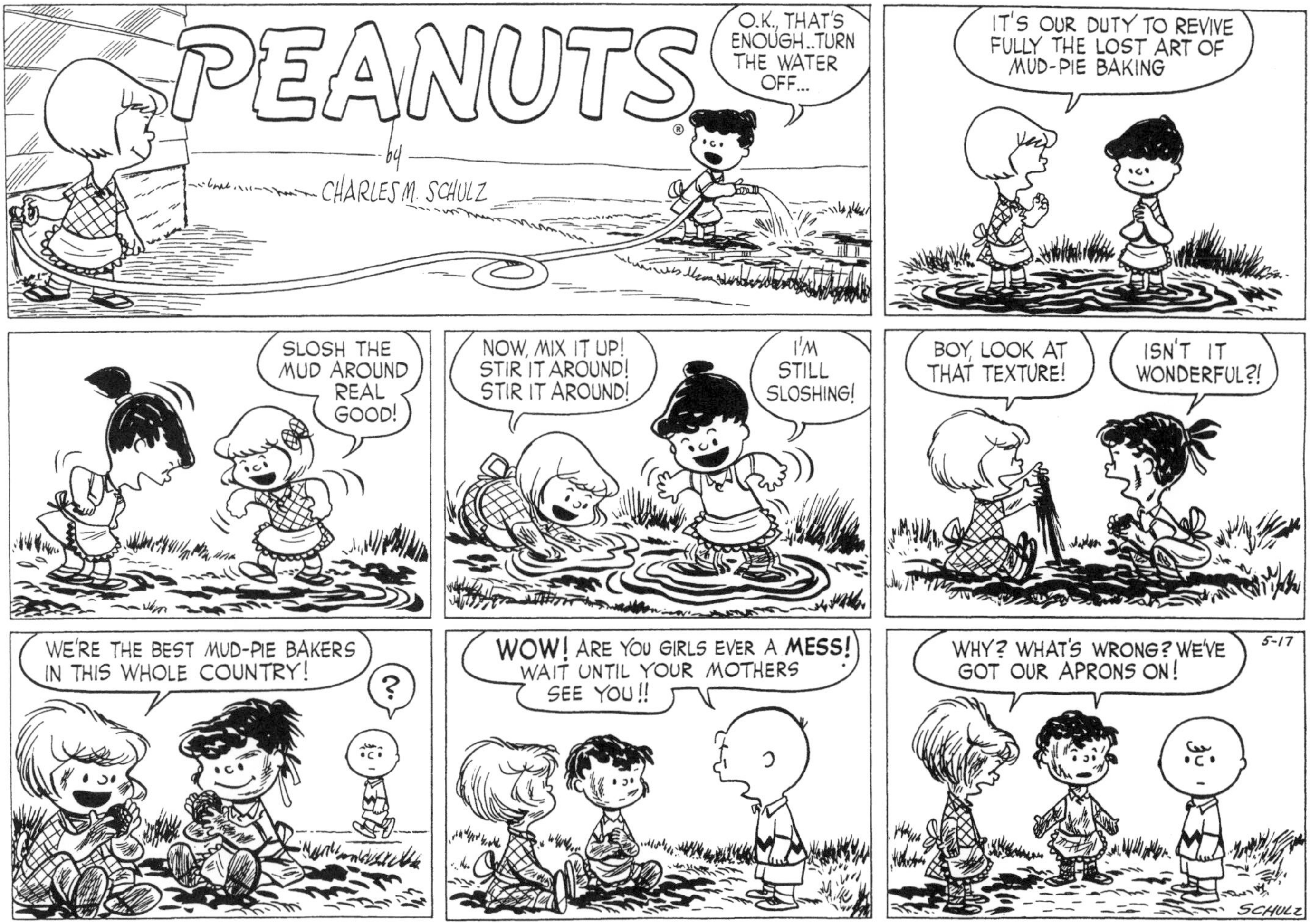
PEANUTS
by CHARLES M. SCHULZ
O.K., THAT'S ENOUGH..TURN THE WATER OFF...
IT'S OUR DUTY TO REVIVE FULLY THE LOST ART OF MUD-PIE BAKING
SLOSH THE MUD AROUND REAL GOOD!
NOW, MIX IT UP! STIR IT AROUND! STIR IT AROUND!
I'M STILL SLOSHING!
BOY, LOOK AT THAT TEXTURE!
ISN'T IT WONDERFUL?!
WE'RE THE BEST MUD-PIE BAKERS IN THIS WHOLE COUNTRY!
?
WOW! ARE YOU GIRLS EVER A MESS! WAIT UNTIL YOUR MOTHERS SEE YOU!!
5-17
WHY? WHAT'S WRONG? WE'VE GOT OUR APRONS ON!
SCHULZ

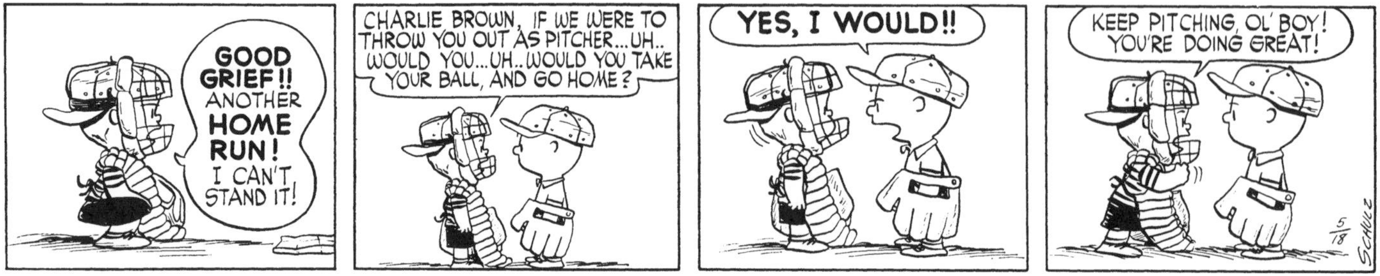
GOOD GRIEF!! ANOTHER HOME RUN! I CAN'T STAND IT!
CHARLIE BROWN, IF WE WERE TO THROW YOU OUT AS PITCHER...UH.. WOULD YOU...UH..WOULD YOU TAKE YOUR BALL, AND GO HOME?
YES, I WOULD!!
KEEP PITCHING, OL' BOY! YOU'RE DOING GREAT!
5/18
SCHULZ

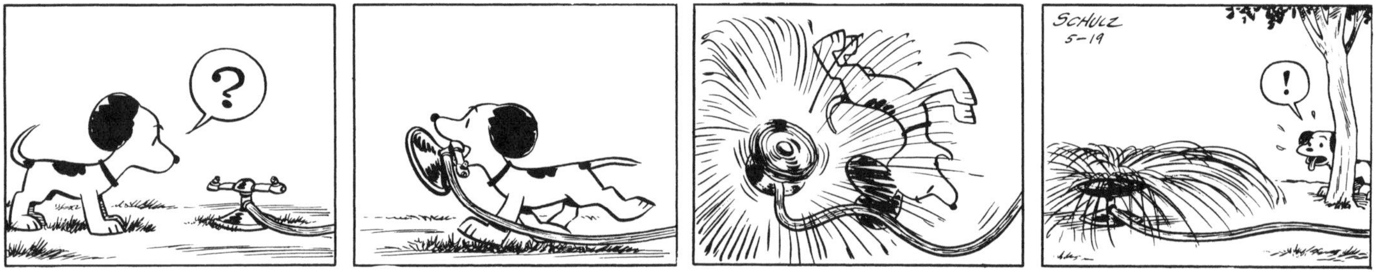
?
SCHULZ
5-19
!

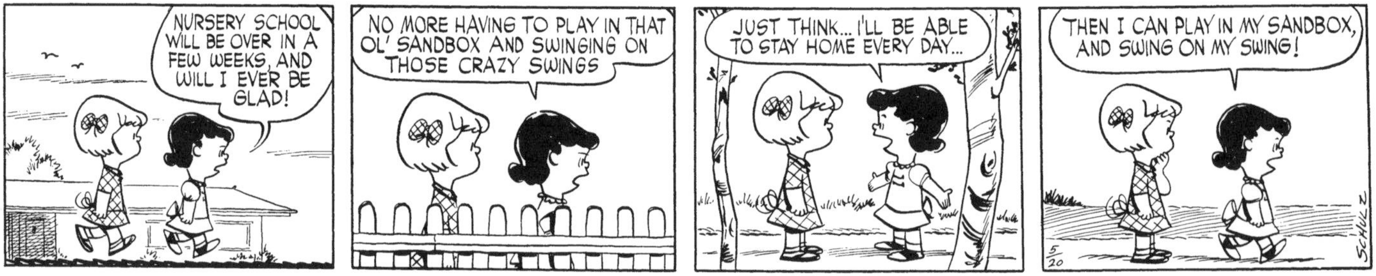
NURSERY SCHOOL WILL BE OVER IN A FEW WEEKS, AND WILL I EVER BE GLAD!
NO MORE HAVING TO PLAY IN THAT OL' SANDBOX AND SWINGING ON THOSE CRAZY SWINGS
JUST THINK... I'LL BE ABLE TO STAY HOME EVERY DAY...
THEN I CAN PLAY IN MY SANDBOX, AND SWING ON MY SWING!
5/20
SCHULZ

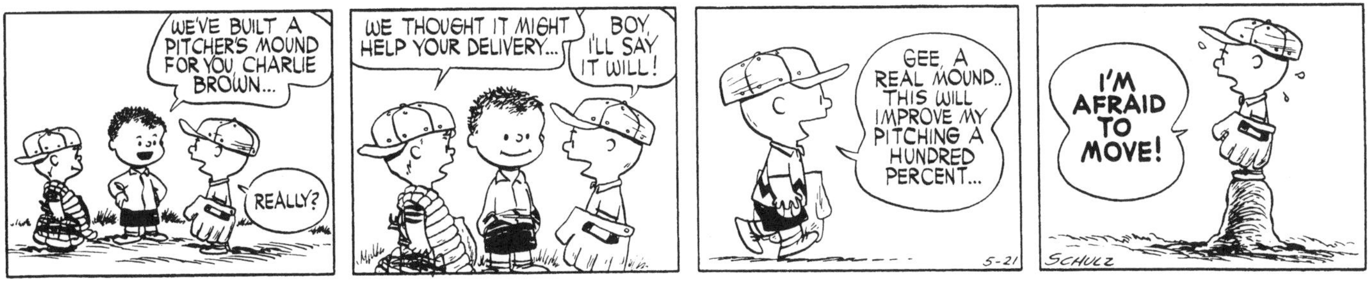
WE'VE BUILT A PITCHER'S MOUND FOR YOU, CHARLIE BROWN...
REALLY?
WE THOUGHT IT MIGHT HELP YOUR DELIVERY...
BOY, I'LL SAY IT WILL!
GEE, A REAL MOUND.. THIS WILL IMPROVE MY PITCHING A HUNDRED PERCENT...
5-21
I'M AFRAID TO MOVE!
SCHULZ

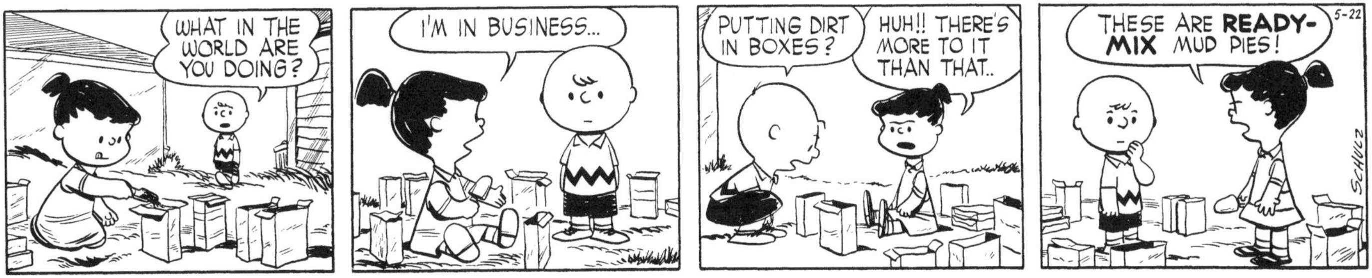
WHAT IN THE WORLD ARE YOU DOING?
I'M IN BUSINESS...
PUTTING DIRT IN BOXES?
HUH!! THERE'S MORE TO IT THAN THAT..
THESE ARE READY-MIX MUD PIES!
5-22
SCHULZ

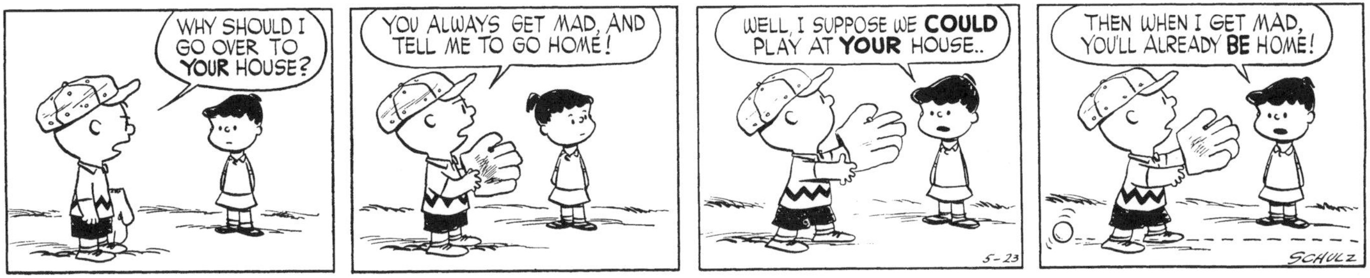
WHY SHOULD I GO OVER TO YOUR HOUSE?
YOU ALWAYS GET MAD, AND TELL ME TO GO HOME!
WELL, I SUPPOSE WE COULD PLAY AT YOUR HOUSE..
5-23
THEN WHEN I GET MAD, YOU'LL ALREADY BE HOME!
SCHULZ

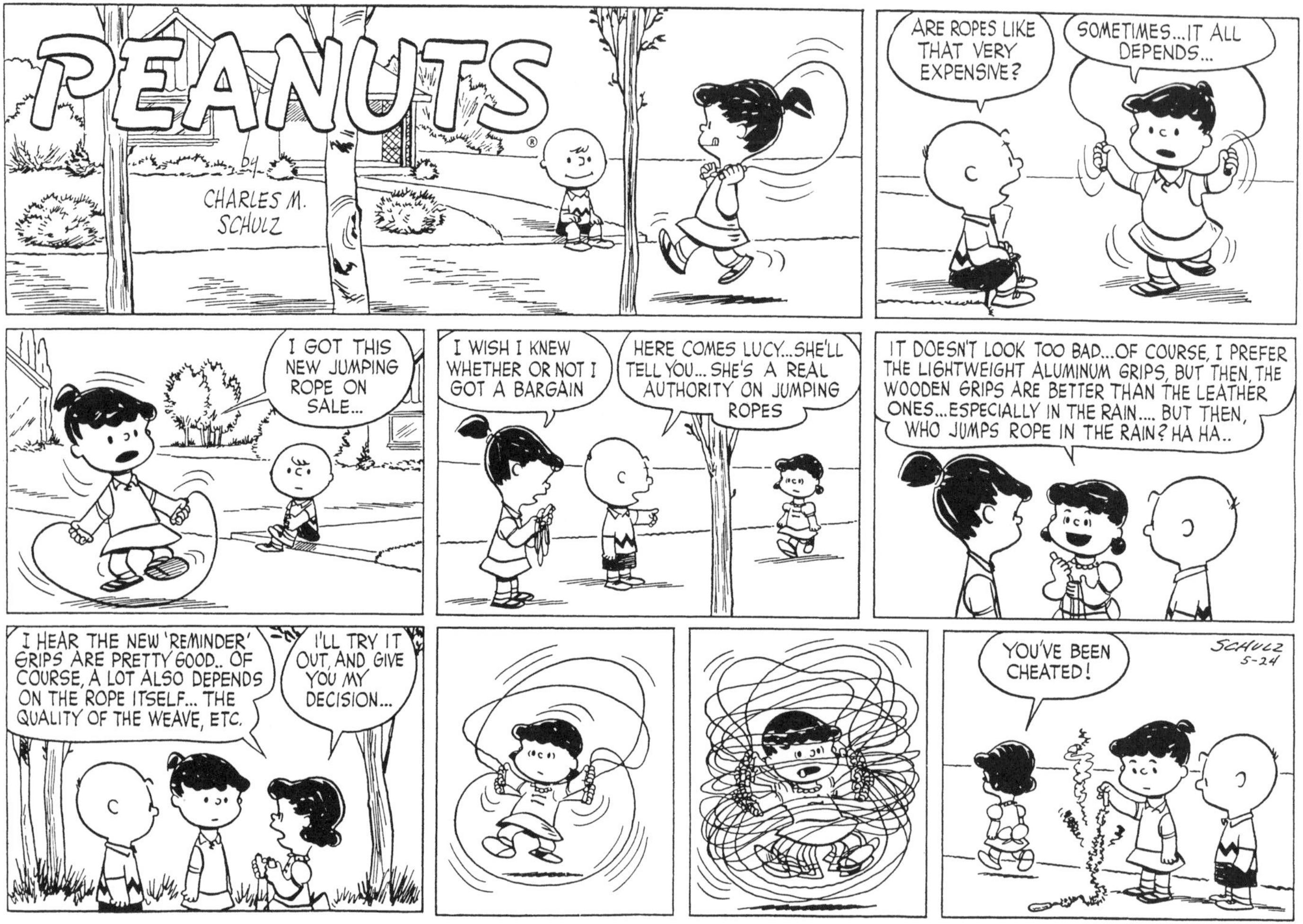
PEANUTS
by CHARLES M. SCHULZ
ARE ROPES LIKE THAT VERY EXPENSIVE?
SOMETIMES...IT ALL DEPENDS...
I GOT THIS NEW JUMPING ROPE ON SALE...
I WISH I KNEW WHETHER OR NOT I GOT A BARGAIN
HERE COMES LUCY...SHE'LL TELL YOU... SHE'S A REAL AUTHORITY ON JUMPING ROPES
IT DOESN'T LOOK TOO BAD...OF COURSE, I PREFER THE LIGHTWEIGHT ALUMINUM GRIPS, BUT THEN, THE WOODEN GRIPS ARE BETTER THAN THE LEATHER ONES...ESPECIALLY IN THE RAIN.... BUT THEN, WHO JUMPS ROPE IN THE RAIN? HA HA..
I HEAR THE NEW 'REMINDER' GRIPS ARE PRETTY GOOD.. OF COURSE, A LOT ALSO DEPENDS ON THE ROPE ITSELF... THE QUALITY OF THE WEAVE, ETC.
I'LL TRY IT OUT, AND GIVE YOU MY DECISION...
YOU'VE BEEN CHEATED!
SCHULZ 5-24

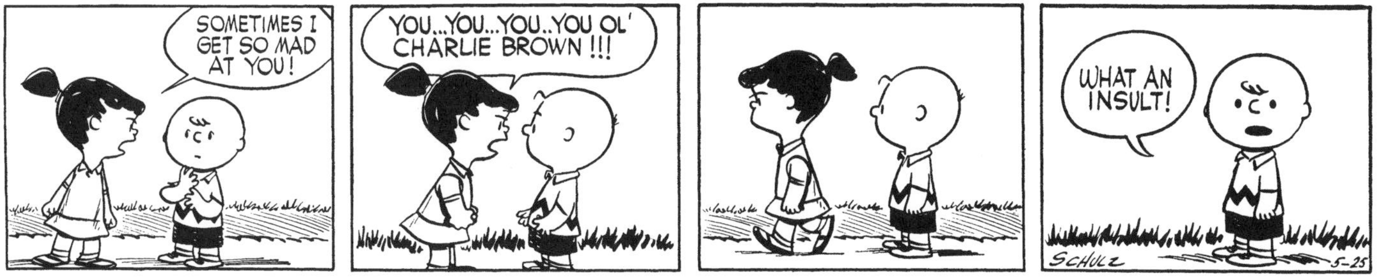
SOMETIMES I GET SO MAD AT YOU!
YOU...YOU...YOU..YOU OL' CHARLIE BROWN !!!
WHAT AN INSULT!
SCHULZ
5-25

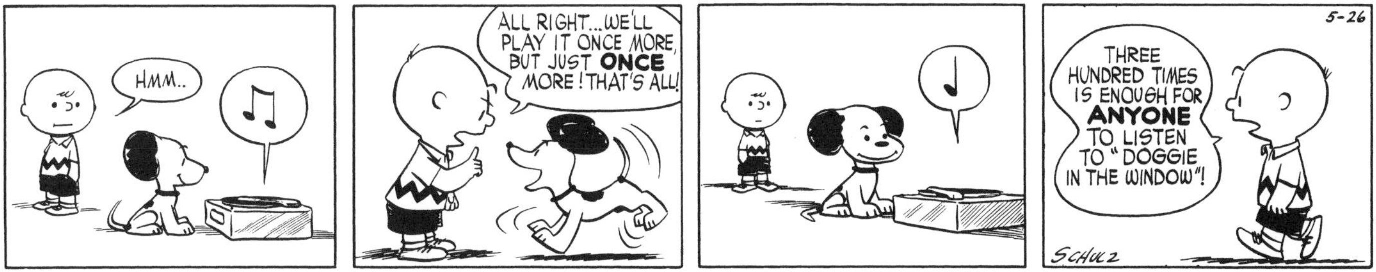
HMM..
ALL RIGHT...WE'LL PLAY IT ONCE MORE, BUT JUST ONCE MORE! THAT'S ALL!
5-26
THREE HUNDRED TIMES IS ENOUGH FOR ANYONE TO LISTEN TO "DOGGIE IN THE WINDOW"!
SCHULZ

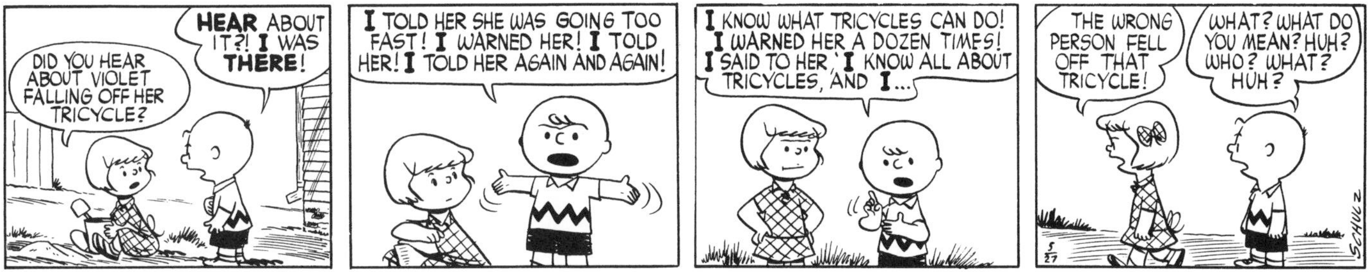
DID YOU HEAR ABOUT VIOLET FALLING OFF HER TRICYCLE?
HEAR ABOUT IT?! I WAS THERE!
I TOLD HER SHE WAS GOING TOO FAST! I WARNED HER! I TOLD HER! I TOLD HER AGAIN AND AGAIN!
I KNOW WHAT TRICYCLES CAN DO! I WARNED HER A DOZEN TIMES! I SAID TO HER, 'I KNOW ALL ABOUT TRICYCLES, AND I...
5/27
THE WRONG PERSON FELL OFF THAT TRICYCLE!
WHAT? WHAT DO YOU MEAN? HUH? WHO? WHAT? HUH?
SCHULZ

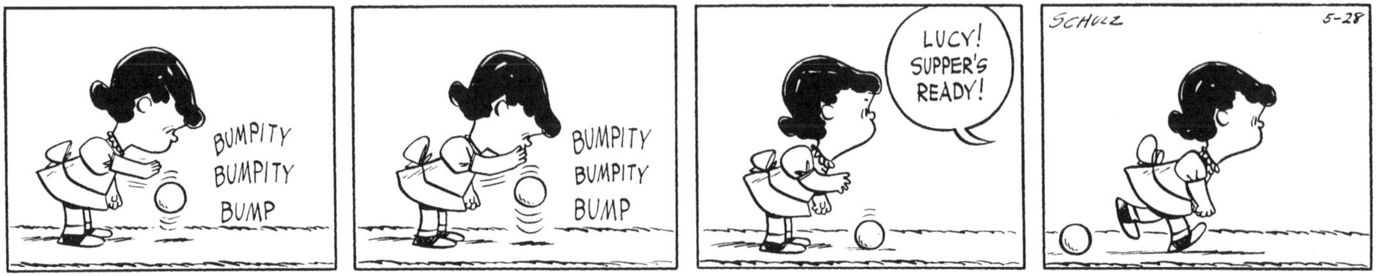
BUMPITY
BUMPITY
BUMP
BUMPITY
BUMPITY
BUMP
LUCY! SUPPER'S READY!
SCHULZ
5-28

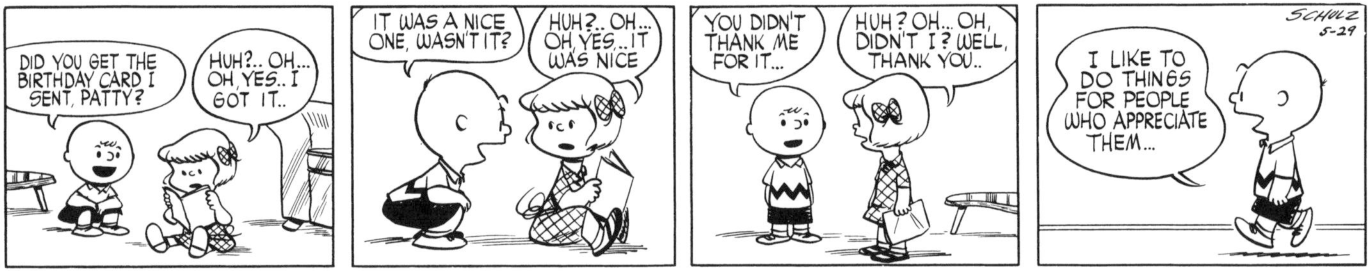
DID YOU GET THE BIRTHDAY CARD I SENT, PATTY?
HUH?.. OH... OH, YES.. I GOT IT..
IT WAS A NICE ONE, WASN'T IT?
HUH?.. OH... OH, YES... IT WAS NICE
YOU DIDN'T THANK ME FOR IT...
HUH? OH... OH, DIDN'T I? WELL, THANK YOU..
SCHULZ
5-29
I LIKE TO DO THINGS FOR PEOPLE WHO APPRECIATE THEM...

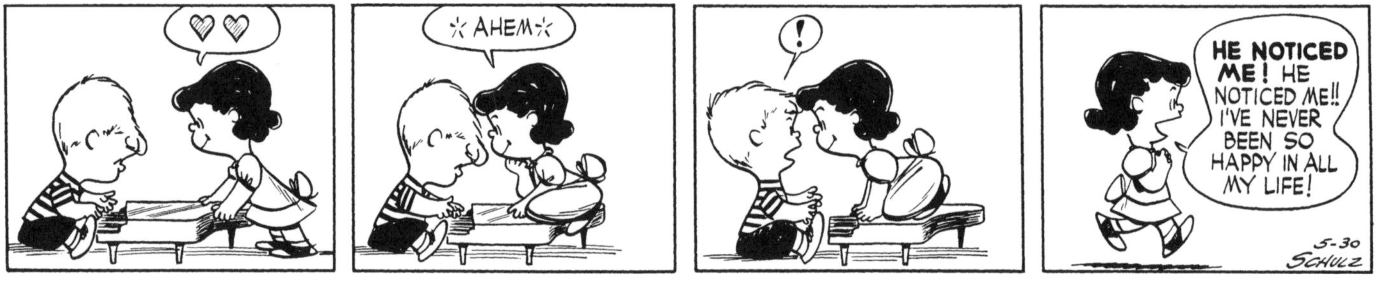
AHEM
!
HE NOTICED ME! HE NOTICED ME!! I'VE NEVER BEEN SO HAPPY IN ALL MY LIFE!
5-30
SCHULZ

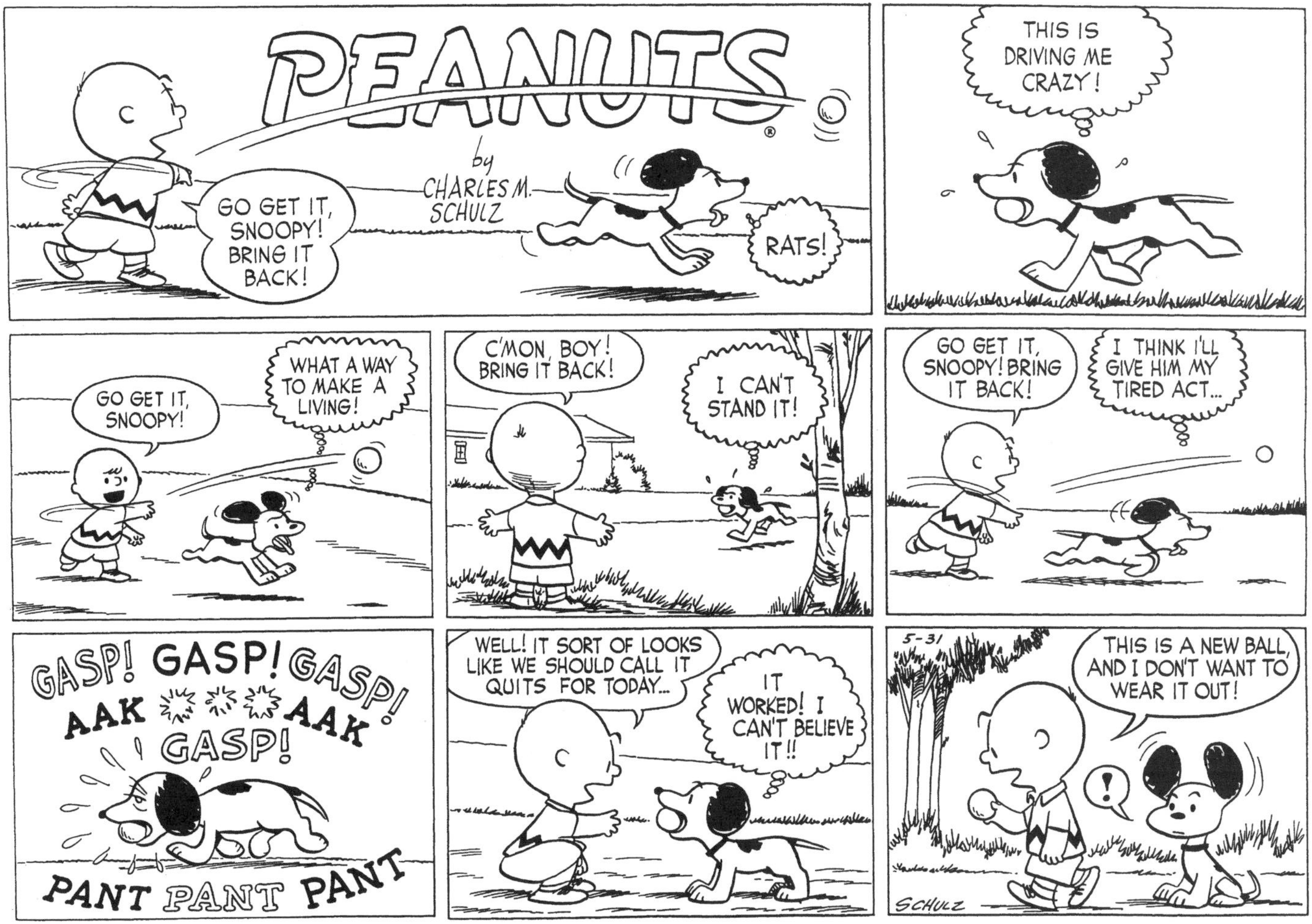
PEANUTS
by CHARLES M. SCHULZ
GO GET IT, SNOOPY! BRING IT BACK!
RATS!
THIS IS DRIVING ME CRAZY!
GO GET IT, SNOOPY!
WHAT A WAY TO MAKE A LIVING!
C'MON, BOY! BRING IT BACK!
I CAN'T STAND IT!
GO GET IT, SNOOPY! BRING IT BACK!
I THINK I'LL GIVE HIM MY TIRED ACT...
GASP! GASP! GASP! AAK AAK GASP!
PANT PANT PANT
WELL! IT SORT OF LOOKS LIKE WE SHOULD CALL IT QUITS FOR TODAY...
IT WORKED! I CAN'T BELIEVE IT!!
5-31
THIS IS A NEW BALL, AND I DON'T WANT TO WEAR IT OUT!
!
SCHULZ

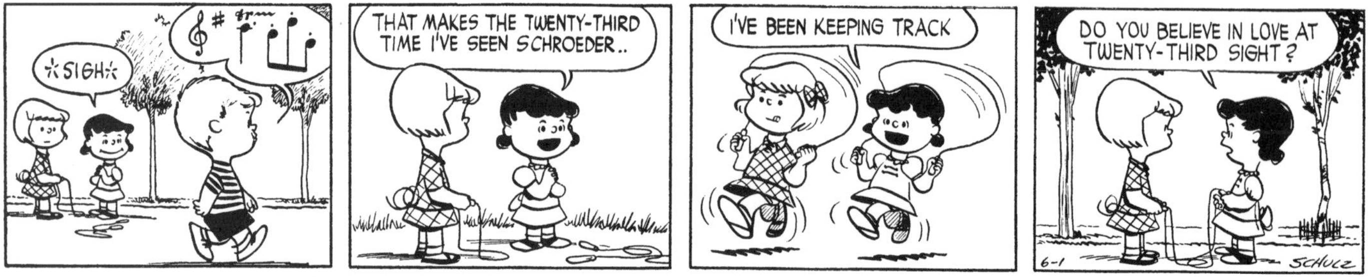
SIGH
THAT MAKES THE TWENTY-THIRD TIME I'VE SEEN SCHROEDER..
I'VE BEEN KEEPING TRACK
DO YOU BELIEVE IN LOVE AT TWENTY-THIRD SIGHT?
6-1
SCHULZ

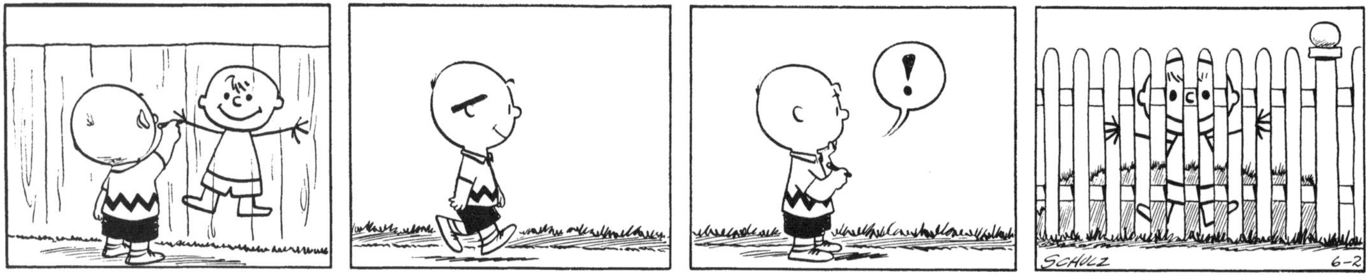
!
SCHULZ
6-2

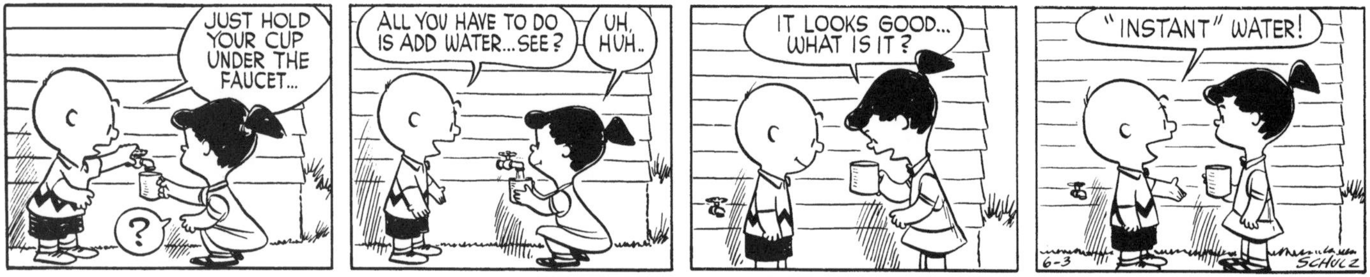
JUST HOLD YOUR CUP UNDER THE FAUCET...
?
ALL YOU HAVE TO DO IS ADD WATER... SEE?
UH, HUH..
IT LOOKS GOOD... WHAT IS IT?
"INSTANT" WATER!
6-3
SCHULZ

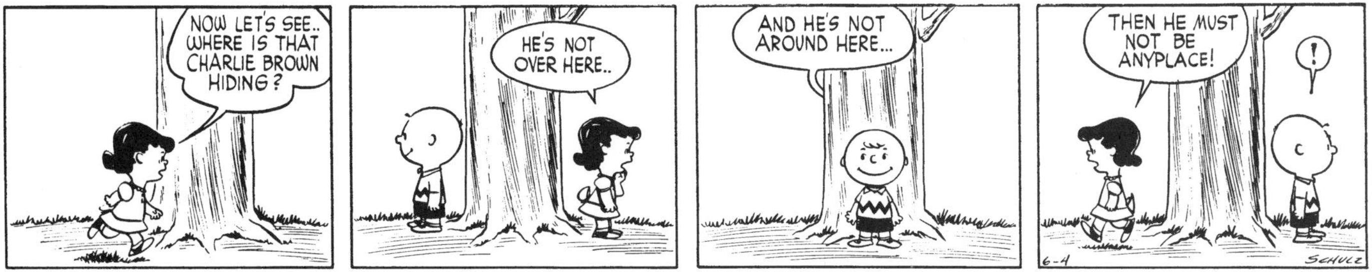
NOW LET'S SEE.. WHERE IS THAT CHARLIE BROWN HIDING?
HE'S NOT OVER HERE..
AND HE'S NOT AROUND HERE...
THEN HE MUST NOT BE ANYPLACE!
!
6-4
SCHULZ

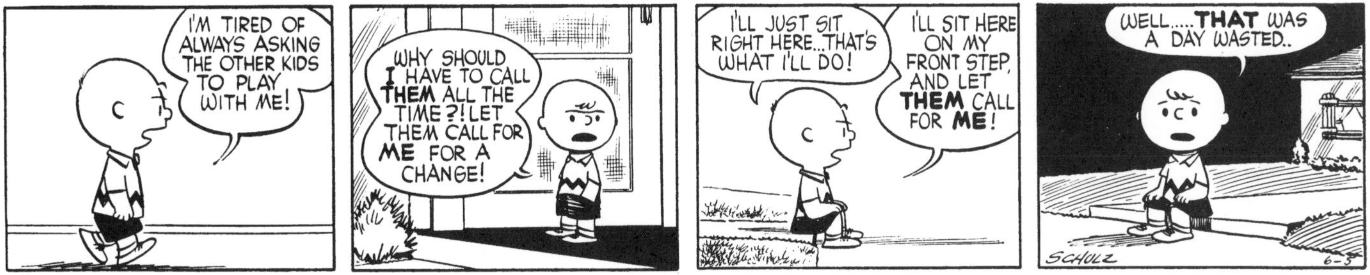
I'M TIRED OF ALWAYS ASKING THE OTHER KIDS TO PLAY WITH ME!
WHY SHOULD I HAVE TO CALL THEM ALL THE TIME?! LET THEM CALL FOR ME FOR A CHANGE!
I'LL JUST SIT RIGHT HERE...THAT'S WHAT I'LL DO!
I'LL SIT HERE ON MY FRONT STEP, AND LET THEM CALL FOR ME!
WELL.....THAT WAS A DAY WASTED..
SCHULZ
6-5

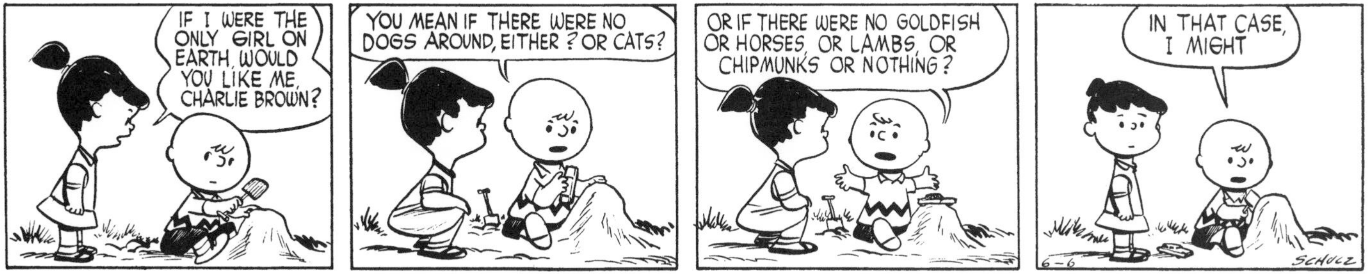
IF I WERE THE ONLY GIRL ON EARTH, WOULD YOU LIKE ME, CHARLIE BROWN?
YOU MEAN IF THERE WERE NO DOGS AROUND, EITHER? OR CATS?
OR IF THERE WERE NO GOLDFISH OR HORSES, OR LAMBS, OR CHIPMUNKS OR NOTHING?
IN THAT CASE, I MIGHT
6-6
SCHULZ

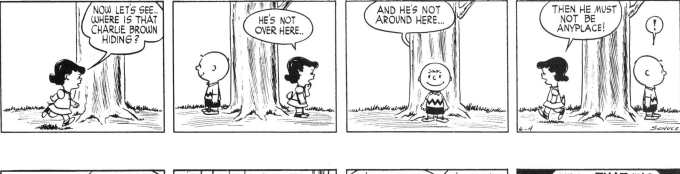

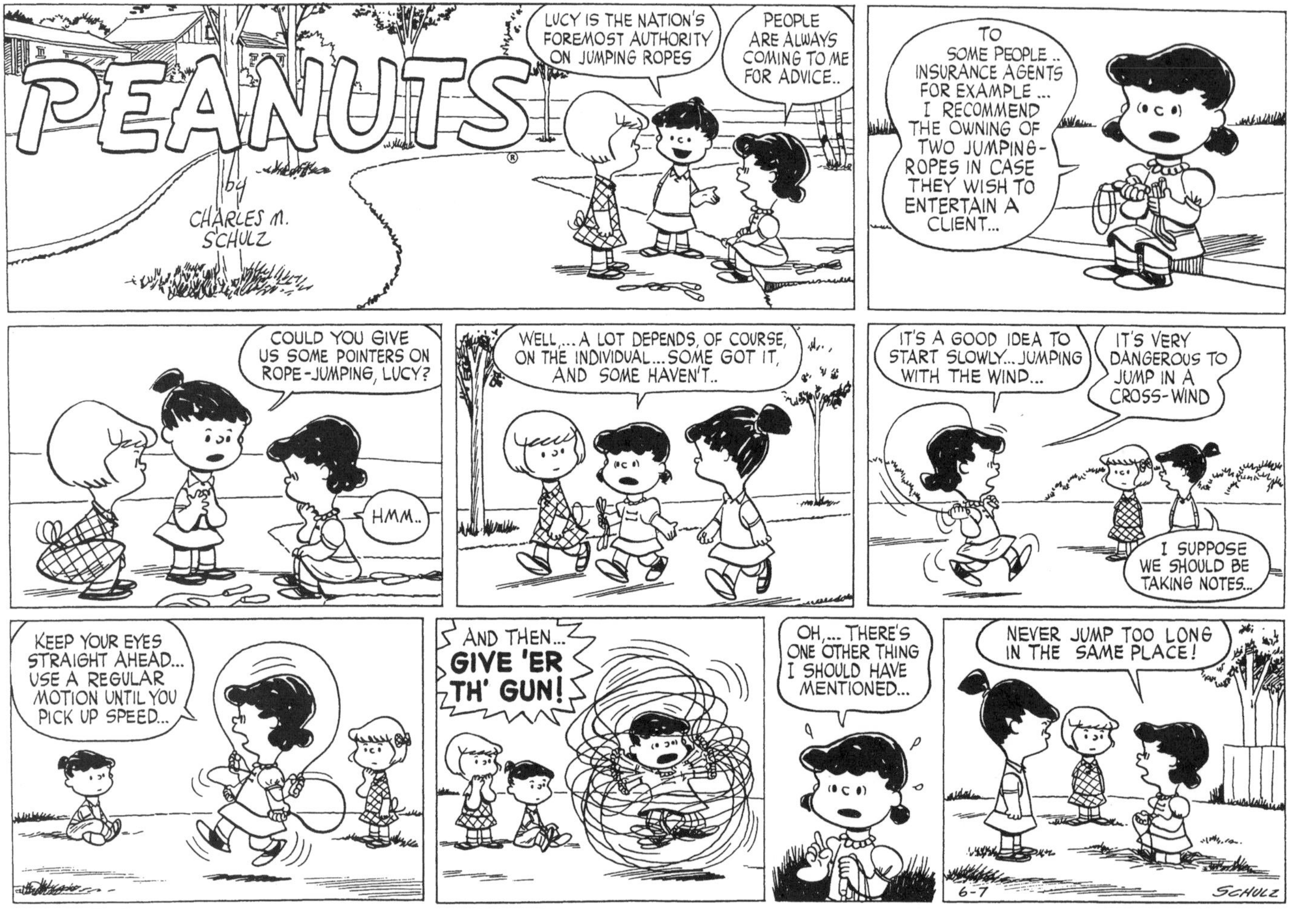
PEANUTS
by CHARLES M. SCHULZ
LUCY IS THE NATION'S FOREMOST AUTHORITY ON JUMPING ROPES
PEOPLE ARE ALWAYS COMING TO ME FOR ADVICE..
TO SOME PEOPLE .. INSURANCE AGENTS FOR EXAMPLE ... I RECOMMEND THE OWNING OF TWO JUMPING-ROPES IN CASE THEY WISH TO ENTERTAIN A CLIENT...
COULD YOU GIVE US SOME POINTERS ON ROPE-JUMPING, LUCY?
HMM..
WELL,... A LOT DEPENDS, OF COURSE, ON THE INDIVIDUAL... SOME GOT IT, AND SOME HAVEN'T..
IT'S A GOOD IDEA TO START SLOWLY... JUMPING WITH THE WIND...
IT'S VERY DANGEROUS TO JUMP IN A CROSS-WIND
I SUPPOSE WE SHOULD BE TAKING NOTES...
KEEP YOUR EYES STRAIGHT AHEAD... USE A REGULAR MOTION UNTIL YOU PICK UP SPEED...
AND THEN... GIVE 'ER TH' GUN!
OH,... THERE'S ONE OTHER THING I SHOULD HAVE MENTIONED...
NEVER JUMP TOO LONG IN THE SAME PLACE!
6-7
SCHULZ

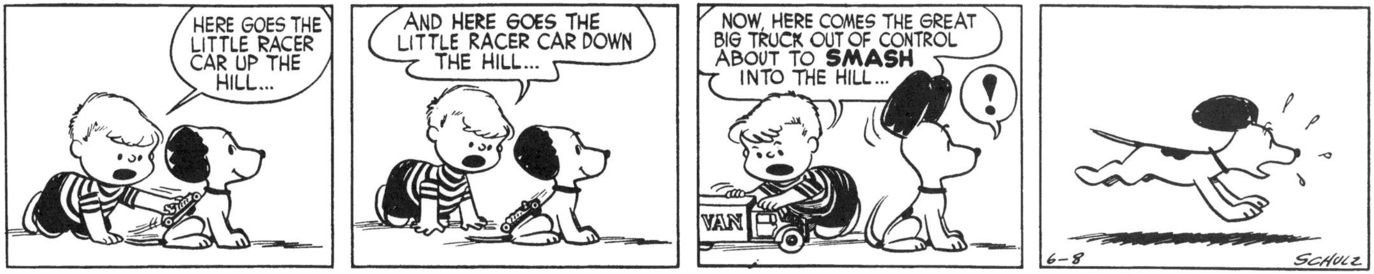
HERE GOES THE LITTLE RACER CAR UP THE HILL...
AND HERE GOES THE LITTLE RACER CAR DOWN THE HILL...
NOW, HERE COMES THE GREAT BIG TRUCK OUT OF CONTROL ABOUT TO **SMASH** INTO THE HILL...
VAN
!
6-8
SCHULZ

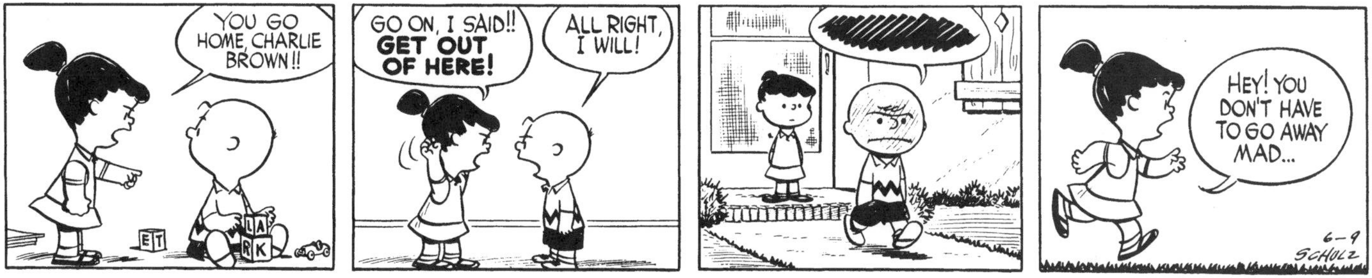
YOU GO HOME, CHARLIE BROWN!!
GO ON, I SAID!! **GET OUT OF HERE!**
ALL RIGHT, I WILL!
HEY! YOU DON'T HAVE TO GO AWAY MAD...
6-9
SCHULZ

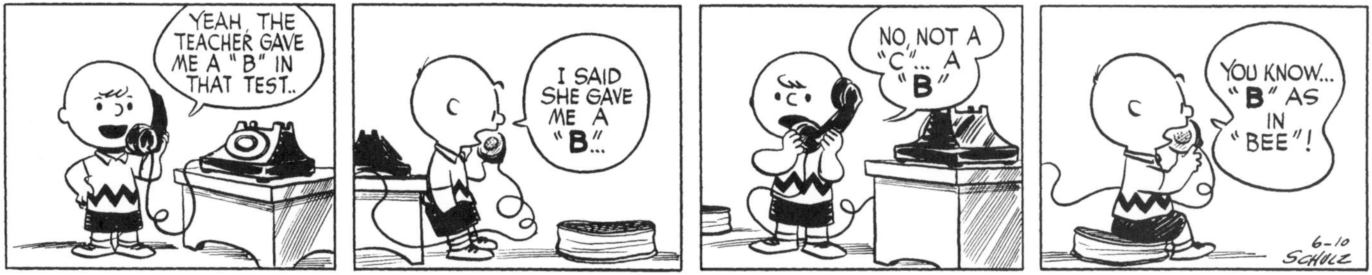
YEAH, THE TEACHER GAVE ME A "B" IN THAT TEST..
I SAID SHE GAVE ME A "**B**"...
NO, NOT A "C"... A "**B**"
YOU KNOW... "**B**" AS IN "BEE"!
6-10
SCHULZ

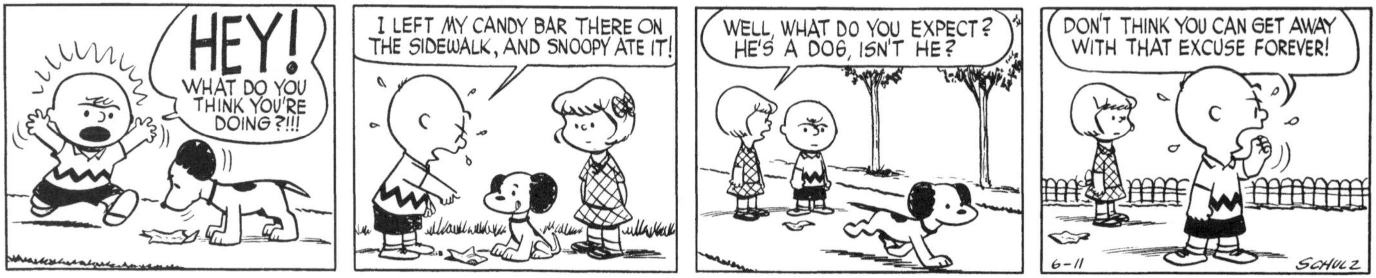
HEY! WHAT DO YOU THINK YOU'RE DOING?!!!
I LEFT MY CANDY BAR THERE ON THE SIDEWALK, AND SNOOPY ATE IT!
WELL, WHAT DO YOU EXPECT? HE'S A DOG, ISN'T HE?
DON'T THINK YOU CAN GET AWAY WITH THAT EXCUSE FOREVER!
6-11
SCHULZ

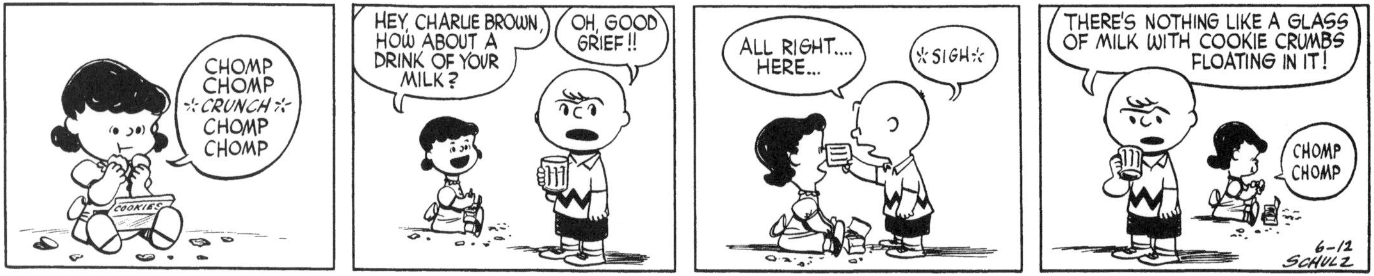
CHOMP CHOMP *CRUNCH* CHOMP CHOMP
COOKIES
HEY, CHARLIE BROWN, HOW ABOUT A DRINK OF YOUR MILK?
OH, GOOD GRIEF!!
ALL RIGHT.... HERE...
SIGH
THERE'S NOTHING LIKE A GLASS OF MILK WITH COOKIE CRUMBS FLOATING IN IT!
CHOMP CHOMP
6-12
SCHULZ

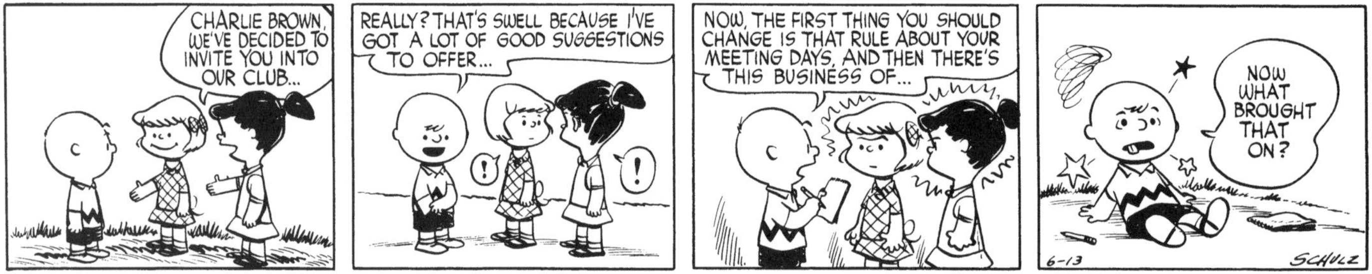
CHARLIE BROWN, WE'VE DECIDED TO INVITE YOU INTO OUR CLUB...
REALLY? THAT'S SWELL BECAUSE I'VE GOT A LOT OF GOOD SUGGESTIONS TO OFFER...
!
!
NOW, THE FIRST THING YOU SHOULD CHANGE IS THAT RULE ABOUT YOUR MEETING DAYS, AND THEN THERE'S THIS BUSINESS OF...
NOW WHAT BROUGHT THAT ON?
6-13
SCHULZ

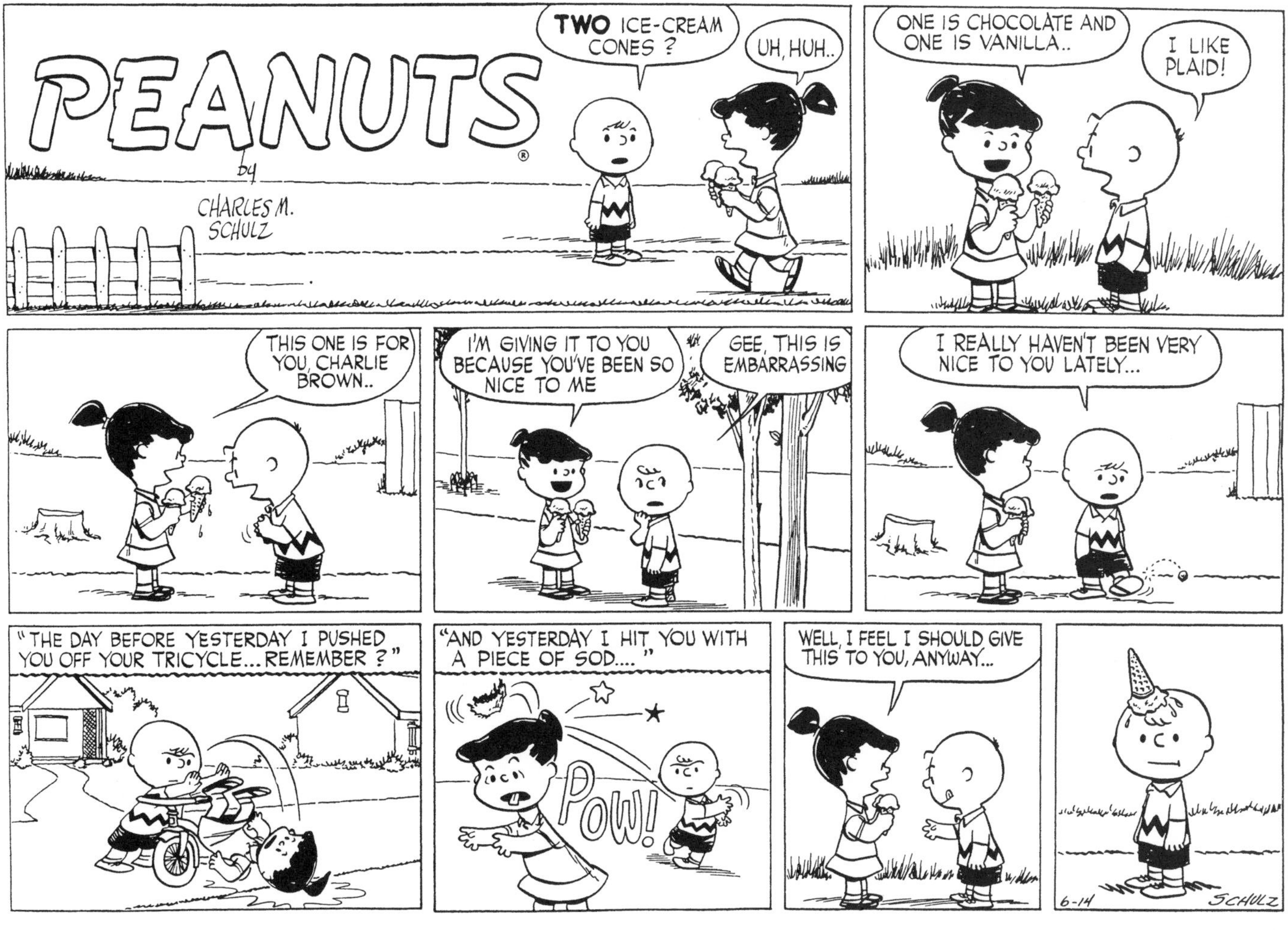
PEANUTS
by CHARLES M. SCHULZ
TWO ICE-CREAM CONES ?
UH, HUH..
ONE IS CHOCOLATE AND ONE IS VANILLA..
I LIKE PLAID!
THIS ONE IS FOR YOU, CHARLIE BROWN..
I'M GIVING IT TO YOU BECAUSE YOU'VE BEEN SO NICE TO ME
GEE, THIS IS EMBARRASSING
I REALLY HAVEN'T BEEN VERY NICE TO YOU LATELY...
"THE DAY BEFORE YESTERDAY I PUSHED YOU OFF YOUR TRICYCLE... REMEMBER ?"
"AND YESTERDAY I HIT YOU WITH A PIECE OF SOD...."
POW!
WELL, I FEEL I SHOULD GIVE THIS TO YOU, ANYWAY...
6-14
SCHULZ

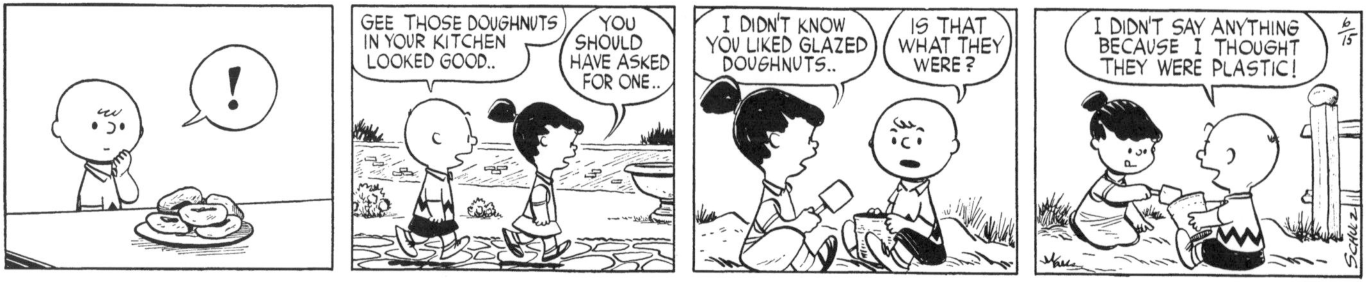
!
GEE THOSE DOUGHNUTS IN YOUR KITCHEN LOOKED GOOD..
YOU SHOULD HAVE ASKED FOR ONE..
I DIDN'T KNOW YOU LIKED GLAZED DOUGHNUTS..
IS THAT WHAT THEY WERE?
I DIDN'T SAY ANYTHING BECAUSE I THOUGHT THEY WERE PLASTIC!
6/15
SCHULZ

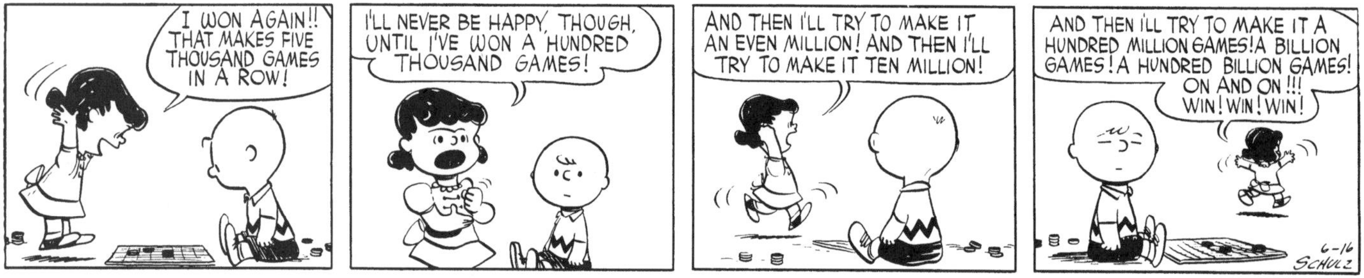
I WON AGAIN!! THAT MAKES FIVE THOUSAND GAMES IN A ROW!
I'LL NEVER BE HAPPY, THOUGH, UNTIL I'VE WON A HUNDRED THOUSAND GAMES!
AND THEN I'LL TRY TO MAKE IT AN EVEN MILLION! AND THEN I'LL TRY TO MAKE IT TEN MILLION!
AND THEN I'LL TRY TO MAKE IT A HUNDRED MILLION GAMES! A BILLION GAMES! A HUNDRED BILLION GAMES! ON AND ON!!! WIN! WIN! WIN!
6-16
SCHULZ

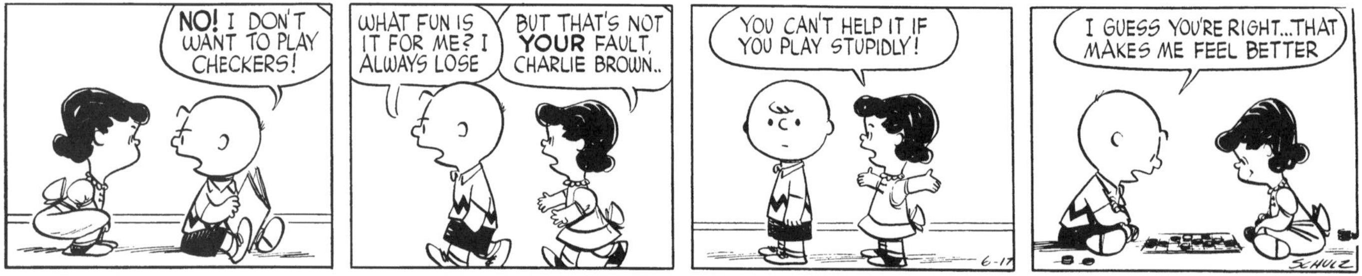
NO! I DON'T WANT TO PLAY CHECKERS!
WHAT FUN IS IT FOR ME? I ALWAYS LOSE
BUT THAT'S NOT **YOUR** FAULT, CHARLIE BROWN..
YOU CAN'T HELP IT IF YOU PLAY STUPIDLY!
6-17
I GUESS YOU'RE RIGHT...THAT MAKES ME FEEL BETTER
SCHULZ

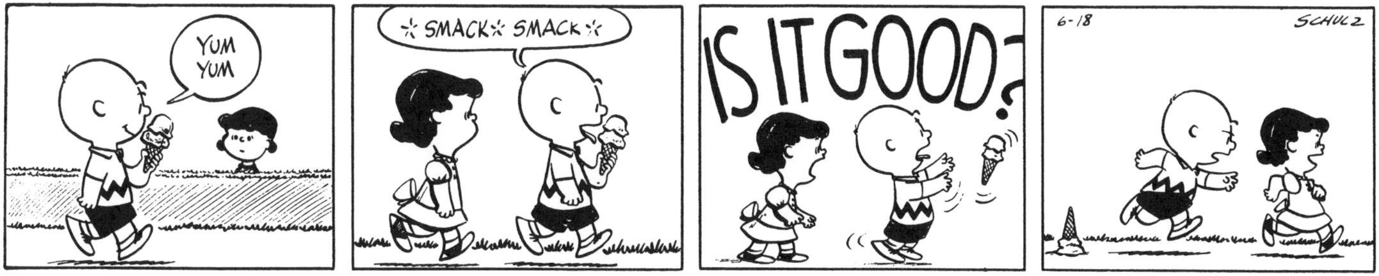
YUM YUM
SMACK SMACK
IS IT GOOD?
6-18
SCHULZ

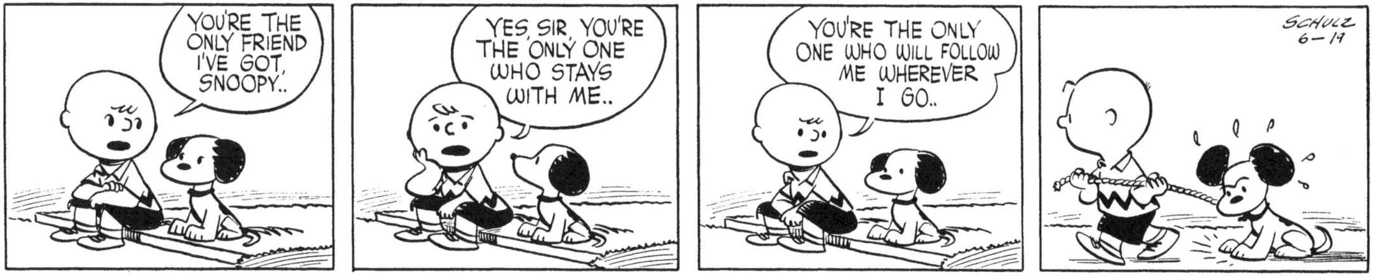
YOU'RE THE ONLY FRIEND I'VE GOT, SNOOPY..
YES, SIR, YOU'RE THE ONLY ONE WHO STAYS WITH ME..
YOU'RE THE ONLY ONE WHO WILL FOLLOW ME WHEREVER I GO..
SCHULZ 6-19

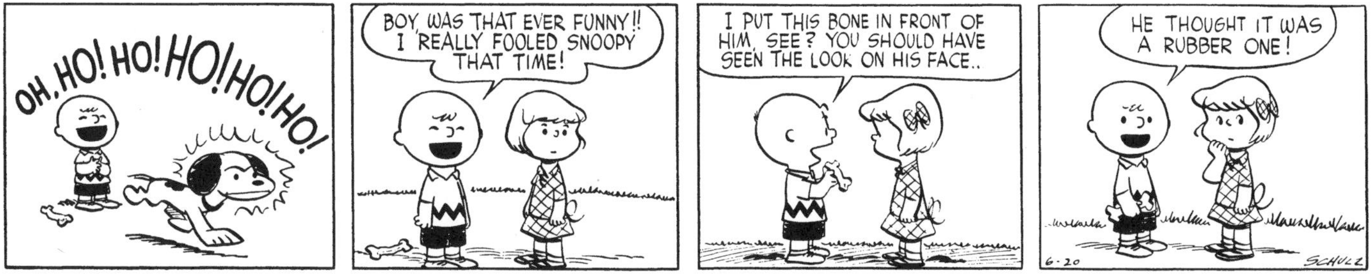
OH, HO! HO! HO! HO! HO!
BOY, WAS THAT EVER FUNNY!! I REALLY FOOLED SNOOPY THAT TIME!
I PUT THIS BONE IN FRONT OF HIM, SEE? YOU SHOULD HAVE SEEN THE LOOK ON HIS FACE..
HE THOUGHT IT WAS A RUBBER ONE!
6-20
SCHULZ

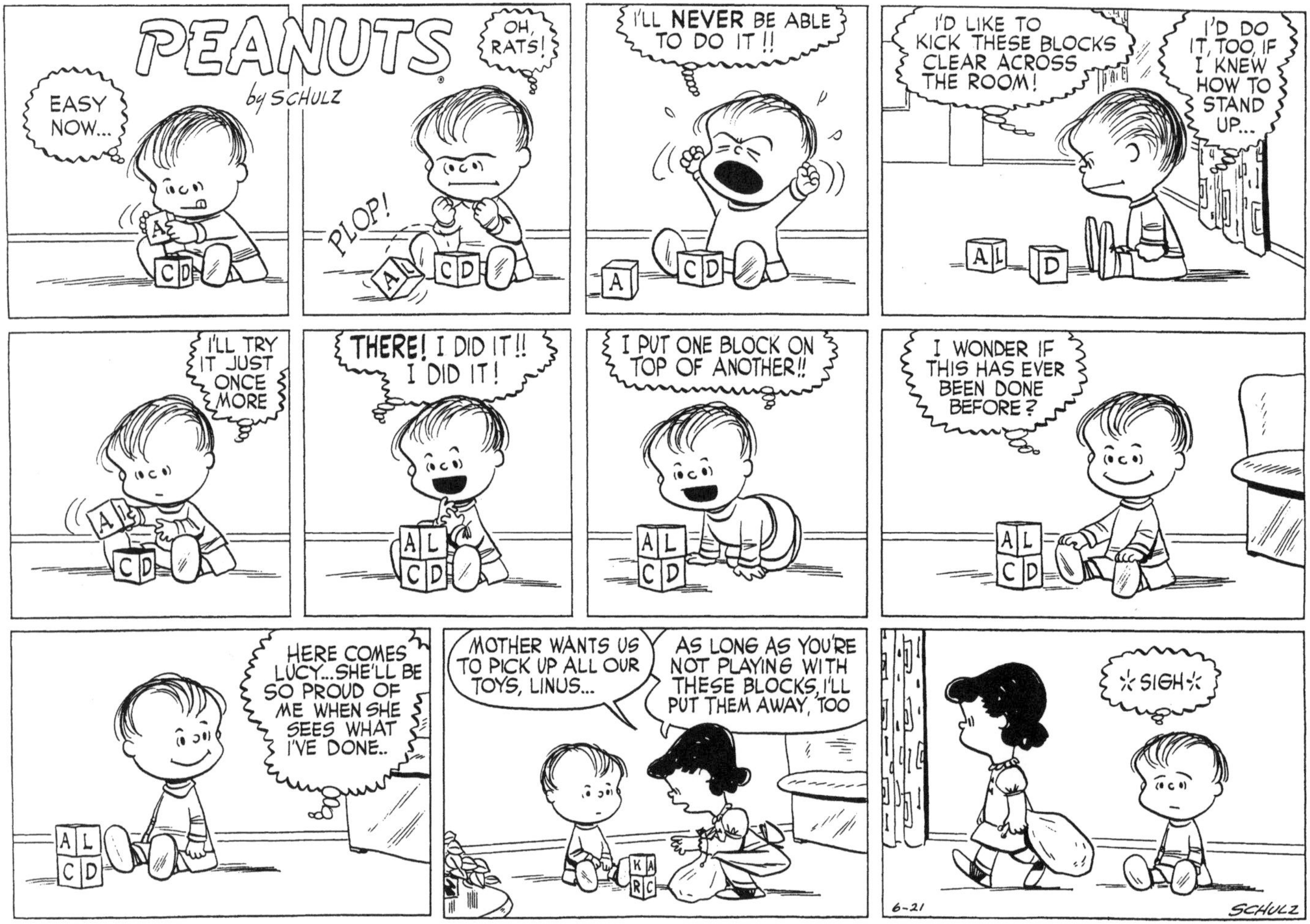
PEANUTS
by SCHULZ
EASY NOW...
OH, RATS!
PLOP!
I'LL NEVER BE ABLE TO DO IT!!
I'D LIKE TO KICK THESE BLOCKS CLEAR ACROSS THE ROOM!
I'D DO IT, TOO, IF I KNEW HOW TO STAND UP...
I'LL TRY IT JUST ONCE MORE
THERE! I DID IT!! I DID IT!
I PUT ONE BLOCK ON TOP OF ANOTHER!!
I WONDER IF THIS HAS EVER BEEN DONE BEFORE?
HERE COMES LUCY...SHE'LL BE SO PROUD OF ME WHEN SHE SEES WHAT I'VE DONE..
MOTHER WANTS US TO PICK UP ALL OUR TOYS, LINUS...
AS LONG AS YOU'RE NOT PLAYING WITH THESE BLOCKS, I'LL PUT THEM AWAY, TOO
SIGH
6-21
SCHULZ

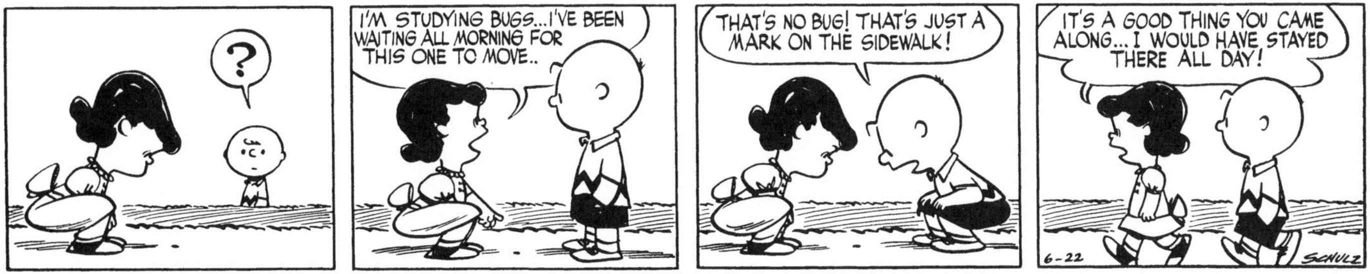
?
I'M STUDYING BUGS...I'VE BEEN WAITING ALL MORNING FOR THIS ONE TO MOVE..
THAT'S NO BUG! THAT'S JUST A MARK ON THE SIDEWALK!
IT'S A GOOD THING YOU CAME ALONG... I WOULD HAVE STAYED THERE ALL DAY!
6-22
SCHULZ

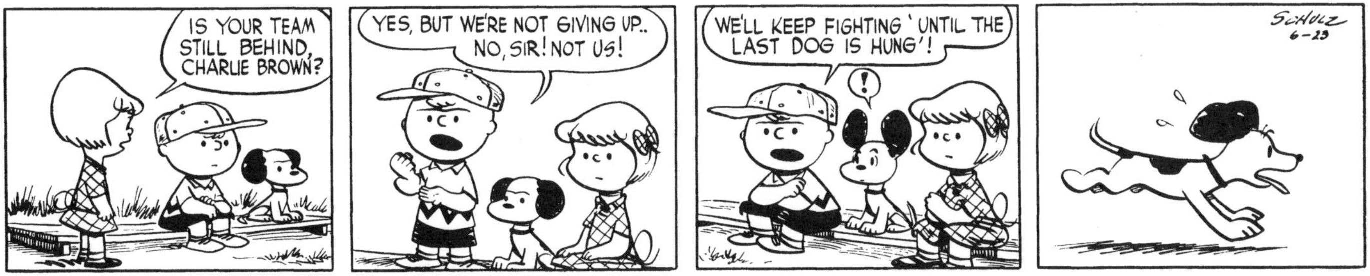
IS YOUR TEAM STILL BEHIND, CHARLIE BROWN?
YES, BUT WE'RE NOT GIVING UP.. NO, SIR! NOT US!
WE'LL KEEP FIGHTING 'UNTIL THE LAST DOG IS HUNG'!
!
SCHULZ
6-23

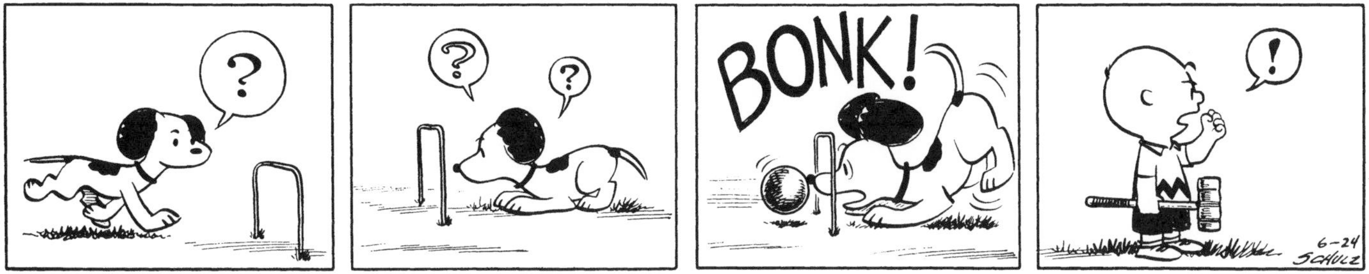
?
?
?
BONK!
!
6-24
SCHULZ

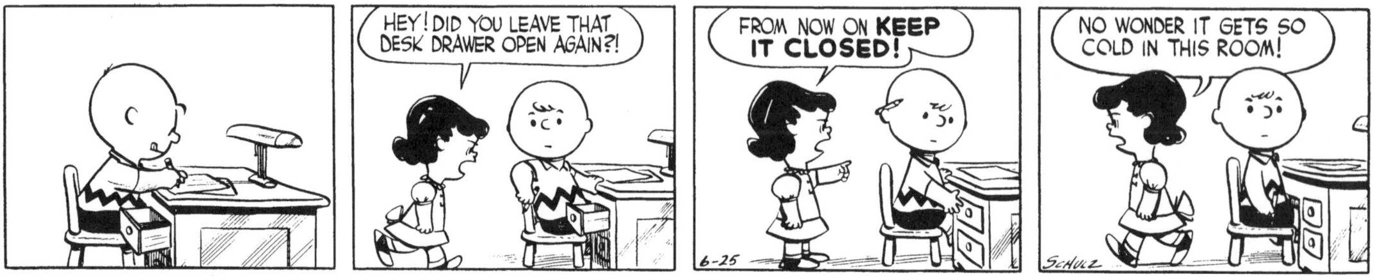
HEY! DID YOU LEAVE THAT DESK DRAWER OPEN AGAIN?!
FROM NOW ON **KEEP IT CLOSED!**
6-25
NO WONDER IT GETS SO COLD IN THIS ROOM!
SCHULZ

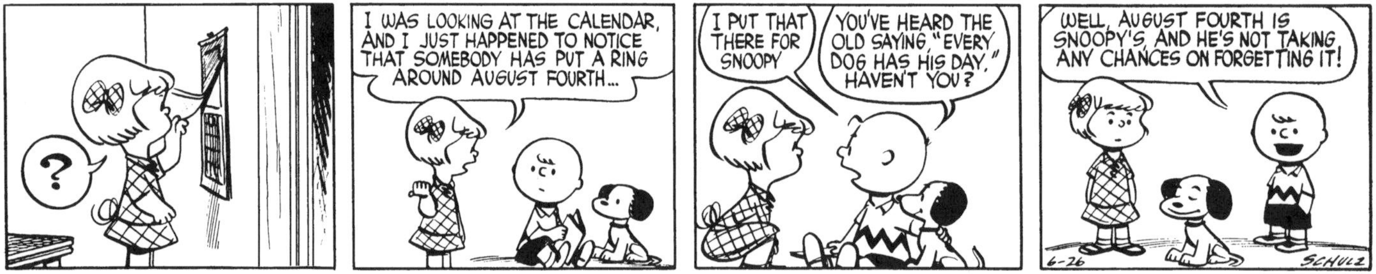
?
I WAS LOOKING AT THE CALENDAR, AND I JUST HAPPENED TO NOTICE THAT SOMEBODY HAS PUT A RING AROUND AUGUST FOURTH...
I PUT THAT THERE FOR SNOOPY
YOU'VE HEARD THE OLD SAYING, "EVERY DOG HAS HIS DAY," HAVEN'T YOU?
WELL, AUGUST FOURTH IS SNOOPY'S, AND HE'S NOT TAKING ANY CHANCES ON FORGETTING IT!
6-26
SCHULZ

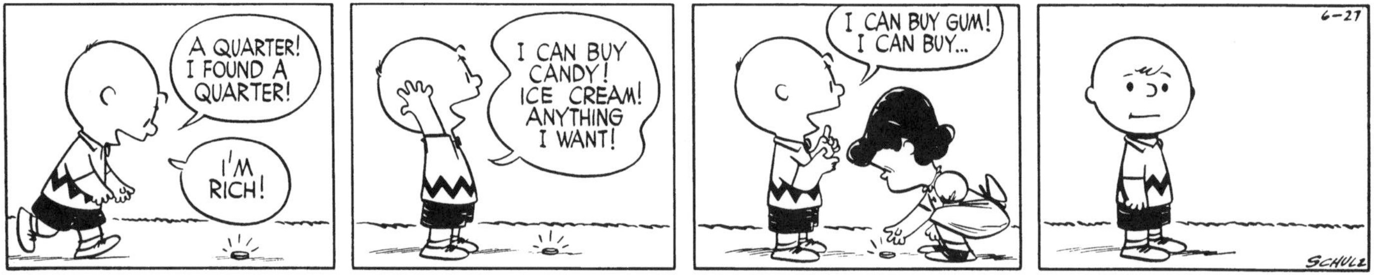
A QUARTER! I FOUND A QUARTER!
I'M RICH!
I CAN BUY CANDY! ICE CREAM! ANYTHING I WANT!
I CAN BUY GUM! I CAN BUY...
6-27
SCHULZ

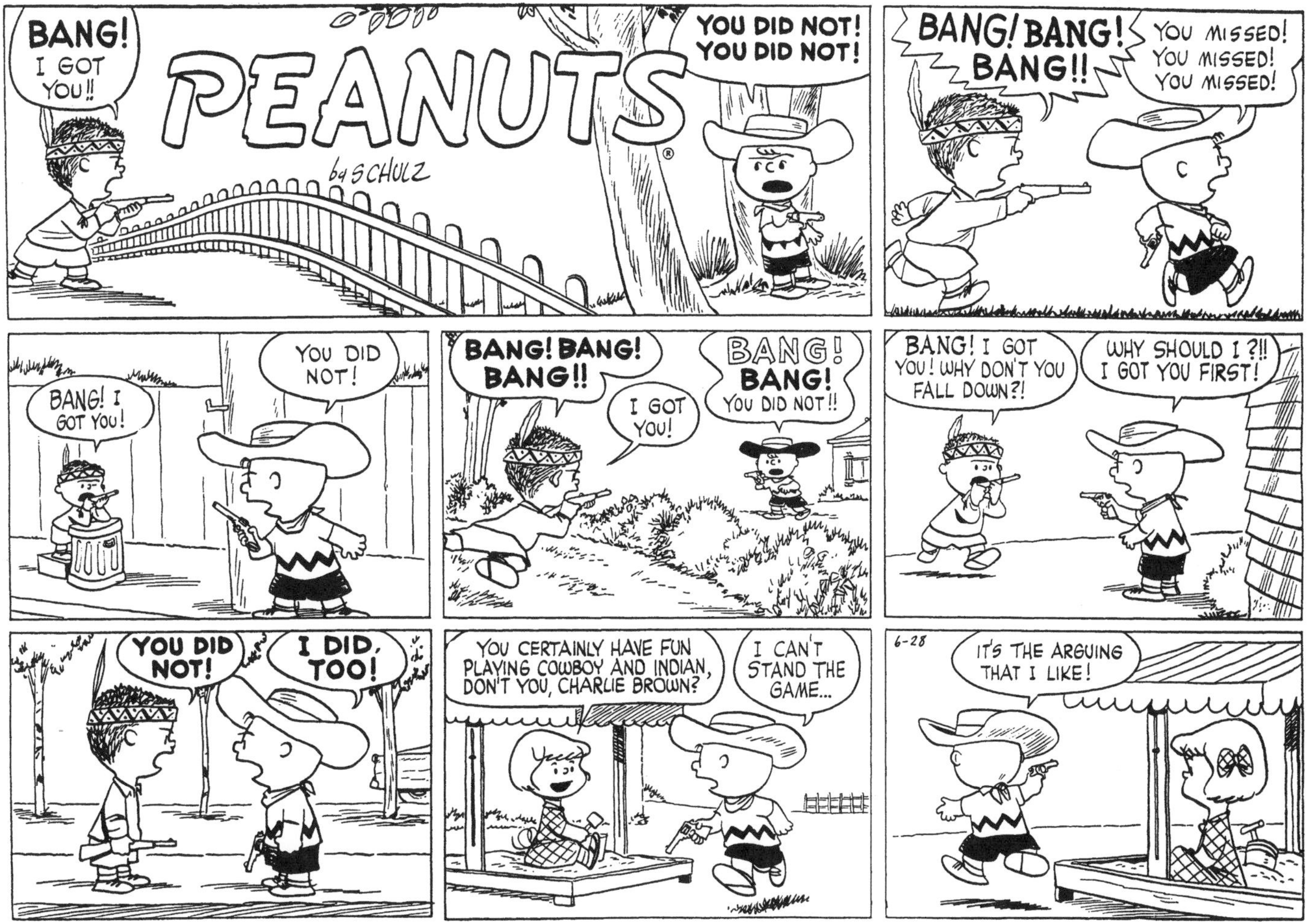
BANG! I GOT YOU!!
PEANUTS
by SCHULZ
YOU DID NOT! YOU DID NOT!
BANG! BANG! BANG!!
YOU MISSED! YOU MISSED! YOU MISSED!
BANG! I GOT YOU!
YOU DID NOT!
BANG! BANG! BANG!!
I GOT YOU!
BANG! BANG! YOU DID NOT!!
BANG! I GOT YOU! WHY DON'T YOU FALL DOWN?!
WHY SHOULD I ?!! I GOT YOU FIRST!
YOU DID NOT!
I DID, TOO!
YOU CERTAINLY HAVE FUN PLAYING COWBOY AND INDIAN, DON'T YOU, CHARLIE BROWN?
I CAN'T STAND THE GAME...
6-28
IT'S THE ARGUING THAT I LIKE!

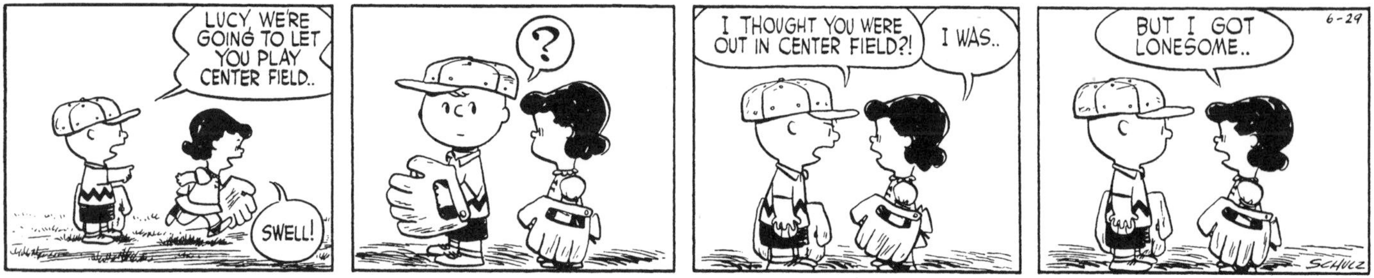
LUCY, WE'RE GOING TO LET YOU PLAY CENTER FIELD..
SWELL!
?
I THOUGHT YOU WERE OUT IN CENTER FIELD?!
I WAS..
BUT I GOT LONESOME..
6-29
SCHULZ

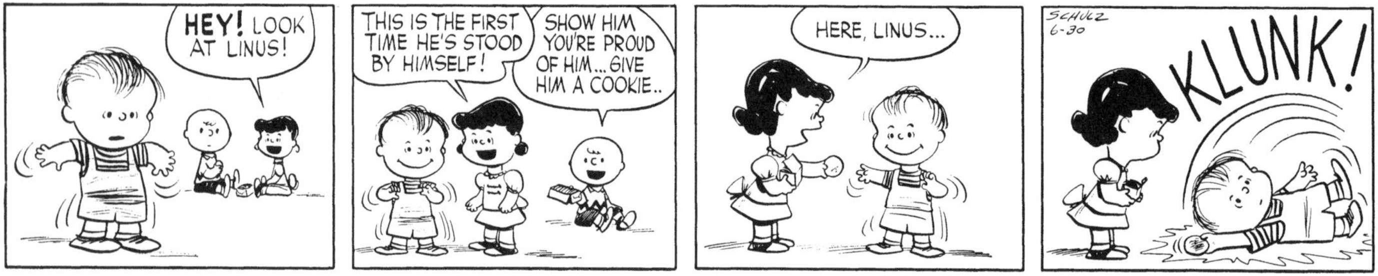
HEY! LOOK AT LINUS!
THIS IS THE FIRST TIME HE'S STOOD BY HIMSELF!
SHOW HIM YOU'RE PROUD OF HIM... GIVE HIM A COOKIE..
HERE, LINUS...
SCHULZ
6-30
KLUNK!

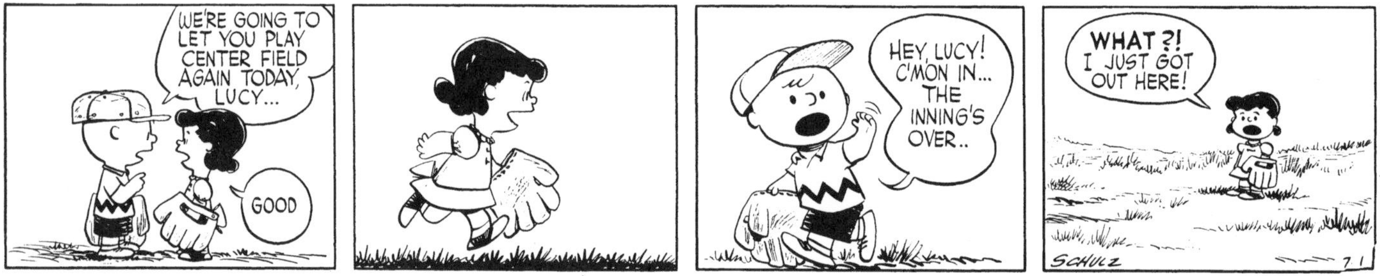
WE'RE GOING TO LET YOU PLAY CENTER FIELD AGAIN TODAY, LUCY...
GOOD
HEY, LUCY! C'MON IN... THE INNING'S OVER..
WHAT?! I JUST GOT OUT HERE!
SCHULZ
7-1

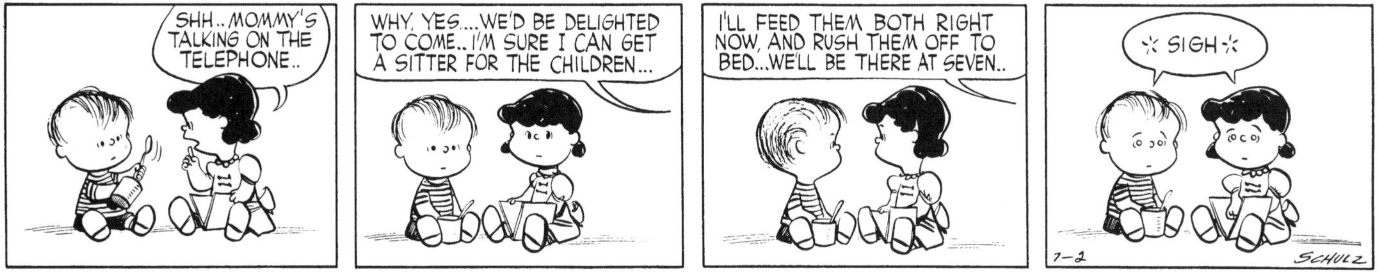
SHH.. MOMMY'S TALKING ON THE TELEPHONE..
WHY, YES....WE'D BE DELIGHTED TO COME.. I'M SURE I CAN GET A SITTER FOR THE CHILDREN...
I'LL FEED THEM BOTH RIGHT NOW, AND RUSH THEM OFF TO BED...WE'LL BE THERE AT SEVEN..
SIGH
7-2
SCHULZ

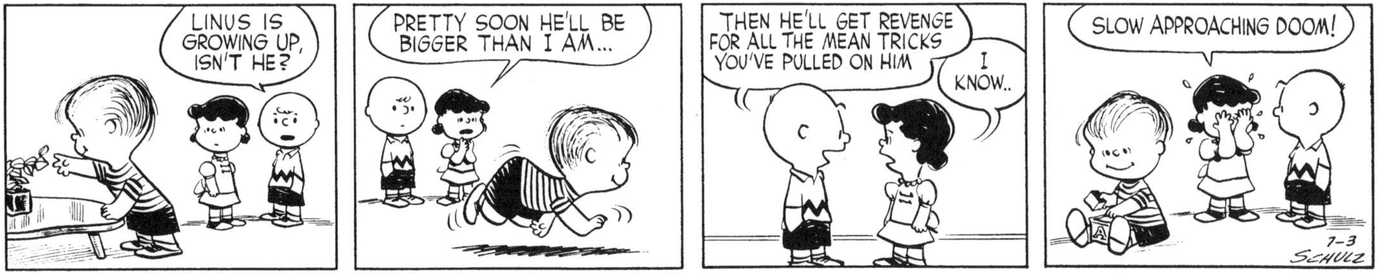
LINUS IS GROWING UP, ISN'T HE?
PRETTY SOON HE'LL BE BIGGER THAN I AM...
THEN HE'LL GET REVENGE FOR ALL THE MEAN TRICKS YOU'VE PULLED ON HIM
I KNOW..
SLOW APPROACHING DOOM!
7-3
SCHULZ

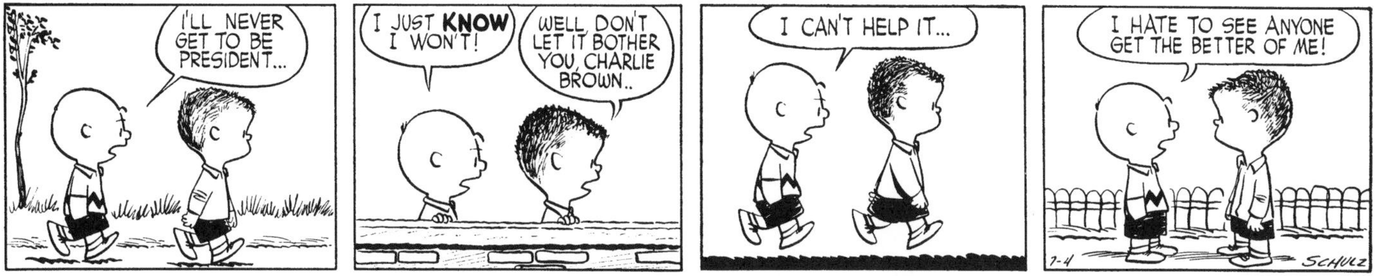
I'LL NEVER GET TO BE PRESIDENT...
I JUST **KNOW** I WON'T!
WELL, DON'T LET IT BOTHER YOU, CHARLIE BROWN..
I CAN'T HELP IT...
I HATE TO SEE ANYONE GET THE BETTER OF ME!
7-4
SCHULZ

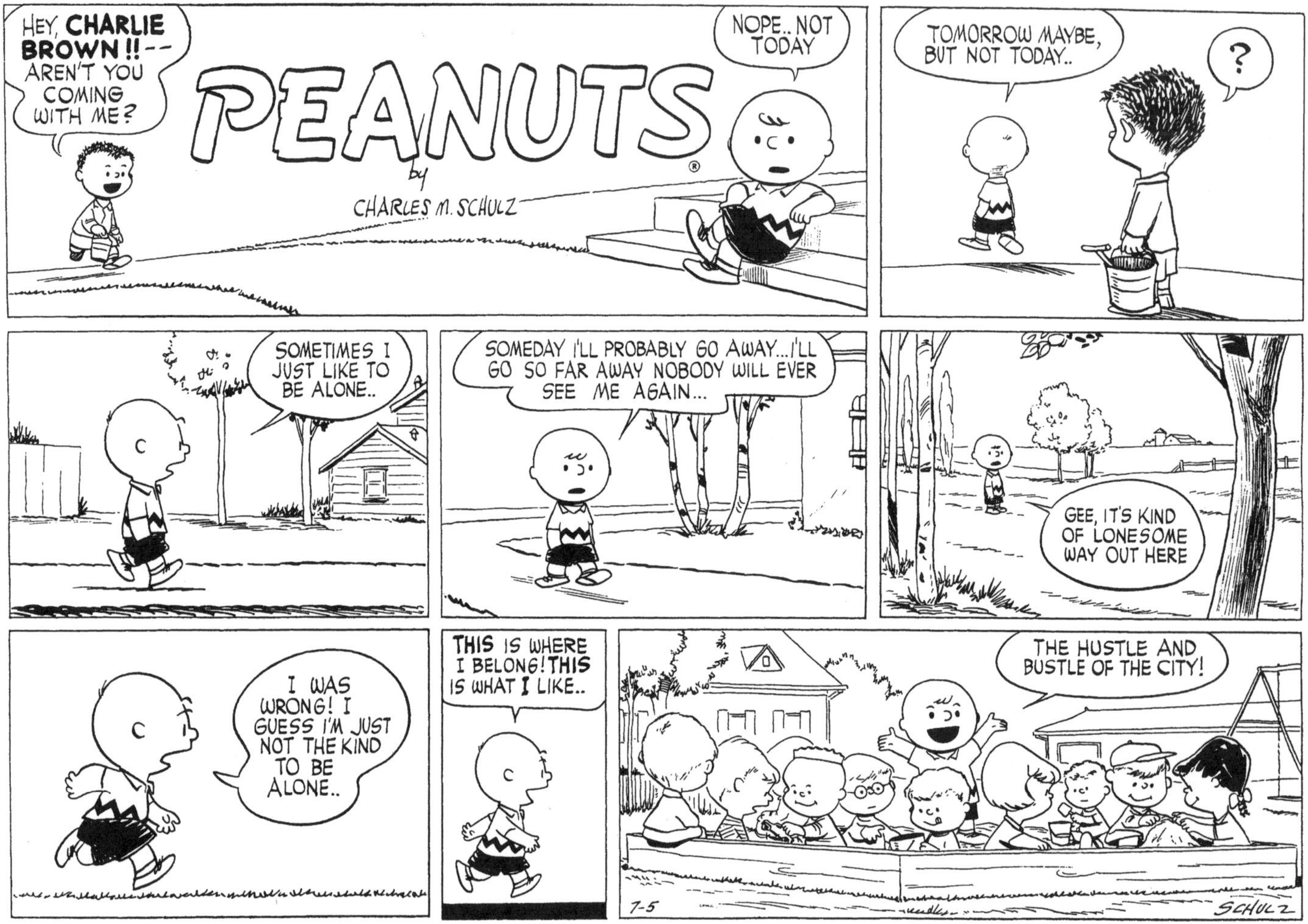
HEY, CHARLIE BROWN!! -- AREN'T YOU COMING WITH ME?
PEANUTS
by CHARLES M. SCHULZ
NOPE.. NOT TODAY
TOMORROW MAYBE, BUT NOT TODAY..
?
SOMETIMES I JUST LIKE TO BE ALONE..
SOMEDAY I'LL PROBABLY GO AWAY...I'LL GO SO FAR AWAY NOBODY WILL EVER SEE ME AGAIN...
GEE, IT'S KIND OF LONESOME WAY OUT HERE
I WAS WRONG! I GUESS I'M JUST NOT THE KIND TO BE ALONE..
THIS IS WHERE I BELONG! THIS IS WHAT I LIKE..
THE HUSTLE AND BUSTLE OF THE CITY!
7-5
SCHULZ

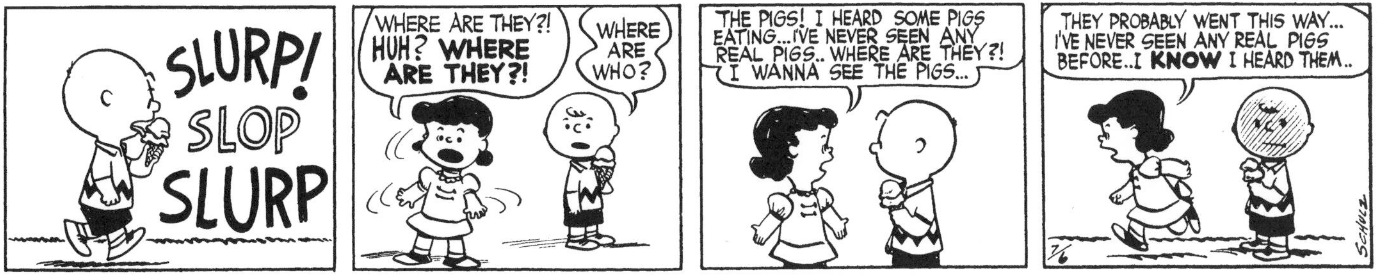
SLURP!
SLOP
SLURP
WHERE ARE THEY?! HUH? WHERE ARE THEY?!
WHERE ARE WHO?
THE PIGS! I HEARD SOME PIGS EATING...I'VE NEVER SEEN ANY REAL PIGS.. WHERE ARE THEY?! I WANNA SEE THE PIGS...
THEY PROBABLY WENT THIS WAY... I'VE NEVER SEEN ANY REAL PIGS BEFORE..I KNOW I HEARD THEM..
7/6
SCHULZ

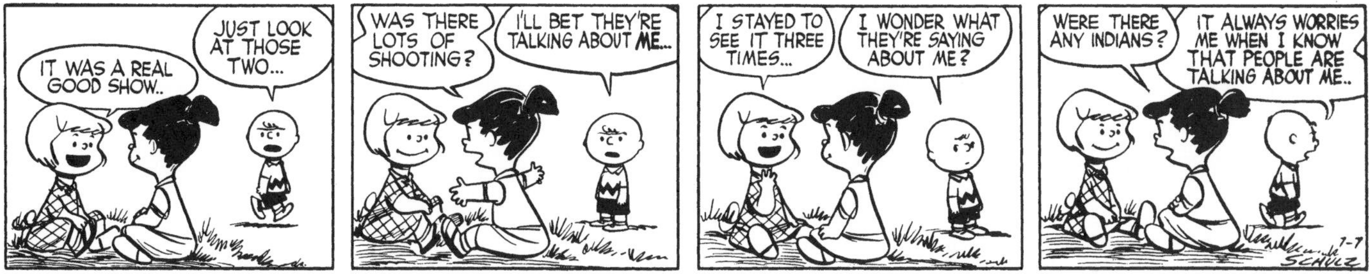
IT WAS A REAL GOOD SHOW..
JUST LOOK AT THOSE TWO...
WAS THERE LOTS OF SHOOTING?
I'LL BET THEY'RE TALKING ABOUT ME...
I STAYED TO SEE IT THREE TIMES...
I WONDER WHAT THEY'RE SAYING ABOUT ME?
WERE THERE ANY INDIANS?
IT ALWAYS WORRIES ME WHEN I KNOW THAT PEOPLE ARE TALKING ABOUT ME..
7-7
SCHULZ

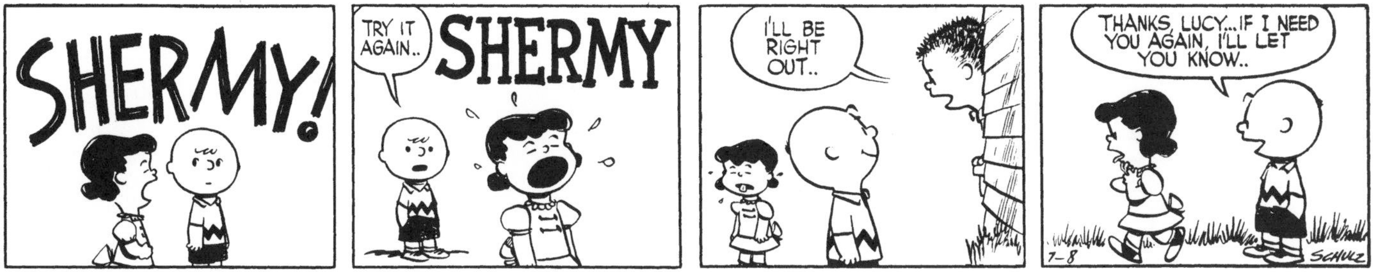
SHERMY!
TRY IT AGAIN..
SHERMY
I'LL BE RIGHT OUT..
THANKS, LUCY...IF I NEED YOU AGAIN, I'LL LET YOU KNOW..
7-8
SCHULZ

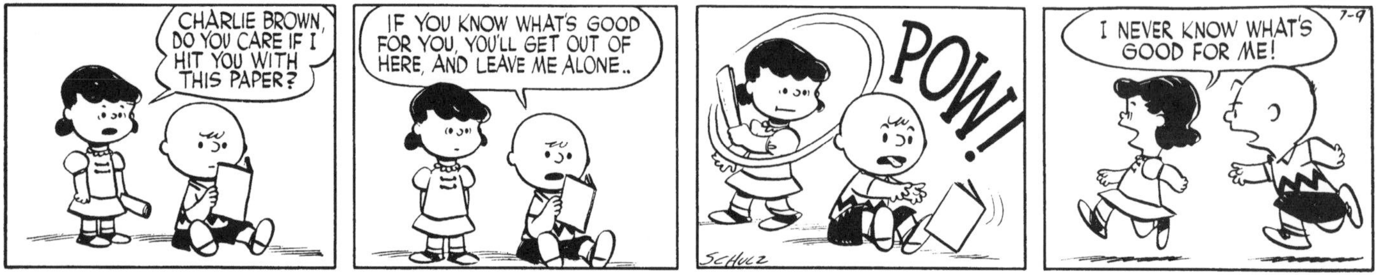
CHARLIE BROWN, DO YOU CARE IF I HIT YOU WITH THIS PAPER?
IF YOU KNOW WHAT'S GOOD FOR YOU, YOU'LL GET OUT OF HERE, AND LEAVE ME ALONE..
POW!
SCHULZ
I NEVER KNOW WHAT'S GOOD FOR ME!
7-9

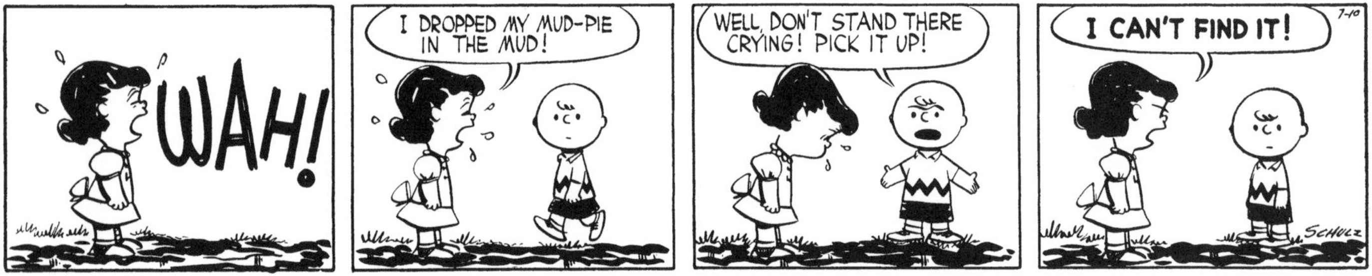
WAH!
I DROPPED MY MUD-PIE IN THE MUD!
WELL, DON'T STAND THERE CRYING! PICK IT UP!
I CAN'T FIND IT!
7-10
SCHULZ

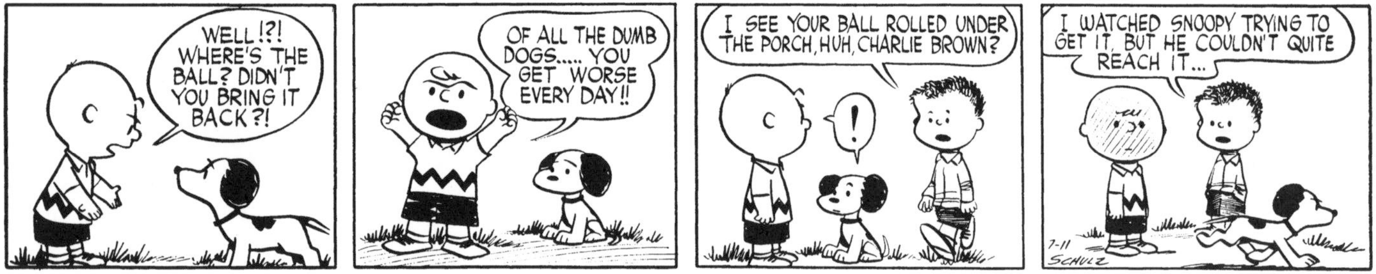
WELL!?! WHERE'S THE BALL? DIDN'T YOU BRING IT BACK?!
SCHULZ
OF ALL THE DUMB DOGS..... YOU GET WORSE EVERY DAY!!
I SEE YOUR BALL ROLLED UNDER THE PORCH, HUH, CHARLIE BROWN?
!
I WATCHED SNOOPY TRYING TO GET IT, BUT HE COULDN'T QUITE REACH IT...
7-11
SCHULZ

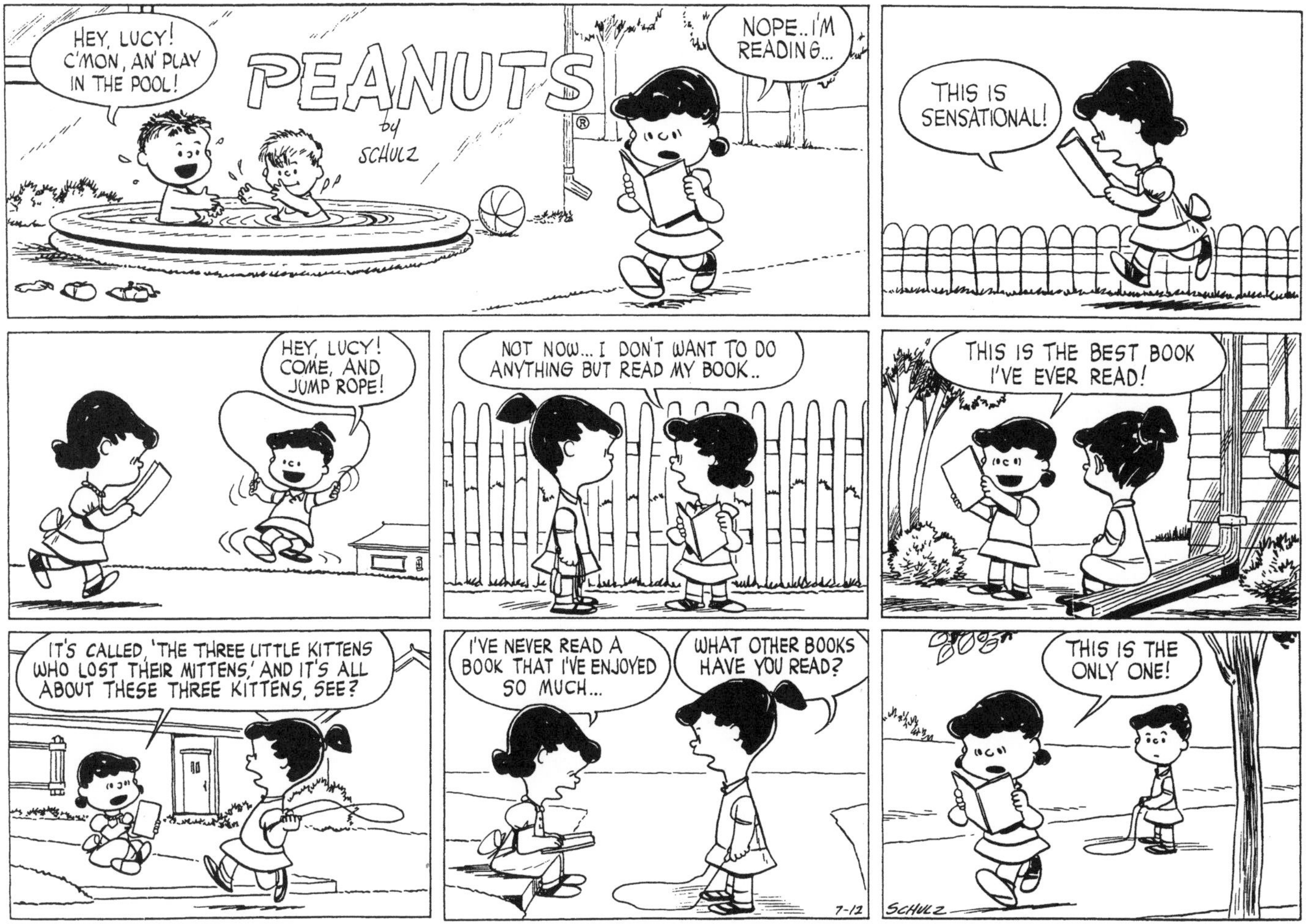
HEY, LUCY! C'MON, AN' PLAY IN THE POOL!
PEANUTS
by SCHULZ
NOPE.. I'M READING...
THIS IS SENSATIONAL!
HEY, LUCY! COME, AND JUMP ROPE!
NOT NOW... I DON'T WANT TO DO ANYTHING BUT READ MY BOOK..
THIS IS THE BEST BOOK I'VE EVER READ!
IT'S CALLED 'THE THREE LITTLE KITTENS WHO LOST THEIR MITTENS,' AND IT'S ALL ABOUT THESE THREE KITTENS, SEE?
I'VE NEVER READ A BOOK THAT I'VE ENJOYED SO MUCH...
WHAT OTHER BOOKS HAVE YOU READ?
THIS IS THE ONLY ONE!
7-12
SCHULZ

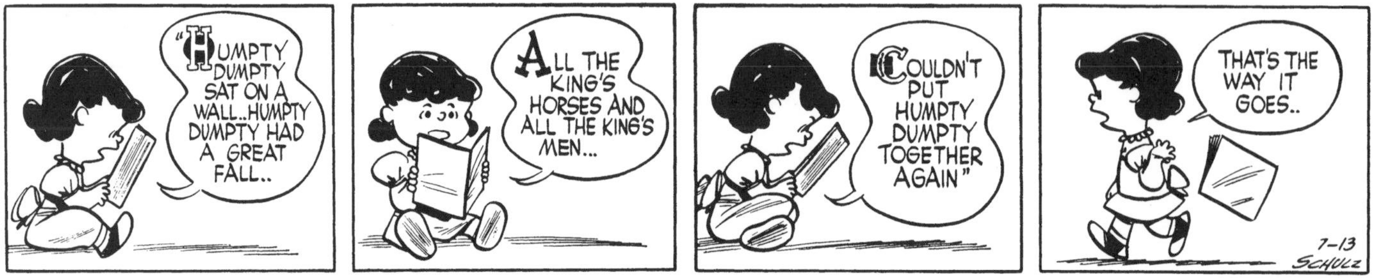
"HUMPTY DUMPTY SAT ON A WALL..HUMPTY DUMPTY HAD A GREAT FALL..
ALL THE KING'S HORSES AND ALL THE KING'S MEN...
COULDN'T PUT HUMPTY DUMPTY TOGETHER AGAIN"
THAT'S THE WAY IT GOES..
7-13
SCHULZ

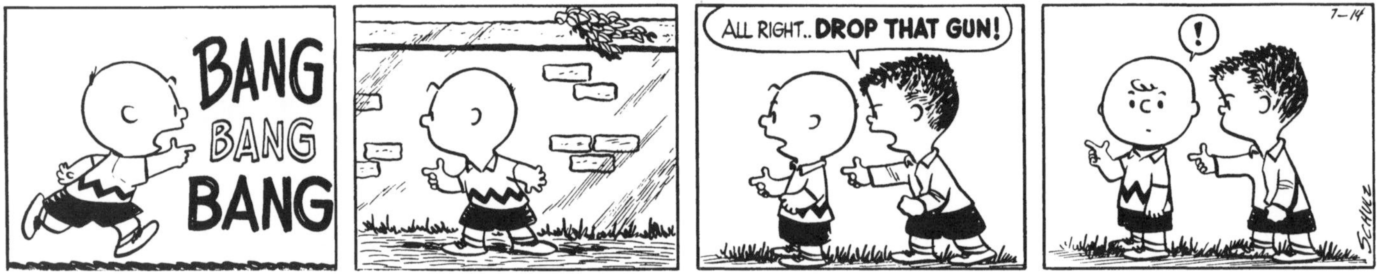
BANG
BANG
BANG
ALL RIGHT.. DROP THAT GUN!
7-14
!
SCHULZ

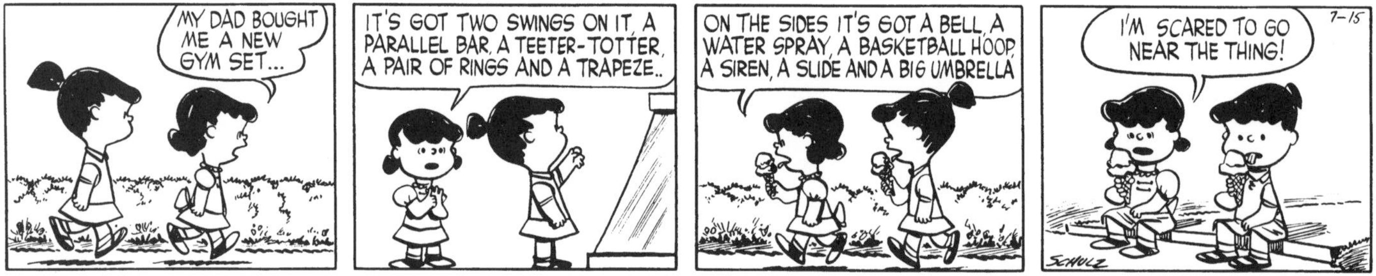
MY DAD BOUGHT ME A NEW GYM SET...
IT'S GOT TWO SWINGS ON IT, A PARALLEL BAR, A TEETER-TOTTER, A PAIR OF RINGS AND A TRAPEZE..
ON THE SIDES IT'S GOT A BELL, A WATER SPRAY, A BASKETBALL HOOP, A SIREN, A SLIDE AND A BIG UMBRELLA
7-15
I'M SCARED TO GO NEAR THE THING!
SCHULZ

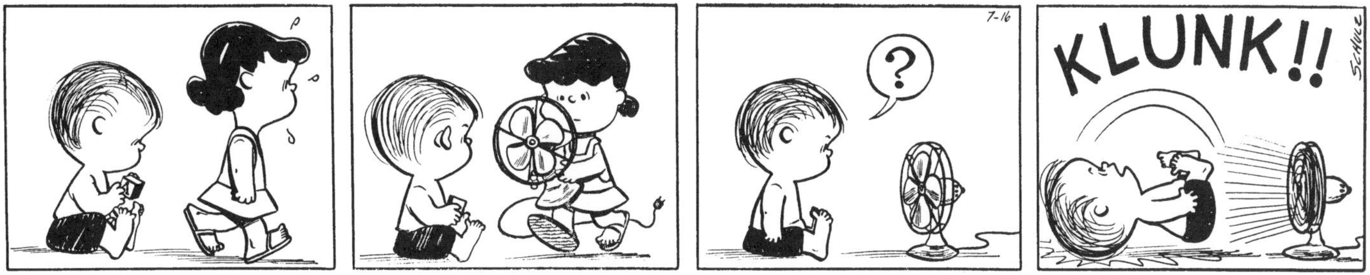
7-16
?
KLUNK!!
SCHULZ

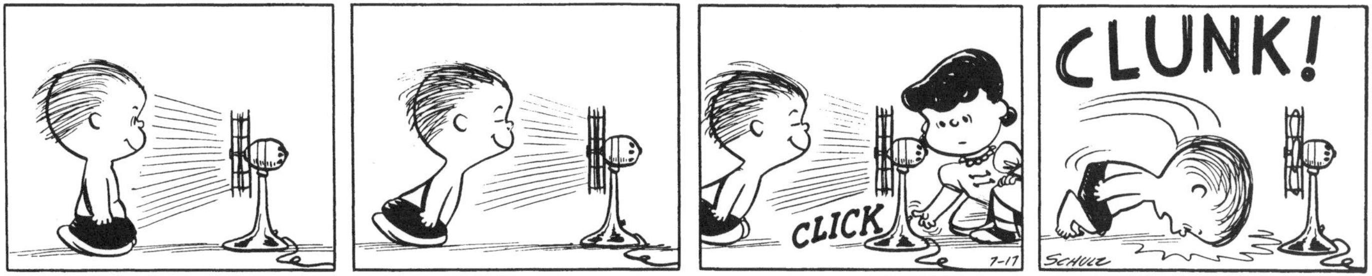
CLICK
7-17
CLUNK!
SCHULZ

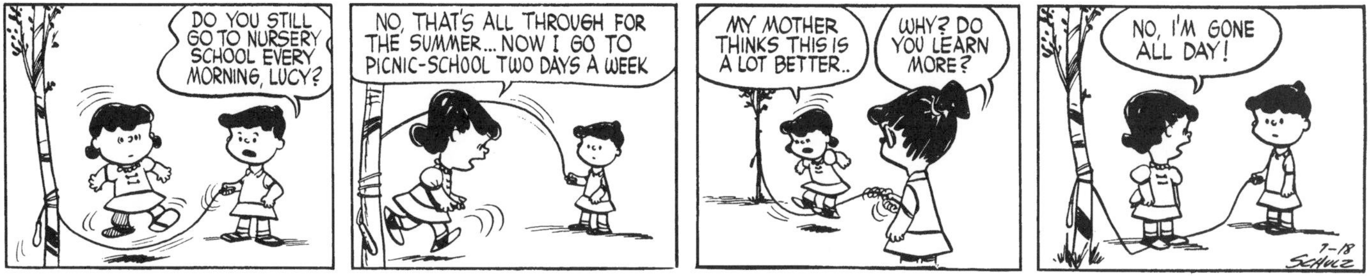
DO YOU STILL GO TO NURSERY SCHOOL EVERY MORNING, LUCY?
NO, THAT'S ALL THROUGH FOR THE SUMMER... NOW I GO TO PICNIC-SCHOOL TWO DAYS A WEEK
MY MOTHER THINKS THIS IS A LOT BETTER..
WHY? DO YOU LEARN MORE?
NO, I'M GONE ALL DAY!
7-18
SCHULZ

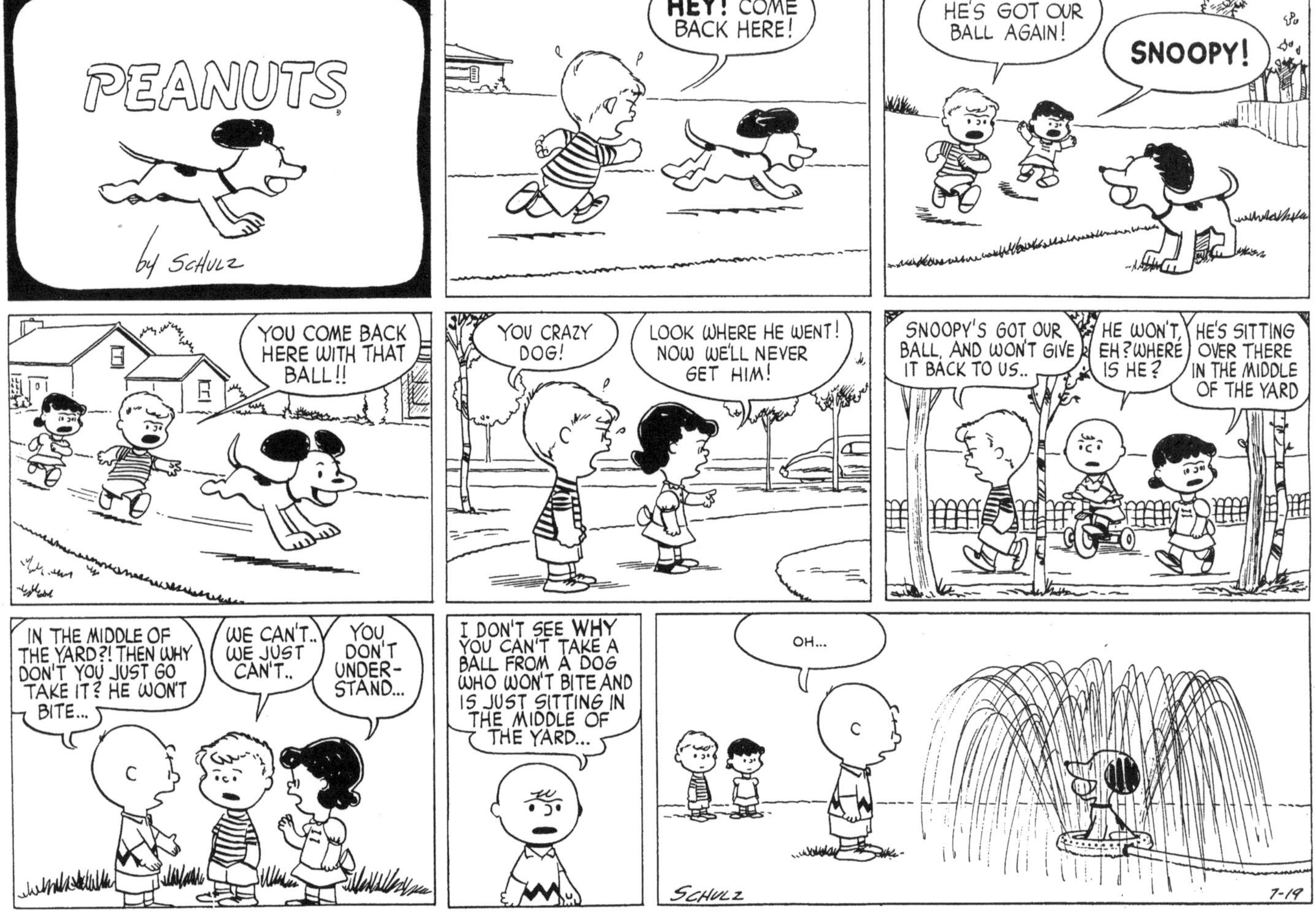
PEANUTS
by SCHULZ
HEY! COME BACK HERE!
HE'S GOT OUR BALL AGAIN!
SNOOPY!
YOU COME BACK HERE WITH THAT BALL!!
YOU CRAZY DOG!
LOOK WHERE HE WENT! NOW WE'LL NEVER GET HIM!
SNOOPY'S GOT OUR BALL, AND WON'T GIVE IT BACK TO US..
HE WON'T, EH? WHERE IS HE?
HE'S SITTING OVER THERE IN THE MIDDLE OF THE YARD
IN THE MIDDLE OF THE YARD?! THEN WHY DON'T YOU JUST GO TAKE IT? HE WON'T BITE...
WE CAN'T.. WE JUST CAN'T..
YOU DON'T UNDER-STAND...
I DON'T SEE WHY YOU CAN'T TAKE A BALL FROM A DOG WHO WON'T BITE AND IS JUST SITTING IN THE MIDDLE OF THE YARD...
OH...
SCHULZ
7-19

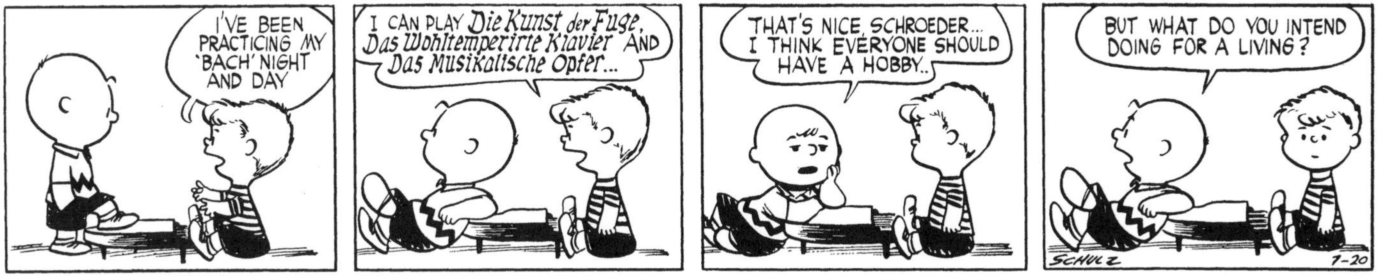
I'VE BEEN PRACTICING MY 'BACH' NIGHT AND DAY
I CAN PLAY Die Kunst der Fuge, Das Wohltemperirte Klavier AND Das Musikalische Opfer...
THAT'S NICE, SCHROEDER... I THINK EVERYONE SHOULD HAVE A HOBBY..
BUT WHAT DO YOU INTEND DOING FOR A LIVING?
SCHULZ
7-20

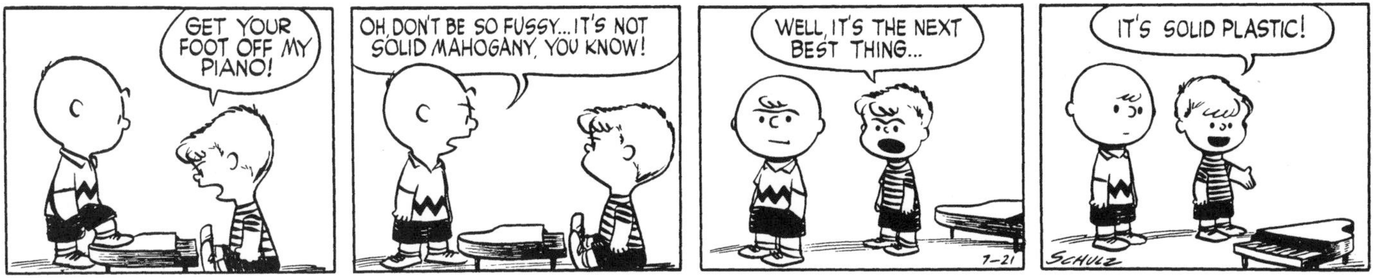
GET YOUR FOOT OFF MY PIANO!
OH, DON'T BE SO FUSSY...IT'S NOT SOLID MAHOGANY, YOU KNOW!
WELL, IT'S THE NEXT BEST THING...
7-21
IT'S SOLID PLASTIC!
SCHULZ

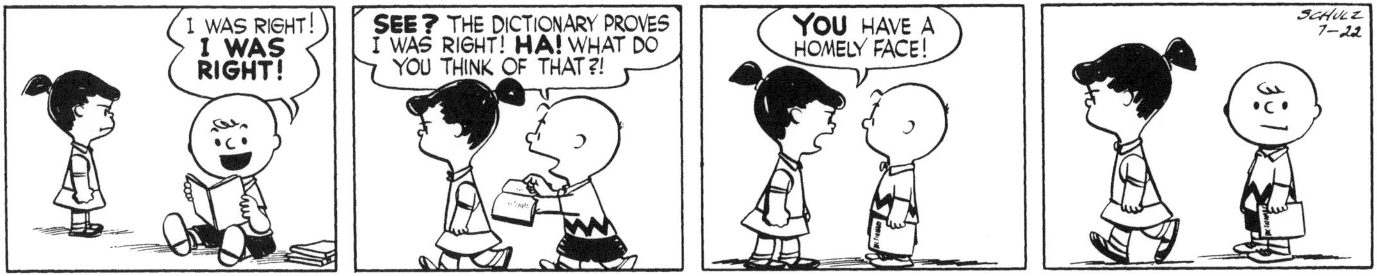
I WAS RIGHT! I WAS RIGHT!
SEE? THE DICTIONARY PROVES I WAS RIGHT! HA! WHAT DO YOU THINK OF THAT?!
YOU HAVE A HOMELY FACE!
SCHULZ 7-22

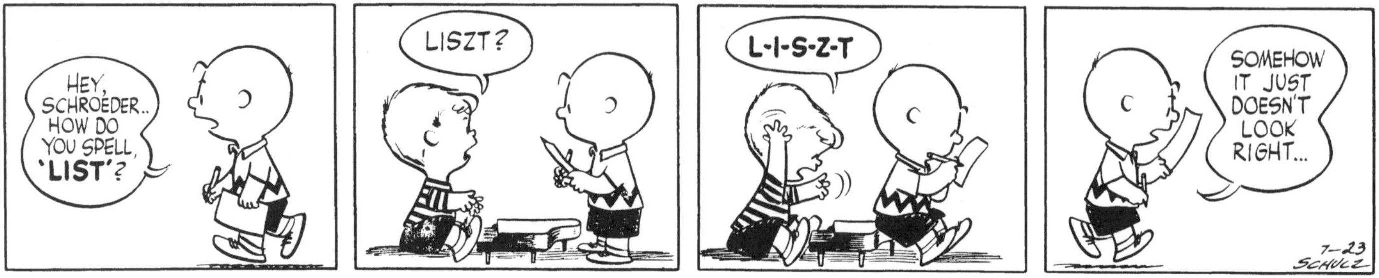
HEY, SCHROEDER.. HOW DO YOU SPELL, 'LIST'?
LISZT?
L-I-S-Z-T
SOMEHOW IT JUST DOESN'T LOOK RIGHT...
7-23
SCHULZ

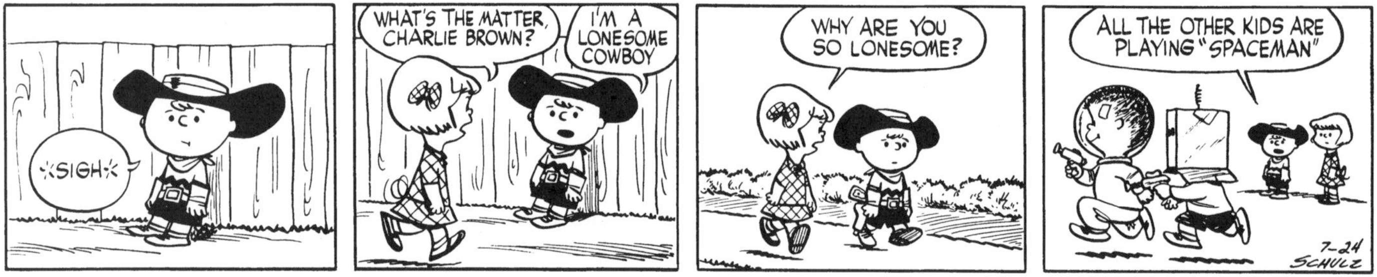
SIGH
WHAT'S THE MATTER, CHARLIE BROWN?
I'M A LONESOME COWBOY
WHY ARE YOU SO LONESOME?
ALL THE OTHER KIDS ARE PLAYING "SPACEMAN"
7-24
SCHULZ

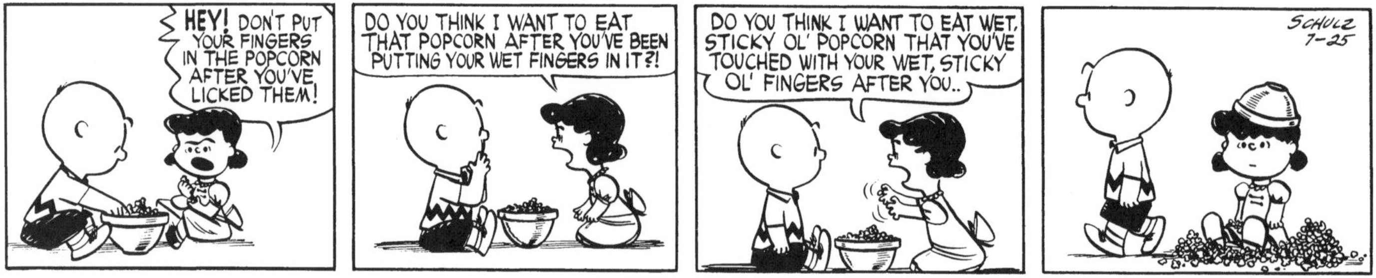
HEY! DON'T PUT YOUR FINGERS IN THE POPCORN AFTER YOU'VE LICKED THEM!
DO YOU THINK I WANT TO EAT THAT POPCORN AFTER YOU'VE BEEN PUTTING YOUR WET FINGERS IN IT?!
DO YOU THINK I WANT TO EAT WET, STICKY OL' POPCORN THAT YOU'VE TOUCHED WITH YOUR WET, STICKY OL' FINGERS AFTER YOU..
SCHULZ
7-25

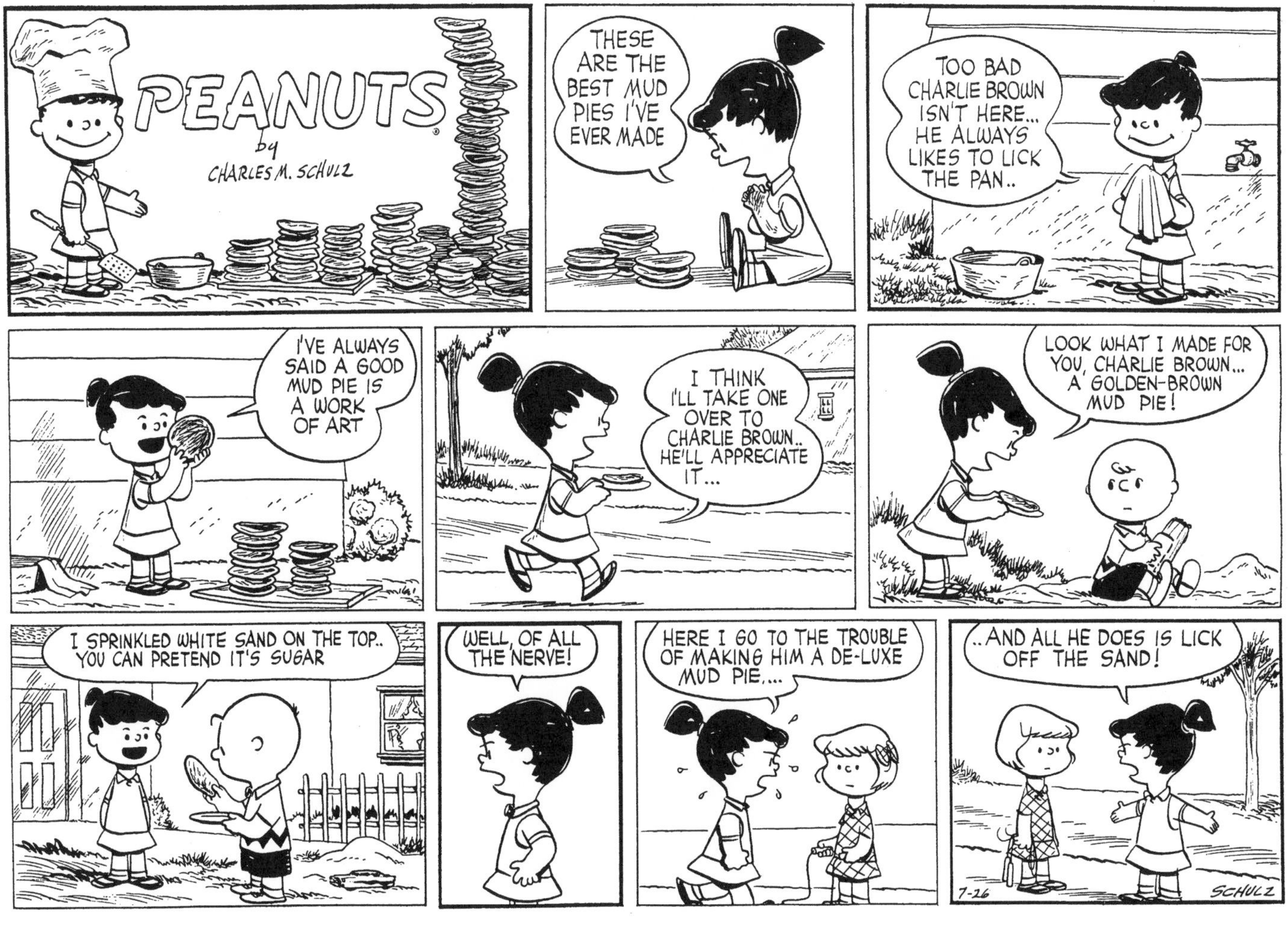
PEANUTS
by CHARLES M. SCHULZ
THESE ARE THE BEST MUD PIES I'VE EVER MADE
TOO BAD CHARLIE BROWN ISN'T HERE... HE ALWAYS LIKES TO LICK THE PAN..
I'VE ALWAYS SAID A GOOD MUD PIE IS A WORK OF ART
I THINK I'LL TAKE ONE OVER TO CHARLIE BROWN.. HE'LL APPRECIATE IT...
LOOK WHAT I MADE FOR YOU, CHARLIE BROWN... A GOLDEN-BROWN MUD PIE!
I SPRINKLED WHITE SAND ON THE TOP.. YOU CAN PRETEND IT'S SUGAR
WELL, OF ALL THE NERVE!
HERE I GO TO THE TROUBLE OF MAKING HIM A DE-LUXE MUD PIE....
..AND ALL HE DOES IS LICK OFF THE SAND!
7-26
SCHULZ

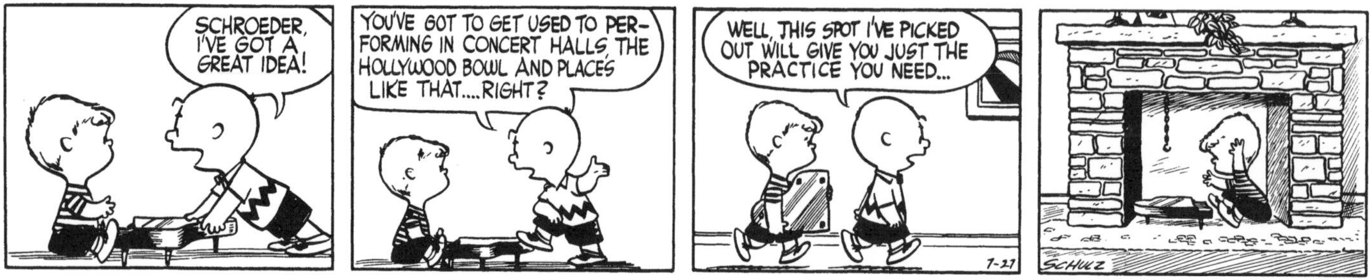
SCHROEDER, I'VE GOT A GREAT IDEA!
YOU'VE GOT TO GET USED TO PERFORMING IN CONCERT HALLS, THE HOLLYWOOD BOWL AND PLACES LIKE THAT....RIGHT?
WELL, THIS SPOT I'VE PICKED OUT WILL GIVE YOU JUST THE PRACTICE YOU NEED...
7-27
SCHULZ

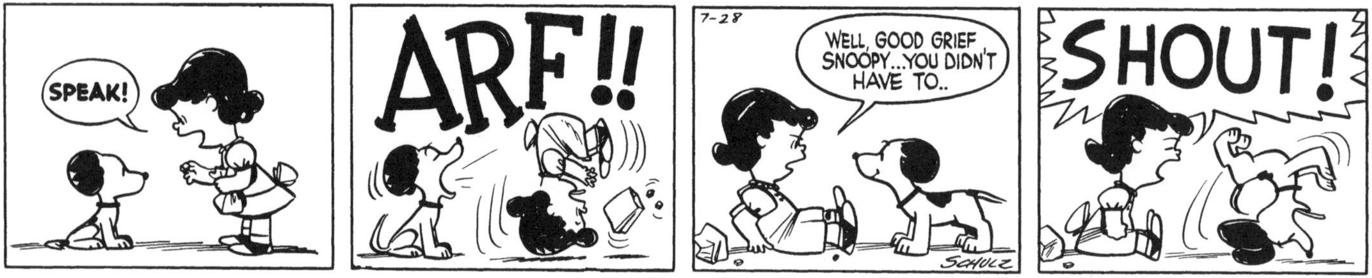
SPEAK!
ARF!!
7-28
WELL, GOOD GRIEF SNOOPY...YOU DIDN'T HAVE TO..
SCHULZ
SHOUT!

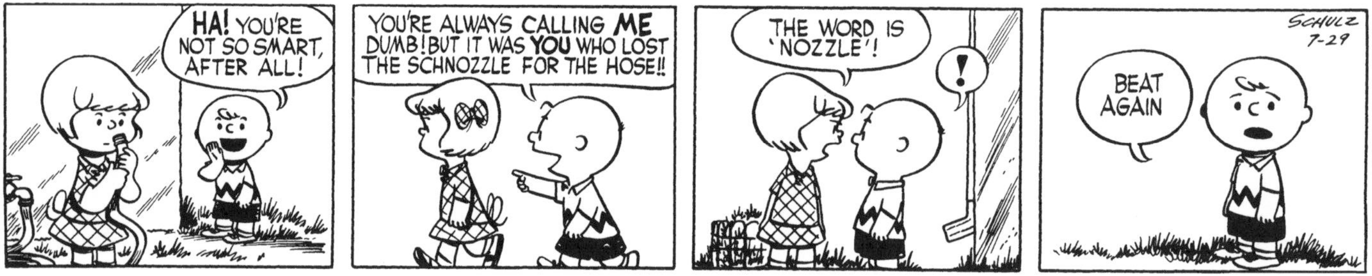
HA! YOU'RE NOT SO SMART, AFTER ALL!
YOU'RE ALWAYS CALLING ME DUMB! BUT IT WAS YOU WHO LOST THE SCHNOZZLE FOR THE HOSE!!
THE WORD IS 'NOZZLE'!
!
SCHULZ 7-29
BEAT AGAIN

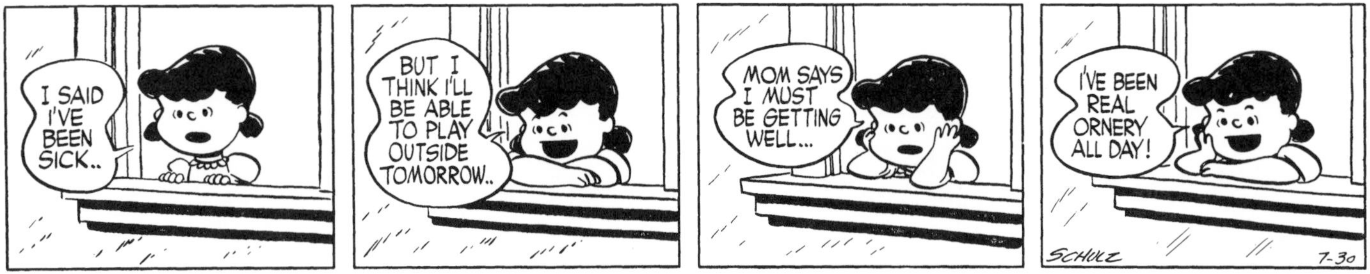
I SAID I'VE BEEN SICK..
BUT I THINK I'LL BE ABLE TO PLAY OUTSIDE TOMORROW..
MOM SAYS I MUST BE GETTING WELL...
I'VE BEEN REAL ORNERY ALL DAY!
SCHULZ
7-30

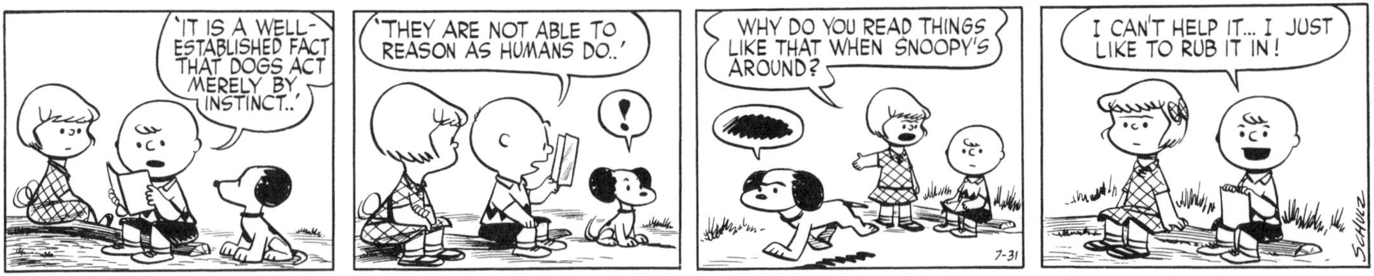
'IT IS A WELL-ESTABLISHED FACT THAT DOGS ACT MERELY BY INSTINCT..'
'THEY ARE NOT ABLE TO REASON AS HUMANS DO..'
!
WHY DO YOU READ THINGS LIKE THAT WHEN SNOOPY'S AROUND?
7-31
I CAN'T HELP IT... I JUST LIKE TO RUB IT IN!
SCHULZ

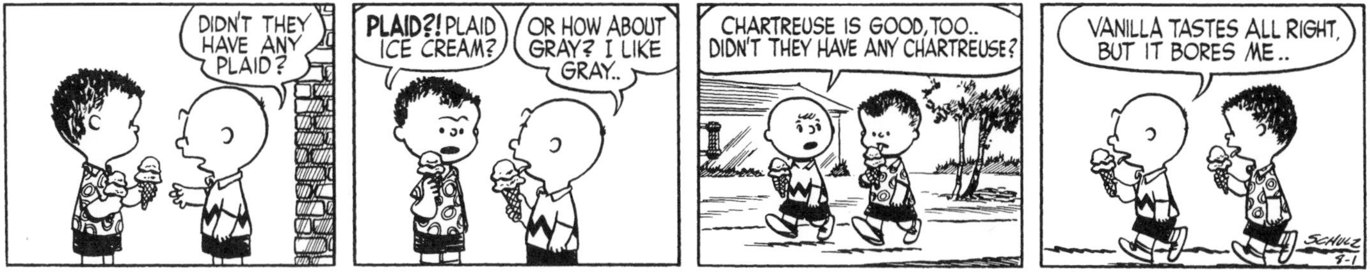
DIDN'T THEY HAVE ANY PLAID?
PLAID?! PLAID ICE CREAM?
OR HOW ABOUT GRAY? I LIKE GRAY..
CHARTREUSE IS GOOD, TOO.. DIDN'T THEY HAVE ANY CHARTREUSE?
VANILLA TASTES ALL RIGHT, BUT IT BORES ME..
SCHULZ
8-1

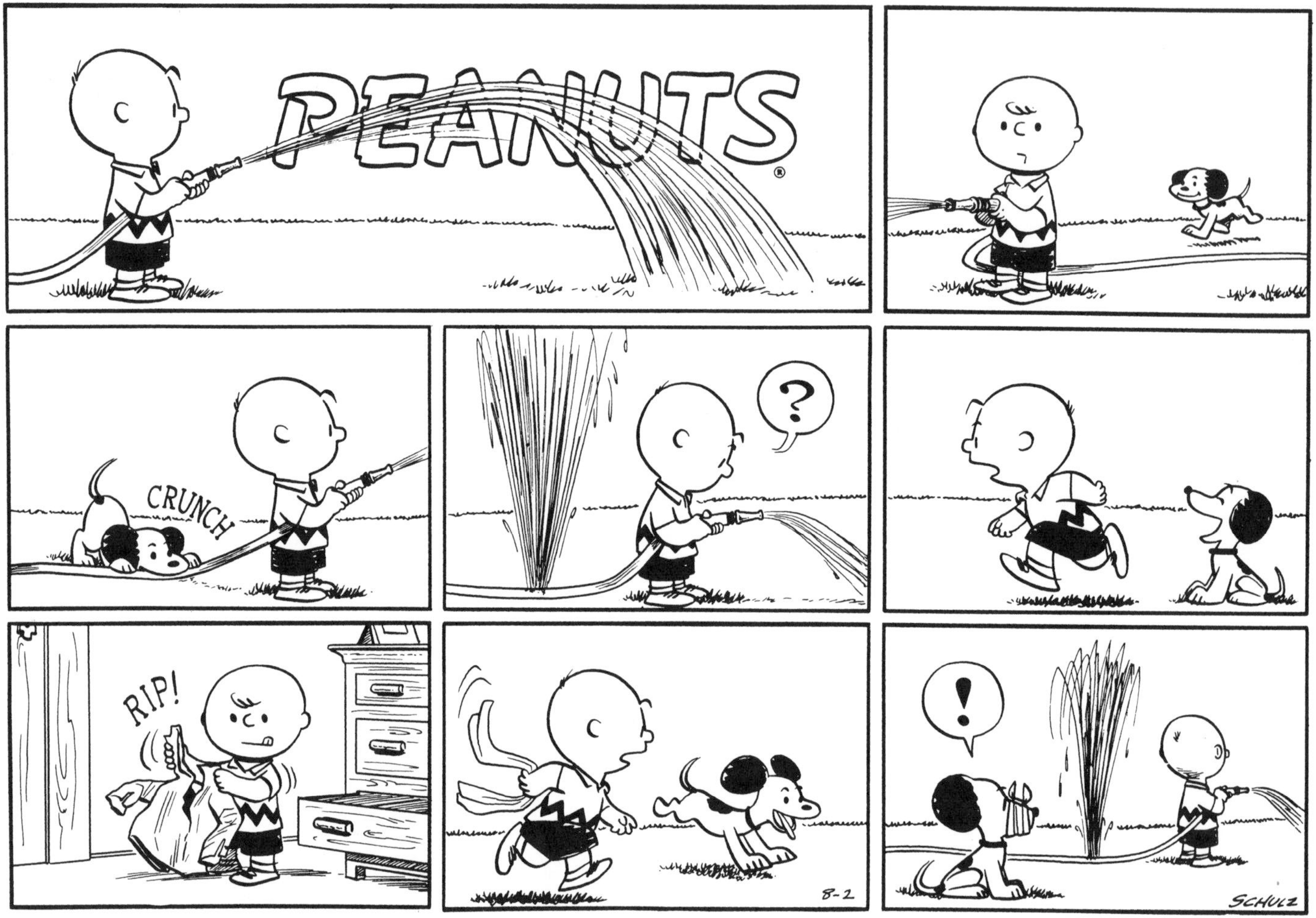
PEANUTS
CRUNCH
?
RIP!
8-2
!
SCHULZ

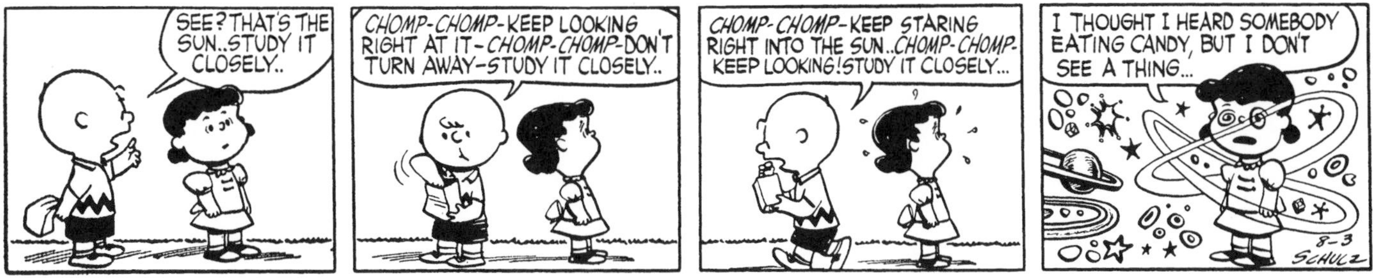

SEE? THAT'S THE SUN..STUDY IT CLOSELY..
CHOMP-CHOMP-KEEP LOOKING RIGHT AT IT-CHOMP-CHOMP-DON'T TURN AWAY-STUDY IT CLOSELY..
CHOMP-CHOMP-KEEP STARING RIGHT INTO THE SUN..CHOMP-CHOMP-KEEP LOOKING! STUDY IT CLOSELY...
I THOUGHT I HEARD SOMEBODY EATING CANDY, BUT I DON'T SEE A THING...
8-3
SCHULZ

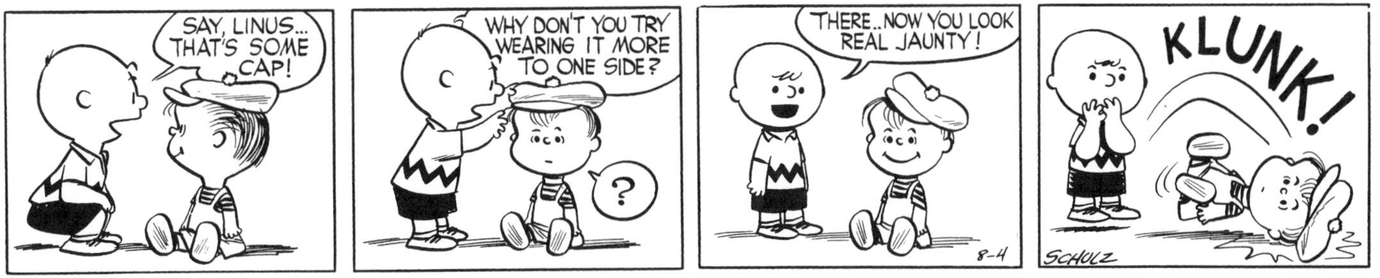

SAY, LINUS... THAT'S SOME CAP!
WHY DON'T YOU TRY WEARING IT MORE TO ONE SIDE?
?
THERE..NOW YOU LOOK REAL JAUNTY!
8-4
KLUNK!
SCHULZ

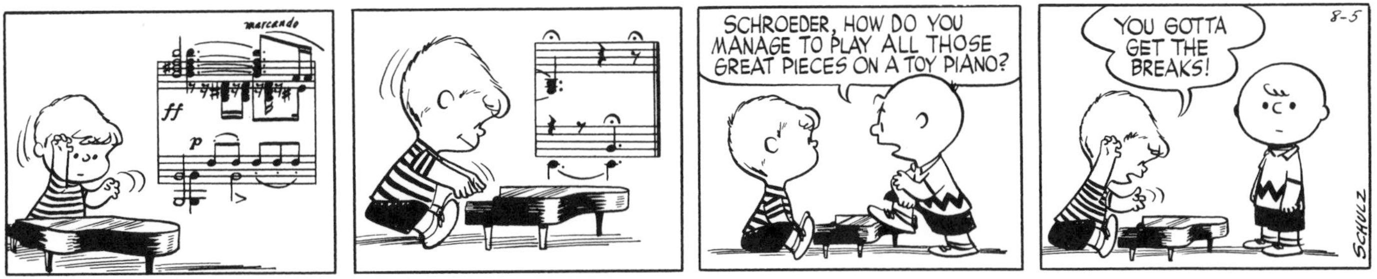

marcando
ff
p
SCHROEDER, HOW DO YOU MANAGE TO PLAY ALL THOSE GREAT PIECES ON A TOY PIANO?
YOU GOTTA GET THE BREAKS!
8-5
SCHULZ

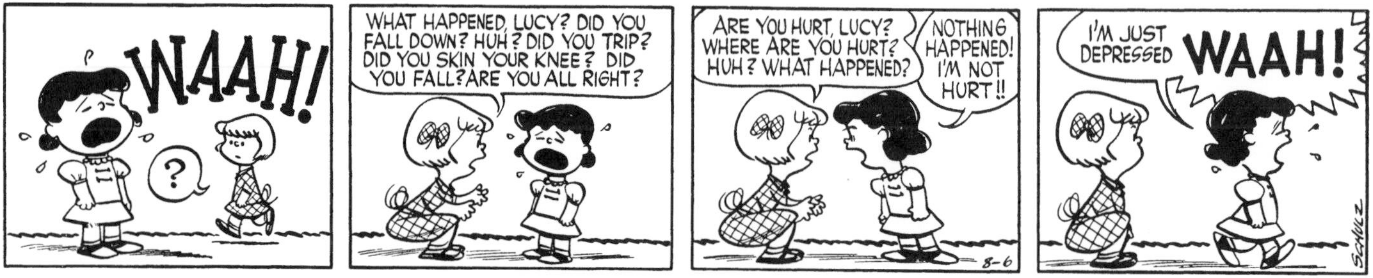
WAAH!
?
WHAT HAPPENED, LUCY? DID YOU FALL DOWN? HUH? DID YOU TRIP? DID YOU SKIN YOUR KNEE? DID YOU FALL? ARE YOU ALL RIGHT?
ARE YOU HURT, LUCY? WHERE ARE YOU HURT? HUH? WHAT HAPPENED?
NOTHING HAPPENED! I'M NOT HURT!!
8-6
I'M JUST DEPRESSED
WAAH!
SCHULZ

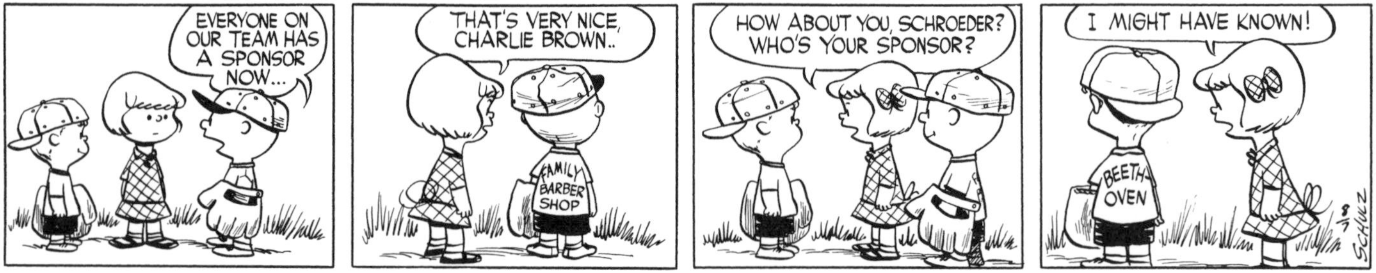
EVERYONE ON OUR TEAM HAS A SPONSOR NOW...
THAT'S VERY NICE, CHARLIE BROWN..
FAMILY BARBER SHOP
HOW ABOUT YOU, SCHROEDER? WHO'S YOUR SPONSOR?
I MIGHT HAVE KNOWN!
BEETH-OVEN
8/7
SCHULZ

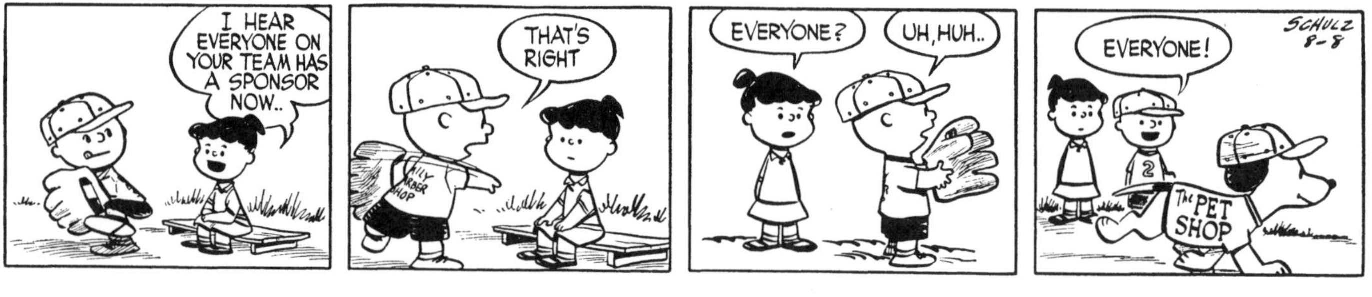
I HEAR EVERYONE ON YOUR TEAM HAS A SPONSOR NOW..
THAT'S RIGHT
EVERYONE?
UH, HUH..
SCHULZ 8-8
EVERYONE!
2
THE PET SHOP

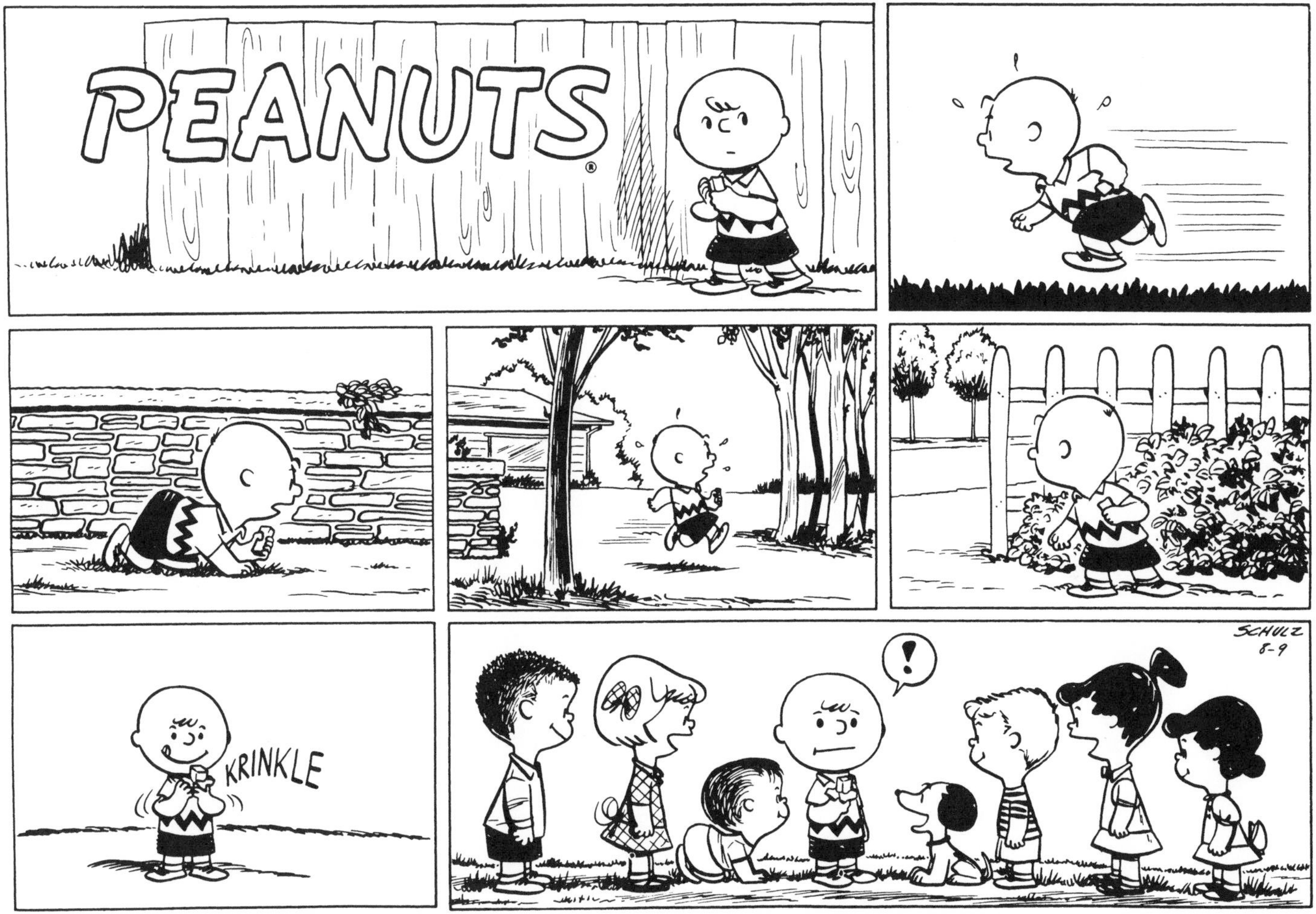
PEANUTS
KRINKLE
!
SCHULZ
8-9

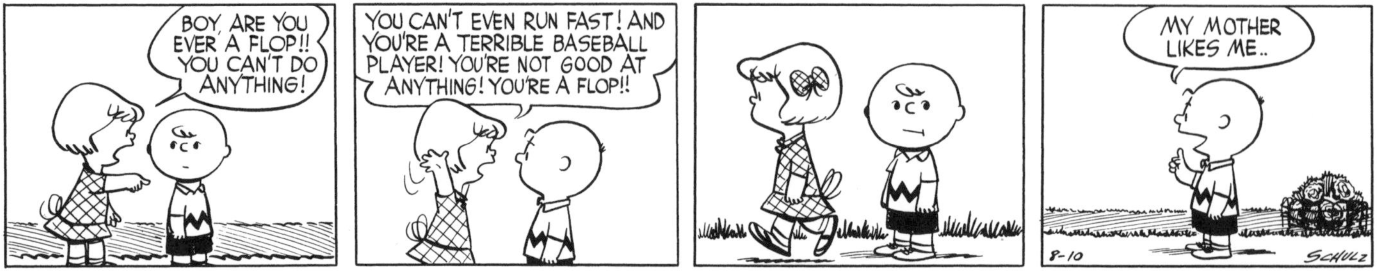
BOY, ARE YOU EVER A FLOP!! YOU CAN'T DO ANYTHING!
YOU CAN'T EVEN RUN FAST! AND YOU'RE A TERRIBLE BASEBALL PLAYER! YOU'RE NOT GOOD AT ANYTHING! YOU'RE A FLOP!!
MY MOTHER LIKES ME..
8-10
SCHULZ

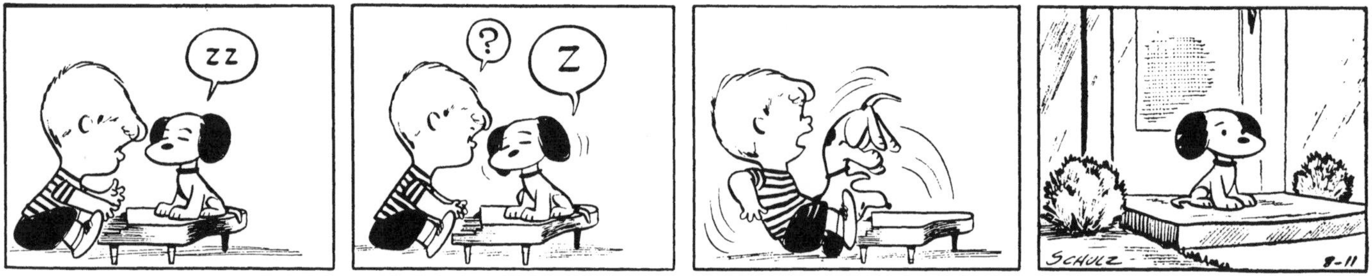
ZZ
?
Z
SCHULZ
8-11

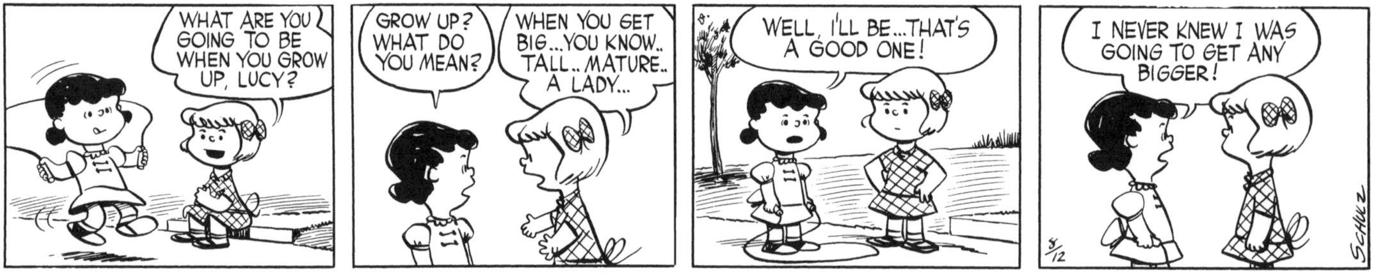
WHAT ARE YOU GOING TO BE WHEN YOU GROW UP, LUCY?
GROW UP? WHAT DO YOU MEAN?
WHEN YOU GET BIG...YOU KNOW.. TALL.. MATURE.. A LADY...
WELL, I'LL BE...THAT'S A GOOD ONE!
I NEVER KNEW I WAS GOING TO GET ANY BIGGER!
8/12
SCHULZ

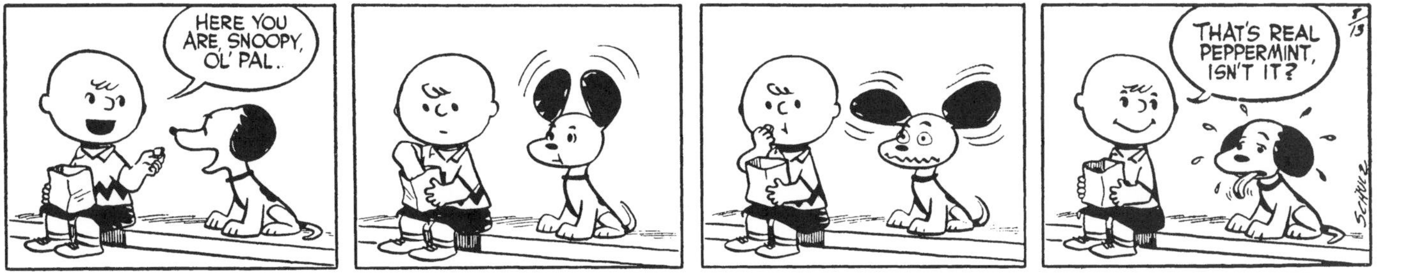
HERE YOU ARE, SNOOPY, OL' PAL..
THAT'S REAL PEPPERMINT, ISN'T IT?
8/13
SCHULZ

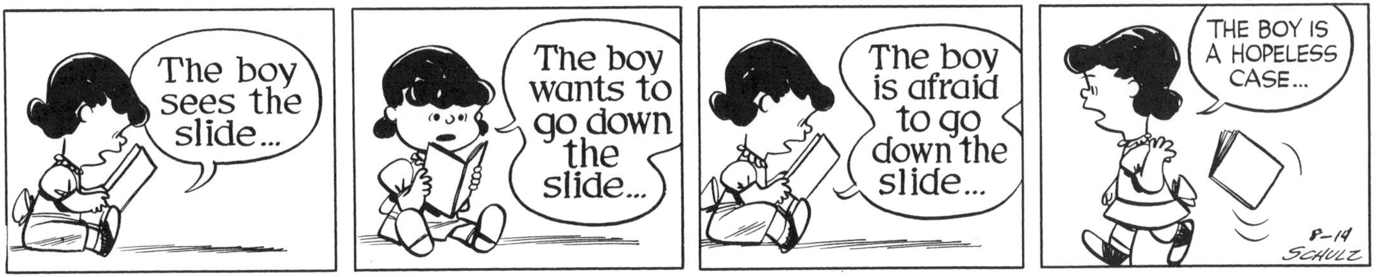
The boy sees the slide...
The boy wants to go down the slide...
The boy is afraid to go down the slide...
THE BOY IS A HOPELESS CASE...
8-14
SCHULZ

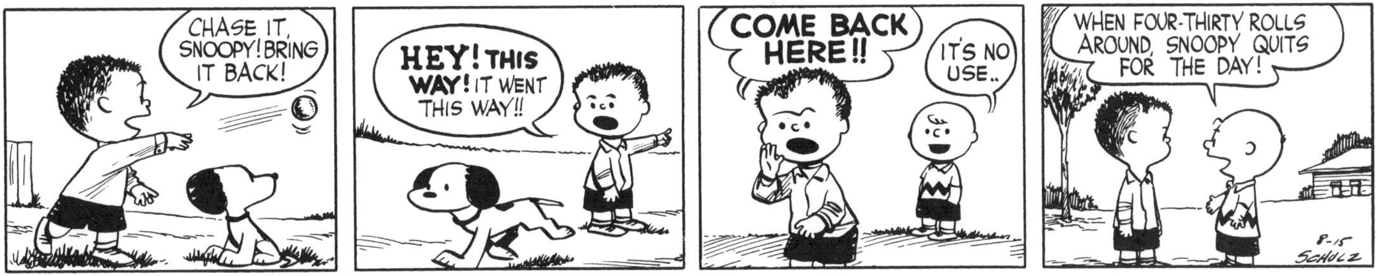
CHASE IT, SNOOPY! BRING IT BACK!
HEY! THIS WAY! IT WENT THIS WAY!!
COME BACK HERE!!
IT'S NO USE..
WHEN FOUR-THIRTY ROLLS AROUND, SNOOPY QUITS FOR THE DAY!
8-15
SCHULZ

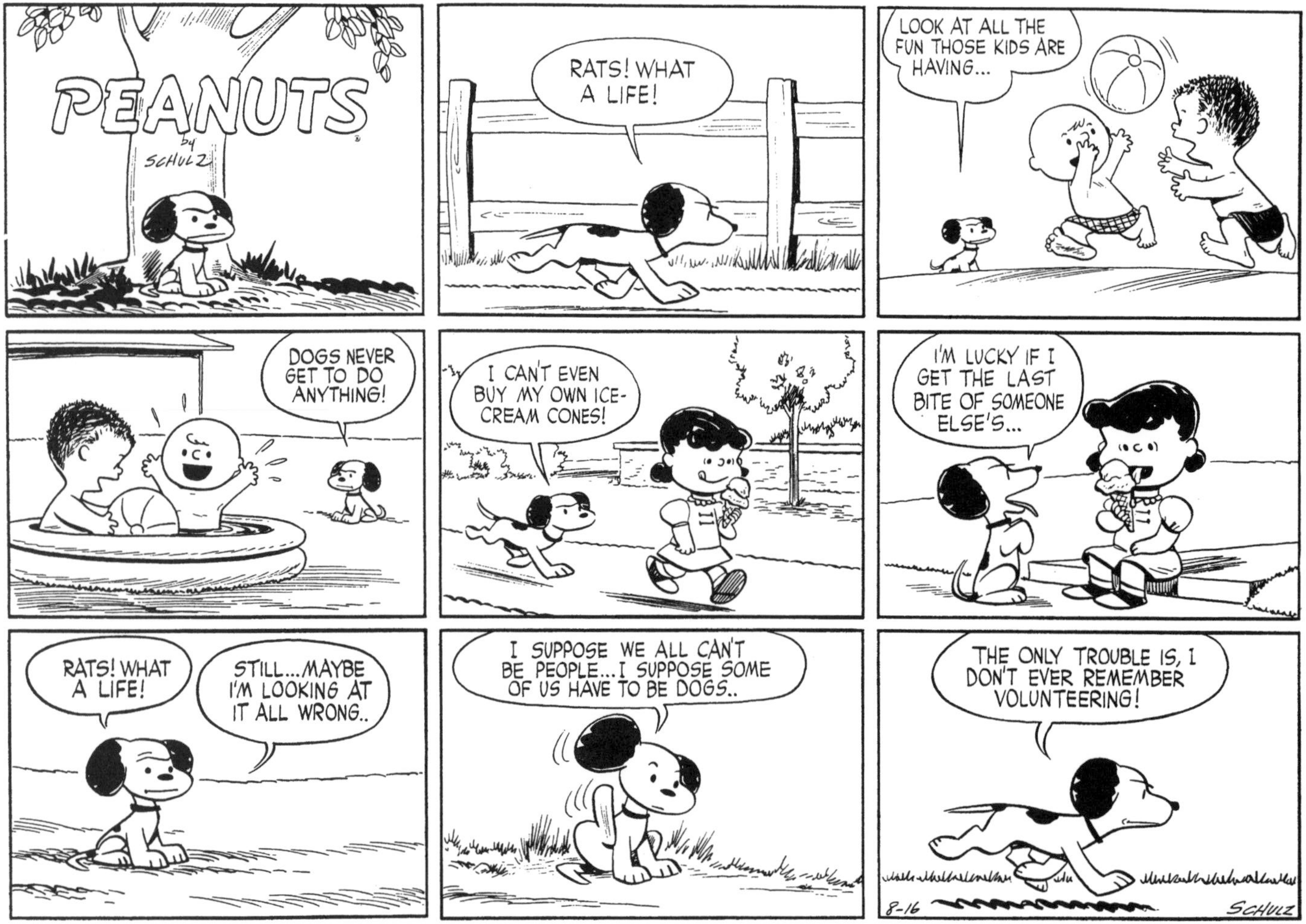
PEANUTS
by SCHULZ
RATS! WHAT A LIFE!
LOOK AT ALL THE FUN THOSE KIDS ARE HAVING...
DOGS NEVER GET TO DO ANYTHING!
I CAN'T EVEN BUY MY OWN ICE-CREAM CONES!
I'M LUCKY IF I GET THE LAST BITE OF SOMEONE ELSE'S...
RATS! WHAT A LIFE!
STILL...MAYBE I'M LOOKING AT IT ALL WRONG..
I SUPPOSE WE ALL CAN'T BE PEOPLE...I SUPPOSE SOME OF US HAVE TO BE DOGS..
THE ONLY TROUBLE IS, I DON'T EVER REMEMBER VOLUNTEERING!
8-16
SCHULZ

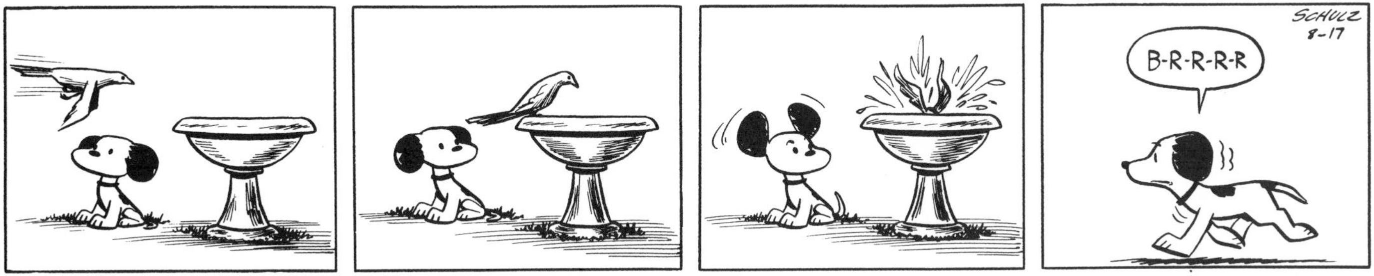
SCHULZ 8-17
B-R-R-R-R

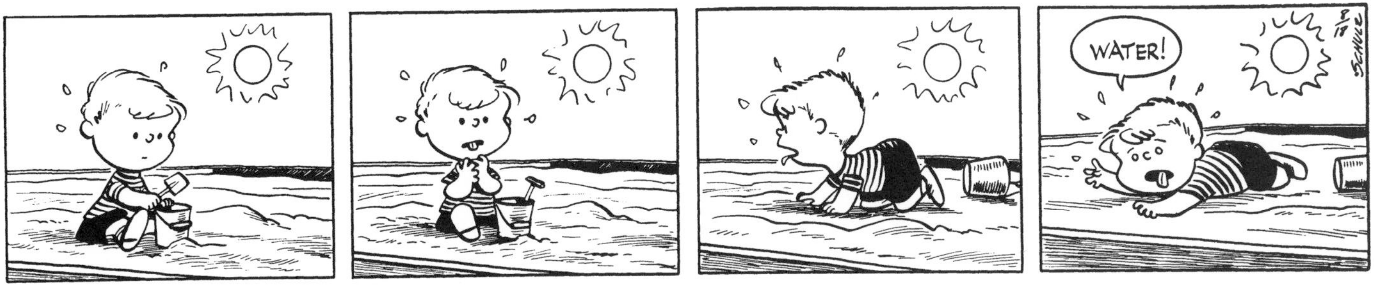
8 18 SCHULZ
WATER!

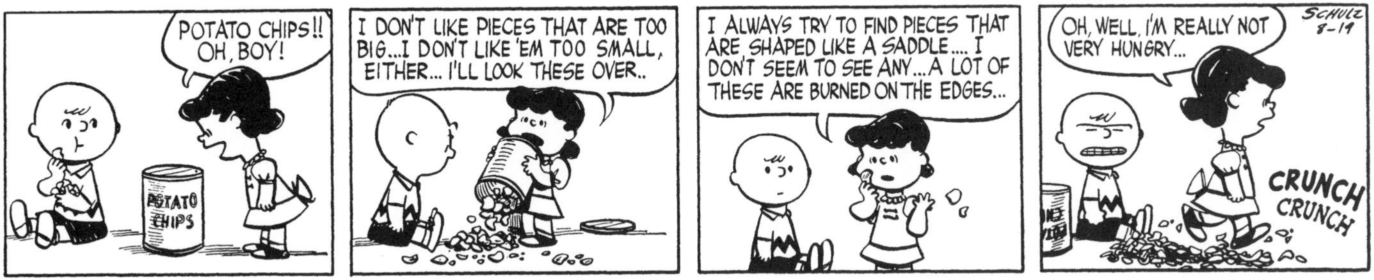
SCHULZ 8-19
POTATO CHIPS!! OH, BOY!
POTATO CHIPS
I DON'T LIKE PIECES THAT ARE TOO BIG...I DON'T LIKE 'EM TOO SMALL, EITHER... I'LL LOOK THESE OVER..
I ALWAYS TRY TO FIND PIECES THAT ARE SHAPED LIKE A SADDLE.... I DON'T SEEM TO SEE ANY...A LOT OF THESE ARE BURNED ON THE EDGES...
OH, WELL, I'M REALLY NOT VERY HUNGRY...
CRUNCH
CRUNCH

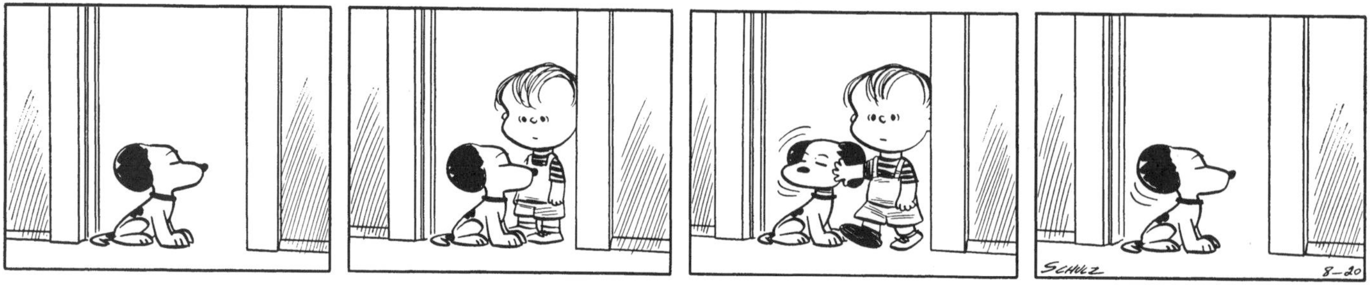
SCHULZ
8-20

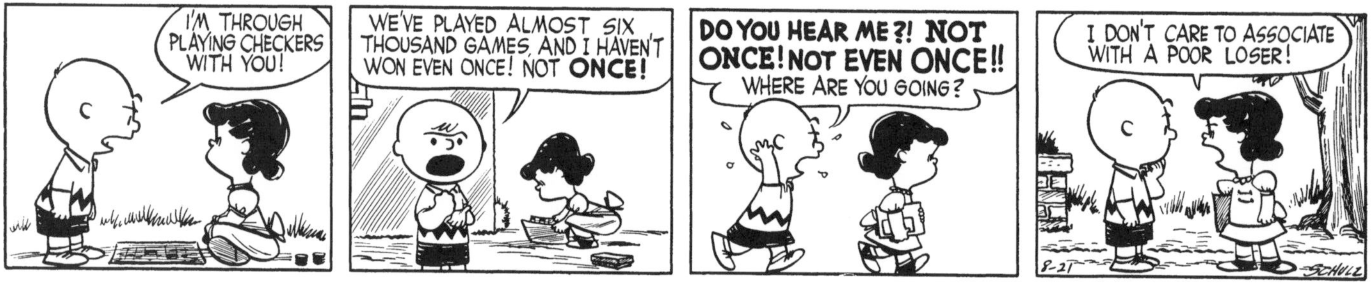
I'M THROUGH PLAYING CHECKERS WITH YOU!
WE'VE PLAYED ALMOST SIX THOUSAND GAMES, AND I HAVEN'T WON EVEN ONCE! NOT ONCE!
DO YOU HEAR ME?! NOT ONCE! NOT EVEN ONCE!!
WHERE ARE YOU GOING?
I DON'T CARE TO ASSOCIATE WITH A POOR LOSER!
8-21
SCHULZ

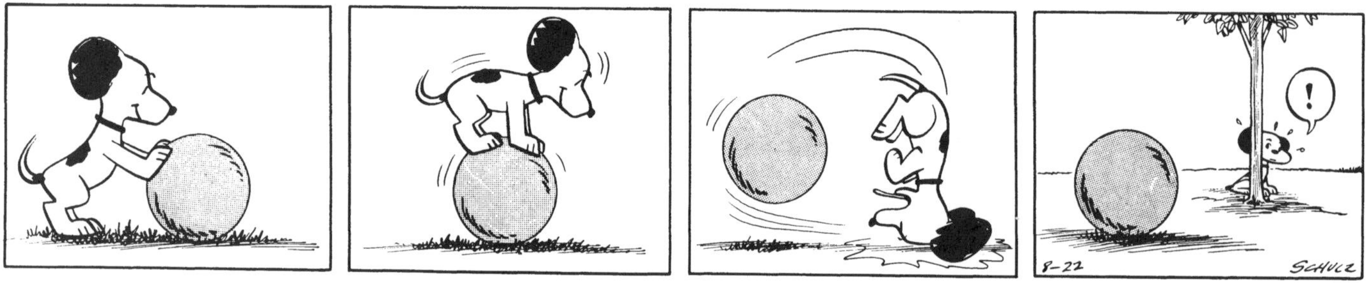
!
8-22
SCHULZ

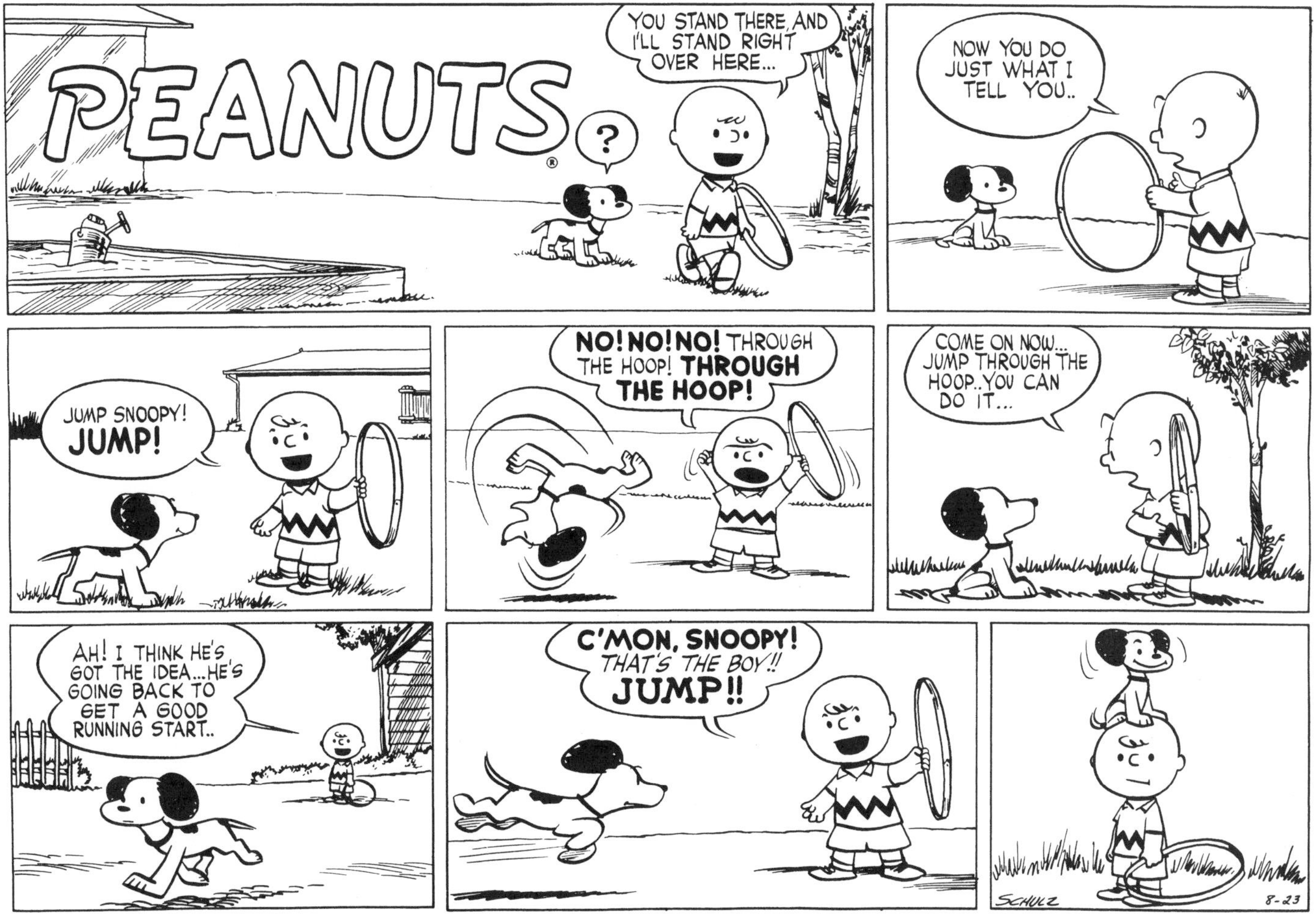
PEANUTS
YOU STAND THERE, AND I'LL STAND RIGHT OVER HERE...
?
NOW YOU DO JUST WHAT I TELL YOU..
JUMP SNOOPY! JUMP!
NO! NO! NO! THROUGH THE HOOP! THROUGH THE HOOP!
COME ON NOW... JUMP THROUGH THE HOOP.. YOU CAN DO IT...
AH! I THINK HE'S GOT THE IDEA...HE'S GOING BACK TO GET A GOOD RUNNING START..
C'MON, SNOOPY! THAT'S THE BOY!! JUMP!!
SCHULZ
8-23

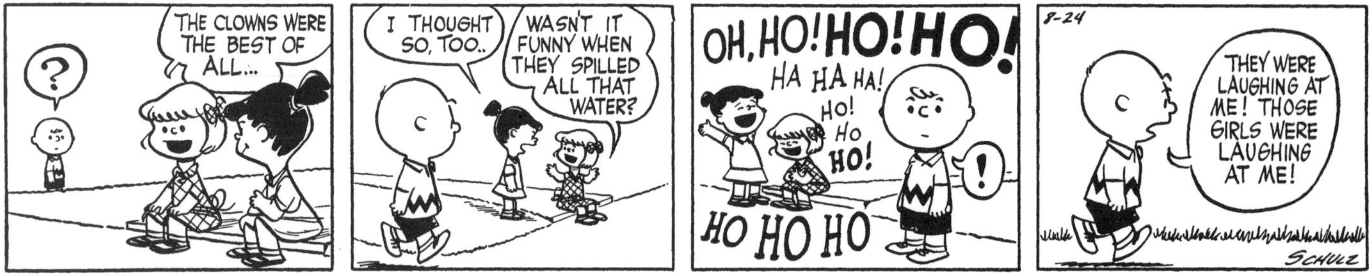
?
THE CLOWNS WERE THE BEST OF ALL...
I THOUGHT SO, TOO..
WASN'T IT FUNNY WHEN THEY SPILLED ALL THAT WATER?
OH, HO! HO! HO!
HA HA HA!
HO! Ho HO!
HO HO HO
!
8-24
THEY WERE LAUGHING AT ME! THOSE GIRLS WERE LAUGHING AT ME!
SCHULZ

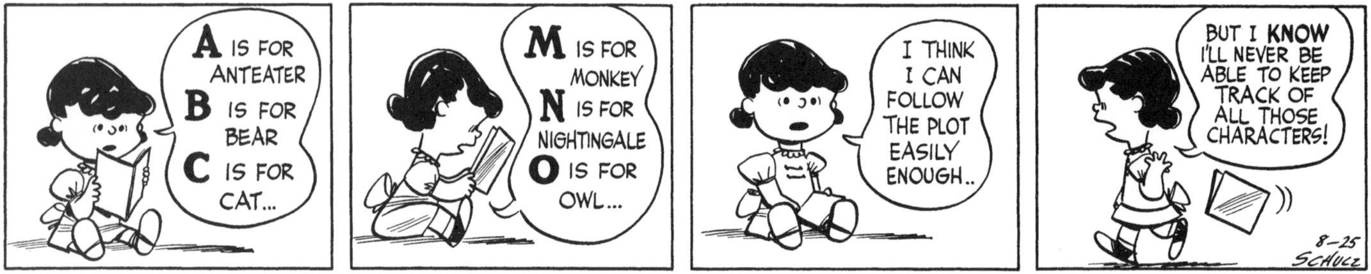
A IS FOR ANTEATER B IS FOR BEAR C IS FOR CAT...
M IS FOR MONKEY N IS FOR NIGHTINGALE O IS FOR OWL...
I THINK I CAN FOLLOW THE PLOT EASILY ENOUGH..
BUT I KNOW I'LL NEVER BE ABLE TO KEEP TRACK OF ALL THOSE CHARACTERS!
8-25
SCHULZ

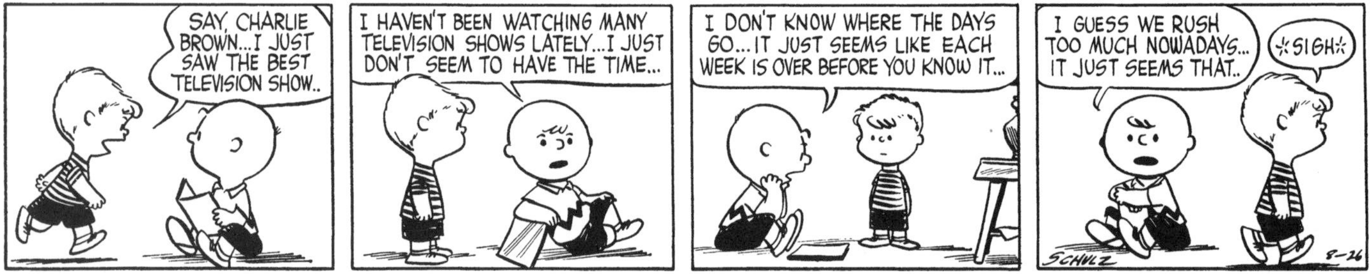
SAY, CHARLIE BROWN...I JUST SAW THE BEST TELEVISION SHOW..
I HAVEN'T BEEN WATCHING MANY TELEVISION SHOWS LATELY...I JUST DON'T SEEM TO HAVE THE TIME...
I DON'T KNOW WHERE THE DAYS GO... IT JUST SEEMS LIKE EACH WEEK IS OVER BEFORE YOU KNOW IT...
I GUESS WE RUSH TOO MUCH NOWADAYS... IT JUST SEEMS THAT..
SIGH
SCHULZ
8-26

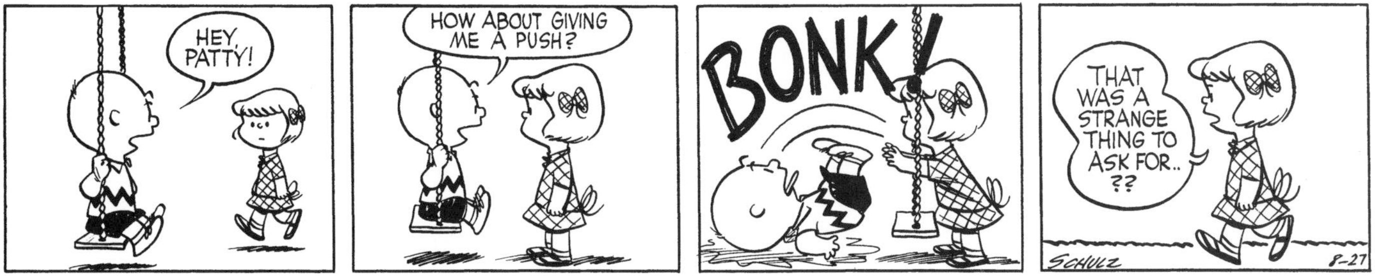
HEY, PATTY!
HOW ABOUT GIVING ME A PUSH?
BONK!
THAT WAS A STRANGE THING TO ASK FOR.. ??
SCHULZ
8-27

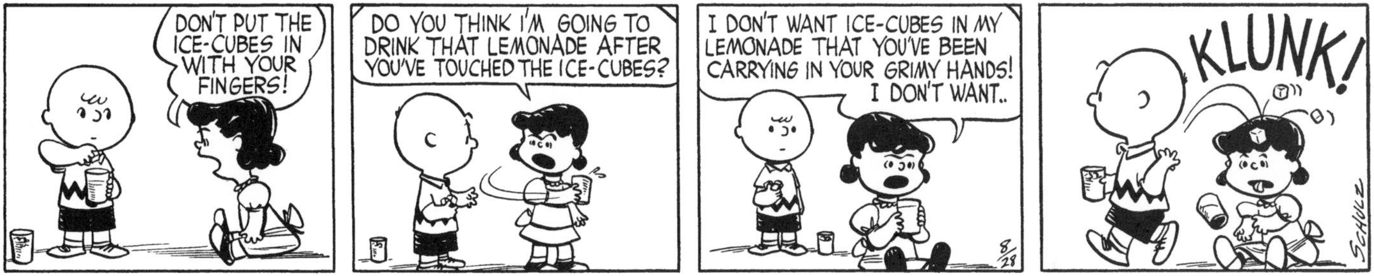
DON'T PUT THE ICE-CUBES IN WITH YOUR FINGERS!
DO YOU THINK I'M GOING TO DRINK THAT LEMONADE AFTER YOU'VE TOUCHED THE ICE-CUBES?
I DON'T WANT ICE-CUBES IN MY LEMONADE THAT YOU'VE BEEN CARRYING IN YOUR GRIMY HANDS! I DON'T WANT..
8/28
KLUNK!
SCHULZ

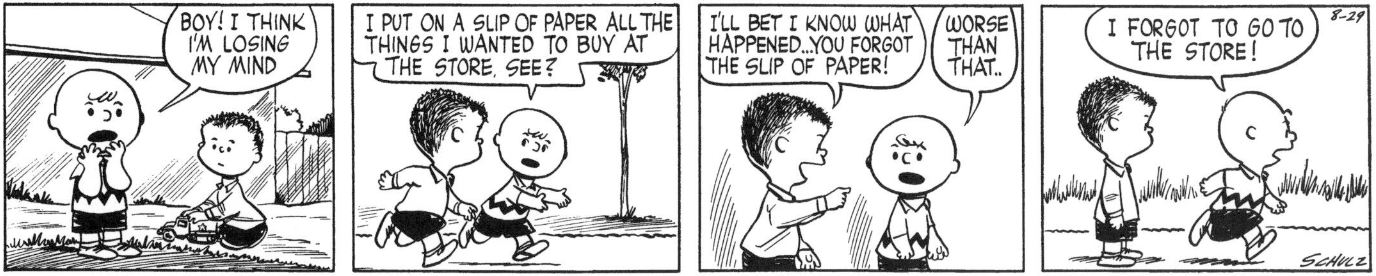
BOY! I THINK I'M LOSING MY MIND
I PUT ON A SLIP OF PAPER ALL THE THINGS I WANTED TO BUY AT THE STORE, SEE?
I'LL BET I KNOW WHAT HAPPENED...YOU FORGOT THE SLIP OF PAPER!
WORSE THAN THAT..
8-29
I FORGOT TO GO TO THE STORE!
SCHULZ

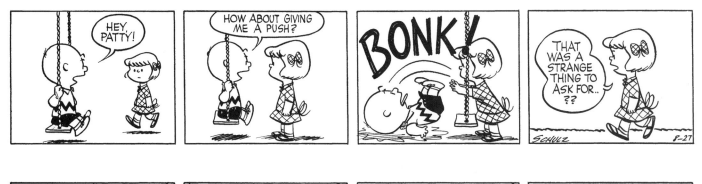

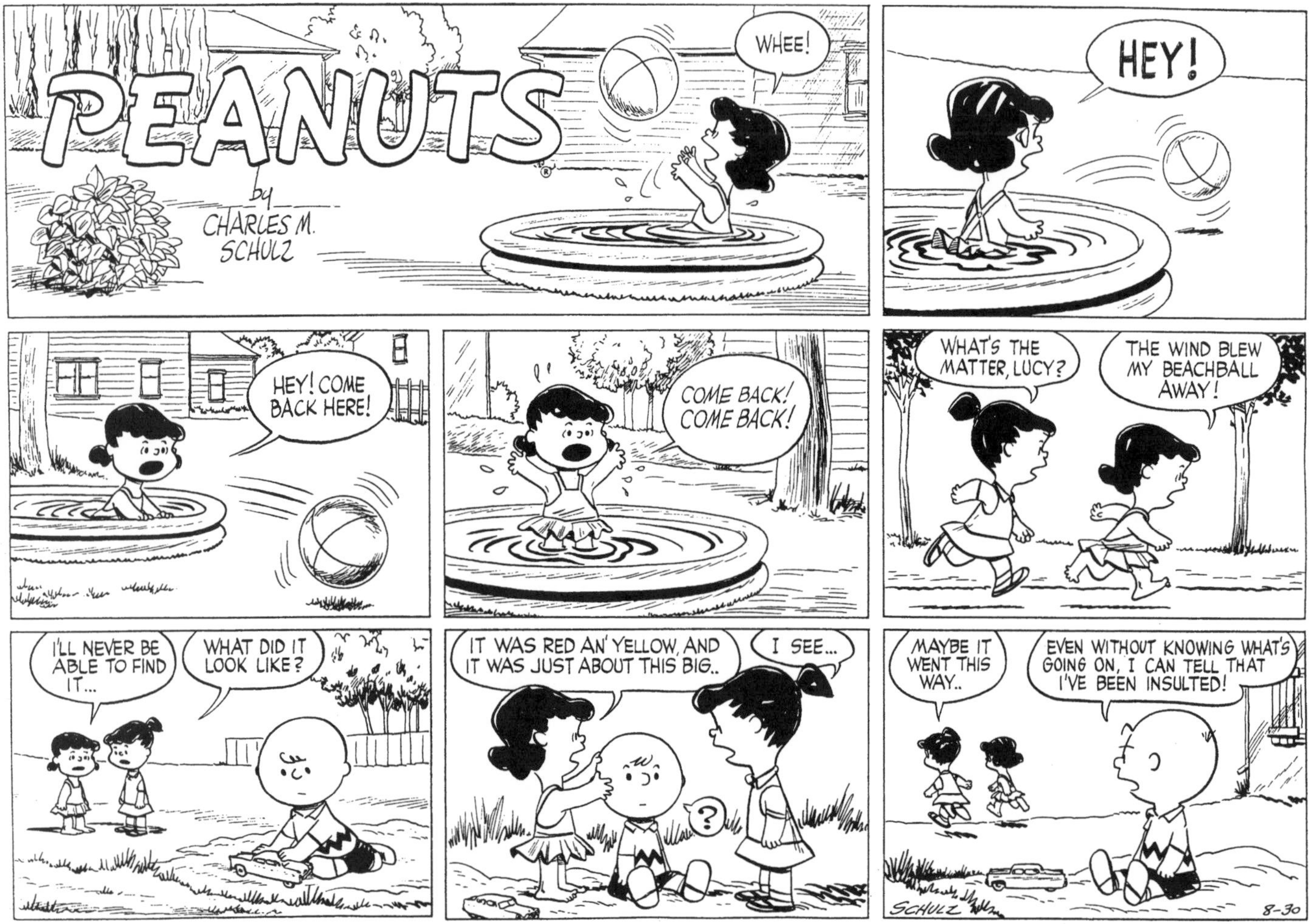
PEANUTS
by CHARLES M. SCHULZ
WHEE!
HEY!
HEY! COME BACK HERE!
COME BACK! COME BACK!
WHAT'S THE MATTER, LUCY?
THE WIND BLEW MY BEACHBALL AWAY!
I'LL NEVER BE ABLE TO FIND IT...
WHAT DID IT LOOK LIKE?
IT WAS RED AN' YELLOW, AND IT WAS JUST ABOUT THIS BIG..
I SEE...
?
MAYBE IT WENT THIS WAY..
EVEN WITHOUT KNOWING WHAT'S GOING ON, I CAN TELL THAT I'VE BEEN INSULTED!
SCHULZ
8-30

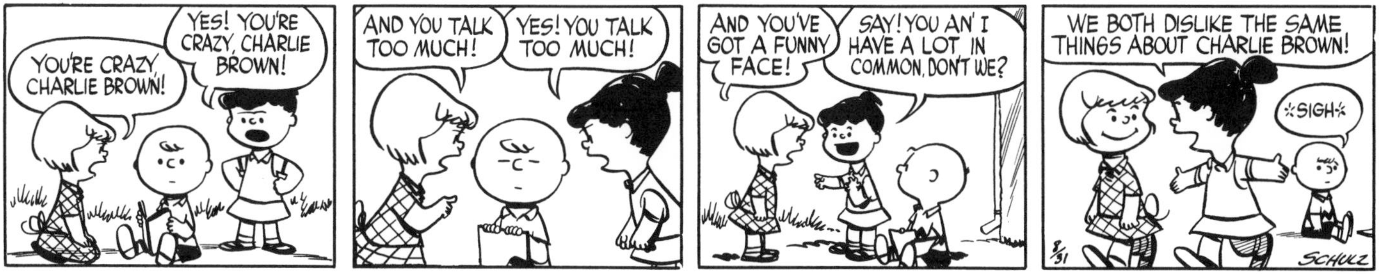
YOU'RE CRAZY, CHARLIE BROWN!
YES! YOU'RE CRAZY, CHARLIE BROWN!
AND YOU TALK TOO MUCH!
YES! YOU TALK TOO MUCH!
AND YOU'VE GOT A FUNNY FACE!
SAY! YOU AN' I HAVE A LOT IN COMMON, DON'T WE?
WE BOTH DISLIKE THE SAME THINGS ABOUT CHARLIE BROWN!
SIGH
8/31
SCHULZ

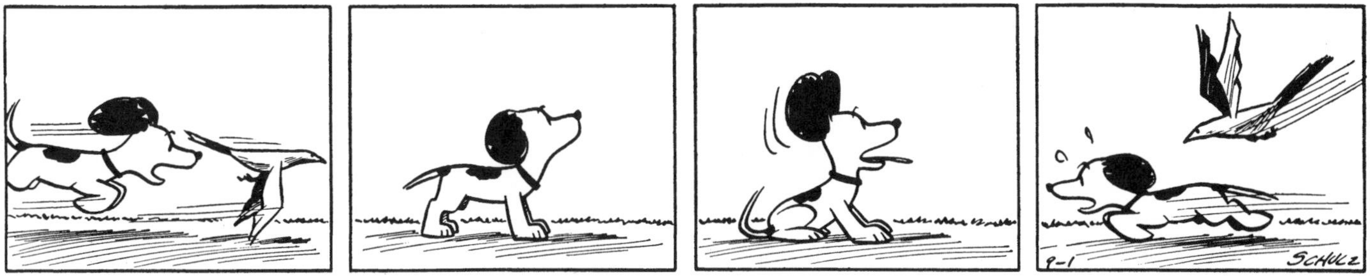
9-1
SCHULZ

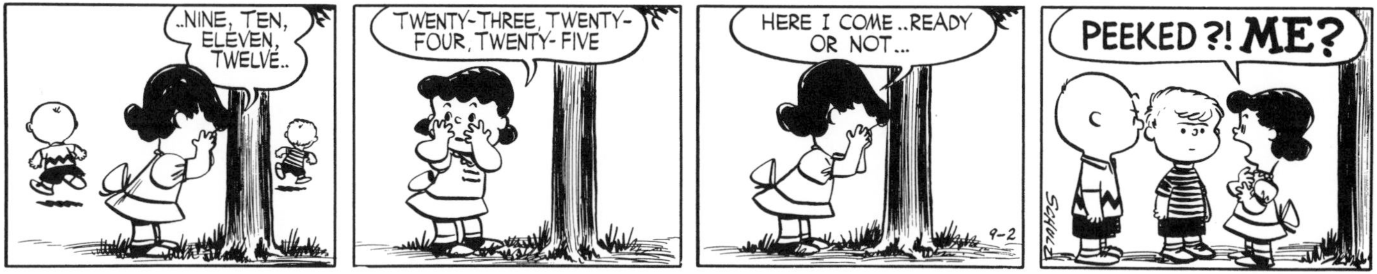
..NINE, TEN, ELEVEN, TWELVE..
TWENTY-THREE, TWENTY-FOUR, TWENTY-FIVE
HERE I COME..READY OR NOT...
9-2
PEEKED ?! ME?
SCHULZ

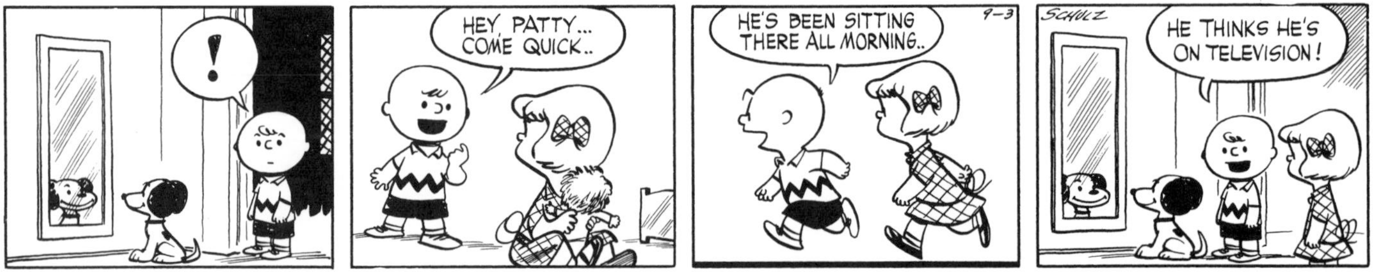
!
HEY PATTY... COME QUICK..
9-3
HE'S BEEN SITTING THERE ALL MORNING..
SCHULZ
HE THINKS HE'S ON TELEVISION!

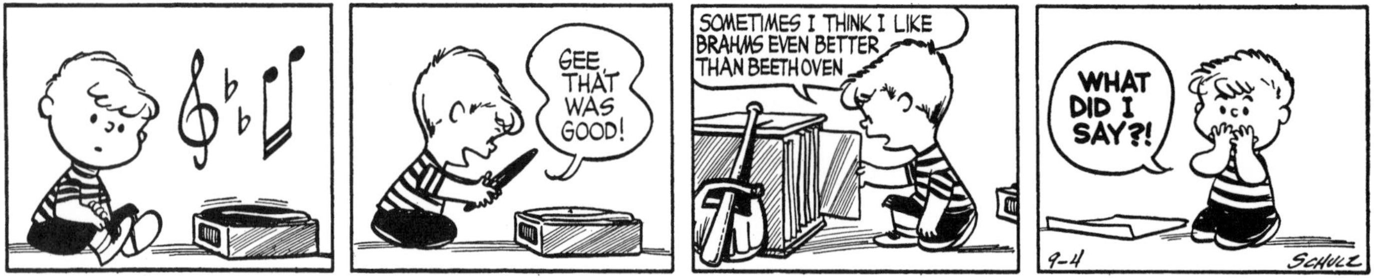
GEE THAT WAS GOOD!
SOMETIMES I THINK I LIKE BRAHMS EVEN BETTER THAN BEETHOVEN
WHAT DID I SAY?!
9-4
SCHULZ

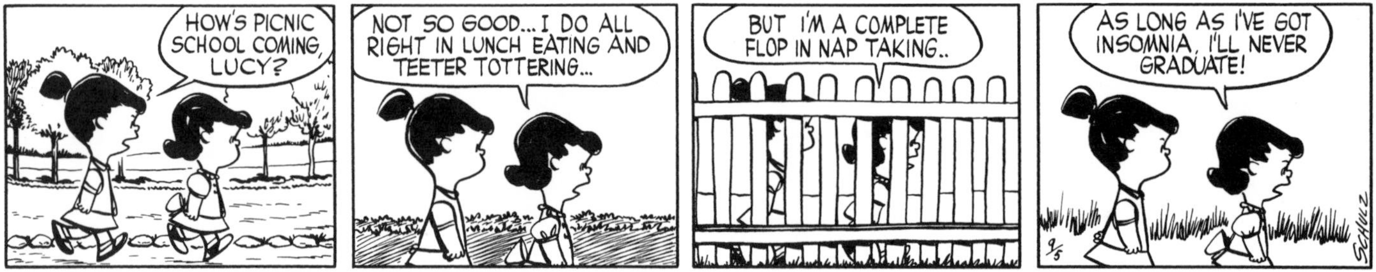
HOW'S PICNIC SCHOOL COMING, LUCY?
NOT SO GOOD... I DO ALL RIGHT IN LUNCH EATING AND TEETER TOTTERING...
BUT I'M A COMPLETE FLOP IN NAP TAKING..
AS LONG AS I'VE GOT INSOMNIA, I'LL NEVER GRADUATE!
9/5
SCHULZ

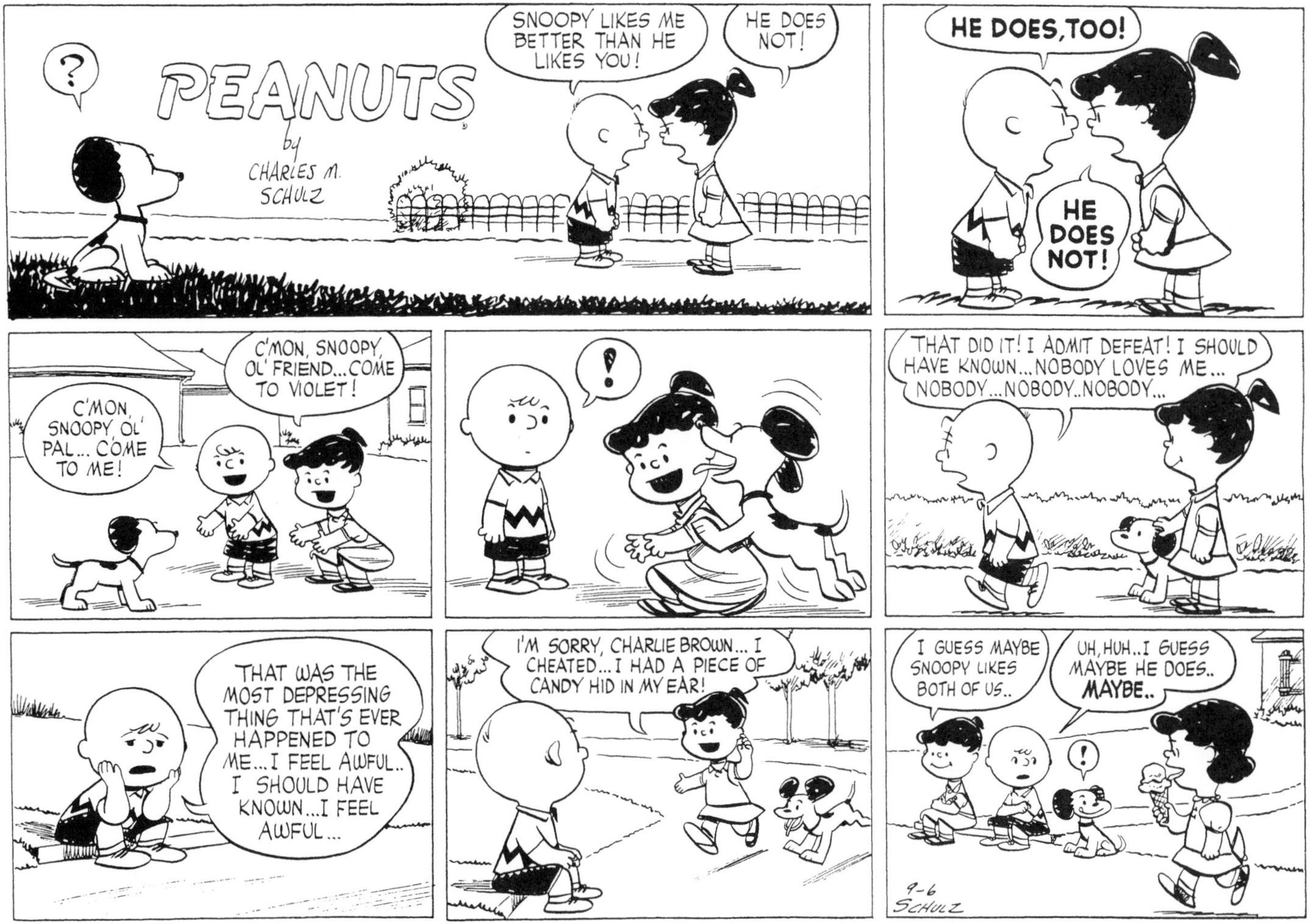
?
PEANUTS
by CHARLES M. SCHULZ
SNOOPY LIKES ME BETTER THAN HE LIKES YOU!
HE DOES NOT!
HE DOES, TOO!
HE DOES NOT!
C'MON, SNOOPY, OL' PAL... COME TO ME!
C'MON, SNOOPY, OL' FRIEND... COME TO VIOLET!
!
THAT DID IT! I ADMIT DEFEAT! I SHOULD HAVE KNOWN... NOBODY LOVES ME... NOBODY... NOBODY.. NOBODY...
THAT WAS THE MOST DEPRESSING THING THAT'S EVER HAPPENED TO ME... I FEEL AWFUL.. I SHOULD HAVE KNOWN... I FEEL AWFUL...
I'M SORRY, CHARLIE BROWN... I CHEATED... I HAD A PIECE OF CANDY HID IN MY EAR!
I GUESS MAYBE SNOOPY LIKES BOTH OF US..
UH, HUH.. I GUESS MAYBE HE DOES.. MAYBE..
!
9-6
SCHULZ

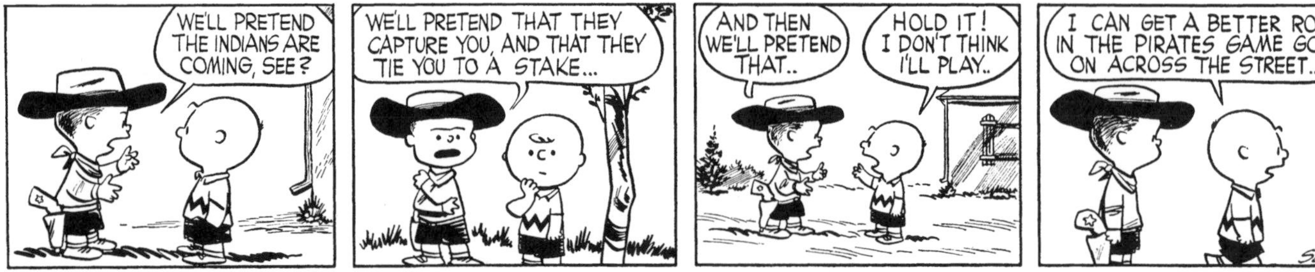
WE'LL PRETEND THE INDIANS ARE COMING, SEE?
WE'LL PRETEND THAT THEY CAPTURE YOU, AND THAT THEY TIE YOU TO A STAKE...
AND THEN WE'LL PRETEND THAT..
HOLD IT! I DON'T THINK I'LL PLAY..
I CAN GET A BETTER ROLE IN THE PIRATES GAME GOING ON ACROSS THE STREET..
9-7
SCHULZ

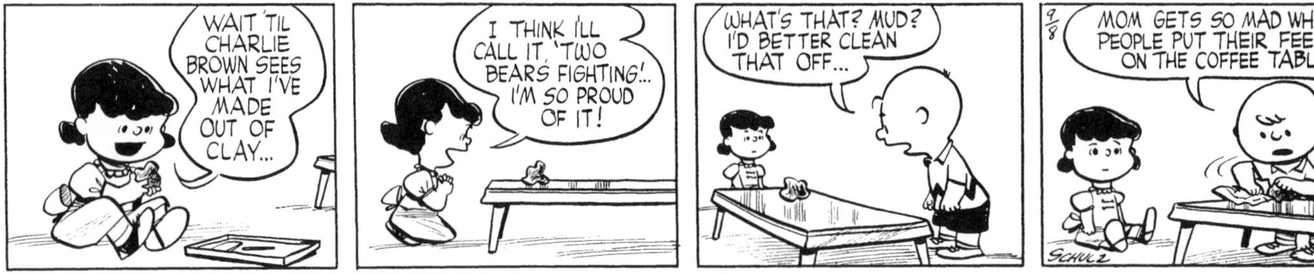
WAIT 'TIL CHARLIE BROWN SEES WHAT I'VE MADE OUT OF CLAY...
I THINK I'LL CALL IT, 'TWO BEARS FIGHTING'.. I'M SO PROUD OF IT!
WHAT'S THAT? MUD? I'D BETTER CLEAN THAT OFF...
9/8
MOM GETS SO MAD WHEN PEOPLE PUT THEIR FEET ON THE COFFEE TABLE..
SCHULZ

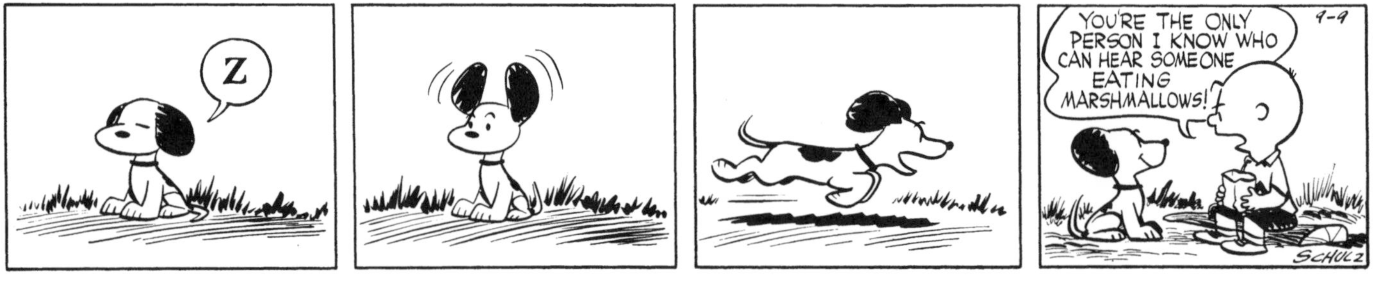
Z
9-9
YOU'RE THE ONLY PERSON I KNOW WHO CAN HEAR SOMEONE EATING MARSHMALLOWS!
SCHULZ

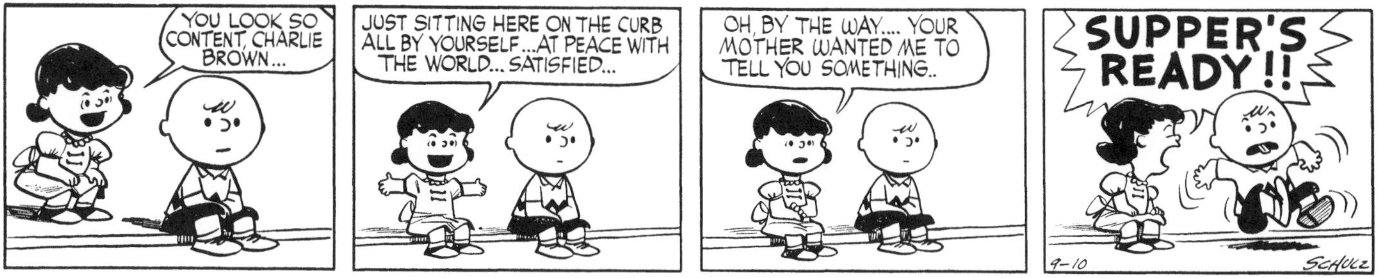
YOU LOOK SO CONTENT, CHARLIE BROWN...
JUST SITTING HERE ON THE CURB ALL BY YOURSELF...AT PEACE WITH THE WORLD... SATISFIED...
OH, BY THE WAY.... YOUR MOTHER WANTED ME TO TELL YOU SOMETHING..
SUPPER'S READY !!
9-10
SCHULZ

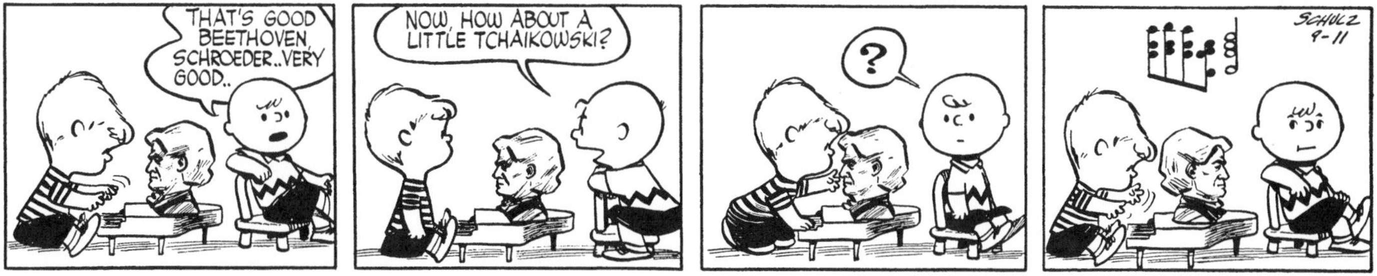
THAT'S GOOD BEETHOVEN, SCHROEDER..VERY GOOD..
NOW, HOW ABOUT A LITTLE TCHAIKOWSKI?
?
SCHULZ 9-11

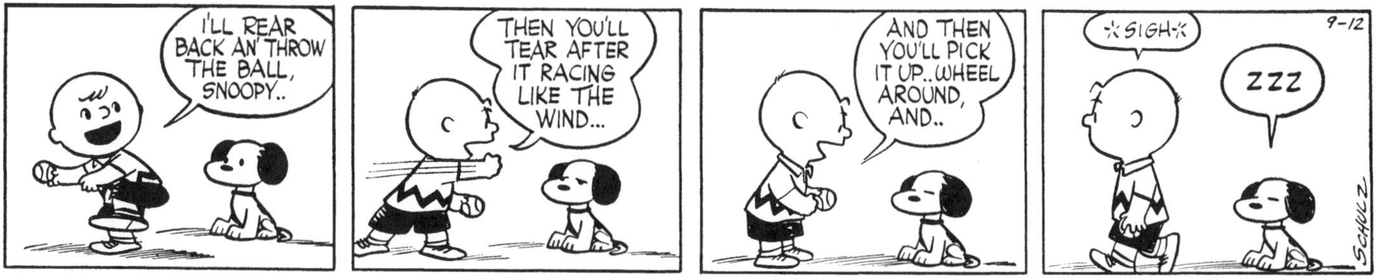
I'LL REAR BACK AN' THROW THE BALL, SNOOPY..
THEN YOU'LL TEAR AFTER IT RACING LIKE THE WIND...
AND THEN YOU'LL PICK IT UP..WHEEL AROUND, AND..
SIGH
ZZZ
9-12
SCHULZ

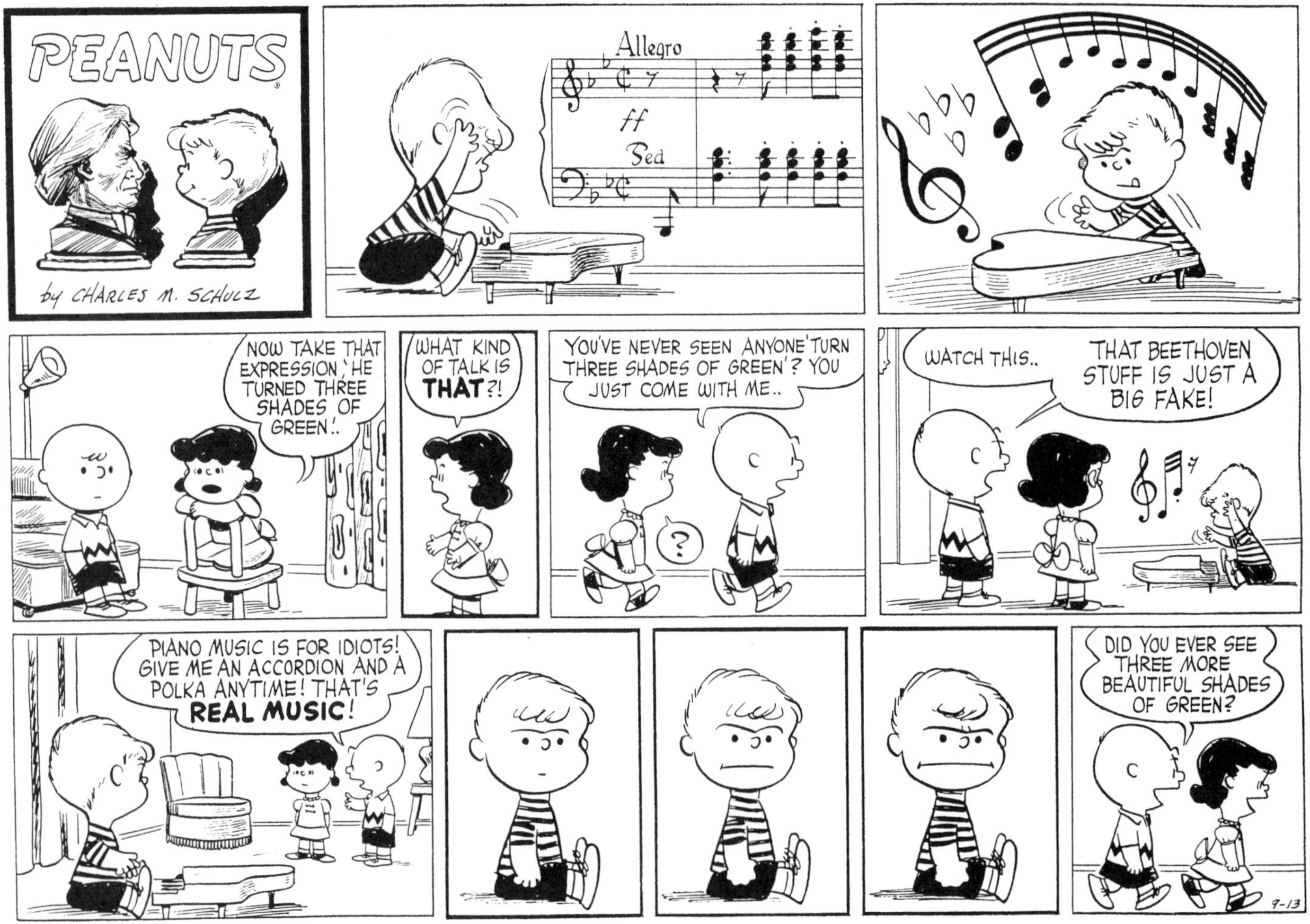
PEANUTS
by CHARLES M. SCHULZ
Allegro
ff
Ped
NOW TAKE THAT EXPRESSION, 'HE TURNED THREE SHADES OF GREEN'..
WHAT KIND OF TALK IS THAT?!
YOU'VE NEVER SEEN ANYONE 'TURN THREE SHADES OF GREEN'? YOU JUST COME WITH ME..
?
WATCH THIS..
THAT BEETHOVEN STUFF IS JUST A BIG FAKE!
PIANO MUSIC IS FOR IDIOTS! GIVE ME AN ACCORDION AND A POLKA ANYTIME! THAT'S REAL MUSIC!
DID YOU EVER SEE THREE MORE BEAUTIFUL SHADES OF GREEN?
9-13

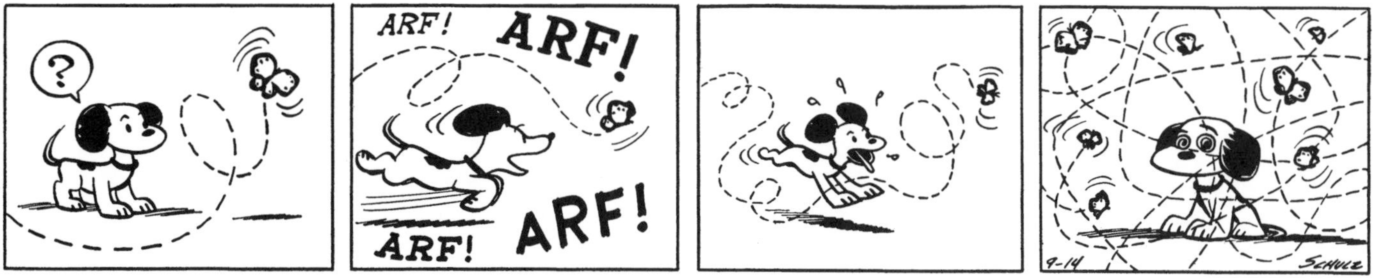
?
ARF!
ARF!
ARF!
ARF!
9-14
SCHULZ

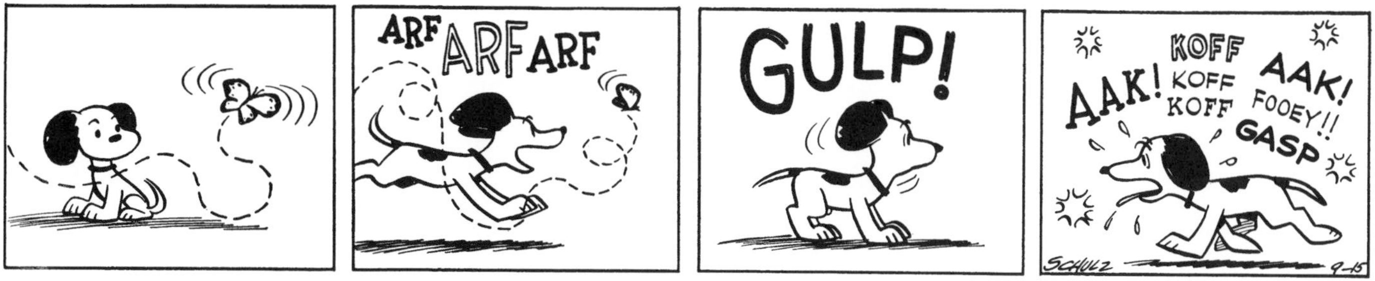
ARF ARF ARF
GULP!
AAK!
KOFF
KOFF
KOFF
AAK!
FOOEY!!
GASP
SCHULZ
9-15

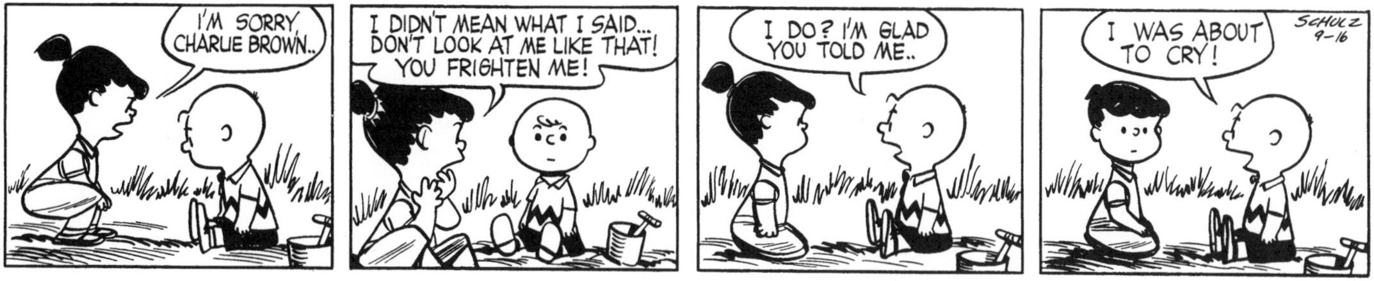
I'M SORRY, CHARLIE BROWN..
I DIDN'T MEAN WHAT I SAID... DON'T LOOK AT ME LIKE THAT! YOU FRIGHTEN ME!
I DO? I'M GLAD YOU TOLD ME..
I WAS ABOUT TO CRY!
SCHULZ 9-16

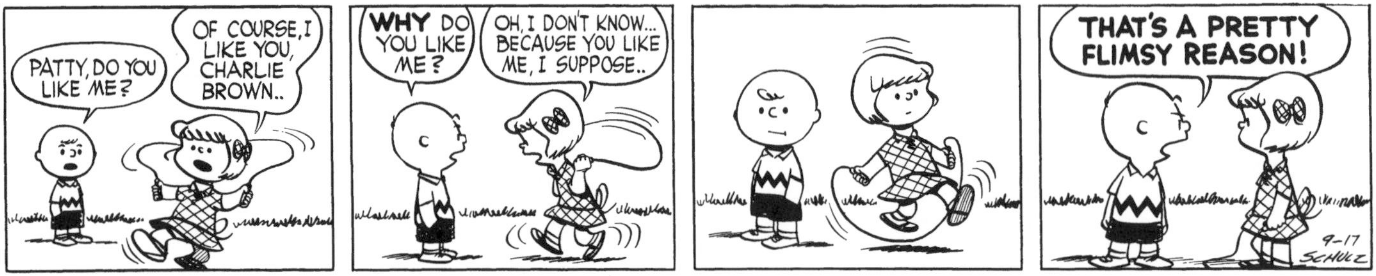
PATTY, DO YOU LIKE ME?
OF COURSE, I LIKE YOU, CHARLIE BROWN..
WHY DO YOU LIKE ME?
OH, I DON'T KNOW... BECAUSE YOU LIKE ME, I SUPPOSE..
THAT'S A PRETTY FLIMSY REASON!
9-17
SCHULZ

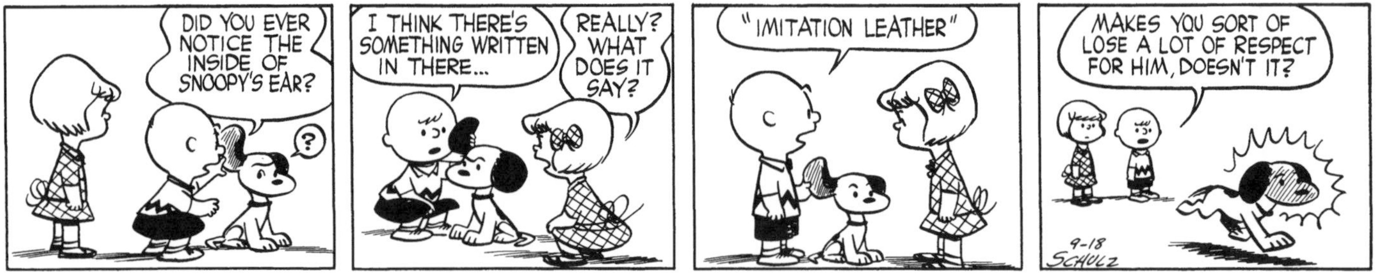
DID YOU EVER NOTICE THE INSIDE OF SNOOPY'S EAR?
?
I THINK THERE'S SOMETHING WRITTEN IN THERE...
REALLY? WHAT DOES IT SAY?
"IMITATION LEATHER"
MAKES YOU SORT OF LOSE A LOT OF RESPECT FOR HIM, DOESN'T IT?
9-18
SCHULZ

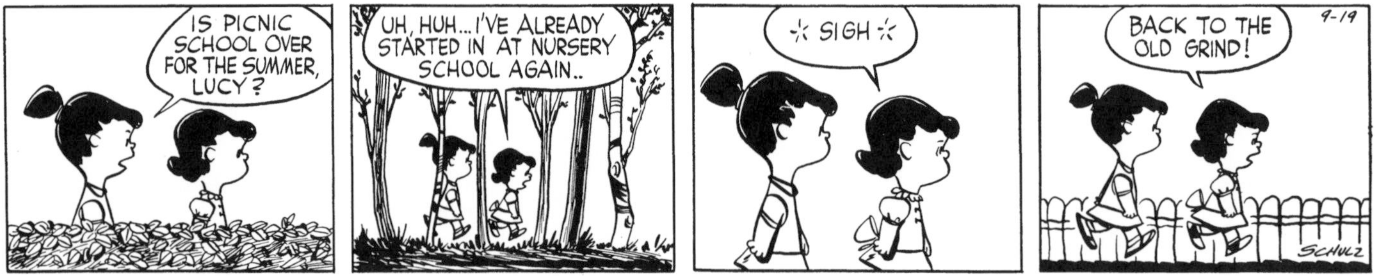
IS PICNIC SCHOOL OVER FOR THE SUMMER, LUCY?
UH, HUH... I'VE ALREADY STARTED IN AT NURSERY SCHOOL AGAIN..
SIGH
BACK TO THE OLD GRIND!
9-19
SCHULZ

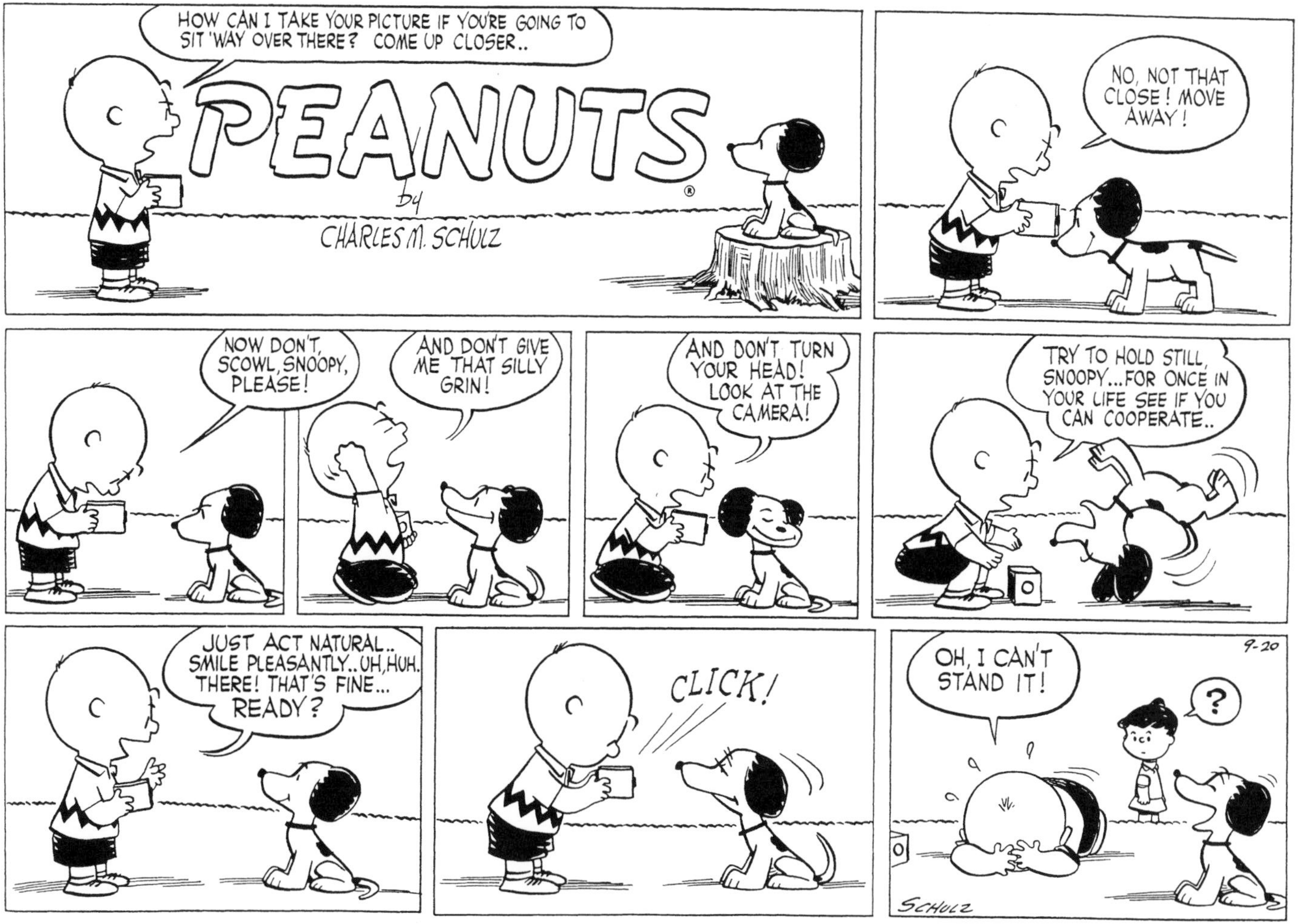
HOW CAN I TAKE YOUR PICTURE IF YOU'RE GOING TO SIT 'WAY OVER THERE? COME UP CLOSER..
PEANUTS
by
CHARLES M. SCHULZ
®
NO, NOT THAT CLOSE! MOVE AWAY!
NOW DON'T, SCOWL, SNOOPY, PLEASE!
AND DON'T GIVE ME THAT SILLY GRIN!
AND DON'T TURN YOUR HEAD! LOOK AT THE CAMERA!
TRY TO HOLD STILL, SNOOPY...FOR ONCE IN YOUR LIFE SEE IF YOU CAN COOPERATE..
JUST ACT NATURAL.. SMILE PLEASANTLY..UH, HUH. THERE! THAT'S FINE... READY?
CLICK!
9-20
OH, I CAN'T STAND IT!
?
SCHULZ

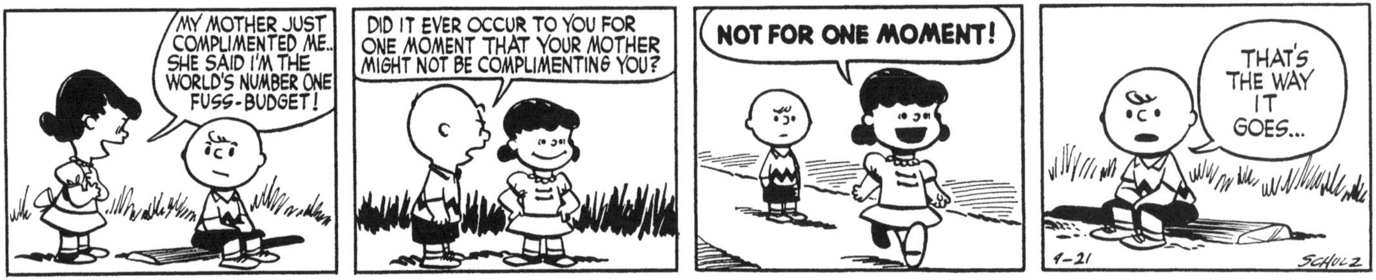
MY MOTHER JUST COMPLIMENTED ME.. SHE SAID I'M THE WORLD'S NUMBER ONE FUSS-BUDGET!
DID IT EVER OCCUR TO YOU FOR ONE MOMENT THAT YOUR MOTHER MIGHT NOT BE COMPLIMENTING YOU?
NOT FOR ONE MOMENT!
THAT'S THE WAY IT GOES...
9-21
SCHULZ

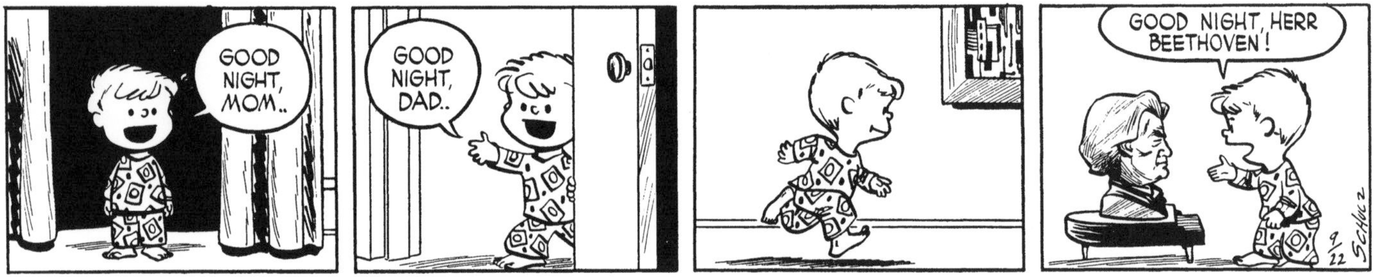
GOOD NIGHT, MOM..
GOOD NIGHT, DAD..
GOOD NIGHT, HERR BEETHOVEN!
SCHULZ
9/22

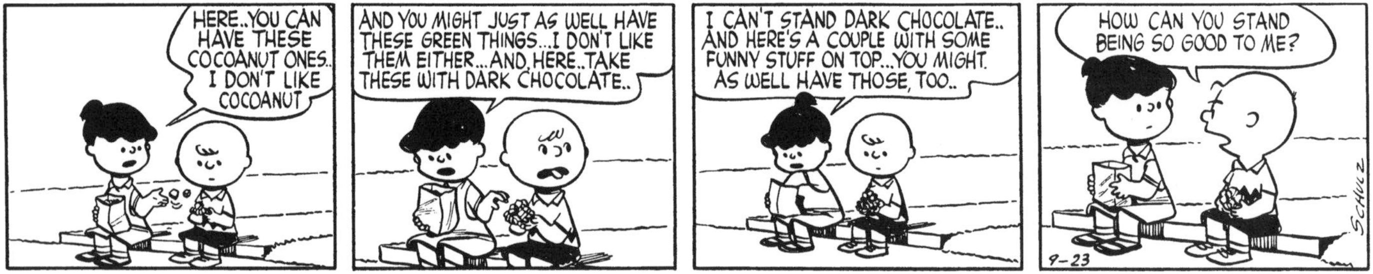
HERE..YOU CAN HAVE THESE COCOANUT ONES.. I DON'T LIKE COCOANUT
AND YOU MIGHT JUST AS WELL HAVE THESE GREEN THINGS...I DON'T LIKE THEM EITHER...AND, HERE..TAKE THESE WITH DARK CHOCOLATE..
I CAN'T STAND DARK CHOCOLATE.. AND HERE'S A COUPLE WITH SOME FUNNY STUFF ON TOP...YOU MIGHT AS WELL HAVE THOSE, TOO..
HOW CAN YOU STAND BEING SO GOOD TO ME?
SCHULZ
9-23

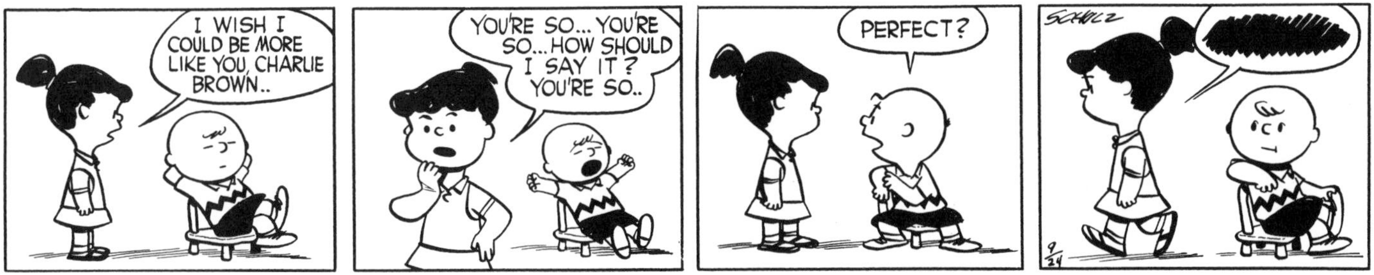
I WISH I COULD BE MORE LIKE YOU, CHARLIE BROWN..
YOU'RE SO... YOU'RE SO...HOW SHOULD I SAY IT? YOU'RE SO..
PERFECT?
SCHULZ
9/24

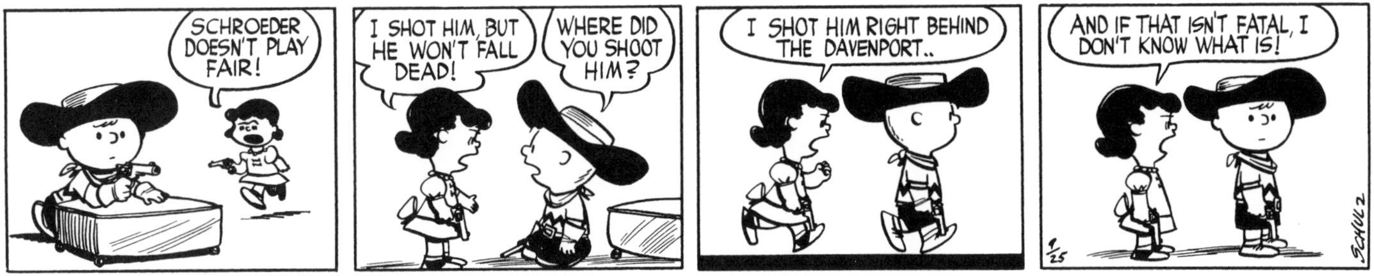
SCHROEDER DOESN'T PLAY FAIR!
I SHOT HIM, BUT HE WON'T FALL DEAD!
WHERE DID YOU SHOOT HIM?
I SHOT HIM RIGHT BEHIND THE DAVENPORT..
AND IF THAT ISN'T FATAL, I DON'T KNOW WHAT IS!
9/25
SCHULZ

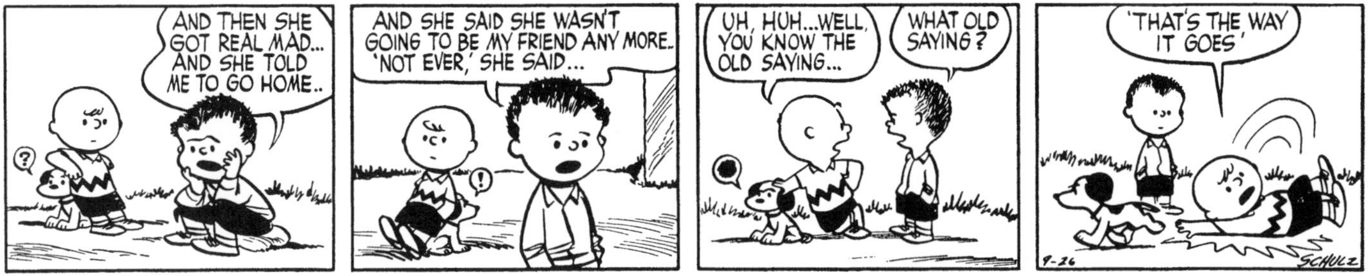
AND THEN SHE GOT REAL MAD... AND SHE TOLD ME TO GO HOME..
AND SHE SAID SHE WASN'T GOING TO BE MY FRIEND ANY MORE.. 'NOT EVER,' SHE SAID...
UH, HUH...WELL, YOU KNOW THE OLD SAYING...
WHAT OLD SAYING?
'THAT'S THE WAY IT GOES'
9-26
SCHULZ

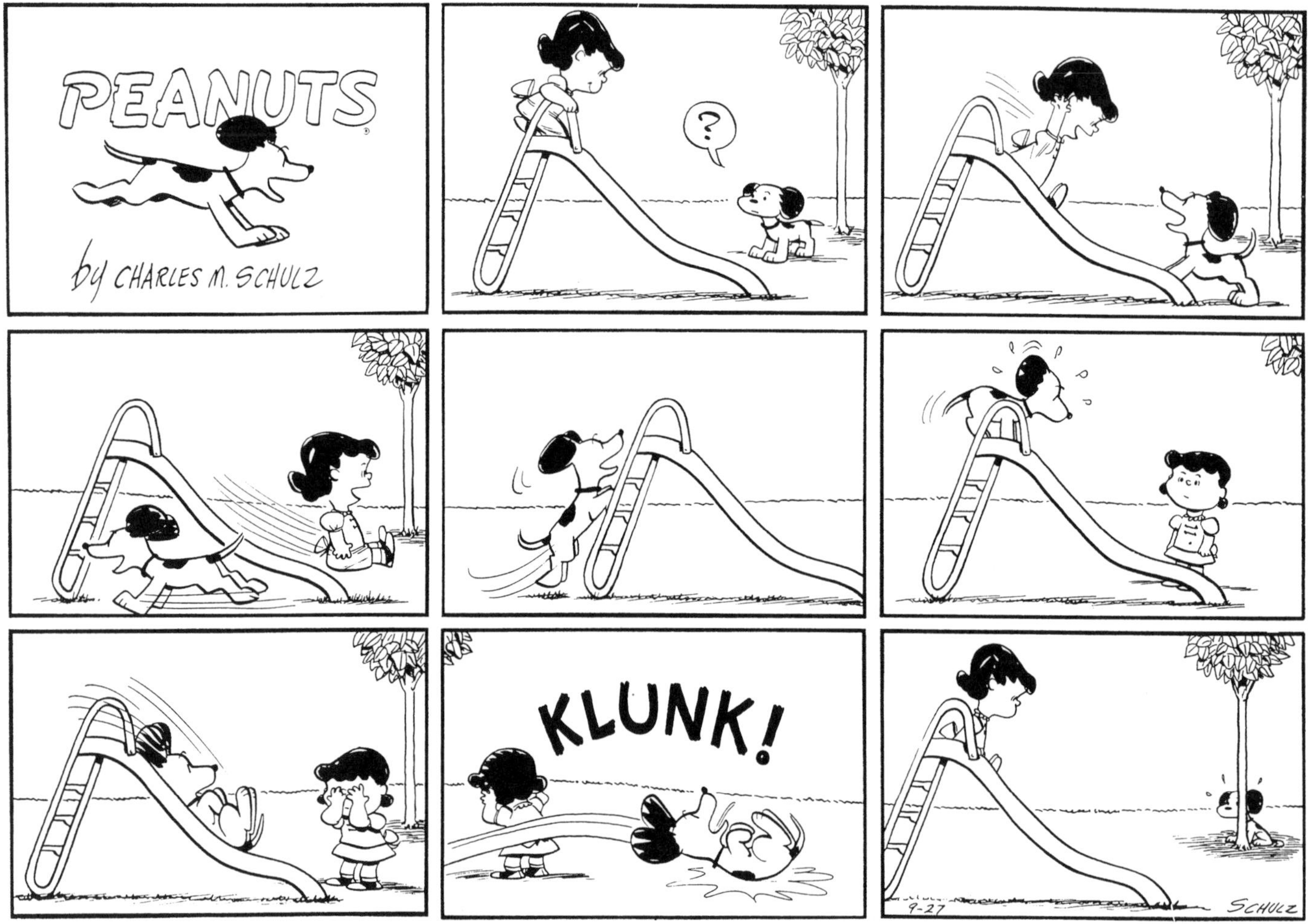
PEANUTS
by CHARLES M. SCHULZ
?
KLUNK!
9-27
SCHULZ

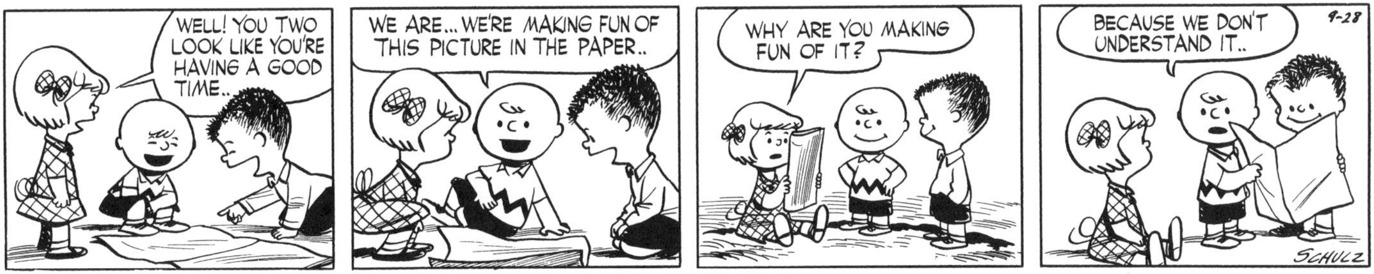
WELL! YOU TWO LOOK LIKE YOU'RE HAVING A GOOD TIME..
WE ARE... WE'RE MAKING FUN OF THIS PICTURE IN THE PAPER..
WHY ARE YOU MAKING FUN OF IT?
BECAUSE WE DON'T UNDERSTAND IT..
9-28
SCHULZ

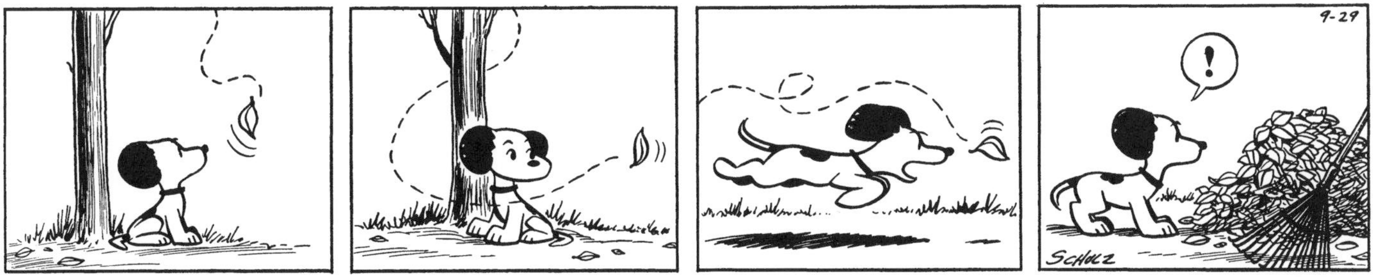
9-29
!
SCHULZ

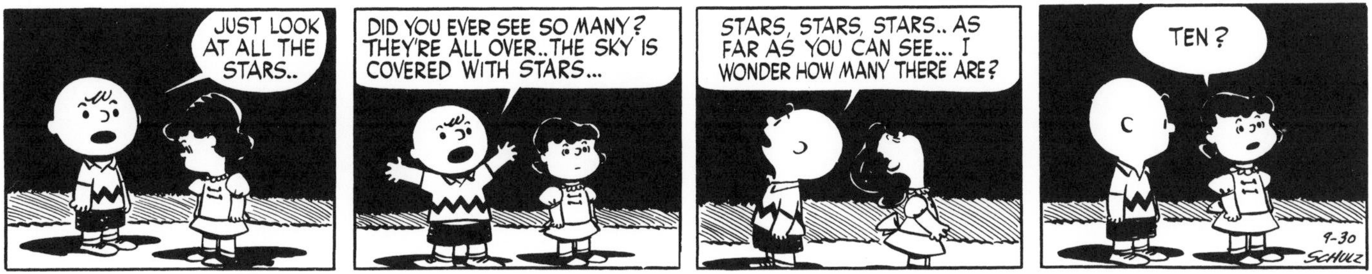
JUST LOOK AT ALL THE STARS..
DID YOU EVER SEE SO MANY? THEY'RE ALL OVER.. THE SKY IS COVERED WITH STARS...
STARS, STARS, STARS.. AS FAR AS YOU CAN SEE... I WONDER HOW MANY THERE ARE?
TEN?
9-30
SCHULZ

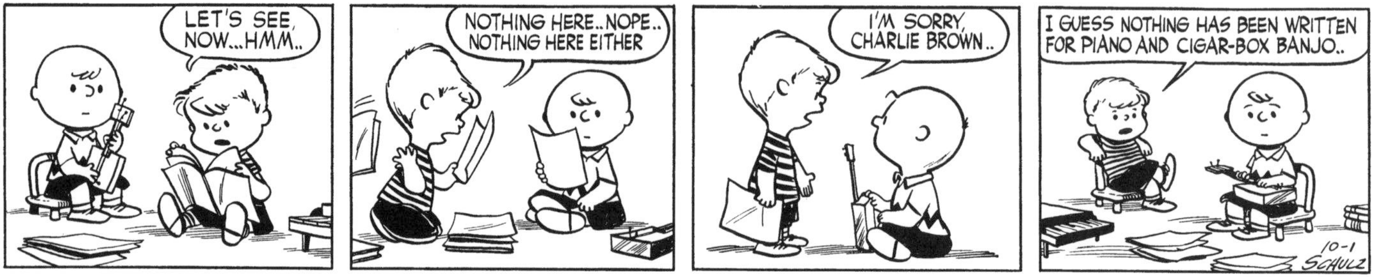
LET'S SEE, NOW...HMM..
NOTHING HERE..NOPE.. NOTHING HERE EITHER
I'M SORRY, CHARLIE BROWN..
I GUESS NOTHING HAS BEEN WRITTEN FOR PIANO AND CIGAR-BOX BANJO..
10-1
SCHULZ

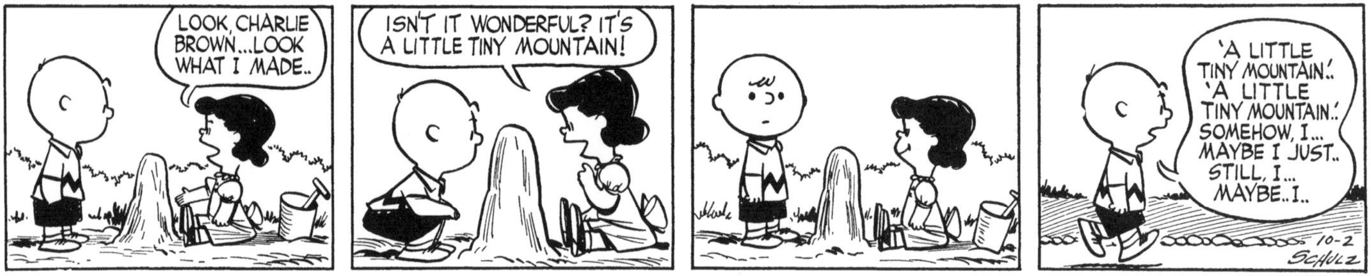
LOOK, CHARLIE BROWN...LOOK WHAT I MADE..
ISN'T IT WONDERFUL? IT'S A LITTLE TINY MOUNTAIN!
'A LITTLE TINY MOUNTAIN!' 'A LITTLE TINY MOUNTAIN!' SOMEHOW, I... MAYBE I JUST.. STILL, I... MAYBE..I..
10-2
SCHULZ

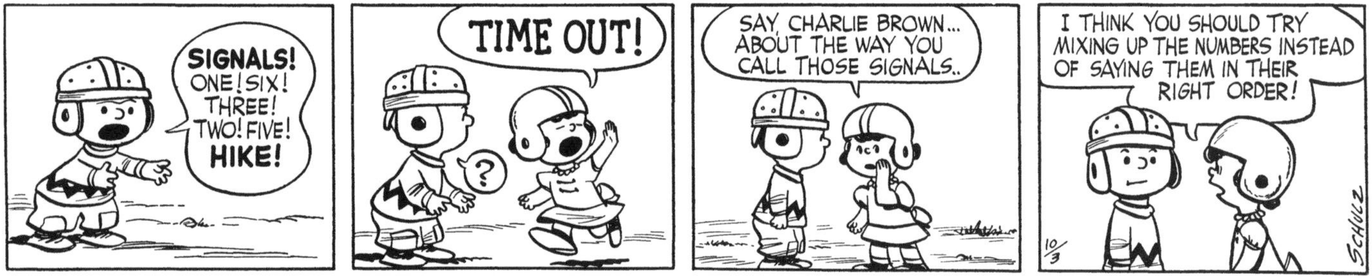
SIGNALS! ONE! SIX! THREE! TWO! FIVE! HIKE!
TIME OUT!
?
SAY, CHARLIE BROWN... ABOUT THE WAY YOU CALL THOSE SIGNALS..
I THINK YOU SHOULD TRY MIXING UP THE NUMBERS INSTEAD OF SAYING THEM IN THEIR RIGHT ORDER!
10/3
SCHULZ

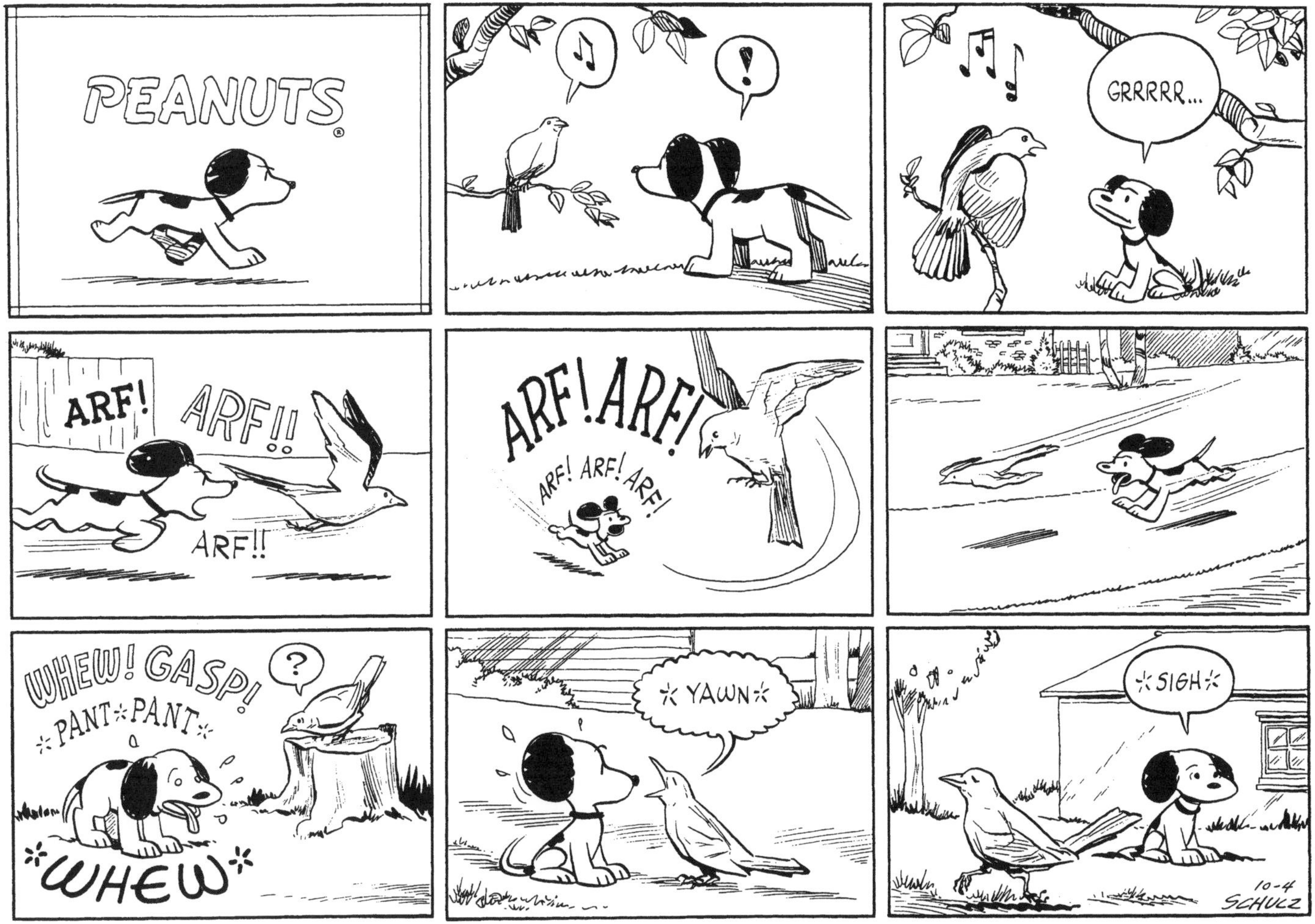
PEANUTS
♪
!
GRRRRR...
ARF!
ARF!!
ARF!!
ARF! ARF!
ARF! ARF! ARF!
WHEW! GASP!
PANT PANT
?
WHEW
YAWN
SIGH
10-4
SCHULZ

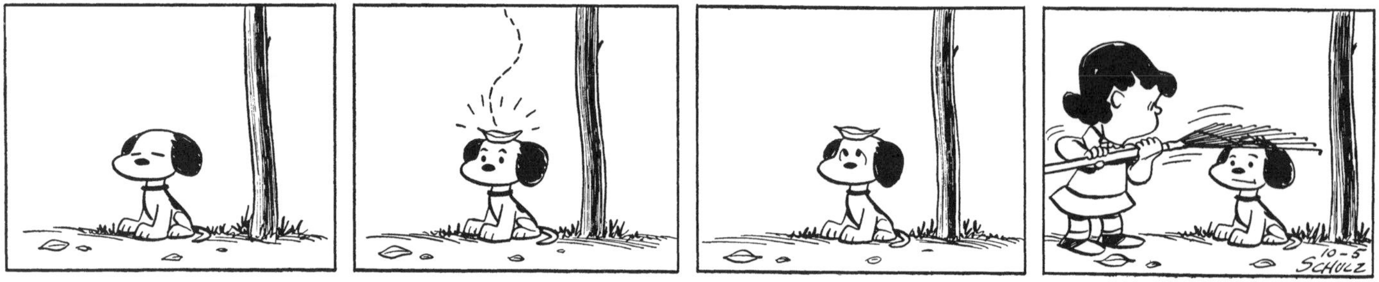
10-5
SCHULZ

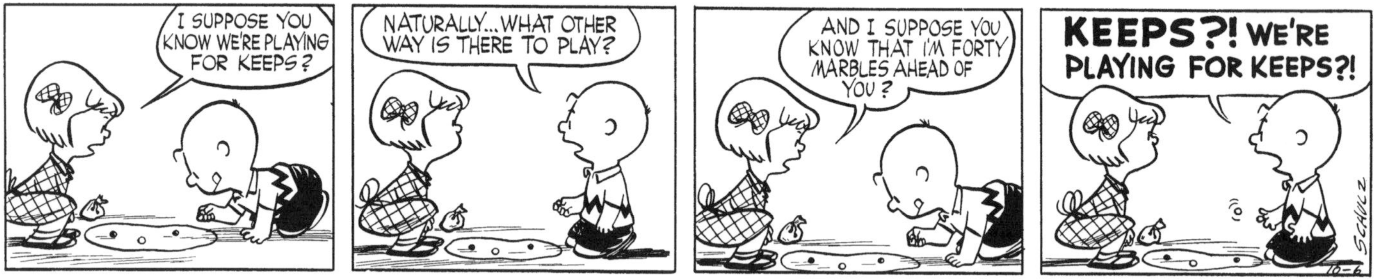
I SUPPOSE YOU KNOW WE'RE PLAYING FOR KEEPS?
NATURALLY...WHAT OTHER WAY IS THERE TO PLAY?
AND I SUPPOSE YOU KNOW THAT I'M FORTY MARBLES AHEAD OF YOU?
KEEPS?! WE'RE PLAYING FOR KEEPS?!
SCHULZ
10-6

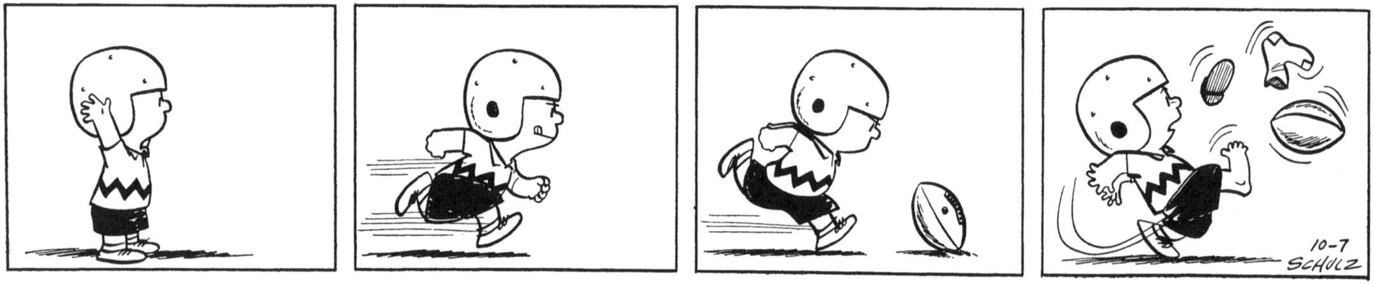
10-7
SCHULZ

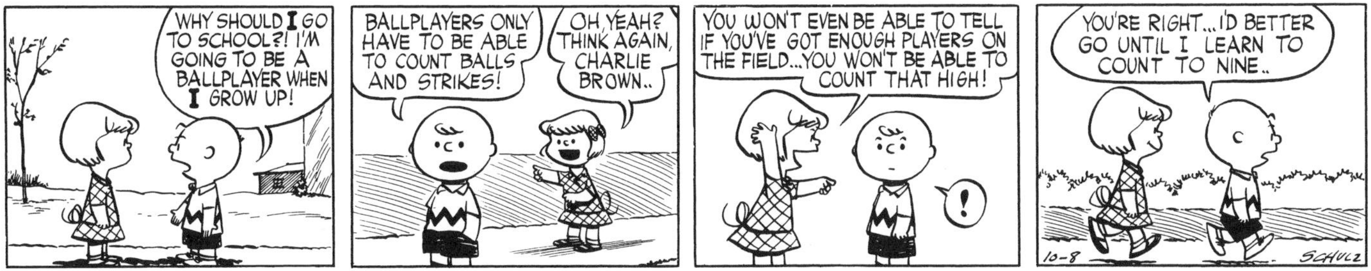
WHY SHOULD I GO TO SCHOOL?! I'M GOING TO BE A BALLPLAYER WHEN I GROW UP!
BALLPLAYERS ONLY HAVE TO BE ABLE TO COUNT BALLS AND STRIKES!
OH YEAH? THINK AGAIN, CHARLIE BROWN..
YOU WON'T EVEN BE ABLE TO TELL IF YOU'VE GOT ENOUGH PLAYERS ON THE FIELD...YOU WON'T BE ABLE TO COUNT THAT HIGH!
!
YOU'RE RIGHT...I'D BETTER GO UNTIL I LEARN TO COUNT TO NINE..
10-8
SCHULZ

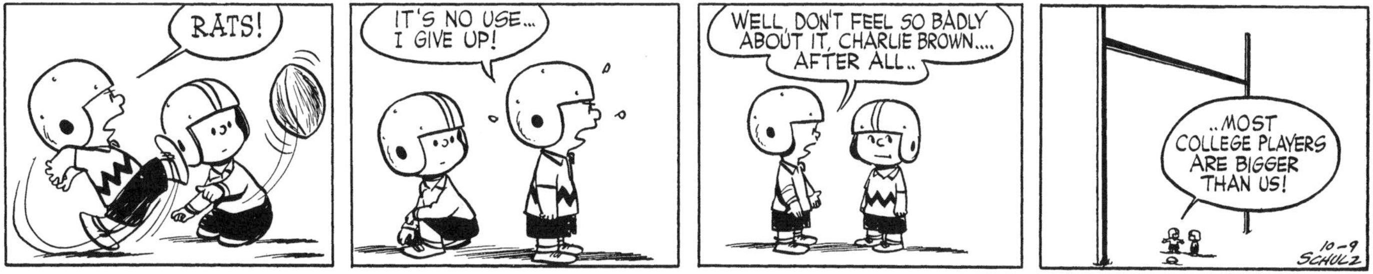
RATS!
IT'S NO USE... I GIVE UP!
WELL, DON'T FEEL SO BADLY ABOUT IT, CHARLIE BROWN.... AFTER ALL..
..MOST COLLEGE PLAYERS ARE BIGGER THAN US!
10-9
SCHULZ

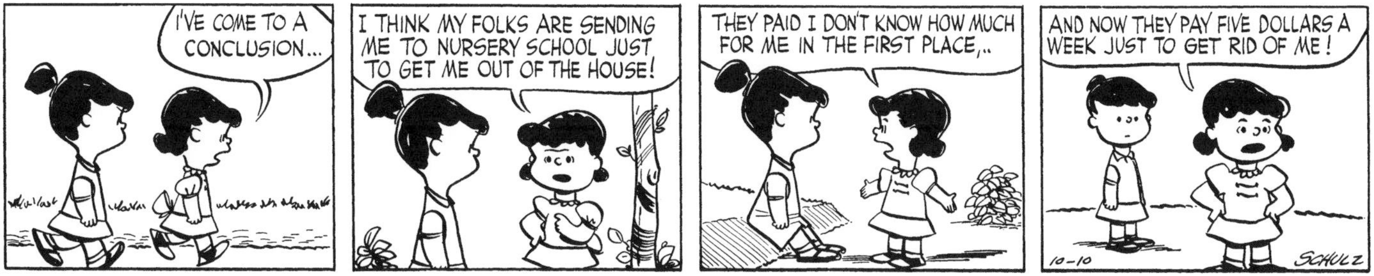
I'VE COME TO A CONCLUSION...
I THINK MY FOLKS ARE SENDING ME TO NURSERY SCHOOL JUST TO GET ME OUT OF THE HOUSE!
THEY PAID I DON'T KNOW HOW MUCH FOR ME IN THE FIRST PLACE,..
AND NOW THEY PAY FIVE DOLLARS A WEEK JUST TO GET RID OF ME!
10-10
SCHULZ

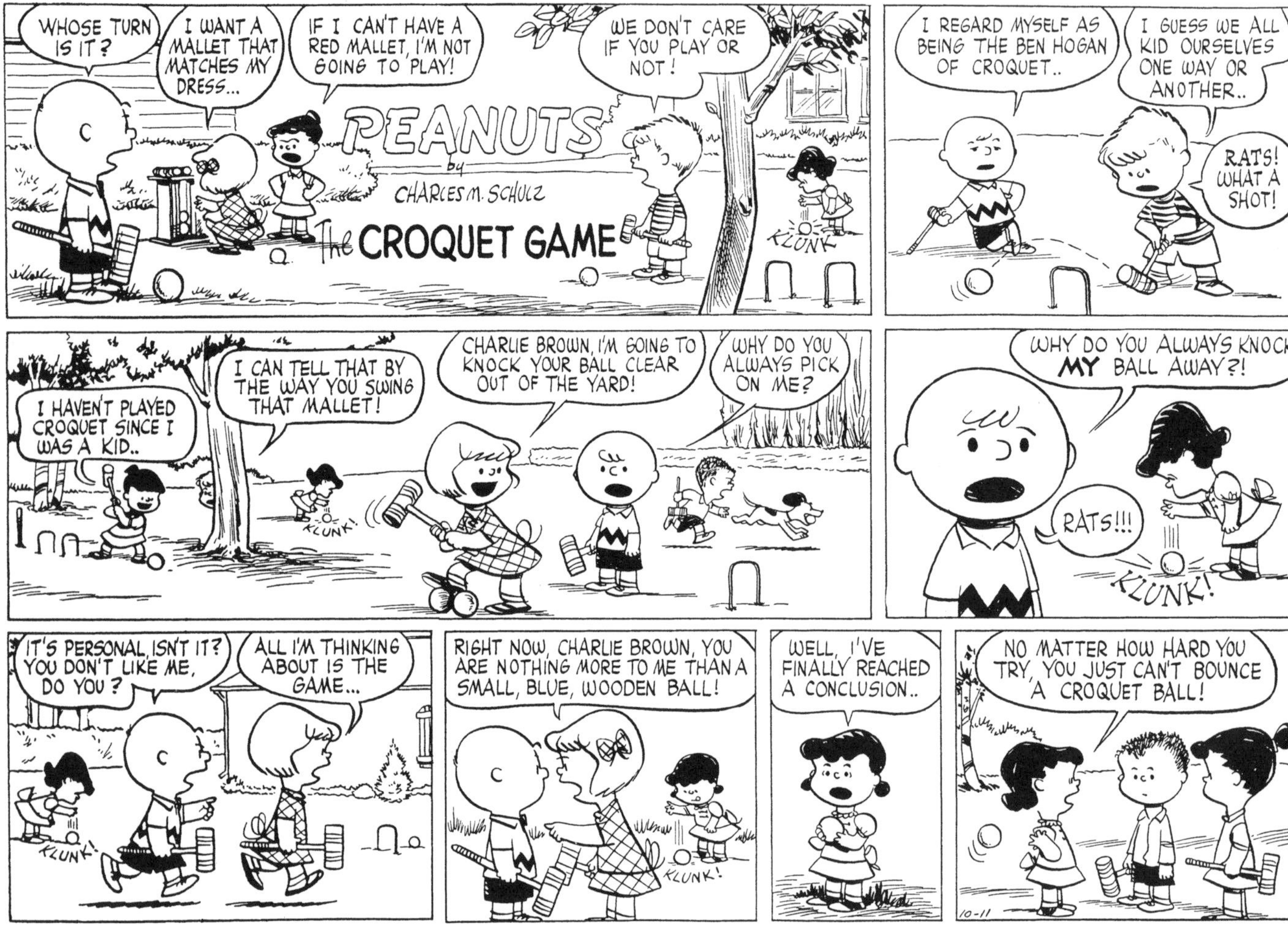
WHOSE TURN IS IT?
I WANT A MALLET THAT MATCHES MY DRESS...
IF I CAN'T HAVE A RED MALLET, I'M NOT GOING TO PLAY!
PEANUTS
by CHARLES M. SCHULZ
The CROQUET GAME
WE DON'T CARE IF YOU PLAY OR NOT!
KLUNK
I REGARD MYSELF AS BEING THE BEN HOGAN OF CROQUET..
I GUESS WE ALL KID OURSELVES ONE WAY OR ANOTHER..
RATS! WHAT A SHOT!
I HAVEN'T PLAYED CROQUET SINCE I WAS A KID..
I CAN TELL THAT BY THE WAY YOU SWING THAT MALLET!
KLUNK!
CHARLIE BROWN, I'M GOING TO KNOCK YOUR BALL CLEAR OUT OF THE YARD!
WHY DO YOU ALWAYS PICK ON ME?
WHY DO YOU ALWAYS KNOCK **MY** BALL AWAY?!
RATS!!!
KLUNK!
IT'S PERSONAL, ISN'T IT? YOU DON'T LIKE ME, DO YOU?
ALL I'M THINKING ABOUT IS THE GAME...
KLUNK!
RIGHT NOW, CHARLIE BROWN, YOU ARE NOTHING MORE TO ME THAN A SMALL, BLUE, WOODEN BALL!
KLUNK!
WELL, I'VE FINALLY REACHED A CONCLUSION..
10-11
NO MATTER HOW HARD YOU TRY, YOU JUST CAN'T BOUNCE A CROQUET BALL!
SCHULZ

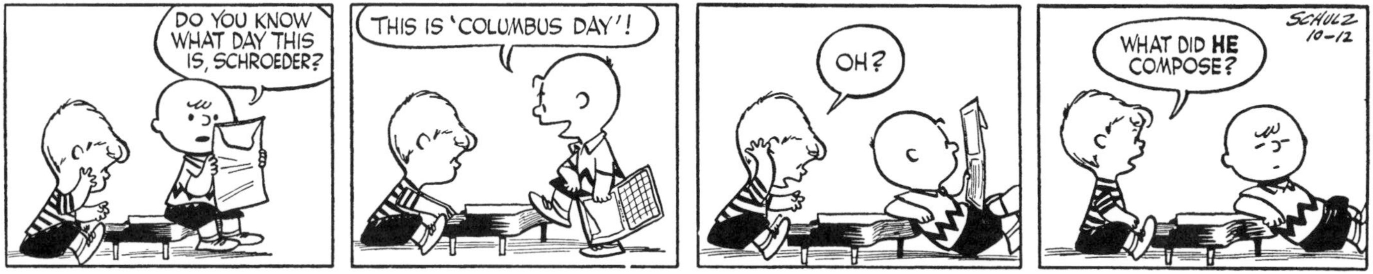
DO YOU KNOW WHAT DAY THIS IS, SCHROEDER?
THIS IS 'COLUMBUS DAY'!
OH?
WHAT DID HE COMPOSE?
SCHULZ 10-12

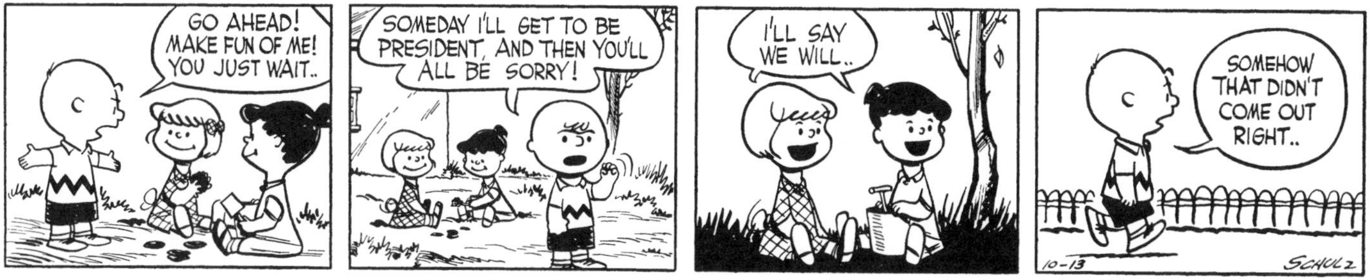
GO AHEAD! MAKE FUN OF ME! YOU JUST WAIT..
SOMEDAY I'LL GET TO BE PRESIDENT, AND THEN YOU'LL ALL BE SORRY!
I'LL SAY WE WILL..
SOMEHOW THAT DIDN'T COME OUT RIGHT..
10-13
SCHULZ

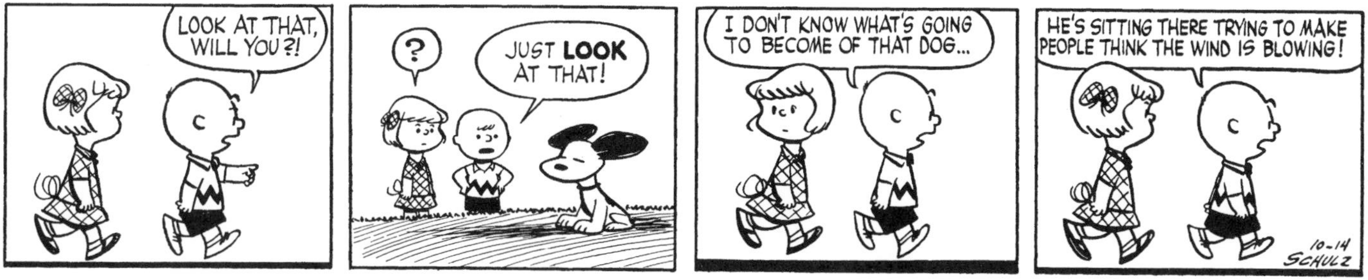
LOOK AT THAT, WILL YOU?!
?
JUST LOOK AT THAT!
I DON'T KNOW WHAT'S GOING TO BECOME OF THAT DOG...
HE'S SITTING THERE TRYING TO MAKE PEOPLE THINK THE WIND IS BLOWING!
10-14 SCHULZ

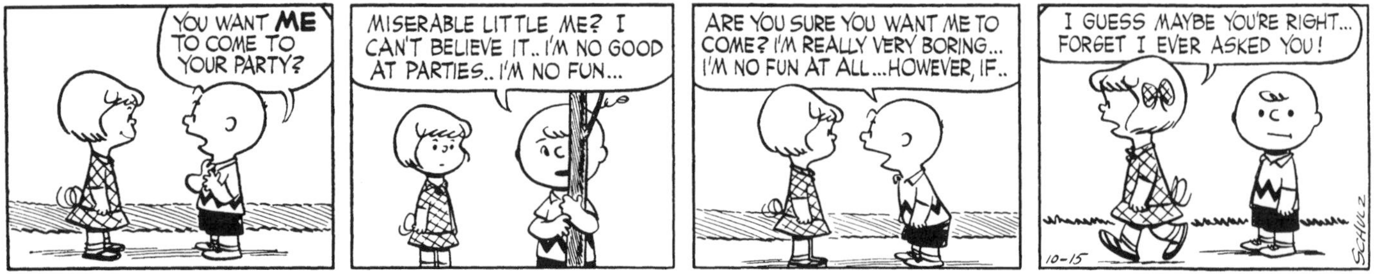
YOU WANT **ME** TO COME TO YOUR PARTY?
MISERABLE LITTLE ME? I CAN'T BELIEVE IT.. I'M NO GOOD AT PARTIES.. I'M NO FUN...
ARE YOU SURE YOU WANT ME TO COME? I'M REALLY VERY BORING... I'M NO FUN AT ALL...HOWEVER, IF..
I GUESS MAYBE YOU'RE RIGHT... FORGET I EVER ASKED YOU!
10-15
SCHULZ

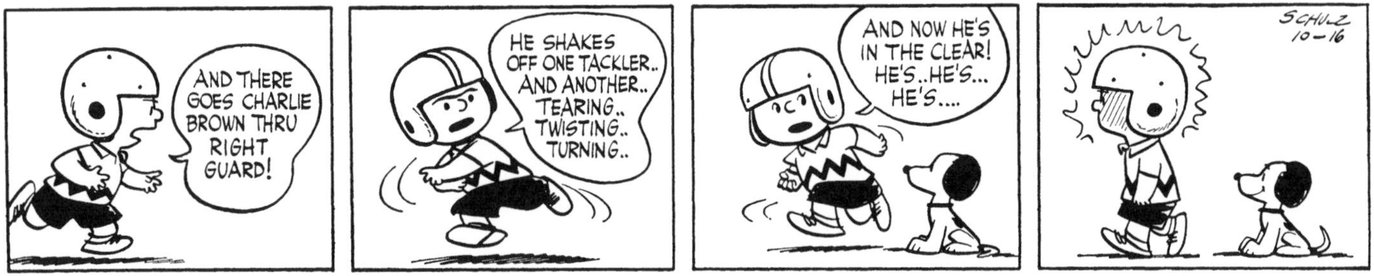
AND THERE GOES CHARLIE BROWN THRU RIGHT GUARD!
HE SHAKES OFF ONE TACKLER.. AND ANOTHER.. TEARING.. TWISTING.. TURNING..
AND NOW HE'S IN THE CLEAR! HE'S..HE'S... HE'S....
SCHULZ
10-16

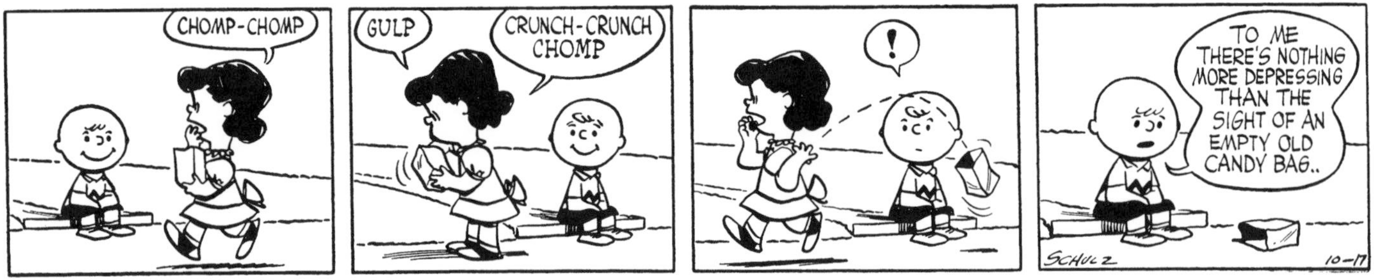
CHOMP-CHOMP
GULP
CRUNCH-CRUNCH CHOMP
!
TO ME THERE'S NOTHING MORE DEPRESSING THAN THE SIGHT OF AN EMPTY OLD CANDY BAG..
SCHULZ
10-17

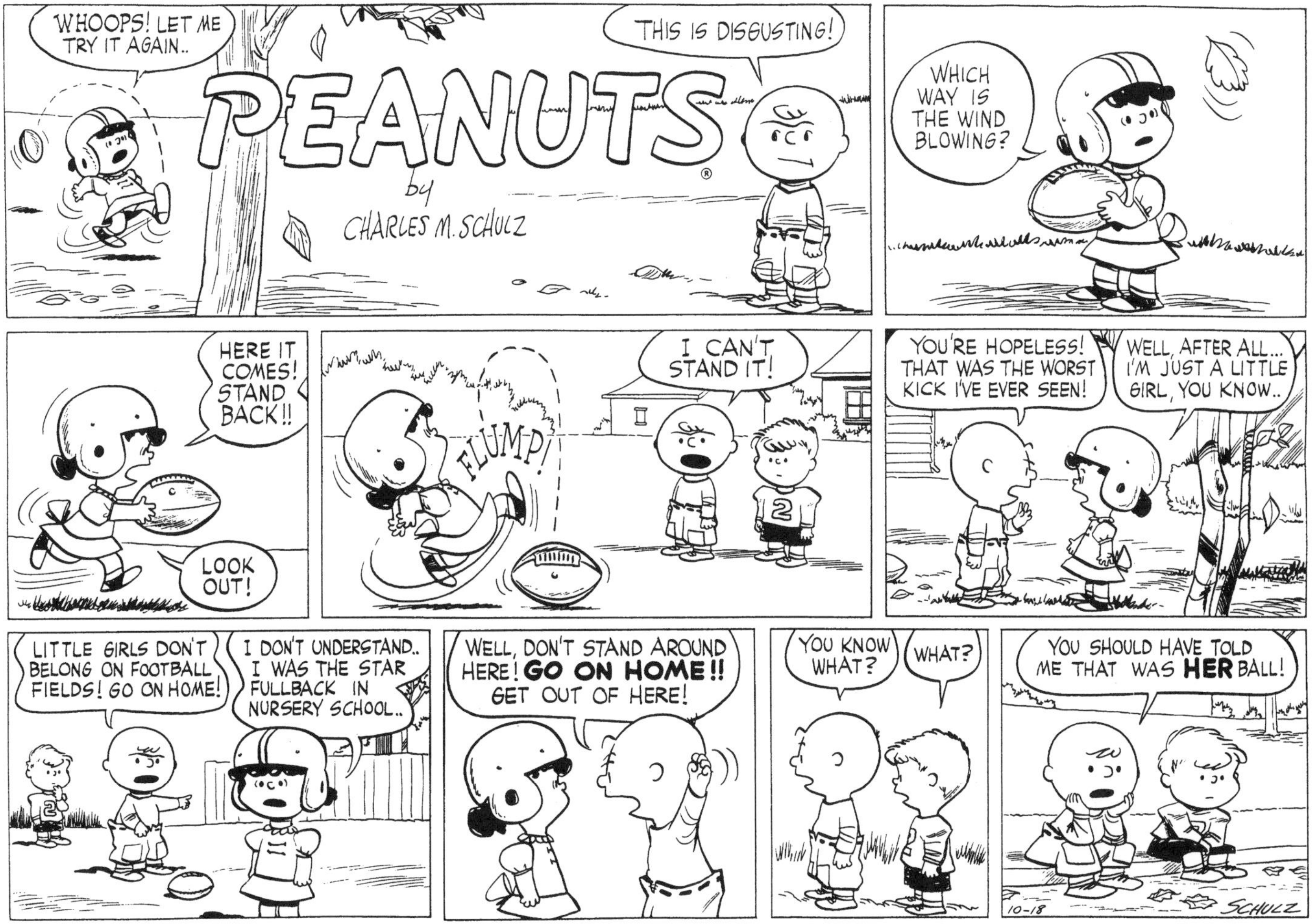
WHOOPS! LET ME TRY IT AGAIN..
PEANUTS®
by CHARLES M. SCHULZ
THIS IS DISGUSTING!
WHICH WAY IS THE WIND BLOWING?
HERE IT COMES! STAND BACK!!
LOOK OUT!
FLUMP!
I CAN'T STAND IT!
2
YOU'RE HOPELESS! THAT WAS THE WORST KICK I'VE EVER SEEN!
WELL, AFTER ALL... I'M JUST A LITTLE GIRL, YOU KNOW..
LITTLE GIRLS DON'T BELONG ON FOOTBALL FIELDS! GO ON HOME!
I DON'T UNDERSTAND.. I WAS THE STAR FULLBACK IN NURSERY SCHOOL..
2
WELL, DON'T STAND AROUND HERE! GO ON HOME!! GET OUT OF HERE!
YOU KNOW WHAT?
WHAT?
YOU SHOULD HAVE TOLD ME THAT WAS HER BALL!
10-18
SCHULZ

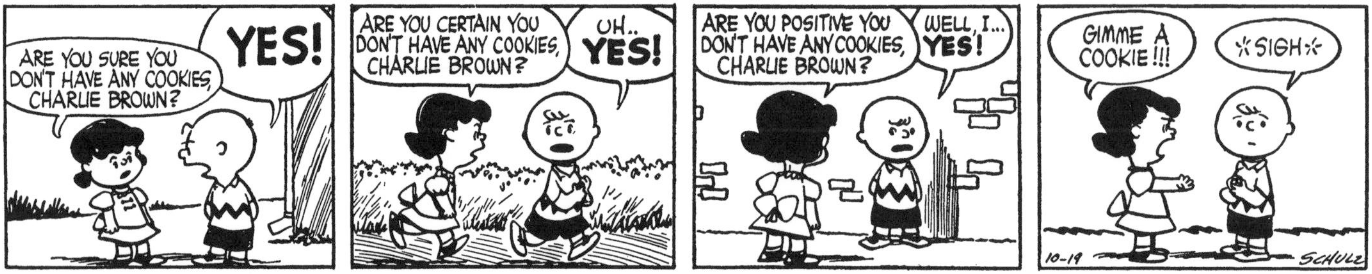
ARE YOU SURE YOU DON'T HAVE ANY COOKIES, CHARLIE BROWN?
YES!
ARE YOU CERTAIN YOU DON'T HAVE ANY COOKIES, CHARLIE BROWN?
UH.. YES!
ARE YOU POSITIVE YOU DON'T HAVE ANY COOKIES, CHARLIE BROWN?
WELL, I... YES!
GIMME A COOKIE!!!
SIGH
10-19
SCHULZ

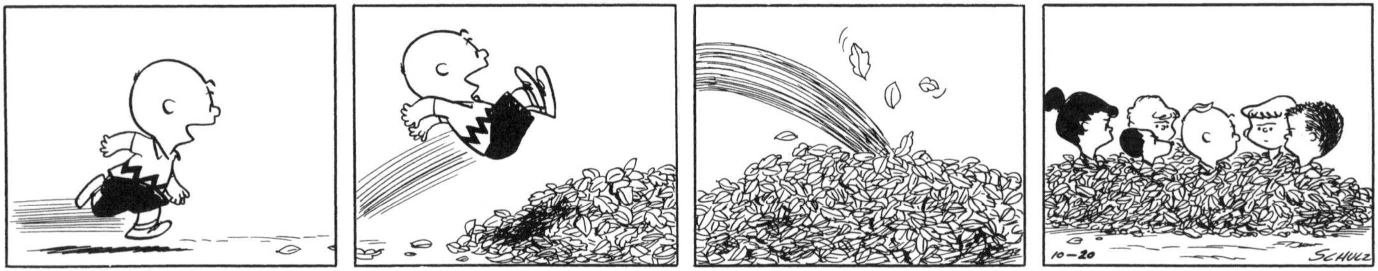
10-20
SCHULZ

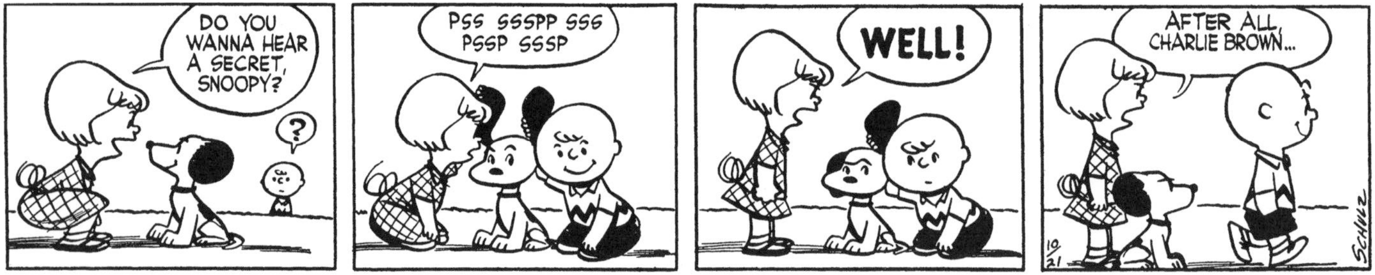
DO YOU WANNA HEAR A SECRET, SNOOPY?
?
PSS SSSPP SSS PSSP SSSP
WELL!
AFTER ALL, CHARLIE BROWN...
10/21
SCHULZ

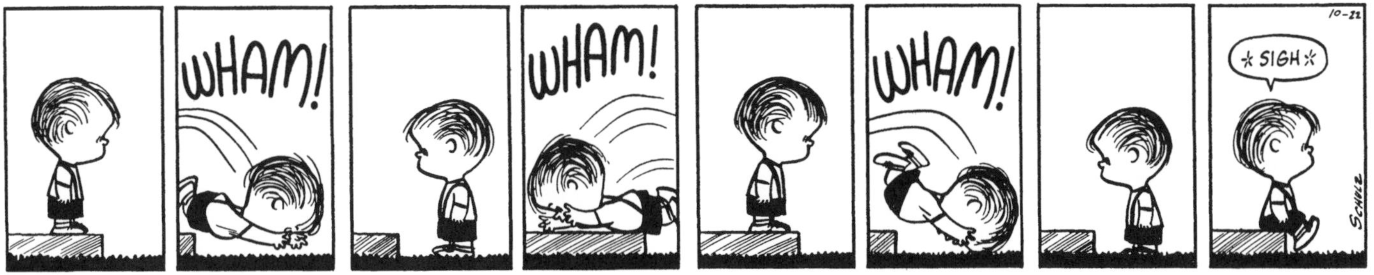
WHAM!
WHAM!
WHAM!
10-22
* SIGH *
SCHULZ

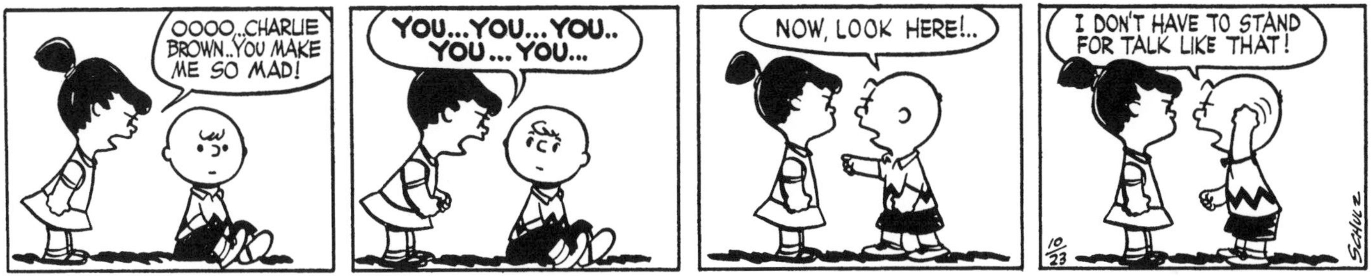
OOOO..CHARLIE BROWN..YOU MAKE ME SO MAD!
YOU...YOU...YOU.. YOU...YOU...
NOW, LOOK HERE!..
I DON'T HAVE TO STAND FOR TALK LIKE THAT!
10/23
SCHULZ

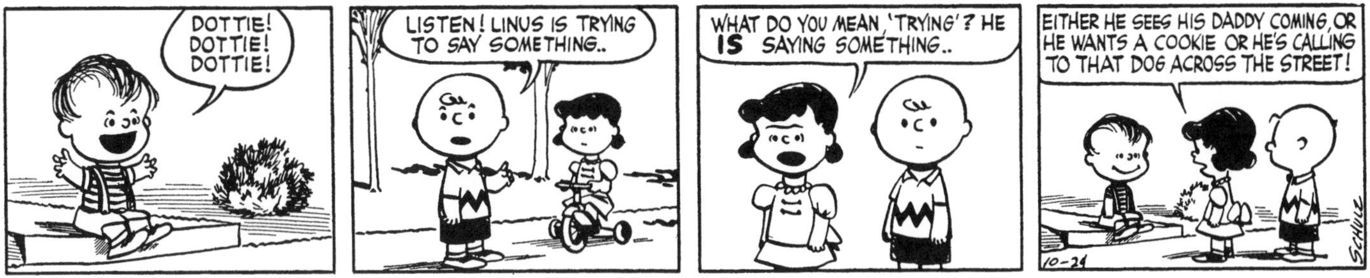
DOTTIE! DOTTIE! DOTTIE!
LISTEN! LINUS IS TRYING TO SAY SOMETHING..
WHAT DO YOU MEAN, 'TRYING'? HE IS SAYING SOMETHING..
EITHER HE SEES HIS DADDY COMING, OR HE WANTS A COOKIE OR HE'S CALLING TO THAT DOG ACROSS THE STREET!
10-24
SCHULZ

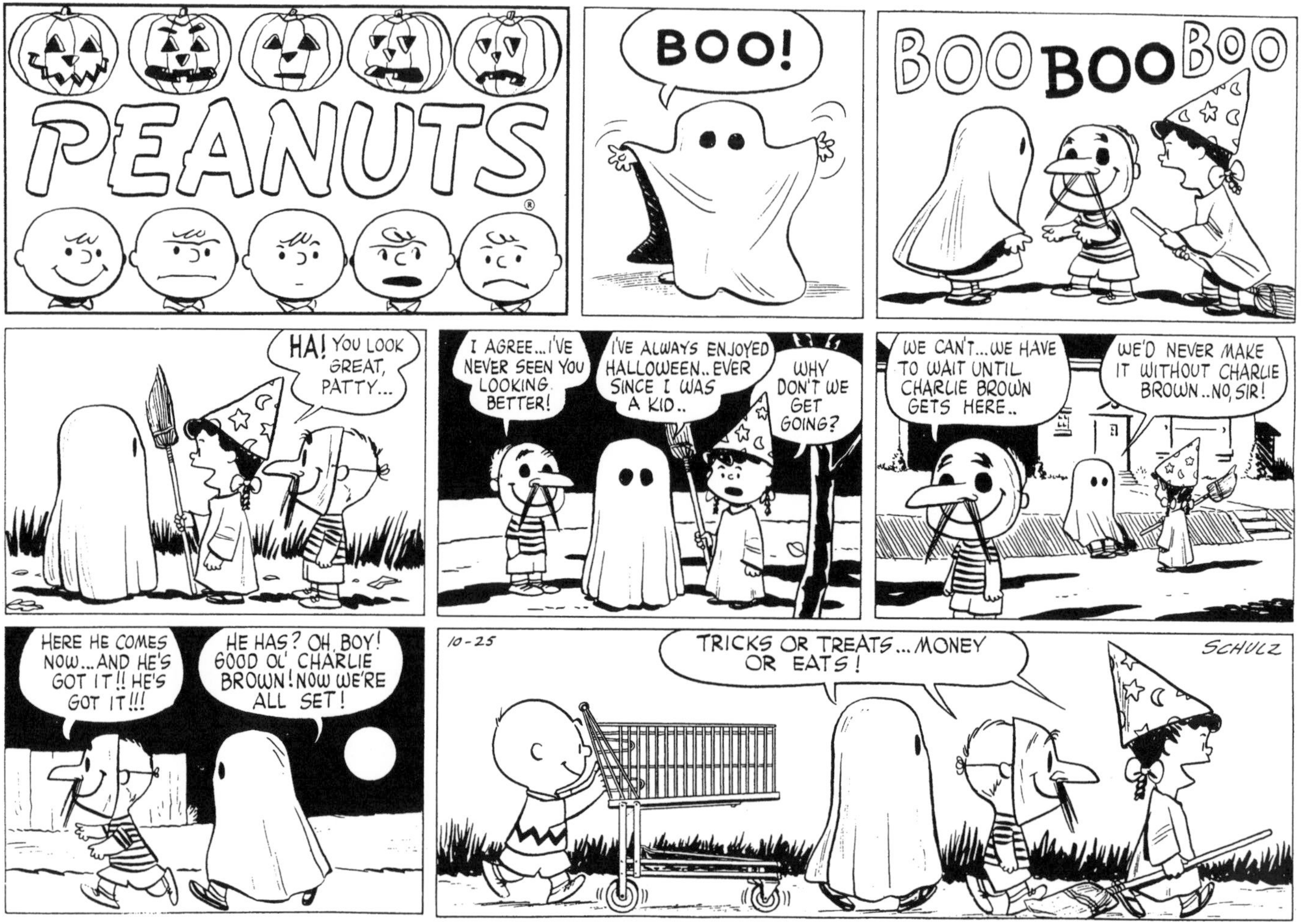
PEANUTS
BOO!
BOO BOO BOO
HA! YOU LOOK GREAT, PATTY...
I AGREE...I'VE NEVER SEEN YOU LOOKING BETTER!
I'VE ALWAYS ENJOYED HALLOWEEN..EVER SINCE I WAS A KID..
WHY DON'T WE GET GOING?
WE CAN'T...WE HAVE TO WAIT UNTIL CHARLIE BROWN GETS HERE..
WE'D NEVER MAKE IT WITHOUT CHARLIE BROWN..NO, SIR!
HERE HE COMES NOW...AND HE'S GOT IT!! HE'S GOT IT!!!
HE HAS? OH, BOY! GOOD OL' CHARLIE BROWN! NOW WE'RE ALL SET!
10-25
TRICKS OR TREATS...MONEY OR EATS!
SCHULZ

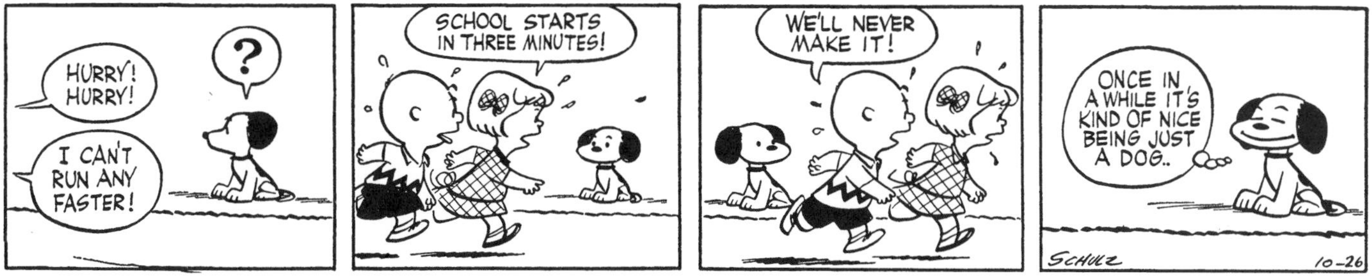
HURRY! HURRY!
I CAN'T RUN ANY FASTER!
?
SCHOOL STARTS IN THREE MINUTES!
WE'LL NEVER MAKE IT!
ONCE IN A WHILE IT'S KIND OF NICE BEING JUST A DOG..
SCHULZ
10-26

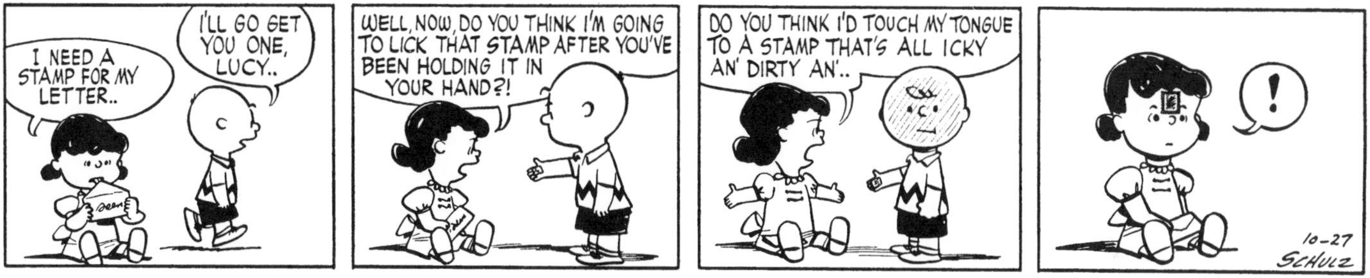
I NEED A STAMP FOR MY LETTER..
I'LL GO GET YOU ONE, LUCY..
WELL, NOW, DO YOU THINK I'M GOING TO LICK THAT STAMP AFTER YOU'VE BEEN HOLDING IT IN YOUR HAND?!
DO YOU THINK I'D TOUCH MY TONGUE TO A STAMP THAT'S ALL ICKY AN' DIRTY AN'..
!
10-27
SCHULZ

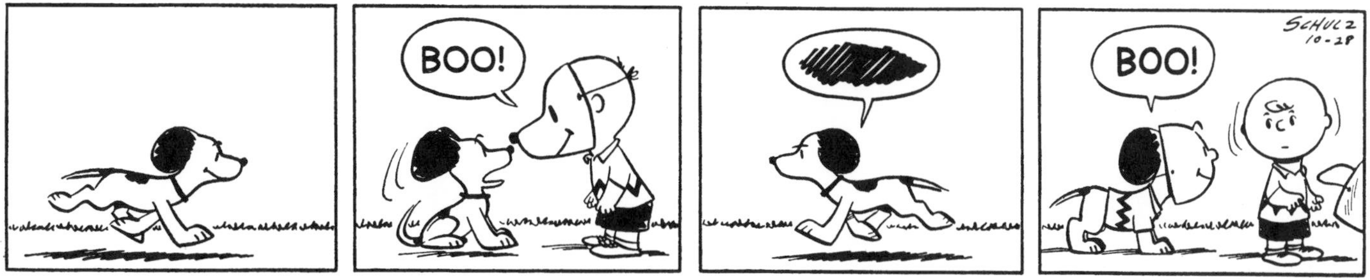
BOO!
SCHULZ
10-28
BOO!

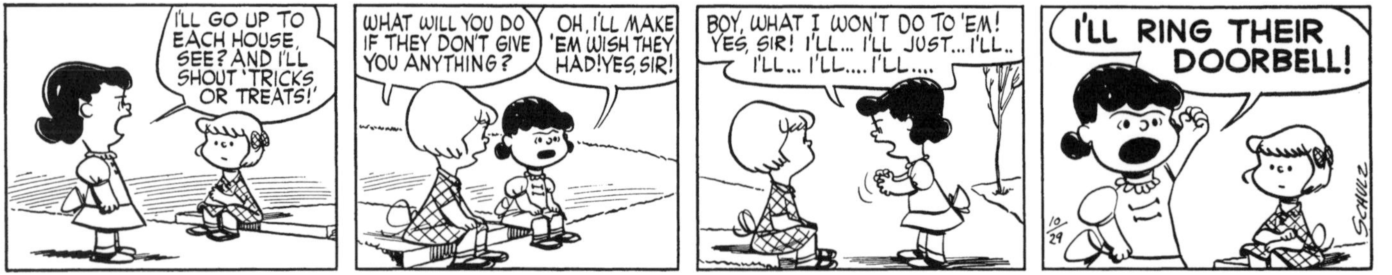
I'LL GO UP TO EACH HOUSE, SEE? AND I'LL SHOUT 'TRICKS OR TREATS!'
WHAT WILL YOU DO IF THEY DON'T GIVE YOU ANYTHING?
OH, I'LL MAKE 'EM WISH THEY HAD! YES, SIR!
BOY, WHAT I WON'T DO TO 'EM! YES, SIR! I'LL... I'LL JUST... I'LL.. I'LL... I'LL.... I'LL....
I'LL RING THEIR DOORBELL!
10/29
SCHULZ

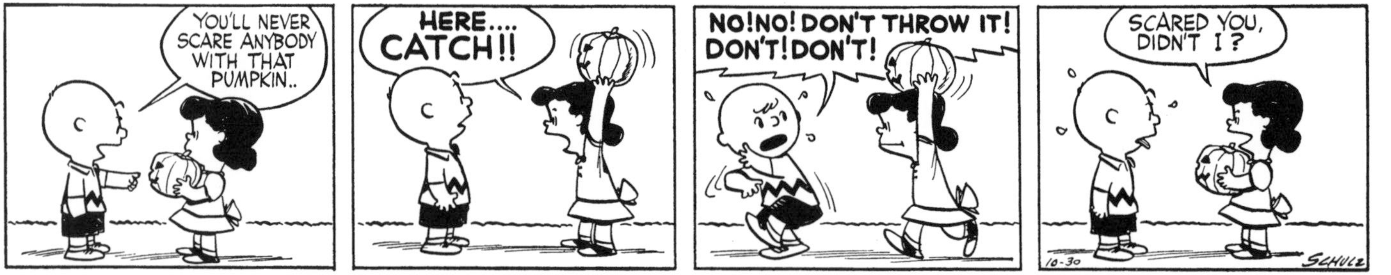
YOU'LL NEVER SCARE ANYBODY WITH THAT PUMPKIN..
HERE.... CATCH!!
NO! NO! DON'T THROW IT! DON'T! DON'T!
SCARED YOU, DIDN'T I?
10-30
SCHULZ

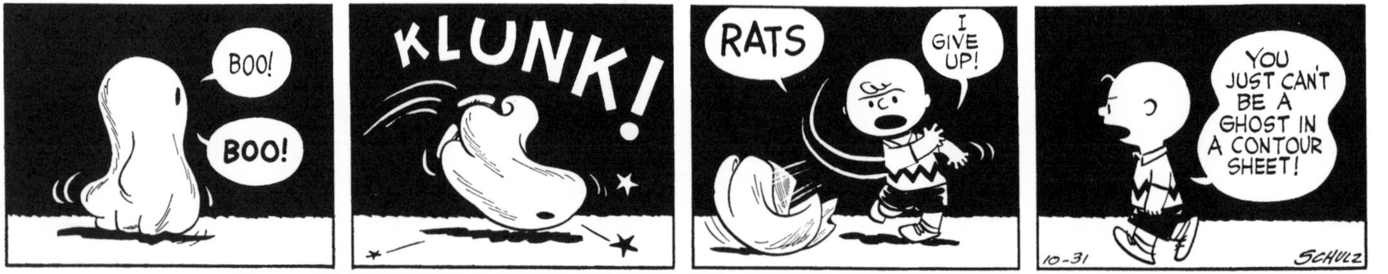
BOO!
BOO!
KLUNK!
RATS
I GIVE UP!
YOU JUST CAN'T BE A GHOST IN A CONTOUR SHEET!
10-31
SCHULZ

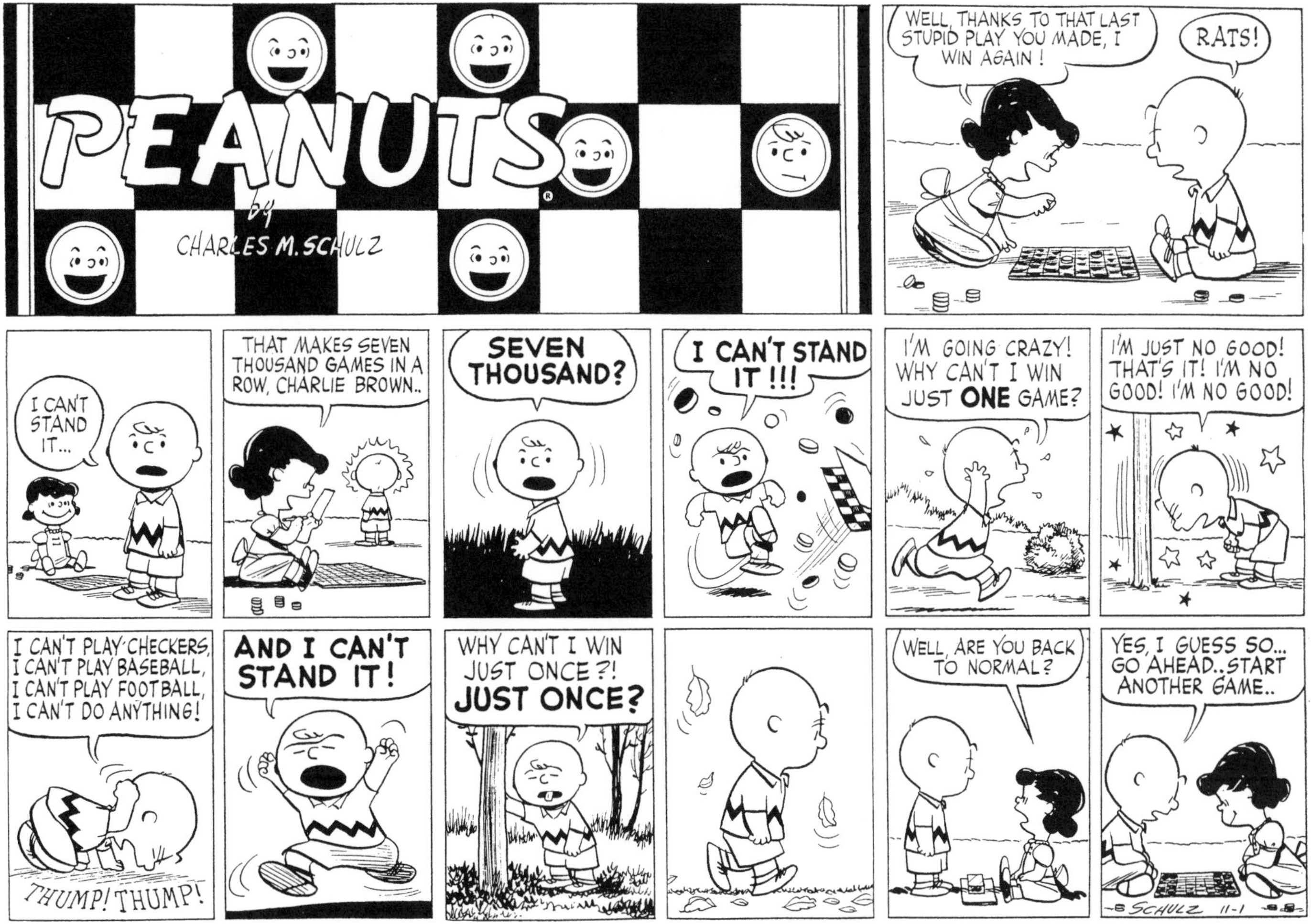
PEANUTS
by
CHARLES M. SCHULZ
WELL, THANKS TO THAT LAST STUPID PLAY YOU MADE, I WIN AGAIN !
RATS!
I CAN'T STAND IT...
THAT MAKES SEVEN THOUSAND GAMES IN A ROW, CHARLIE BROWN..
SEVEN THOUSAND?
I CAN'T STAND IT !!!
I'M GOING CRAZY! WHY CAN'T I WIN JUST ONE GAME?
I'M JUST NO GOOD! THAT'S IT! I'M NO GOOD! I'M NO GOOD!
I CAN'T PLAY CHECKERS, I CAN'T PLAY BASEBALL, I CAN'T PLAY FOOTBALL, I CAN'T DO ANYTHING!
THUMP! THUMP!
AND I CAN'T STAND IT!
WHY CAN'T I WIN JUST ONCE?! JUST ONCE?
WELL, ARE YOU BACK TO NORMAL?
YES, I GUESS SO... GO AHEAD..START ANOTHER GAME..
SCHULZ 11-1

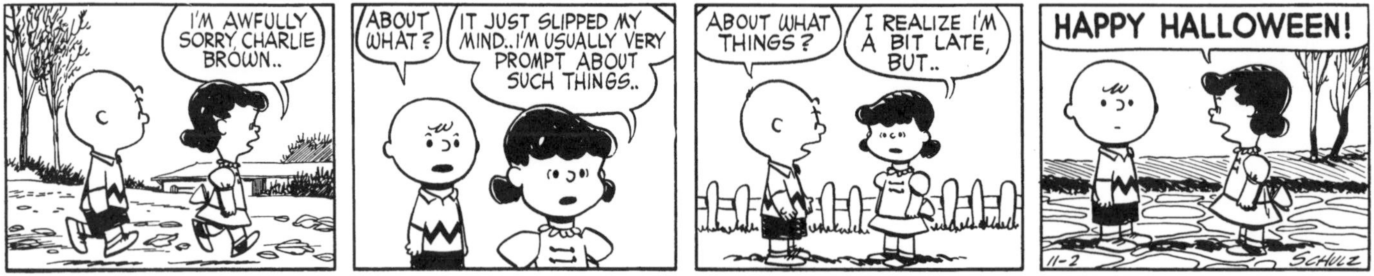
I'M AWFULLY SORRY, CHARLIE BROWN..
ABOUT WHAT?
IT JUST SLIPPED MY MIND..I'M USUALLY VERY PROMPT ABOUT SUCH THINGS..
ABOUT WHAT THINGS?
I REALIZE I'M A BIT LATE, BUT..
HAPPY HALLOWEEN!
11-2
SCHULZ

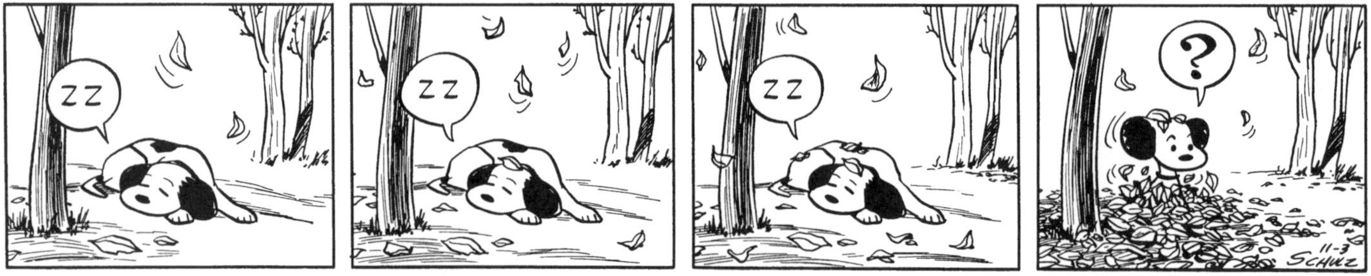
ZZ
ZZ
ZZ
?
11-3
SCHULZ

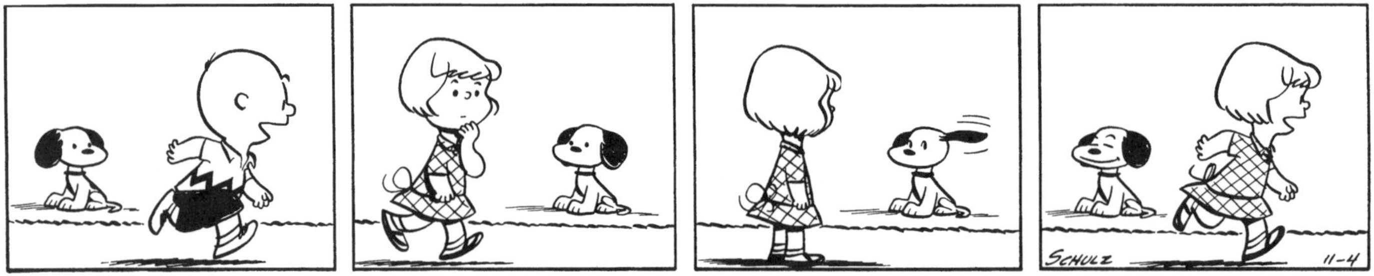
SCHULZ
11-4

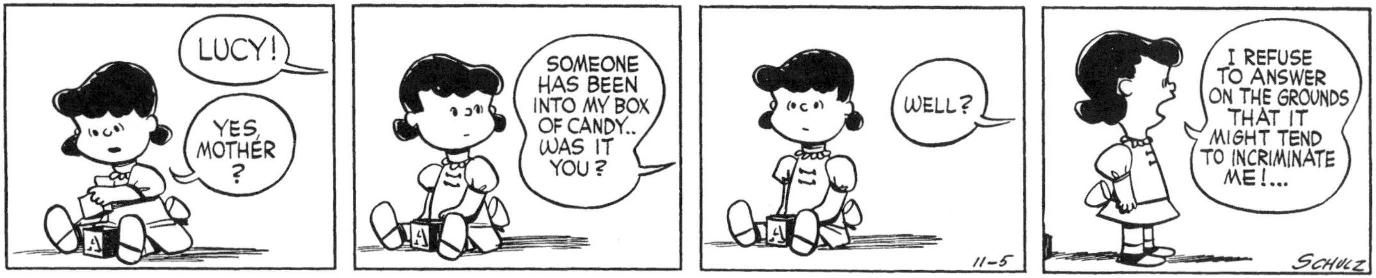
LUCY!
YES, MOTHER ?
SOMEONE HAS BEEN INTO MY BOX OF CANDY.. WAS IT YOU ?
WELL ?
I REFUSE TO ANSWER ON THE GROUNDS THAT IT MIGHT TEND TO INCRIMINATE ME!...
11-5
SCHULZ

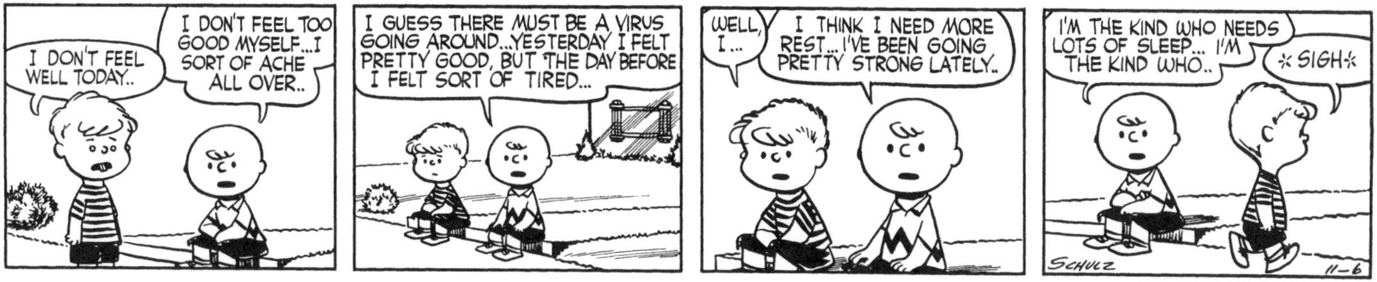
I DON'T FEEL WELL TODAY..
I DON'T FEEL TOO GOOD MYSELF...I SORT OF ACHE ALL OVER..
I GUESS THERE MUST BE A VIRUS GOING AROUND...YESTERDAY I FELT PRETTY GOOD, BUT THE DAY BEFORE I FELT SORT OF TIRED...
WELL, I...
I THINK I NEED MORE REST...I'VE BEEN GOING PRETTY STRONG LATELY..
I'M THE KIND WHO NEEDS LOTS OF SLEEP... I'M THE KIND WHO..
SIGH
SCHULZ
11-6

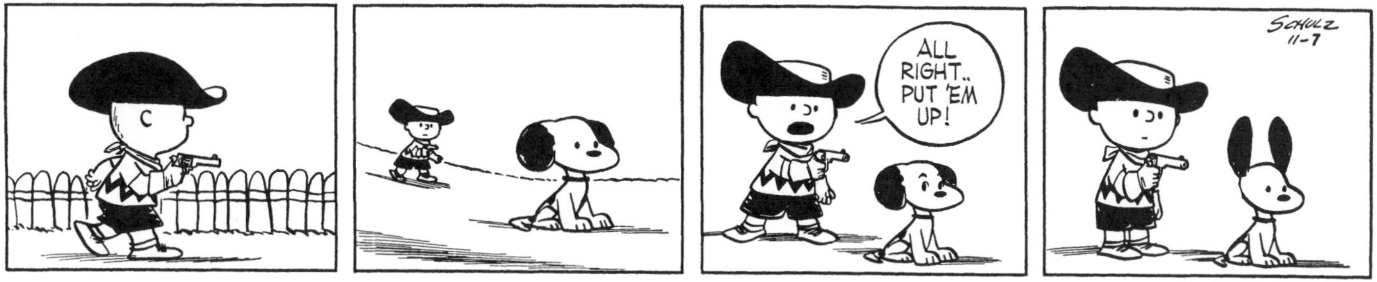
ALL RIGHT.. PUT 'EM UP!
SCHULZ
11-7

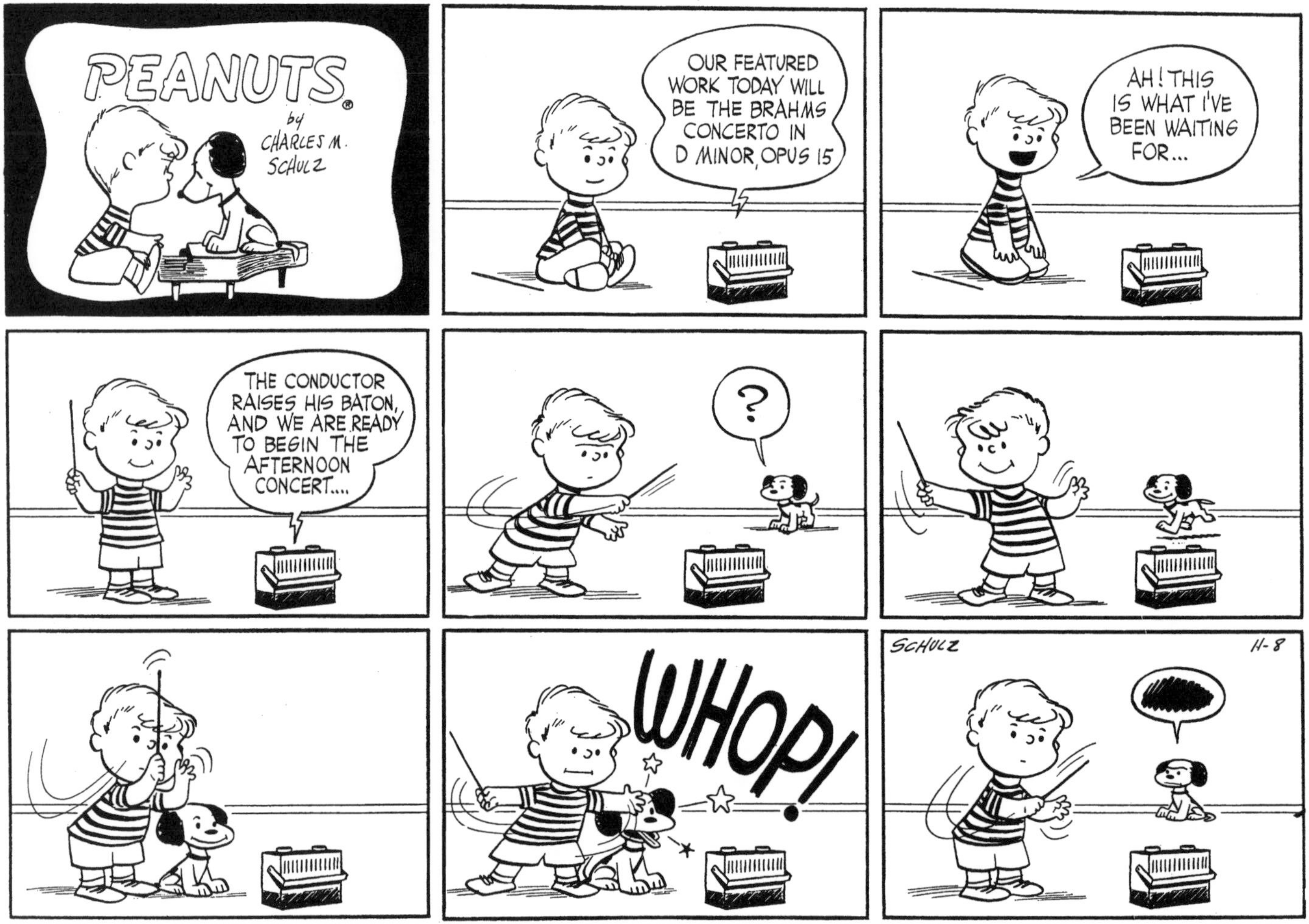
PEANUTS
by CHARLES M. SCHULZ
OUR FEATURED WORK TODAY WILL BE THE BRAHMS CONCERTO IN D MINOR, OPUS 15
AH! THIS IS WHAT I'VE BEEN WAITING FOR...
THE CONDUCTOR RAISES HIS BATON, AND WE ARE READY TO BEGIN THE AFTERNOON CONCERT....
?
WHOP!
SCHULZ
11-8

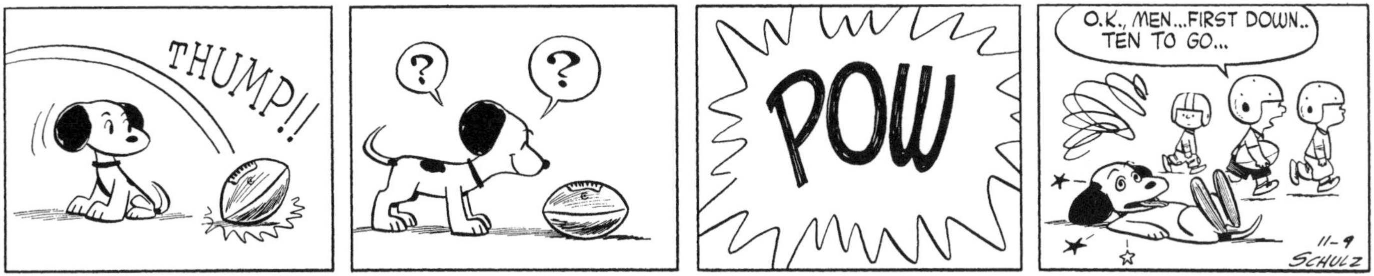
THUMP!!
?
?
POW
O.K., MEN...FIRST DOWN.. TEN TO GO...
11-9
SCHULZ

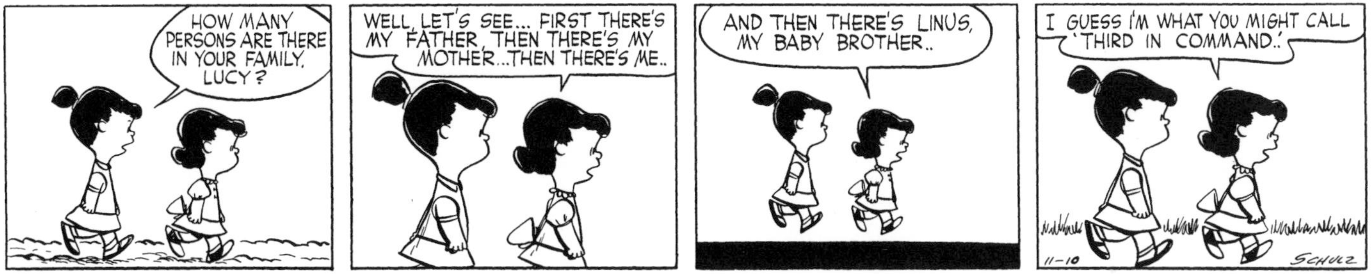
HOW MANY PERSONS ARE THERE IN YOUR FAMILY, LUCY?
WELL, LET'S SEE... FIRST THERE'S MY FATHER, THEN THERE'S MY MOTHER...THEN THERE'S ME..
AND THEN THERE'S LINUS, MY BABY BROTHER..
I GUESS I'M WHAT YOU MIGHT CALL 'THIRD IN COMMAND.'
11-10
SCHULZ

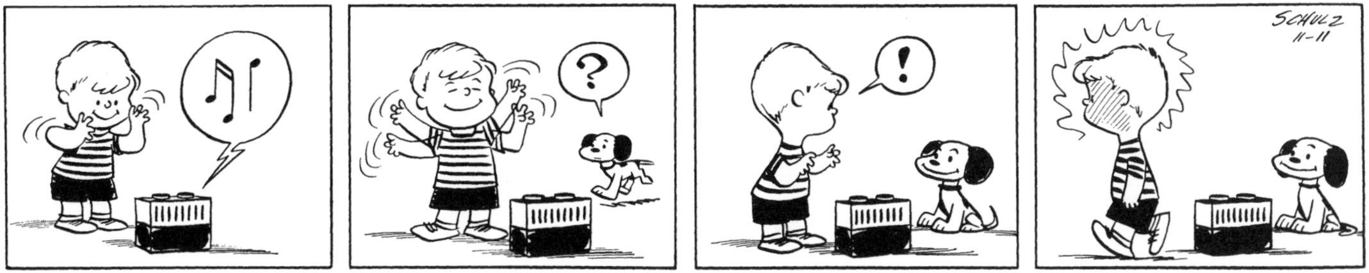
?
!
SCHULZ
11-11

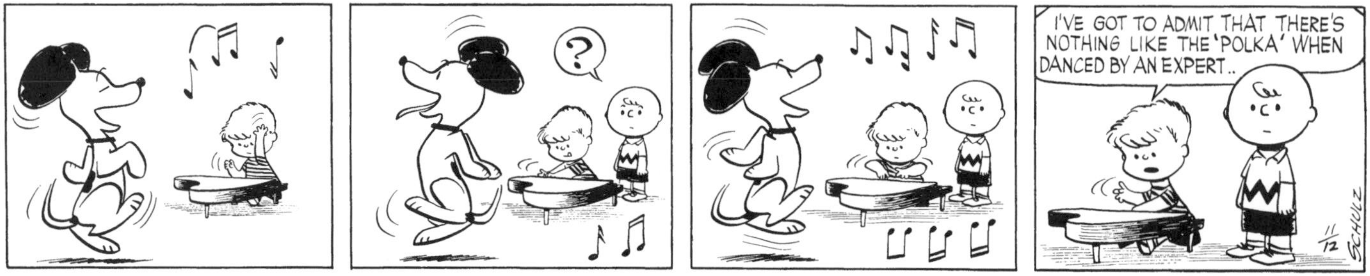
I'VE GOT TO ADMIT THAT THERE'S NOTHING LIKE THE 'POLKA' WHEN DANCED BY AN EXPERT..
11/12
SCHULZ

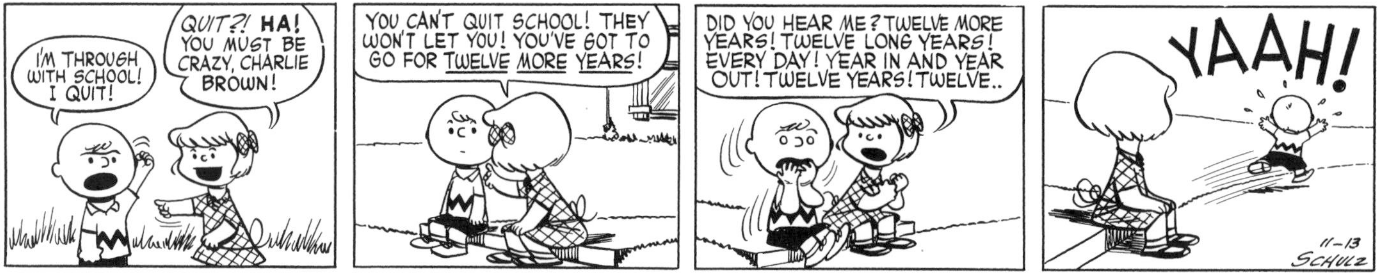
I'M THROUGH WITH SCHOOL! I QUIT!
QUIT?! HA! YOU MUST BE CRAZY, CHARLIE BROWN!
YOU CAN'T QUIT SCHOOL! THEY WON'T LET YOU! YOU'VE GOT TO GO FOR TWELVE MORE YEARS!
DID YOU HEAR ME? TWELVE MORE YEARS! TWELVE LONG YEARS! EVERY DAY! YEAR IN AND YEAR OUT! TWELVE YEARS! TWELVE..
YAAH!
11-13
SCHULZ

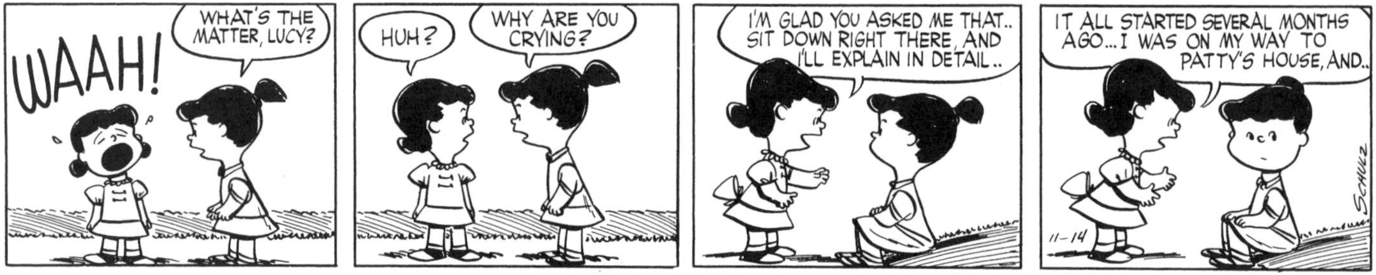
WAAH!
WHAT'S THE MATTER, LUCY?
HUH?
WHY ARE YOU CRYING?
I'M GLAD YOU ASKED ME THAT.. SIT DOWN RIGHT THERE, AND I'LL EXPLAIN IN DETAIL..
IT ALL STARTED SEVERAL MONTHS AGO... I WAS ON MY WAY TO PATTY'S HOUSE, AND..
11-14
SCHULZ

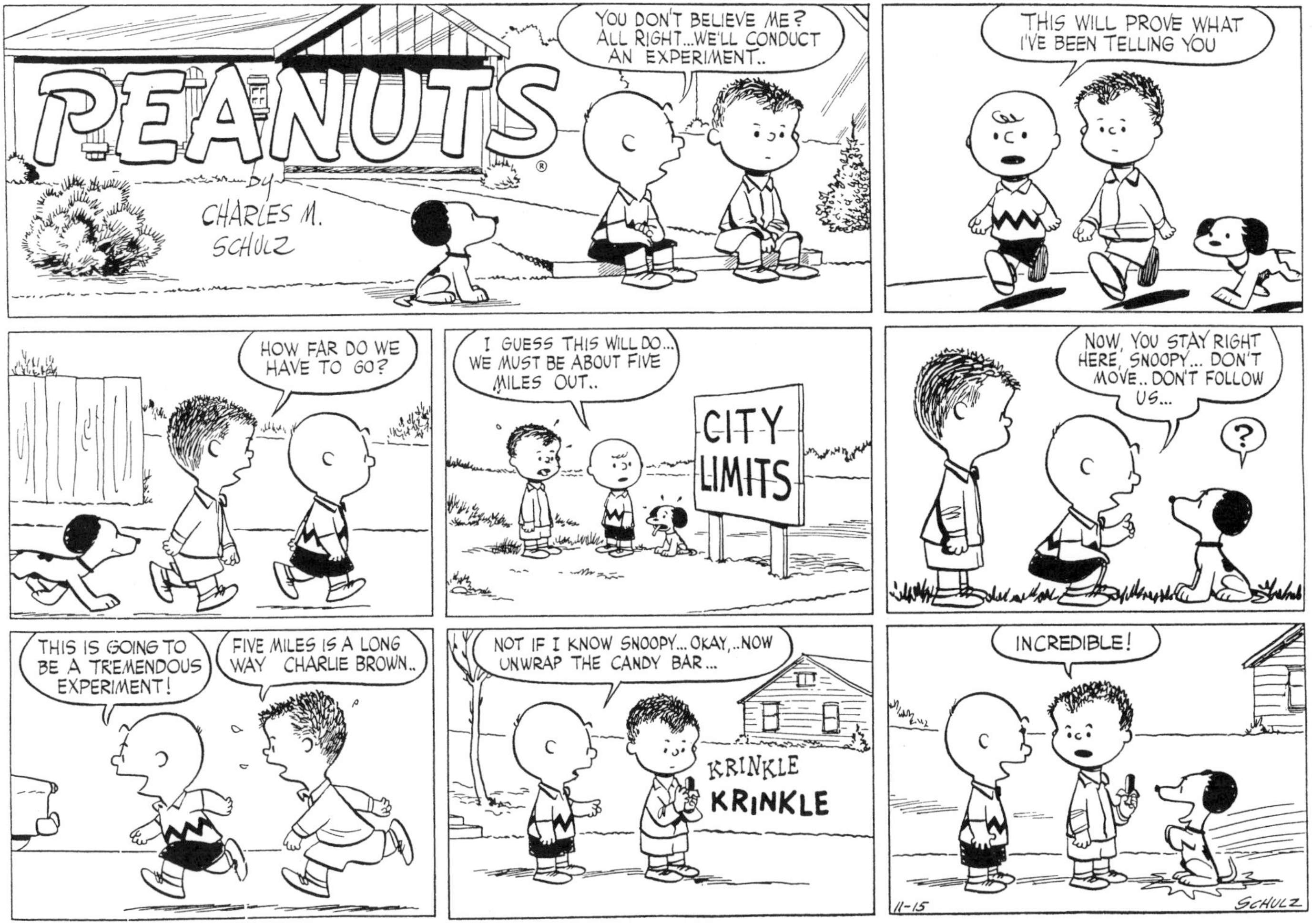
PEANUTS
by CHARLES M. SCHULZ
YOU DON'T BELIEVE ME? ALL RIGHT...WE'LL CONDUCT AN EXPERIMENT..
THIS WILL PROVE WHAT I'VE BEEN TELLING YOU
HOW FAR DO WE HAVE TO GO?
I GUESS THIS WILL DO... WE MUST BE ABOUT FIVE MILES OUT..
CITY LIMITS
NOW, YOU STAY RIGHT HERE, SNOOPY... DON'T MOVE.. DON'T FOLLOW US...
?
THIS IS GOING TO BE A TREMENDOUS EXPERIMENT!
FIVE MILES IS A LONG WAY CHARLIE BROWN..
NOT IF I KNOW SNOOPY... OKAY,..NOW UNWRAP THE CANDY BAR...
KRINKLE
KRINKLE
INCREDIBLE!
11-15
SCHULZ

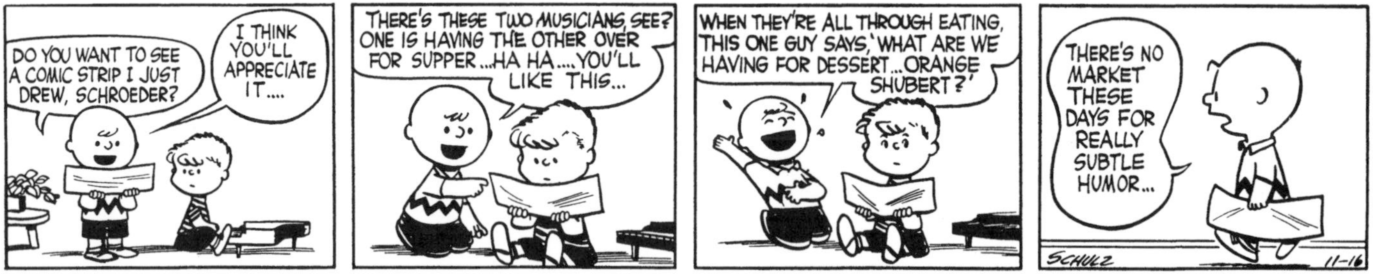
DO YOU WANT TO SEE A COMIC STRIP I JUST DREW, SCHROEDER?
I THINK YOU'LL APPRECIATE IT....
THERE'S THESE TWO MUSICIANS, SEE? ONE IS HAVING THE OTHER OVER FOR SUPPER...HA HA....YOU'LL LIKE THIS...
WHEN THEY'RE ALL THROUGH EATING, THIS ONE GUY SAYS, 'WHAT ARE WE HAVING FOR DESSERT...ORANGE SHUBERT?'
THERE'S NO MARKET THESE DAYS FOR REALLY SUBTLE HUMOR...
SCHULZ
11-16

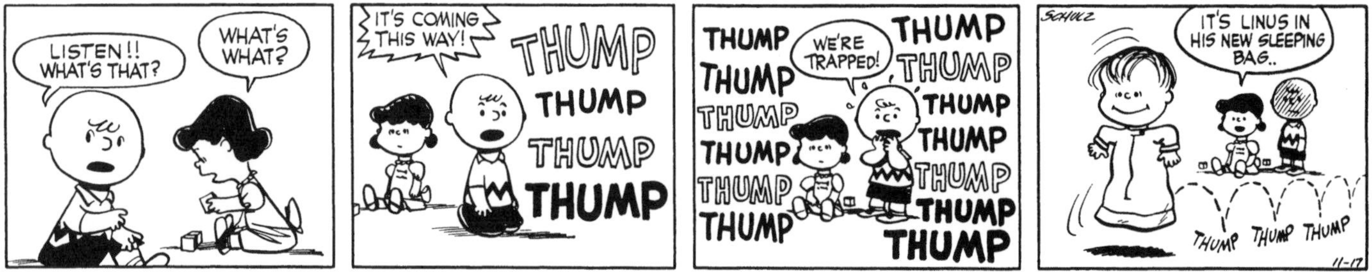
LISTEN!! WHAT'S THAT?
WHAT'S WHAT?
IT'S COMING THIS WAY!
THUMP
THUMP
THUMP
THUMP
THUMP
THUMP
THUMP
THUMP
THUMP
THUMP
WE'RE TRAPPED!
THUMP
THUMP
THUMP
THUMP
THUMP
THUMP
THUMP
SCHULZ
IT'S LINUS IN HIS NEW SLEEPING BAG..
THUMP THUMP THUMP
11-17

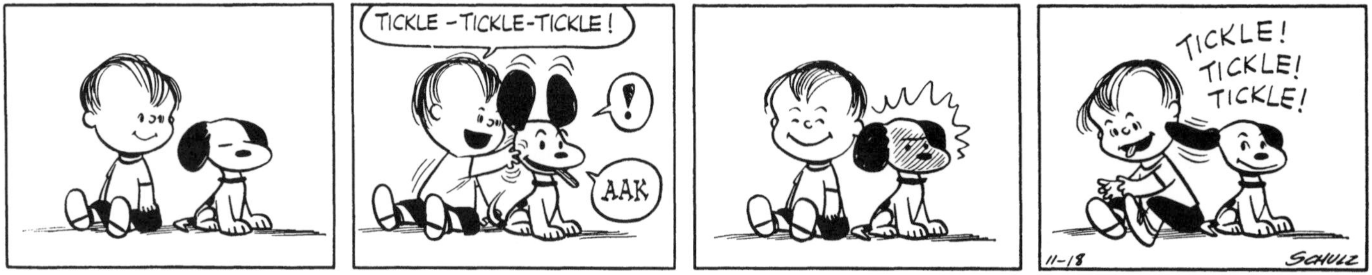
TICKLE -TICKLE-TICKLE!
!
AAK
TICKLE! TICKLE! TICKLE!
11-18
SCHULZ

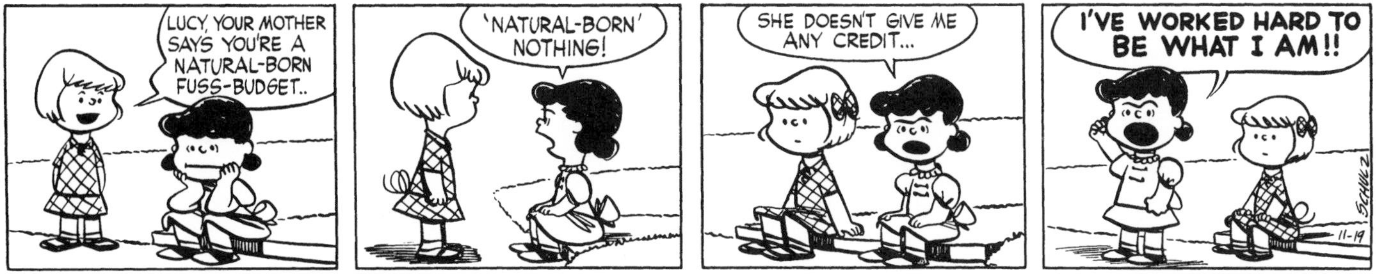
LUCY, YOUR MOTHER SAYS YOU'RE A NATURAL-BORN FUSS-BUDGET..
'NATURAL-BORN' NOTHING!
SHE DOESN'T GIVE ME ANY CREDIT...
I'VE WORKED HARD TO BE WHAT I AM!!
SCHULZ
11-19

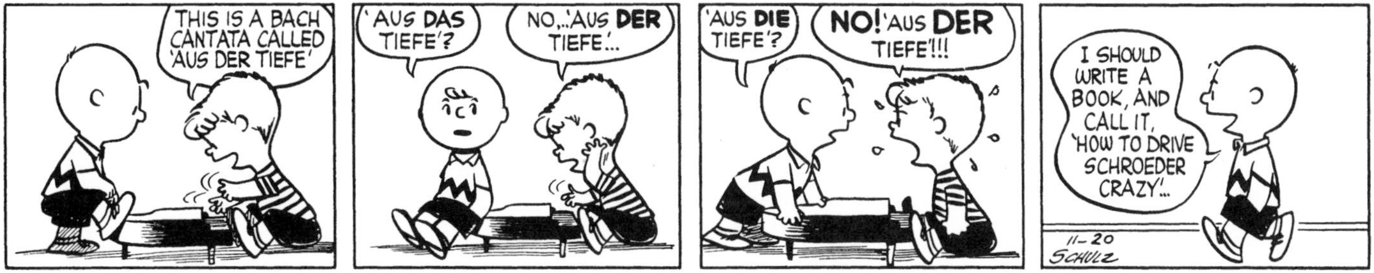
THIS IS A BACH CANTATA CALLED 'AUS DER TIEFE'
'AUS DAS TIEFE'?
NO,..'AUS DER TIEFE'...
'AUS DIE TIEFE'?
NO! 'AUS DER TIEFE'!!!
I SHOULD WRITE A BOOK, AND CALL IT, 'HOW TO DRIVE SCHROEDER CRAZY'...
11-20
SCHULZ

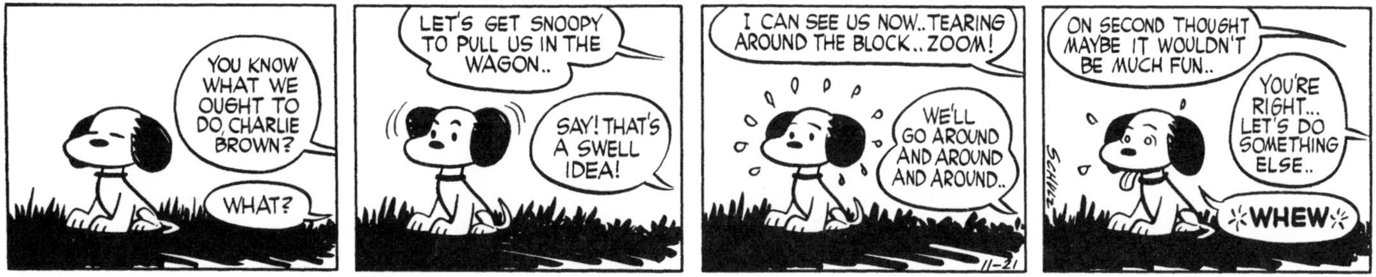
YOU KNOW WHAT WE OUGHT TO DO, CHARLIE BROWN?
WHAT?
LET'S GET SNOOPY TO PULL US IN THE WAGON..
SAY! THAT'S A SWELL IDEA!
I CAN SEE US NOW.. TEARING AROUND THE BLOCK.. ZOOM!
WE'LL GO AROUND AND AROUND AND AROUND..
SCHULZ
11-21
ON SECOND THOUGHT MAYBE IT WOULDN'T BE MUCH FUN..
YOU'RE RIGHT... LET'S DO SOMETHING ELSE..
WHEW

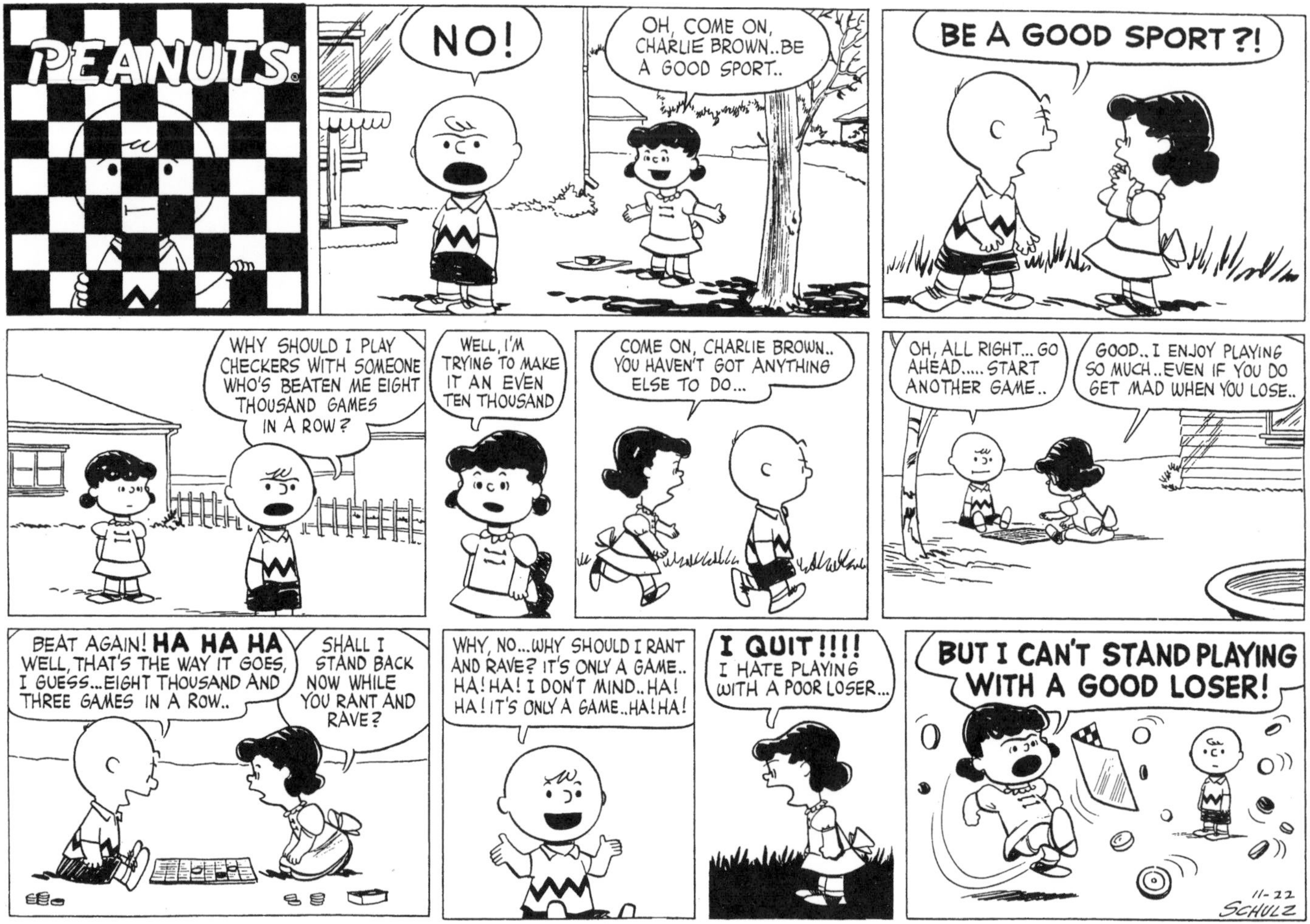
PEANUTS
NO!
OH, COME ON, CHARLIE BROWN..BE A GOOD SPORT..
BE A GOOD SPORT?!
WHY SHOULD I PLAY CHECKERS WITH SOMEONE WHO'S BEATEN ME EIGHT THOUSAND GAMES IN A ROW?
WELL, I'M TRYING TO MAKE IT AN EVEN TEN THOUSAND
COME ON, CHARLIE BROWN.. YOU HAVEN'T GOT ANYTHING ELSE TO DO...
OH, ALL RIGHT... GO AHEAD..... START ANOTHER GAME..
GOOD.. I ENJOY PLAYING SO MUCH..EVEN IF YOU DO GET MAD WHEN YOU LOSE..
BEAT AGAIN! HA HA HA WELL, THAT'S THE WAY IT GOES, I GUESS...EIGHT THOUSAND AND THREE GAMES IN A ROW..
SHALL I STAND BACK NOW WHILE YOU RANT AND RAVE?
WHY, NO...WHY SHOULD I RANT AND RAVE? IT'S ONLY A GAME.. HA! HA! I DON'T MIND..HA! HA! IT'S ONLY A GAME..HA! HA!
I QUIT!!!! I HATE PLAYING WITH A POOR LOSER...
BUT I CAN'T STAND PLAYING WITH A GOOD LOSER!
11-22
SCHULZ

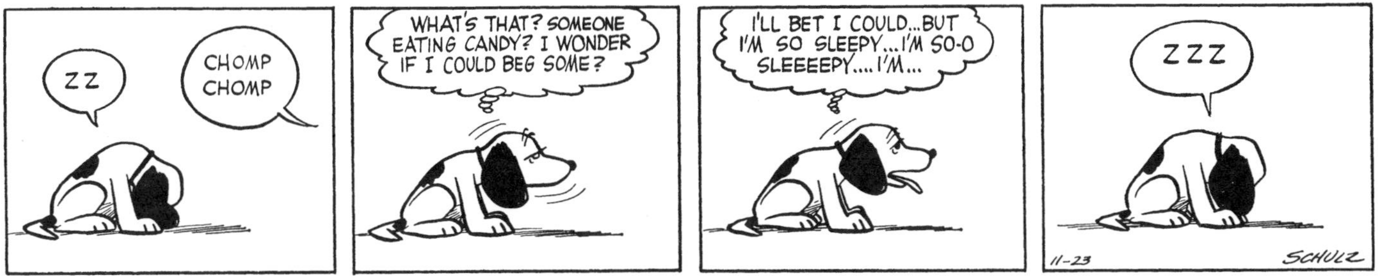
ZZ
CHOMP CHOMP
WHAT'S THAT? SOMEONE EATING CANDY? I WONDER IF I COULD BEG SOME?
I'LL BET I COULD...BUT I'M SO SLEEPY...I'M SO-O SLEEEEPY....I'M...
ZZZ
11-23
SCHULZ

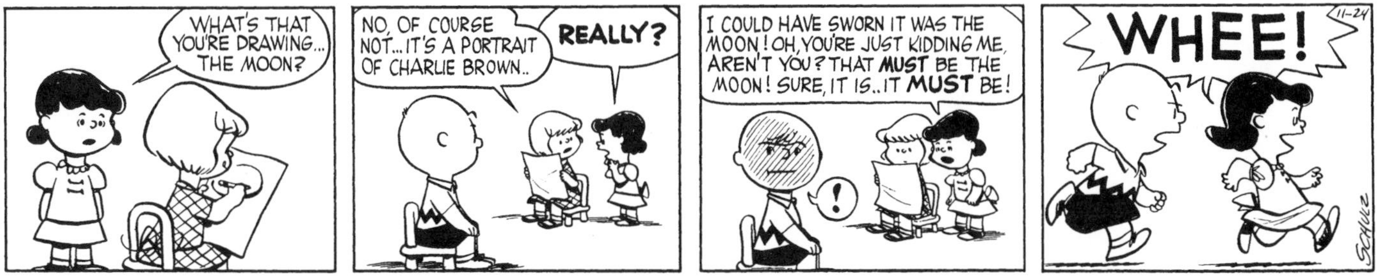
WHAT'S THAT YOU'RE DRAWING... THE MOON?
NO, OF COURSE NOT...IT'S A PORTRAIT OF CHARLIE BROWN..
REALLY?
I COULD HAVE SWORN IT WAS THE MOON! OH, YOU'RE JUST KIDDING ME, AREN'T YOU? THAT MUST BE THE MOON! SURE, IT IS..IT MUST BE!
!
WHEE!
11-24
SCHULZ

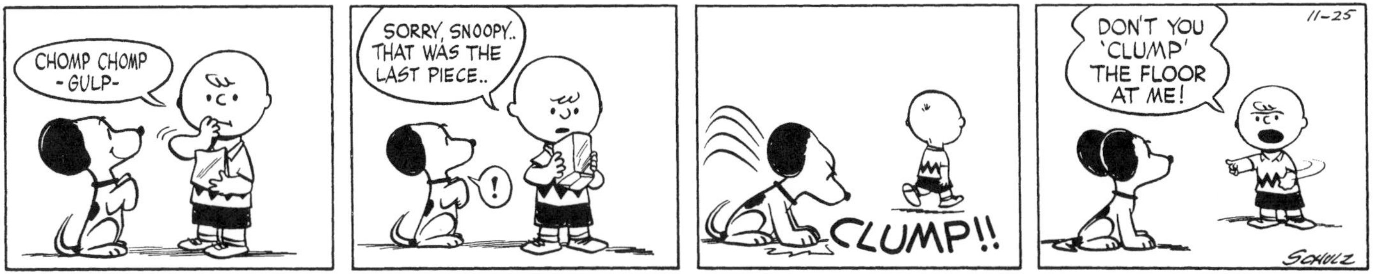
CHOMP CHOMP -GULP-
SORRY, SNOOPY.. THAT WAS THE LAST PIECE..
!
CLUMP!!
11-25
DON'T YOU 'CLUMP' THE FLOOR AT ME!
SCHULZ

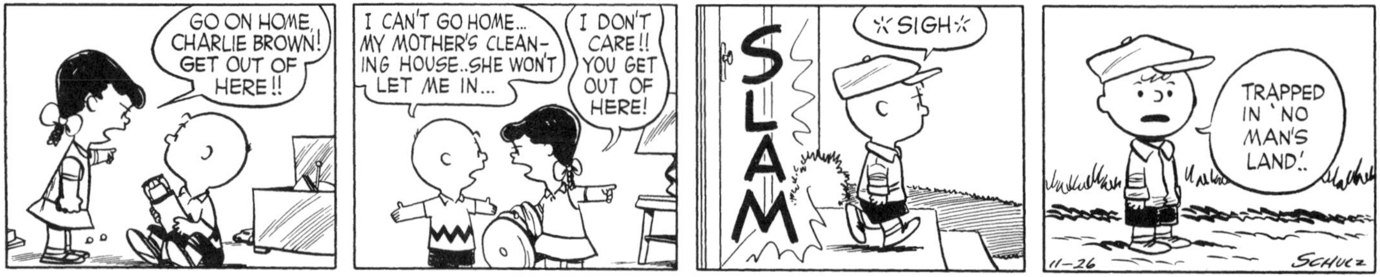
GO ON HOME, CHARLIE BROWN! GET OUT OF HERE!!
I CAN'T GO HOME... MY MOTHER'S CLEANING HOUSE..SHE WON'T LET ME IN...
I DON'T CARE!! YOU GET OUT OF HERE!
SLAM
SIGH
TRAPPED IN 'NO MAN'S LAND'.
11-26
SCHULZ

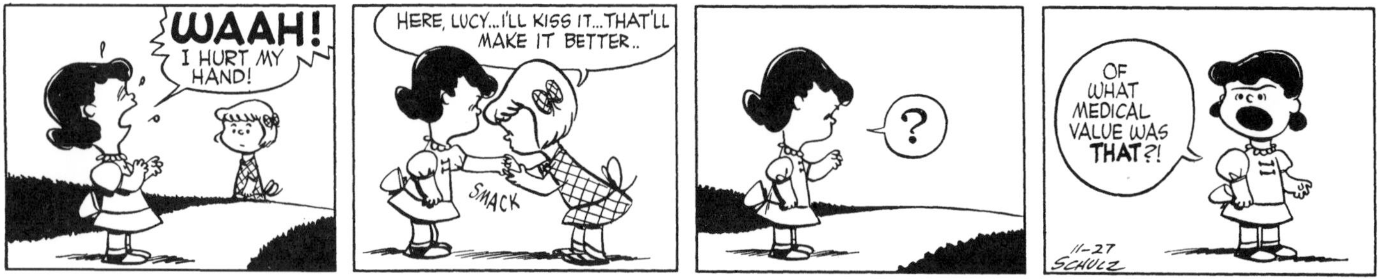
WAAH! I HURT MY HAND!
HERE, LUCY...I'LL KISS IT...THAT'LL MAKE IT BETTER..
SMACK
?
OF WHAT MEDICAL VALUE WAS THAT?!
11-27
SCHULZ

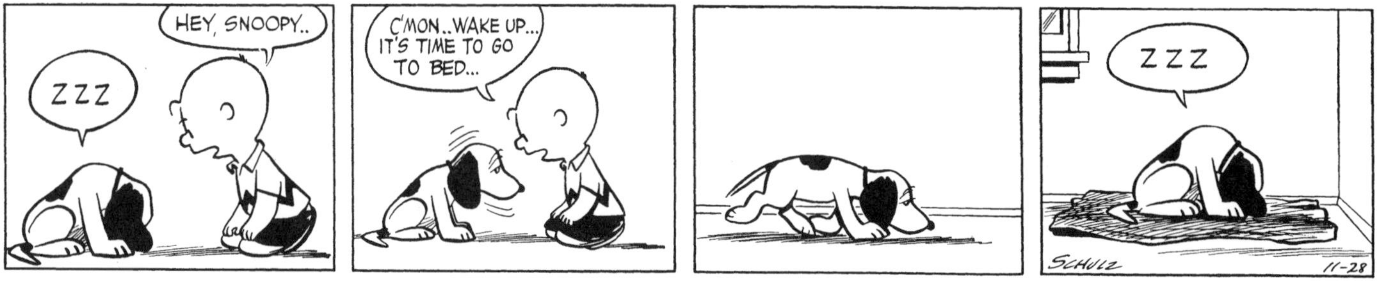
HEY, SNOOPY..
ZZZ
C'MON..WAKE UP... IT'S TIME TO GO TO BED...
ZZZ
SCHULZ
11-28

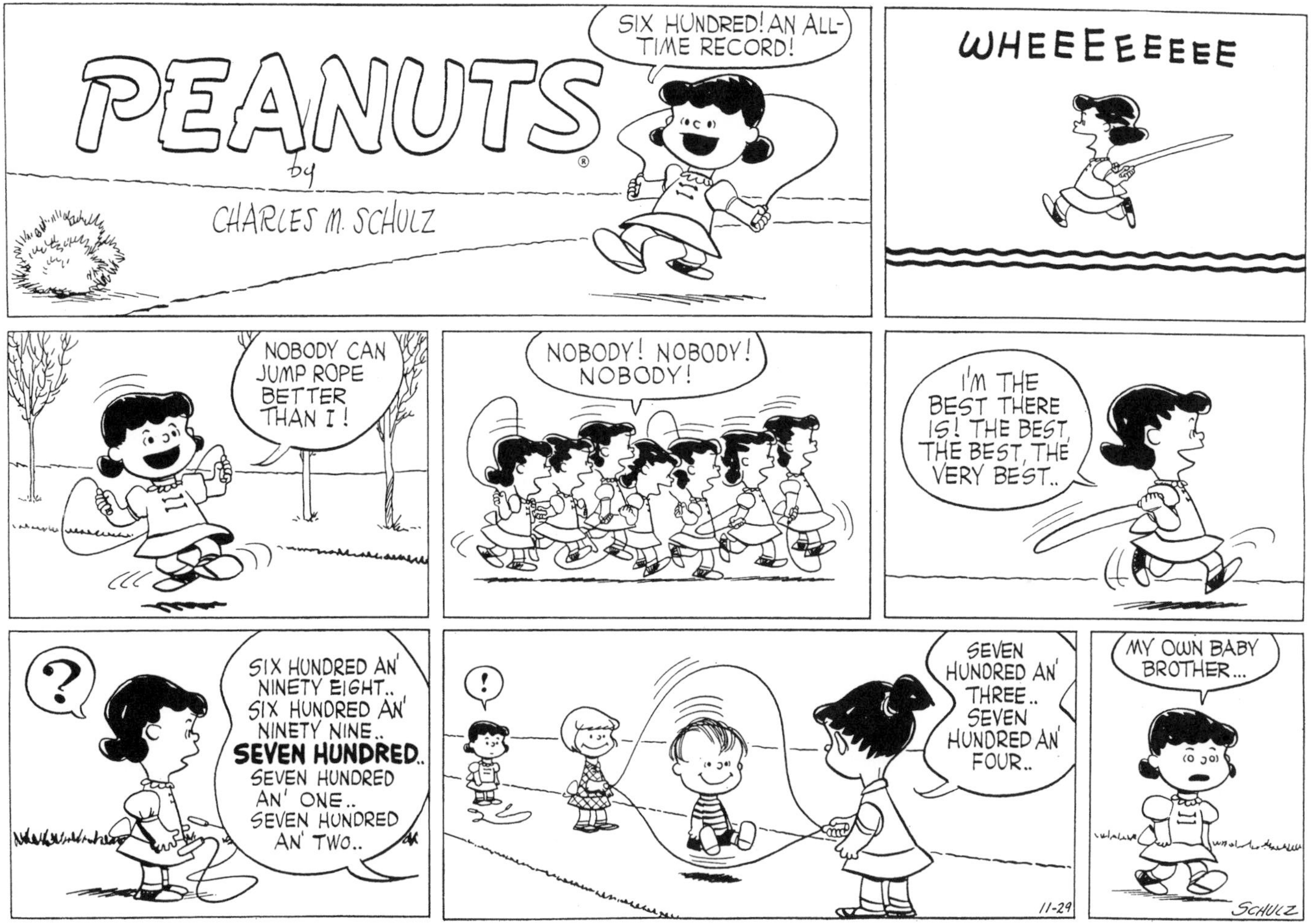
PEANUTS
by
CHARLES M. SCHULZ
SIX HUNDRED! AN ALL-TIME RECORD!
WHEEEEEEEEE
NOBODY CAN JUMP ROPE BETTER THAN I!
NOBODY! NOBODY! NOBODY!
I'M THE BEST THERE IS! THE BEST, THE BEST, THE VERY BEST..
?
SIX HUNDRED AN' NINETY EIGHT.. SIX HUNDRED AN' NINETY NINE.. **SEVEN HUNDRED**.. SEVEN HUNDRED AN' ONE.. SEVEN HUNDRED AN' TWO..
!
SEVEN HUNDRED AN' THREE.. SEVEN HUNDRED AN' FOUR..
11-29
MY OWN BABY BROTHER...
SCHULZ

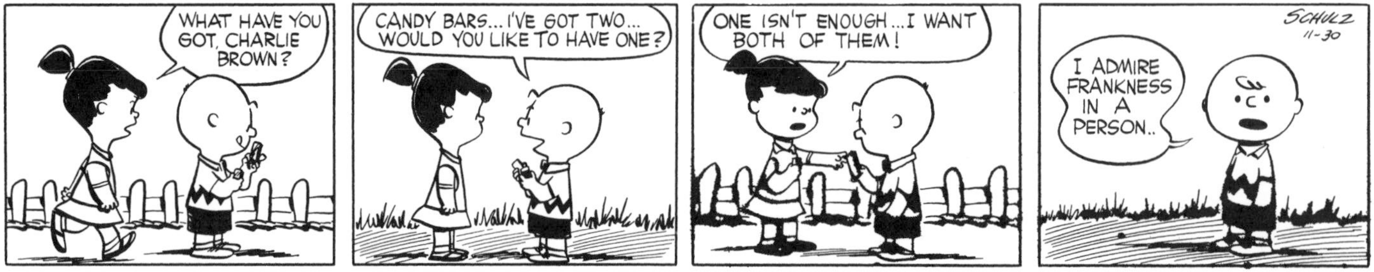
WHAT HAVE YOU GOT, CHARLIE BROWN?
CANDY BARS... I'VE GOT TWO... WOULD YOU LIKE TO HAVE ONE?
ONE ISN'T ENOUGH... I WANT BOTH OF THEM!
SCHULZ 11-30
I ADMIRE FRANKNESS IN A PERSON..

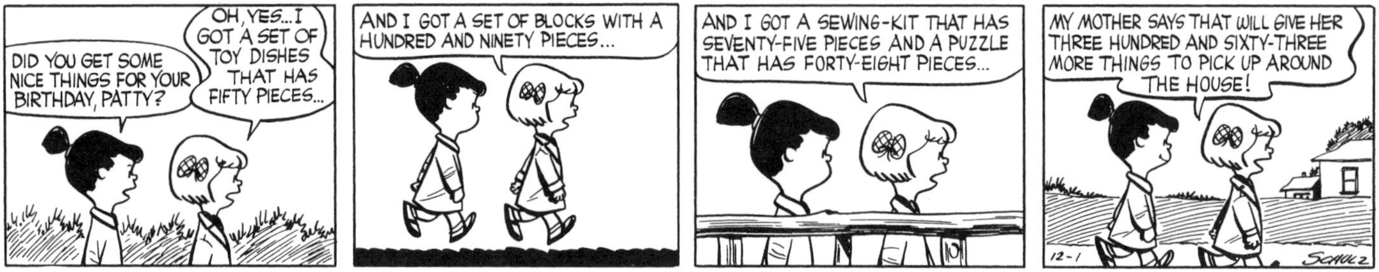
DID YOU GET SOME NICE THINGS FOR YOUR BIRTHDAY, PATTY?
OH, YES... I GOT A SET OF TOY DISHES THAT HAS FIFTY PIECES...
AND I GOT A SET OF BLOCKS WITH A HUNDRED AND NINETY PIECES...
AND I GOT A SEWING-KIT THAT HAS SEVENTY-FIVE PIECES AND A PUZZLE THAT HAS FORTY-EIGHT PIECES...
MY MOTHER SAYS THAT WILL GIVE HER THREE HUNDRED AND SIXTY-THREE MORE THINGS TO PICK UP AROUND THE HOUSE!
12-1
SCHULZ

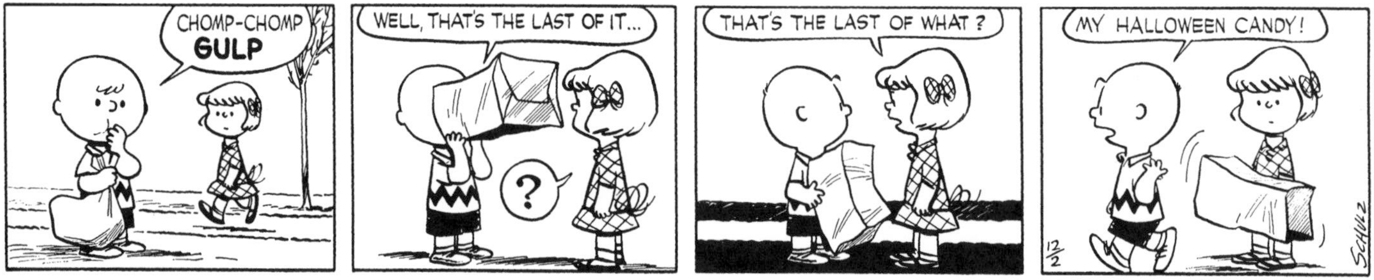
CHOMP-CHOMP
GULP
WELL, THAT'S THE LAST OF IT...
?
THAT'S THE LAST OF WHAT?
MY HALLOWEEN CANDY!
12/2
SCHULZ

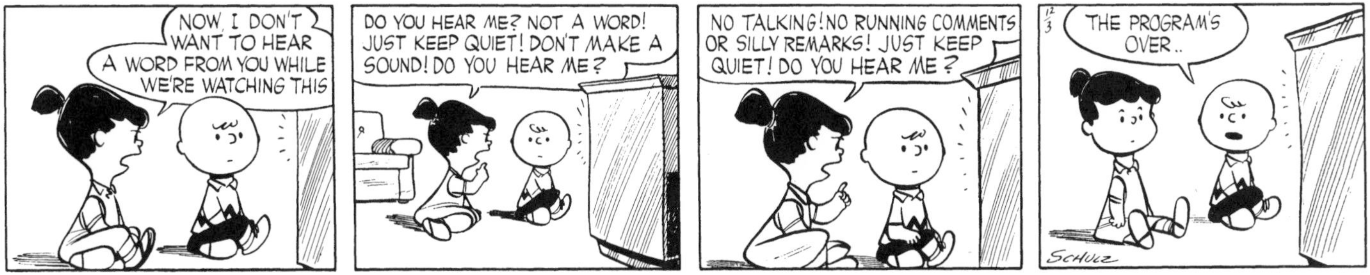
NOW, I DON'T WANT TO HEAR A WORD FROM YOU WHILE WE'RE WATCHING THIS
DO YOU HEAR ME? NOT A WORD! JUST KEEP QUIET! DON'T MAKE A SOUND! DO YOU HEAR ME?
NO TALKING! NO RUNNING COMMENTS OR SILLY REMARKS! JUST KEEP QUIET! DO YOU HEAR ME?
12/3
THE PROGRAM'S OVER..
SCHULZ

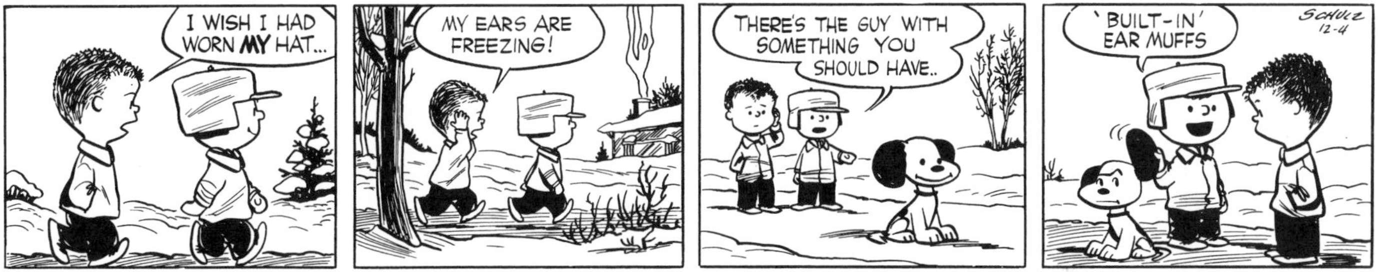
I WISH I HAD WORN MY HAT...
MY EARS ARE FREEZING!
THERE'S THE GUY WITH SOMETHING YOU SHOULD HAVE..
'BUILT-IN' EAR MUFFS
SCHULZ 12-4

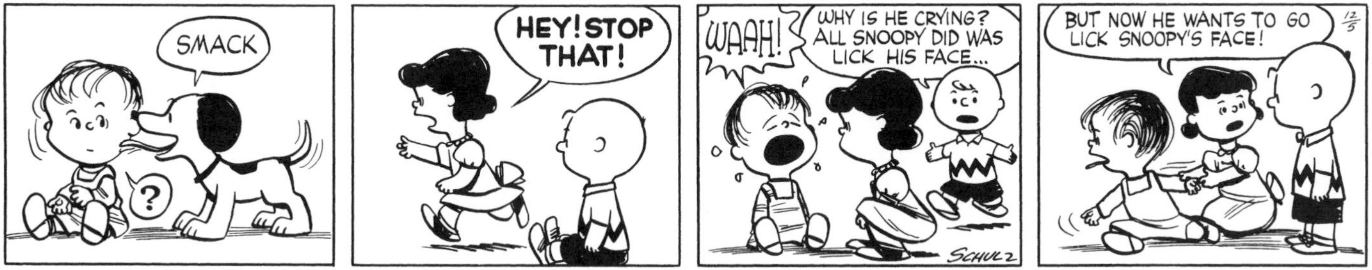
SMACK
?
HEY! STOP THAT!
WAAH!
WHY IS HE CRYING? ALL SNOOPY DID WAS LICK HIS FACE...
SCHULZ
BUT NOW HE WANTS TO GO LICK SNOOPY'S FACE!
12/5

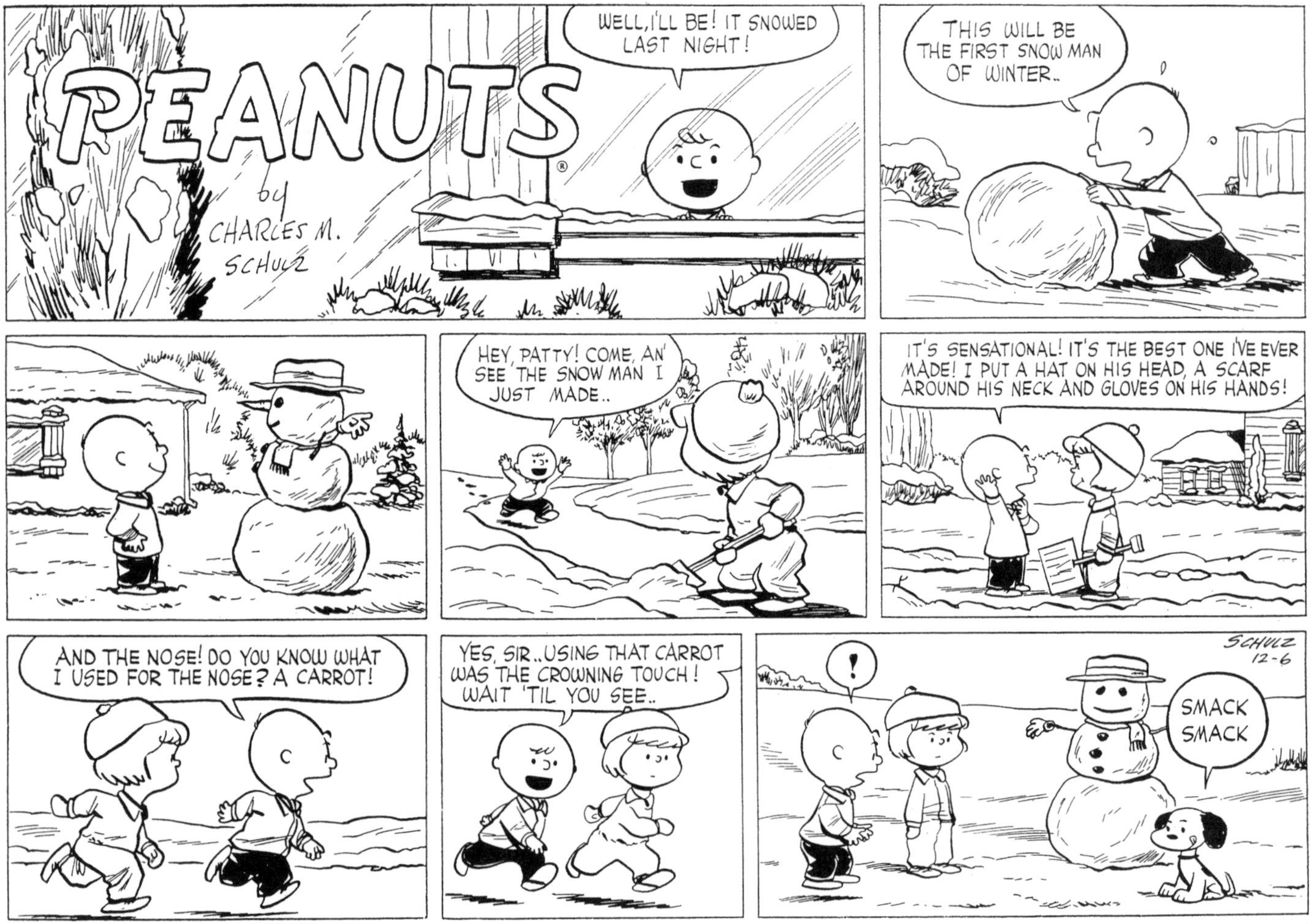
PEANUTS
by CHARLES M. SCHULZ
WELL, I'LL BE! IT SNOWED LAST NIGHT!
THIS WILL BE THE FIRST SNOW MAN OF WINTER..
HEY, PATTY! COME AN' SEE THE SNOW MAN I JUST MADE..
IT'S SENSATIONAL! IT'S THE BEST ONE I'VE EVER MADE! I PUT A HAT ON HIS HEAD, A SCARF AROUND HIS NECK AND GLOVES ON HIS HANDS!
AND THE NOSE! DO YOU KNOW WHAT I USED FOR THE NOSE? A CARROT!
YES, SIR..USING THAT CARROT WAS THE CROWNING TOUCH! WAIT 'TIL YOU SEE..
!
SMACK SMACK
SCHULZ 12-6

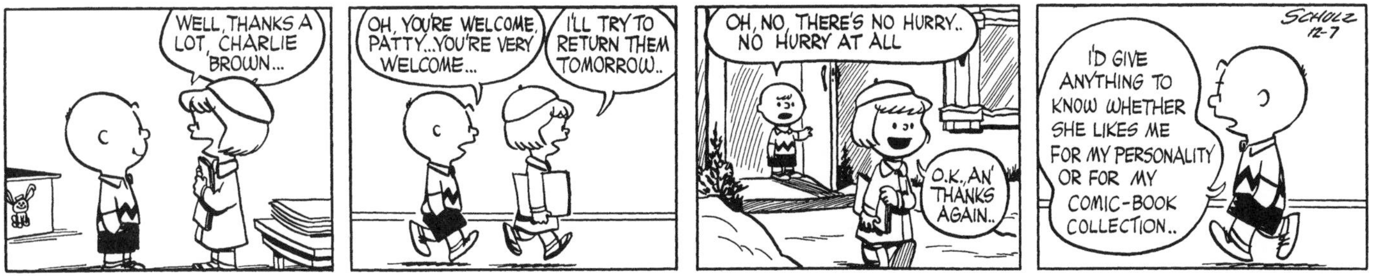
WELL, THANKS A LOT, CHARLIE BROWN...
OH, YOU'RE WELCOME, PATTY...YOU'RE VERY WELCOME...
I'LL TRY TO RETURN THEM TOMORROW..
OH, NO, THERE'S NO HURRY.. NO HURRY AT ALL
O.K., AN' THANKS AGAIN..
SCHULZ 12-7
I'D GIVE ANYTHING TO KNOW WHETHER SHE LIKES ME FOR MY PERSONALITY OR FOR MY COMIC-BOOK COLLECTION..

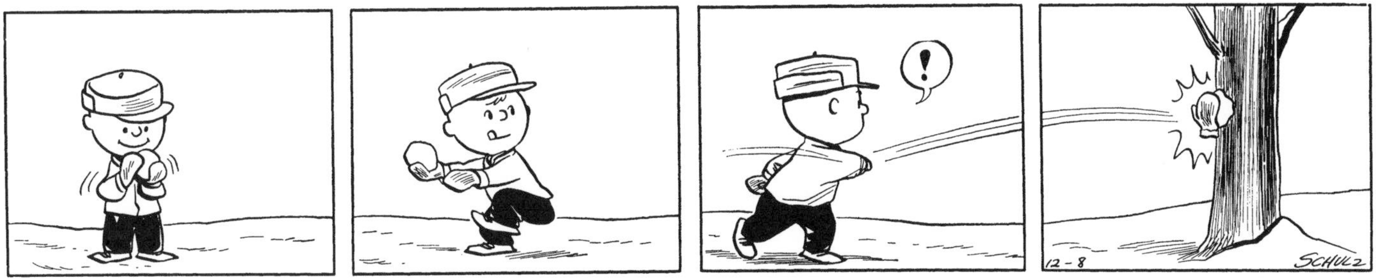
!
12-8
SCHULZ

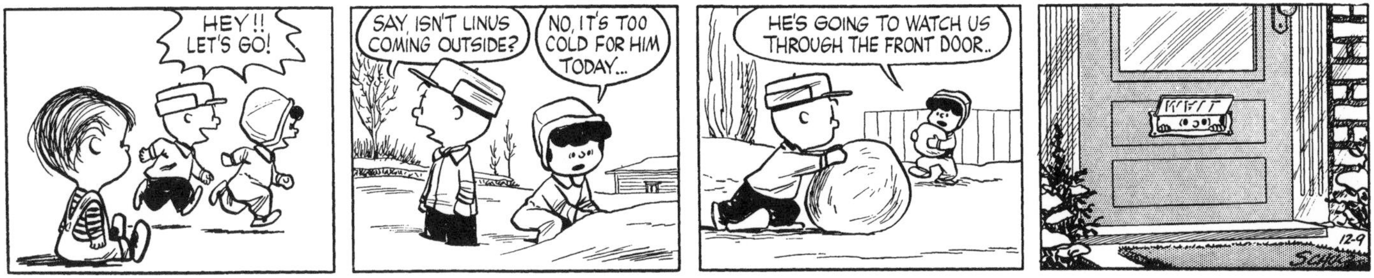
HEY!! LET'S GO!
SAY, ISN'T LINUS COMING OUTSIDE?
NO, IT'S TOO COLD FOR HIM TODAY...
HE'S GOING TO WATCH US THROUGH THE FRONT DOOR..
12-9

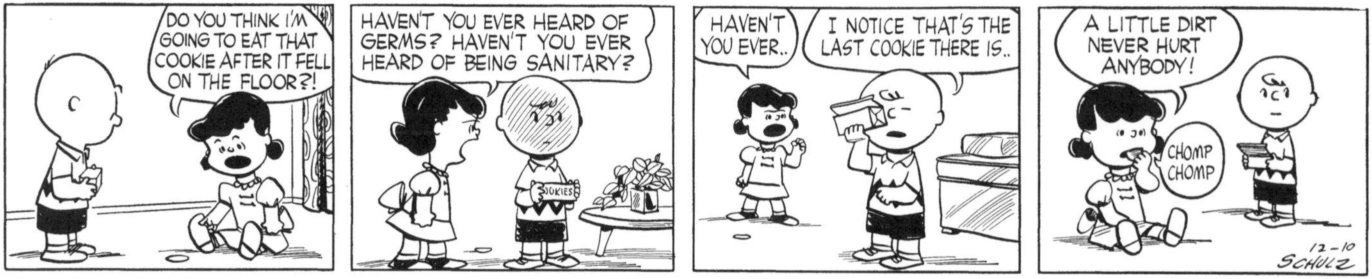
DO YOU THINK I'M GOING TO EAT THAT COOKIE AFTER IT FELL ON THE FLOOR?!
HAVEN'T YOU EVER HEARD OF GERMS? HAVEN'T YOU EVER HEARD OF BEING SANITARY?
HAVEN'T YOU EVER..
I NOTICE THAT'S THE LAST COOKIE THERE IS..
A LITTLE DIRT NEVER HURT ANYBODY!
CHOMP CHOMP
12-10
SCHULZ

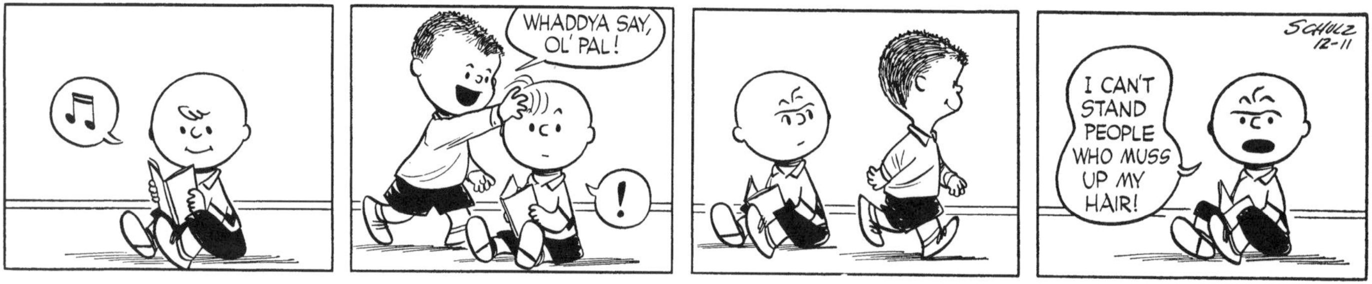
WHADDYA SAY, OL' PAL!
!
SCHULZ
12-11
I CAN'T STAND PEOPLE WHO MUSS UP MY HAIR!

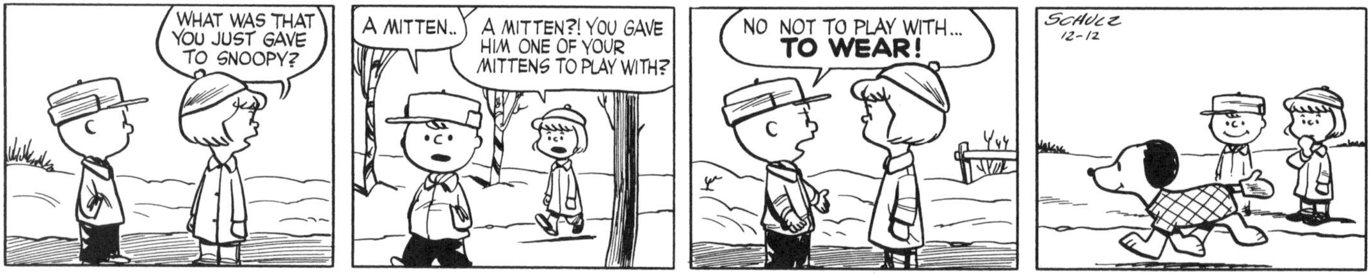
WHAT WAS THAT YOU JUST GAVE TO SNOOPY?
A MITTEN..
A MITTEN?! YOU GAVE HIM ONE OF YOUR MITTENS TO PLAY WITH?
NO NOT TO PLAY WITH... **TO WEAR!**
SCHULZ
12-12

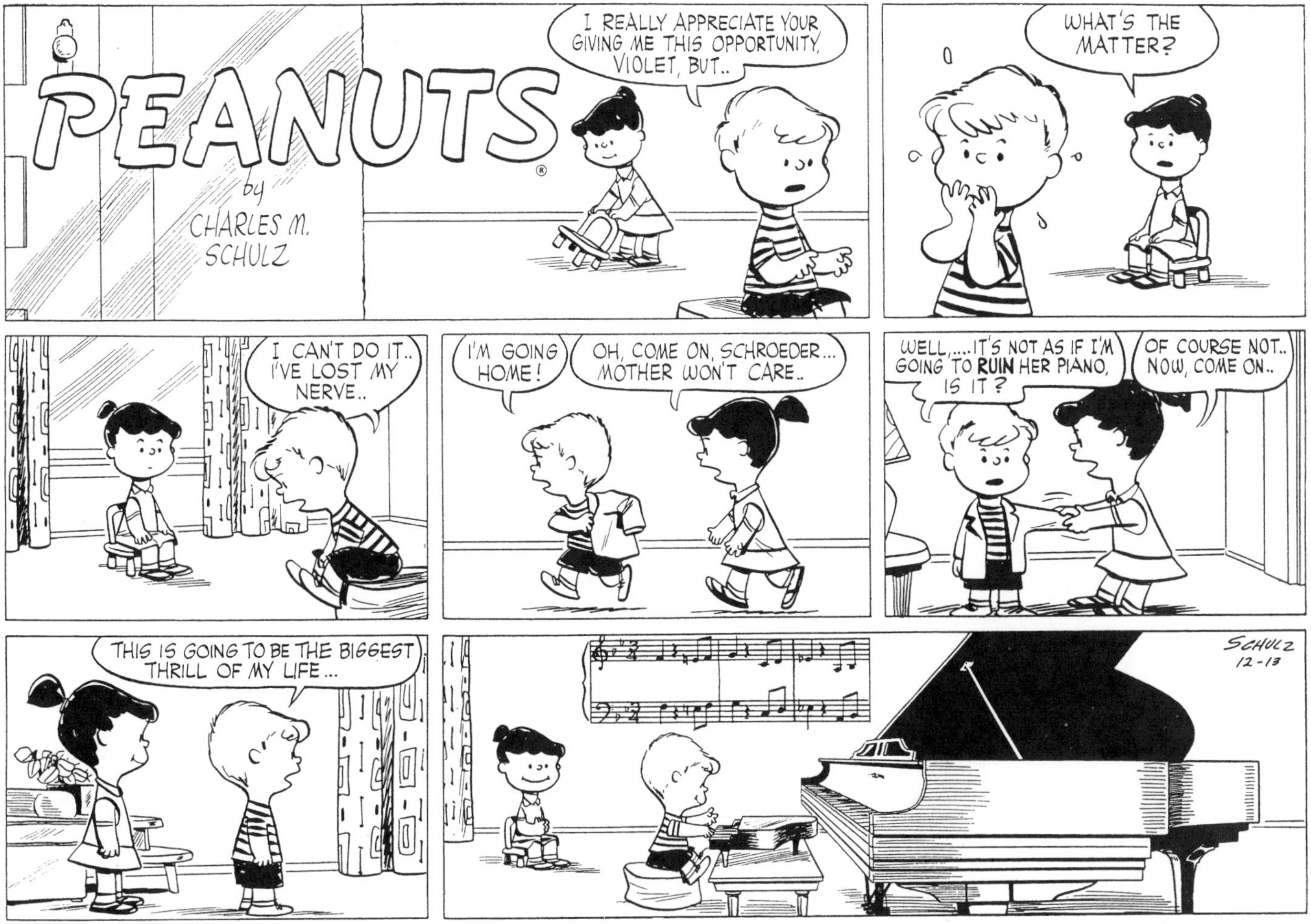
PEANUTS
by CHARLES M. SCHULZ
I REALLY APPRECIATE YOUR GIVING ME THIS OPPORTUNITY, VIOLET, BUT..
WHAT'S THE MATTER?
I CAN'T DO IT.. I'VE LOST MY NERVE..
I'M GOING HOME!
OH, COME ON, SCHROEDER... MOTHER WON'T CARE..
WELL,....IT'S NOT AS IF I'M GOING TO RUIN HER PIANO, IS IT?
OF COURSE NOT.. NOW, COME ON..
THIS IS GOING TO BE THE BIGGEST THRILL OF MY LIFE...
SCHULZ 12-13

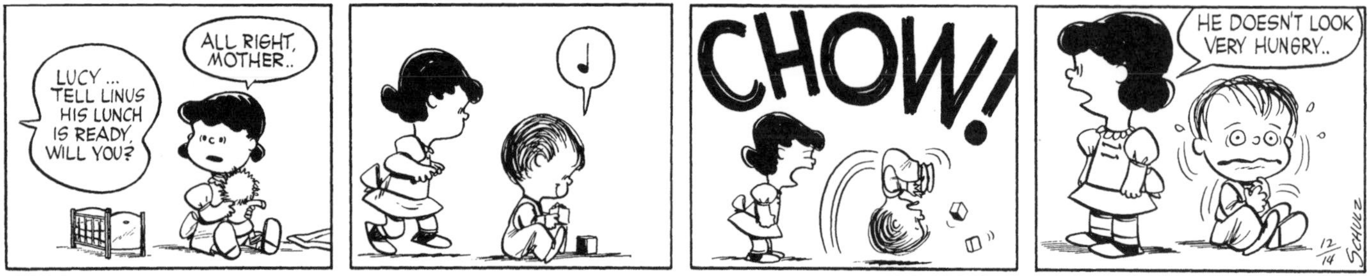
LUCY ... TELL LINUS HIS LUNCH IS READY, WILL YOU?
ALL RIGHT, MOTHER..
CHOW!!
HE DOESN'T LOOK VERY HUNGRY..
12/14
SCHULZ

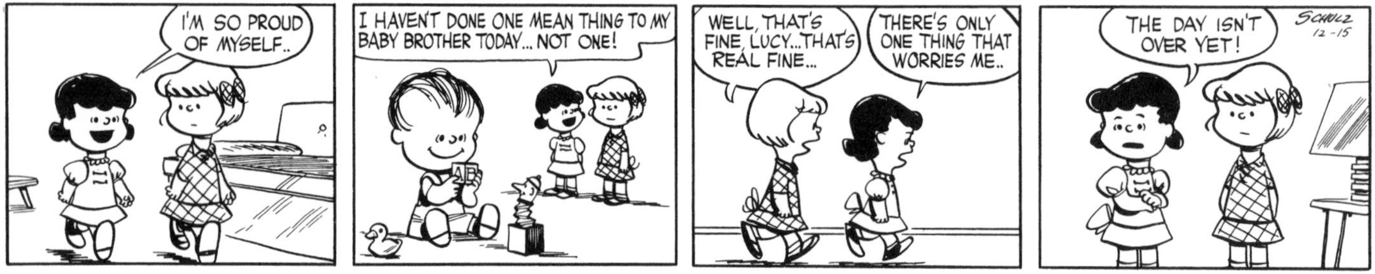
I'M SO PROUD OF MYSELF..
I HAVEN'T DONE ONE MEAN THING TO MY BABY BROTHER TODAY... NOT ONE!
WELL, THAT'S FINE, LUCY...THAT'S REAL FINE...
THERE'S ONLY ONE THING THAT WORRIES ME..
THE DAY ISN'T OVER YET!
SCHULZ
12-15

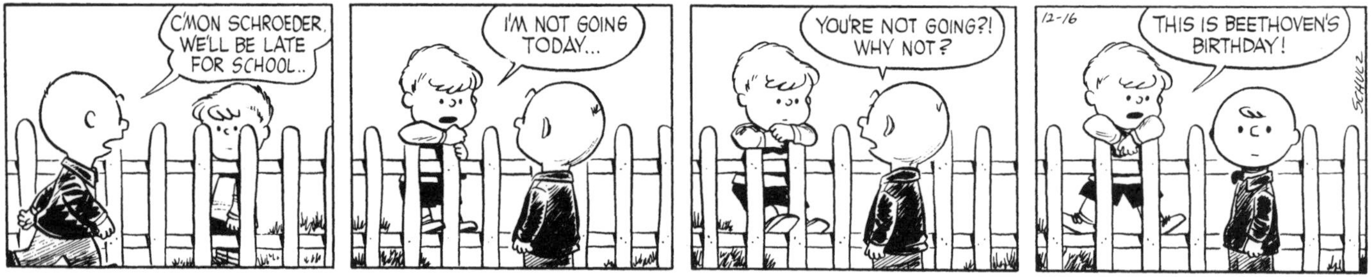
C'MON SCHROEDER, WE'LL BE LATE FOR SCHOOL..
I'M NOT GOING TODAY...
YOU'RE NOT GOING?! WHY NOT?
12-16
THIS IS BEETHOVEN'S BIRTHDAY!
SCHULZ

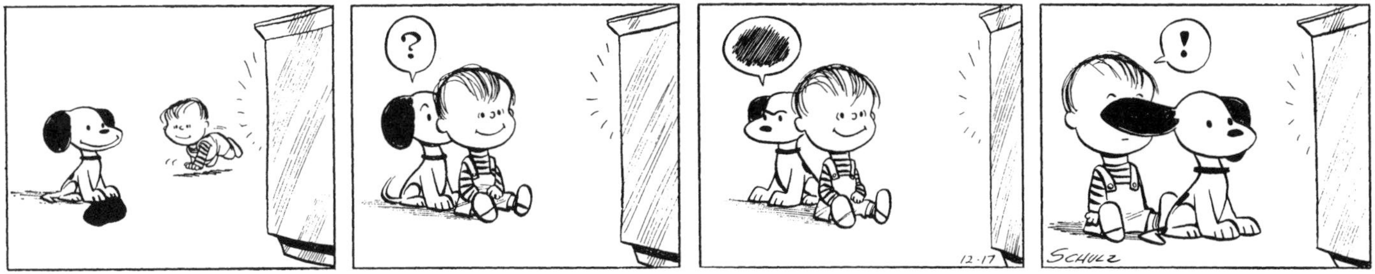
?
!
12-17
SCHULZ

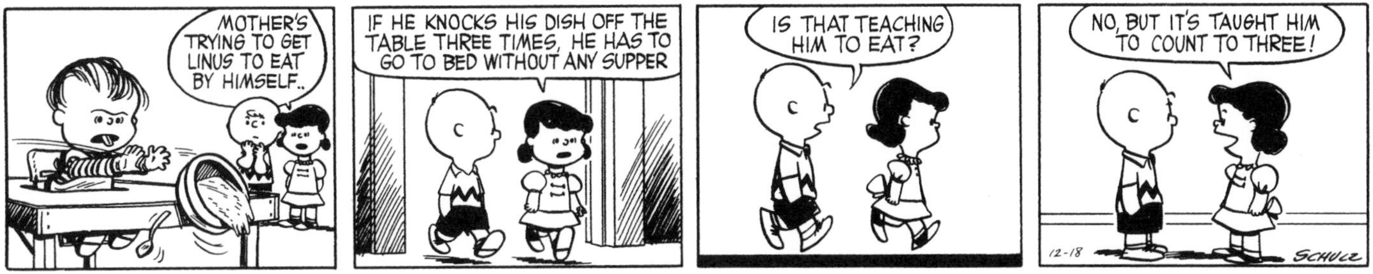
MOTHER'S TRYING TO GET LINUS TO EAT BY HIMSELF..
IF HE KNOCKS HIS DISH OFF THE TABLE THREE TIMES, HE HAS TO GO TO BED WITHOUT ANY SUPPER
IS THAT TEACHING HIM TO EAT?
NO, BUT IT'S TAUGHT HIM TO COUNT TO THREE!
12-18
SCHULZ

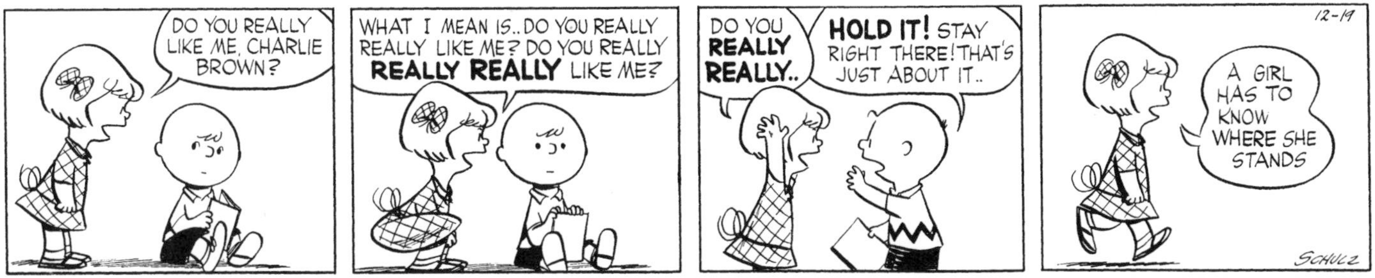
DO YOU REALLY LIKE ME, CHARLIE BROWN?
WHAT I MEAN IS..DO YOU REALLY REALLY LIKE ME? DO YOU REALLY REALLY REALLY LIKE ME?
DO YOU REALLY REALLY..
HOLD IT! STAY RIGHT THERE! THAT'S JUST ABOUT IT..
12-19
A GIRL HAS TO KNOW WHERE SHE STANDS
SCHULZ

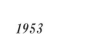

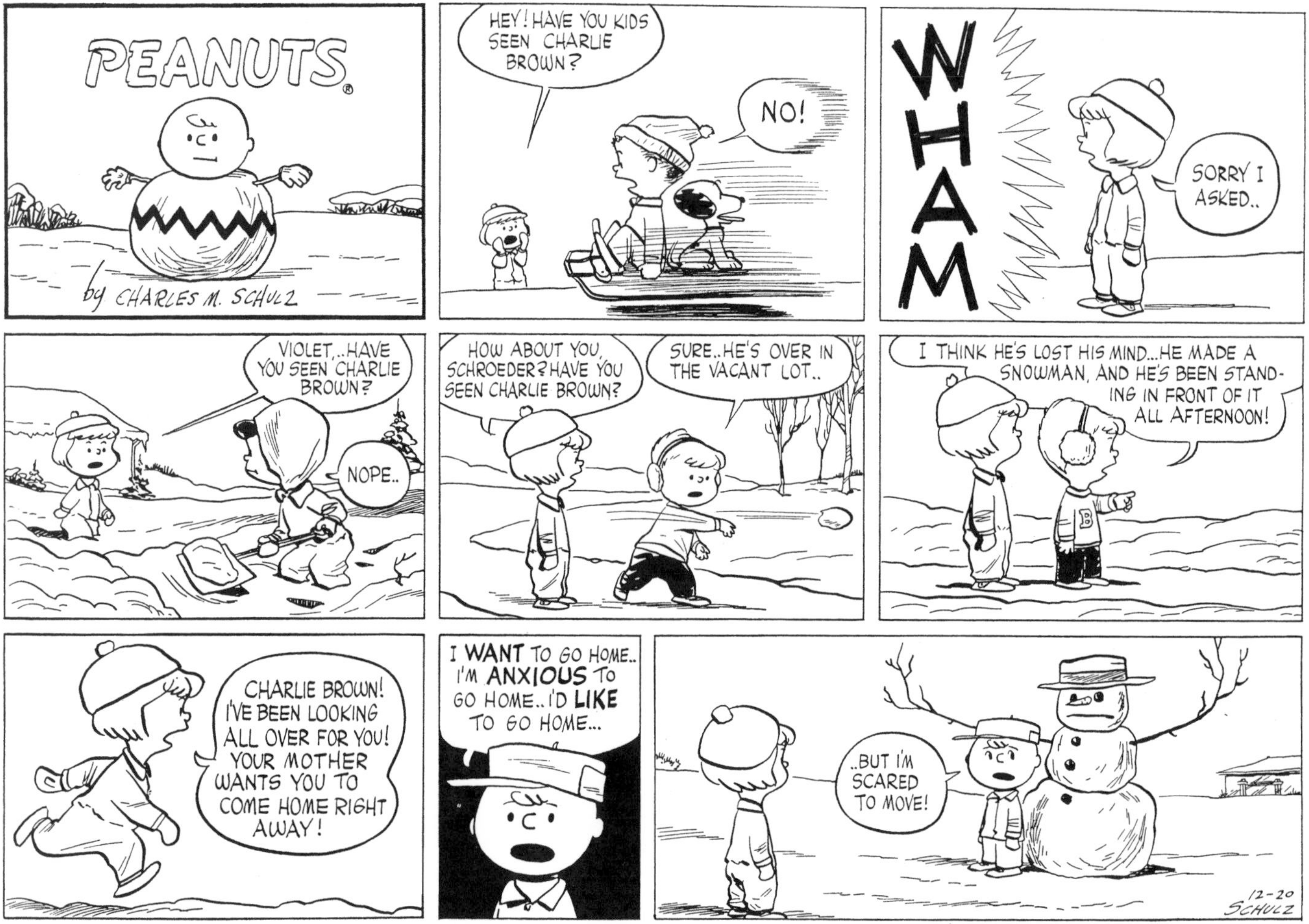
PEANUTS®
by CHARLES M. SCHULZ
HEY! HAVE YOU KIDS SEEN CHARLIE BROWN?
NO!
WHAM
SORRY I ASKED..
VIOLET,..HAVE YOU SEEN CHARLIE BROWN?
NOPE..
HOW ABOUT YOU, SCHROEDER? HAVE YOU SEEN CHARLIE BROWN?
SURE..HE'S OVER IN THE VACANT LOT..
I THINK HE'S LOST HIS MIND...HE MADE A SNOWMAN, AND HE'S BEEN STANDING IN FRONT OF IT ALL AFTERNOON!
CHARLIE BROWN! I'VE BEEN LOOKING ALL OVER FOR YOU! YOUR MOTHER WANTS YOU TO COME HOME RIGHT AWAY!
I WANT TO GO HOME.. I'M ANXIOUS TO GO HOME..I'D LIKE TO GO HOME...
..BUT I'M SCARED TO MOVE!
12-20
SCHULZ

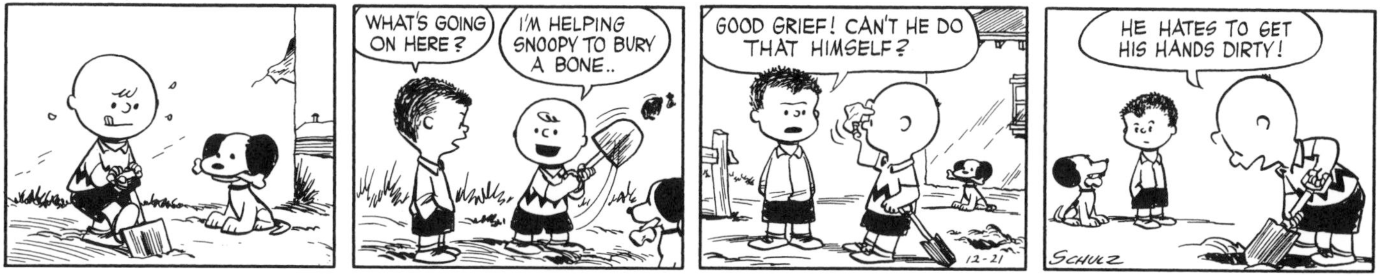
WHAT'S GOING ON HERE?
I'M HELPING SNOOPY TO BURY A BONE..
GOOD GRIEF! CAN'T HE DO THAT HIMSELF?
12-21
HE HATES TO GET HIS HANDS DIRTY!
SCHULZ

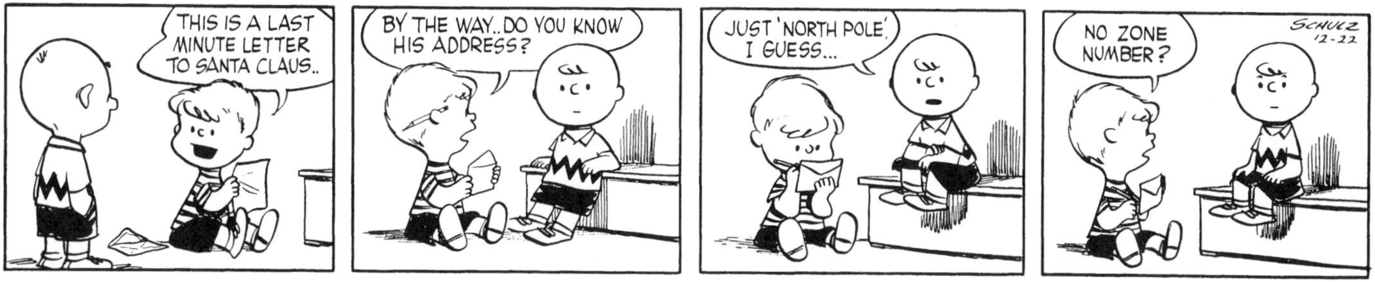
THIS IS A LAST MINUTE LETTER TO SANTA CLAUS..
BY THE WAY..DO YOU KNOW HIS ADDRESS?
JUST 'NORTH POLE', I GUESS...
SCHULZ 12-22
NO ZONE NUMBER?

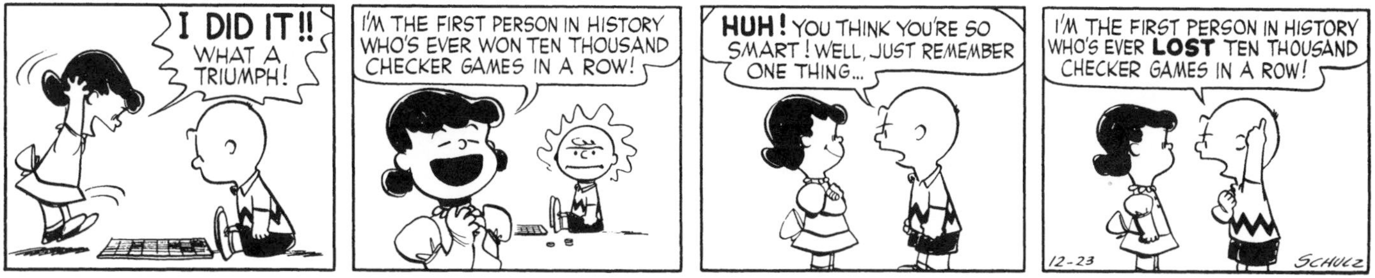
I DID IT!! WHAT A TRIUMPH!
I'M THE FIRST PERSON IN HISTORY WHO'S EVER WON TEN THOUSAND CHECKER GAMES IN A ROW!
HUH! YOU THINK YOU'RE SO SMART! WELL, JUST REMEMBER ONE THING...
I'M THE FIRST PERSON IN HISTORY WHO'S EVER LOST TEN THOUSAND CHECKER GAMES IN A ROW!
12-23
SCHULZ

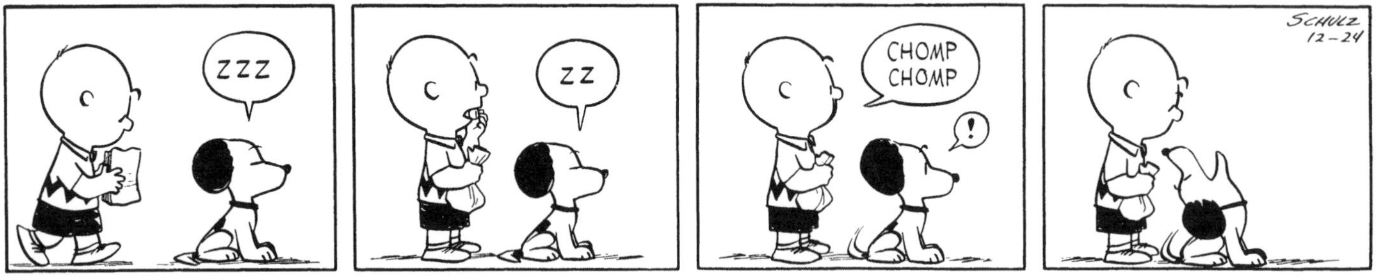
ZZZ
ZZ
CHOMP CHOMP
!
SCHULZ 12-24

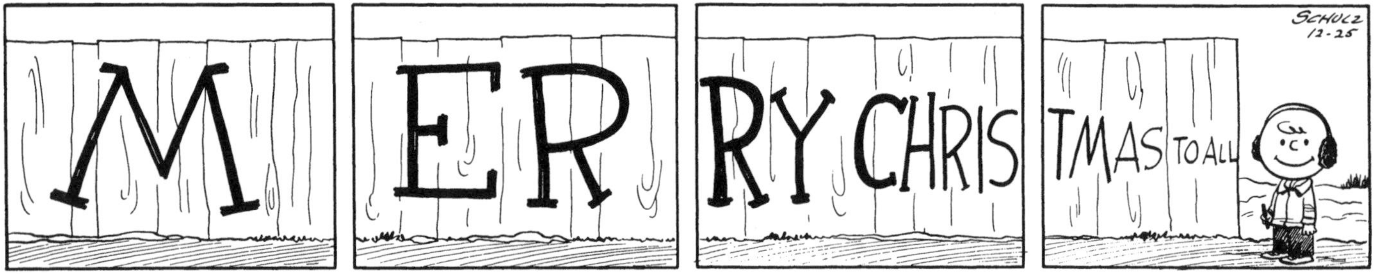
M
ER
RY CHRIS
TMAS TO ALL
SCHULZ 12-25

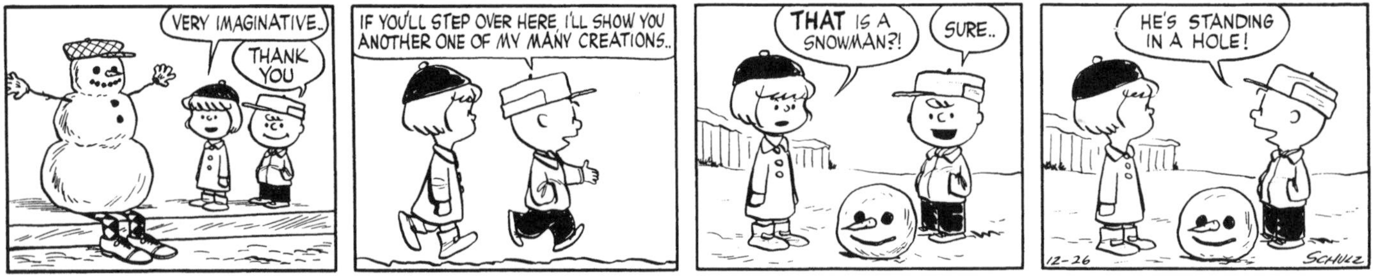
VERY IMAGINATIVE..
THANK YOU
IF YOU'LL STEP OVER HERE, I'LL SHOW YOU ANOTHER ONE OF MY MANY CREATIONS..
THAT IS A SNOWMAN?!
SURE..
HE'S STANDING IN A HOLE!
12-26
SCHULZ

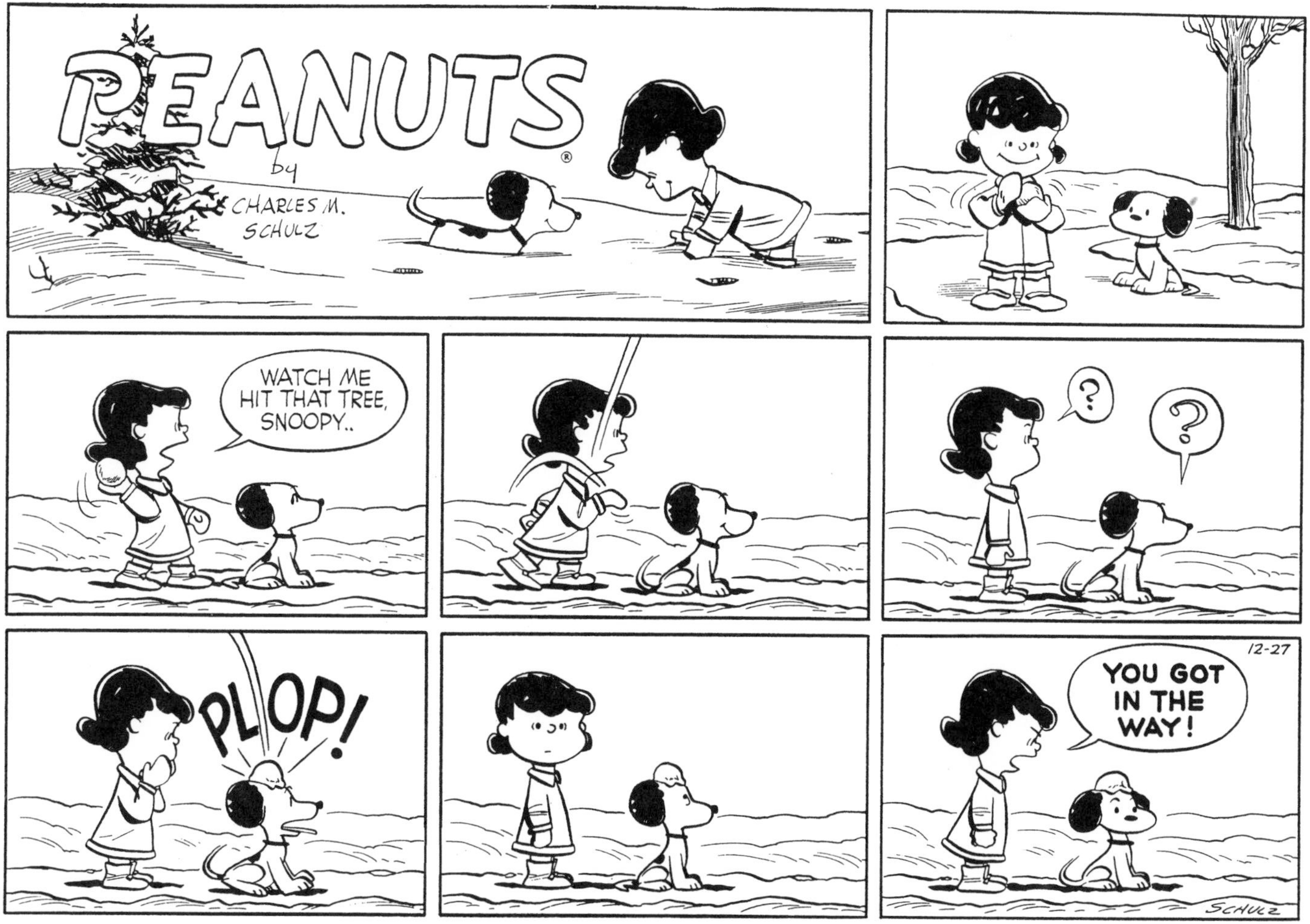
PEANUTS
by CHARLES M. SCHULZ
WATCH ME HIT THAT TREE, SNOOPY..
?
?
PLOP!
12-27
YOU GOT IN THE WAY!
SCHULZ

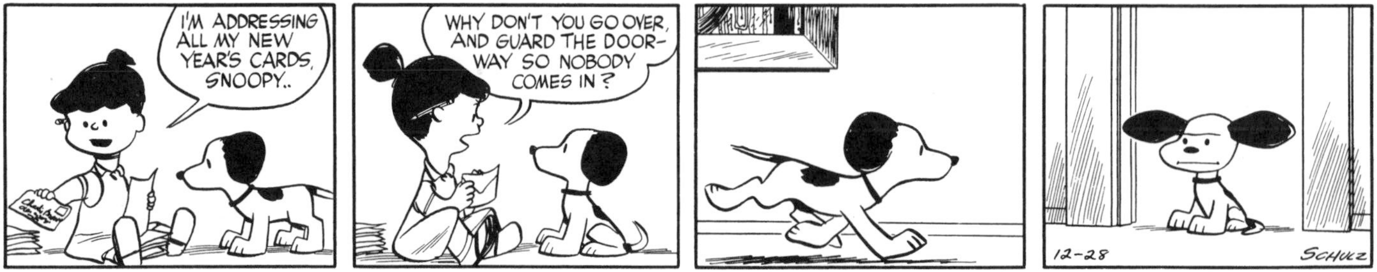
I'M ADDRESSING ALL MY NEW YEAR'S CARDS, SNOOPY..
WHY DON'T YOU GO OVER, AND GUARD THE DOORWAY SO NOBODY COMES IN?
12-28
SCHULZ

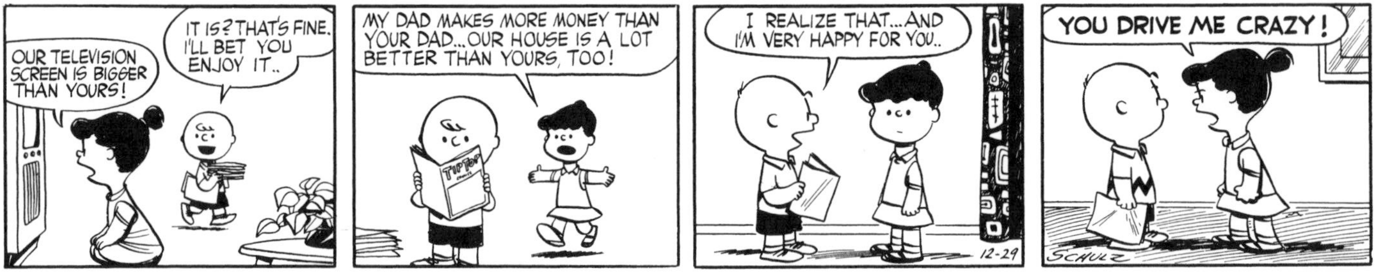
OUR TELEVISION SCREEN IS BIGGER THAN YOURS!
IT IS? THAT'S FINE. I'LL BET YOU ENJOY IT..
MY DAD MAKES MORE MONEY THAN YOUR DAD...OUR HOUSE IS A LOT BETTER THAN YOURS, TOO!
I REALIZE THAT...AND I'M VERY HAPPY FOR YOU..
12-29
YOU DRIVE ME CRAZY!
SCHULZ

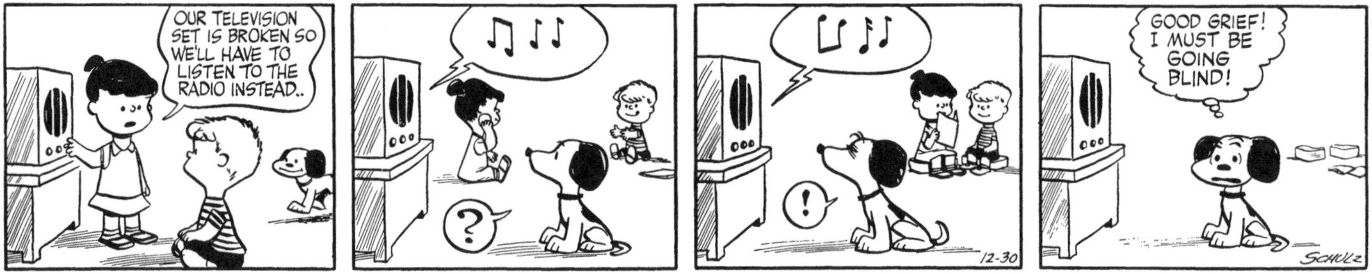
OUR TELEVISION SET IS BROKEN SO WE'LL HAVE TO LISTEN TO THE RADIO INSTEAD..
?
!
12-30
GOOD GRIEF! I MUST BE GOING BLIND!
SCHULZ

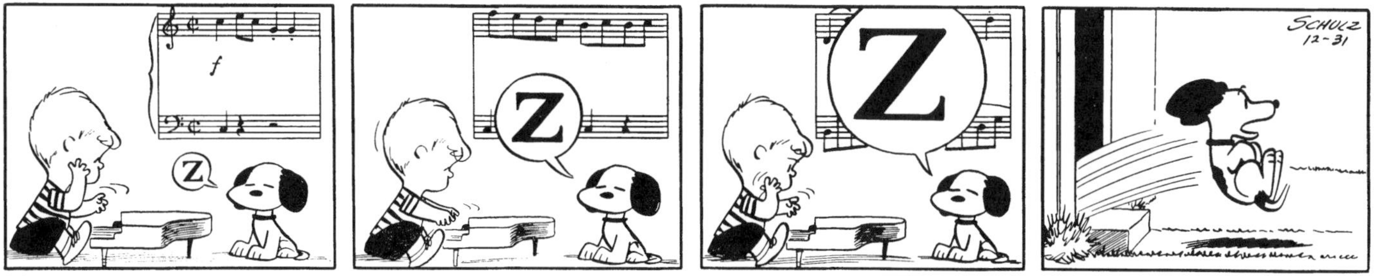
Z
Z
Z
SCHULZ 12-31

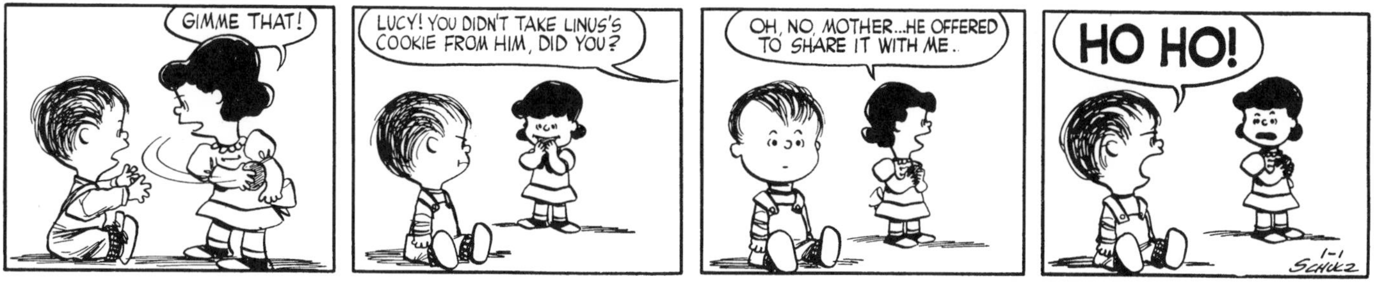
GIMME THAT!
LUCY! YOU DIDN'T TAKE LINUS'S COOKIE FROM HIM, DID YOU?
OH, NO, MOTHER...HE OFFERED TO SHARE IT WITH ME..
HO HO!
1-1 SCHULZ

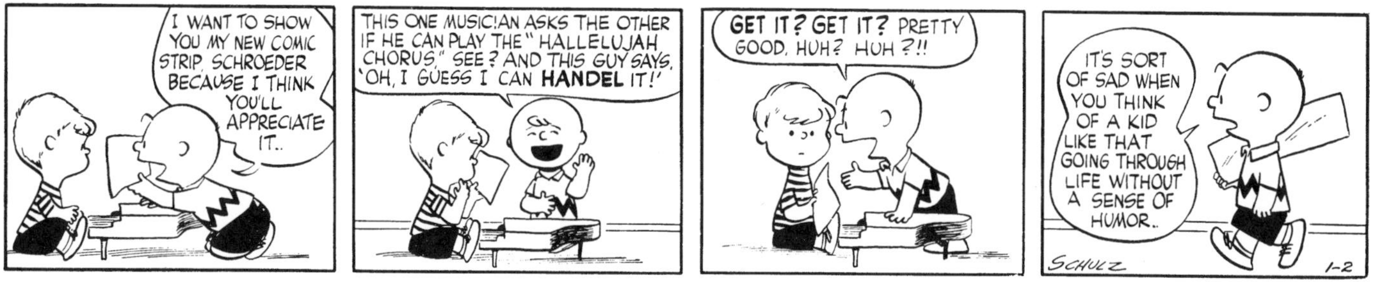
I WANT TO SHOW YOU MY NEW COMIC STRIP, SCHROEDER BECAUSE I THINK YOU'LL APPRECIATE IT..
THIS ONE MUSICIAN ASKS THE OTHER IF HE CAN PLAY THE "HALLELUJAH CHORUS," SEE? AND THIS GUY SAYS, 'OH, I GUESS I CAN HANDEL IT!'
GET IT? GET IT? PRETTY GOOD, HUH? HUH?!!
IT'S SORT OF SAD WHEN YOU THINK OF A KID LIKE THAT GOING THROUGH LIFE WITHOUT A SENSE OF HUMOR..
SCHULZ 1-2

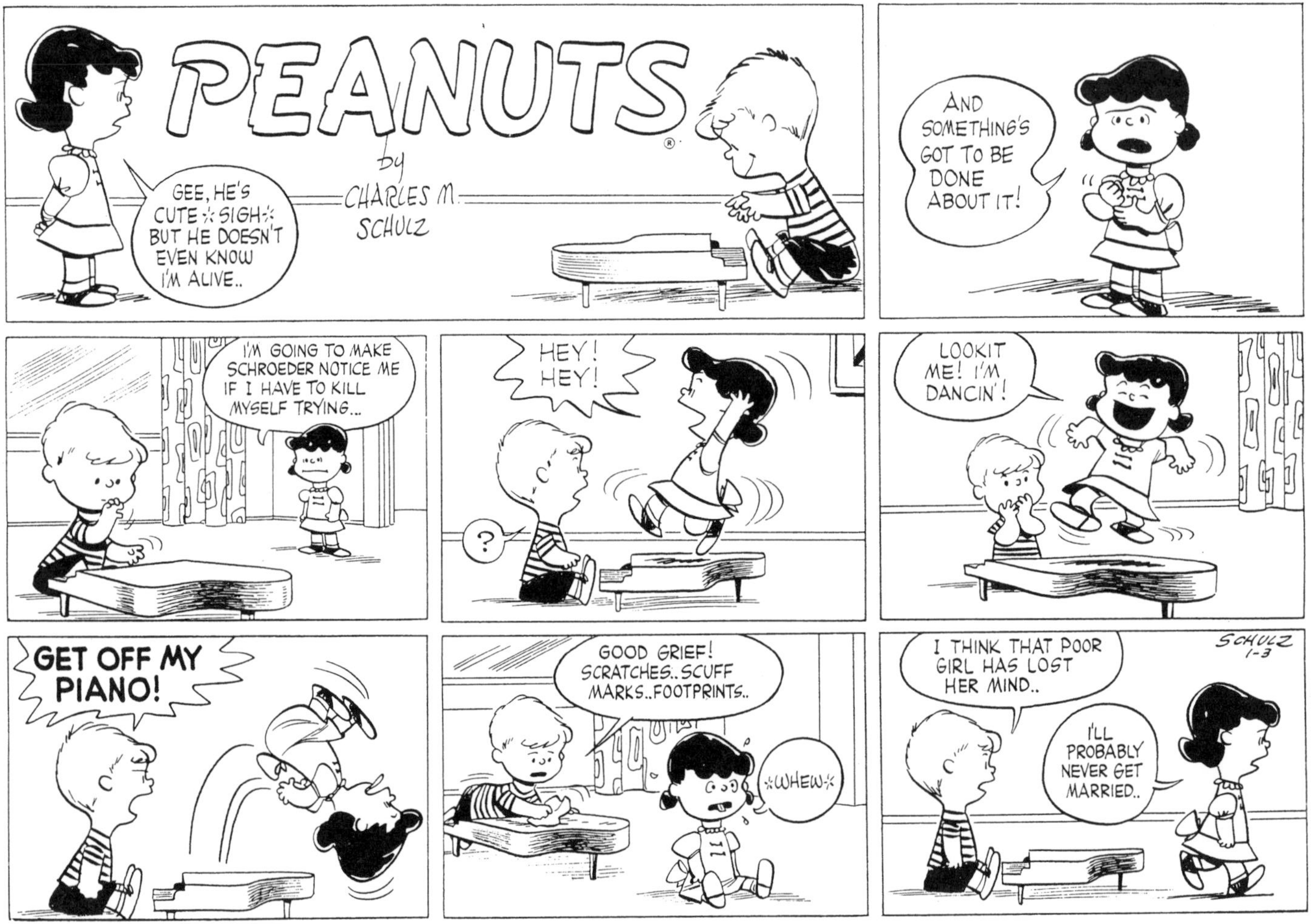
PEANUTS
by CHARLES M. SCHULZ
GEE, HE'S CUTE *SIGH* BUT HE DOESN'T EVEN KNOW I'M ALIVE..
AND SOMETHING'S GOT TO BE DONE ABOUT IT!
I'M GOING TO MAKE SCHROEDER NOTICE ME IF I HAVE TO KILL MYSELF TRYING...
HEY! HEY!
?
LOOKIT ME! I'M DANCIN'!
GET OFF MY PIANO!
GOOD GRIEF! SCRATCHES..SCUFF MARKS..FOOTPRINTS..
WHEW
SCHULZ 1-3
I THINK THAT POOR GIRL HAS LOST HER MIND..
I'LL PROBABLY NEVER GET MARRIED..

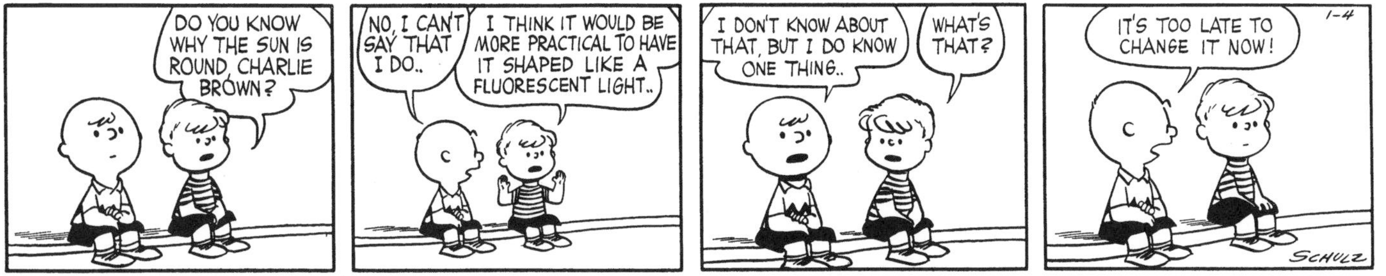
DO YOU KNOW WHY THE SUN IS ROUND, CHARLIE BROWN?
NO, I CAN'T SAY THAT I DO..
I THINK IT WOULD BE MORE PRACTICAL TO HAVE IT SHAPED LIKE A FLUORESCENT LIGHT..
I DON'T KNOW ABOUT THAT, BUT I DO KNOW ONE THING..
WHAT'S THAT?
IT'S TOO LATE TO CHANGE IT NOW!
1-4
SCHULZ

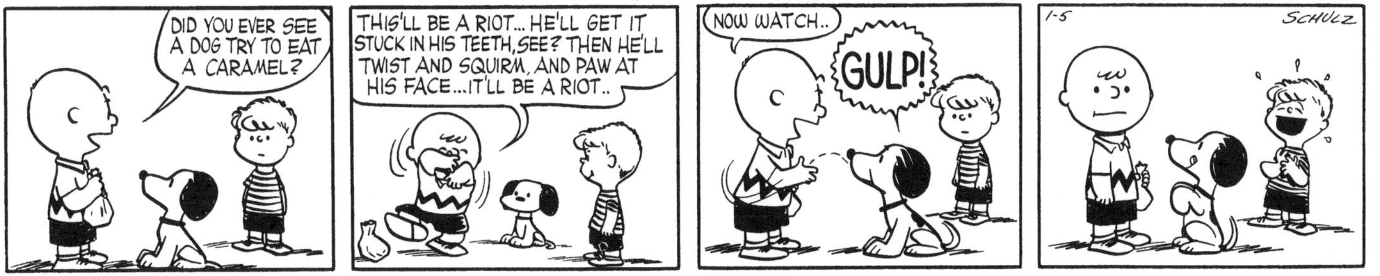
DID YOU EVER SEE A DOG TRY TO EAT A CARAMEL?
THIS'LL BE A RIOT... HE'LL GET IT STUCK IN HIS TEETH, SEE? THEN HE'LL TWIST AND SQUIRM, AND PAW AT HIS FACE...IT'LL BE A RIOT..
NOW WATCH..
GULP!
1-5
SCHULZ

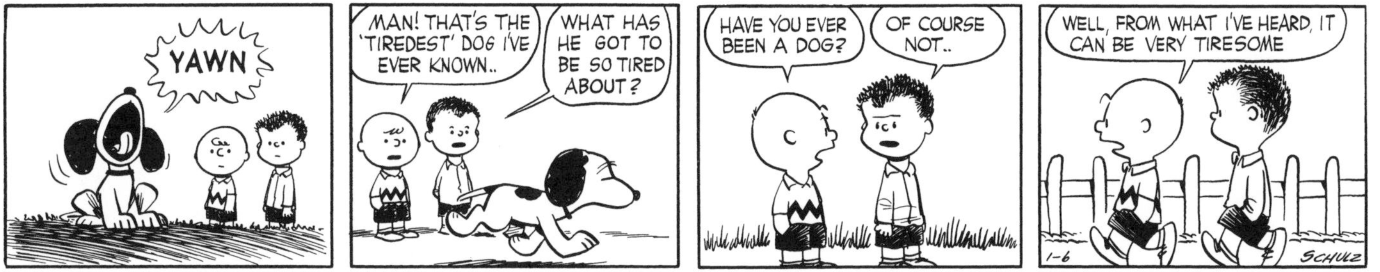
YAWN
MAN! THAT'S THE 'TIREDEST' DOG I'VE EVER KNOWN..
WHAT HAS HE GOT TO BE SO TIRED ABOUT?
HAVE YOU EVER BEEN A DOG?
OF COURSE NOT..
WELL, FROM WHAT I'VE HEARD, IT CAN BE VERY TIRESOME
1-6
SCHULZ

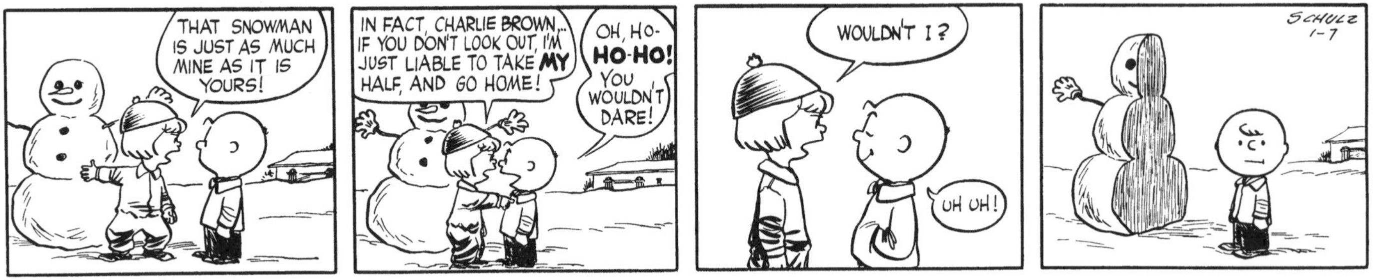
THAT SNOWMAN IS JUST AS MUCH MINE AS IT IS YOURS!
IN FACT, CHARLIE BROWN... IF YOU DON'T LOOK OUT, I'M JUST LIABLE TO TAKE MY HALF, AND GO HOME!
OH, HO- HO-HO! YOU WOULDN'T DARE!
WOULDN'T I?
UH UH!
SCHULZ 1-7

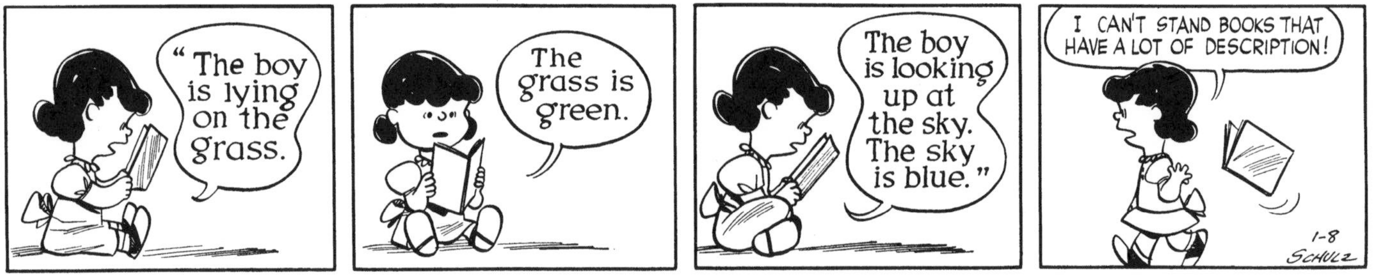
"The boy is lying on the grass.
The grass is green.
The boy is looking up at the sky. The sky is blue."
I CAN'T STAND BOOKS THAT HAVE A LOT OF DESCRIPTION!
1-8 SCHULZ

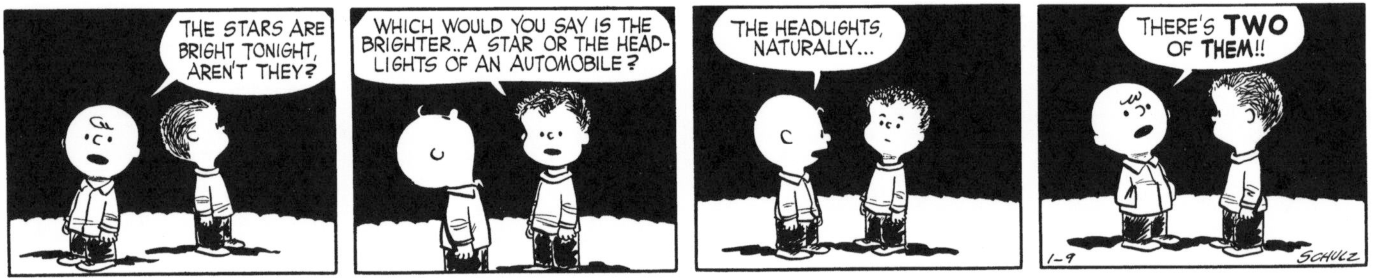
THE STARS ARE BRIGHT TONIGHT, AREN'T THEY?
WHICH WOULD YOU SAY IS THE BRIGHTER..A STAR OR THE HEAD-LIGHTS OF AN AUTOMOBILE?
THE HEADLIGHTS, NATURALLY...
THERE'S TWO OF THEM!!
1-9
SCHULZ

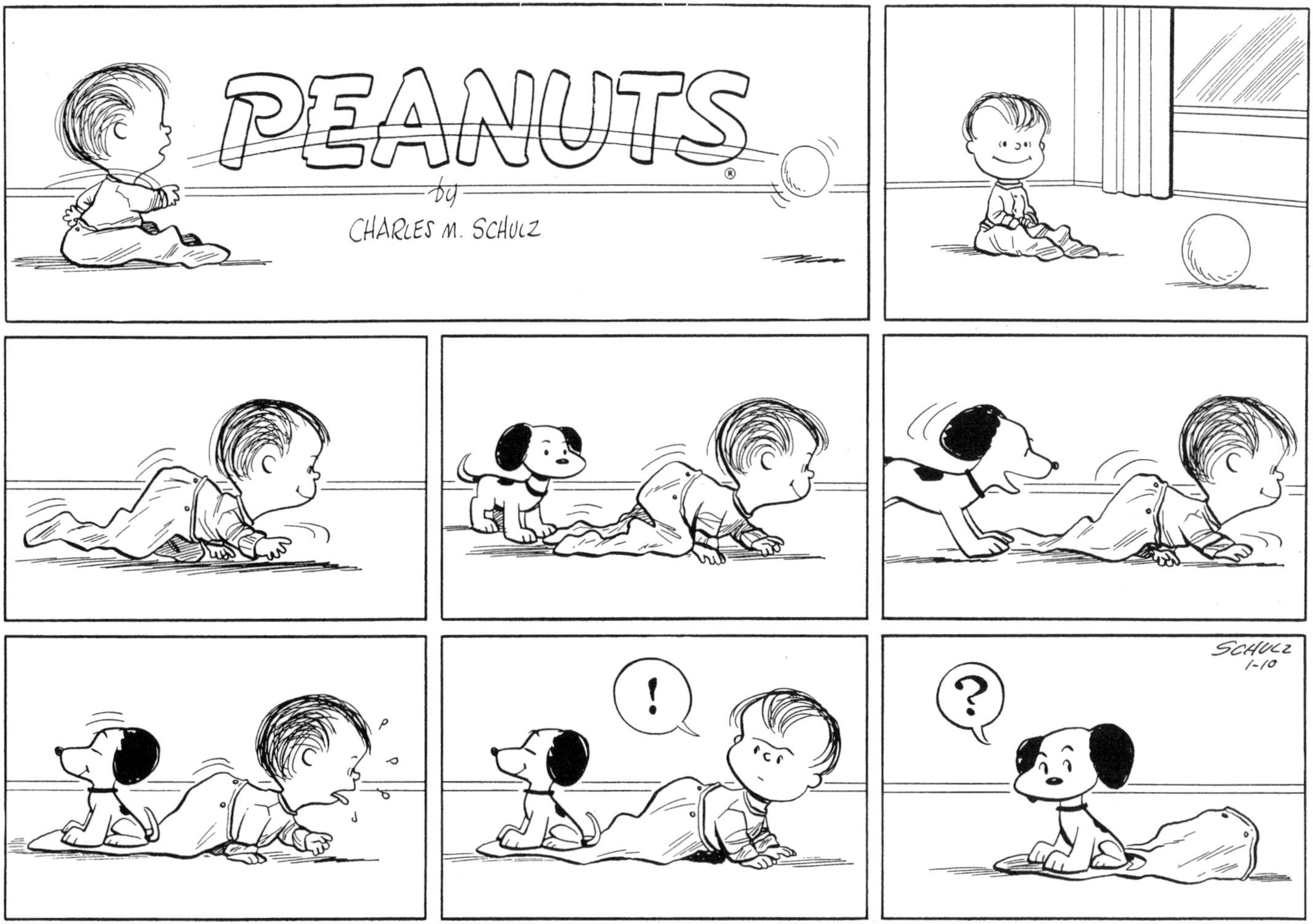
PEANUTS
by
CHARLES M. SCHULZ
!
?
SCHULZ
1-10

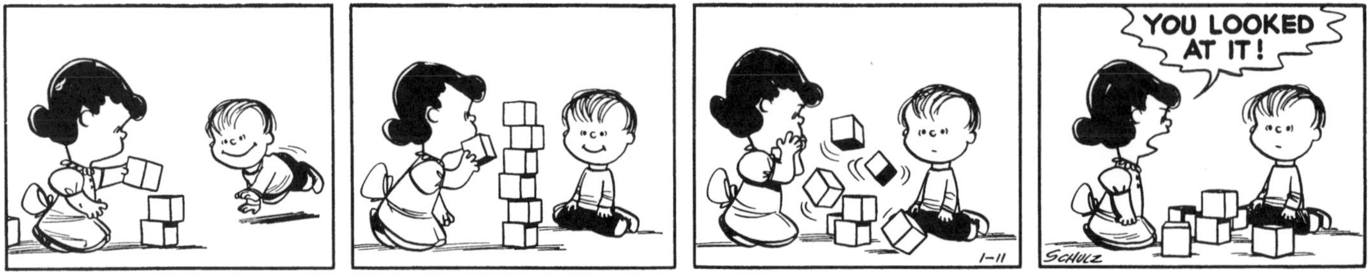
1-11
SCHULZ
YOU LOOKED AT IT!

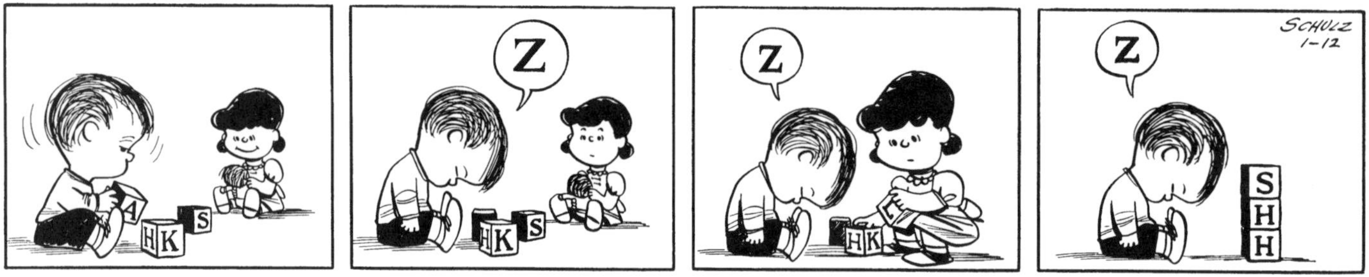
Z
Z
SCHULZ 1-12
Z

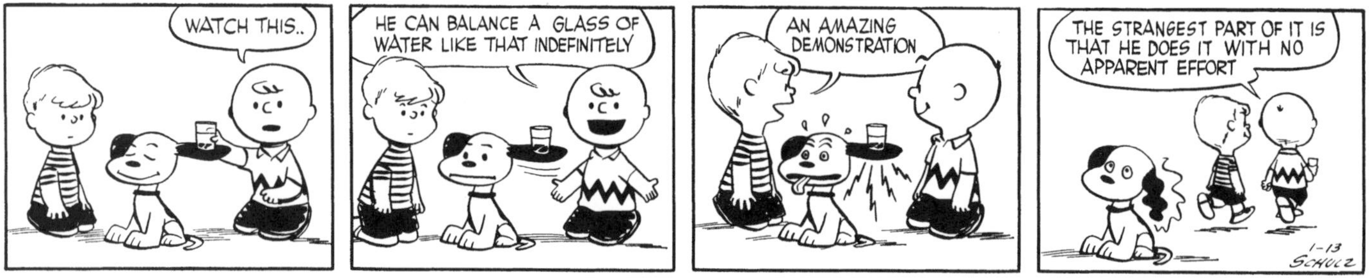
WATCH THIS..
HE CAN BALANCE A GLASS OF WATER LIKE THAT INDEFINITELY
AN AMAZING DEMONSTRATION
THE STRANGEST PART OF IT IS THAT HE DOES IT WITH NO APPARENT EFFORT
1-13 SCHULZ

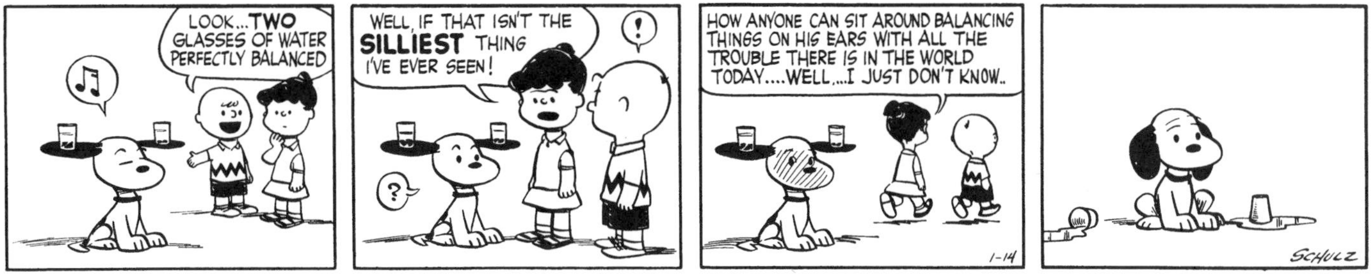
LOOK...TWO GLASSES OF WATER PERFECTLY BALANCED
WELL, IF THAT ISN'T THE SILLIEST THING I'VE EVER SEEN!
!
?
HOW ANYONE CAN SIT AROUND BALANCING THINGS ON HIS EARS WITH ALL THE TROUBLE THERE IS IN THE WORLD TODAY....WELL,...I JUST DON'T KNOW..
1-14
SCHULZ

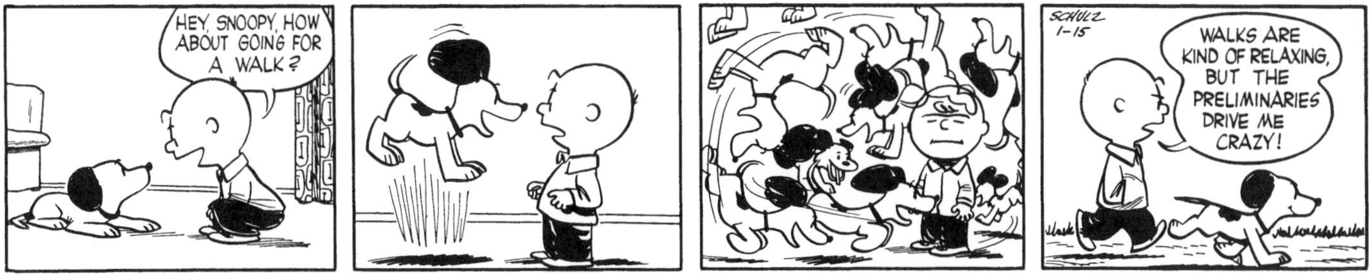
HEY, SNOOPY, HOW ABOUT GOING FOR A WALK?
SCHULZ
1-15
WALKS ARE KIND OF RELAXING, BUT THE PRELIMINARIES DRIVE ME CRAZY!

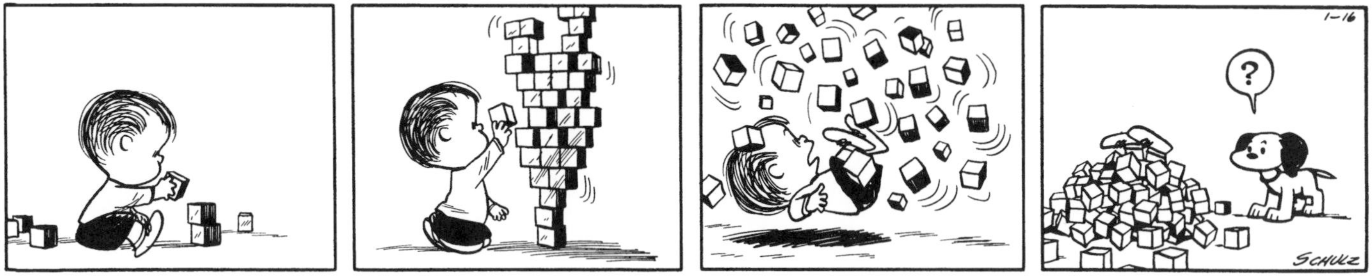
1-16
?
SCHULZ

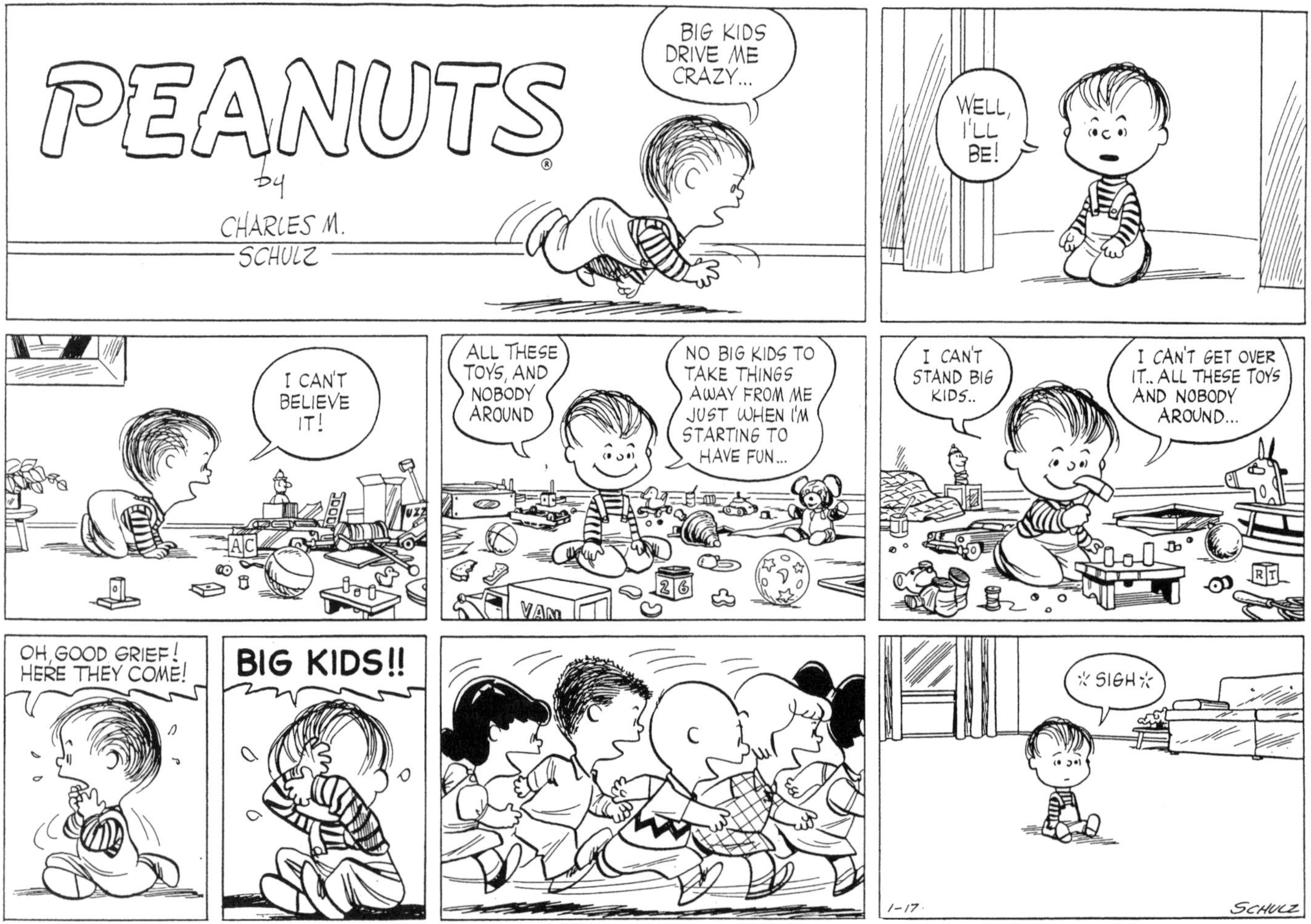
PEANUTS
by
CHARLES M. SCHULZ
BIG KIDS DRIVE ME CRAZY...
WELL, I'LL BE!
I CAN'T BELIEVE IT!
ALL THESE TOYS, AND NOBODY AROUND
NO BIG KIDS TO TAKE THINGS AWAY FROM ME JUST WHEN I'M STARTING TO HAVE FUN...
I CAN'T STAND BIG KIDS..
I CAN'T GET OVER IT.. ALL THESE TOYS AND NOBODY AROUND...
OH, GOOD GRIEF! HERE THEY COME!
BIG KIDS!!
SIGH
1-17
SCHULZ

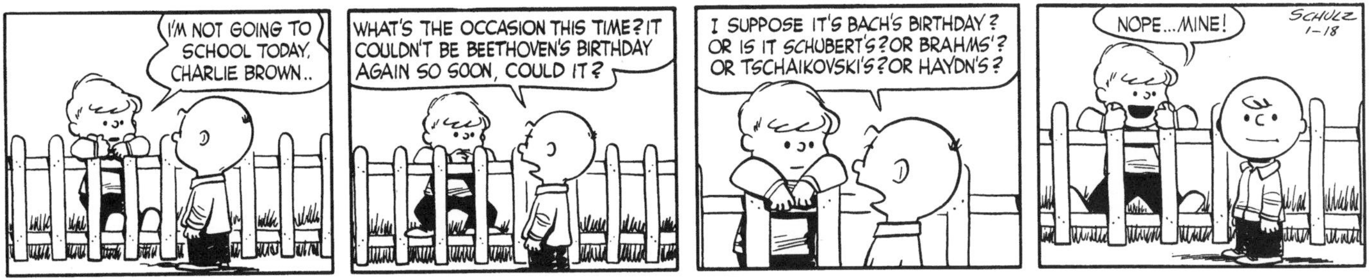
I'M NOT GOING TO SCHOOL TODAY, CHARLIE BROWN..
WHAT'S THE OCCASION THIS TIME? IT COULDN'T BE BEETHOVEN'S BIRTHDAY AGAIN SO SOON, COULD IT?
I SUPPOSE IT'S BACH'S BIRTHDAY? OR IS IT SCHUBERT'S? OR BRAHMS'? OR TSCHAIKOVSKI'S? OR HAYDN'S?
NOPE...MINE!
SCHULZ 1-18

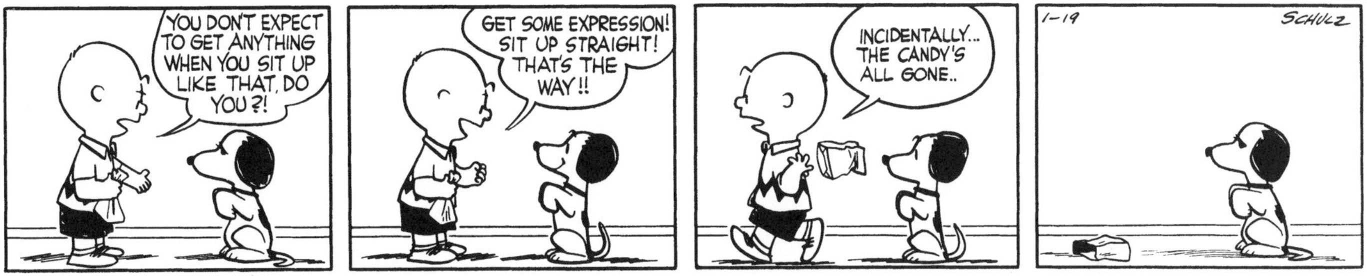
YOU DON'T EXPECT TO GET ANYTHING WHEN YOU SIT UP LIKE THAT, DO YOU?!
GET SOME EXPRESSION! SIT UP STRAIGHT! THAT'S THE WAY!!
INCIDENTALLY... THE CANDY'S ALL GONE..
1-19
SCHULZ

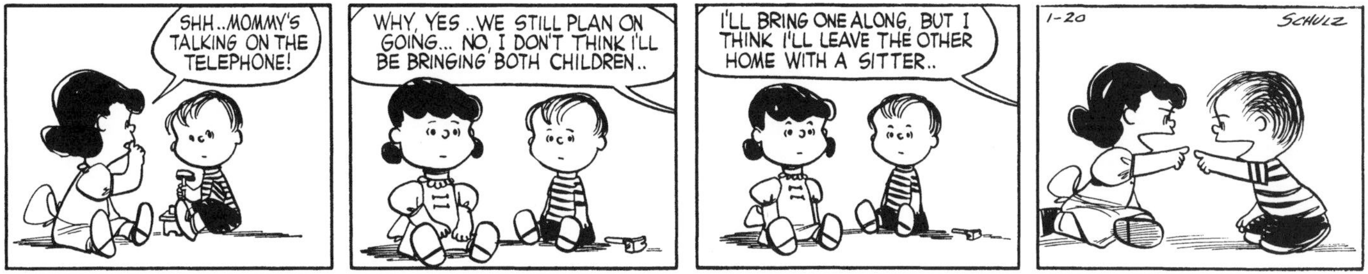
SHH..MOMMY'S TALKING ON THE TELEPHONE!
WHY, YES..WE STILL PLAN ON GOING... NO, I DON'T THINK I'LL BE BRINGING BOTH CHILDREN..
I'LL BRING ONE ALONG, BUT I THINK I'LL LEAVE THE OTHER HOME WITH A SITTER..
1-20
SCHULZ

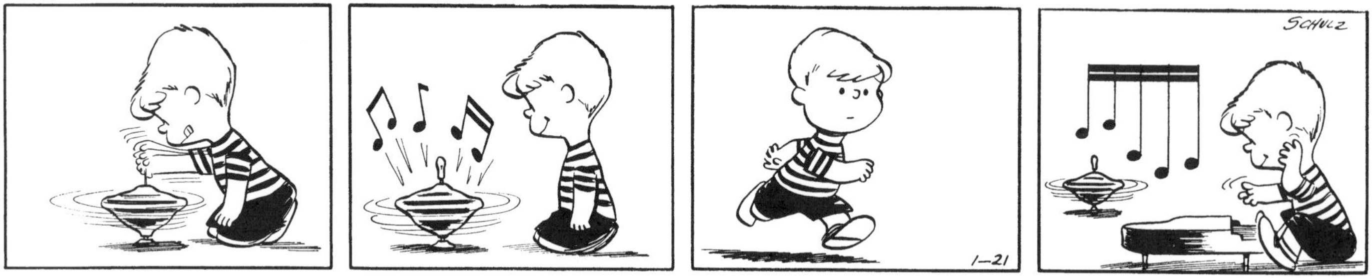
1-21
SCHULZ

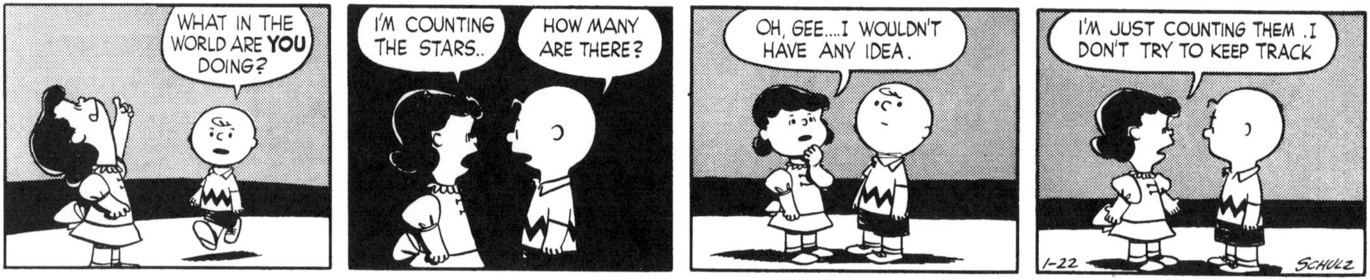
WHAT IN THE WORLD ARE **YOU** DOING?
I'M COUNTING THE STARS..
HOW MANY ARE THERE?
OH, GEE....I WOULDN'T HAVE ANY IDEA.
I'M JUST COUNTING THEM .I DON'T TRY TO KEEP TRACK
1-22
SCHULZ

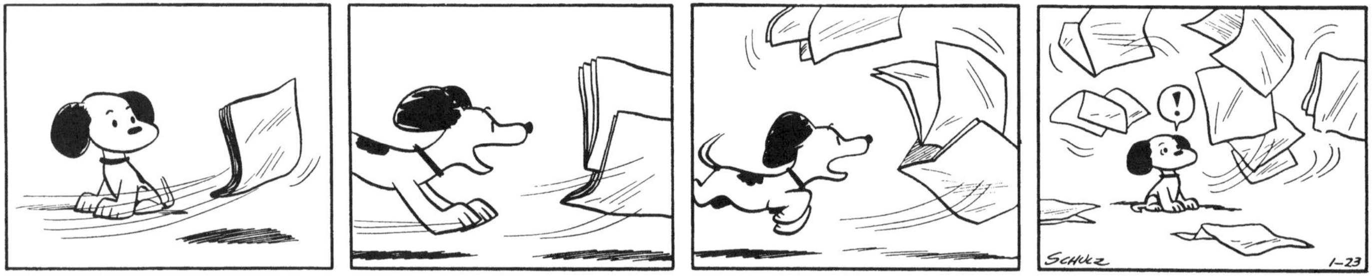
!
SCHULZ
1-23

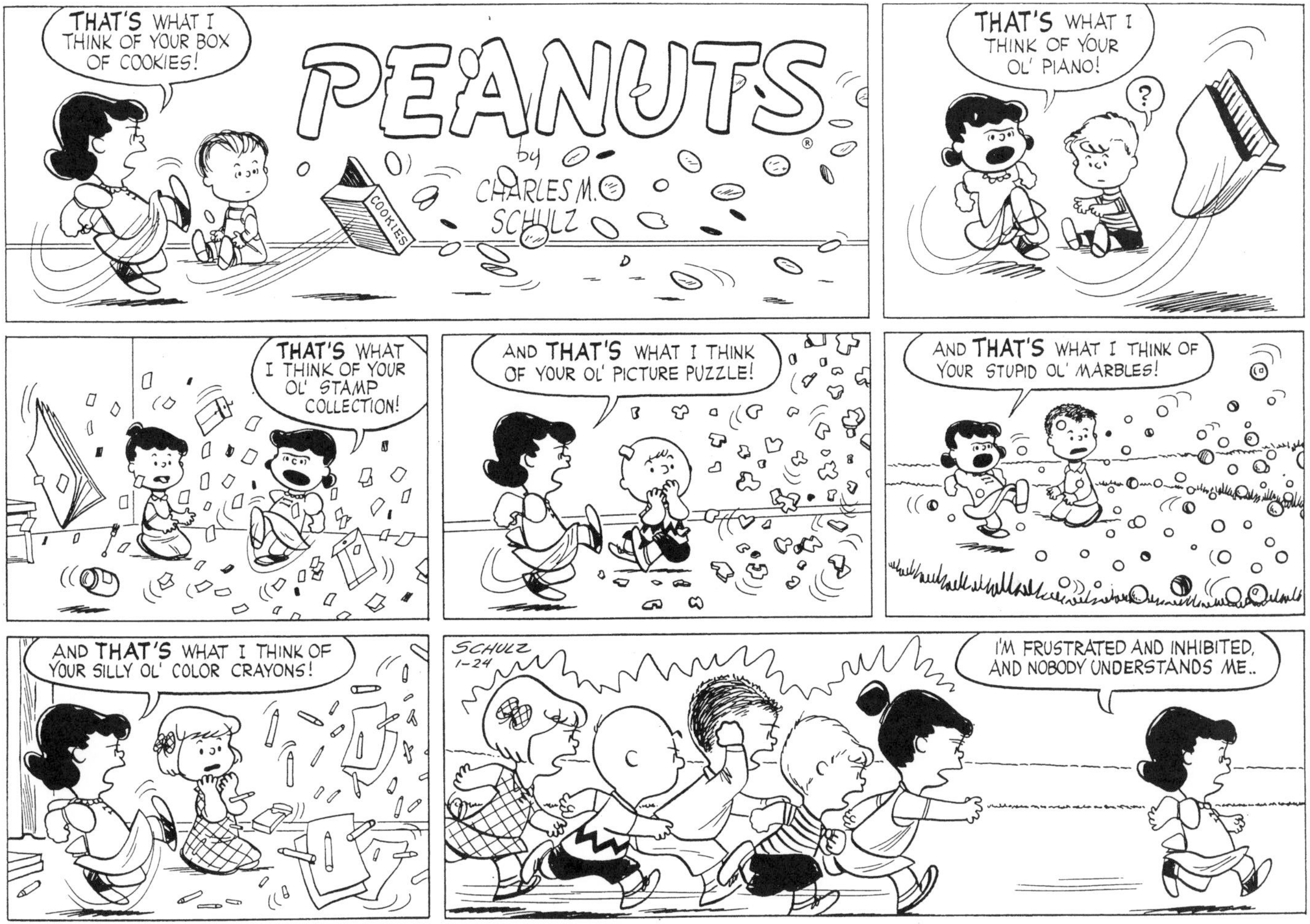
THAT'S WHAT I THINK OF YOUR BOX OF COOKIES!
PEANUTS
by CHARLES M. SCHULZ
COOKIES
THAT'S WHAT I THINK OF YOUR OL' PIANO!
?
THAT'S WHAT I THINK OF YOUR OL' STAMP COLLECTION!
AND THAT'S WHAT I THINK OF YOUR OL' PICTURE PUZZLE!
AND THAT'S WHAT I THINK OF YOUR STUPID OL' MARBLES!
AND THAT'S WHAT I THINK OF YOUR SILLY OL' COLOR CRAYONS!
SCHULZ 1-24
I'M FRUSTRATED AND INHIBITED, AND NOBODY UNDERSTANDS ME..

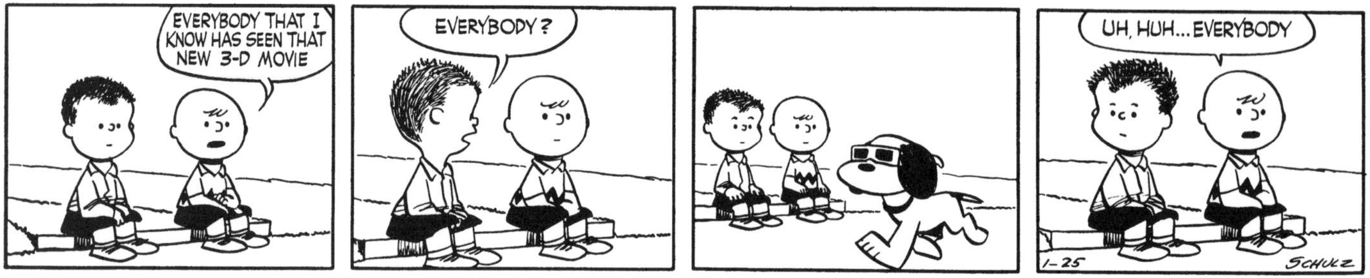
EVERYBODY THAT I KNOW HAS SEEN THAT NEW 3-D MOVIE
EVERYBODY?
UH, HUH...EVERYBODY
1-25
SCHULZ

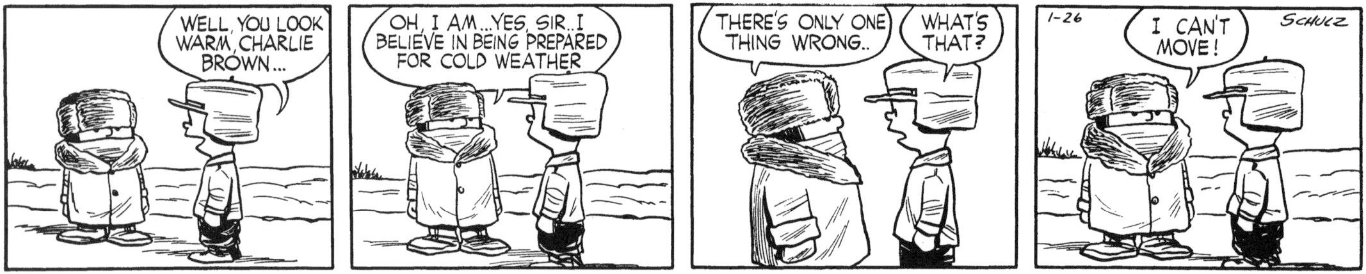
WELL, YOU LOOK WARM, CHARLIE BROWN...
OH, I AM...YES, SIR..I BELIEVE IN BEING PREPARED FOR COLD WEATHER
THERE'S ONLY ONE THING WRONG..
WHAT'S THAT?
1-26
SCHULZ
I CAN'T MOVE!

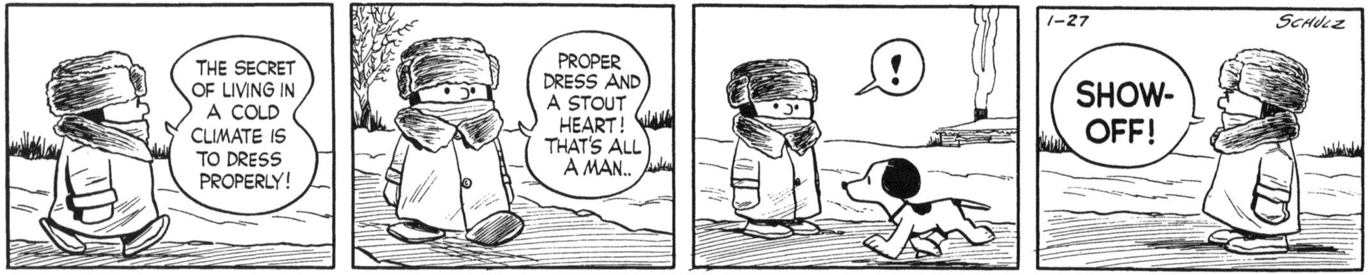
THE SECRET OF LIVING IN A COLD CLIMATE IS TO DRESS PROPERLY!
PROPER DRESS AND A STOUT HEART! THAT'S ALL A MAN..
!
1-27
SCHULZ
SHOW-OFF!

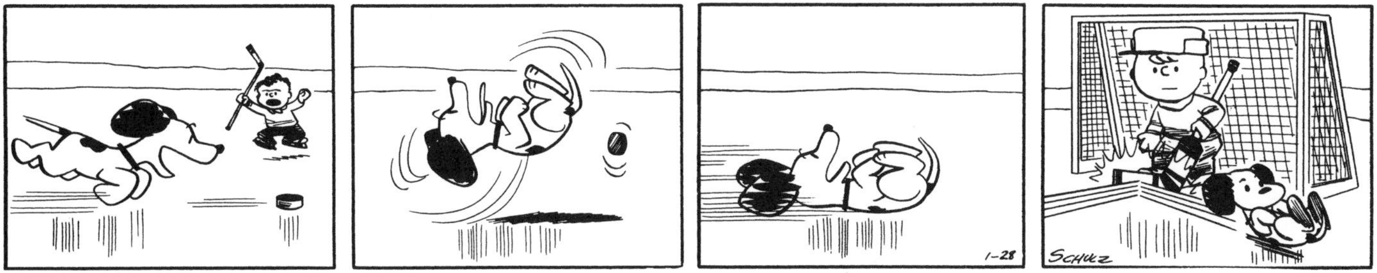
1-28
SCHULZ

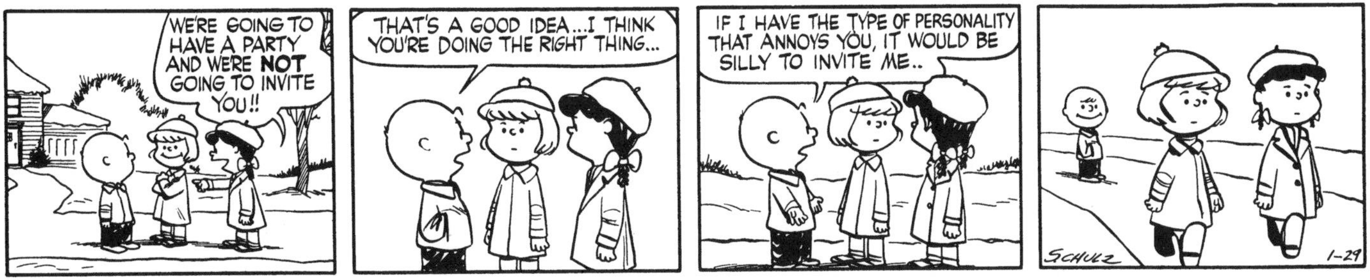
WE'RE GOING TO HAVE A PARTY AND WE'RE **NOT** GOING TO INVITE YOU!!
THAT'S A GOOD IDEA...I THINK YOU'RE DOING THE RIGHT THING...
IF I HAVE THE TYPE OF PERSONALITY THAT ANNOYS YOU, IT WOULD BE SILLY TO INVITE ME..
SCHULZ
1-29

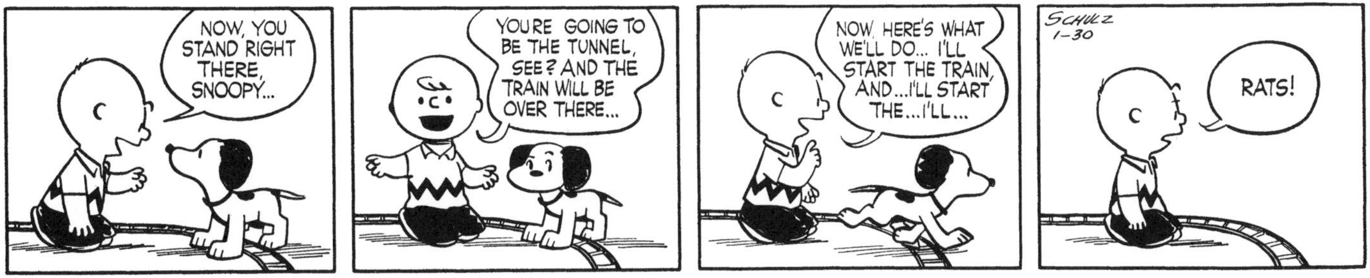
NOW, YOU STAND RIGHT THERE, SNOOPY...
YOU'RE GOING TO BE THE TUNNEL, SEE? AND THE TRAIN WILL BE OVER THERE...
NOW, HERE'S WHAT WE'LL DO... I'LL START THE TRAIN, AND...I'LL START THE...I'LL...
SCHULZ
1-30
RATS!

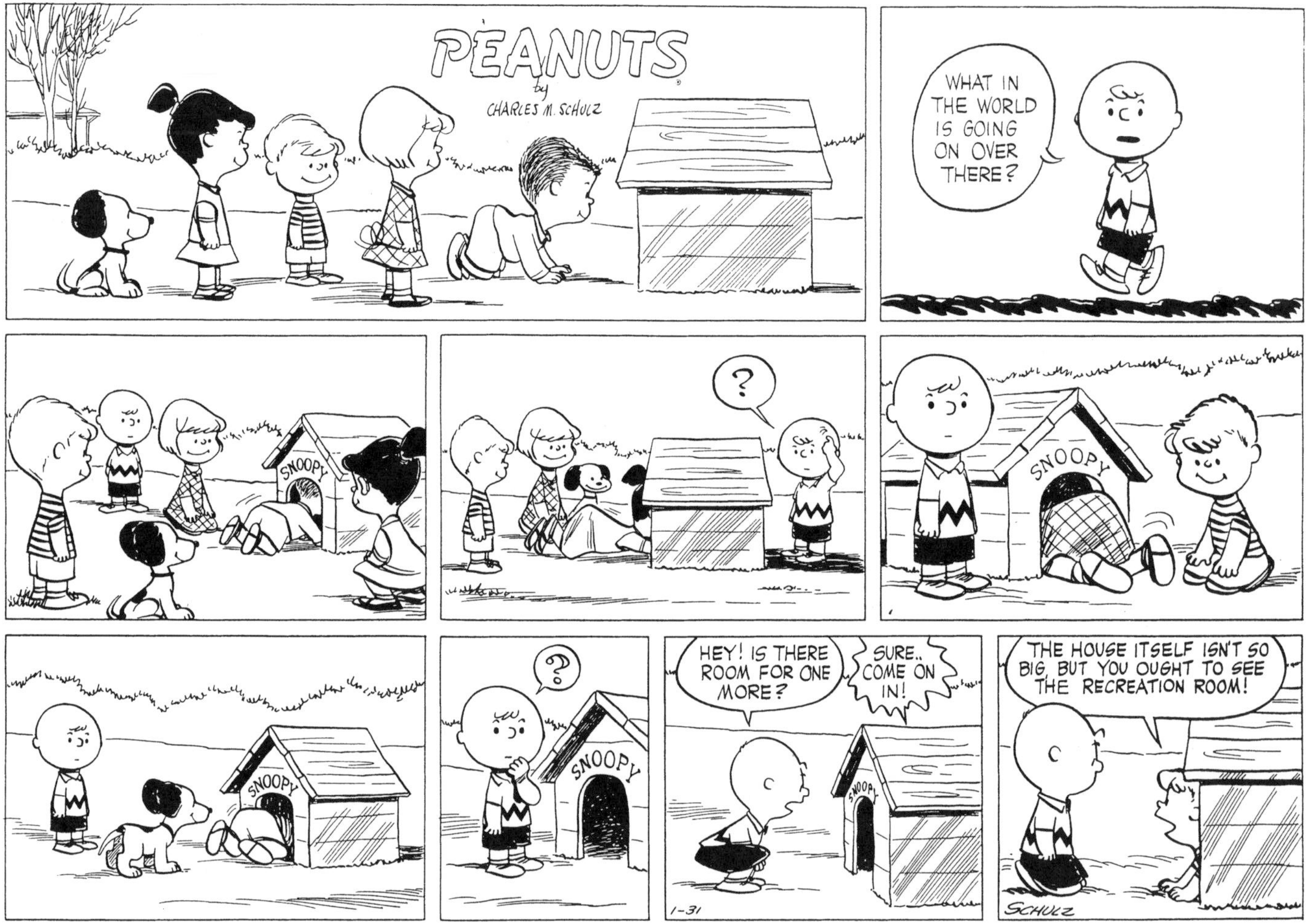
PEANUTS
by
CHARLES M. SCHULZ
WHAT IN THE WORLD IS GOING ON OVER THERE?
?
SNOOPY
?
HEY! IS THERE ROOM FOR ONE MORE?
SURE.. COME ON IN!
THE HOUSE ITSELF ISN'T SO BIG, BUT YOU OUGHT TO SEE THE RECREATION ROOM!
1-31
SCHULZ

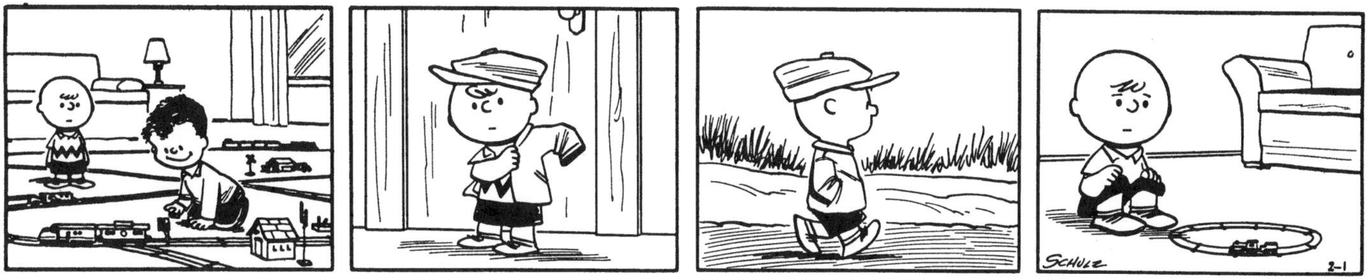
SCHULZ
2-1

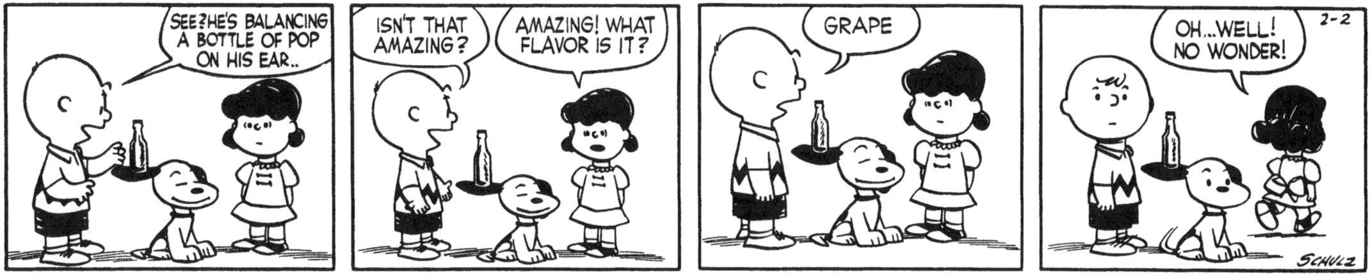
SEE? HE'S BALANCING A BOTTLE OF POP ON HIS EAR..
ISN'T THAT AMAZING?
AMAZING! WHAT FLAVOR IS IT?
GRAPE
2-2
OH...WELL! NO WONDER!
SCHULZ

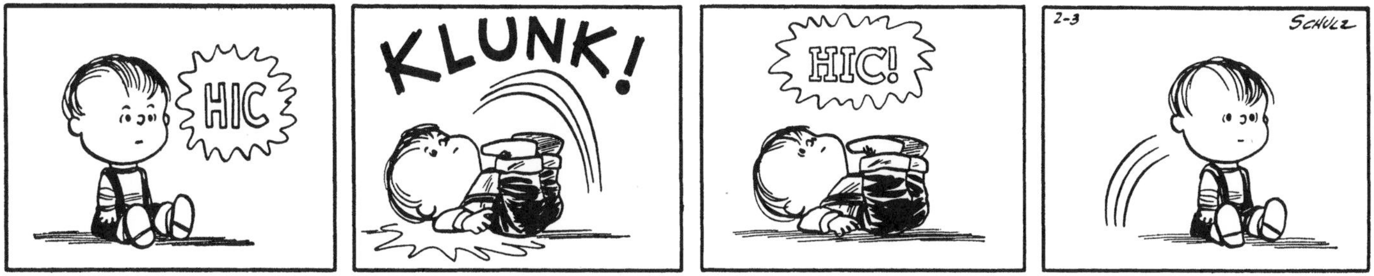
HIC
KLUNK!
HIC!
2-3
SCHULZ

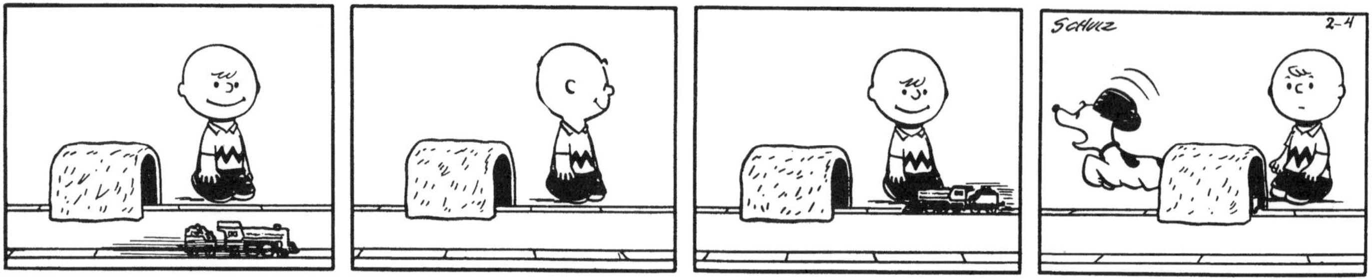
SCHULZ
2-4

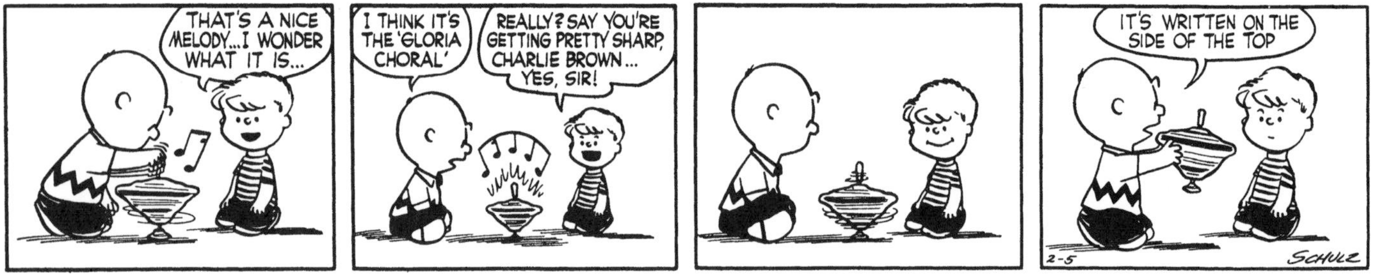
THAT'S A NICE MELODY...I WONDER WHAT IT IS...
I THINK IT'S THE 'GLORIA CHORAL'
REALLY? SAY YOU'RE GETTING PRETTY SHARP, CHARLIE BROWN... YES, SIR!
IT'S WRITTEN ON THE SIDE OF THE TOP
2-5
SCHULZ

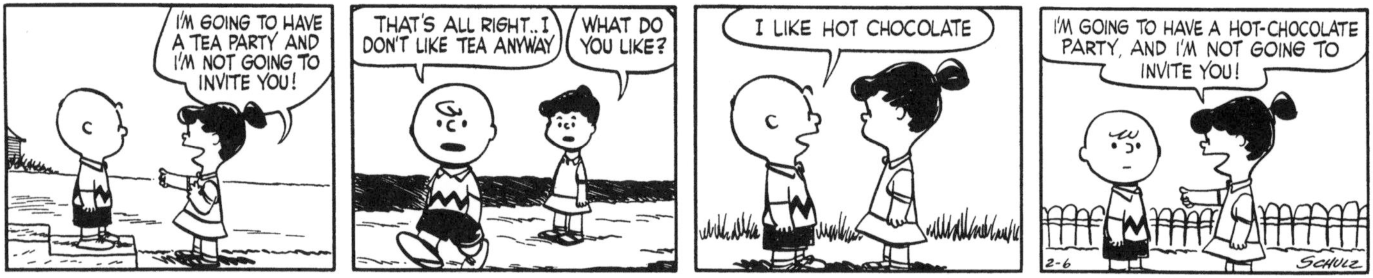
I'M GOING TO HAVE A TEA PARTY AND I'M NOT GOING TO INVITE YOU!
THAT'S ALL RIGHT..I DON'T LIKE TEA ANYWAY
WHAT DO YOU LIKE?
I LIKE HOT CHOCOLATE
I'M GOING TO HAVE A HOT-CHOCOLATE PARTY, AND I'M NOT GOING TO INVITE YOU!
2-6
SCHULZ

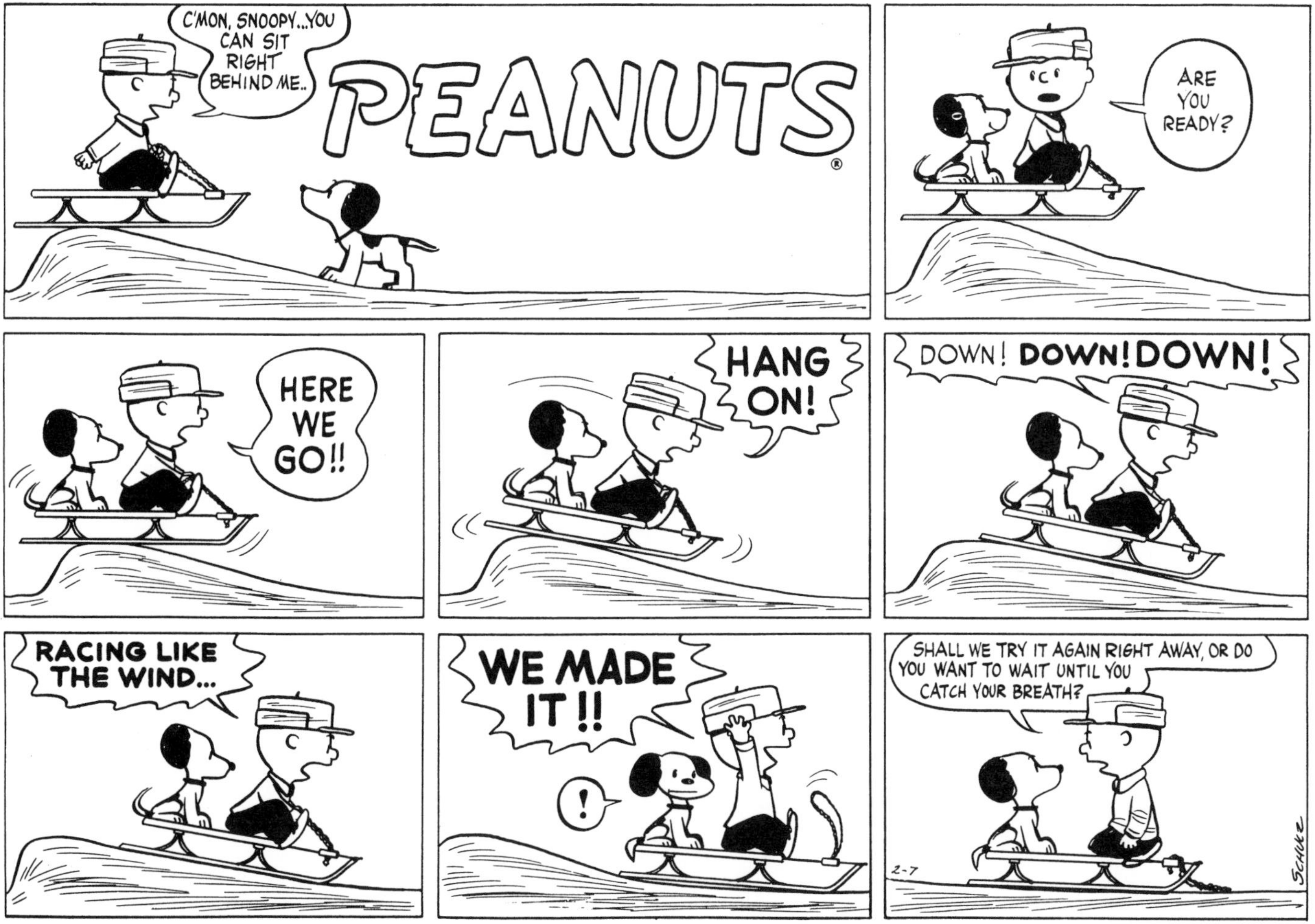
C'MON, SNOOPY...YOU CAN SIT RIGHT BEHIND ME..
PEANUTS
ARE YOU READY?
HERE WE GO!!
HANG ON!
DOWN! DOWN! DOWN!
RACING LIKE THE WIND...
WE MADE IT!!
!
SHALL WE TRY IT AGAIN RIGHT AWAY, OR DO YOU WANT TO WAIT UNTIL YOU CATCH YOUR BREATH?
2-7
SCHULZ

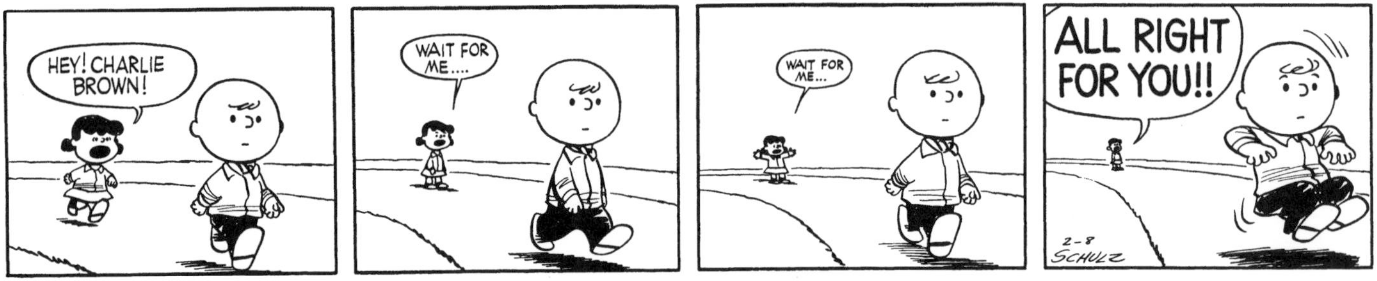
HEY! CHARLIE BROWN!
WAIT FOR ME....
WAIT FOR ME...
ALL RIGHT FOR YOU!!
2-8
SCHULZ

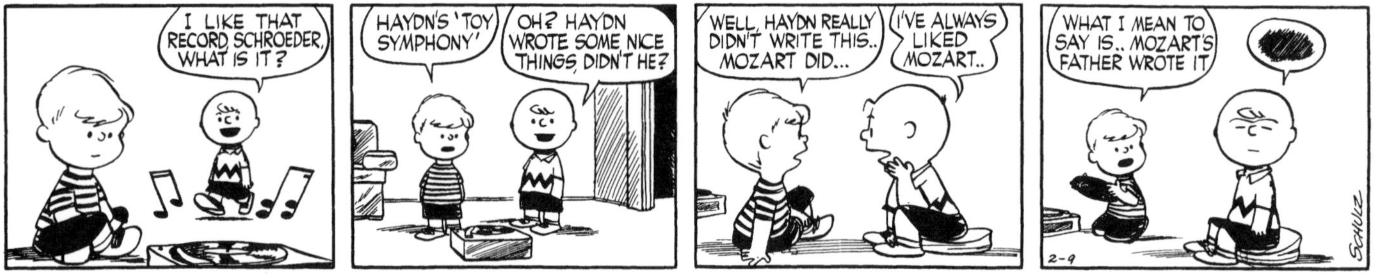
I LIKE THAT RECORD, SCHROEDER, WHAT IS IT?
HAYDN'S 'TOY SYMPHONY'
OH? HAYDN WROTE SOME NICE THINGS, DIDN'T HE?
WELL, HAYDN REALLY DIDN'T WRITE THIS.. MOZART DID...
I'VE ALWAYS LIKED MOZART..
WHAT I MEAN TO SAY IS.. MOZART'S FATHER WROTE IT
2-9
SCHULZ

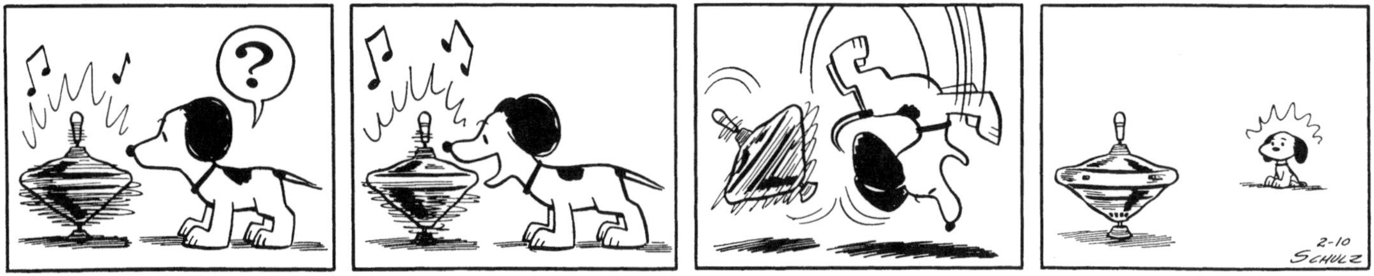
?
2-10
SCHULZ

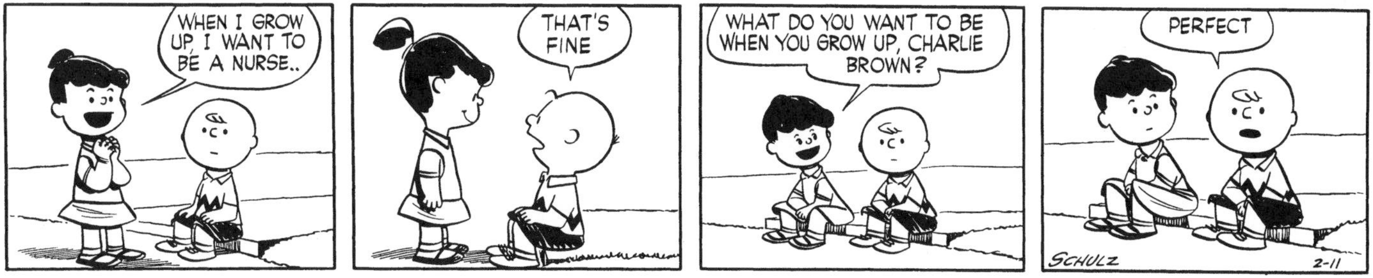
WHEN I GROW UP, I WANT TO BE A NURSE..
THAT'S FINE
WHAT DO YOU WANT TO BE WHEN YOU GROW UP, CHARLIE BROWN?
PERFECT
SCHULZ
2-11

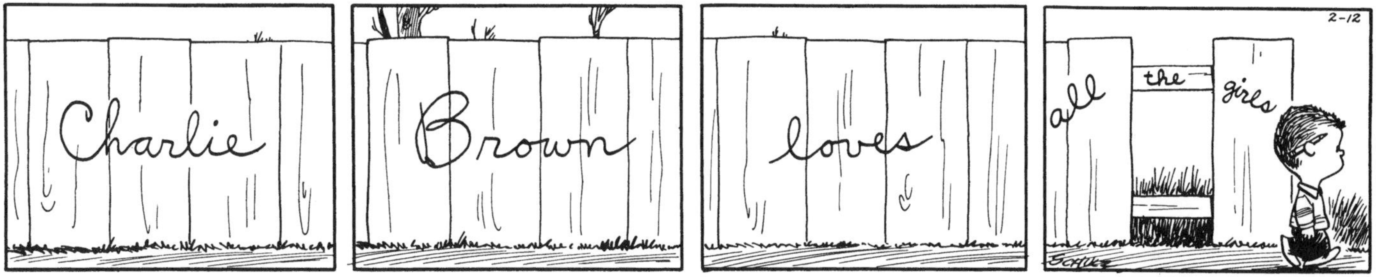
Charlie
Brown
loves
all
the
girls
2-12
SCHULZ

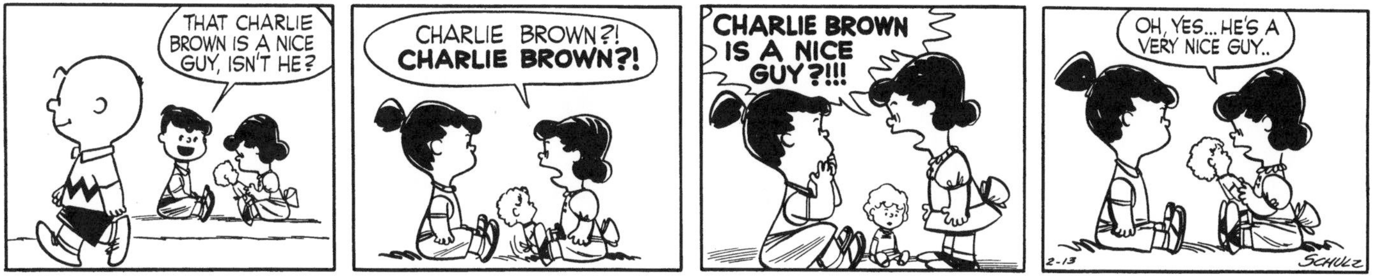
THAT CHARLIE BROWN IS A NICE GUY, ISN'T HE?
CHARLIE BROWN?! CHARLIE BROWN?!
CHARLIE BROWN IS A NICE GUY?!!!
OH, YES... HE'S A VERY NICE GUY..
2-13
SCHULZ

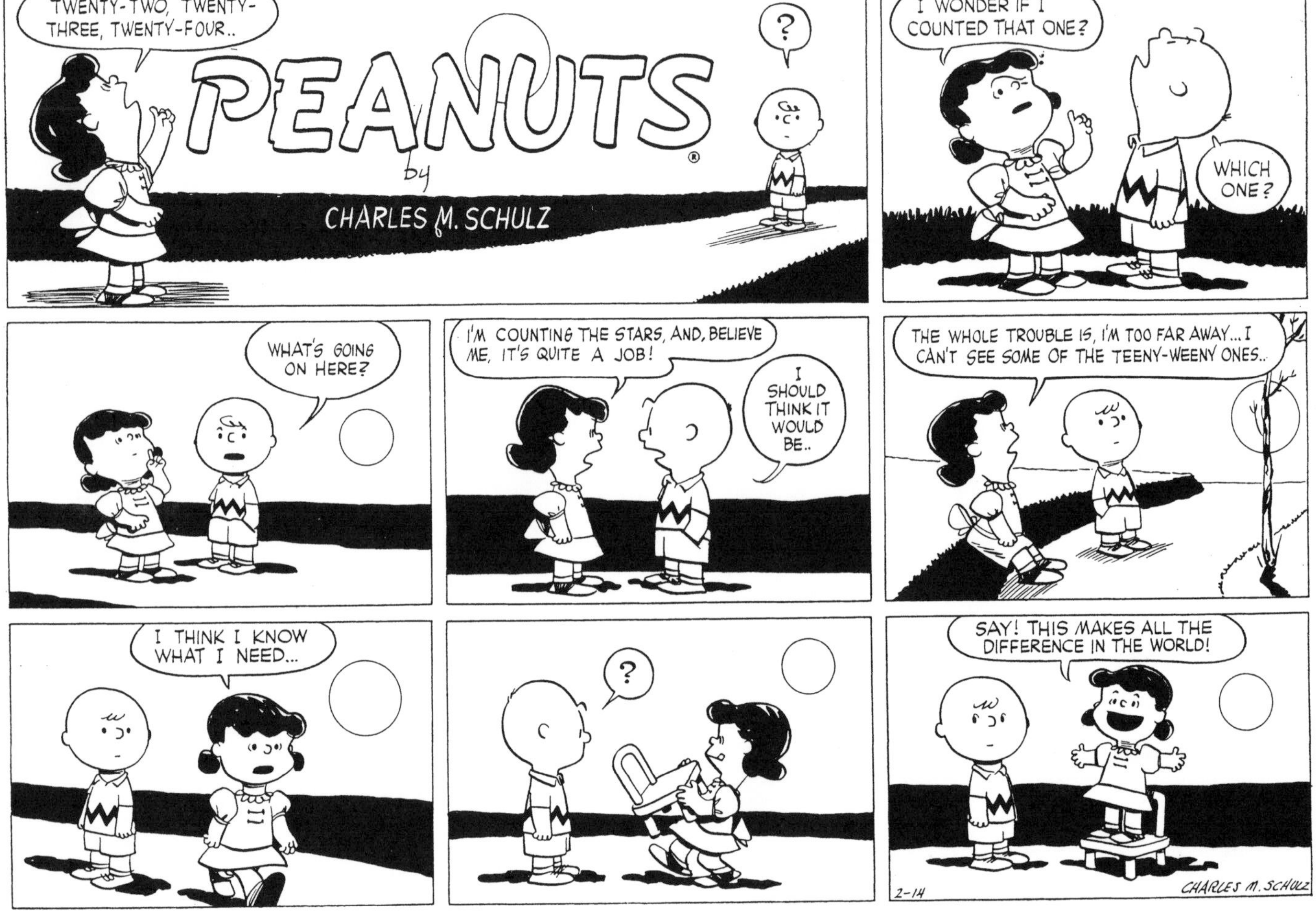
TWENTY-TWO, TWENTY-THREE, TWENTY-FOUR..
PEANUTS
by
CHARLES M. SCHULZ
?
I WONDER IF I COUNTED THAT ONE?
WHICH ONE?
WHAT'S GOING ON HERE?
I'M COUNTING THE STARS, AND, BELIEVE ME, IT'S QUITE A JOB!
I SHOULD THINK IT WOULD BE..
THE WHOLE TROUBLE IS, I'M TOO FAR AWAY... I CAN'T SEE SOME OF THE TEENY-WEENY ONES..
I THINK I KNOW WHAT I NEED...
?
SAY! THIS MAKES ALL THE DIFFERENCE IN THE WORLD!
2-14
CHARLES M. SCHULZ

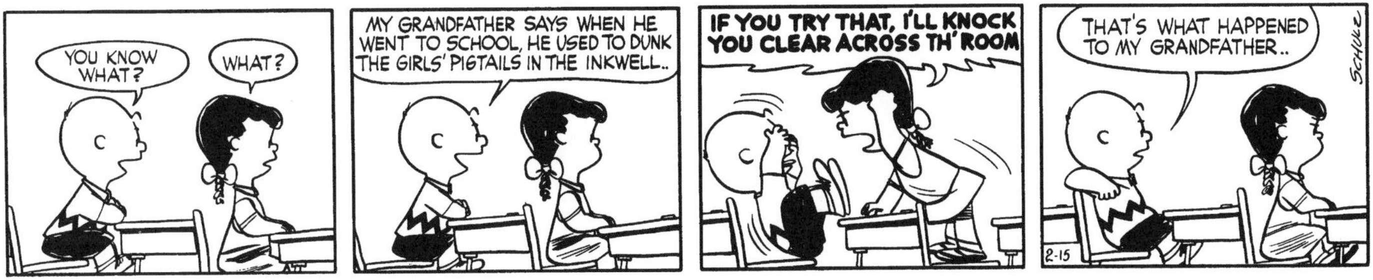
YOU KNOW WHAT?
WHAT?
MY GRANDFATHER SAYS WHEN HE WENT TO SCHOOL, HE USED TO DUNK THE GIRLS' PIGTAILS IN THE INKWELL..
IF YOU TRY THAT, I'LL KNOCK YOU CLEAR ACROSS TH' ROOM
THAT'S WHAT HAPPENED TO MY GRANDFATHER..
SCHULZ
2-15

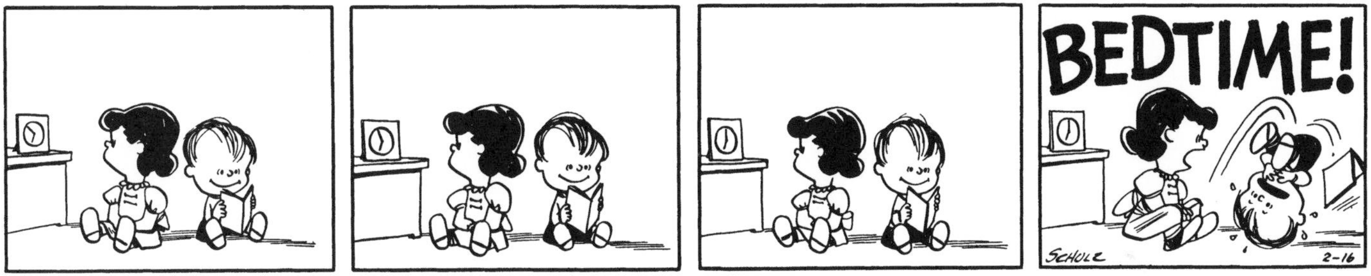
BEDTIME!
SCHULZ
2-16

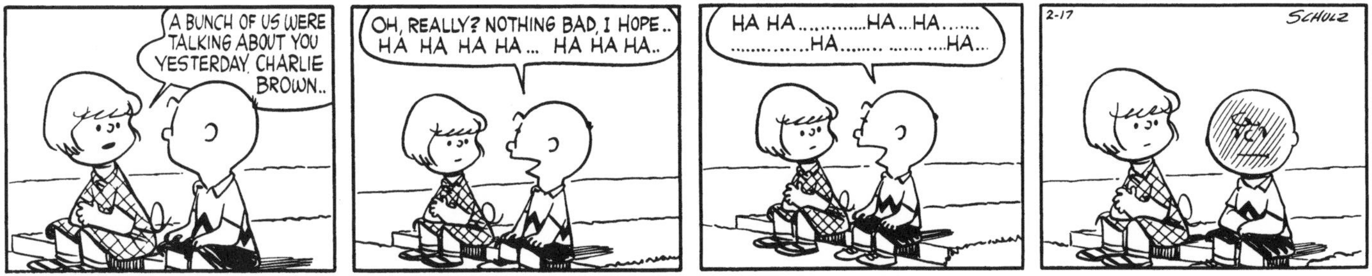
A BUNCH OF US WERE TALKING ABOUT YOU YESTERDAY, CHARLIE BROWN..
OH, REALLY? NOTHING BAD, I HOPE.. HA HA HA HA... HA HA HA..
HA HA.............HA...HA....... ....HA......... ....HA...
2-17
SCHULZ

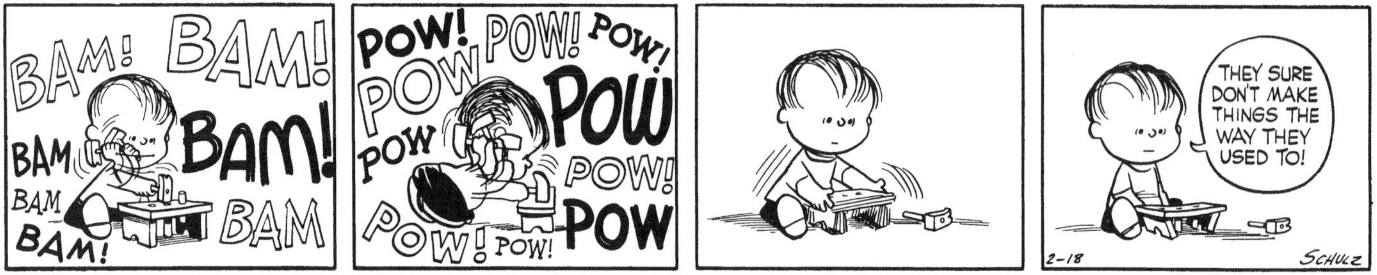
BAM! BAM!
BAM BAM!
BAM
BAM
BAM!
BAM
POW! POW! POW!
POW
POW
POW
POW!
POW! POW!
POW
THEY SURE DON'T MAKE THINGS THE WAY THEY USED TO!
2-18
SCHULZ

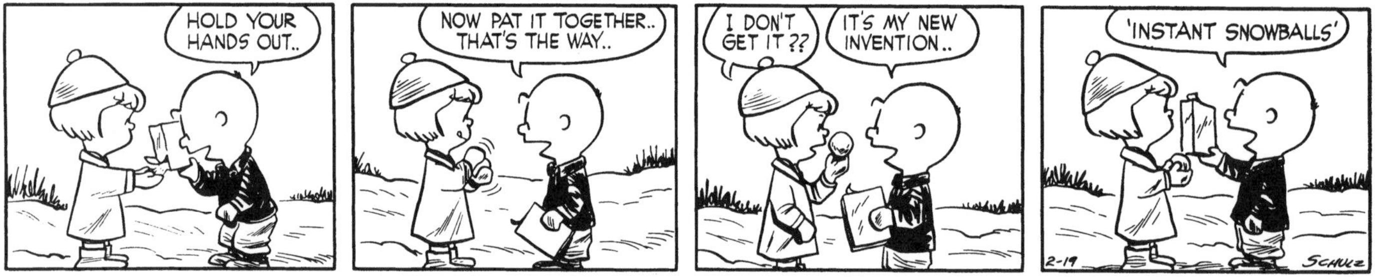
HOLD YOUR HANDS OUT..
NOW PAT IT TOGETHER.. THAT'S THE WAY..
I DON'T GET IT ??
IT'S MY NEW INVENTION..
'INSTANT SNOWBALLS'
2-19
SCHULZ

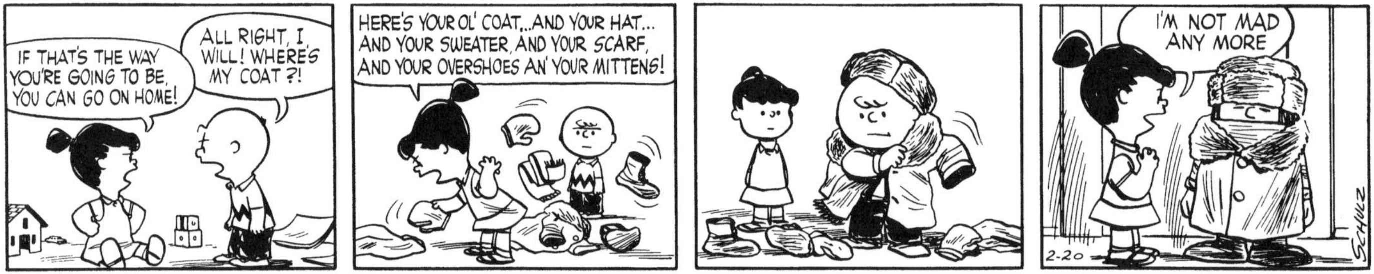
IF THAT'S THE WAY YOU'RE GOING TO BE, YOU CAN GO ON HOME!
ALL RIGHT, I WILL! WHERE'S MY COAT ?!
HERE'S YOUR OL' COAT...AND YOUR HAT... AND YOUR SWEATER, AND YOUR SCARF, AND YOUR OVERSHOES AN' YOUR MITTENS!
I'M NOT MAD ANY MORE
2-20
SCHULZ

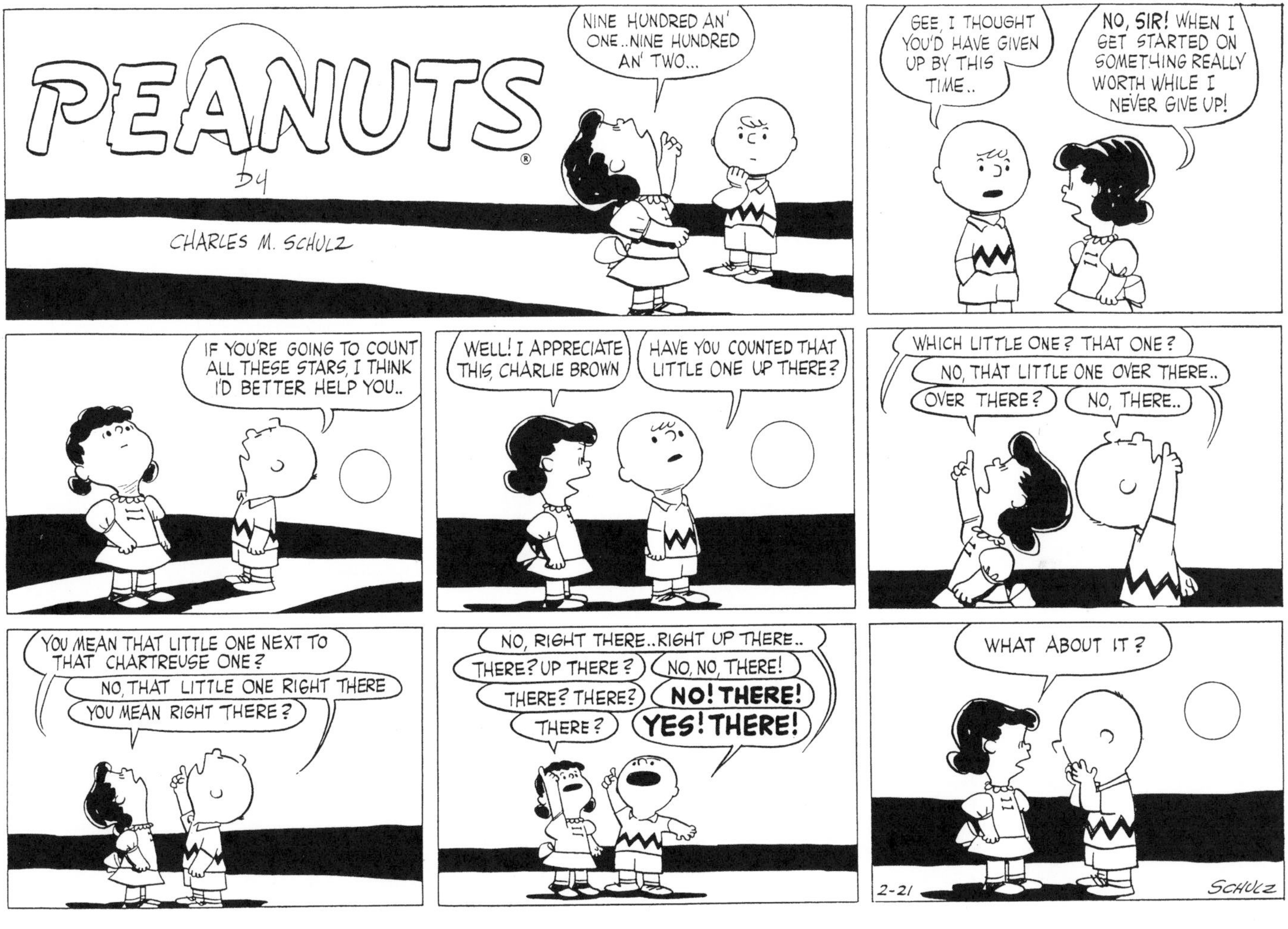
PEANUTS
by
CHARLES M. SCHULZ
NINE HUNDRED AN' ONE..NINE HUNDRED AN' TWO...
GEE, I THOUGHT YOU'D HAVE GIVEN UP BY THIS TIME..
NO, SIR! WHEN I GET STARTED ON SOMETHING REALLY WORTH WHILE I NEVER GIVE UP!
IF YOU'RE GOING TO COUNT ALL THESE STARS, I THINK I'D BETTER HELP YOU..
WELL! I APPRECIATE THIS, CHARLIE BROWN
HAVE YOU COUNTED THAT LITTLE ONE UP THERE?
WHICH LITTLE ONE? THAT ONE?
NO, THAT LITTLE ONE OVER THERE..
OVER THERE?
NO, THERE..
YOU MEAN THAT LITTLE ONE NEXT TO THAT CHARTREUSE ONE?
NO, THAT LITTLE ONE RIGHT THERE
YOU MEAN RIGHT THERE?
NO, RIGHT THERE..RIGHT UP THERE..
THERE? UP THERE?
NO, NO, THERE!
THERE? THERE?
NO! THERE!
THERE?
YES! THERE!
WHAT ABOUT IT?
2-21
SCHULZ

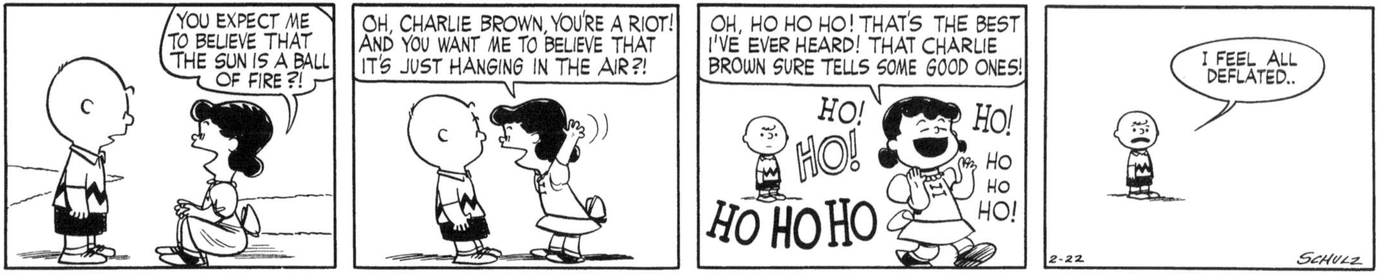
YOU EXPECT ME TO BELIEVE THAT THE SUN IS A BALL OF FIRE?!
OH, CHARLIE BROWN, YOU'RE A RIOT! AND YOU WANT ME TO BELIEVE THAT IT'S JUST HANGING IN THE AIR?!
OH, HO HO HO! THAT'S THE BEST I'VE EVER HEARD! THAT CHARLIE BROWN SURE TELLS SOME GOOD ONES!
HO! HO! HO HO HO HO! HO HO HO!
I FEEL ALL DEFLATED..
2-22
SCHULZ

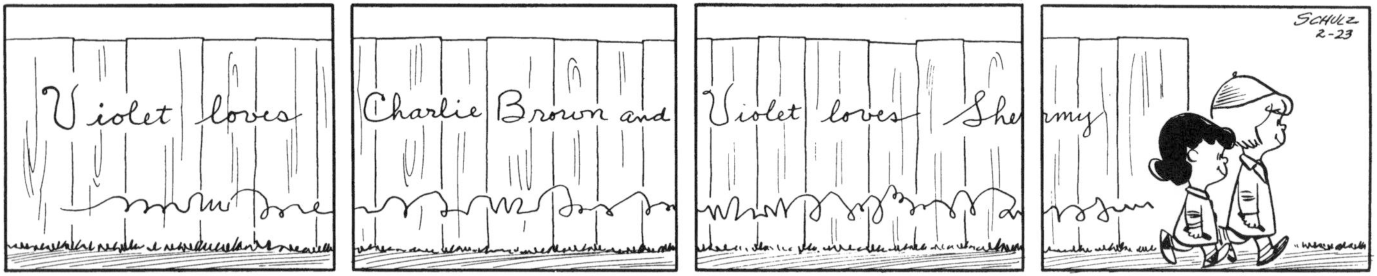
Violet loves
Charlie Brown and
Violet loves She
rmy
SCHULZ 2-23

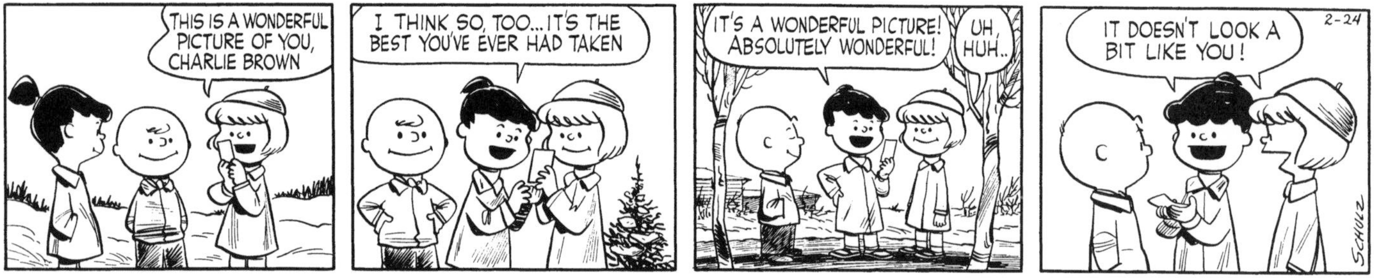
THIS IS A WONDERFUL PICTURE OF YOU, CHARLIE BROWN
I THINK SO, TOO... IT'S THE BEST YOU'VE EVER HAD TAKEN
IT'S A WONDERFUL PICTURE! ABSOLUTELY WONDERFUL!
UH, HUH..
IT DOESN'T LOOK A BIT LIKE YOU!
2-24
SCHULZ

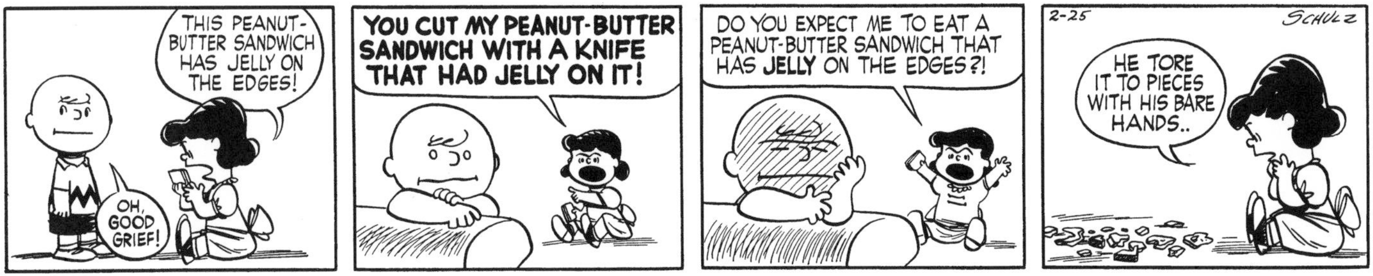
THIS PEANUT-BUTTER SANDWICH HAS JELLY ON THE EDGES!
OH, GOOD GRIEF!
YOU CUT MY PEANUT-BUTTER SANDWICH WITH A KNIFE THAT HAD JELLY ON IT!
DO YOU EXPECT ME TO EAT A PEANUT-BUTTER SANDWICH THAT HAS JELLY ON THE EDGES?!
2-25
SCHULZ
HE TORE IT TO PIECES WITH HIS BARE HANDS..

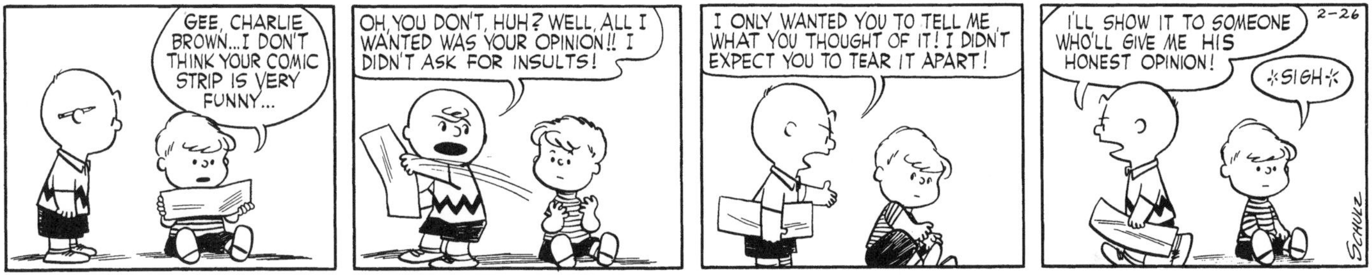
GEE, CHARLIE BROWN...I DON'T THINK YOUR COMIC STRIP IS VERY FUNNY...
OH, YOU DON'T, HUH? WELL, ALL I WANTED WAS YOUR OPINION!! I DIDN'T ASK FOR INSULTS!
I ONLY WANTED YOU TO TELL ME WHAT YOU THOUGHT OF IT! I DIDN'T EXPECT YOU TO TEAR IT APART!
2-26
I'LL SHOW IT TO SOMEONE WHO'LL GIVE ME HIS HONEST OPINION!
SIGH
SCHULZ

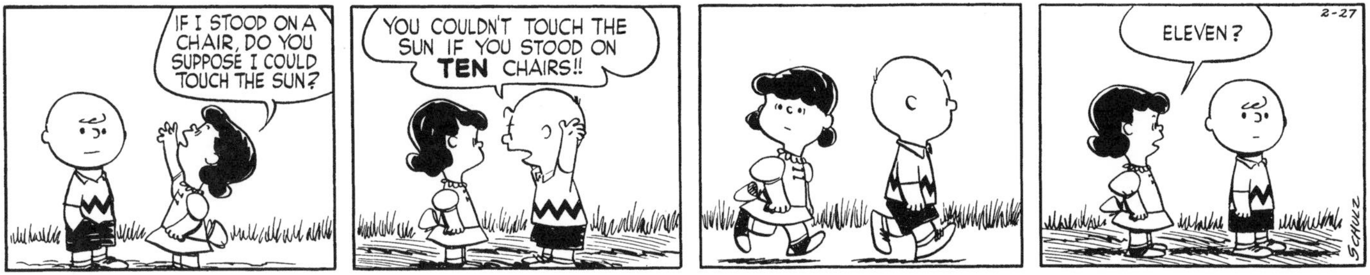
IF I STOOD ON A CHAIR, DO YOU SUPPOSE I COULD TOUCH THE SUN?
YOU COULDN'T TOUCH THE SUN IF YOU STOOD ON TEN CHAIRS!!
2-27
ELEVEN?
SCHULZ

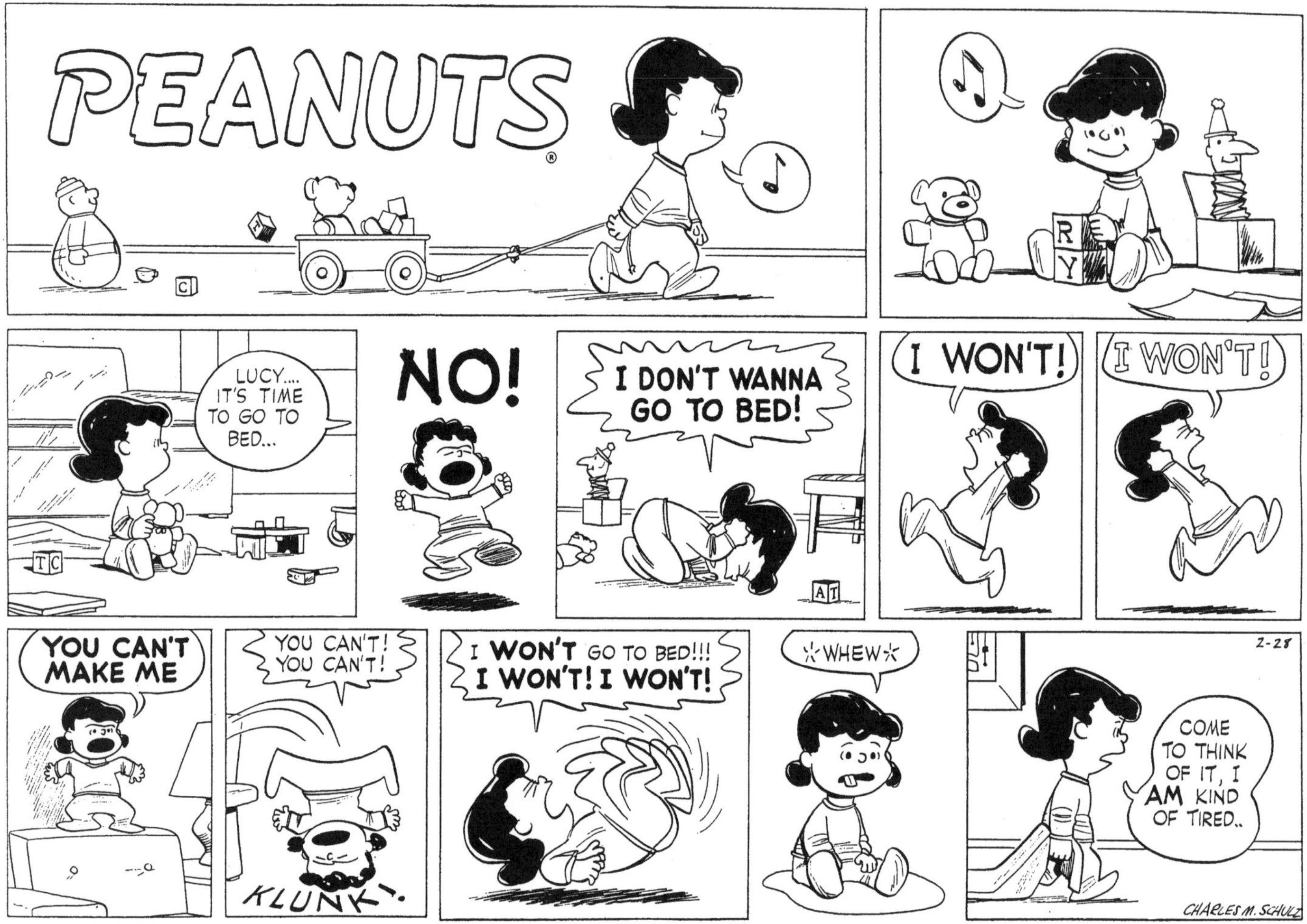
PEANUTS
♪
♪
R
Y
TC
LUCY.... IT'S TIME TO GO TO BED...
NO!
I DON'T WANNA GO TO BED!
AT
I WON'T!
I WON'T!
YOU CAN'T MAKE ME
YOU CAN'T! YOU CAN'T!
KLUNK!
I WON'T GO TO BED!!! I WON'T! I WON'T!
WHEW
2-28
COME TO THINK OF IT, I AM KIND OF TIRED..
CHARLES M. SCHULZ

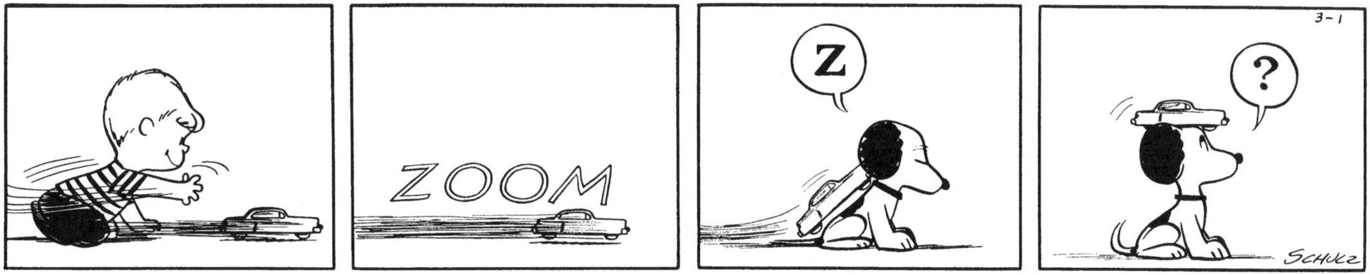
ZOOM
Z
3-1
?
SCHULZ

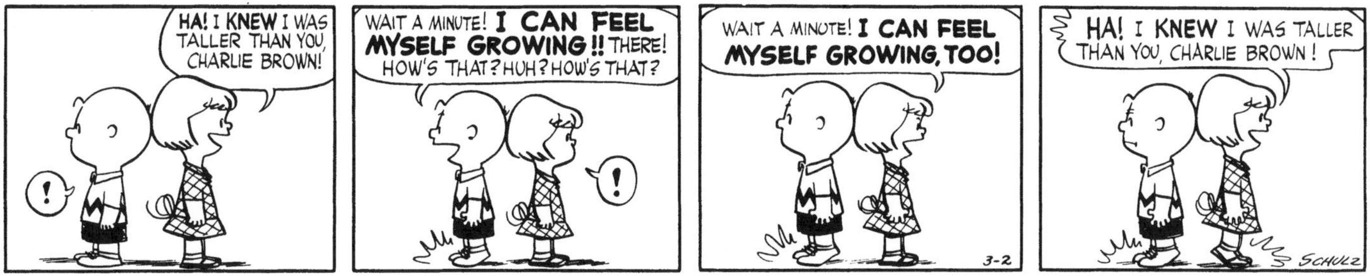
HA! I KNEW I WAS TALLER THAN YOU, CHARLIE BROWN!
!
WAIT A MINUTE! I CAN FEEL MYSELF GROWING!! THERE! HOW'S THAT? HUH? HOW'S THAT?
!
WAIT A MINUTE! I CAN FEEL MYSELF GROWING, TOO!
3-2
HA! I KNEW I WAS TALLER THAN YOU, CHARLIE BROWN!
SCHULZ

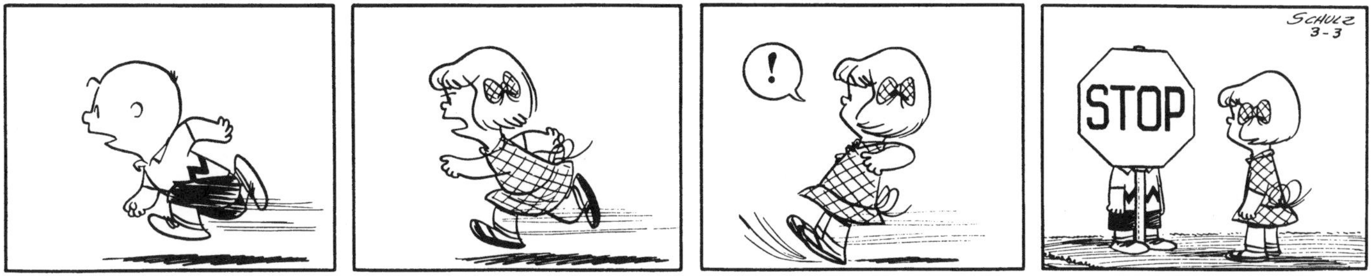
!
SCHULZ
3-3
STOP

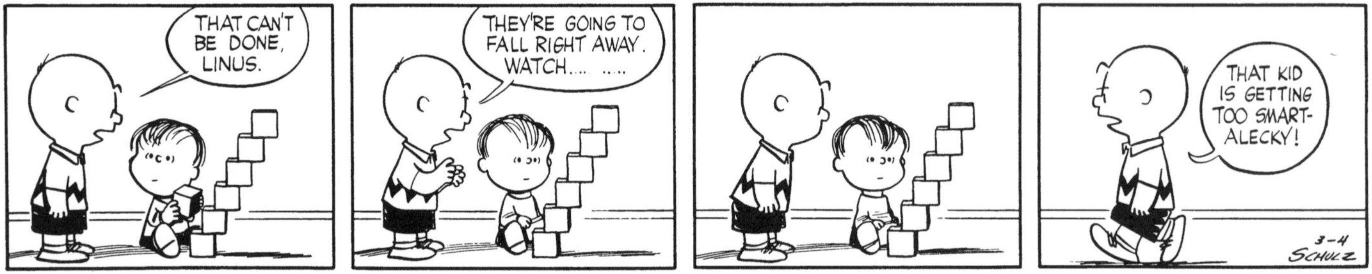
THAT CAN'T BE DONE, LINUS.
THEY'RE GOING TO FALL RIGHT AWAY. WATCH..... .....
THAT KID IS GETTING TOO SMART-ALECKY!
3-4
SCHULZ

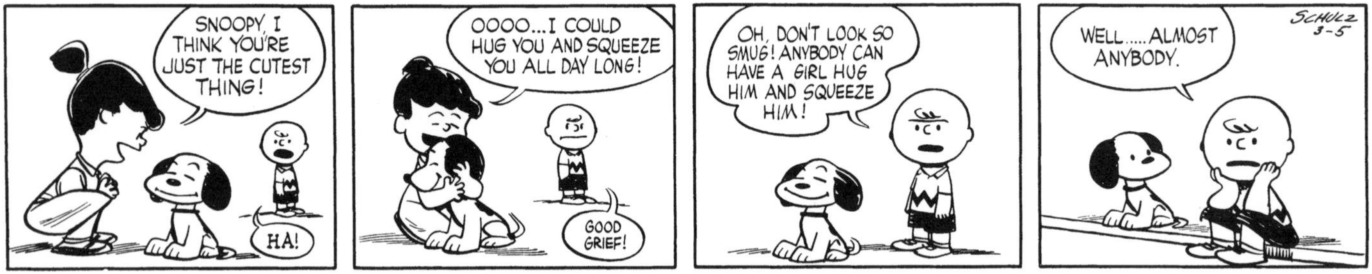
SNOOPY, I THINK YOU'RE JUST THE CUTEST THING!
HA!
OOOO...I COULD HUG YOU AND SQUEEZE YOU ALL DAY LONG!
GOOD GRIEF!
OH, DON'T LOOK SO SMUG! ANYBODY CAN HAVE A GIRL HUG HIM AND SQUEEZE HIM!
SCHULZ
3-5
WELL.....ALMOST ANYBODY.

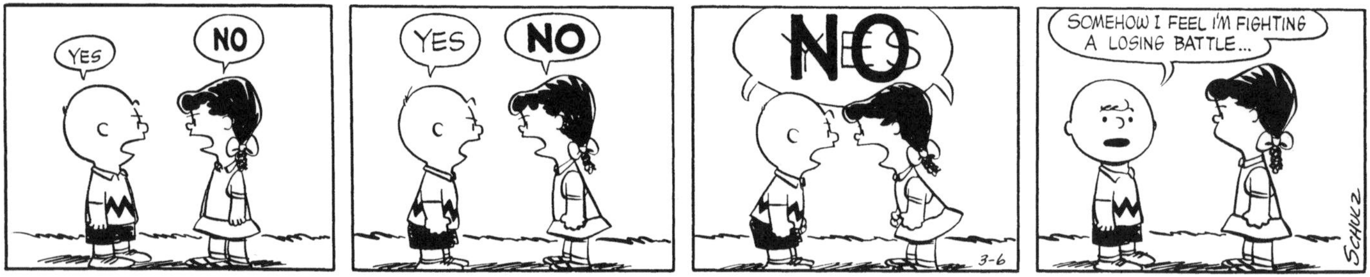
YES
NO
YES
NO
NO
3-6
SOMEHOW I FEEL I'M FIGHTING A LOSING BATTLE...
SCHULZ

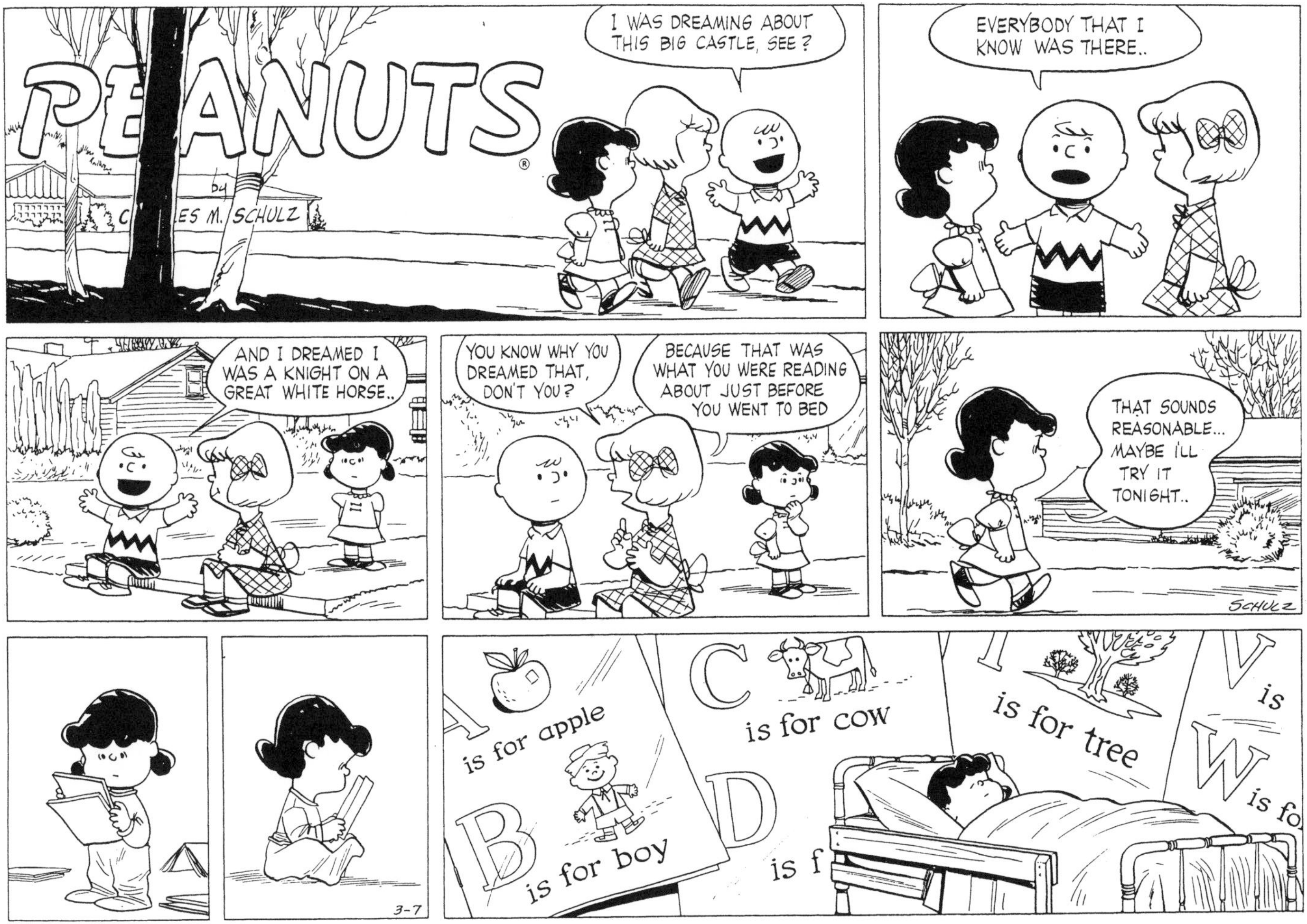
PEANUTS
by CHARLES M. SCHULZ
I WAS DREAMING ABOUT THIS BIG CASTLE, SEE?
EVERYBODY THAT I KNOW WAS THERE..
AND I DREAMED I WAS A KNIGHT ON A GREAT WHITE HORSE..
YOU KNOW WHY YOU DREAMED THAT, DON'T YOU?
BECAUSE THAT WAS WHAT YOU WERE READING ABOUT JUST BEFORE YOU WENT TO BED
THAT SOUNDS REASONABLE... MAYBE I'LL TRY IT TONIGHT..
SCHULZ
3-7
is for apple
B is for boy
C is for cow
D is f
is for tree
V is
W is fo

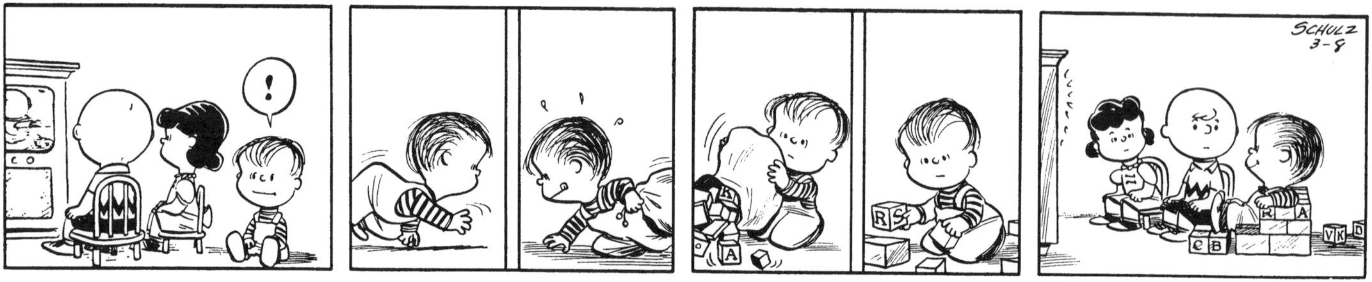
!
SCHULZ 3-8

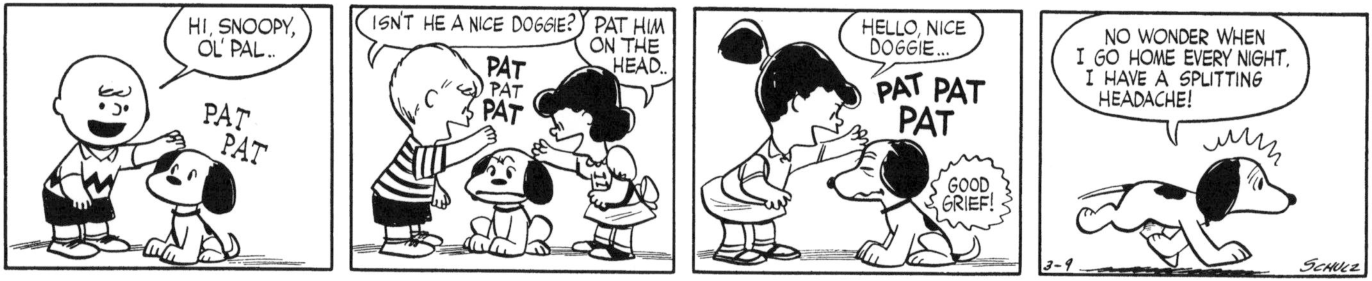
HI, SNOOPY, OL' PAL..
PAT PAT
ISN'T HE A NICE DOGGIE?
PAT PAT PAT
PAT HIM ON THE HEAD..
HELLO, NICE DOGGIE...
PAT PAT PAT
GOOD GRIEF!
NO WONDER WHEN I GO HOME EVERY NIGHT, I HAVE A SPLITTING HEADACHE!
3-9
SCHULZ

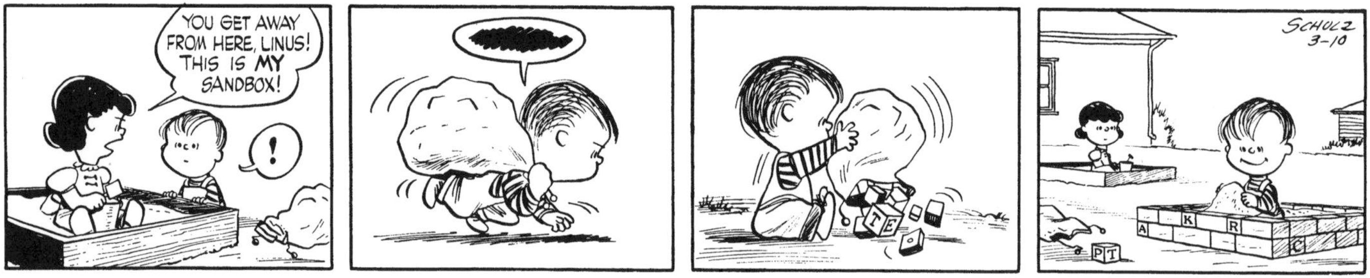
YOU GET AWAY FROM HERE, LINUS! THIS IS MY SANDBOX!
!
SCHULZ 3-10

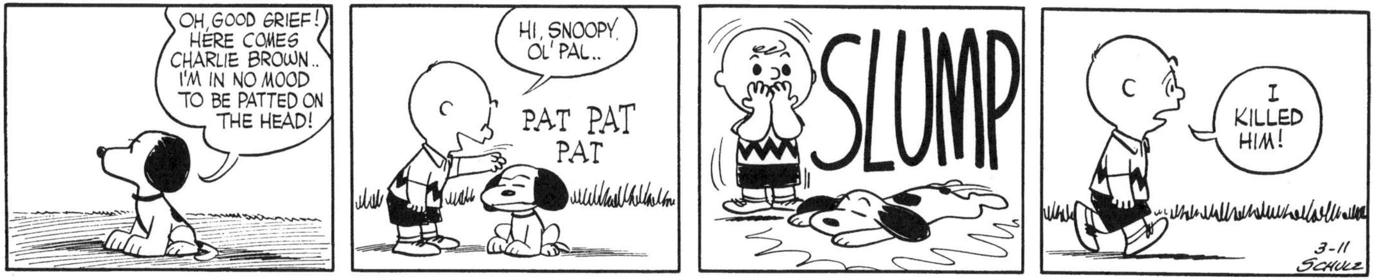
OH, GOOD GRIEF! HERE COMES CHARLIE BROWN.. I'M IN NO MOOD TO BE PATTED ON THE HEAD!
HI, SNOOPY, OL' PAL..
PAT PAT PAT
SLUMP
I KILLED HIM!
3-11
SCHULZ

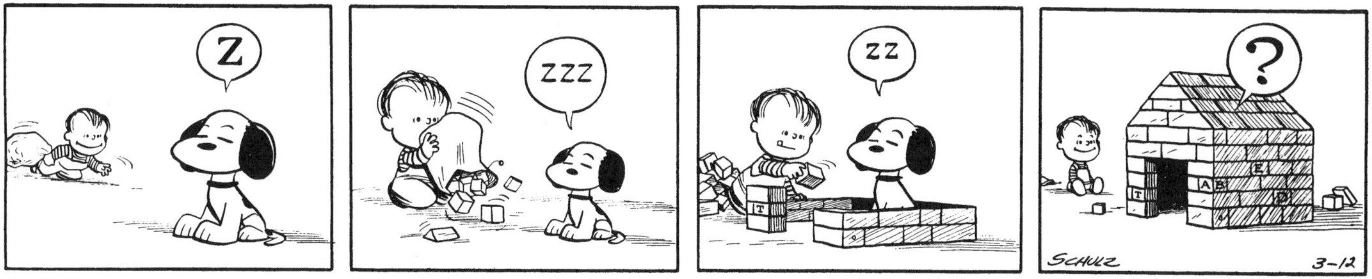
Z
ZZZ
ZZ
?
SCHULZ
3-12

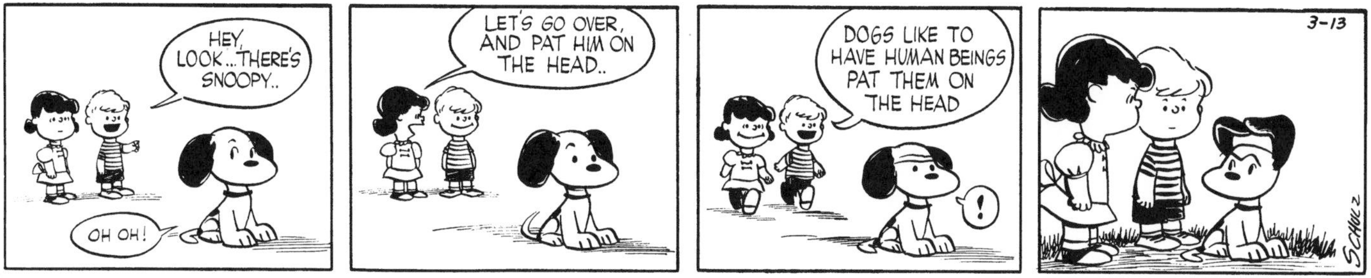
HEY, LOOK...THERE'S SNOOPY..
OH OH!
LET'S GO OVER, AND PAT HIM ON THE HEAD..
DOGS LIKE TO HAVE HUMAN BEINGS PAT THEM ON THE HEAD
!
3-13
SCHULZ

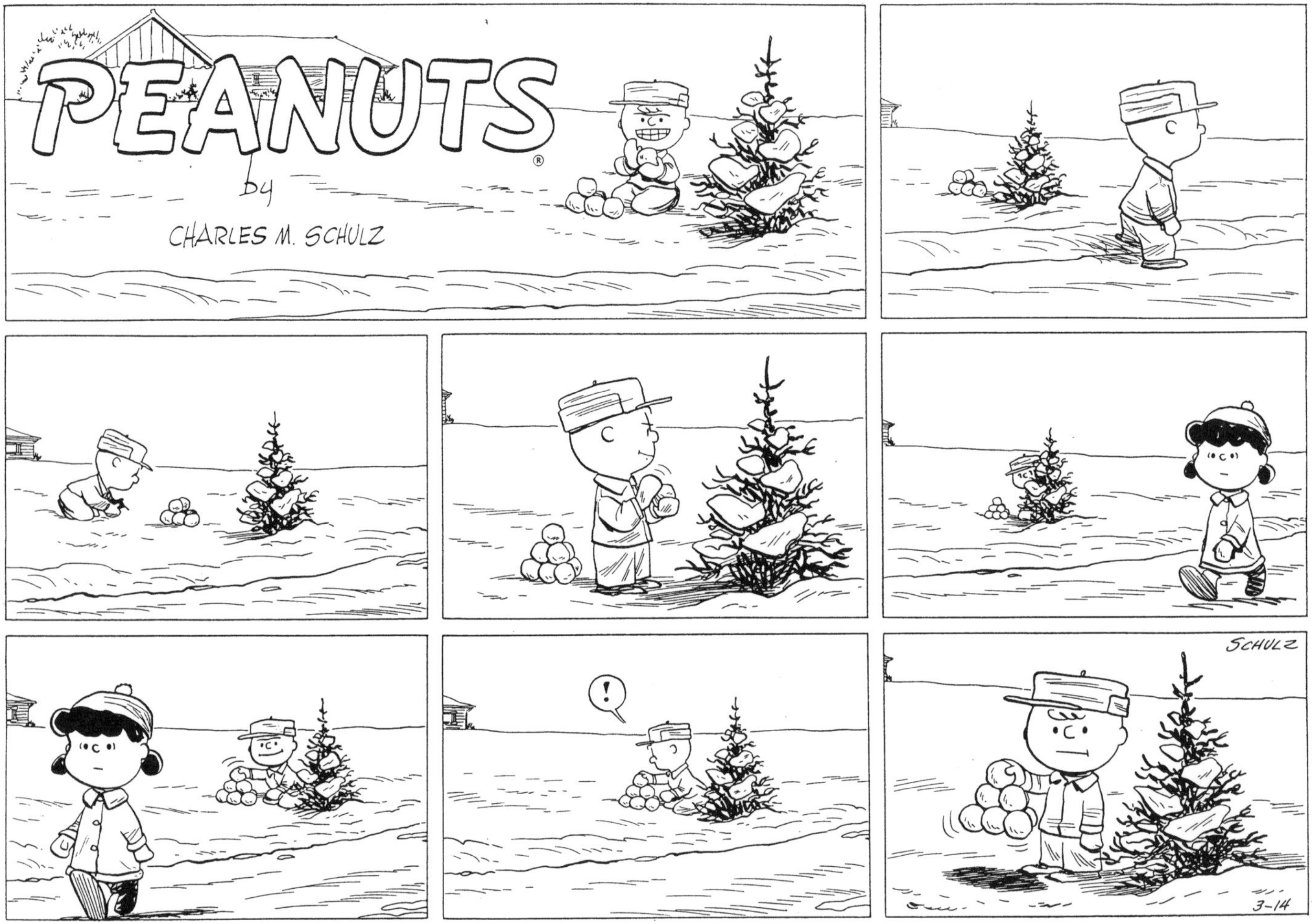
PEANUTS
by
CHARLES M. SCHULZ
!
SCHULZ
3-14

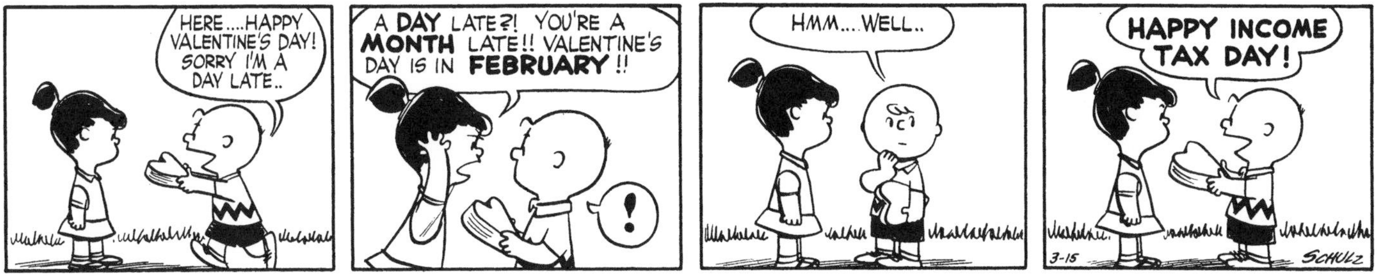
HERE....HAPPY VALENTINE'S DAY! SORRY I'M A DAY LATE..
A **DAY** LATE?! YOU'RE A **MONTH** LATE!! VALENTINE'S DAY IS IN **FEBRUARY** !!
!
HMM....WELL..
HAPPY INCOME TAX DAY!
3-15
SCHULZ

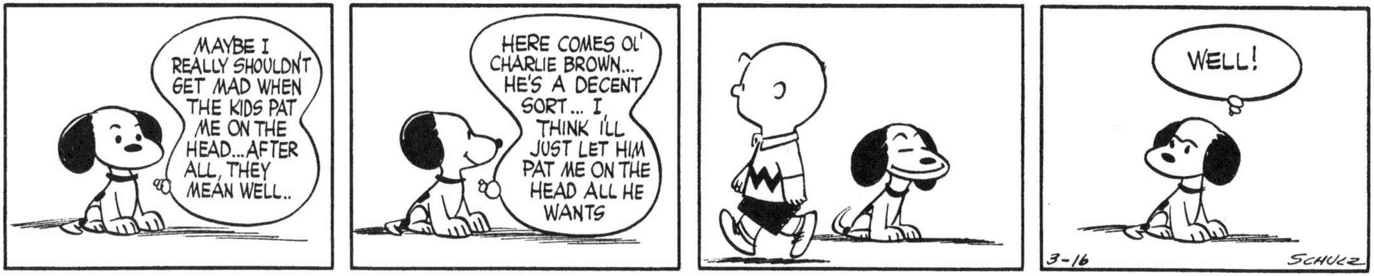
MAYBE I REALLY SHOULDN'T GET MAD WHEN THE KIDS PAT ME ON THE HEAD...AFTER ALL, THEY MEAN WELL..
HERE COMES OL' CHARLIE BROWN... HE'S A DECENT SORT... I THINK I'LL JUST LET HIM PAT ME ON THE HEAD ALL HE WANTS
WELL!
3-16
SCHULZ

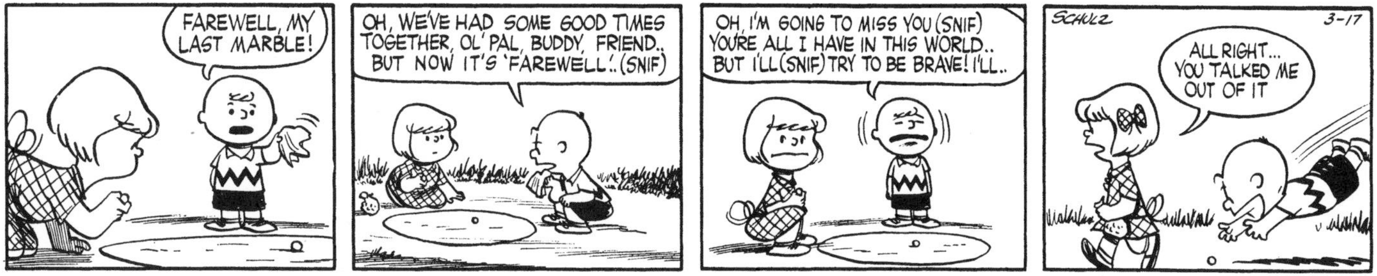
FAREWELL, MY LAST MARBLE!
OH, WE'VE HAD SOME GOOD TIMES TOGETHER, OL' PAL, BUDDY, FRIEND.. BUT NOW IT'S 'FAREWELL'.. (SNIF)
OH, I'M GOING TO MISS YOU (SNIF) YOU'RE ALL I HAVE IN THIS WORLD.. BUT I'LL (SNIF) TRY TO BE BRAVE! I'LL..
SCHULZ
3-17
ALL RIGHT... YOU TALKED ME OUT OF IT

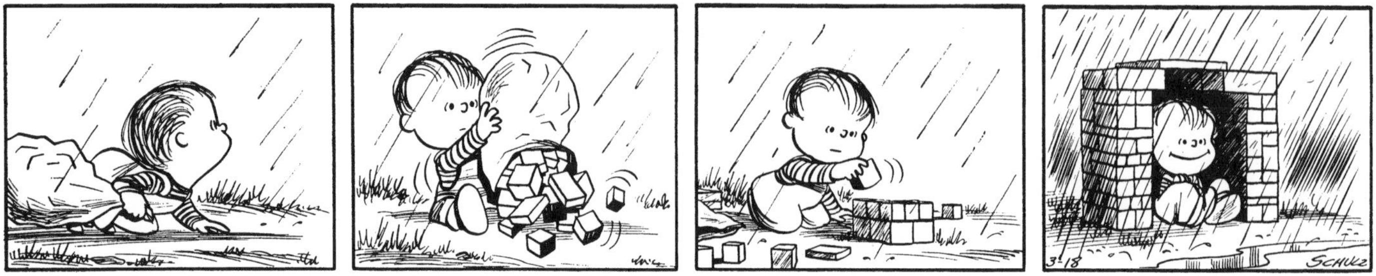
3-18
SCHULZ

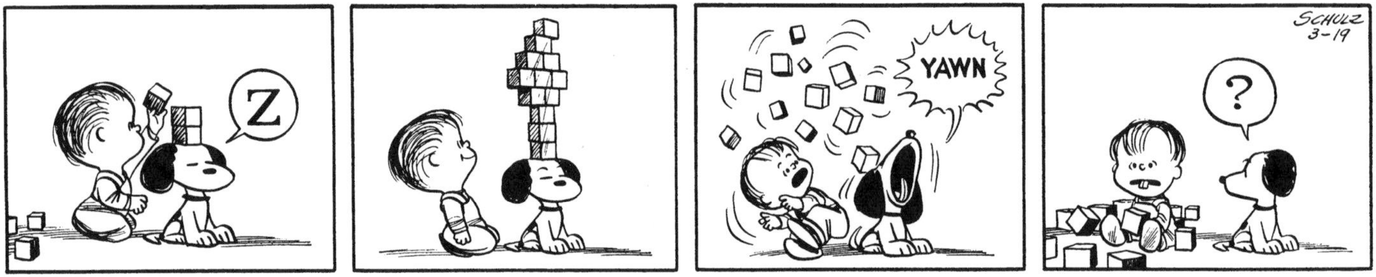
SCHULZ
3-19
Z
YAWN
?

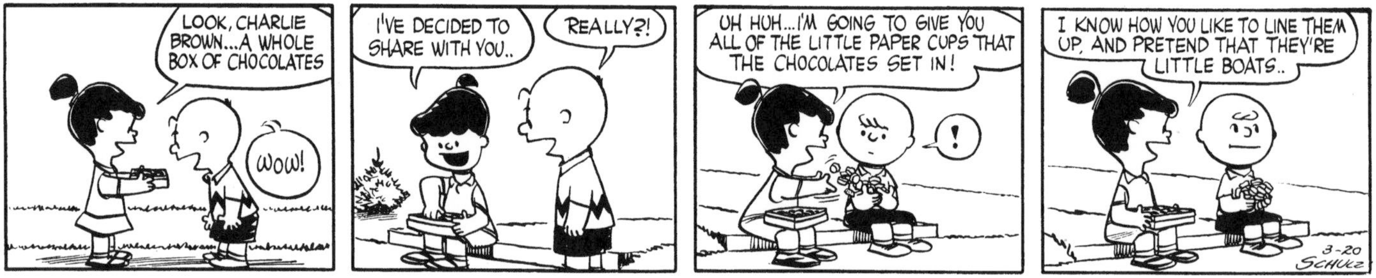
LOOK, CHARLIE BROWN...A WHOLE BOX OF CHOCOLATES
WOW!
I'VE DECIDED TO SHARE WITH YOU..
REALLY?!
UH HUH...I'M GOING TO GIVE YOU ALL OF THE LITTLE PAPER CUPS THAT THE CHOCOLATES SET IN!
!
I KNOW HOW YOU LIKE TO LINE THEM UP, AND PRETEND THAT THEY'RE LITTLE BOATS..
3-20
SCHULZ

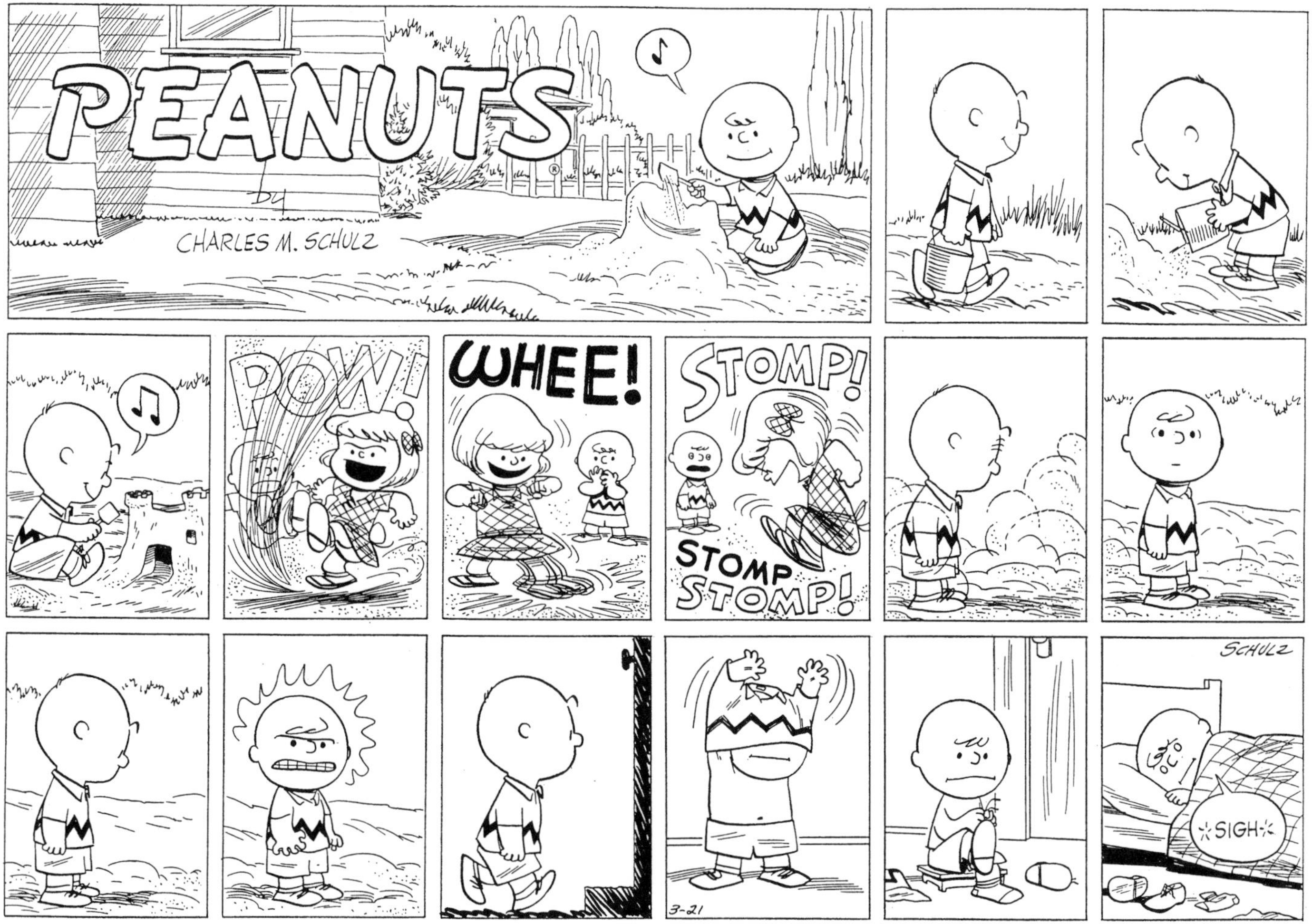
PEANUTS
by
CHARLES M. SCHULZ
POW!
WHEE!
STOMP!
STOMP
STOMP!
SCHULZ
3-21
SIGH

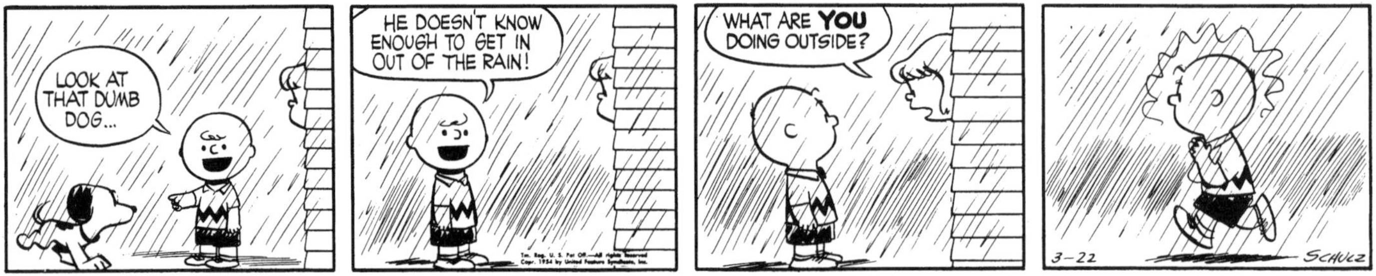
LOOK AT THAT DUMB DOG...
HE DOESN'T KNOW ENOUGH TO GET IN OUT OF THE RAIN!
Tm. Reg. U. S. Pat. Off.—All rights reserved Copr. 1954 by United Feature Syndicate, Inc.
WHAT ARE **YOU** DOING OUTSIDE?
3-22
SCHULZ

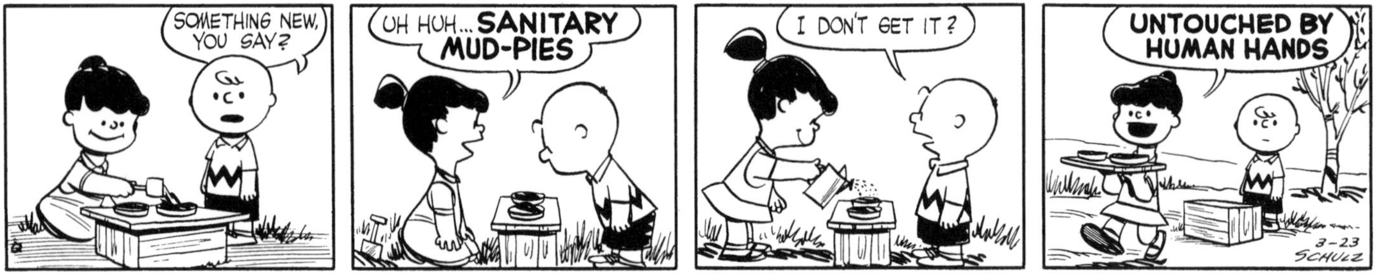
SOMETHING NEW, YOU SAY?
UH HUH... **SANITARY MUD-PIES**
I DON'T GET IT?
UNTOUCHED BY HUMAN HANDS
3-23
SCHULZ

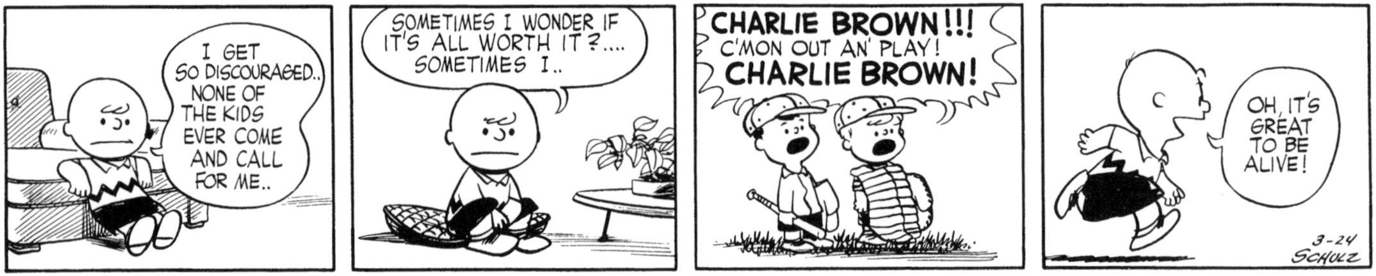
I GET SO DISCOURAGED.. NONE OF THE KIDS EVER COME AND CALL FOR ME..
SOMETIMES I WONDER IF IT'S ALL WORTH IT?.... SOMETIMES I..
CHARLIE BROWN!!!
C'MON OUT AN' PLAY!
CHARLIE BROWN!
OH, IT'S GREAT TO BE ALIVE!
3-24
SCHULZ

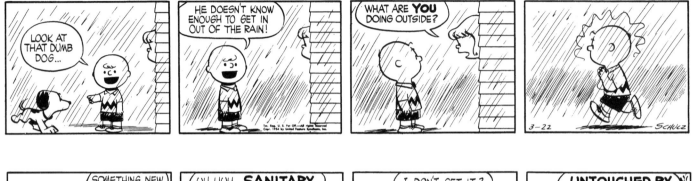

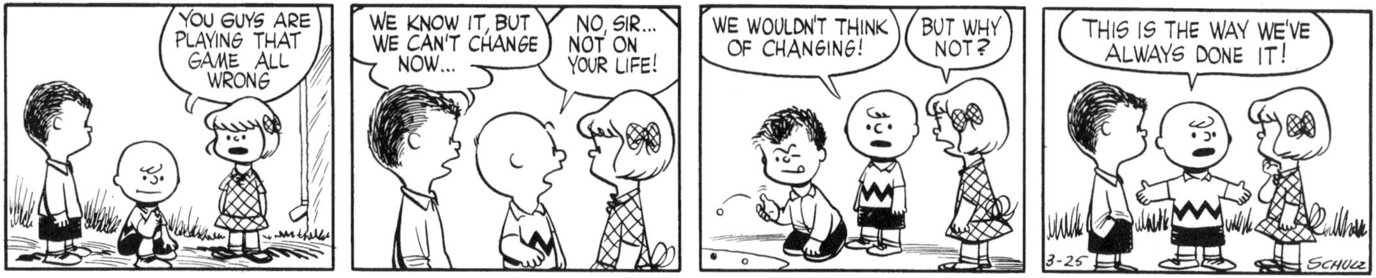
YOU GUYS ARE PLAYING THAT GAME ALL WRONG
WE KNOW IT, BUT WE CAN'T CHANGE NOW...
NO, SIR... NOT ON YOUR LIFE!
WE WOULDN'T THINK OF CHANGING!
BUT WHY NOT?
THIS IS THE WAY WE'VE ALWAYS DONE IT!
3-25
SCHULZ

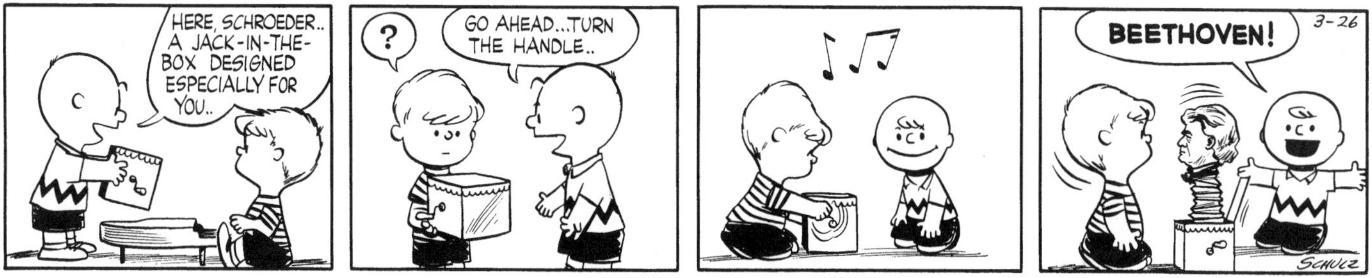
HERE, SCHROEDER.. A JACK-IN-THE-BOX DESIGNED ESPECIALLY FOR YOU..
?
GO AHEAD...TURN THE HANDLE..
BEETHOVEN!
3-26
SCHULZ

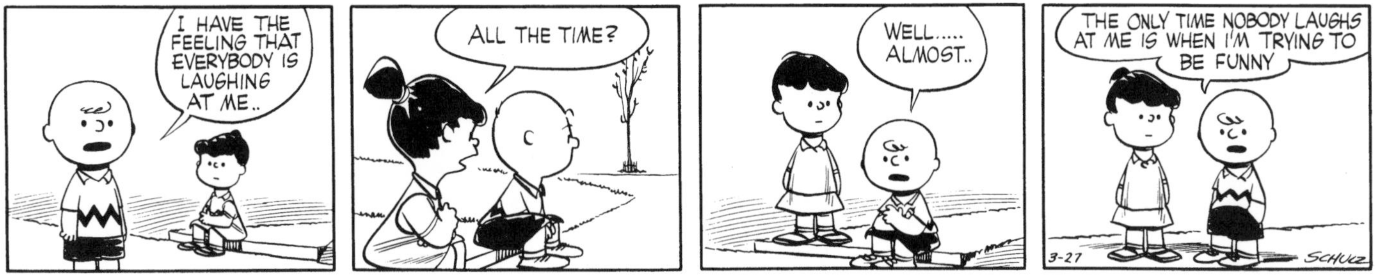
I HAVE THE FEELING THAT EVERYBODY IS LAUGHING AT ME..
ALL THE TIME?
WELL..... ALMOST..
THE ONLY TIME NOBODY LAUGHS AT ME IS WHEN I'M TRYING TO BE FUNNY
3-27
SCHULZ

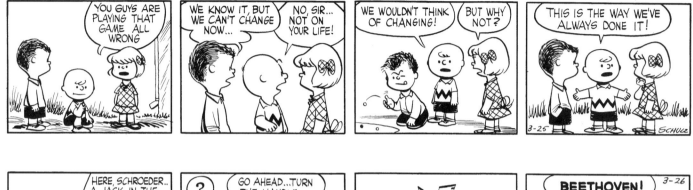

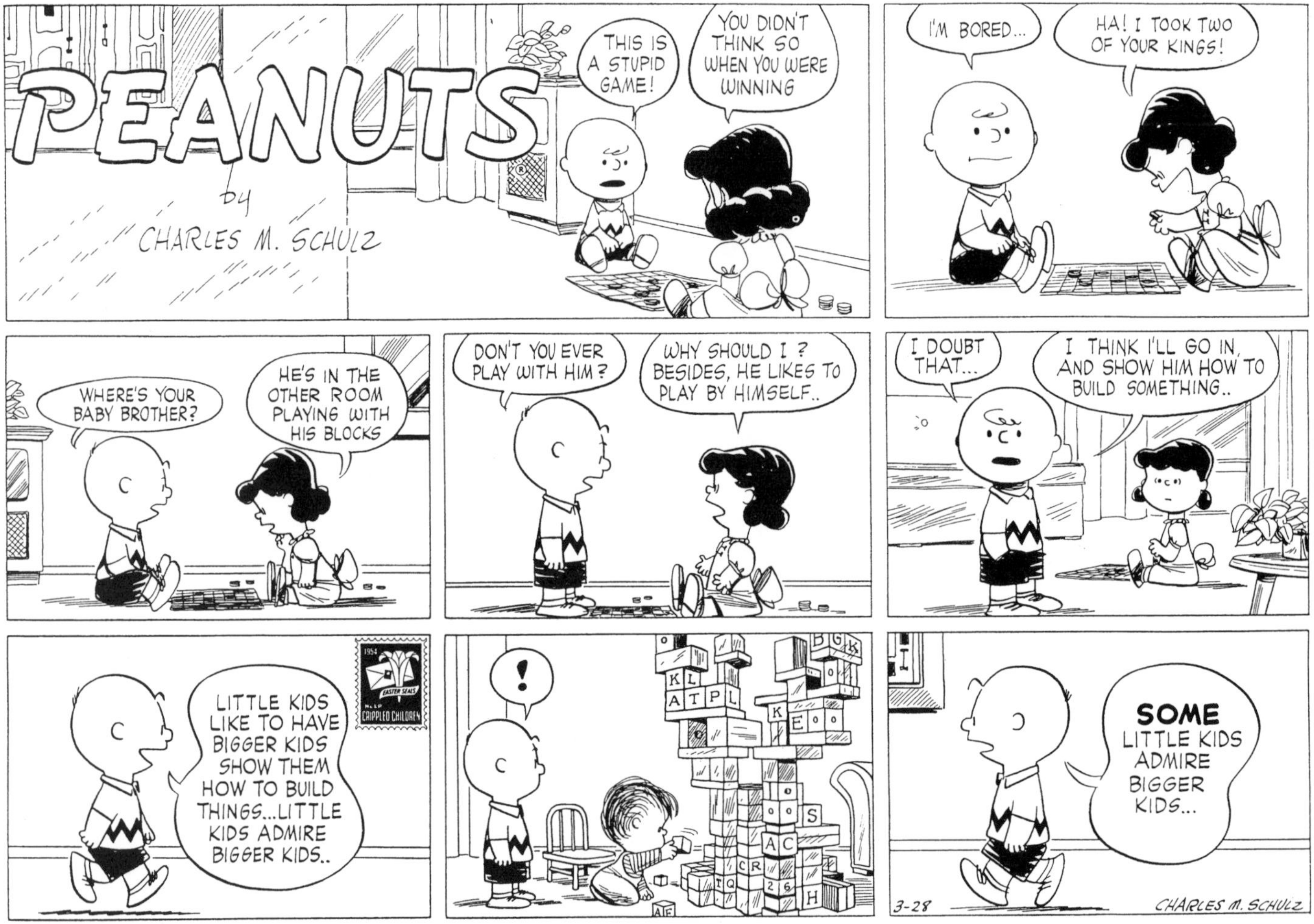
PEANUTS
by
CHARLES M. SCHULZ
THIS IS A STUPID GAME!
YOU DIDN'T THINK SO WHEN YOU WERE WINNING
I'M BORED...
HA! I TOOK TWO OF YOUR KINGS!
WHERE'S YOUR BABY BROTHER?
HE'S IN THE OTHER ROOM PLAYING WITH HIS BLOCKS
DON'T YOU EVER PLAY WITH HIM?
WHY SHOULD I ? BESIDES, HE LIKES TO PLAY BY HIMSELF..
I DOUBT THAT...
I THINK I'LL GO IN, AND SHOW HIM HOW TO BUILD SOMETHING..
LITTLE KIDS LIKE TO HAVE BIGGER KIDS SHOW THEM HOW TO BUILD THINGS...LITTLE KIDS ADMIRE BIGGER KIDS..
1954
EASTER SEALS
HELP
CRIPPLED CHILDREN
!
SOME LITTLE KIDS ADMIRE BIGGER KIDS...
3-28
CHARLES M. SCHULZ

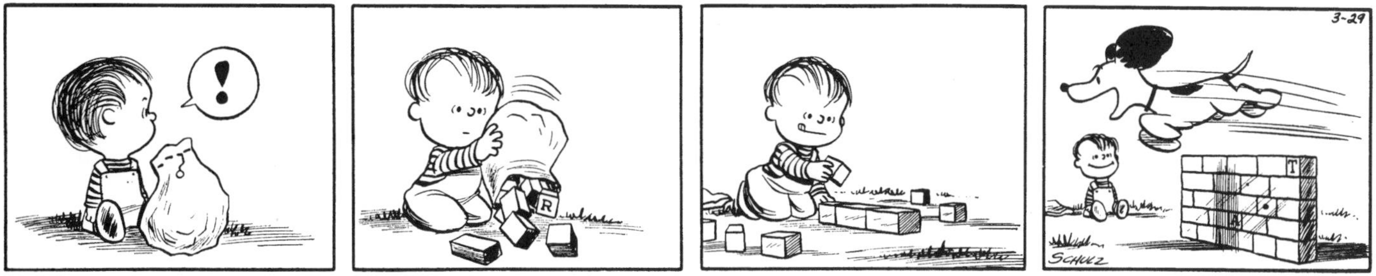
!
R
3-29
T
A
SCHULZ

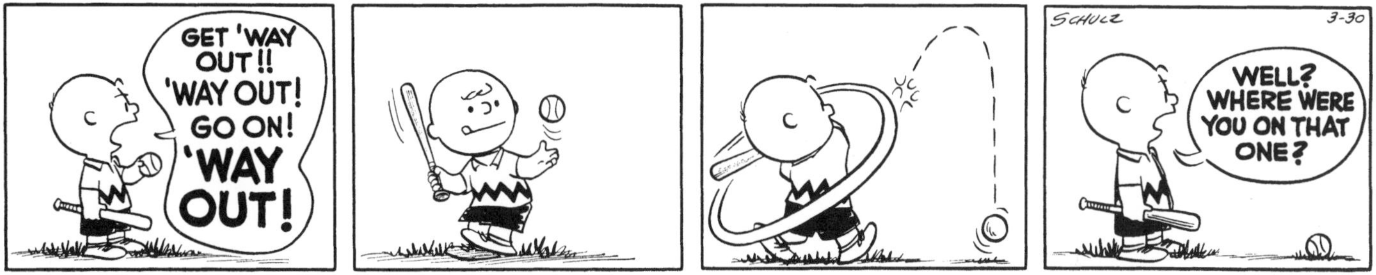
GET 'WAY OUT!! 'WAY OUT! GO ON! 'WAY OUT!
SCHULZ
3-30
WELL? WHERE WERE YOU ON THAT ONE?

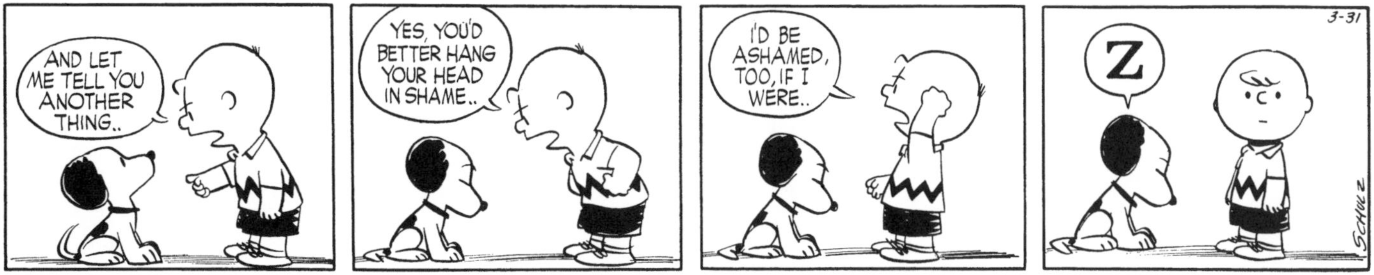
AND LET ME TELL YOU ANOTHER THING..
YES, YOU'D BETTER HANG YOUR HEAD IN SHAME..
I'D BE ASHAMED, TOO, IF I WERE..
3-31
Z
SCHULZ

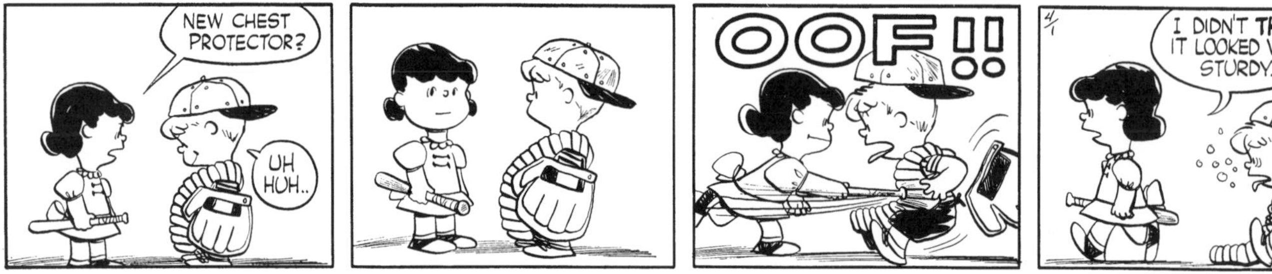
NEW CHEST PROTECTOR?
UH HUH..
OOF!!
4/1
I DIDN'T THINK IT LOOKED VERY STURDY..
SCHULZ

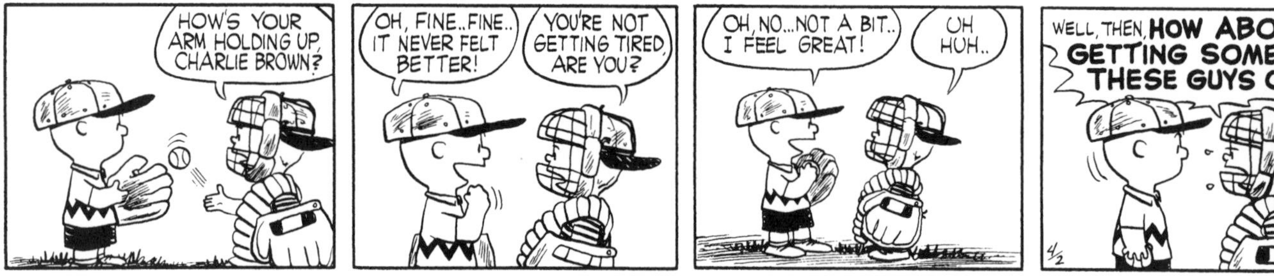
HOW'S YOUR ARM HOLDING UP, CHARLIE BROWN?
OH, FINE..FINE.. IT NEVER FELT BETTER!
YOU'RE NOT GETTING TIRED, ARE YOU?
OH, NO...NOT A BIT.. I FEEL GREAT!
UH HUH..
WELL, THEN, HOW ABOUT GETTING SOME OF THESE GUYS OUT?
4/2
SCHULZ

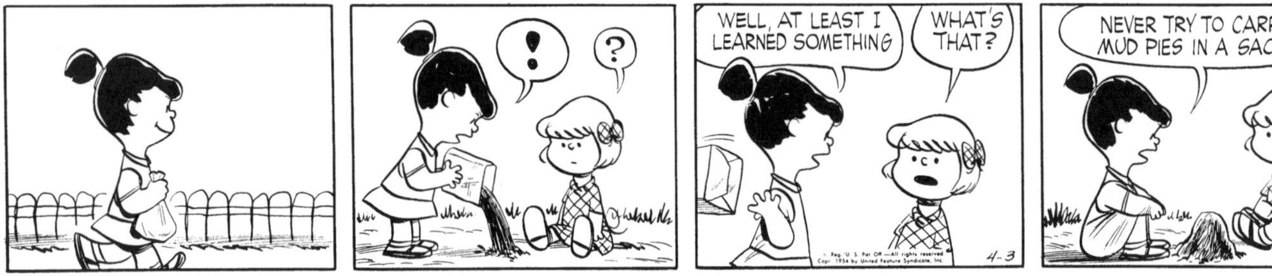
!
?
WELL, AT LEAST I LEARNED SOMETHING
WHAT'S THAT?
4-3
NEVER TRY TO CARRY MUD PIES IN A SACK!
SCHULZ

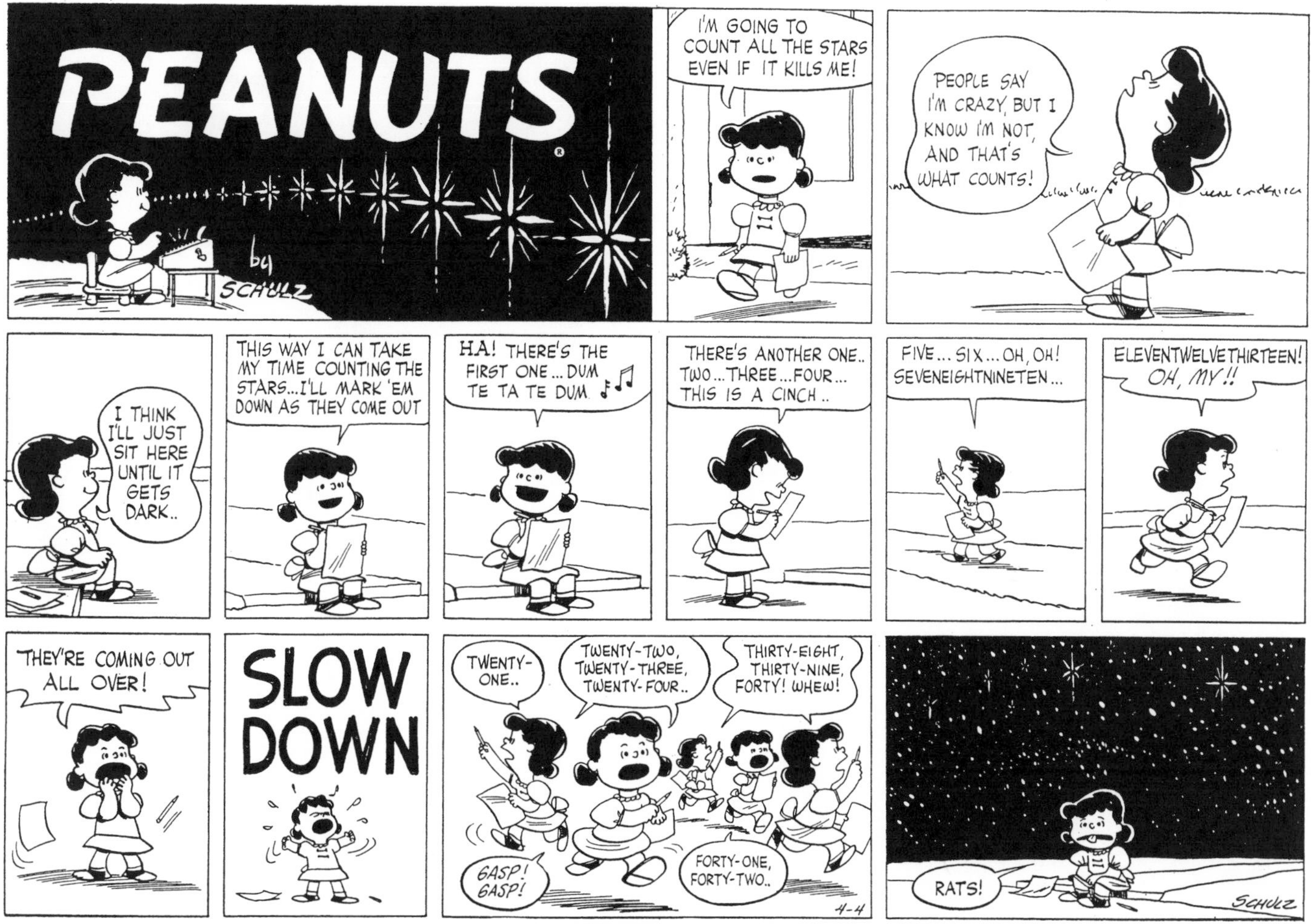
PEANUTS
by SCHULZ
I'M GOING TO COUNT ALL THE STARS EVEN IF IT KILLS ME!
PEOPLE SAY I'M CRAZY, BUT I KNOW I'M NOT, AND THAT'S WHAT COUNTS!
I THINK I'LL JUST SIT HERE UNTIL IT GETS DARK..
THIS WAY I CAN TAKE MY TIME COUNTING THE STARS...I'LL MARK 'EM DOWN AS THEY COME OUT
HA! THERE'S THE FIRST ONE ... DUM TE TA TE DUM
THERE'S ANOTHER ONE.. TWO ... THREE ... FOUR ... THIS IS A CINCH ..
FIVE ... SIX ... OH, OH! SEVENEIGHTNINETEN ...
ELEVENTWELVETHIRTEEN! OH, MY!!
THEY'RE COMING OUT ALL OVER!
SLOW DOWN
TWENTY-ONE..
TWENTY-TWO, TWENTY-THREE, TWENTY-FOUR..
THIRTY-EIGHT, THIRTY-NINE, FORTY! WHEW!
GASP! GASP!
FORTY-ONE, FORTY-TWO..
4-4
RATS!
SCHULZ

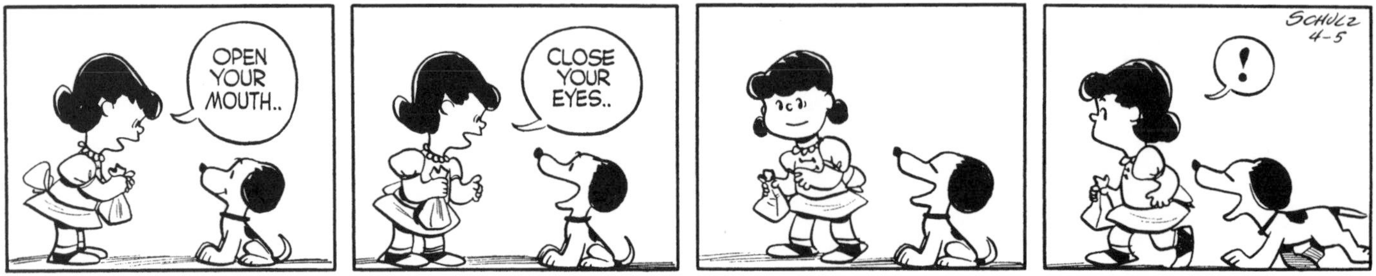
OPEN YOUR MOUTH..
CLOSE YOUR EYES..
SCHULZ 4-5
!

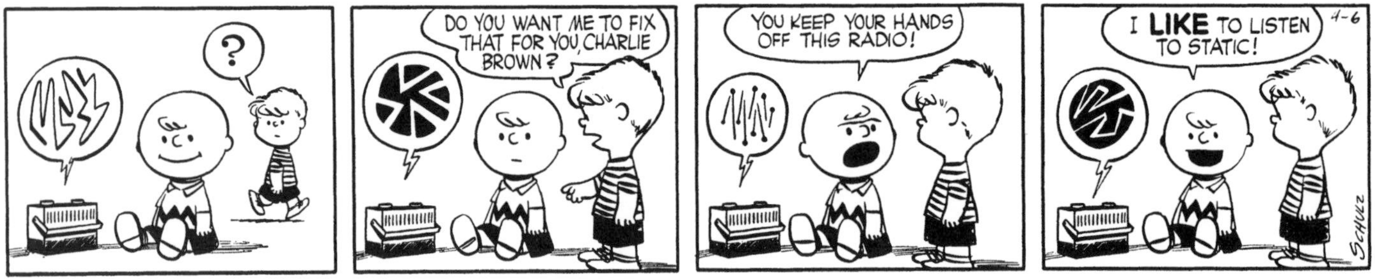
?
DO YOU WANT ME TO FIX THAT FOR YOU, CHARLIE BROWN?
YOU KEEP YOUR HANDS OFF THIS RADIO!
4-6
I **LIKE** TO LISTEN TO STATIC!
SCHULZ

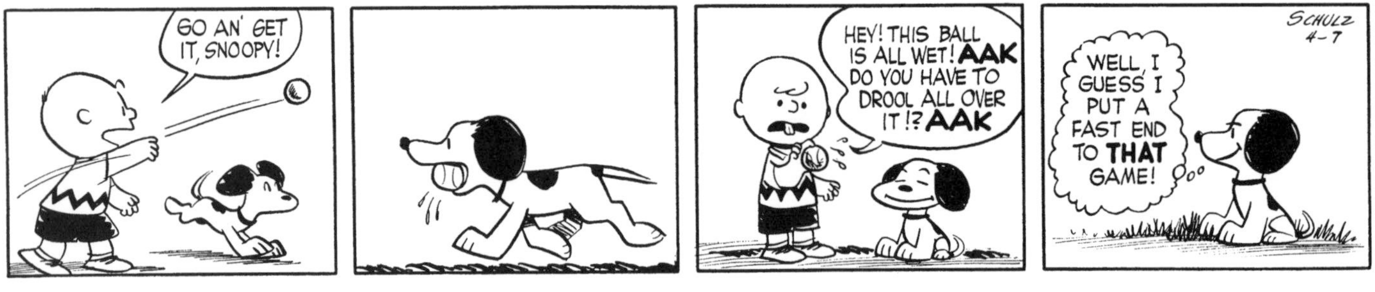
GO AN' GET IT, SNOOPY!
HEY! THIS BALL IS ALL WET! **AAK** DO YOU HAVE TO DROOL ALL OVER IT!? **AAK**
SCHULZ 4-7
WELL, I GUESS I PUT A FAST END TO **THAT** GAME!

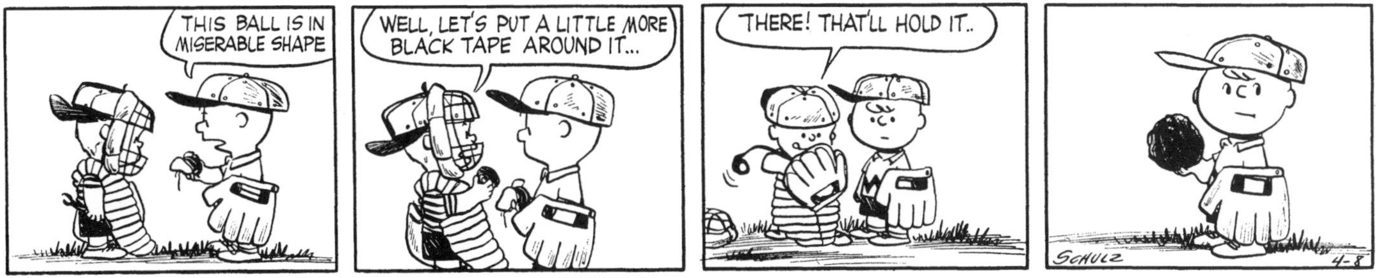
THIS BALL IS IN MISERABLE SHAPE
WELL, LET'S PUT A LITTLE MORE BLACK TAPE AROUND IT...
THERE! THAT'LL HOLD IT..
SCHULZ
4-8

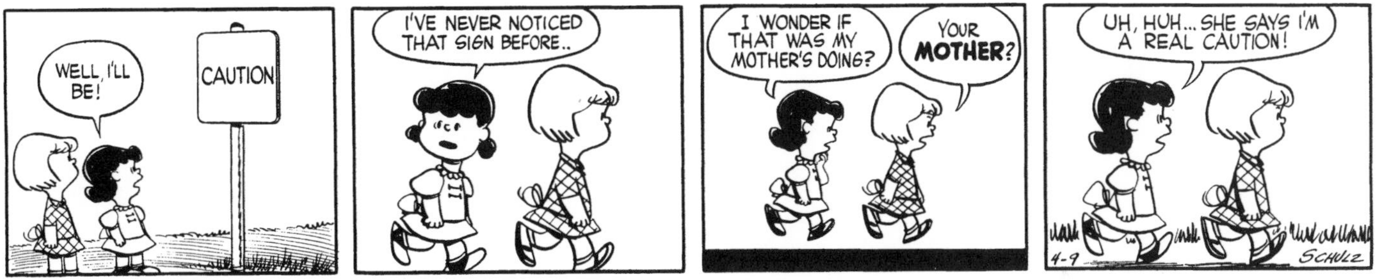
WELL, I'LL BE!
CAUTION
I'VE NEVER NOTICED THAT SIGN BEFORE..
I WONDER IF THAT WAS MY MOTHER'S DOING?
YOUR **MOTHER**?
UH, HUH... SHE SAYS I'M A REAL CAUTION!
4-9
SCHULZ

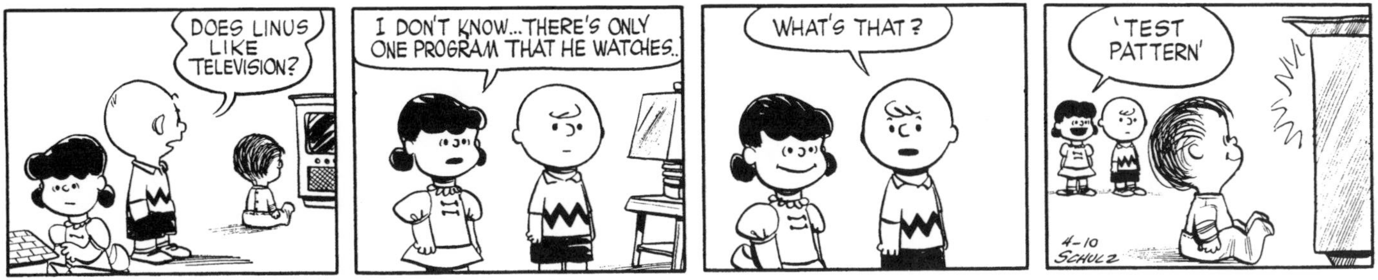
DOES LINUS LIKE TELEVISION?
I DON'T KNOW...THERE'S ONLY ONE PROGRAM THAT HE WATCHES..
WHAT'S THAT?
'TEST PATTERN'
4-10
SCHULZ

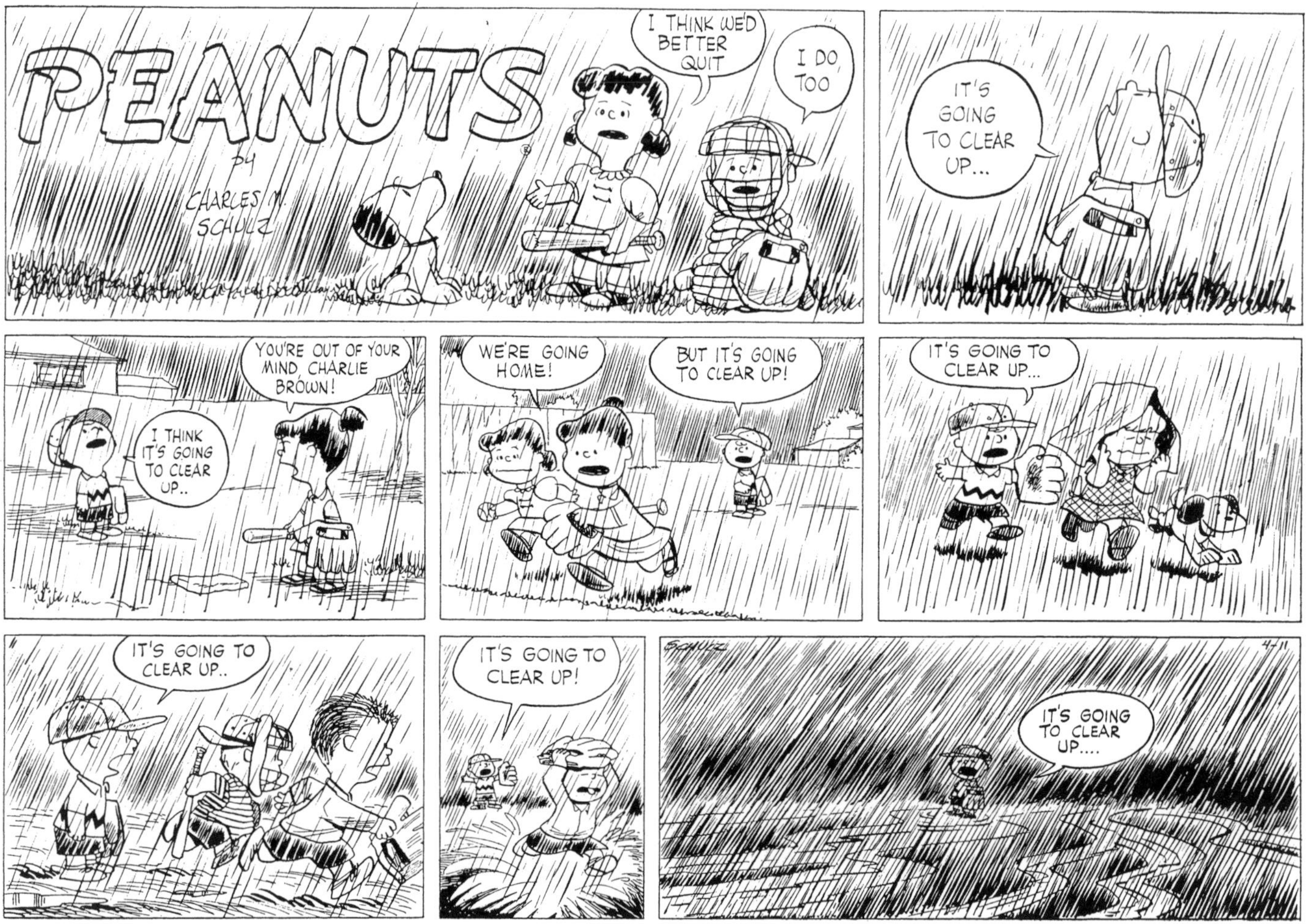
PEANUTS
by
CHARLES M. SCHULZ
I THINK WE'D BETTER QUIT
I DO, TOO
IT'S GOING TO CLEAR UP...
YOU'RE OUT OF YOUR MIND, CHARLIE BROWN!
I THINK IT'S GOING TO CLEAR UP..
WE'RE GOING HOME!
BUT IT'S GOING TO CLEAR UP!
IT'S GOING TO CLEAR UP...
IT'S GOING TO CLEAR UP..
IT'S GOING TO CLEAR UP!
SCHULZ
4-11
IT'S GOING TO CLEAR UP....

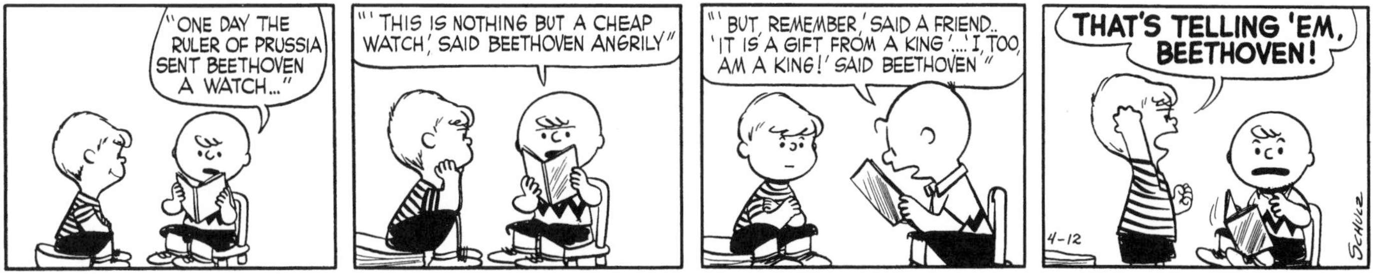
"ONE DAY THE RULER OF PRUSSIA SENT BEETHOVEN A WATCH..."
"'THIS IS NOTHING BUT A CHEAP WATCH,' SAID BEETHOVEN ANGRILY"
"'BUT, REMEMBER,' SAID A FRIEND.. 'IT IS A GIFT FROM A KING'...'I, TOO, AM A KING!' SAID BEETHOVEN"
THAT'S TELLING 'EM, BEETHOVEN!
4-12
SCHULZ

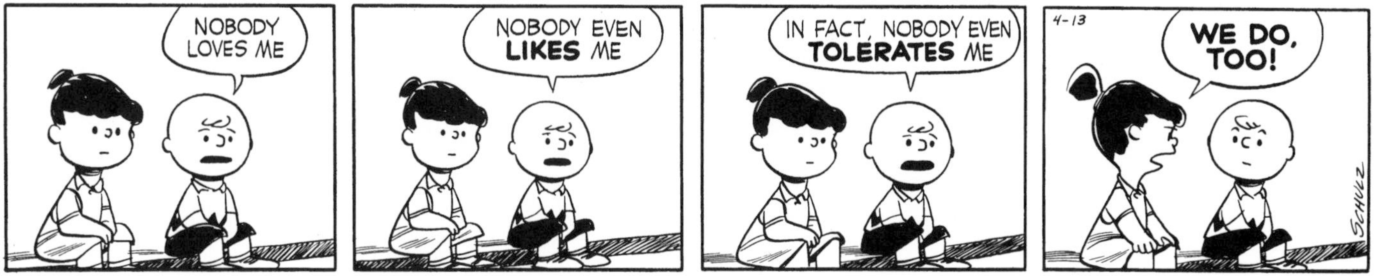
NOBODY LOVES ME
NOBODY EVEN **LIKES** ME
IN FACT, NOBODY EVEN **TOLERATES** ME
4-13
WE DO, TOO!
SCHULZ

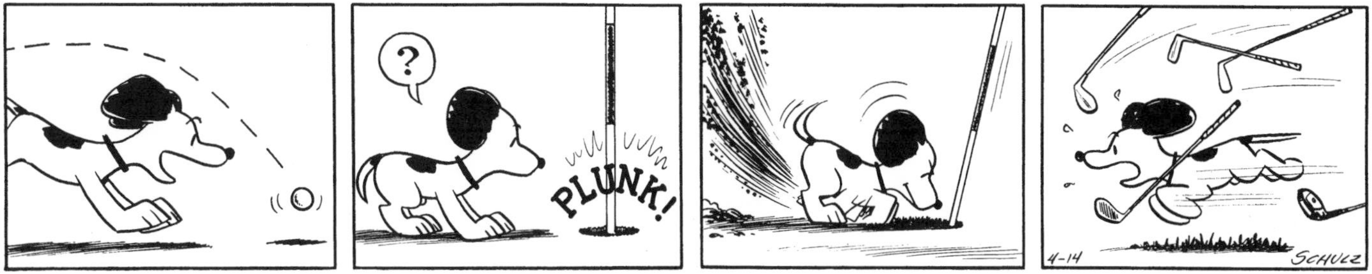
?
PLUNK!
4-14
SCHULZ

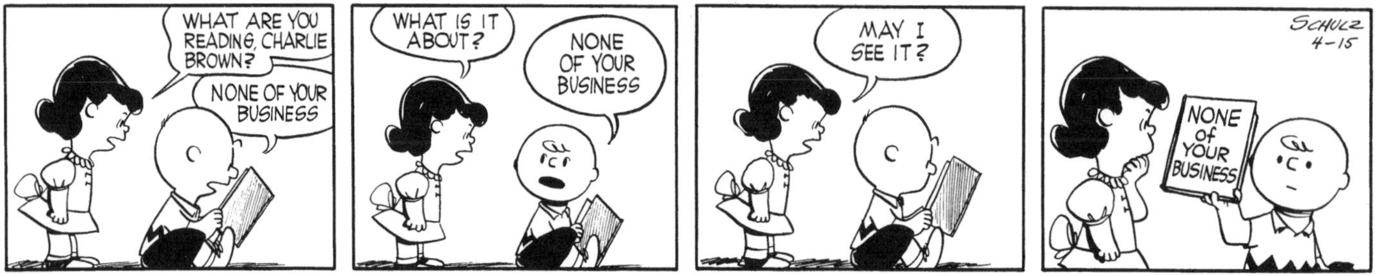
WHAT ARE YOU READING, CHARLIE BROWN?
NONE OF YOUR BUSINESS
WHAT IS IT ABOUT?
NONE OF YOUR BUSINESS
MAY I SEE IT?
SCHULZ 4-15
NONE of YOUR BUSINESS

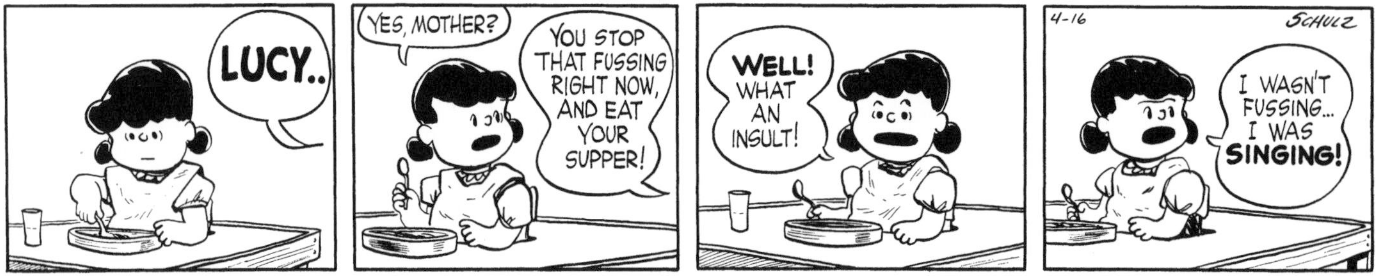
LUCY..
YES, MOTHER?
YOU STOP THAT FUSSING RIGHT NOW, AND EAT YOUR SUPPER!
WELL! WHAT AN INSULT!
4-16
SCHULZ
I WASN'T FUSSING... I WAS SINGING!

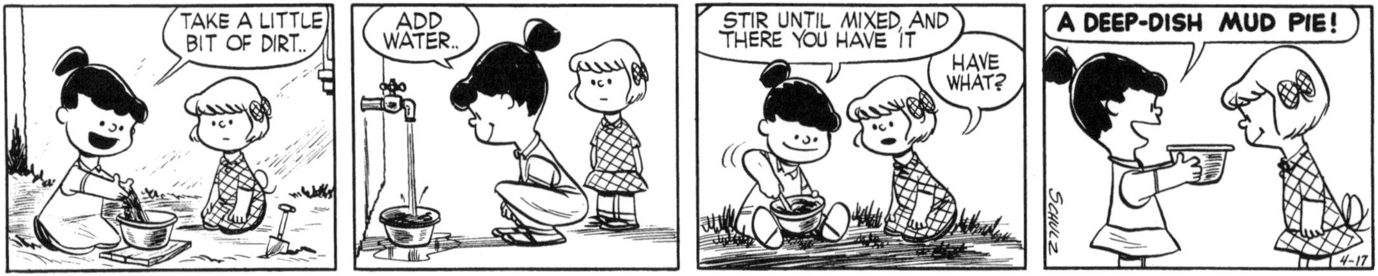
TAKE A LITTLE BIT OF DIRT..
ADD WATER..
STIR UNTIL MIXED, AND THERE YOU HAVE IT
HAVE WHAT?
A DEEP-DISH MUD PIE!
SCHULZ
4-17

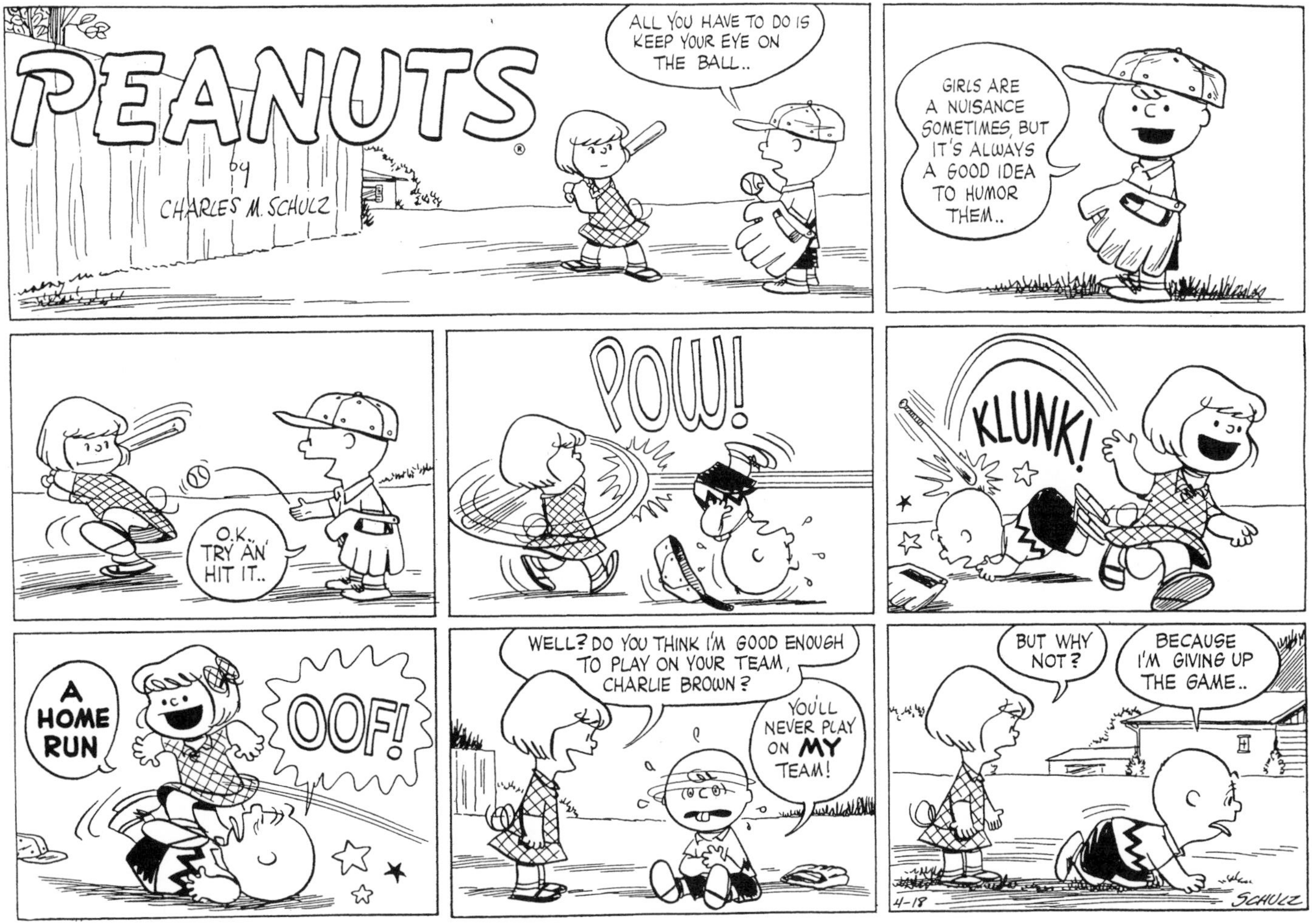
PEANUTS®
by
CHARLES M. SCHULZ
ALL YOU HAVE TO DO IS KEEP YOUR EYE ON THE BALL..
GIRLS ARE A NUISANCE SOMETIMES, BUT IT'S ALWAYS A GOOD IDEA TO HUMOR THEM..
O.K.. TRY AN' HIT IT..
POW!
KLUNK!
A HOME RUN
OOF!
WELL? DO YOU THINK I'M GOOD ENOUGH TO PLAY ON YOUR TEAM, CHARLIE BROWN?
YOU'LL NEVER PLAY ON MY TEAM!
BUT WHY NOT?
BECAUSE I'M GIVING UP THE GAME..
4-18
SCHULZ

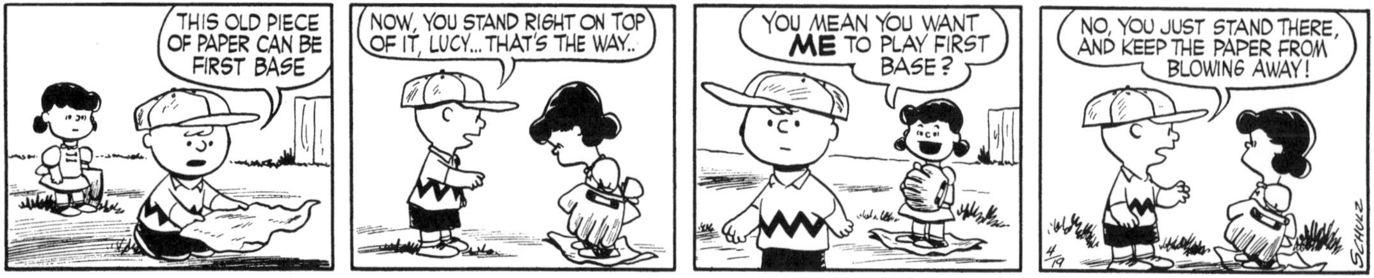
THIS OLD PIECE OF PAPER CAN BE FIRST BASE
NOW, YOU STAND RIGHT ON TOP OF IT, LUCY... THAT'S THE WAY..
YOU MEAN YOU WANT **ME** TO PLAY FIRST BASE?
NO, YOU JUST STAND THERE, AND KEEP THE PAPER FROM BLOWING AWAY!
SCHULZ
4/19

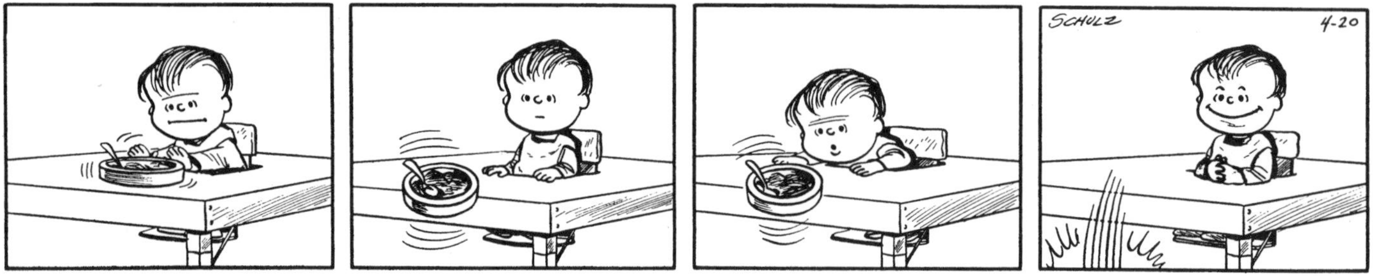
SCHULZ
4-20

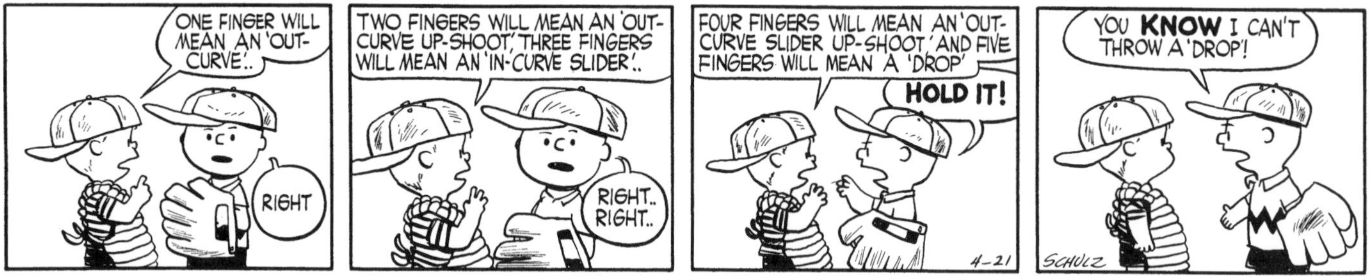
ONE FINGER WILL MEAN AN 'OUT-CURVE'..
RIGHT
TWO FINGERS WILL MEAN AN 'OUT-CURVE UP-SHOOT,' THREE FINGERS WILL MEAN AN 'IN-CURVE SLIDER'..
RIGHT.. RIGHT..
FOUR FINGERS WILL MEAN AN 'OUT-CURVE SLIDER UP-SHOOT,' AND FIVE FINGERS WILL MEAN A 'DROP'
HOLD IT!
4-21
YOU **KNOW** I CAN'T THROW A 'DROP'!
SCHULZ

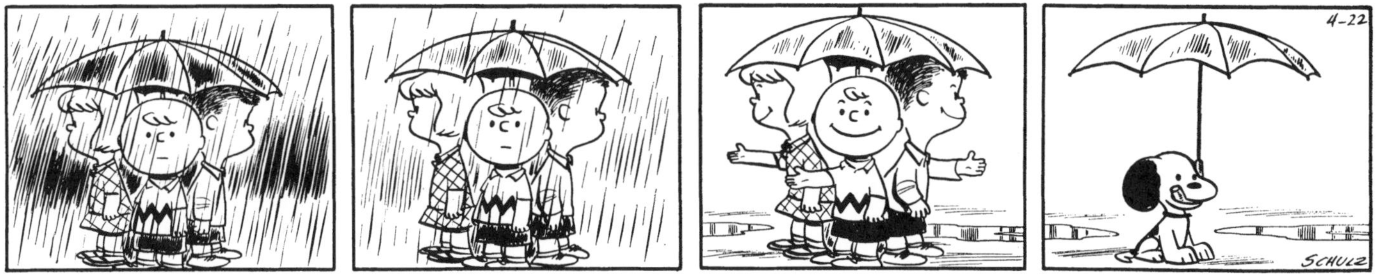
4-22
SCHULZ

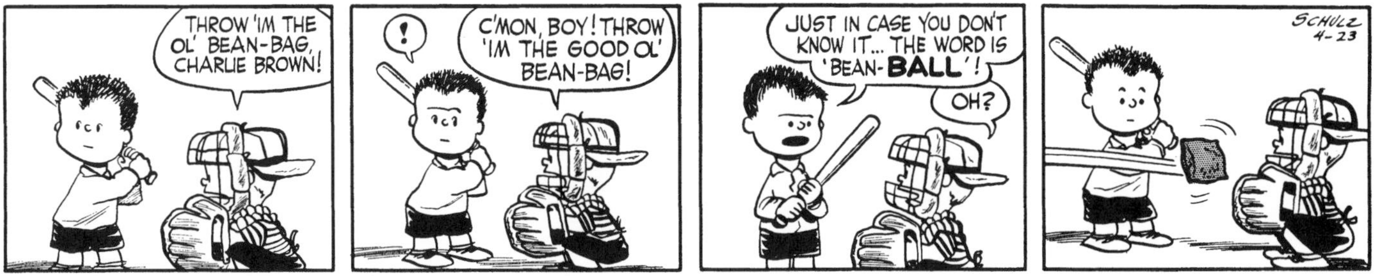
THROW 'IM THE OL' BEAN-BAG, CHARLIE BROWN!
!
C'MON, BOY! THROW 'IM THE GOOD OL' BEAN-BAG!
JUST IN CASE YOU DON'T KNOW IT... THE WORD IS 'BEAN-**BALL**'!
OH?
SCHULZ
4-23

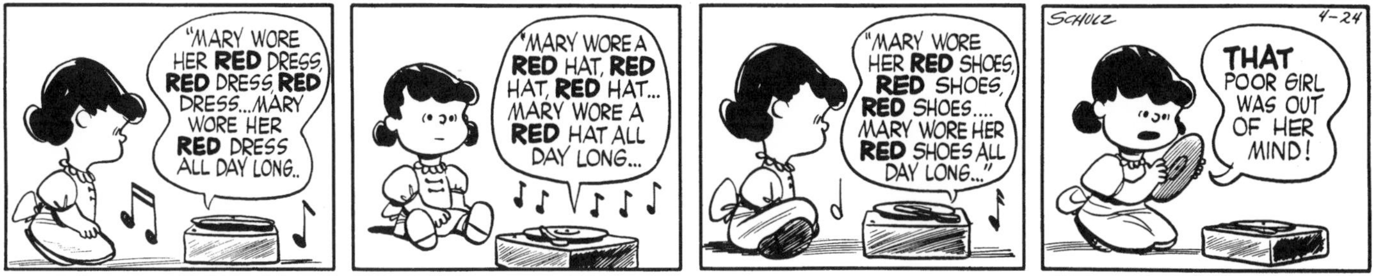
"MARY WORE HER **RED** DRESS, **RED** DRESS, **RED** DRESS...MARY WORE HER **RED** DRESS ALL DAY LONG..
"MARY WORE A **RED** HAT, **RED** HAT, **RED** HAT... MARY WORE A **RED** HAT ALL DAY LONG...
"MARY WORE HER **RED** SHOES, **RED** SHOES, **RED** SHOES.... MARY WORE HER **RED** SHOES ALL DAY LONG..."
SCHULZ
4-24
THAT POOR GIRL WAS OUT OF HER MIND!

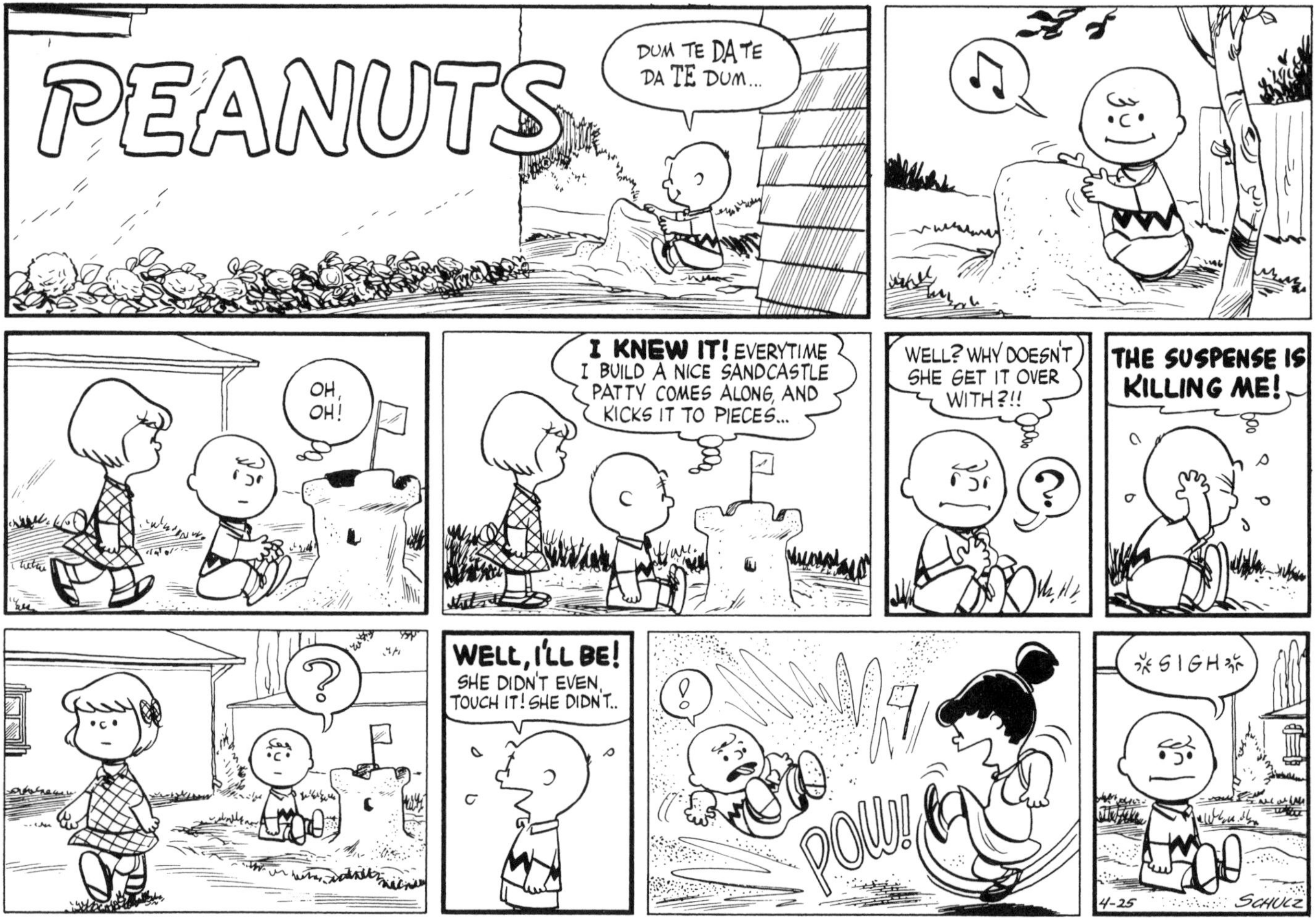
PEANUTS
DUM TE DA TE DA TE DUM...
OH, OH!
I KNEW IT! EVERYTIME I BUILD A NICE SANDCASTLE PATTY COMES ALONG, AND KICKS IT TO PIECES...
WELL? WHY DOESN'T SHE GET IT OVER WITH?!!
?
THE SUSPENSE IS KILLING ME!
?
WELL, I'LL BE! SHE DIDN'T EVEN TOUCH IT! SHE DIDN'T..
!
POW!
SIGH
4-25
SCHULZ

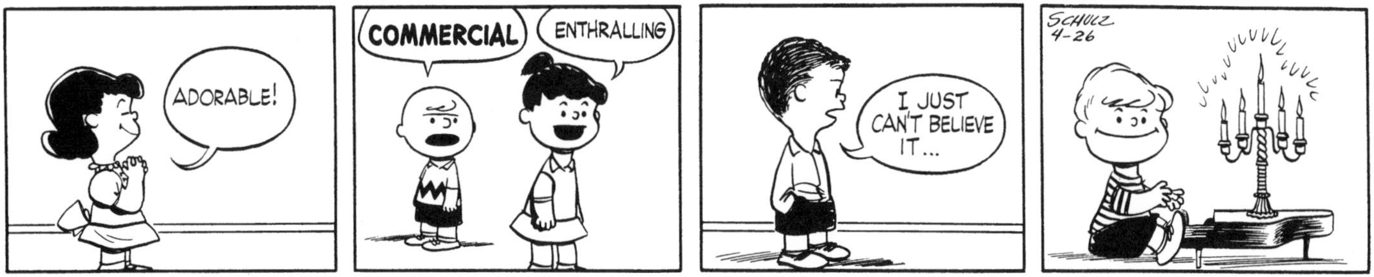
ADORABLE!
COMMERCIAL
ENTHRALLING
I JUST CAN'T BELIEVE IT...
SCHULZ 4-26

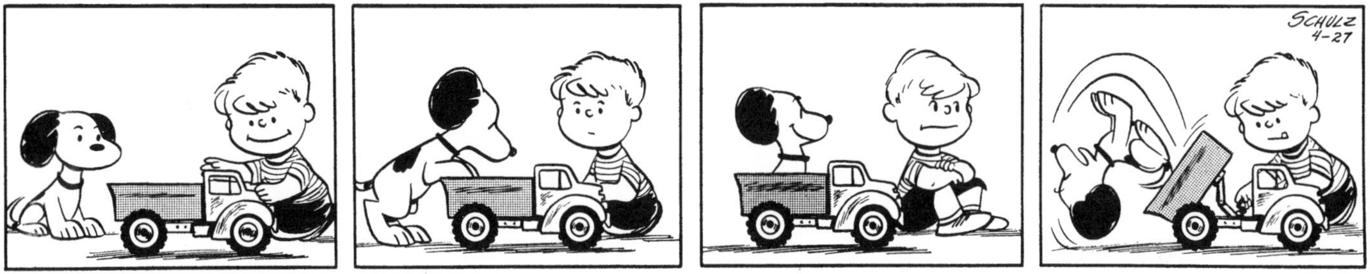
SCHULZ 4-27

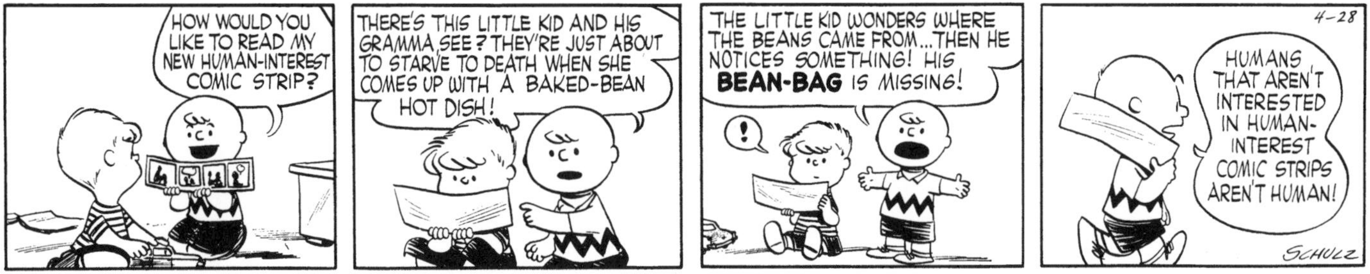
HOW WOULD YOU LIKE TO READ MY NEW HUMAN-INTEREST COMIC STRIP?
THERE'S THIS LITTLE KID AND HIS GRAMMA, SEE? THEY'RE JUST ABOUT TO STARVE TO DEATH WHEN SHE COMES UP WITH A BAKED-BEAN HOT DISH!
THE LITTLE KID WONDERS WHERE THE BEANS CAME FROM...THEN HE NOTICES SOMETHING! HIS BEAN-BAG IS MISSING!
!
4-28
HUMANS THAT AREN'T INTERESTED IN HUMAN-INTEREST COMIC STRIPS AREN'T HUMAN!
SCHULZ

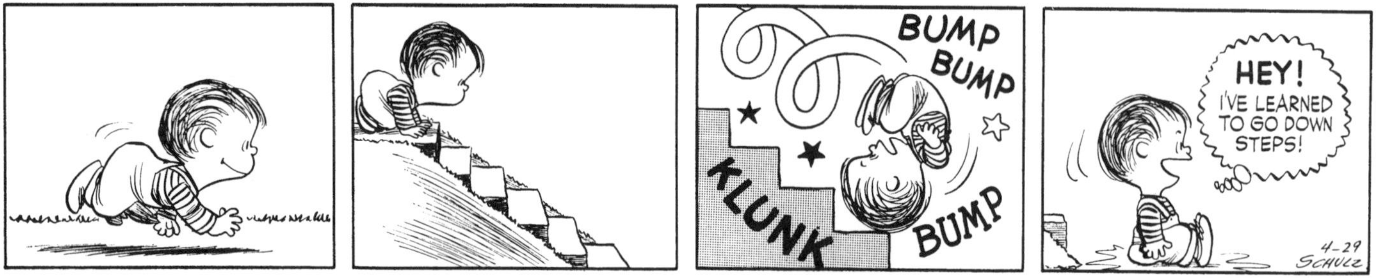
BUMP
BUMP
KLUNK
BUMP
HEY!
I'VE LEARNED TO GO DOWN STEPS!
4-29
SCHULZ

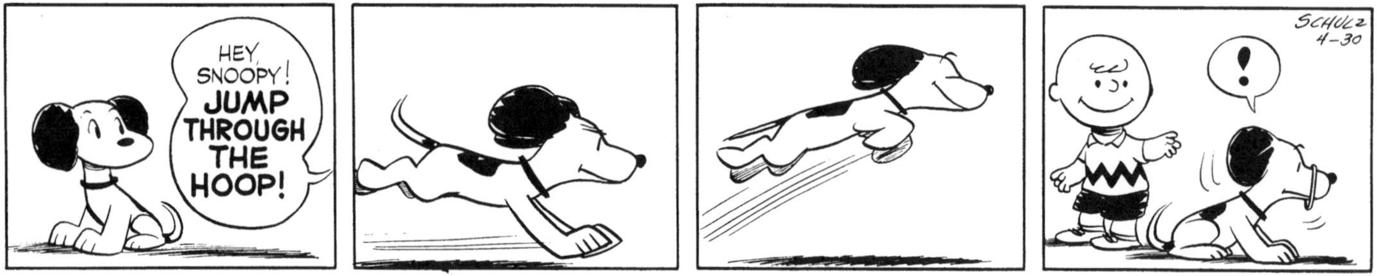
HEY, SNOOPY! **JUMP THROUGH THE HOOP!**
SCHULZ
4-30
!

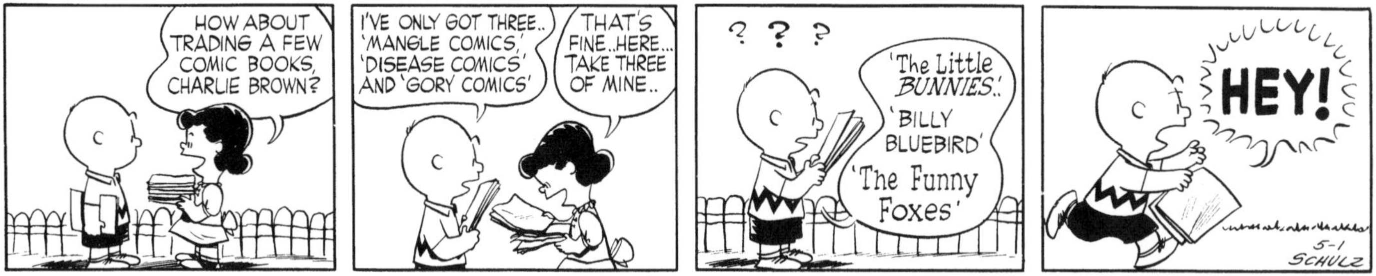
HOW ABOUT TRADING A FEW COMIC BOOKS, CHARLIE BROWN?
I'VE ONLY GOT THREE.. 'MANGLE COMICS,' 'DISEASE COMICS' AND 'GORY COMICS'
THAT'S FINE..HERE... TAKE THREE OF MINE..
? ? ?
'The Little *BUNNIES*.' 'BILLY BLUEBIRD' 'The Funny Foxes'
HEY!
5-1
SCHULZ

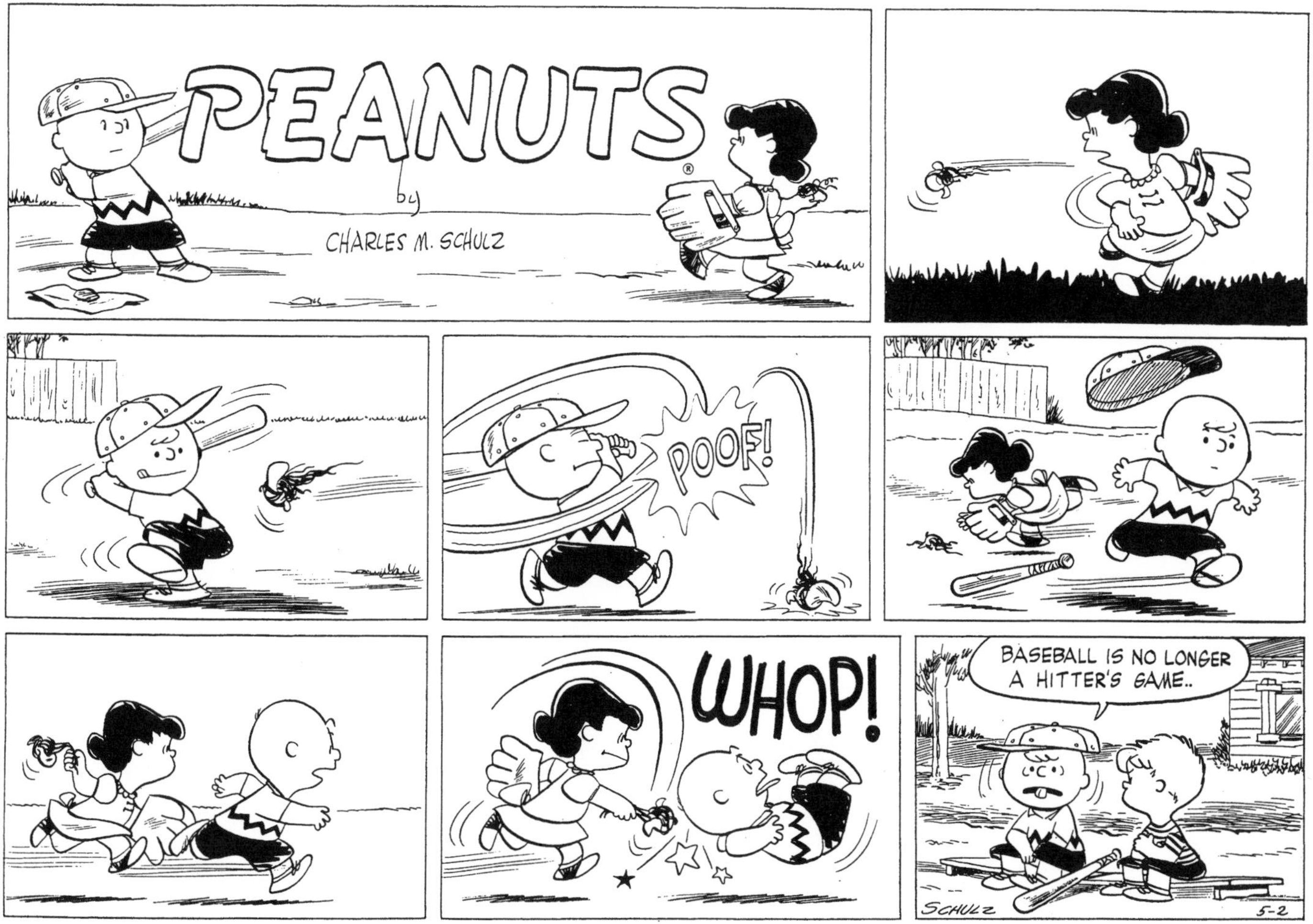
PEANUTS
by
CHARLES M. SCHULZ
POOF!
WHOP!
BASEBALL IS NO LONGER
A HITTER'S GAME..
SCHULZ
5-2

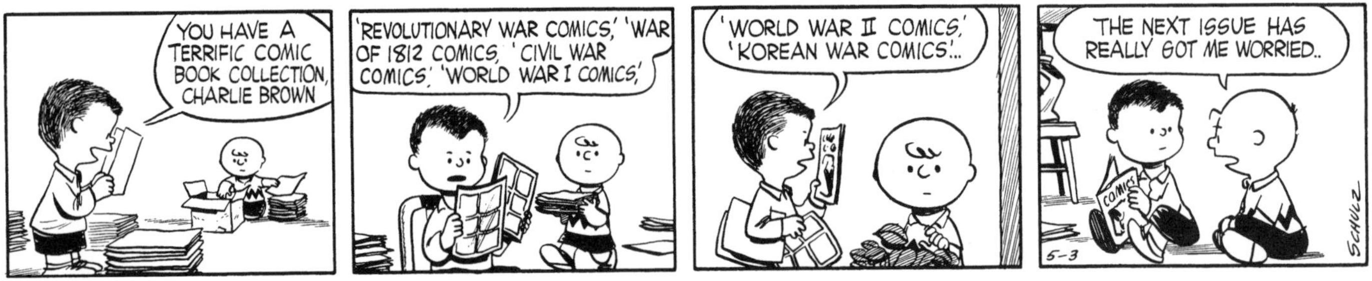
YOU HAVE A TERRIFIC COMIC BOOK COLLECTION, CHARLIE BROWN
'REVOLUTIONARY WAR COMICS,' 'WAR OF 1812 COMICS,' 'CIVIL WAR COMICS,' 'WORLD WAR I COMICS,'
'WORLD WAR II COMICS,' 'KOREAN WAR COMICS'...
THE NEXT ISSUE HAS REALLY GOT ME WORRIED..
COMICS
5-3
SCHULZ

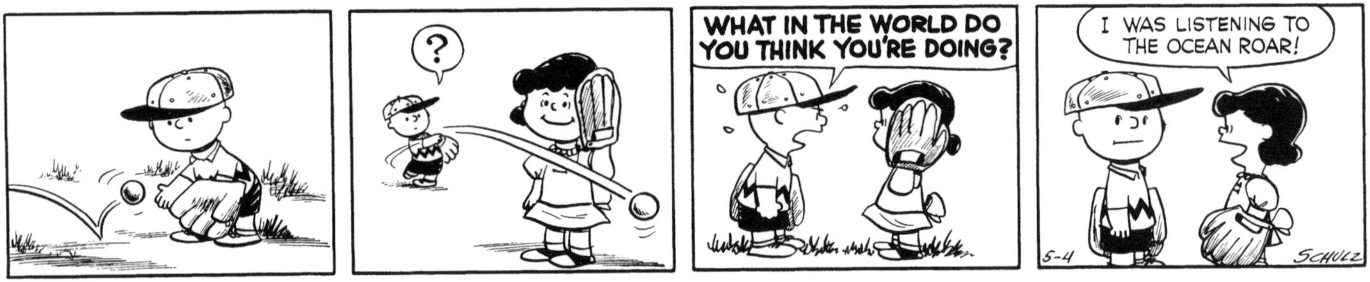
?
WHAT IN THE WORLD DO YOU THINK YOU'RE DOING?
I WAS LISTENING TO THE OCEAN ROAR!
5-4
SCHULZ

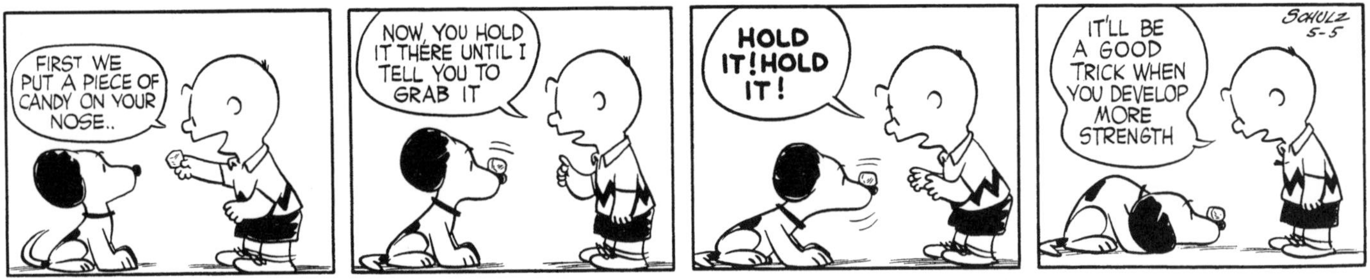
FIRST WE PUT A PIECE OF CANDY ON YOUR NOSE..
NOW, YOU HOLD IT THERE UNTIL I TELL YOU TO GRAB IT
HOLD IT! HOLD IT!
SCHULZ 5-5
IT'LL BE A GOOD TRICK WHEN YOU DEVELOP MORE STRENGTH

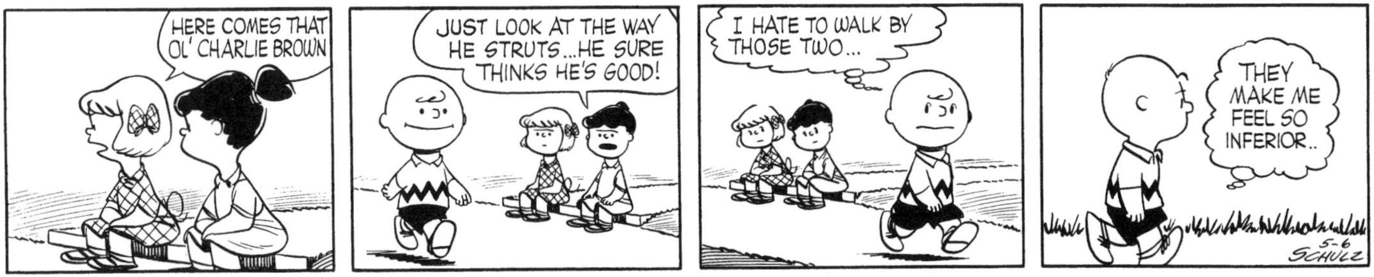
HERE COMES THAT OL' CHARLIE BROWN
JUST LOOK AT THE WAY HE STRUTS...HE SURE THINKS HE'S GOOD!
I HATE TO WALK BY THOSE TWO...
THEY MAKE ME FEEL SO INFERIOR..
5-6 SCHULZ

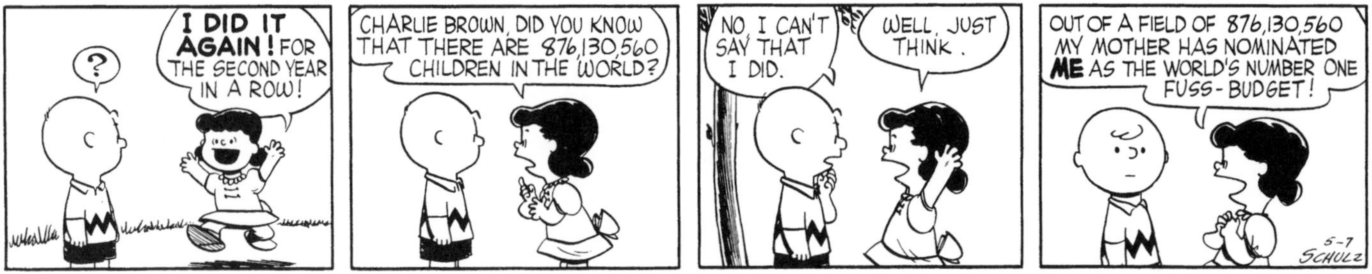
?
I DID IT AGAIN! FOR THE SECOND YEAR IN A ROW!
CHARLIE BROWN, DID YOU KNOW THAT THERE ARE 876,130,560 CHILDREN IN THE WORLD?
NO, I CAN'T SAY THAT I DID.
WELL, JUST THINK.
OUT OF A FIELD OF 876,130,560 MY MOTHER HAS NOMINATED ME AS THE WORLD'S NUMBER ONE FUSS-BUDGET!
5-7 SCHULZ

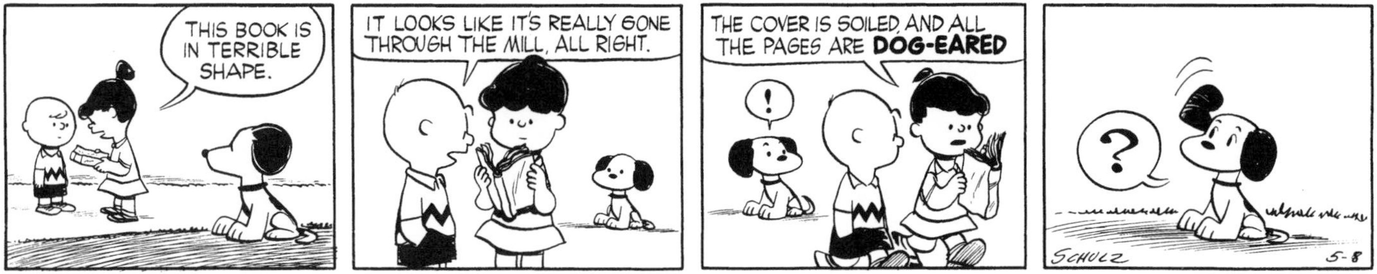
THIS BOOK IS IN TERRIBLE SHAPE.
IT LOOKS LIKE IT'S REALLY GONE THROUGH THE MILL, ALL RIGHT.
!
THE COVER IS SOILED, AND ALL THE PAGES ARE DOG-EARED
?
SCHULZ 5-8

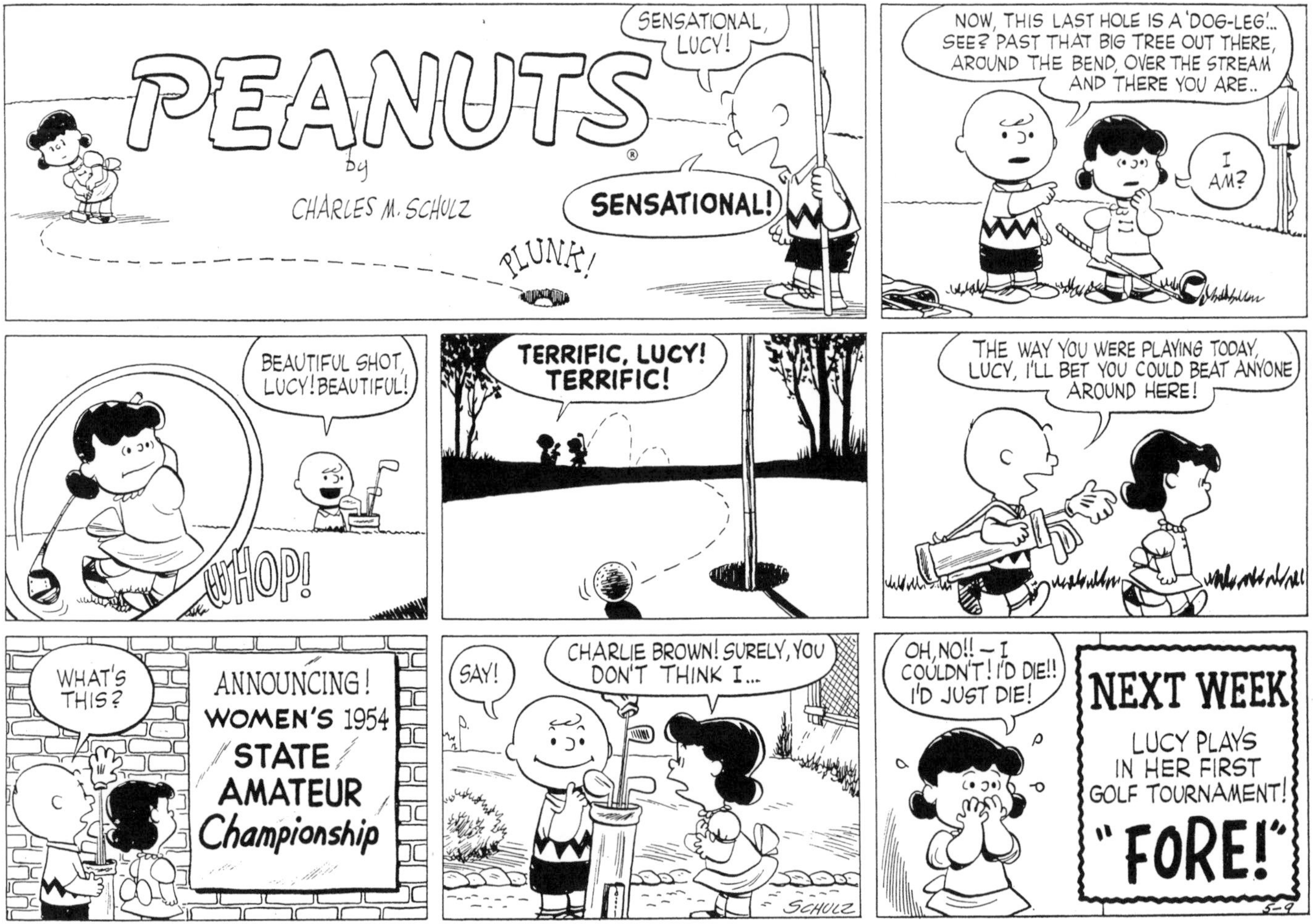
SENSATIONAL, LUCY!
PEANUTS®
by CHARLES M. SCHULZ
SENSATIONAL!
PLUNK!
NOW, THIS LAST HOLE IS A 'DOG-LEG'.. SEE? PAST THAT BIG TREE OUT THERE, AROUND THE BEND, OVER THE STREAM AND THERE YOU ARE..
I AM?
BEAUTIFUL SHOT, LUCY! BEAUTIFUL!
WHOP!
TERRIFIC, LUCY! TERRIFIC!
THE WAY YOU WERE PLAYING TODAY, LUCY, I'LL BET YOU COULD BEAT ANYONE AROUND HERE!
WHAT'S THIS?
ANNOUNCING! WOMEN'S 1954 STATE AMATEUR Championship
SAY!
CHARLIE BROWN! SURELY, YOU DON'T THINK I...
SCHULZ
OH, NO!! – I COULDN'T! I'D DIE!! I'D JUST DIE!
NEXT WEEK
LUCY PLAYS IN HER FIRST GOLF TOURNAMENT!
"FORE!"
5-9

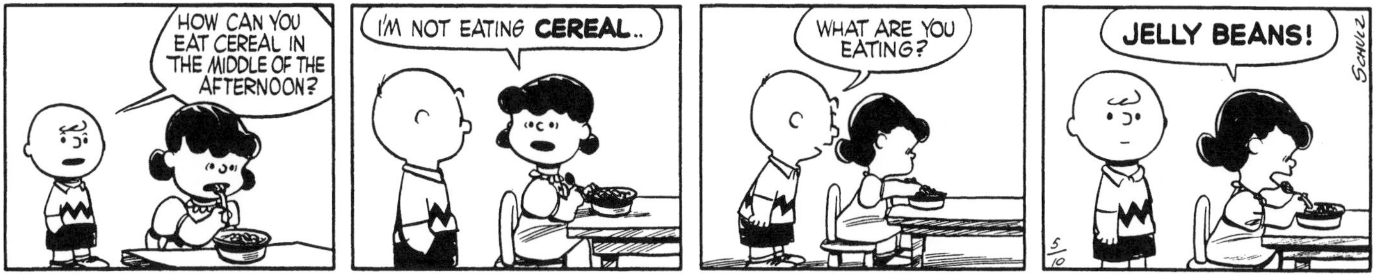
HOW CAN YOU EAT CEREAL IN THE MIDDLE OF THE AFTERNOON?
I'M NOT EATING CEREAL..
WHAT ARE YOU EATING?
JELLY BEANS!
SCHULZ
5/10

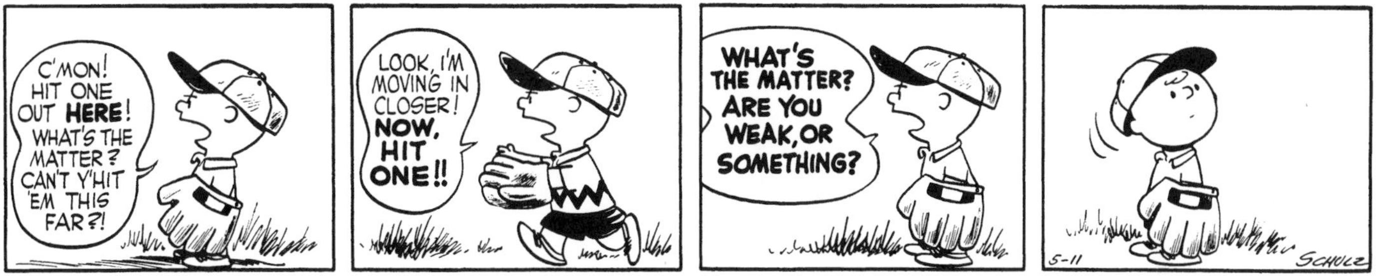
C'MON! HIT ONE OUT HERE! WHAT'S THE MATTER? CAN'T Y'HIT 'EM THIS FAR?!
LOOK, I'M MOVING IN CLOSER! NOW, HIT ONE!!
WHAT'S THE MATTER? ARE YOU WEAK, OR SOMETHING?
5-11
SCHULZ

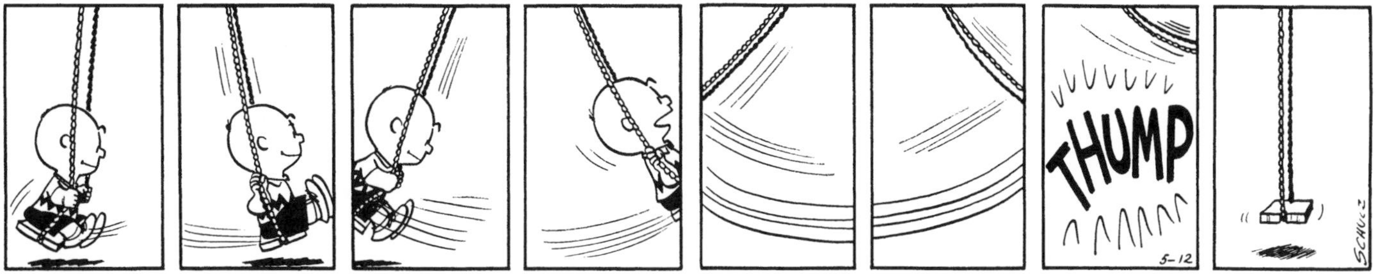
THUMP
5-12
SCHULZ

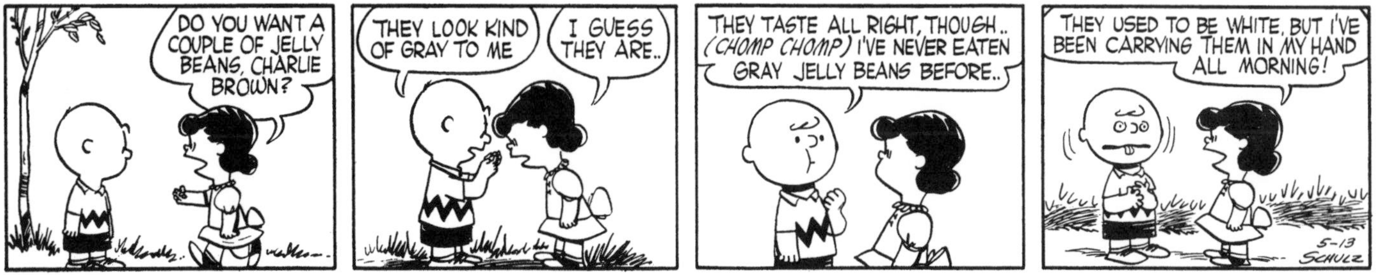
DO YOU WANT A COUPLE OF JELLY BEANS, CHARLIE BROWN?
THEY LOOK KIND OF GRAY TO ME
I GUESS THEY ARE..
THEY TASTE ALL RIGHT, THOUGH.. (CHOMP CHOMP) I'VE NEVER EATEN GRAY JELLY BEANS BEFORE..
THEY USED TO BE WHITE, BUT I'VE BEEN CARRYING THEM IN MY HAND ALL MORNING!
5-13
SCHULZ

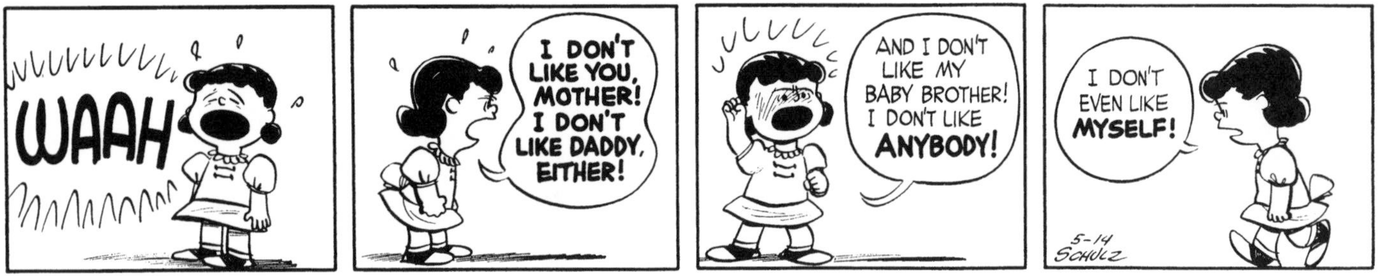
WAAH
I DON'T LIKE YOU, MOTHER! I DON'T LIKE DADDY, EITHER!
AND I DON'T LIKE MY BABY BROTHER! I DON'T LIKE ANYBODY!
I DON'T EVEN LIKE MYSELF!
5-14
SCHULZ

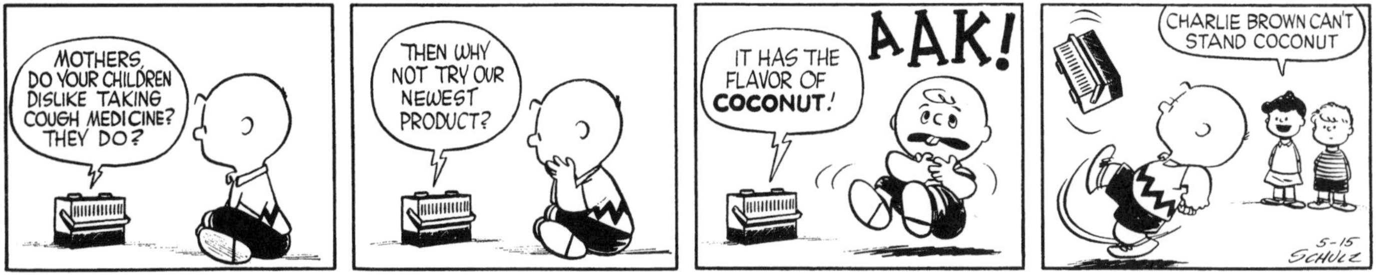
MOTHERS, DO YOUR CHILDREN DISLIKE TAKING COUGH MEDICINE? THEY DO?
THEN WHY NOT TRY OUR NEWEST PRODUCT?
IT HAS THE FLAVOR OF COCONUT!
AAK!
CHARLIE BROWN CAN'T STAND COCONUT
5-15
SCHULZ

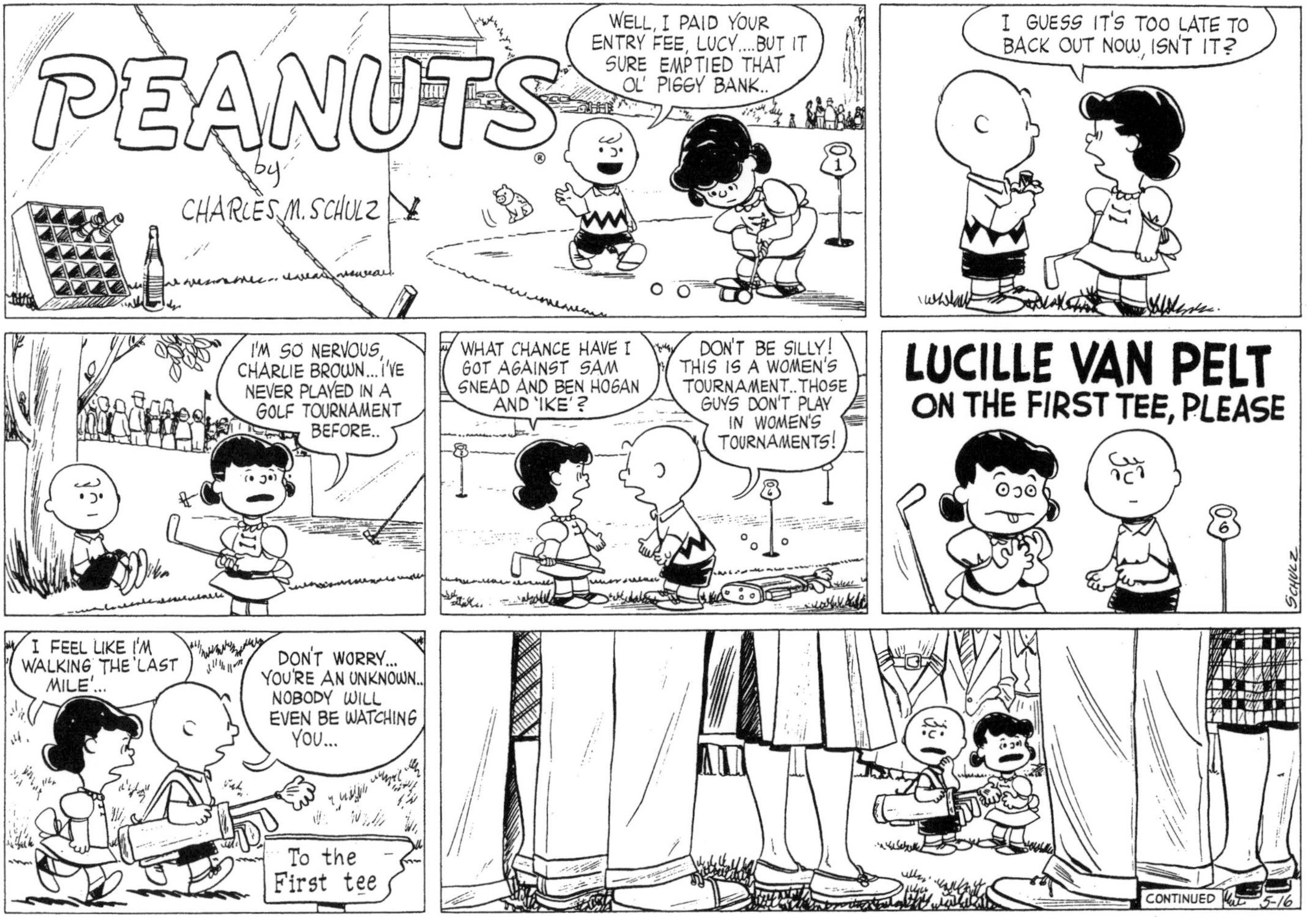
PEANUTS
by CHARLES M. SCHULZ
WELL, I PAID YOUR ENTRY FEE, LUCY....BUT IT SURE EMPTIED THAT OL' PIGGY BANK..
I GUESS IT'S TOO LATE TO BACK OUT NOW, ISN'T IT?
I'M SO NERVOUS, CHARLIE BROWN...I'VE NEVER PLAYED IN A GOLF TOURNAMENT BEFORE..
WHAT CHANCE HAVE I GOT AGAINST SAM SNEAD AND BEN HOGAN AND 'IKE'?
DON'T BE SILLY! THIS IS A WOMEN'S TOURNAMENT..THOSE GUYS DON'T PLAY IN WOMEN'S TOURNAMENTS!
LUCILLE VAN PELT ON THE FIRST TEE, PLEASE
I FEEL LIKE I'M WALKING THE 'LAST MILE'...
DON'T WORRY... YOU'RE AN UNKNOWN.. NOBODY WILL EVEN BE WATCHING YOU...
To the First tee
CONTINUED
5-16

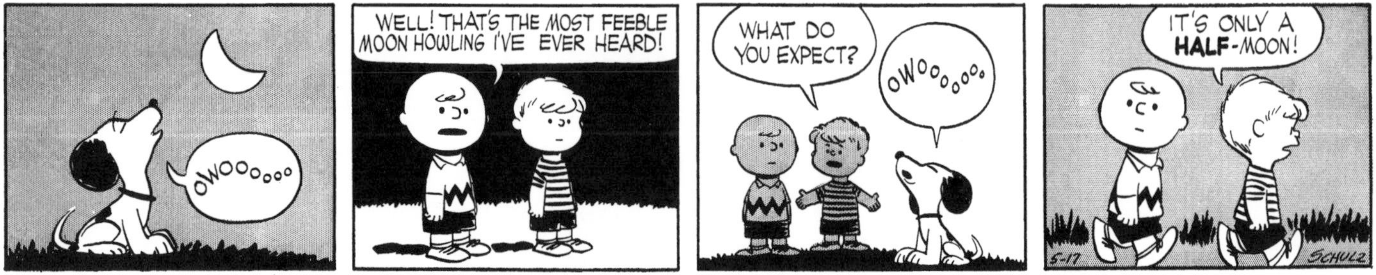
OWOOoooo
WELL! THAT'S THE MOST FEEBLE MOON HOWLING I'VE EVER HEARD!
WHAT DO YOU EXPECT?
OWOOoooooo
IT'S ONLY A **HALF**-MOON!
5-17
SCHULZ

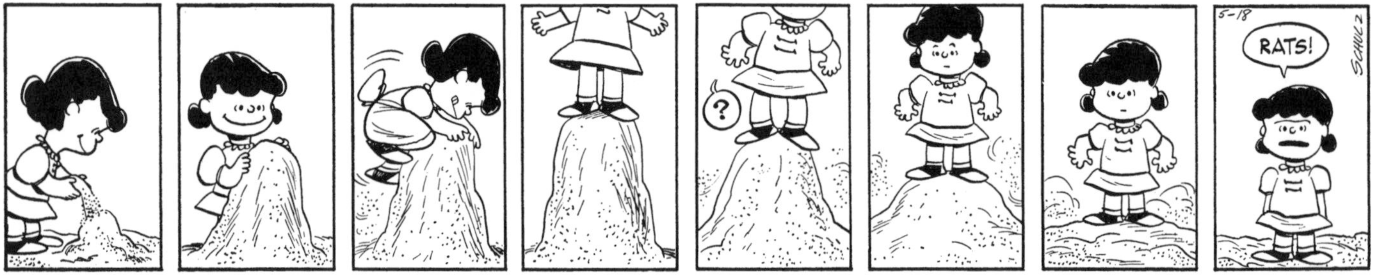
?
5-18
SCHULZ
RATS!

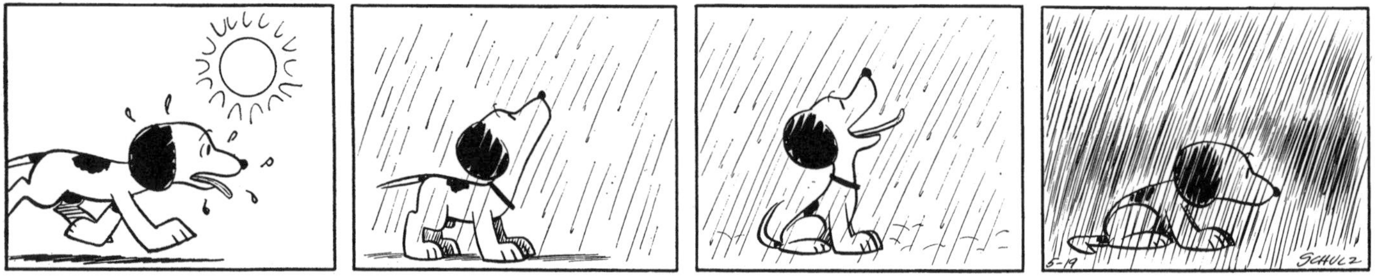
5-19
SCHULZ

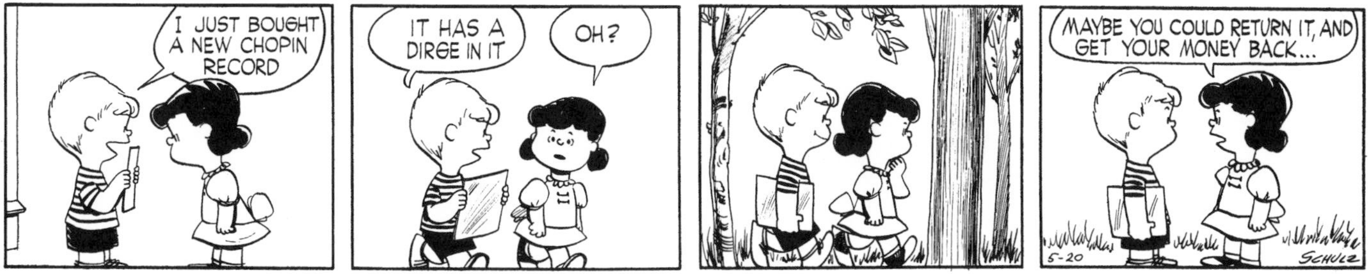
I JUST BOUGHT A NEW CHOPIN RECORD
IT HAS A DIRGE IN IT
OH?
MAYBE YOU COULD RETURN IT, AND GET YOUR MONEY BACK...
5-20
SCHULZ

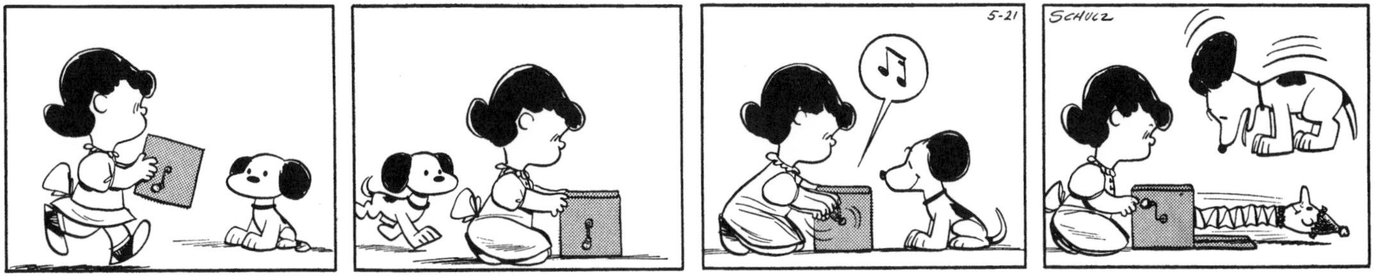
5-21
SCHULZ

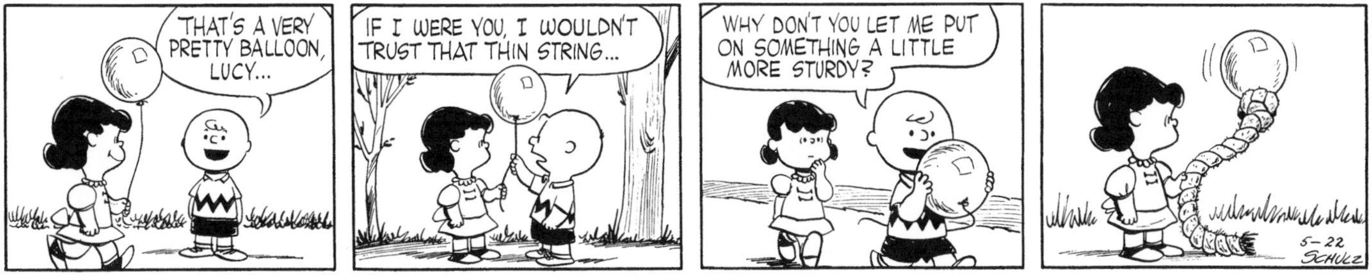
THAT'S A VERY PRETTY BALLOON, LUCY...
IF I WERE YOU, I WOULDN'T TRUST THAT THIN STRING...
WHY DON'T YOU LET ME PUT ON SOMETHING A LITTLE MORE STURDY?
5-22
SCHULZ

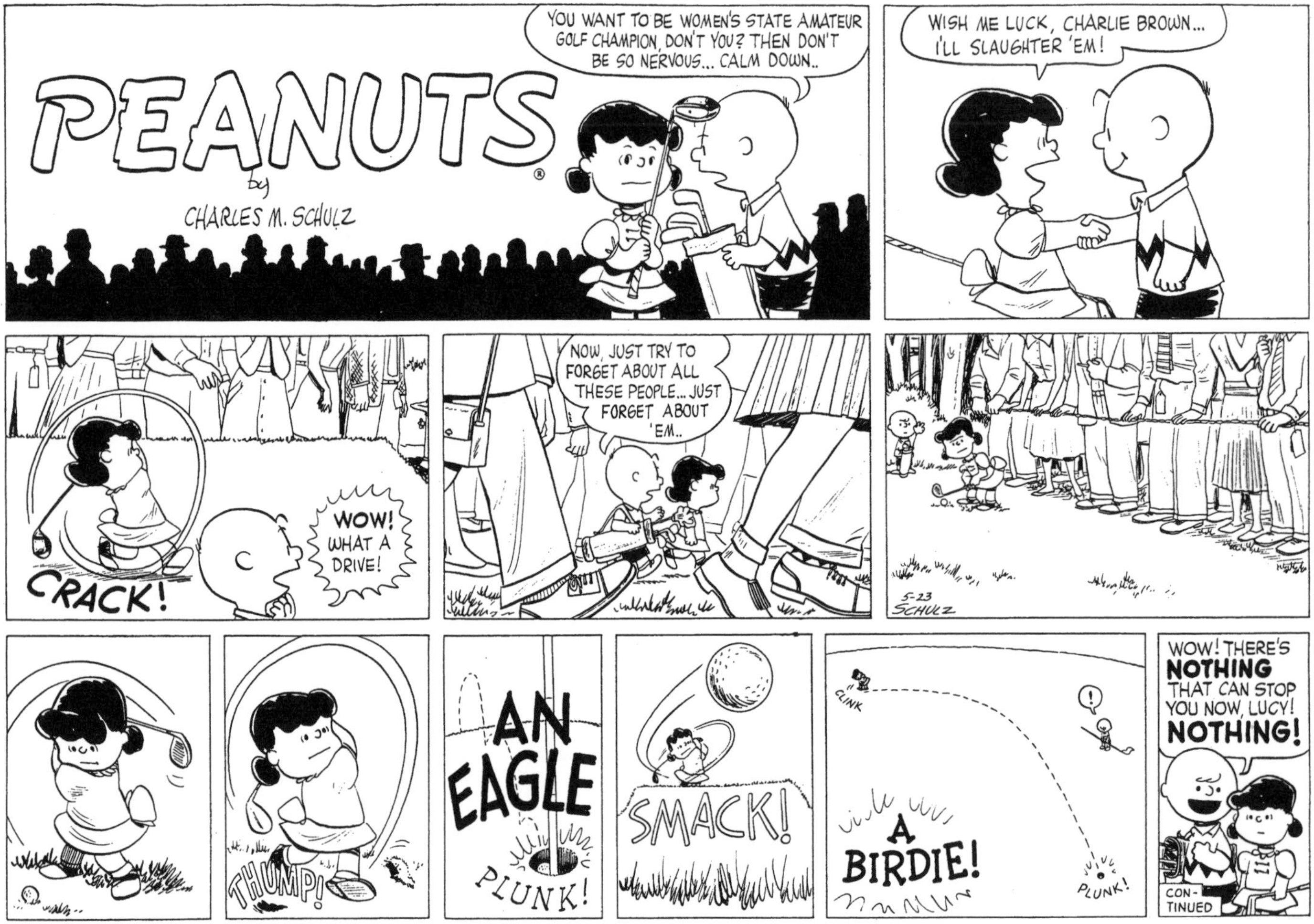

PEANUTS
by CHARLES M. SCHULZ
YOU WANT TO BE WOMEN'S STATE AMATEUR GOLF CHAMPION, DON'T YOU? THEN DON'T BE SO NERVOUS... CALM DOWN..
WISH ME LUCK, CHARLIE BROWN... I'LL SLAUGHTER 'EM!
CRACK!
WOW! WHAT A DRIVE!
NOW, JUST TRY TO FORGET ABOUT ALL THESE PEOPLE... JUST FORGET ABOUT 'EM..
5-23
SCHULZ
THUMP!
AN EAGLE
PLUNK!
SMACK!
CLINK
!
A BIRDIE!
PLUNK!
WOW! THERE'S NOTHING THAT CAN STOP YOU NOW, LUCY! NOTHING!
CON-TINUED

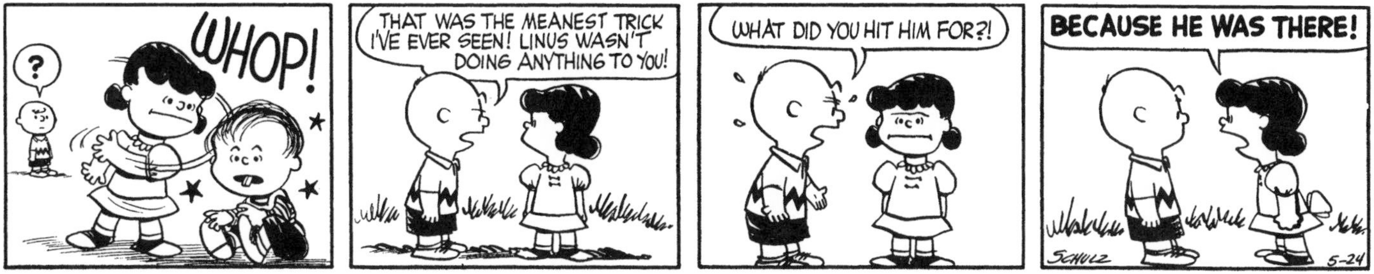
?
WHOP!
THAT WAS THE MEANEST TRICK I'VE EVER SEEN! LINUS WASN'T DOING ANYTHING TO YOU!
WHAT DID YOU HIT HIM FOR?!
BECAUSE HE WAS THERE!
SCHULZ
5-24

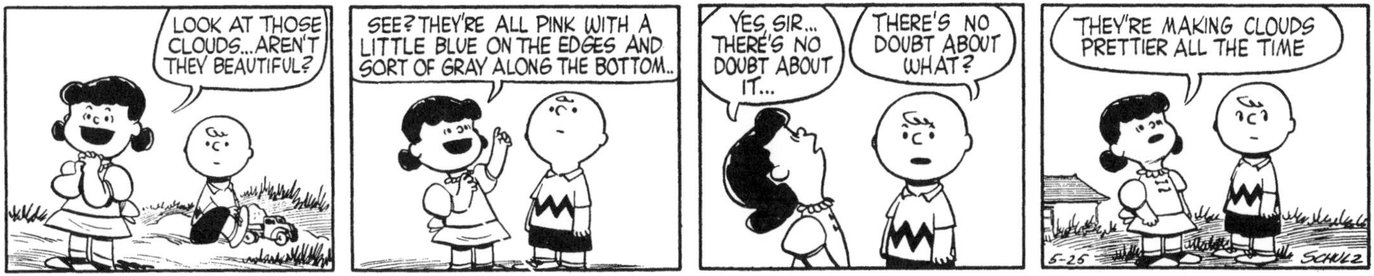
LOOK AT THOSE CLOUDS...AREN'T THEY BEAUTIFUL?
SEE? THEY'RE ALL PINK WITH A LITTLE BLUE ON THE EDGES AND SORT OF GRAY ALONG THE BOTTOM..
YES, SIR... THERE'S NO DOUBT ABOUT IT...
THERE'S NO DOUBT ABOUT WHAT?
THEY'RE MAKING CLOUDS PRETTIER ALL THE TIME
5-25
SCHULZ

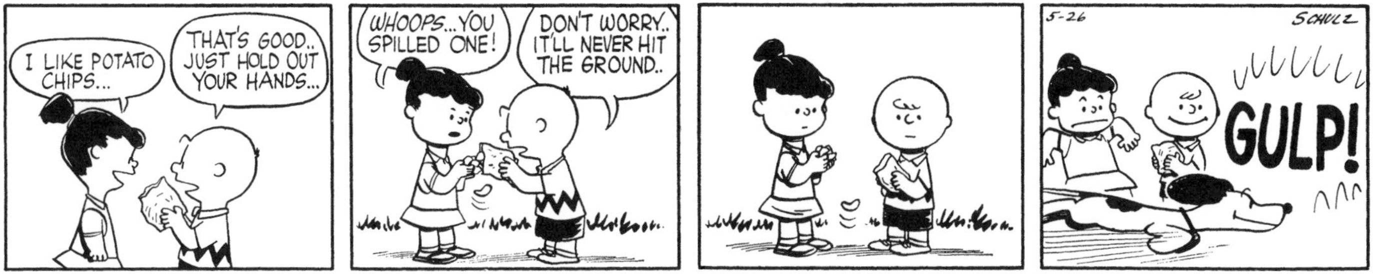
I LIKE POTATO CHIPS...
THAT'S GOOD.. JUST HOLD OUT YOUR HANDS...
WHOOPS...YOU SPILLED ONE!
DON'T WORRY.. IT'LL NEVER HIT THE GROUND..
5-26
SCHULZ
GULP!

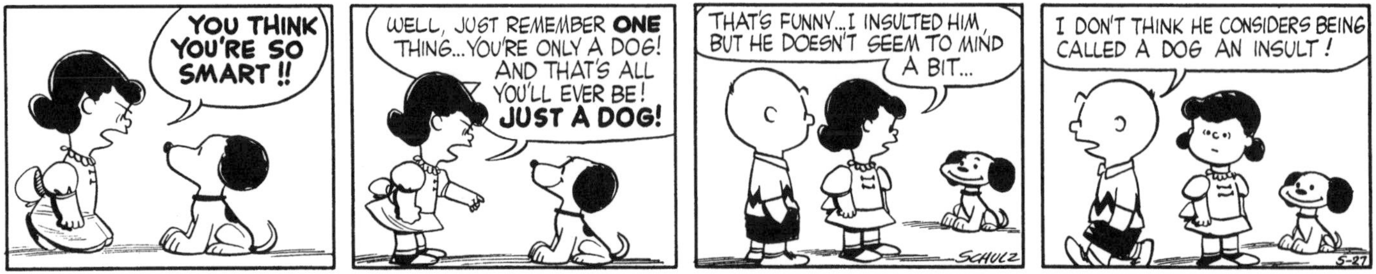
YOU THINK YOU'RE SO SMART !!
WELL, JUST REMEMBER ONE THING... YOU'RE ONLY A DOG! AND THAT'S ALL YOU'LL EVER BE! JUST A DOG!
THAT'S FUNNY... I INSULTED HIM, BUT HE DOESN'T SEEM TO MIND A BIT...
SCHULZ
I DON'T THINK HE CONSIDERS BEING CALLED A DOG AN INSULT!
5-27

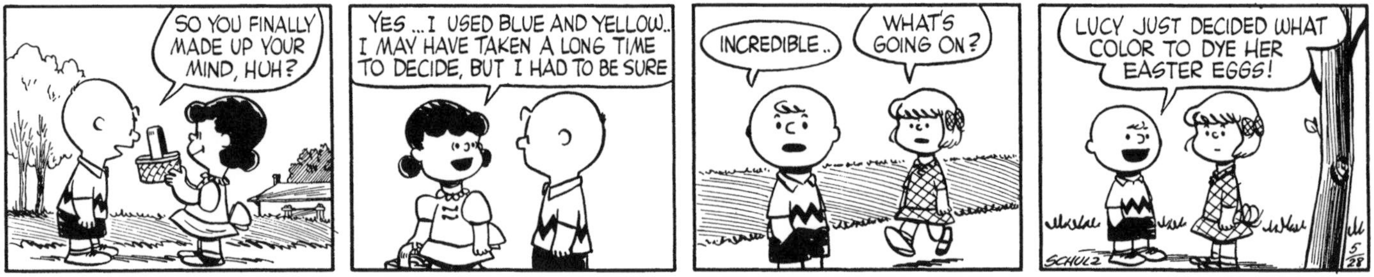
SO YOU FINALLY MADE UP YOUR MIND, HUH?
YES ... I USED BLUE AND YELLOW.. I MAY HAVE TAKEN A LONG TIME TO DECIDE, BUT I HAD TO BE SURE
INCREDIBLE ..
WHAT'S GOING ON?
LUCY JUST DECIDED WHAT COLOR TO DYE HER EASTER EGGS!
SCHULZ
5 28

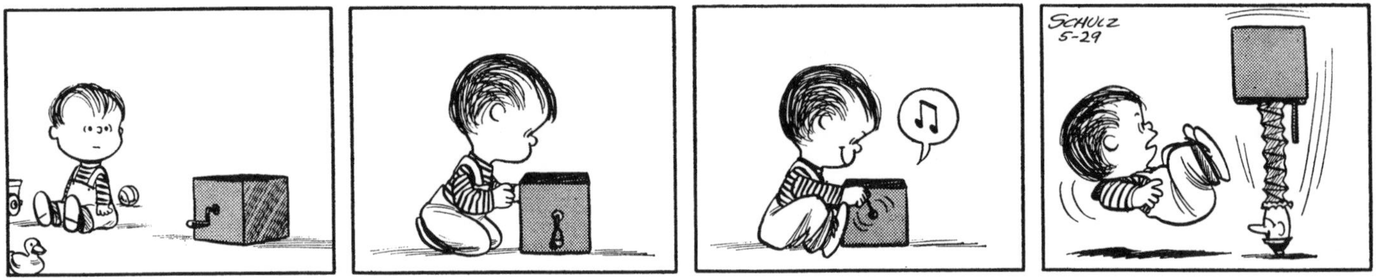
SCHULZ 5-29

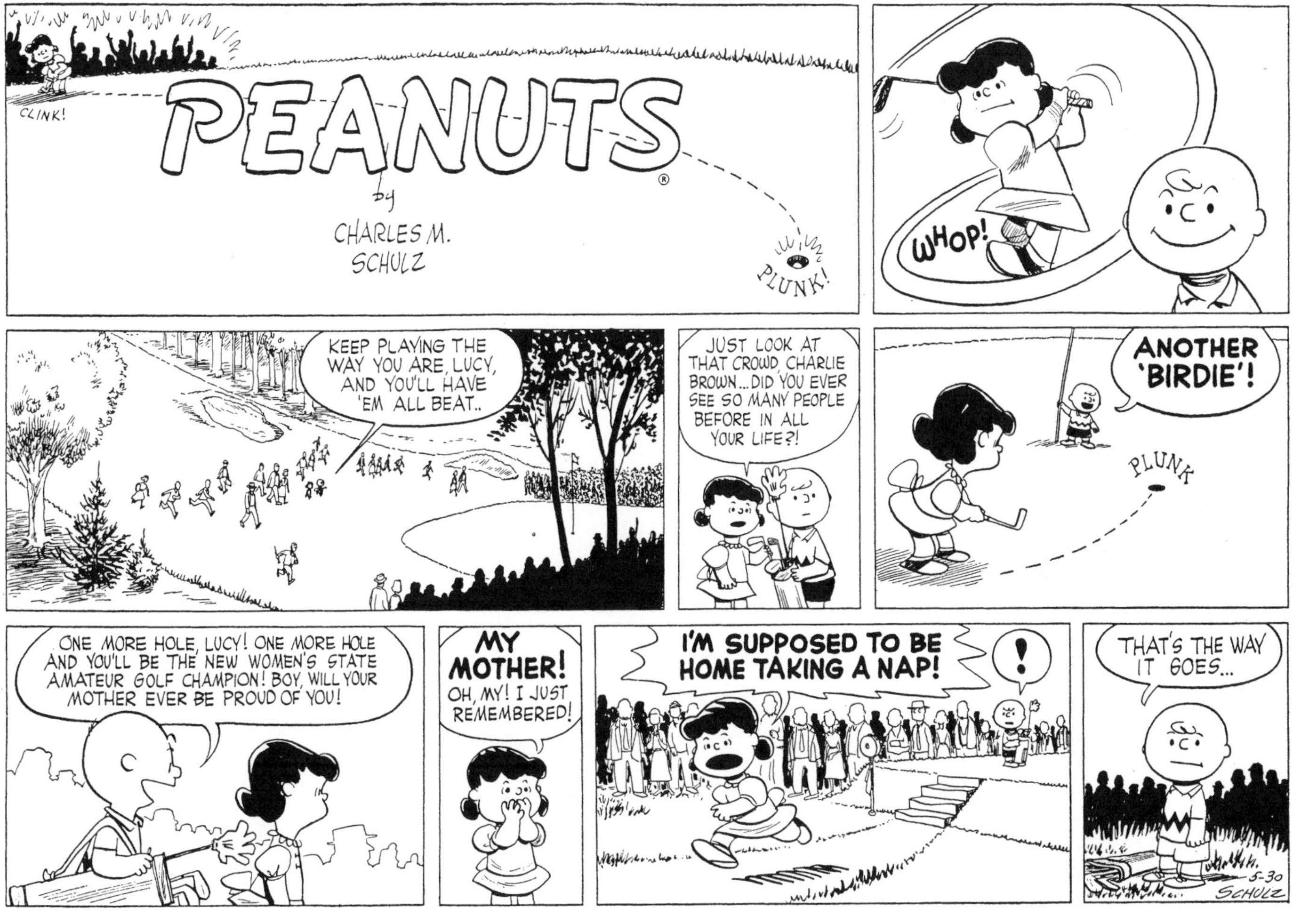
CLINK!
PEANUTS
by
CHARLES M. SCHULZ
PLUNK!
WHOP!
KEEP PLAYING THE WAY YOU ARE, LUCY, AND YOU'LL HAVE 'EM ALL BEAT..
JUST LOOK AT THAT CROWD, CHARLIE BROWN... DID YOU EVER SEE SO MANY PEOPLE BEFORE IN ALL YOUR LIFE?!
ANOTHER 'BIRDIE'!
PLUNK
ONE MORE HOLE, LUCY! ONE MORE HOLE AND YOU'LL BE THE NEW WOMEN'S STATE AMATEUR GOLF CHAMPION! BOY, WILL YOUR MOTHER EVER BE PROUD OF YOU!
MY MOTHER!
OH, MY! I JUST REMEMBERED!
I'M SUPPOSED TO BE HOME TAKING A NAP!
!
THAT'S THE WAY IT GOES...
5-30
SCHULZ

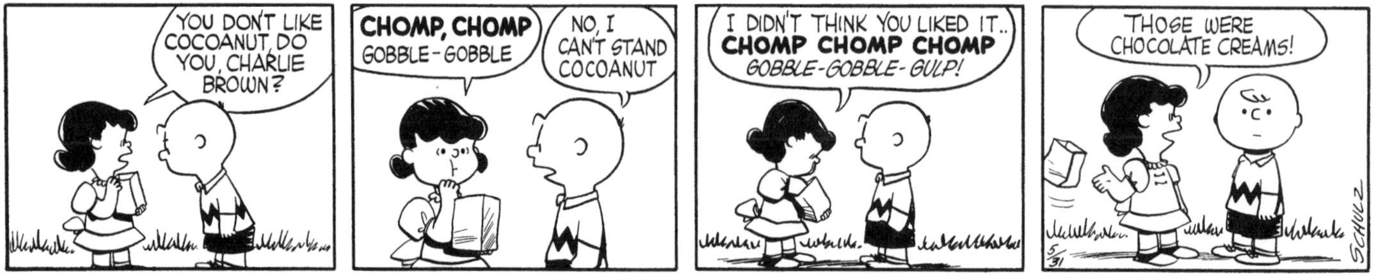
YOU DON'T LIKE COCOANUT, DO YOU, CHARLIE BROWN?
CHOMP, CHOMP GOBBLE-GOBBLE
NO, I CAN'T STAND COCOANUT
I DIDN'T THINK YOU LIKED IT.. CHOMP CHOMP CHOMP GOBBLE-GOBBLE-GULP!
THOSE WERE CHOCOLATE CREAMS!
5/31
SCHULZ

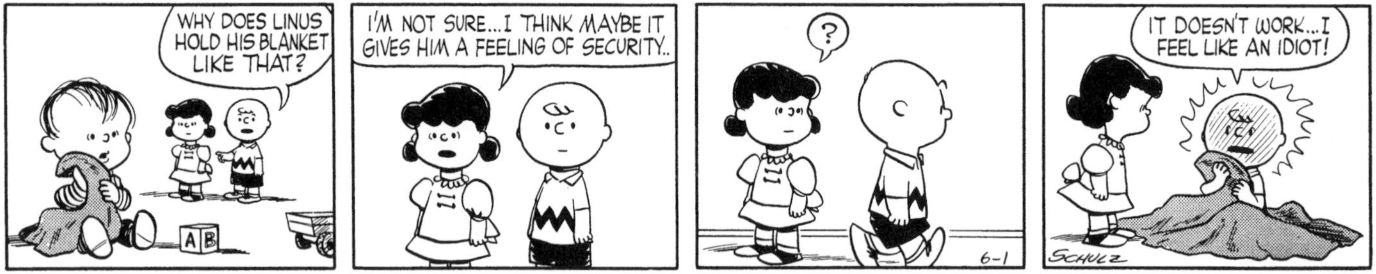
WHY DOES LINUS HOLD HIS BLANKET LIKE THAT?
A B
I'M NOT SURE...I THINK MAYBE IT GIVES HIM A FEELING OF SECURITY..
?
6-1
IT DOESN'T WORK...I FEEL LIKE AN IDIOT!
SCHULZ

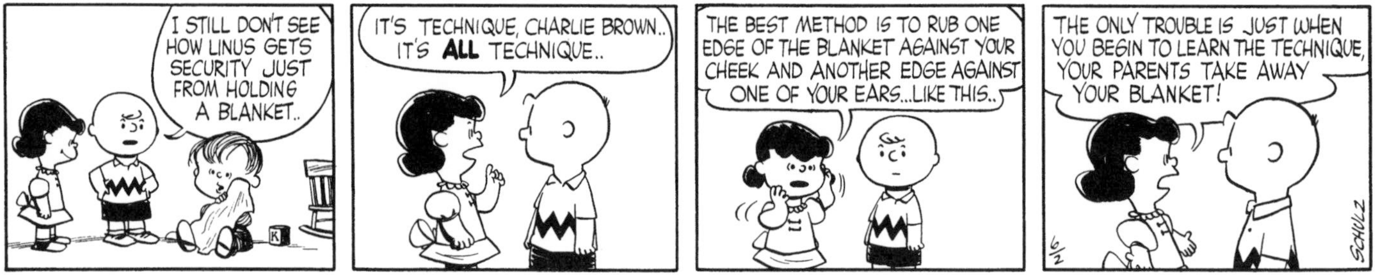
I STILL DON'T SEE HOW LINUS GETS SECURITY JUST FROM HOLDING A BLANKET..
K
IT'S TECHNIQUE, CHARLIE BROWN.. IT'S ALL TECHNIQUE..
THE BEST METHOD IS TO RUB ONE EDGE OF THE BLANKET AGAINST YOUR CHEEK AND ANOTHER EDGE AGAINST ONE OF YOUR EARS...LIKE THIS..
THE ONLY TROUBLE IS JUST WHEN YOU BEGIN TO LEARN THE TECHNIQUE, YOUR PARENTS TAKE AWAY YOUR BLANKET!
6/2
SCHULZ

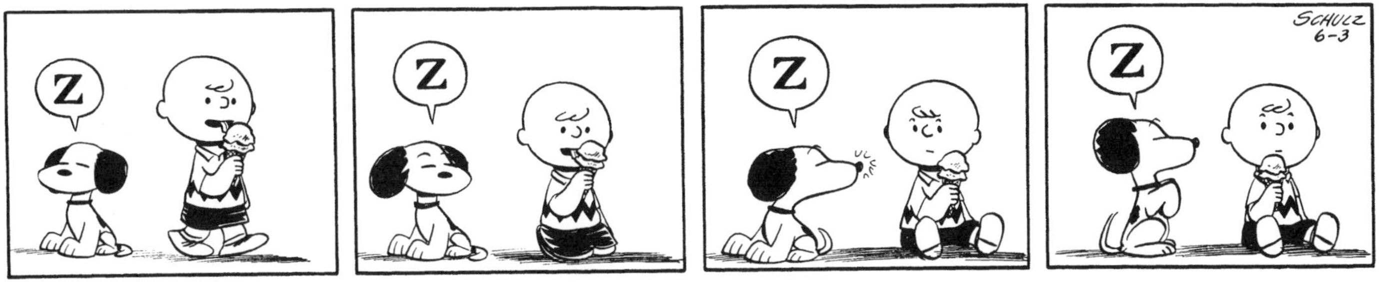
Z
Z
Z
Z
SCHULZ 6-3

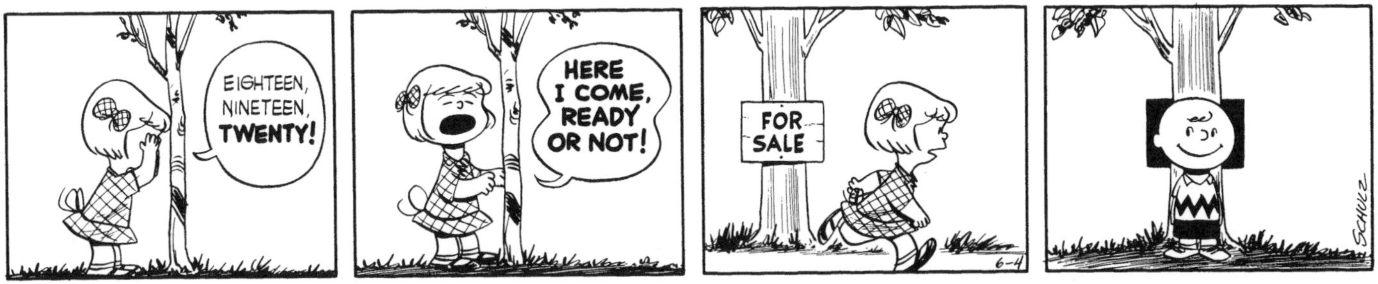
EIGHTEEN, NINETEEN, TWENTY!
HERE I COME, READY OR NOT!
FOR SALE
6-4
SCHULZ

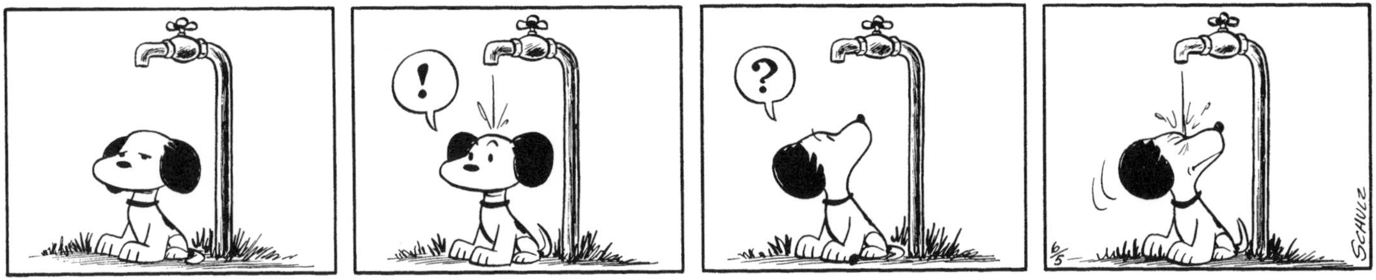
!
?
6/5
SCHULZ

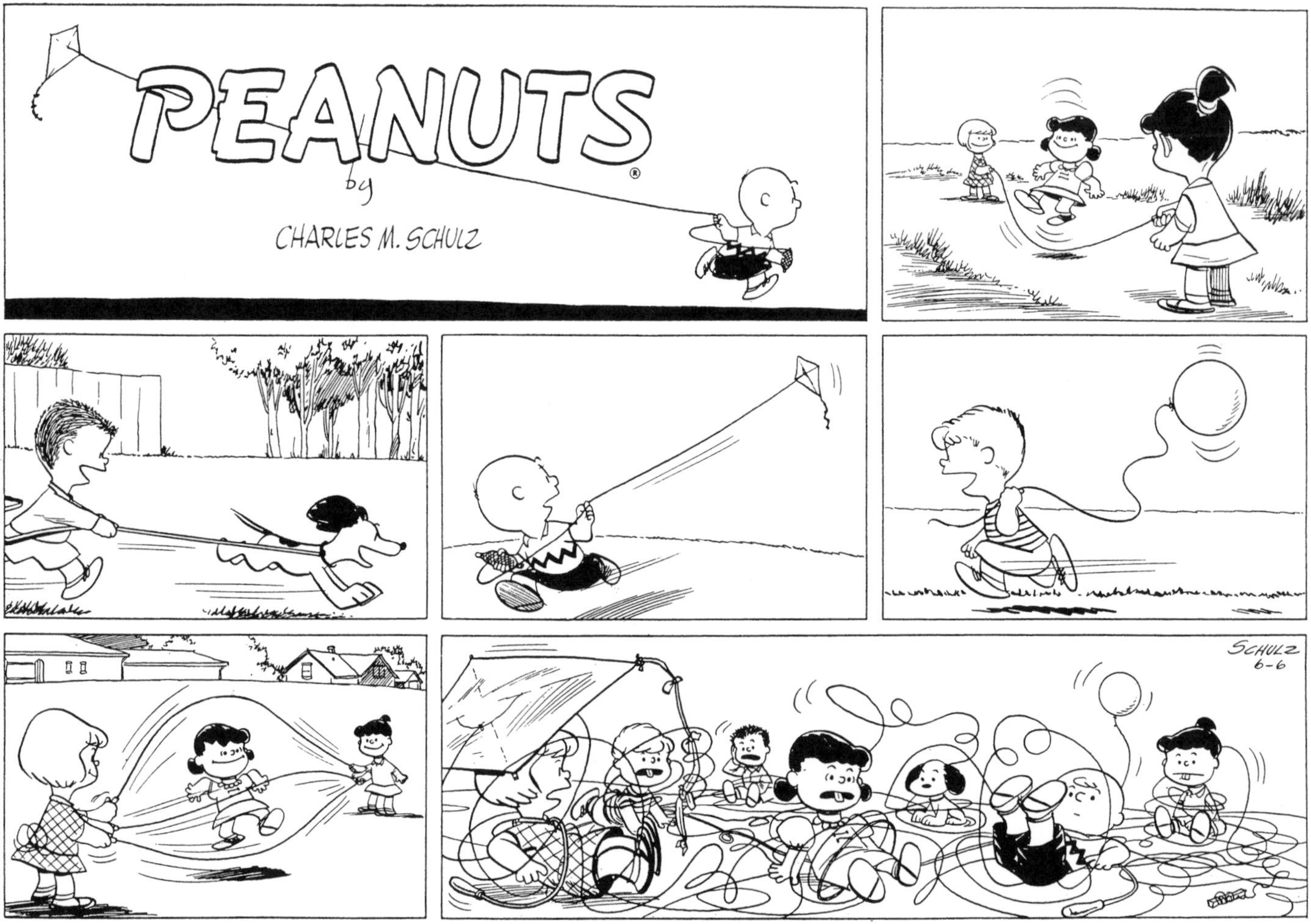
PEANUTS
by
CHARLES M. SCHULZ
SCHULZ
6-6

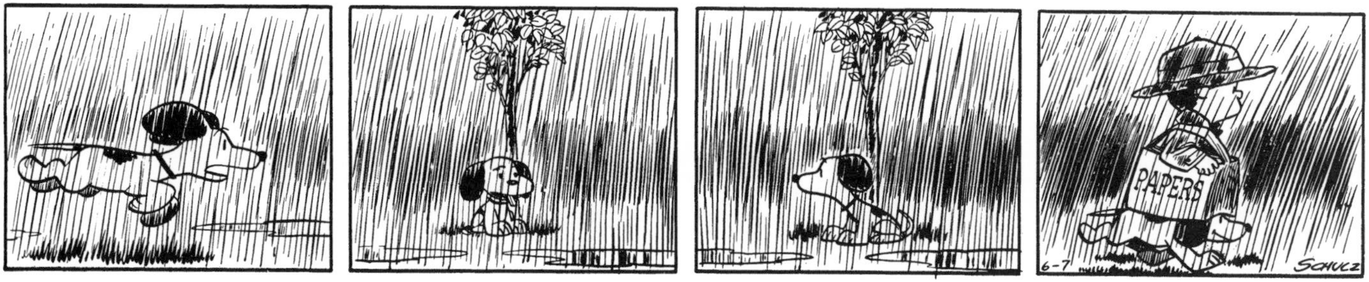
PAPERS
6-7
SCHULZ

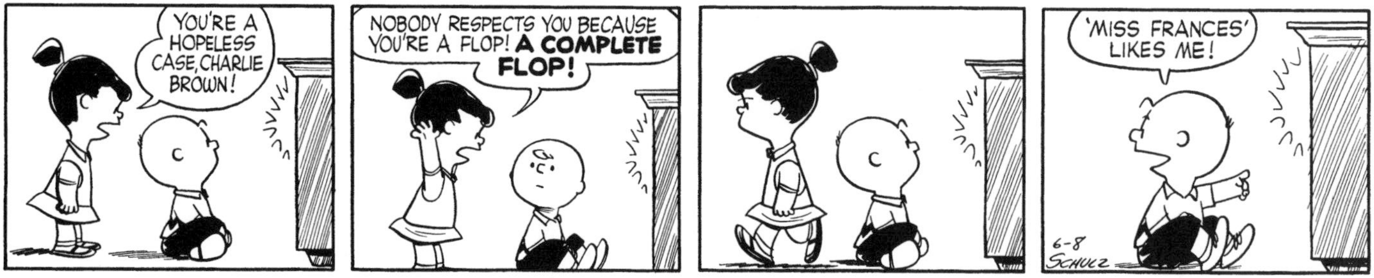
YOU'RE A HOPELESS CASE, CHARLIE BROWN!
NOBODY RESPECTS YOU BECAUSE YOU'RE A FLOP! **A COMPLETE FLOP!**
'MISS FRANCES' LIKES ME!
6-8
SCHULZ

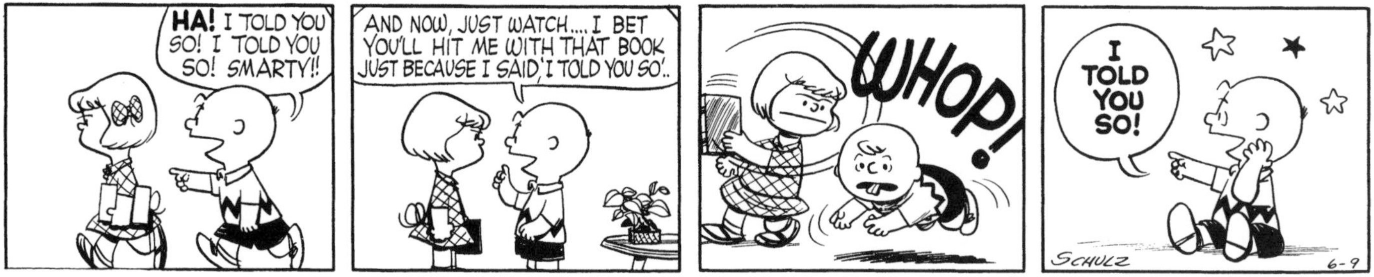
HA! I TOLD YOU SO! I TOLD YOU SO! SMARTY!!
AND NOW, JUST WATCH.... I BET YOU'LL HIT ME WITH THAT BOOK JUST BECAUSE I SAID,'I TOLD YOU SO'..
WHOP!
I TOLD YOU SO!
SCHULZ
6-9

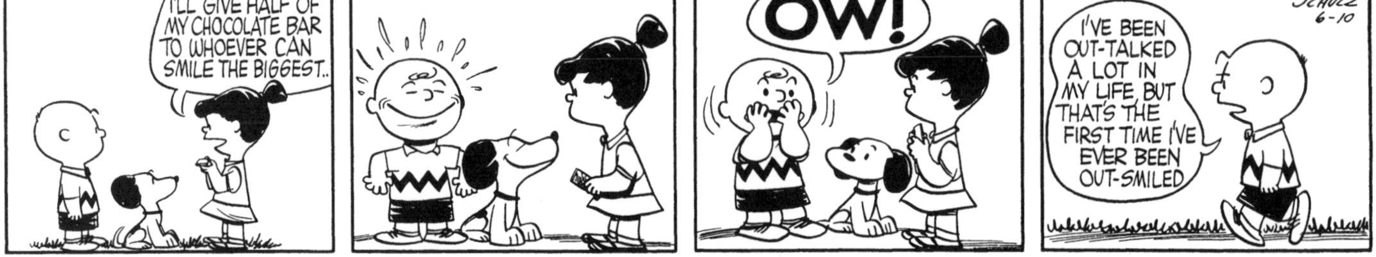
I'LL GIVE HALF OF MY CHOCOLATE BAR TO WHOEVER CAN SMILE THE BIGGEST..
OW!
SCHULZ 6-10
I'VE BEEN OUT-TALKED A LOT IN MY LIFE, BUT THAT'S THE FIRST TIME I'VE EVER BEEN OUT-SMILED

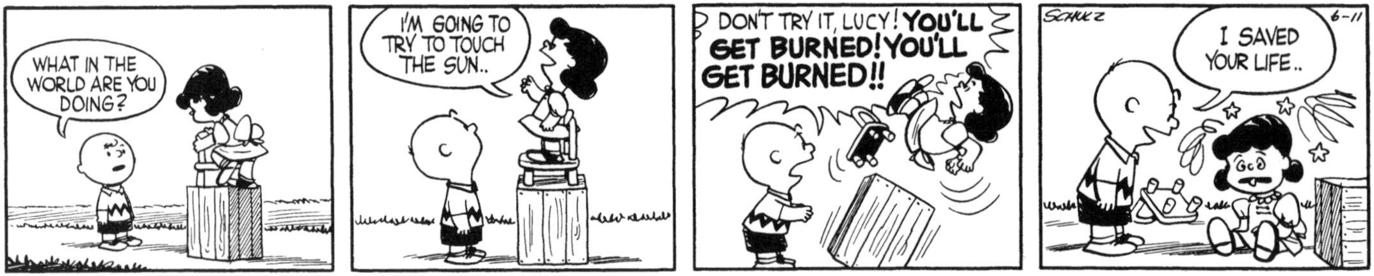
WHAT IN THE WORLD ARE YOU DOING?
I'M GOING TO TRY TO TOUCH THE SUN..
DON'T TRY IT, LUCY! YOU'LL GET BURNED! YOU'LL GET BURNED!!
SCHULZ 6-11
I SAVED YOUR LIFE..

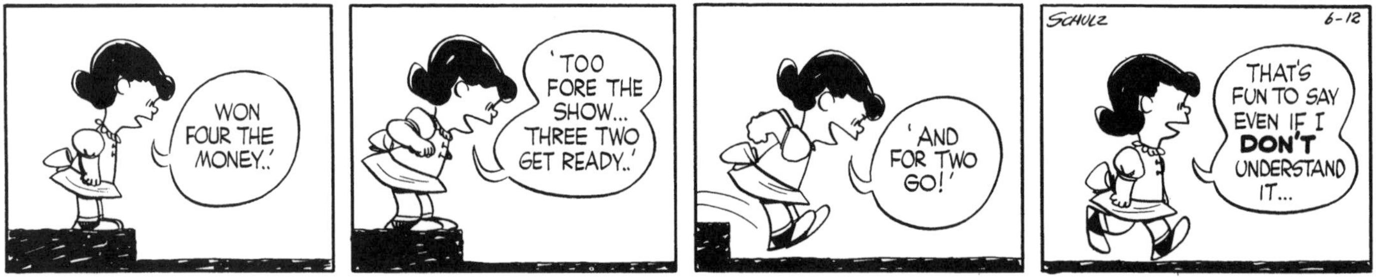
WON FOUR THE MONEY..'
'TOO FORE THE SHOW... THREE TWO GET READY..'
'AND FOR TWO GO!'
SCHULZ 6-12
THAT'S FUN TO SAY EVEN IF I DON'T UNDERSTAND IT...

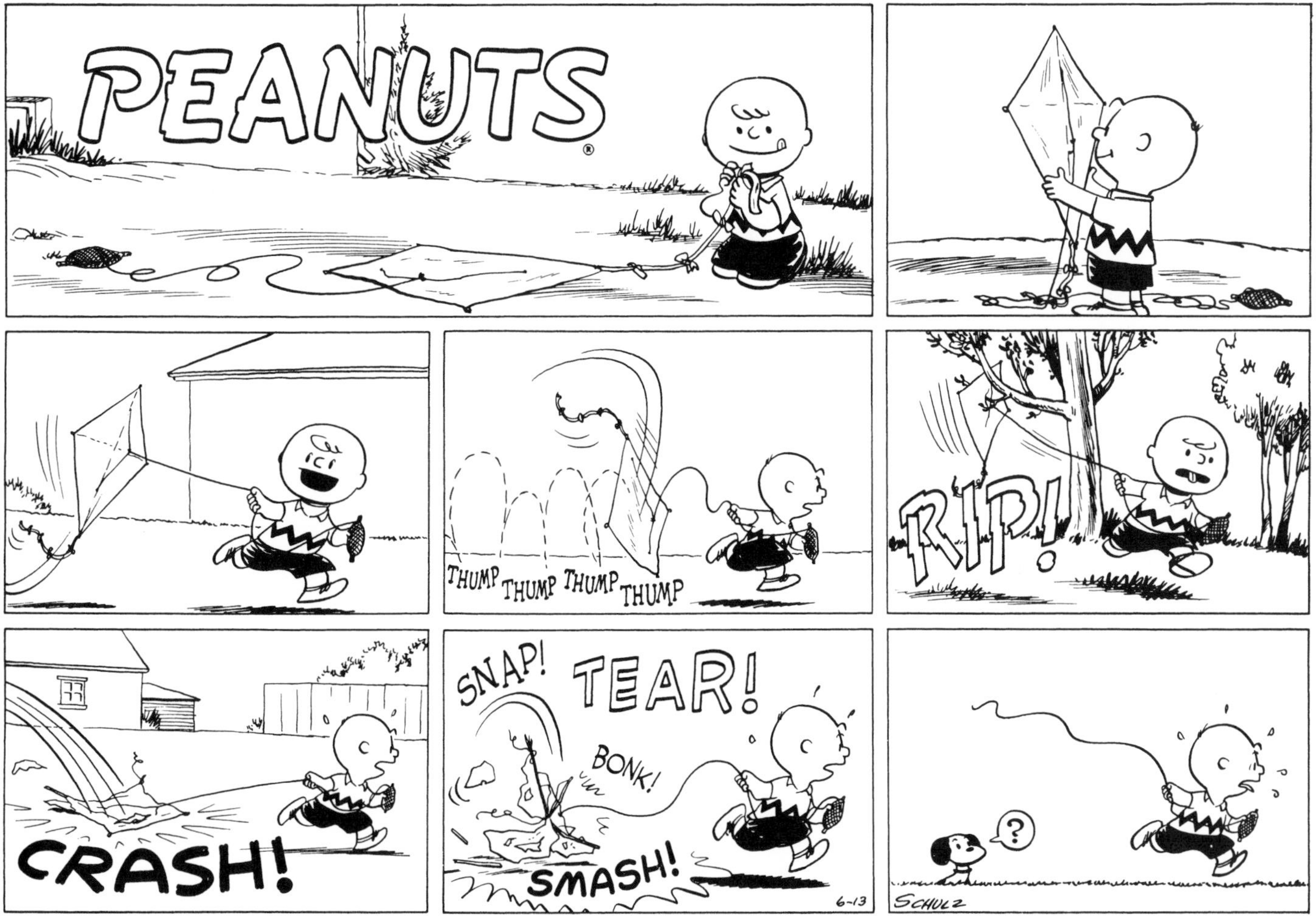
PEANUTS
THUMP THUMP THUMP THUMP
RIP!
CRASH!
SNAP! TEAR!
BONK!
SMASH!
6-13
?
SCHULZ

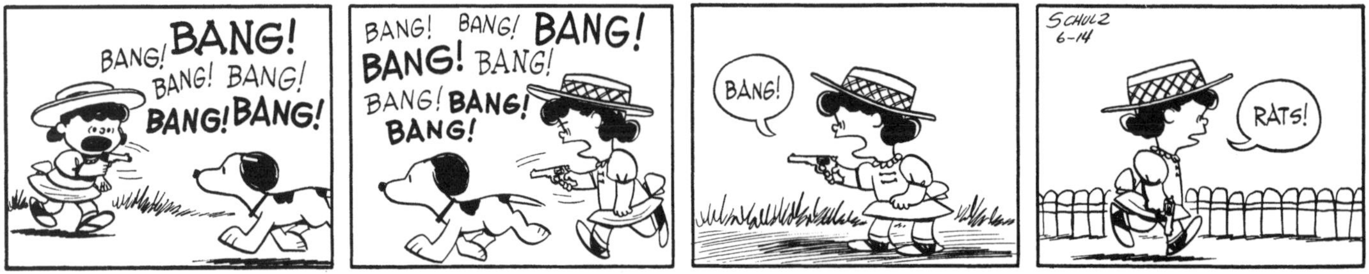
BANG! BANG! BANG! BANG! BANG! BANG!
BANG! BANG! BANG! BANG! BANG! BANG! BANG! BANG!
BANG!
SCHULZ 6-14
RATS!

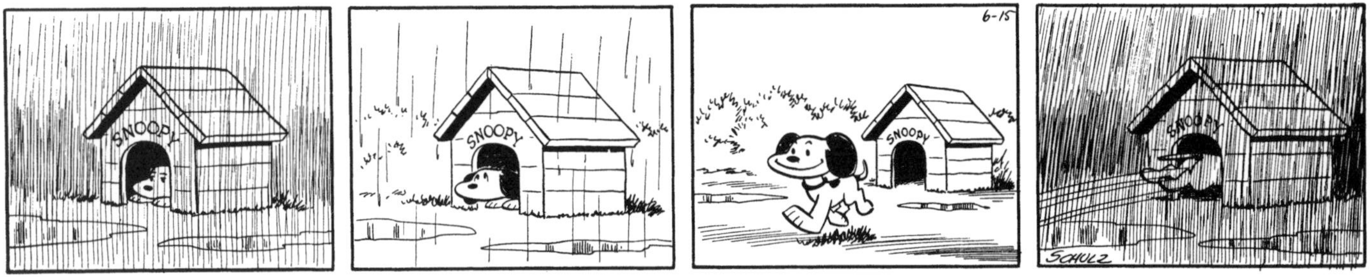
SNOOPY
SNOOPY
6-15
SNOOPY
SNOOPY
SCHULZ

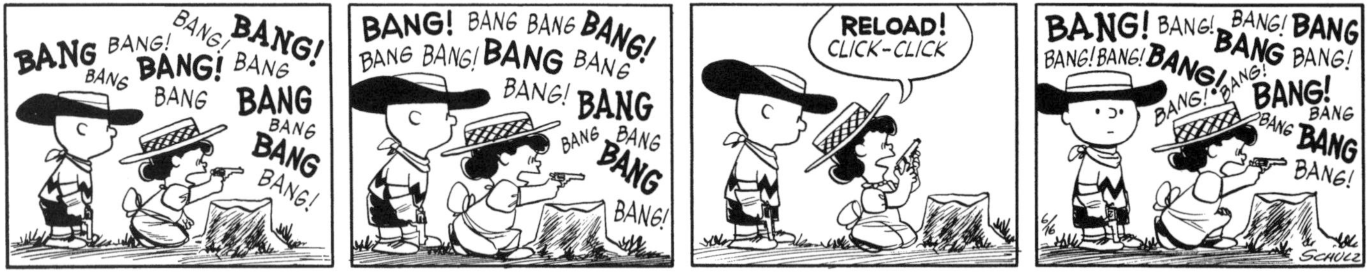
BANG BANG! BANG! BANG! BANG BANG! BANG BANG BANG BANG BANG BANG!
BANG! BANG BANG BANG! BANG BANG! BANG BANG BANG! BANG BANG BANG BANG!
RELOAD! CLICK-CLICK
BANG! BANG! BANG! BANG BANG! BANG! BANG BANG! BANG! BANG! BANG! BANG! BANG BANG BANG BANG!
6/16
SCHULZ

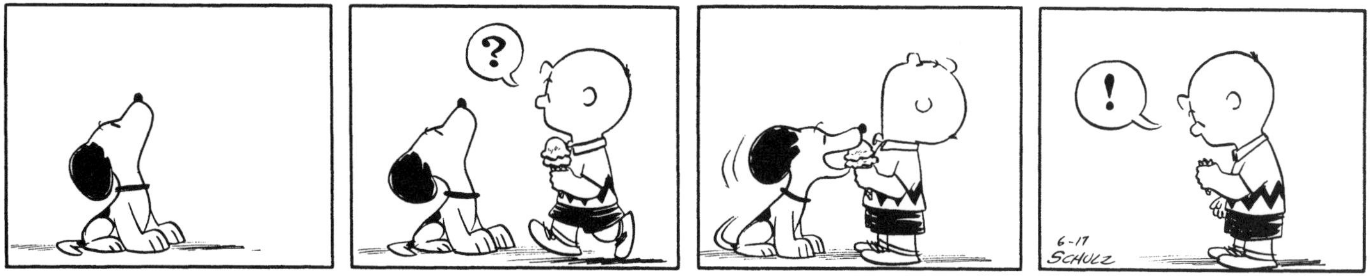
?
!
6-17
SCHULZ

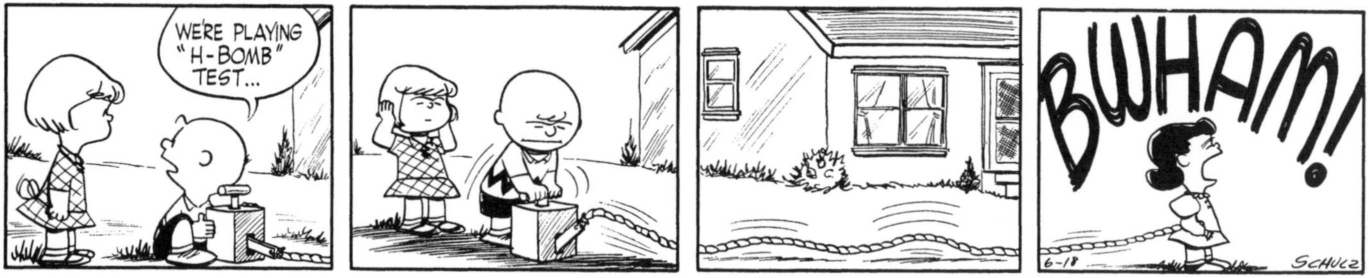
WE'RE PLAYING "H-BOMB" TEST...
BWHAM!
6-18
SCHULZ

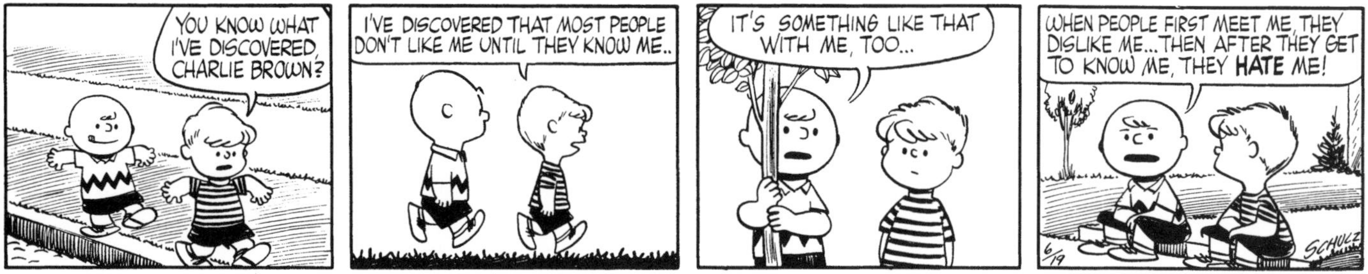
YOU KNOW WHAT I'VE DISCOVERED, CHARLIE BROWN?
I'VE DISCOVERED THAT MOST PEOPLE DON'T LIKE ME UNTIL THEY KNOW ME..
IT'S SOMETHING LIKE THAT WITH ME, TOO...
WHEN PEOPLE FIRST MEET ME, THEY DISLIKE ME...THEN AFTER THEY GET TO KNOW ME, THEY **HATE** ME!
6/19
SCHULZ

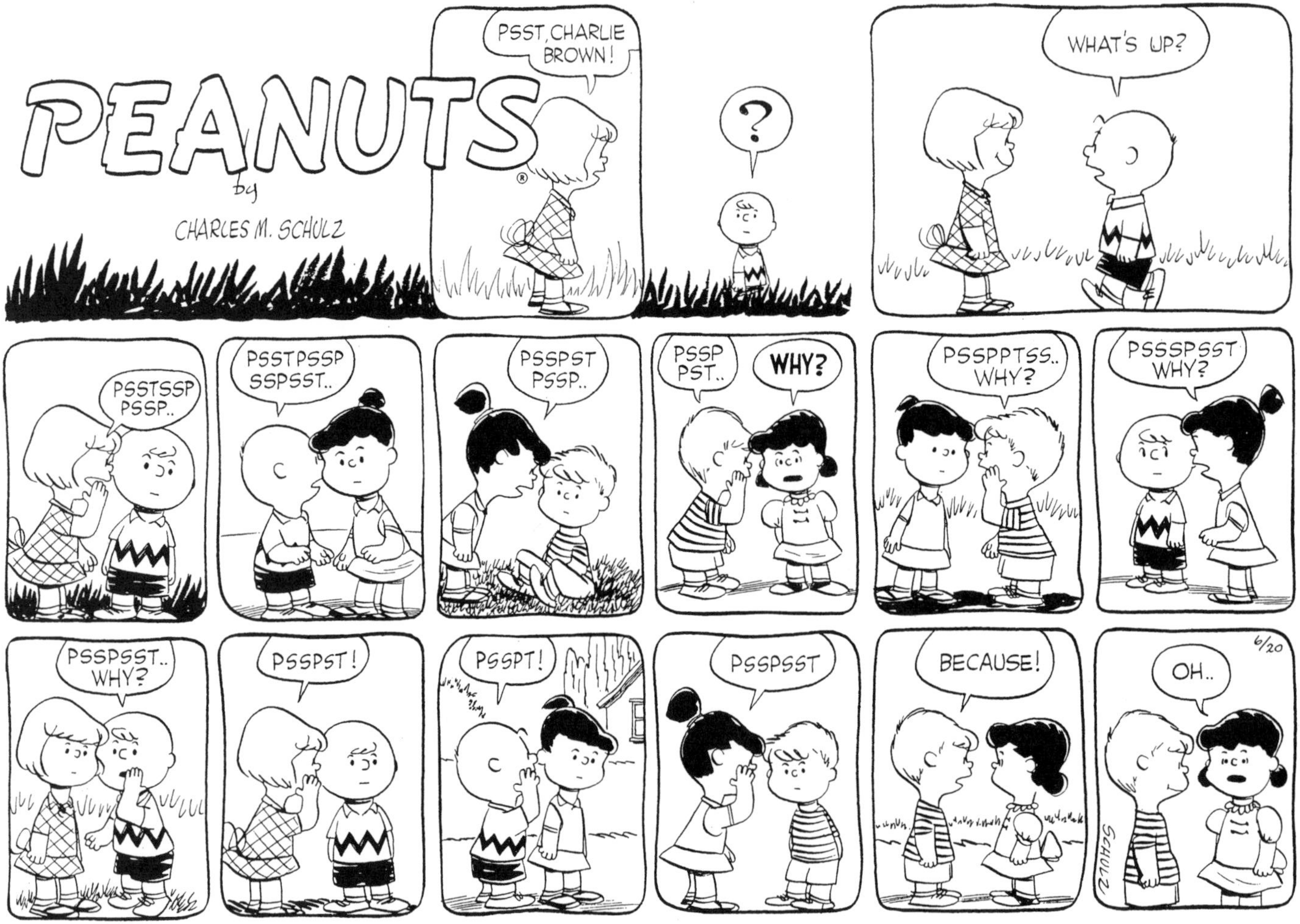
PEANUTS
by
CHARLES M. SCHULZ
PSST, CHARLIE BROWN!
?
WHAT'S UP?
PSSTSSP PSSP..
PSSTPSSP SSPSST..
PSSPST PSSP..
PSSP PST..
WHY?
PSSPPTSS.. WHY?
PSSSPSST WHY?
PSSPSST.. WHY?
PSSPST!
PSSPT!
PSSPSST
BECAUSE!
OH..
6/20
SCHULZ

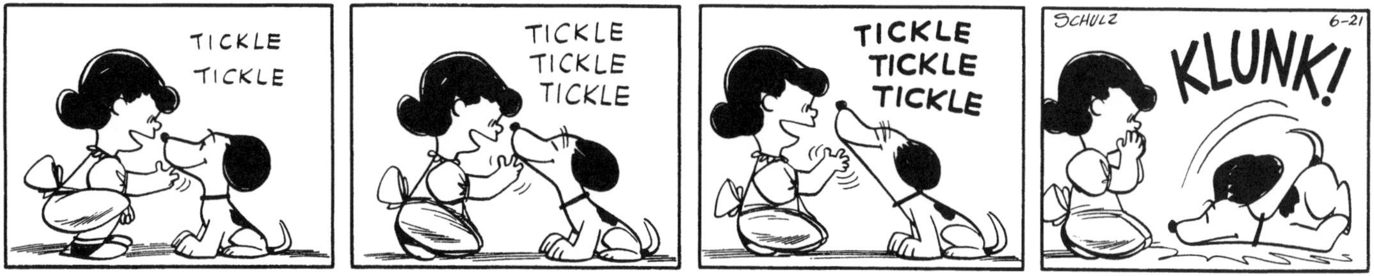
TICKLE TICKLE
TICKLE TICKLE TICKLE
TICKLE TICKLE TICKLE
SCHULZ
6-21
KLUNK!

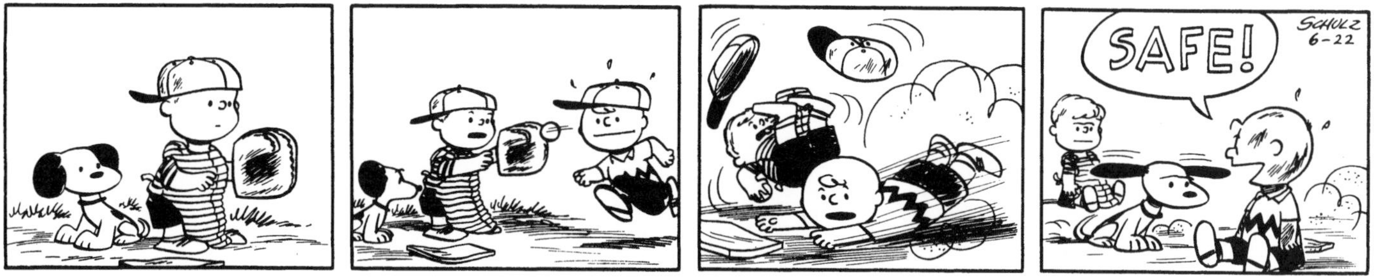
SAFE!
SCHULZ 6-22

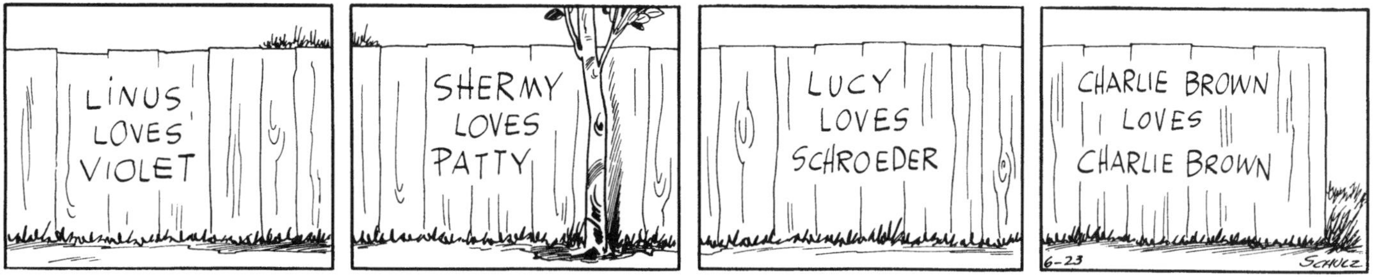
LINUS LOVES VIOLET
SHERMY LOVES PATTY
LUCY LOVES SCHROEDER
CHARLIE BROWN LOVES CHARLIE BROWN
6-23
SCHULZ

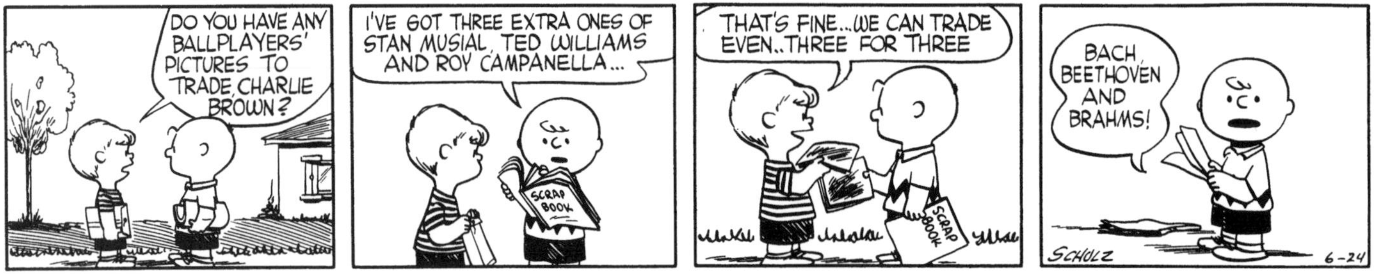
DO YOU HAVE ANY BALLPLAYERS' PICTURES TO TRADE, CHARLIE BROWN?
I'VE GOT THREE EXTRA ONES OF STAN MUSIAL, TED WILLIAMS AND ROY CAMPANELLA...
SCRAP BOOK
THAT'S FINE...WE CAN TRADE EVEN..THREE FOR THREE
SCRAP BOOK
BACH, BEETHOVEN AND BRAHMS!
SCHULZ
6-24

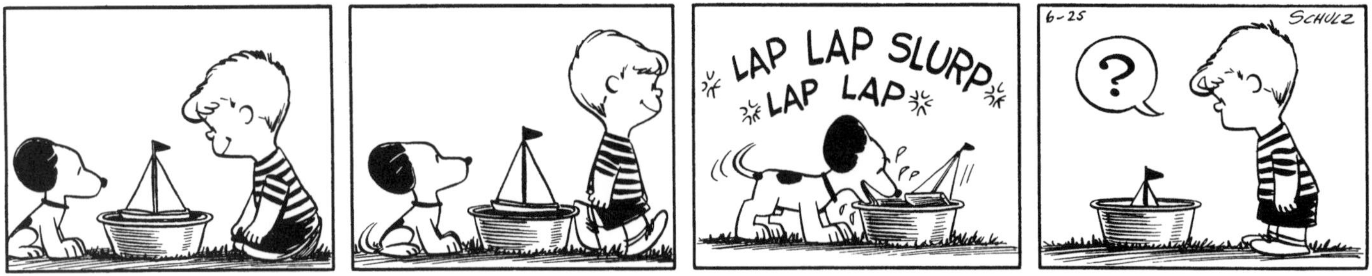
LAP LAP SLURP
LAP LAP
6-25
SCHULZ
?

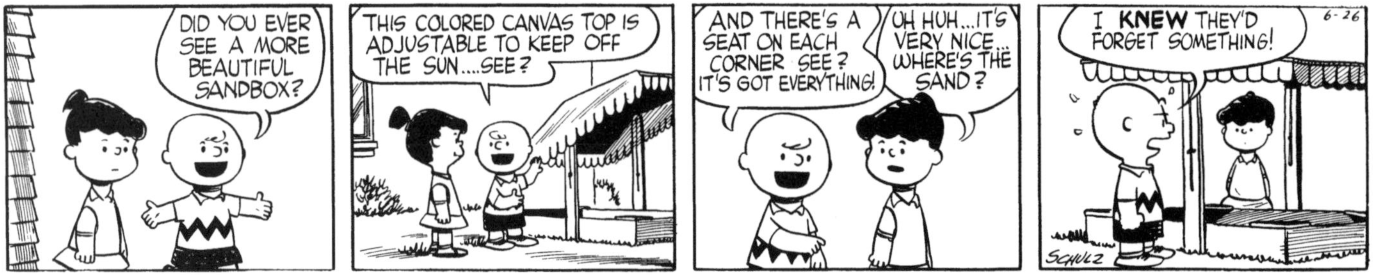
DID YOU EVER SEE A MORE BEAUTIFUL SANDBOX?
THIS COLORED CANVAS TOP IS ADJUSTABLE TO KEEP OFF THE SUN....SEE?
AND THERE'S A SEAT ON EACH CORNER SEE? IT'S GOT EVERYTHING!
UH HUH...IT'S VERY NICE... WHERE'S THE SAND?
I KNEW THEY'D FORGET SOMETHING!
6-26
SCHULZ

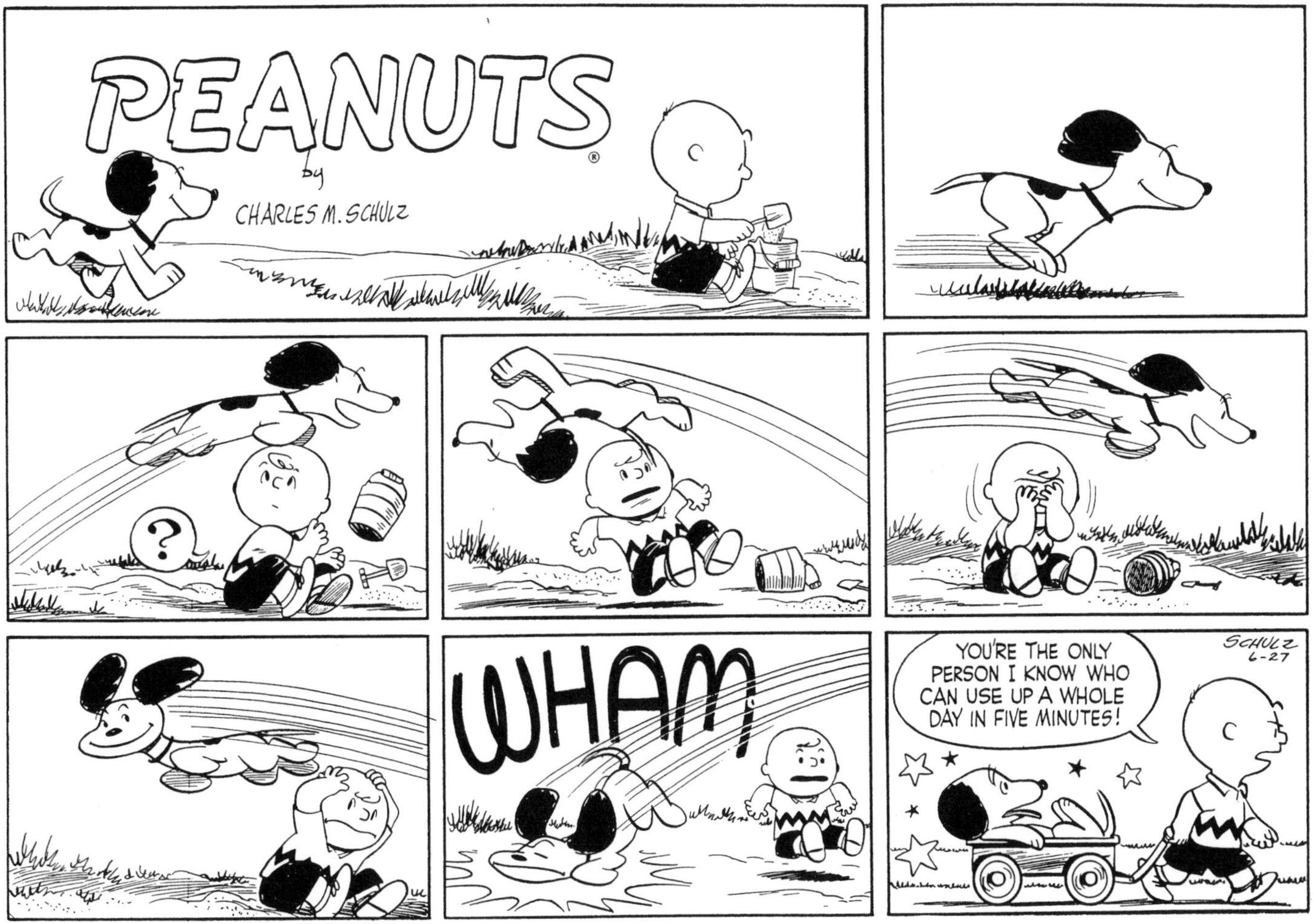
PEANUTS
by
CHARLES M. SCHULZ
WHAM
YOU'RE THE ONLY PERSON I KNOW WHO CAN USE UP A WHOLE DAY IN FIVE MINUTES!
SCHULZ 6-27

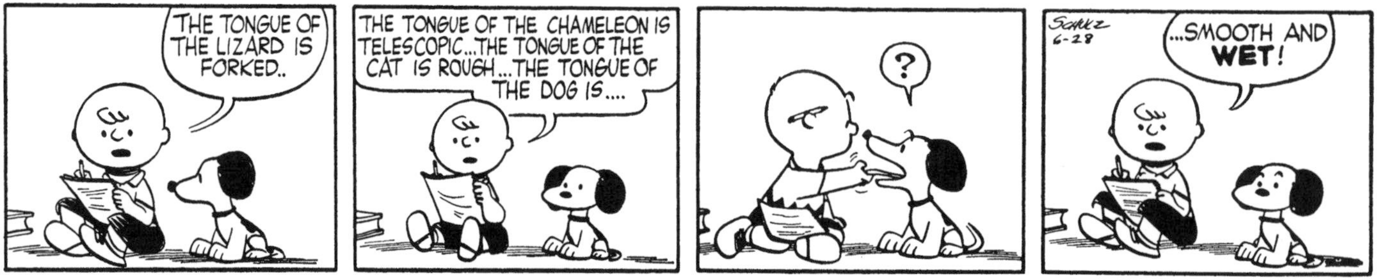
THE TONGUE OF THE LIZARD IS FORKED..
THE TONGUE OF THE CHAMELEON IS TELESCOPIC...THE TONGUE OF THE CAT IS ROUGH...THE TONGUE OF THE DOG IS....
?
SCHULZ 6-28
...SMOOTH AND WET!

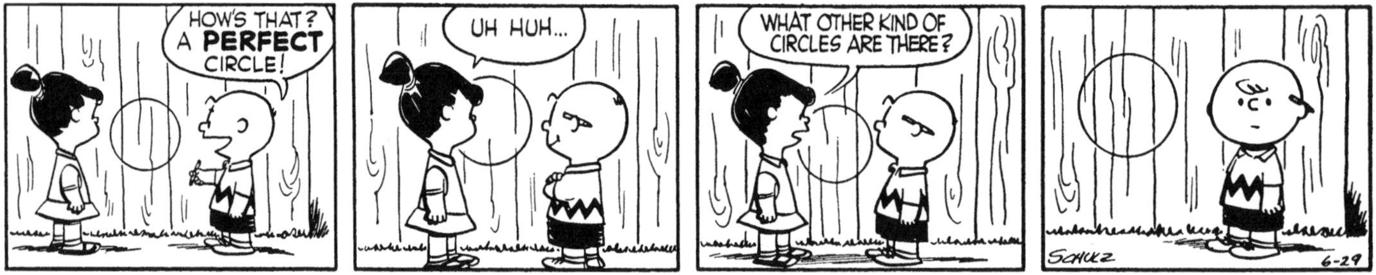
HOW'S THAT? A PERFECT CIRCLE!
UH HUH...
WHAT OTHER KIND OF CIRCLES ARE THERE?
SCHULZ
6-29

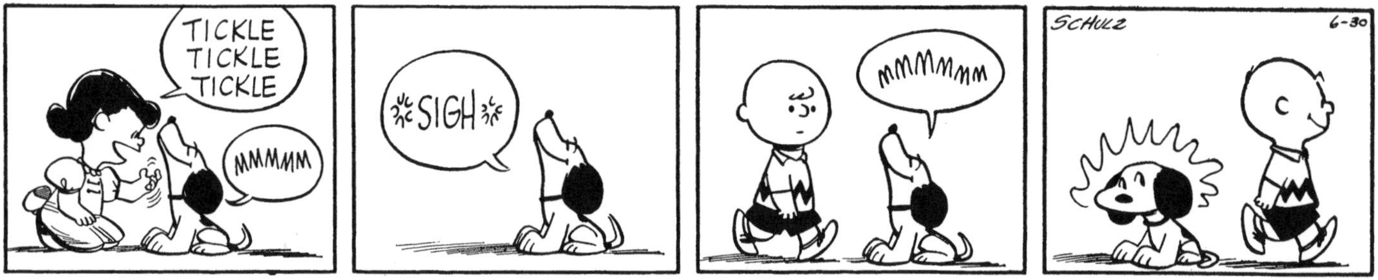
TICKLE TICKLE TICKLE
MMMMM
SIGH
MMMMMMM
SCHULZ
6-30

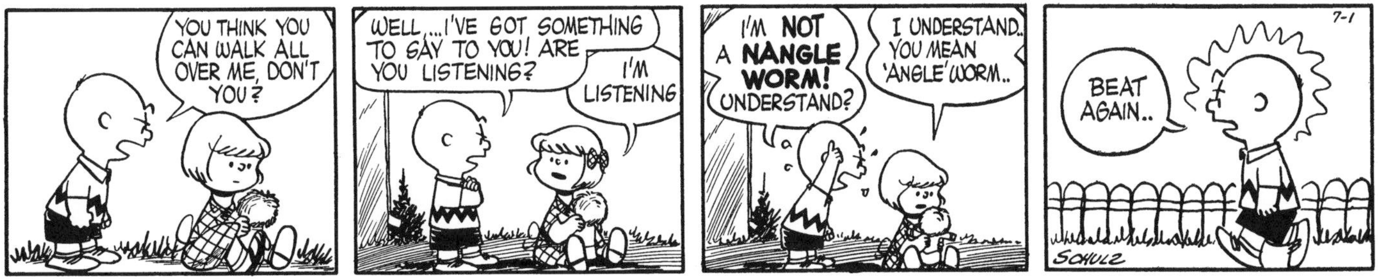
YOU THINK YOU CAN WALK ALL OVER ME, DON'T YOU?
WELL,...I'VE GOT SOMETHING TO SAY TO YOU! ARE YOU LISTENING?
I'M LISTENING
I'M NOT A NANGLE WORM! UNDERSTAND?
I UNDERSTAND.. YOU MEAN 'ANGLE' WORM..
7-1
BEAT AGAIN..
SCHULZ

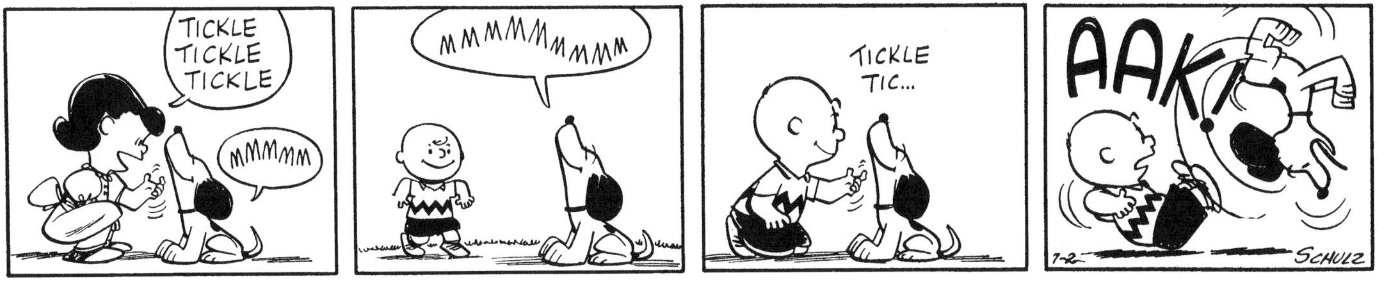
TICKLE TICKLE TICKLE
MMMMM
MMMMMMMMMMM
TICKLE TIC...
AAK!
7-2
SCHULZ

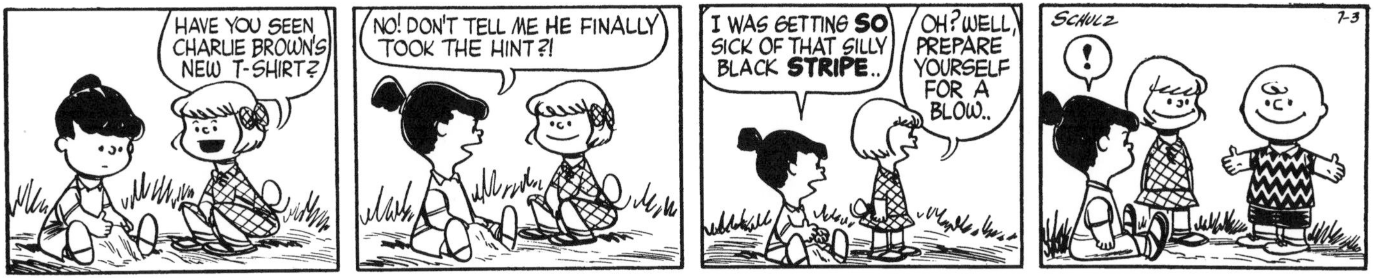
HAVE YOU SEEN CHARLIE BROWN'S NEW T-SHIRT?
NO! DON'T TELL ME HE FINALLY TOOK THE HINT?!
I WAS GETTING SO SICK OF THAT SILLY BLACK STRIPE..
OH? WELL, PREPARE YOURSELF FOR A BLOW..
SCHULZ
7-3
!

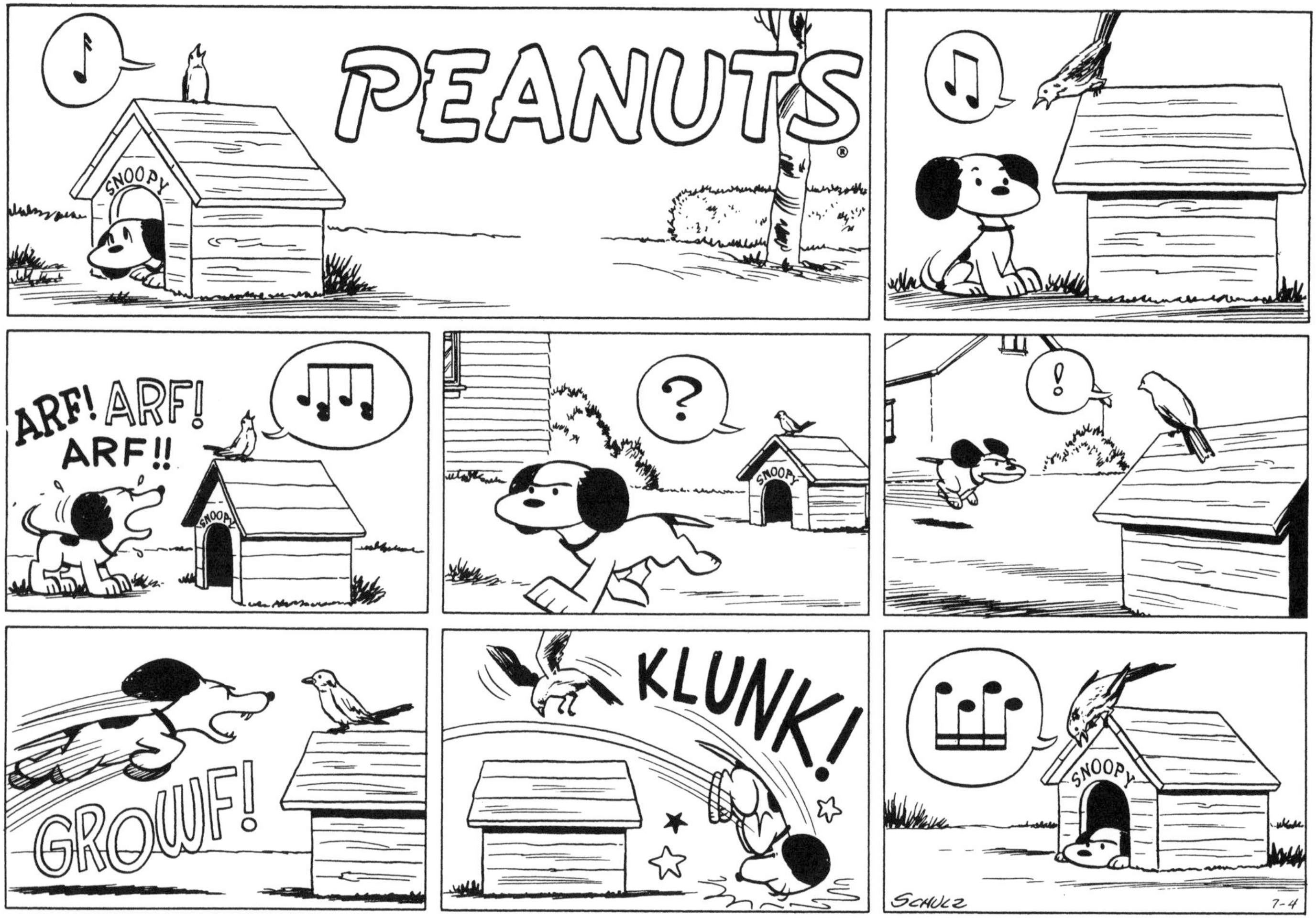
PEANUTS®
SNOOPY
ARF! ARF!
ARF!!
SNOOPY
?
SNOOPY
!
GROWF!
KLUNK!
SNOOPY
SCHULZ
7-4

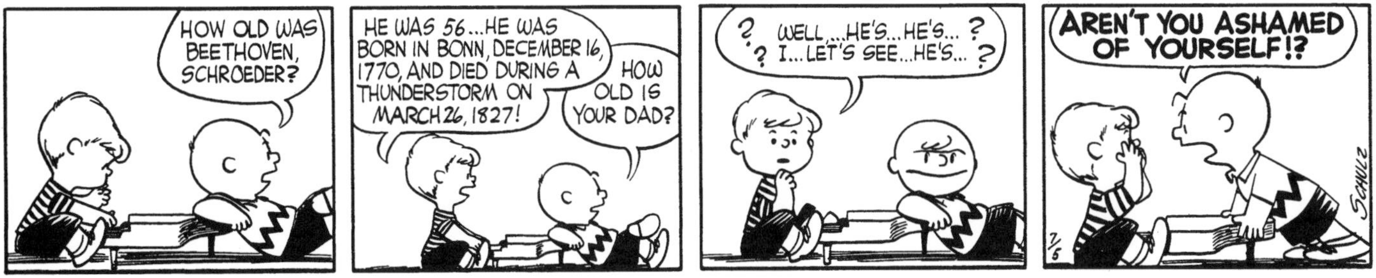
HOW OLD WAS BEETHOVEN, SCHROEDER?
HE WAS 56...HE WAS BORN IN BONN, DECEMBER 16, 1770, AND DIED DURING A THUNDERSTORM ON MARCH 26, 1827!
HOW OLD IS YOUR DAD?
? ? WELL,...HE'S...HE'S... ? I...LET'S SEE...HE'S... ?
AREN'T YOU ASHAMED OF YOURSELF!?
SCHULZ
7/5

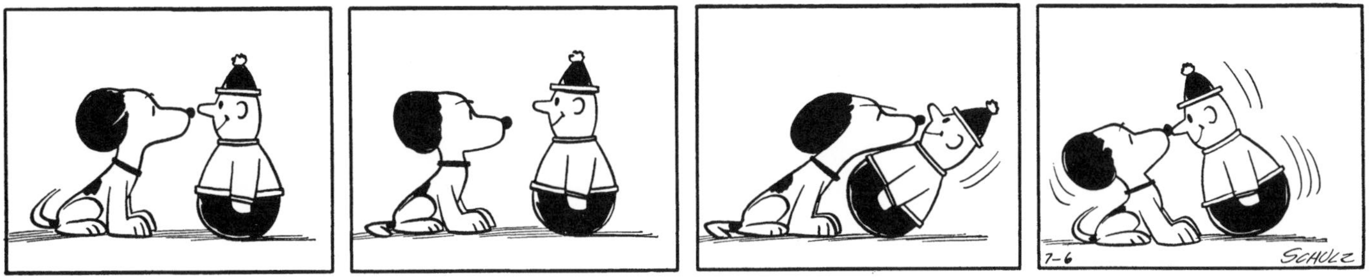
7-6
SCHULZ

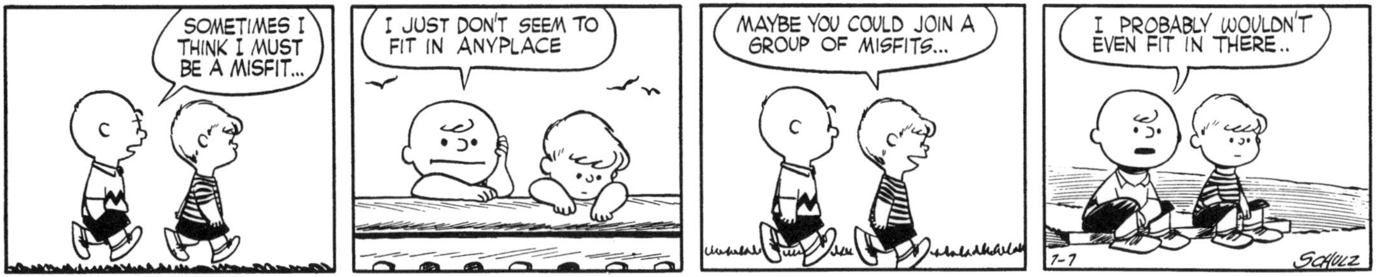
SOMETIMES I THINK I MUST BE A MISFIT...
I JUST DON'T SEEM TO FIT IN ANYPLACE
MAYBE YOU COULD JOIN A GROUP OF MISFITS...
I PROBABLY WOULDN'T EVEN FIT IN THERE..
7-7
SCHULZ

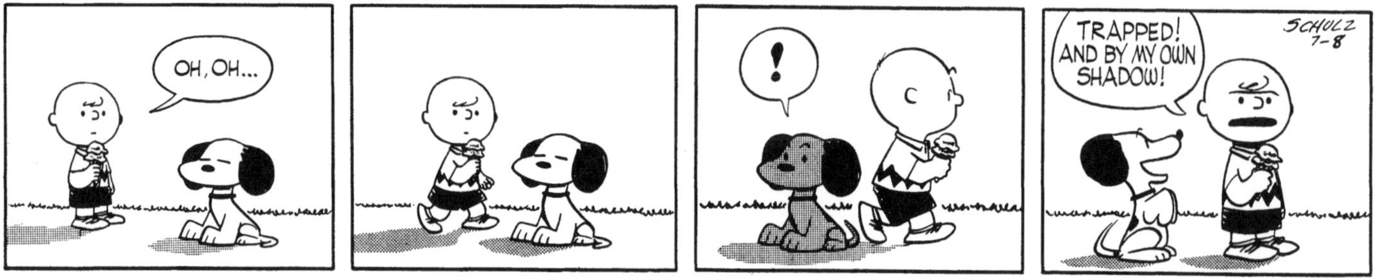
OH, OH...
!
TRAPPED! AND BY MY OWN SHADOW!
SCHULZ 7-8

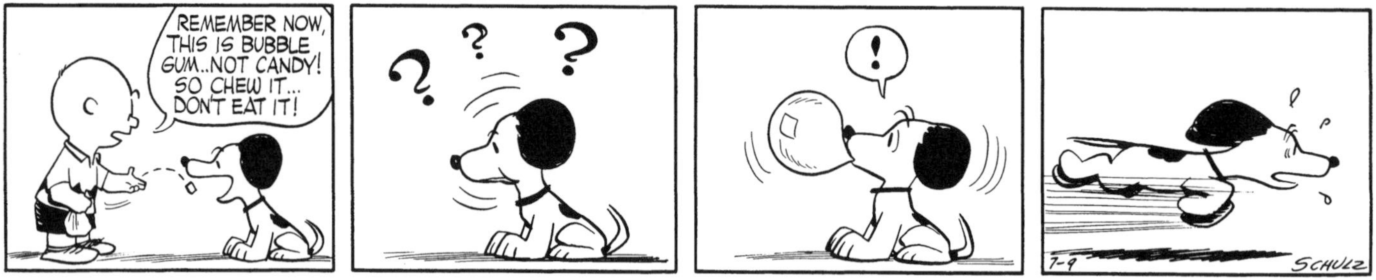
REMEMBER NOW, THIS IS BUBBLE GUM..NOT CANDY! SO CHEW IT... DON'T EAT IT!
? ? ?
!
7-9
SCHULZ

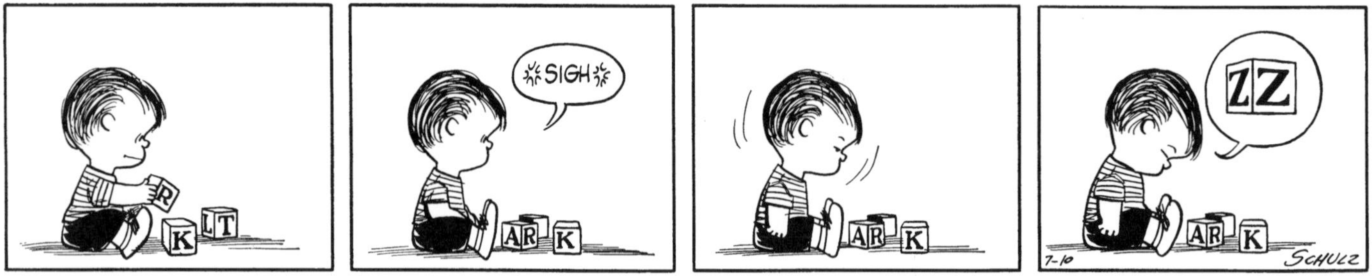
R
K
LT
SIGH
AR
K
AR
K
ZZ
AR
K
7-10
SCHULZ

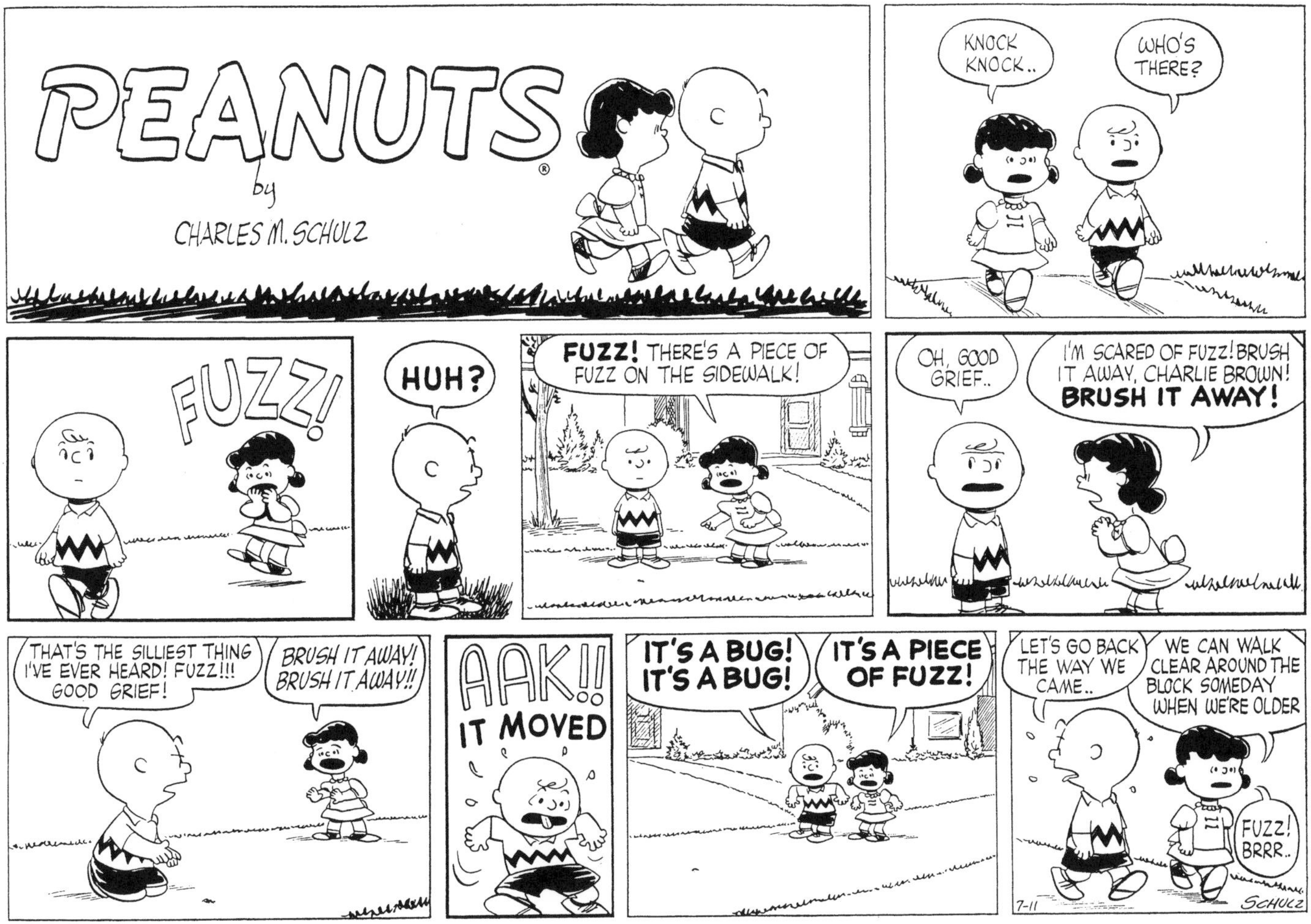
PEANUTS
by
CHARLES M. SCHULZ
KNOCK KNOCK..
WHO'S THERE?
FUZZ!
HUH?
FUZZ! THERE'S A PIECE OF FUZZ ON THE SIDEWALK!
OH, GOOD GRIEF..
I'M SCARED OF FUZZ! BRUSH IT AWAY, CHARLIE BROWN! BRUSH IT AWAY!
THAT'S THE SILLIEST THING I'VE EVER HEARD! FUZZ!!! GOOD GRIEF!
BRUSH IT AWAY! BRUSH IT AWAY!!
AAK!!
IT MOVED
IT'S A BUG! IT'S A BUG!
IT'S A PIECE OF FUZZ!
LET'S GO BACK THE WAY WE CAME..
WE CAN WALK CLEAR AROUND THE BLOCK SOMEDAY WHEN WE'RE OLDER
FUZZ! BRRR..
7-11
SCHULZ

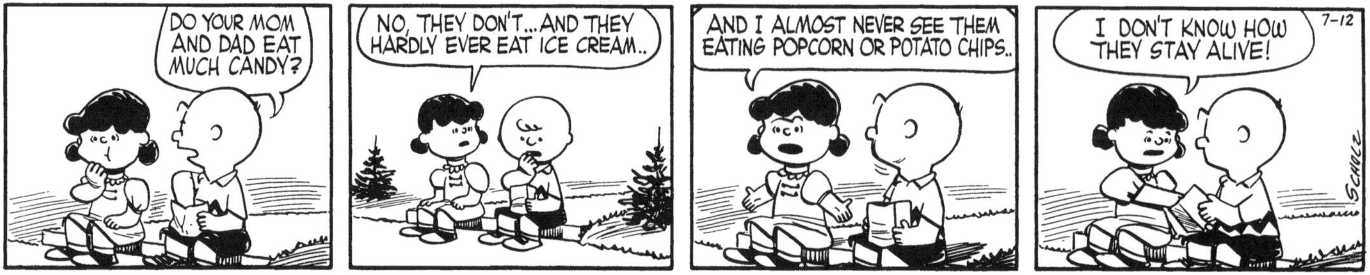
DO YOUR MOM AND DAD EAT MUCH CANDY?
NO, THEY DON'T...AND THEY HARDLY EVER EAT ICE CREAM..
AND I ALMOST NEVER SEE THEM EATING POPCORN OR POTATO CHIPS..
I DON'T KNOW HOW THEY STAY ALIVE!
7-12
SCHULZ

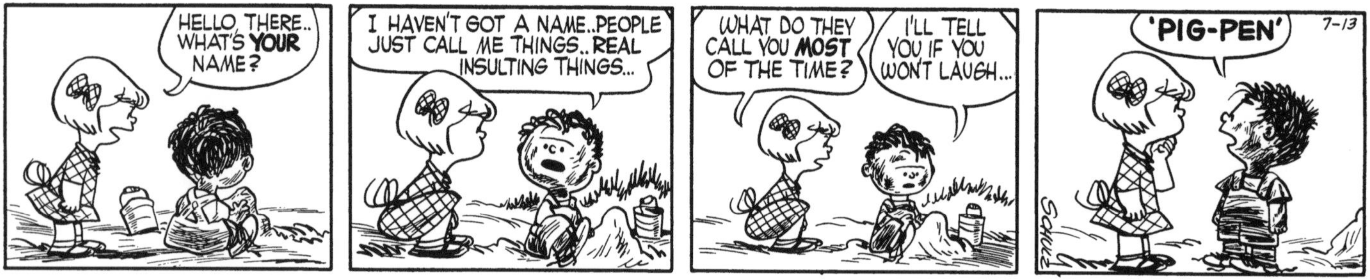
HELLO THERE.. WHAT'S **YOUR** NAME?
I HAVEN'T GOT A NAME..PEOPLE JUST CALL ME THINGS..**REAL** INSULTING THINGS...
WHAT DO THEY CALL YOU **MOST** OF THE TIME?
I'LL TELL YOU IF YOU WON'T LAUGH...
'PIG-PEN'
7-13
SCHULZ

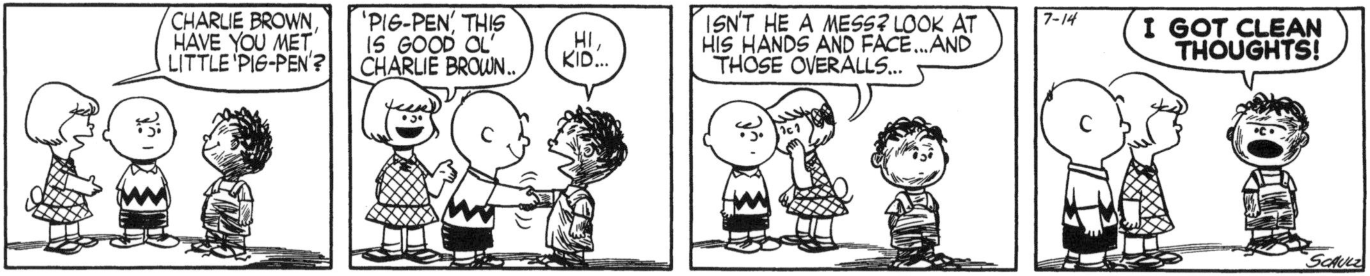
CHARLIE BROWN, HAVE YOU MET LITTLE 'PIG-PEN'?
'PIG-PEN', THIS IS GOOD OL' CHARLIE BROWN..
HI, KID...
ISN'T HE A MESS? LOOK AT HIS HANDS AND FACE...AND THOSE OVERALLS...
7-14
I GOT CLEAN THOUGHTS!
SCHULZ

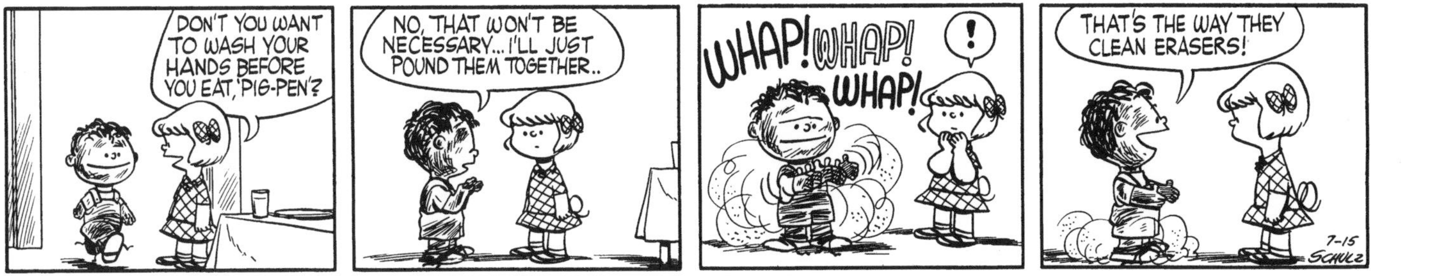
DON'T YOU WANT TO WASH YOUR HANDS BEFORE YOU EAT, 'PIG-PEN'?
NO, THAT WON'T BE NECESSARY... I'LL JUST POUND THEM TOGETHER..
WHAP! WHAP! WHAP!
!
THAT'S THE WAY THEY CLEAN ERASERS!
7-15
SCHULZ

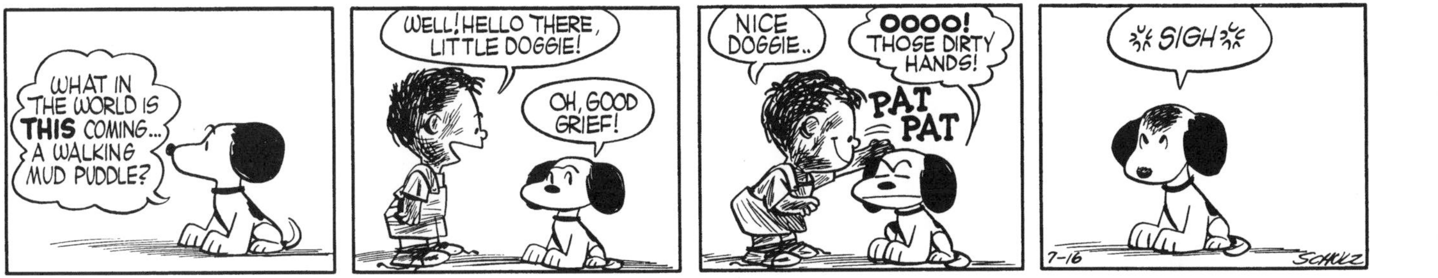
WHAT IN THE WORLD IS **THIS** COMING... A WALKING MUD PUDDLE?
WELL! HELLO THERE, LITTLE DOGGIE!
OH, GOOD GRIEF!
NICE DOGGIE..
OOOO! THOSE DIRTY HANDS!
PAT PAT
SIGH
7-16
SCHULZ

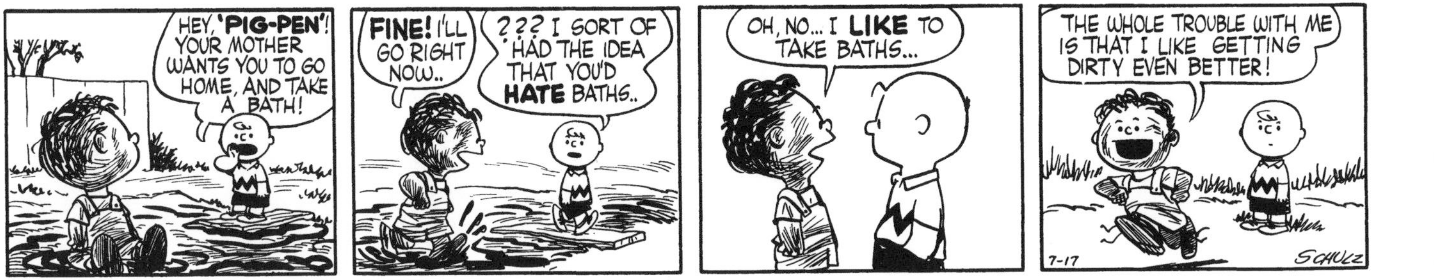
HEY, **'PIG-PEN'**! YOUR MOTHER WANTS YOU TO GO HOME, AND TAKE A BATH!
FINE! I'LL GO RIGHT NOW..
??? I SORT OF HAD THE IDEA THAT YOU'D **HATE** BATHS..
OH, NO... I **LIKE** TO TAKE BATHS...
THE WHOLE TROUBLE WITH ME IS THAT I LIKE GETTING DIRTY EVEN BETTER!
7-17
SCHULZ

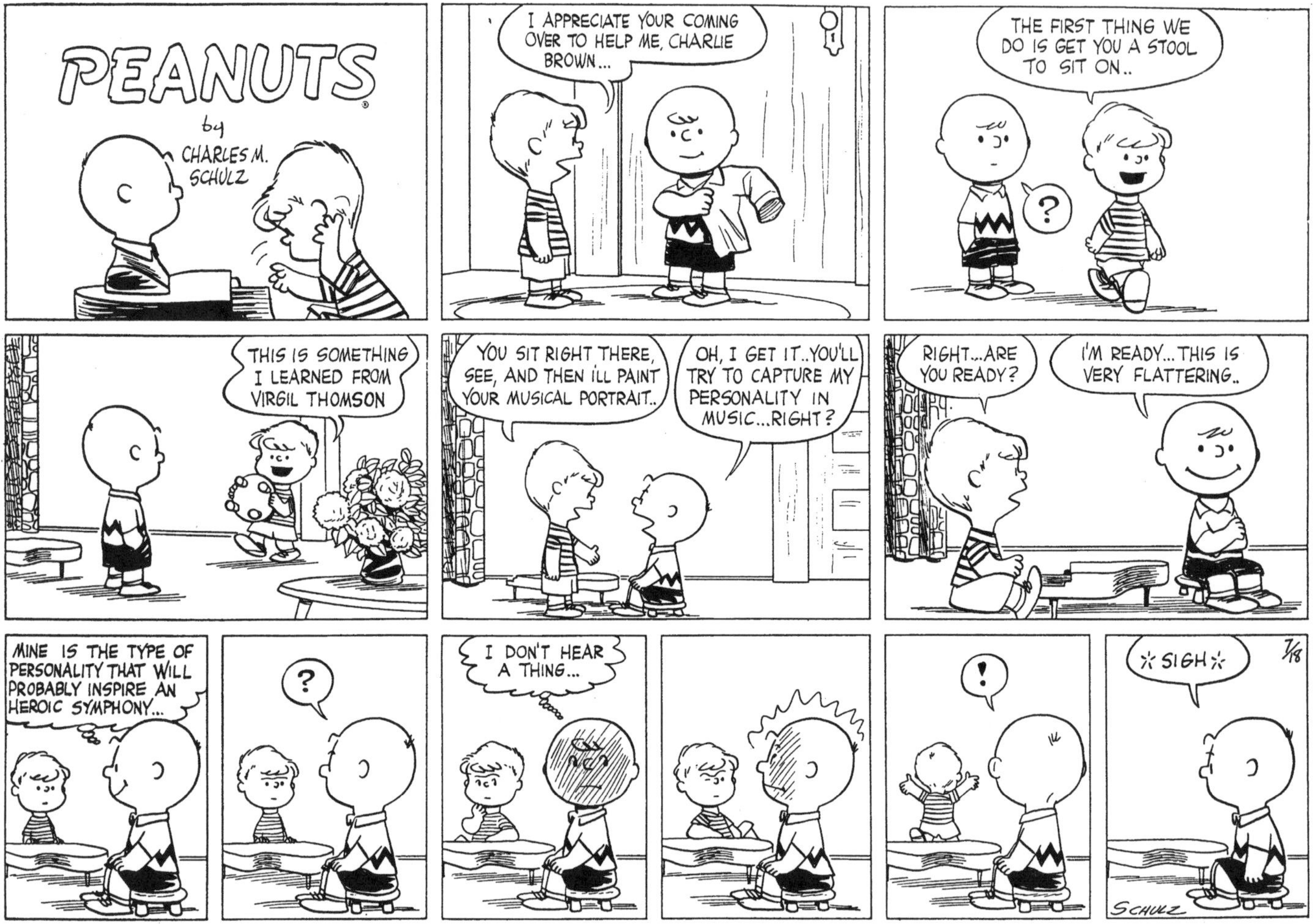
PEANUTS
by CHARLES M. SCHULZ
I APPRECIATE YOUR COMING OVER TO HELP ME, CHARLIE BROWN...
THE FIRST THING WE DO IS GET YOU A STOOL TO SIT ON..
?
THIS IS SOMETHING I LEARNED FROM VIRGIL THOMSON
YOU SIT RIGHT THERE, SEE, AND THEN I'LL PAINT YOUR MUSICAL PORTRAIT..
OH, I GET IT..YOU'LL TRY TO CAPTURE MY PERSONALITY IN MUSIC...RIGHT?
RIGHT...ARE YOU READY?
I'M READY...THIS IS VERY FLATTERING..
MINE IS THE TYPE OF PERSONALITY THAT WILL PROBABLY INSPIRE AN HEROIC SYMPHONY...
?
I DON'T HEAR A THING...
!
SIGH
7/18
SCHULZ

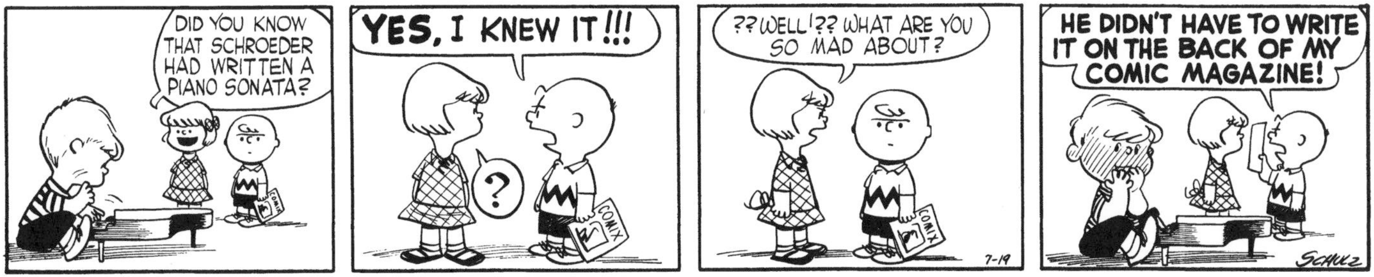
DID YOU KNOW THAT SCHROEDER HAD WRITTEN A PIANO SONATA?
COMIX
YES, I KNEW IT!!!
?
COMIX
??WELL!?? WHAT ARE YOU SO MAD ABOUT?
COMIX
7-19
HE DIDN'T HAVE TO WRITE IT ON THE BACK OF MY COMIC MAGAZINE!
SCHULZ

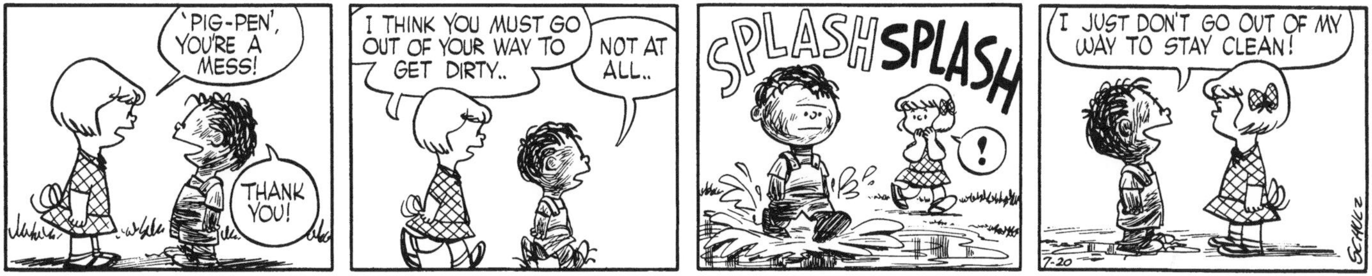
'PIG-PEN', YOU'RE A MESS!
THANK YOU!
I THINK YOU MUST GO OUT OF YOUR WAY TO GET DIRTY..
NOT AT ALL..
SPLASH
SPLASH
!
I JUST DON'T GO OUT OF MY WAY TO STAY CLEAN!
7-20
SCHULZ

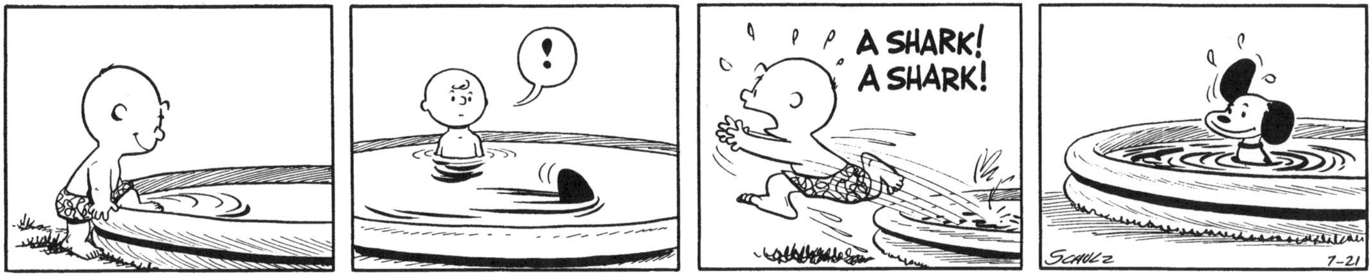
!
A SHARK! A SHARK!
SCHULZ
7-21

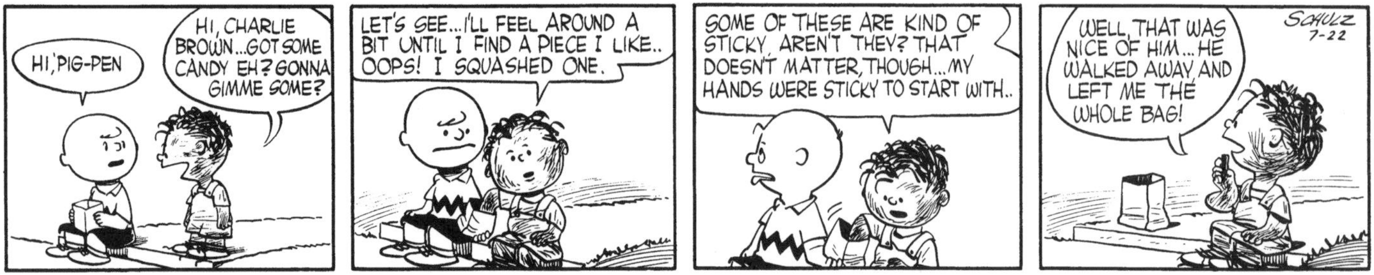
HI, PIG-PEN
HI, CHARLIE BROWN...GOT SOME CANDY EH? GONNA GIMME SOME?
LET'S SEE...I'LL FEEL AROUND A BIT UNTIL I FIND A PIECE I LIKE.. OOPS! I SQUASHED ONE.
SOME OF THESE ARE KIND OF STICKY, AREN'T THEY? THAT DOESN'T MATTER, THOUGH...MY HANDS WERE STICKY TO START WITH..
WELL, THAT WAS NICE OF HIM...HE WALKED AWAY, AND LEFT ME THE WHOLE BAG!
SCHULZ 7-22

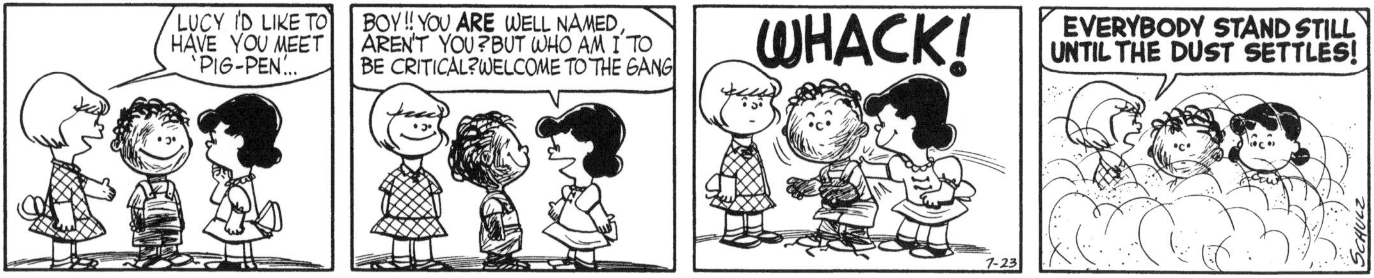
LUCY I'D LIKE TO HAVE YOU MEET 'PIG-PEN'...
BOY!! YOU ARE WELL NAMED, AREN'T YOU? BUT WHO AM I TO BE CRITICAL? WELCOME TO THE GANG
WHACK!
7-23
EVERYBODY STAND STILL UNTIL THE DUST SETTLES!
SCHULZ

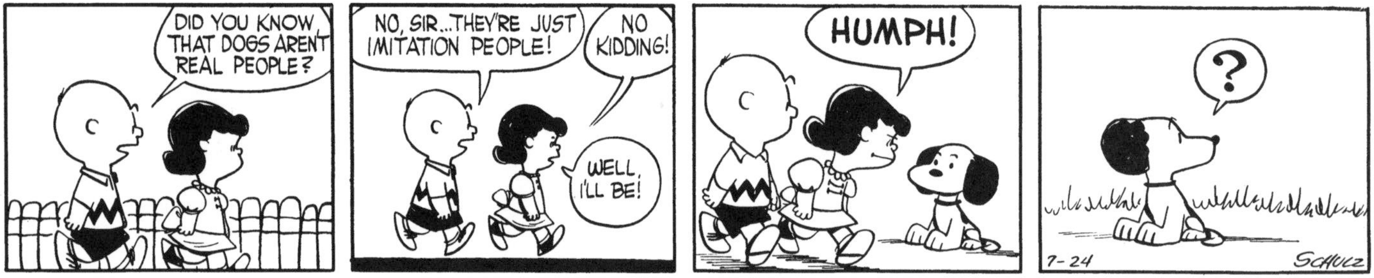
DID YOU KNOW THAT DOGS AREN'T REAL PEOPLE?
NO, SIR...THEY'RE JUST IMITATION PEOPLE!
NO KIDDING!
WELL, I'LL BE!
HUMPH!
?
7-24
SCHULZ

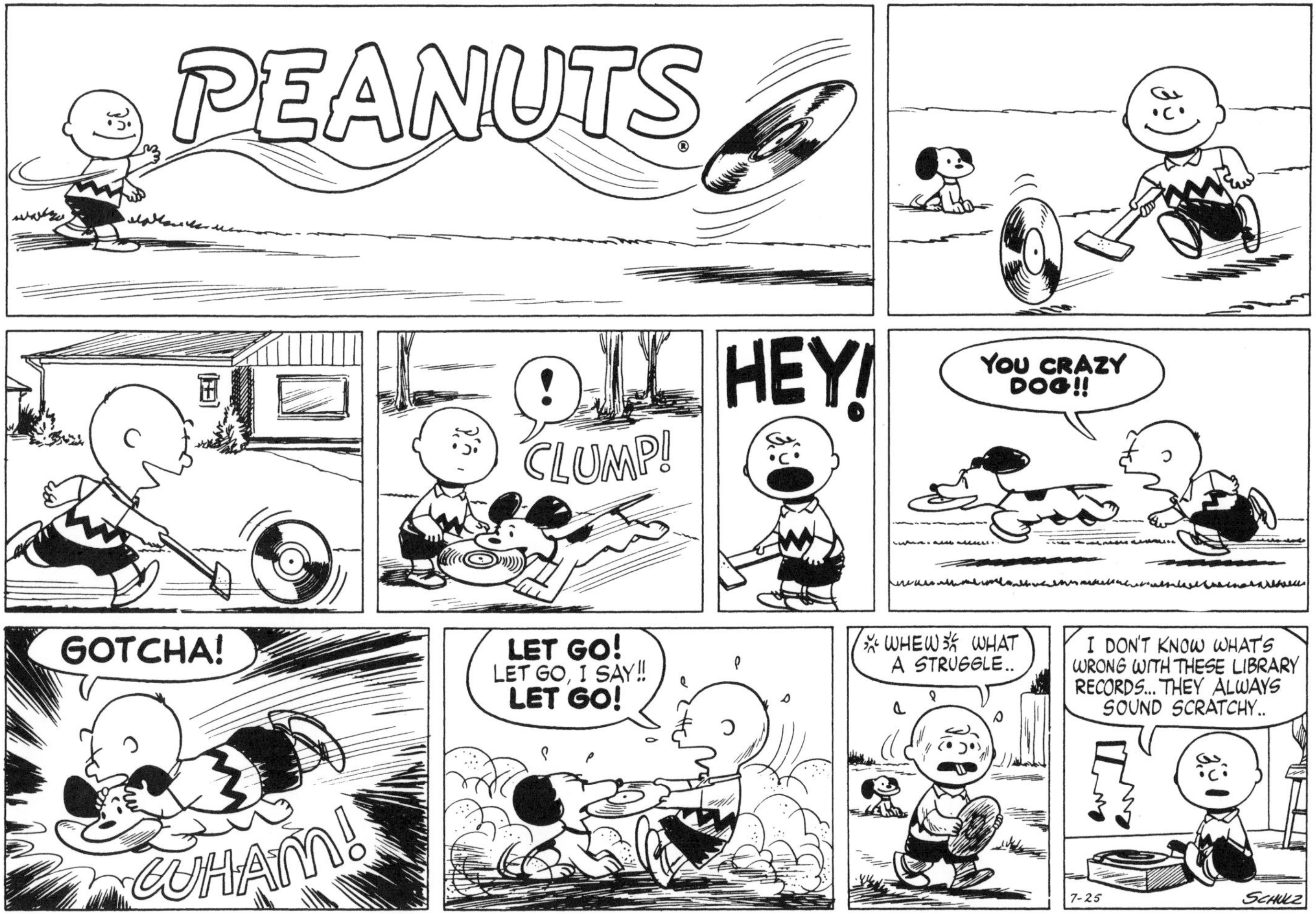
PEANUTS
!
CLUMP!
HEY!
YOU CRAZY DOG!!
GOTCHA!
WHAM!
LET GO! LET GO, I SAY!! LET GO!
WHEW WHAT A STRUGGLE..
I DON'T KNOW WHAT'S WRONG WITH THESE LIBRARY RECORDS... THEY ALWAYS SOUND SCRATCHY..
7-25
SCHULZ

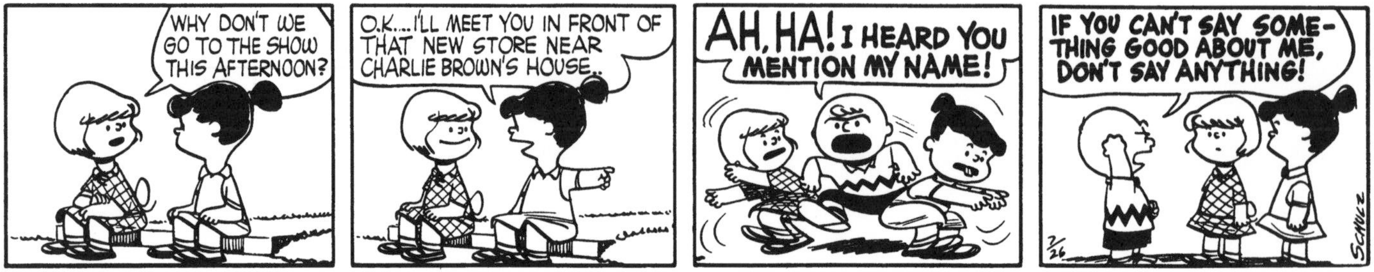
WHY DON'T WE GO TO THE SHOW THIS AFTERNOON?
O.K....I'LL MEET YOU IN FRONT OF THAT NEW STORE NEAR CHARLIE BROWN'S HOUSE..
AH, HA! I HEARD YOU MENTION MY NAME!
IF YOU CAN'T SAY SOMETHING GOOD ABOUT ME, DON'T SAY ANYTHING!
7/26
SCHULZ

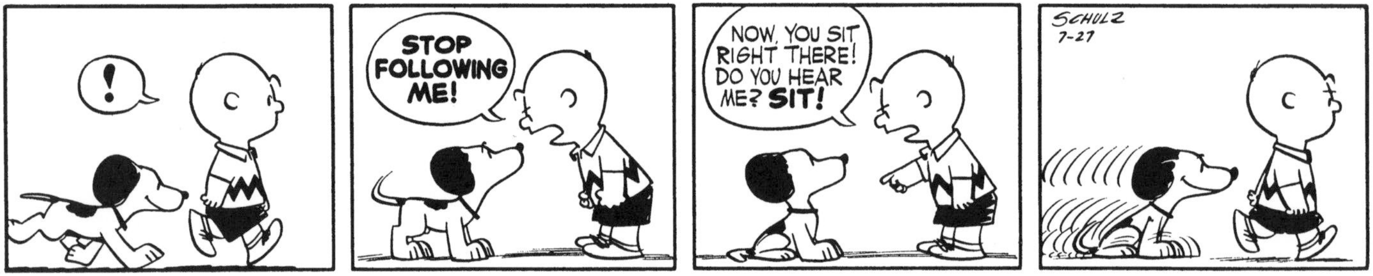
!
STOP FOLLOWING ME!
NOW, YOU SIT RIGHT THERE! DO YOU HEAR ME? SIT!
SCHULZ
7-27

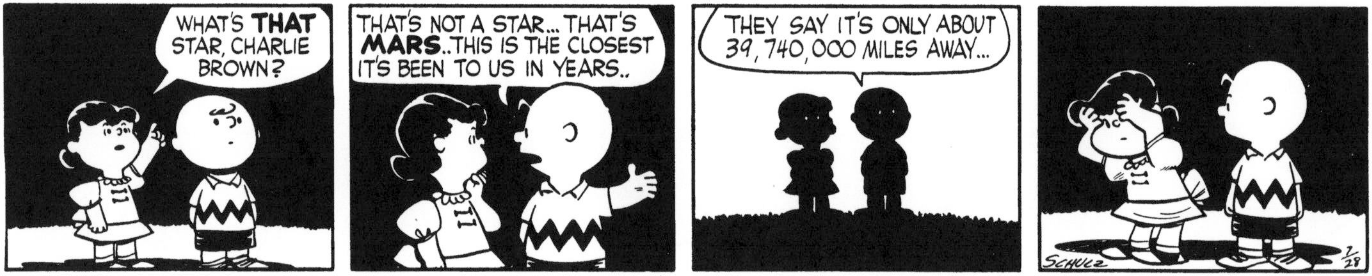
WHAT'S THAT STAR, CHARLIE BROWN?
THAT'S NOT A STAR... THAT'S MARS..THIS IS THE CLOSEST IT'S BEEN TO US IN YEARS..
THEY SAY IT'S ONLY ABOUT 39,740,000 MILES AWAY...
SCHULZ
7/28

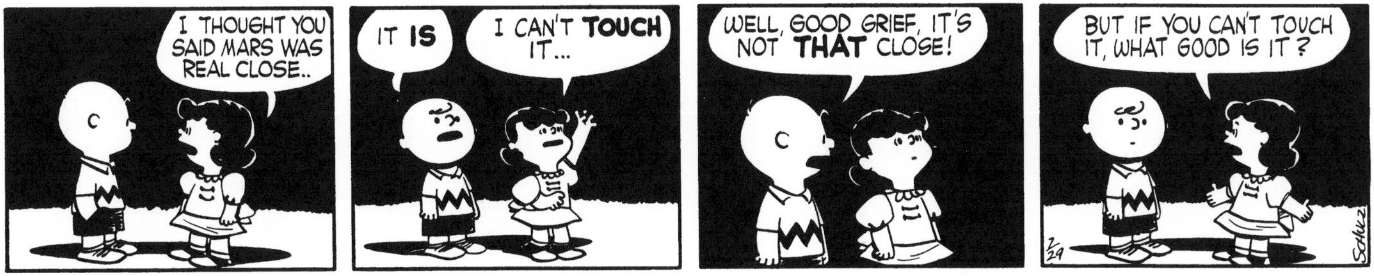
I THOUGHT YOU SAID MARS WAS REAL CLOSE..
IT IS
I CAN'T TOUCH IT...
WELL, GOOD GRIEF, IT'S NOT THAT CLOSE!
BUT IF YOU CAN'T TOUCH IT, WHAT GOOD IS IT?
7/29
SCHULZ

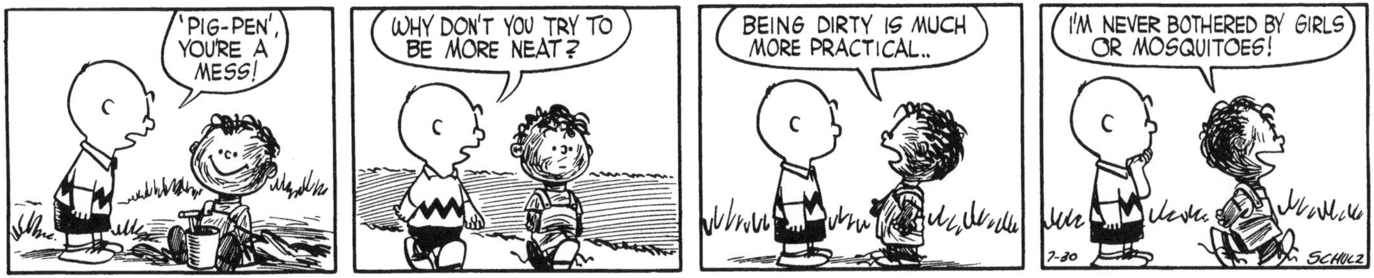
'PIG-PEN', YOU'RE A MESS!
WHY DON'T YOU TRY TO BE MORE NEAT?
BEING DIRTY IS MUCH MORE PRACTICAL..
I'M NEVER BOTHERED BY GIRLS OR MOSQUITOES!
7-30
SCHULZ

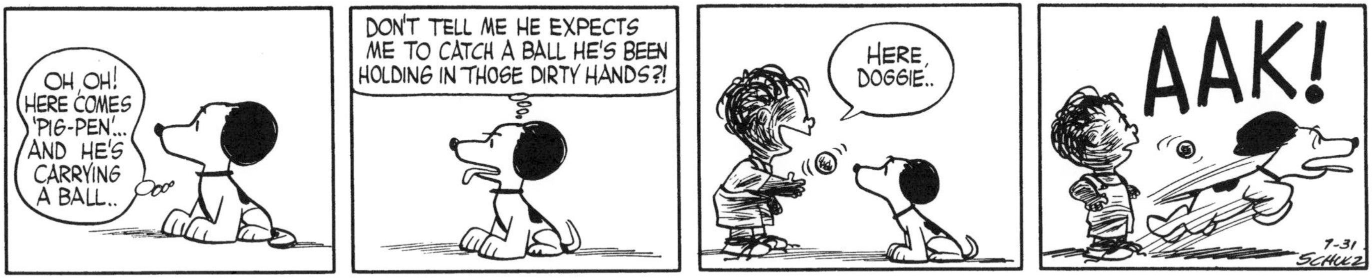
OH, OH! HERE COMES 'PIG-PEN'... AND HE'S CARRYING A BALL..
DON'T TELL ME HE EXPECTS ME TO CATCH A BALL HE'S BEEN HOLDING IN THOSE DIRTY HANDS?!
HERE, DOGGIE..
AAK!
7-31
SCHULZ

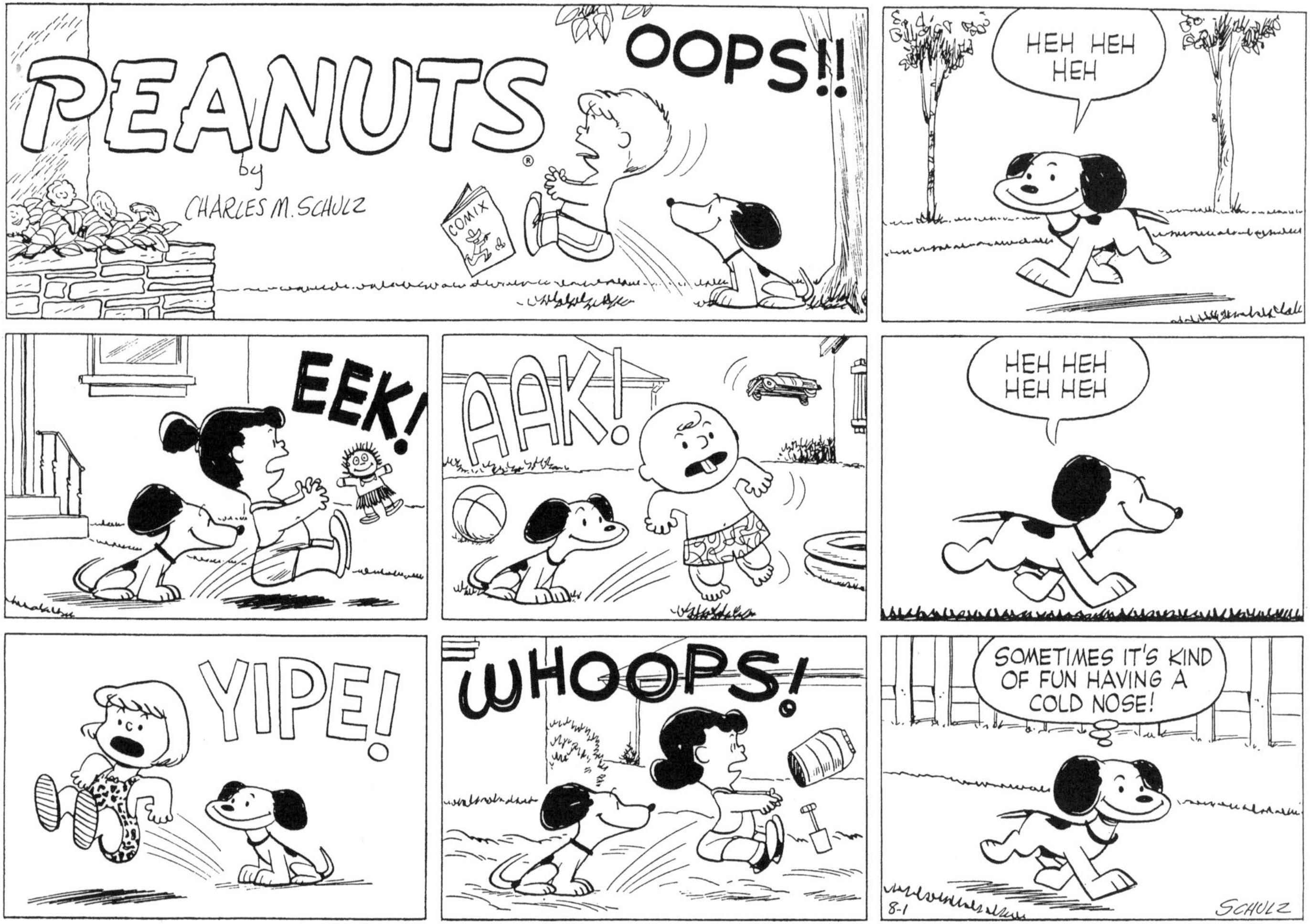
PEANUTS
by
CHARLES M. SCHULZ
OOPS!!
COMIX
HEH HEH
HEH
EEK!
AAK!
HEH HEH
HEH HEH
YIPE!
WHOOPS!
SOMETIMES IT'S KIND
OF FUN HAVING A
COLD NOSE!
8-1
SCHULZ

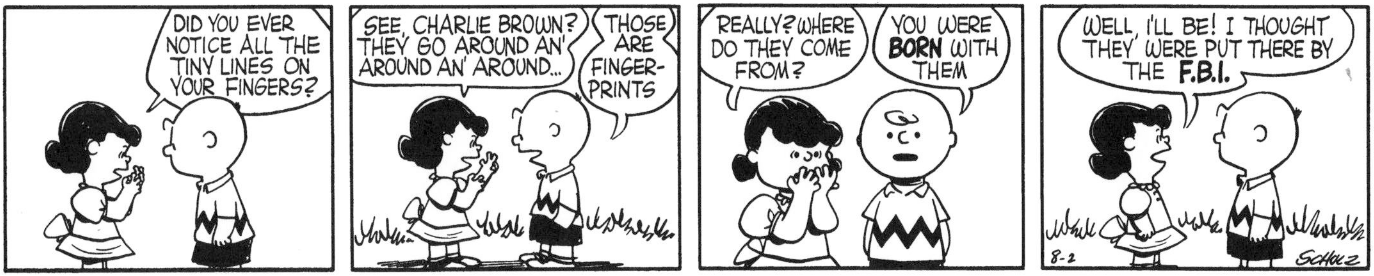
DID YOU EVER NOTICE ALL THE TINY LINES ON YOUR FINGERS?
SEE, CHARLIE BROWN? THEY GO AROUND AN' AROUND AN' AROUND...
THOSE ARE FINGER-PRINTS
REALLY? WHERE DO THEY COME FROM?
YOU WERE BORN WITH THEM
WELL, I'LL BE! I THOUGHT THEY WERE PUT THERE BY THE F.B.I.
8-2
SCHULZ

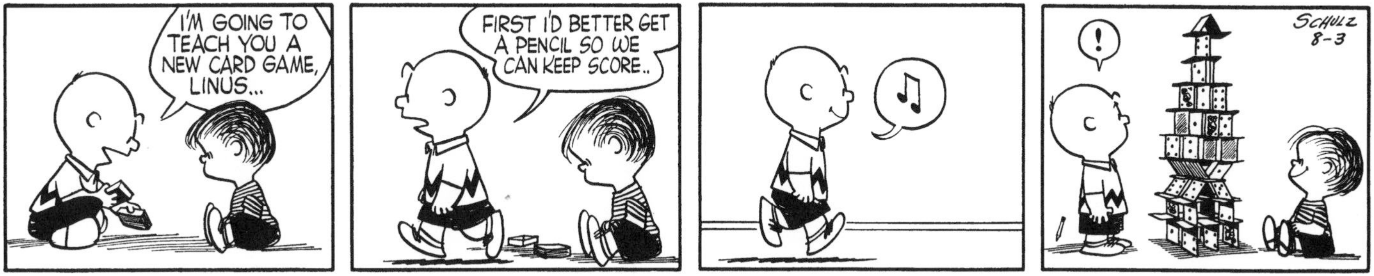
I'M GOING TO TEACH YOU A NEW CARD GAME, LINUS...
FIRST I'D BETTER GET A PENCIL SO WE CAN KEEP SCORE..
!
SCHULZ 8-3

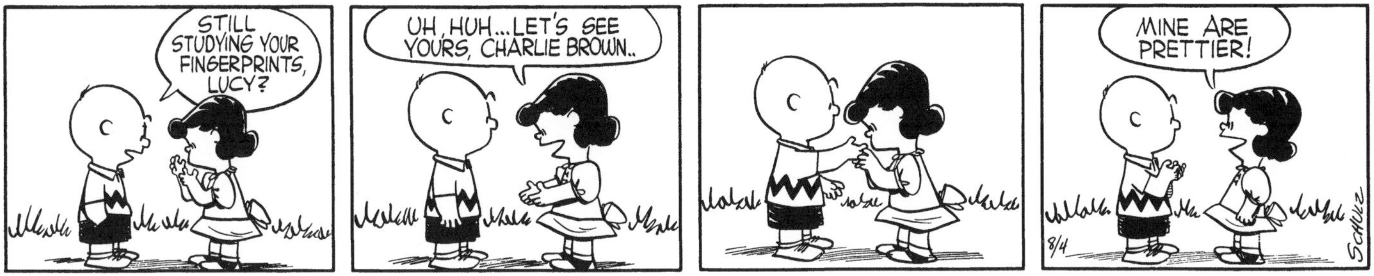
STILL STUDYING YOUR FINGERPRINTS, LUCY?
UH, HUH...LET'S SEE YOURS, CHARLIE BROWN..
MINE ARE PRETTIER!
8/4
SCHULZ

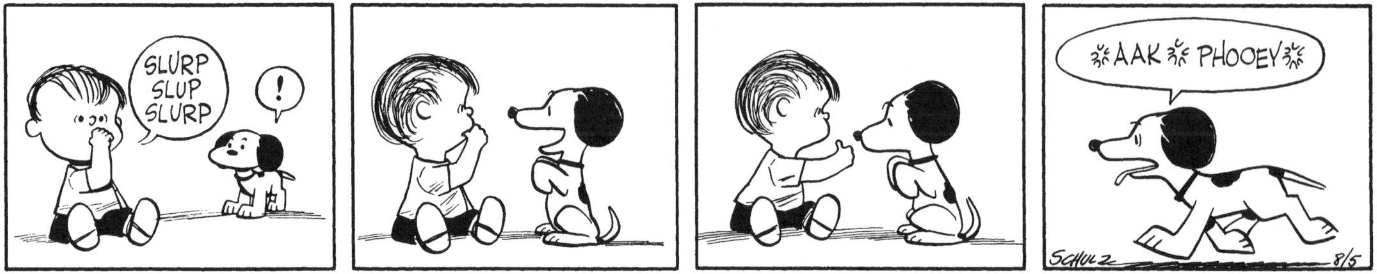
SLURP SLUP SLURP
!
AAK PHOOEY
SCHULZ 8/5

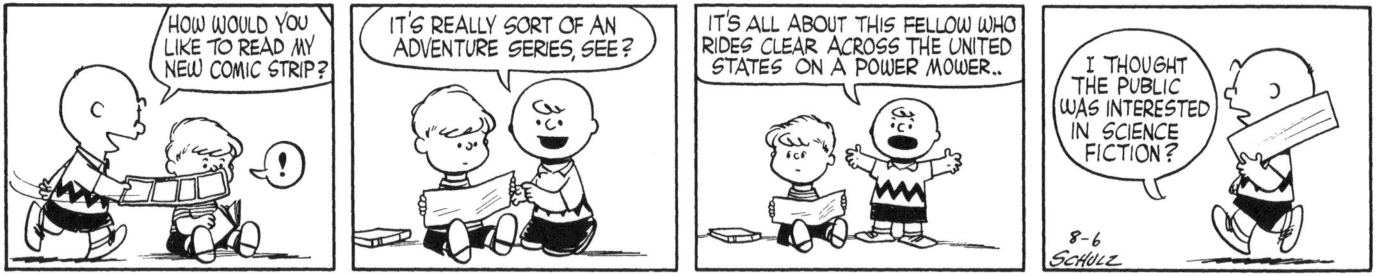
HOW WOULD YOU LIKE TO READ MY NEW COMIC STRIP?
!
IT'S REALLY SORT OF AN ADVENTURE SERIES, SEE?
IT'S ALL ABOUT THIS FELLOW WHO RIDES CLEAR ACROSS THE UNITED STATES ON A POWER MOWER..
I THOUGHT THE PUBLIC WAS INTERESTED IN SCIENCE FICTION?
8-6
SCHULZ

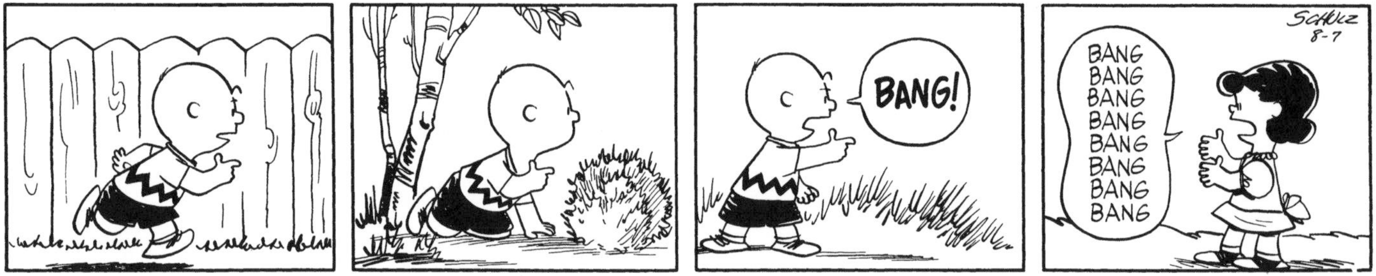
BANG!
SCHULZ 8-7
BANG BANG BANG BANG BANG BANG BANG BANG BANG

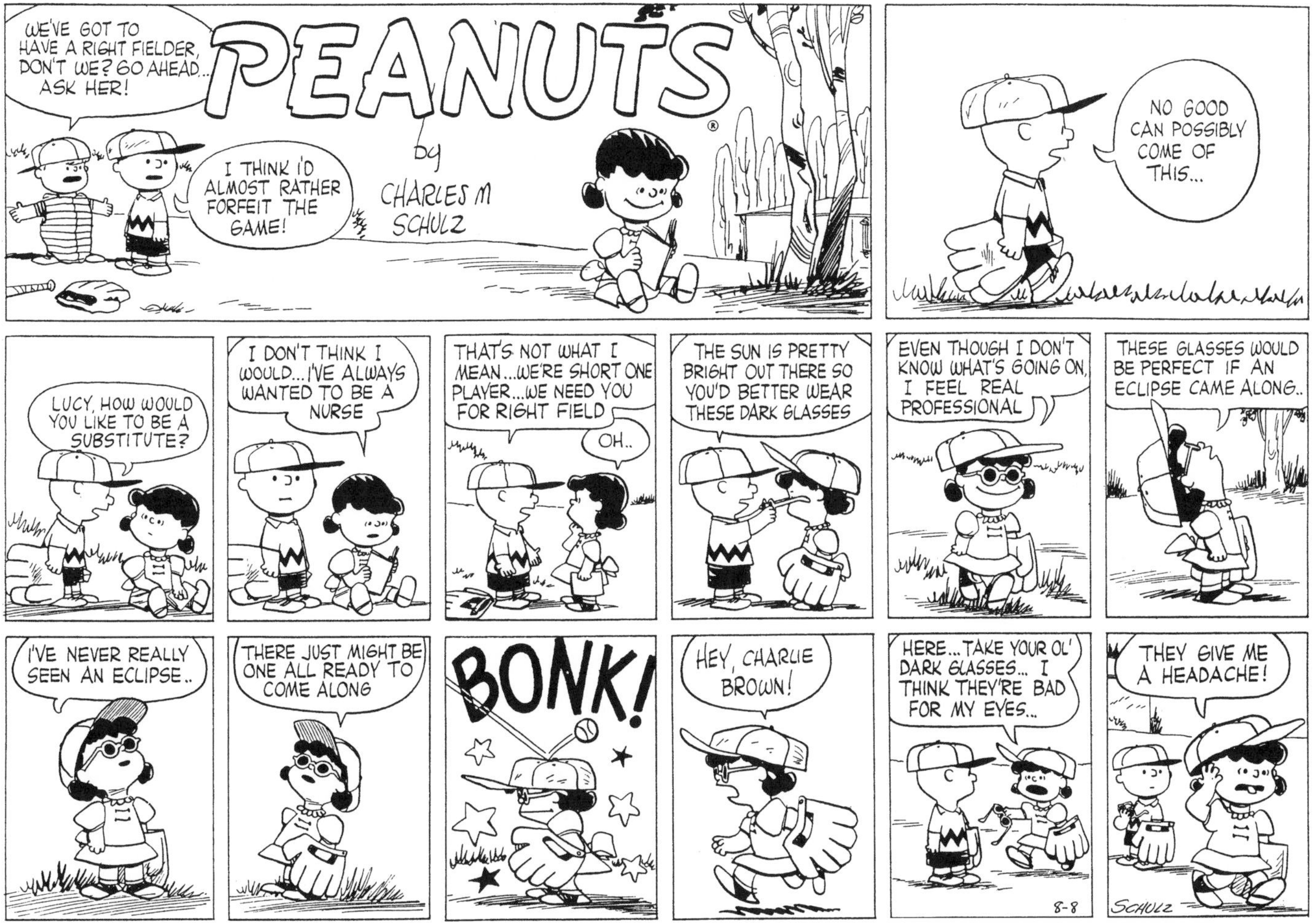
WE'VE GOT TO HAVE A RIGHT FIELDER, DON'T WE? GO AHEAD... ASK HER!
PEANUTS
®
by CHARLES M SCHULZ
I THINK I'D ALMOST RATHER FORFEIT THE GAME!
NO GOOD CAN POSSIBLY COME OF THIS...
LUCY, HOW WOULD YOU LIKE TO BE A SUBSTITUTE?
I DON'T THINK I WOULD... I'VE ALWAYS WANTED TO BE A NURSE
THAT'S NOT WHAT I MEAN... WE'RE SHORT ONE PLAYER... WE NEED YOU FOR RIGHT FIELD
OH..
THE SUN IS PRETTY BRIGHT OUT THERE SO YOU'D BETTER WEAR THESE DARK GLASSES
EVEN THOUGH I DON'T KNOW WHAT'S GOING ON, I FEEL REAL PROFESSIONAL
THESE GLASSES WOULD BE PERFECT IF AN ECLIPSE CAME ALONG..
I'VE NEVER REALLY SEEN AN ECLIPSE..
THERE JUST MIGHT BE ONE ALL READY TO COME ALONG
BONK!
HEY, CHARLIE BROWN!
HERE... TAKE YOUR OL' DARK GLASSES... I THINK THEY'RE BAD FOR MY EYES...
8-8
THEY GIVE ME A HEADACHE!
SCHULZ

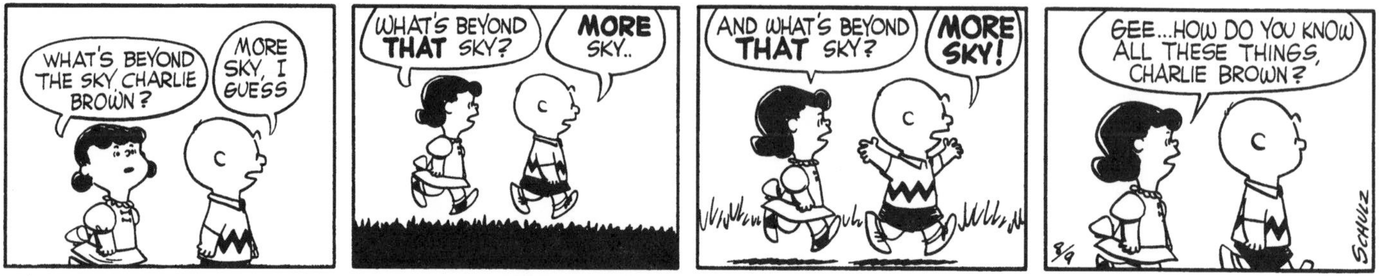
WHAT'S BEYOND THE SKY, CHARLIE BROWN?
MORE SKY, I GUESS
WHAT'S BEYOND **THAT** SKY?
MORE SKY..
AND WHAT'S BEYOND **THAT** SKY?
MORE SKY!
GEE...HOW DO YOU KNOW ALL THESE THINGS, CHARLIE BROWN?
8/9
SCHULZ

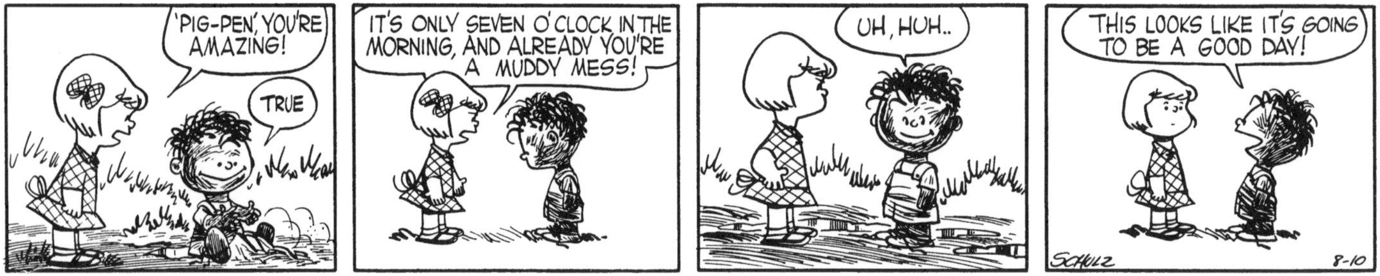
'PIG-PEN,' YOU'RE AMAZING!
TRUE
IT'S ONLY SEVEN O'CLOCK IN THE MORNING, AND ALREADY YOU'RE A MUDDY MESS!
UH, HUH..
THIS LOOKS LIKE IT'S GOING TO BE A GOOD DAY!
SCHULZ
8-10

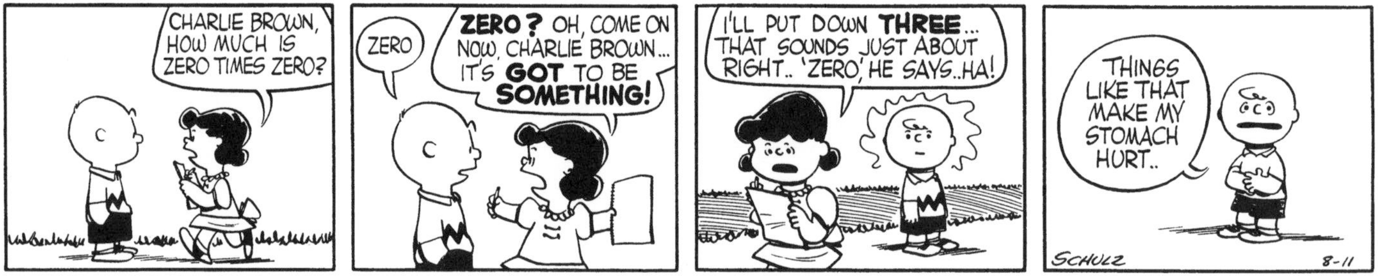
CHARLIE BROWN, HOW MUCH IS ZERO TIMES ZERO?
ZERO
ZERO? OH, COME ON NOW, CHARLIE BROWN... IT'S **GOT** TO BE **SOMETHING!**
I'LL PUT DOWN **THREE**... THAT SOUNDS JUST ABOUT RIGHT.. 'ZERO,' HE SAYS..HA!
THINGS LIKE THAT MAKE MY STOMACH HURT..
SCHULZ
8-11

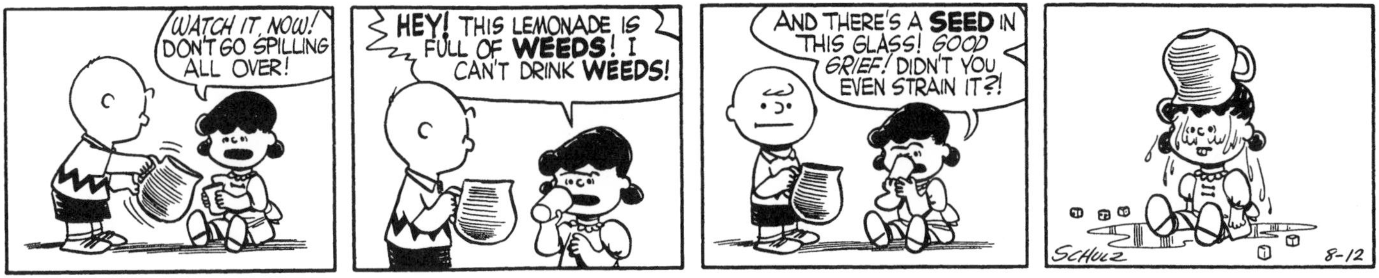
WATCH IT, NOW! DON'T GO SPILLING ALL OVER!
HEY! THIS LEMONADE IS FULL OF WEEDS! I CAN'T DRINK WEEDS!
AND THERE'S A SEED IN THIS GLASS! GOOD GRIEF! DIDN'T YOU EVEN STRAIN IT?!
SCHULZ
8-12

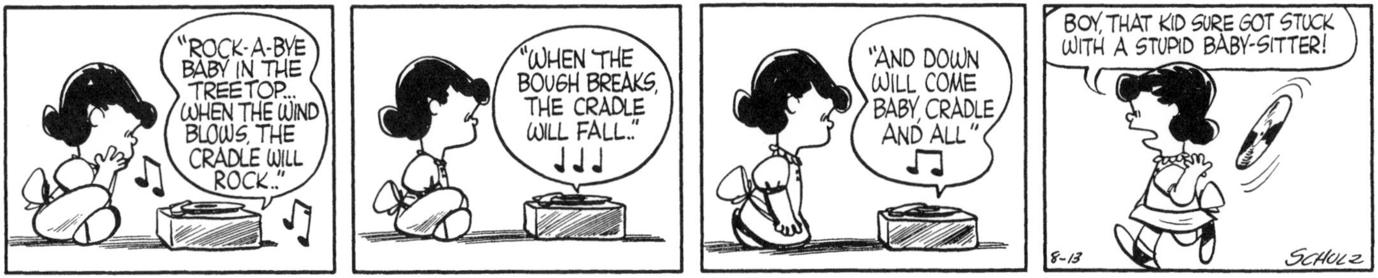
"ROCK-A-BYE BABY IN THE TREETOP... WHEN THE WIND BLOWS, THE CRADLE WILL ROCK.."
"WHEN THE BOUGH BREAKS, THE CRADLE WILL FALL.."
"AND DOWN WILL COME BABY, CRADLE AND ALL"
BOY, THAT KID SURE GOT STUCK WITH A STUPID BABY-SITTER!
8-13
SCHULZ

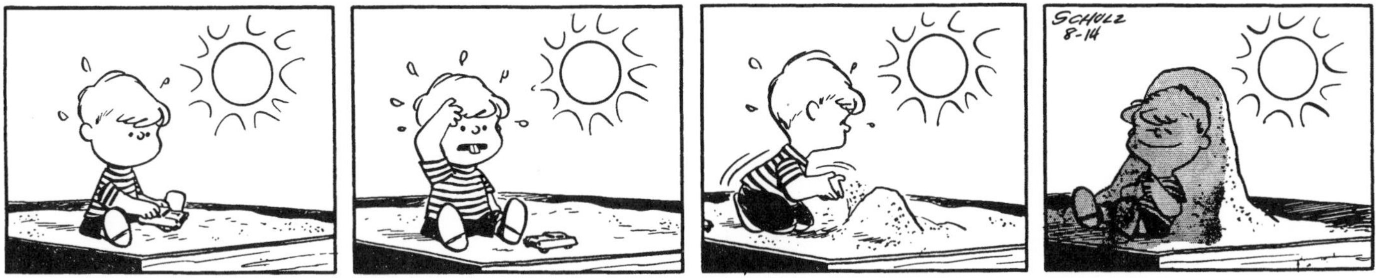
SCHULZ
8-14

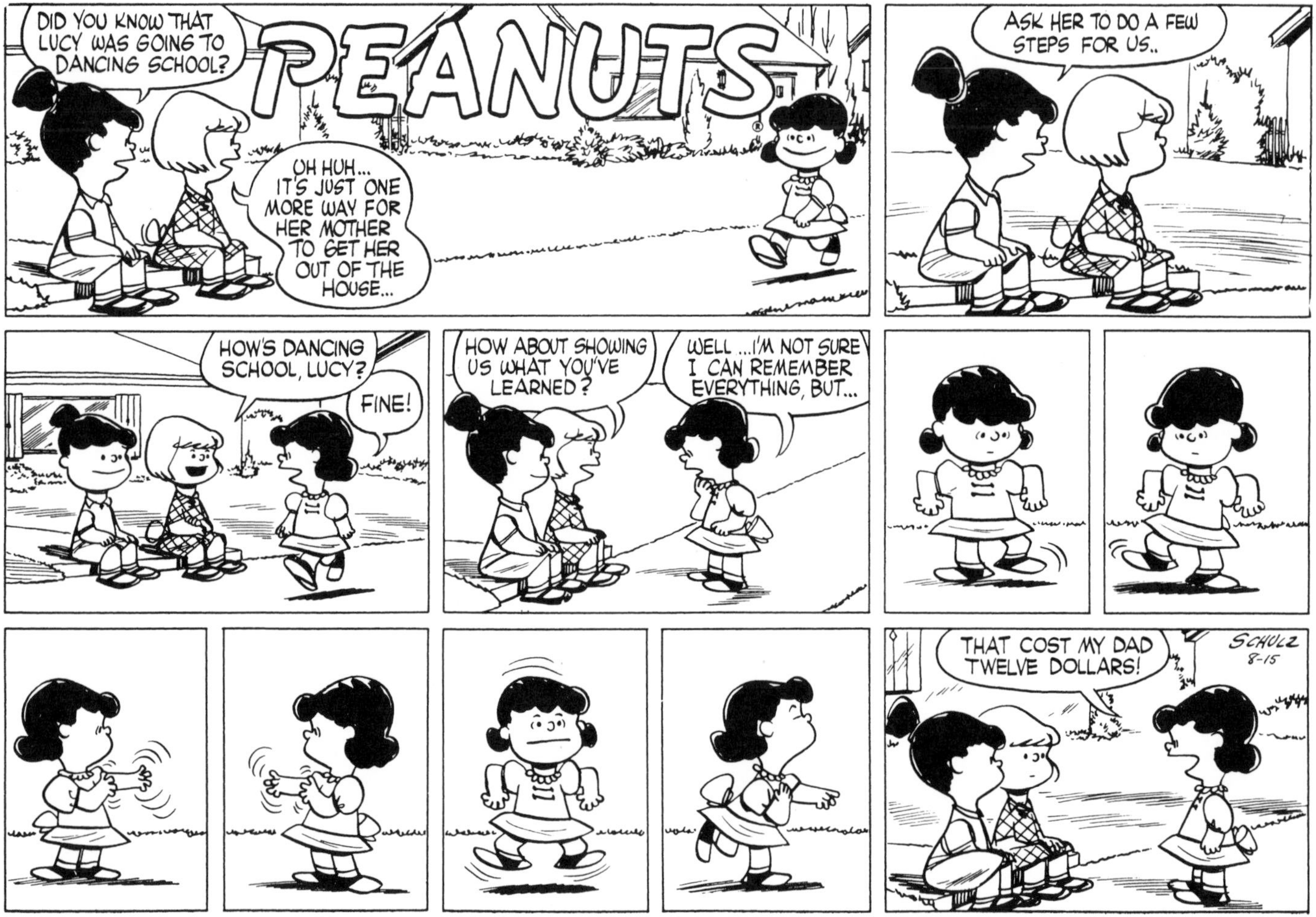
DID YOU KNOW THAT LUCY WAS GOING TO DANCING SCHOOL?
PEANUTS
UH HUH... IT'S JUST ONE MORE WAY FOR HER MOTHER TO GET HER OUT OF THE HOUSE...
ASK HER TO DO A FEW STEPS FOR US..
HOW'S DANCING SCHOOL, LUCY?
FINE!
HOW ABOUT SHOWING US WHAT YOU'VE LEARNED?
WELL ...I'M NOT SURE I CAN REMEMBER EVERYTHING, BUT...
THAT COST MY DAD TWELVE DOLLARS!
SCHULZ 8-15

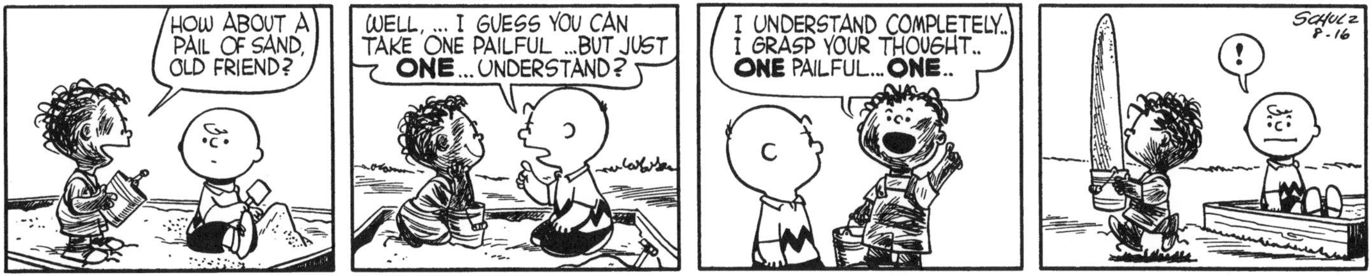
HOW ABOUT A PAIL OF SAND, OLD FRIEND?
WELL, ... I GUESS YOU CAN TAKE ONE PAILFUL ...BUT JUST **ONE**... UNDERSTAND?
I UNDERSTAND COMPLETELY.. I GRASP YOUR THOUGHT.. **ONE** PAILFUL...**ONE**..
!
SCHULZ 8-16

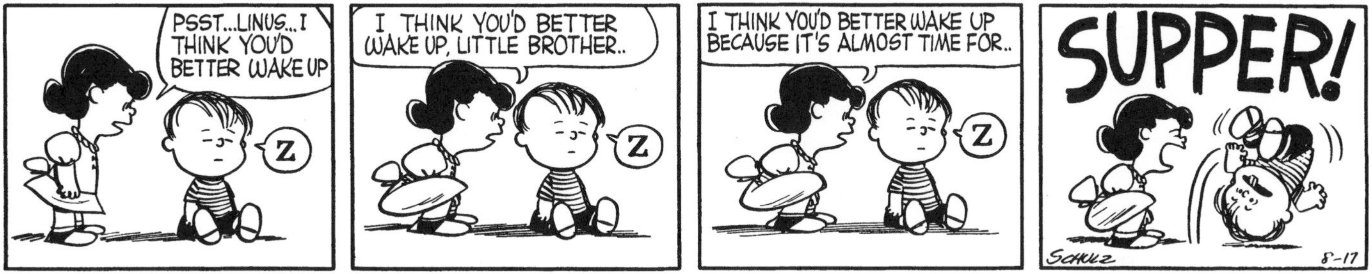
PSST...LINUS...I THINK YOU'D BETTER WAKE UP
Z
I THINK YOU'D BETTER WAKE UP, LITTLE BROTHER..
Z
I THINK YOU'D BETTER WAKE UP BECAUSE IT'S ALMOST TIME FOR..
Z
SUPPER!
SCHULZ 8-17

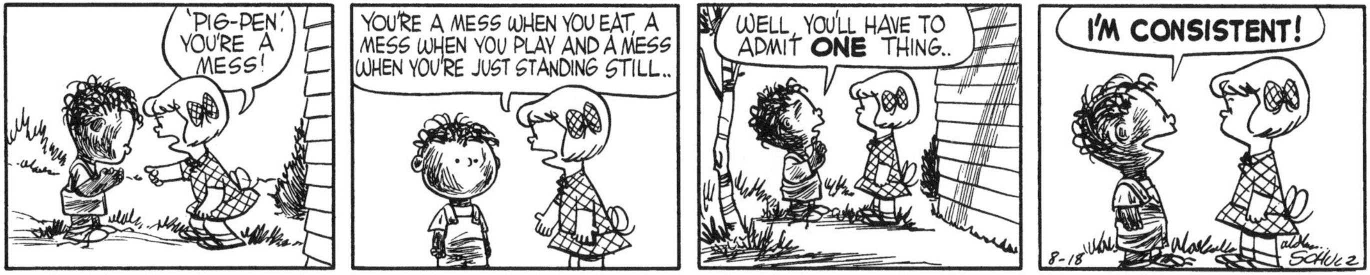
'PIG-PEN', YOU'RE A MESS!
YOU'RE A MESS WHEN YOU EAT, A MESS WHEN YOU PLAY AND A MESS WHEN YOU'RE JUST STANDING STILL..
WELL, YOU'LL HAVE TO ADMIT **ONE** THING..
I'M CONSISTENT!
8-18 SCHULZ

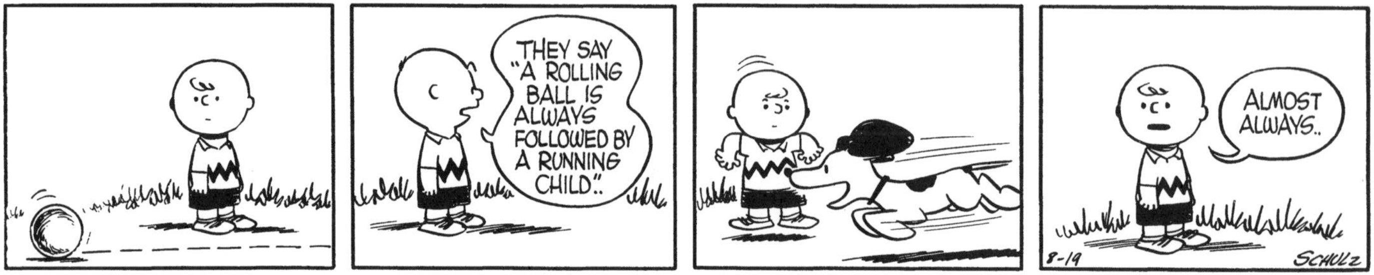
THEY SAY "A ROLLING BALL IS ALWAYS FOLLOWED BY A RUNNING CHILD"..
ALMOST ALWAYS..
8-19
SCHULZ

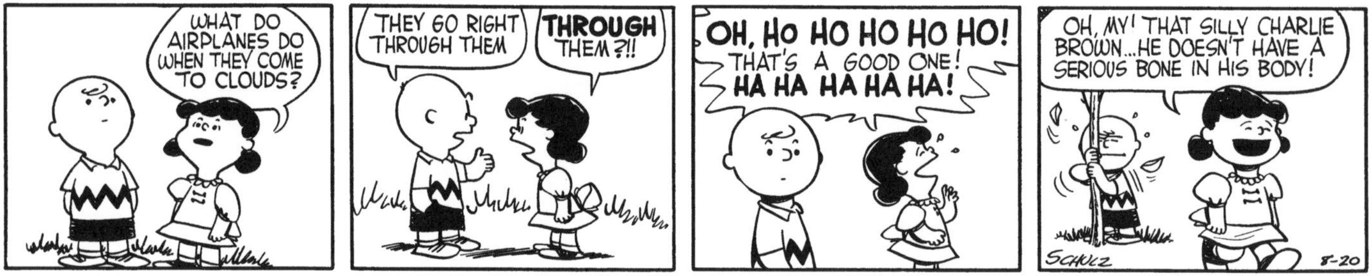
WHAT DO AIRPLANES DO WHEN THEY COME TO CLOUDS?
THEY GO RIGHT THROUGH THEM
THROUGH THEM?!!
OH, HO HO HO HO HO! THAT'S A GOOD ONE! HA HA HA HA HA!
OH, MY! THAT SILLY CHARLIE BROWN...HE DOESN'T HAVE A SERIOUS BONE IN HIS BODY!
SCHULZ
8-20

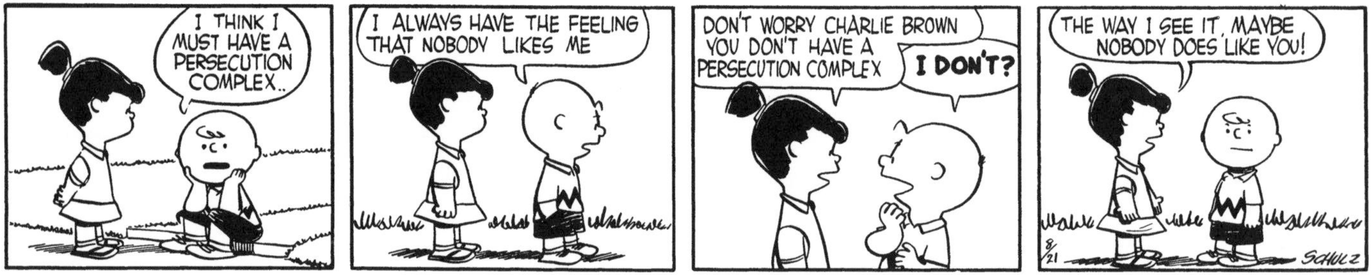
I THINK I MUST HAVE A PERSECUTION COMPLEX..
I ALWAYS HAVE THE FEELING THAT NOBODY LIKES ME
DON'T WORRY CHARLIE BROWN YOU DON'T HAVE A PERSECUTION COMPLEX
I DON'T?
THE WAY I SEE IT, MAYBE NOBODY DOES LIKE YOU!
8/21
SCHULZ

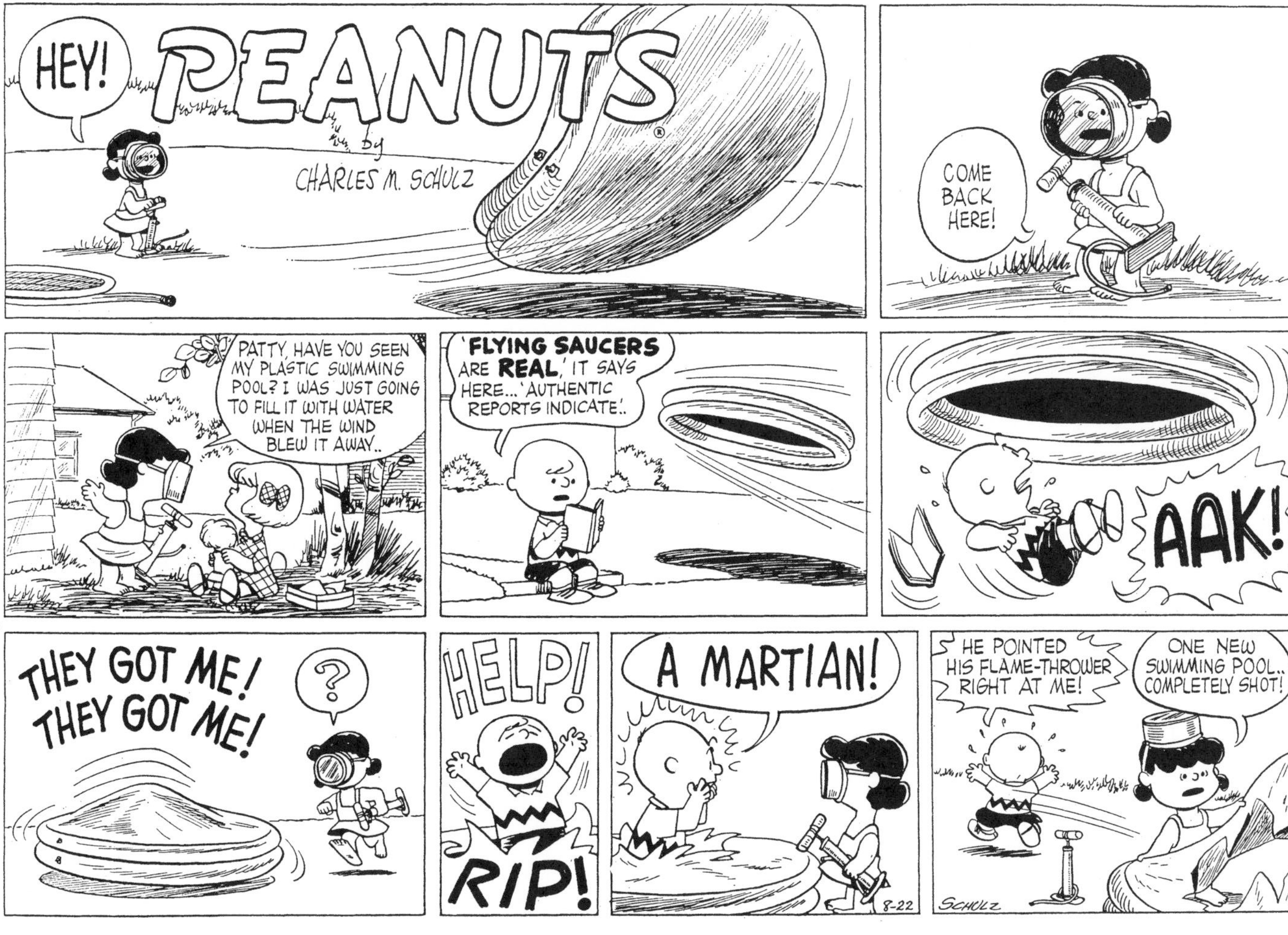
HEY!
PEANUTS
by CHARLES M. SCHULZ
COME BACK HERE!
PATTY, HAVE YOU SEEN MY PLASTIC SWIMMING POOL? I WAS JUST GOING TO FILL IT WITH WATER WHEN THE WIND BLEW IT AWAY..
'FLYING SAUCERS ARE REAL,' IT SAYS HERE...'AUTHENTIC REPORTS INDICATE'..
AAK!
THEY GOT ME! THEY GOT ME!
?
HELP!
RIP!
A MARTIAN!
8-22
HE POINTED HIS FLAME-THROWER RIGHT AT ME!
ONE NEW SWIMMING POOL.. COMPLETELY SHOT!
SCHULZ

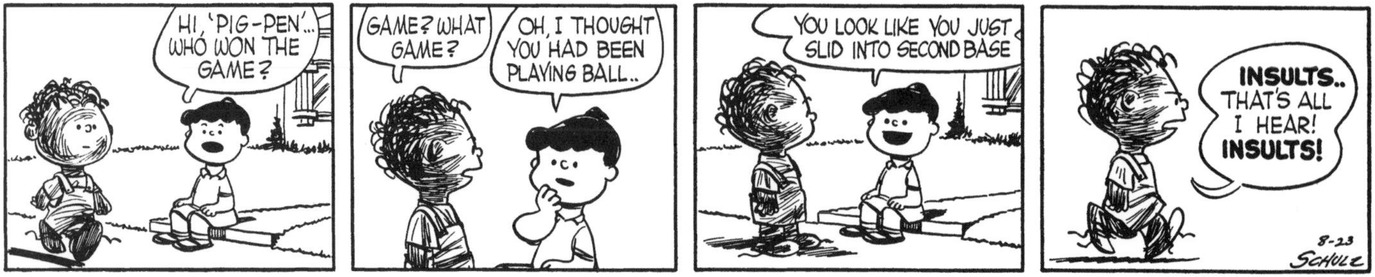
HI, 'PIG-PEN'... WHO WON THE GAME?
GAME? WHAT GAME?
OH, I THOUGHT YOU HAD BEEN PLAYING BALL..
YOU LOOK LIKE YOU JUST SLID INTO SECOND BASE
INSULTS.. THAT'S ALL I HEAR! **INSULTS!**
8-23
SCHULZ

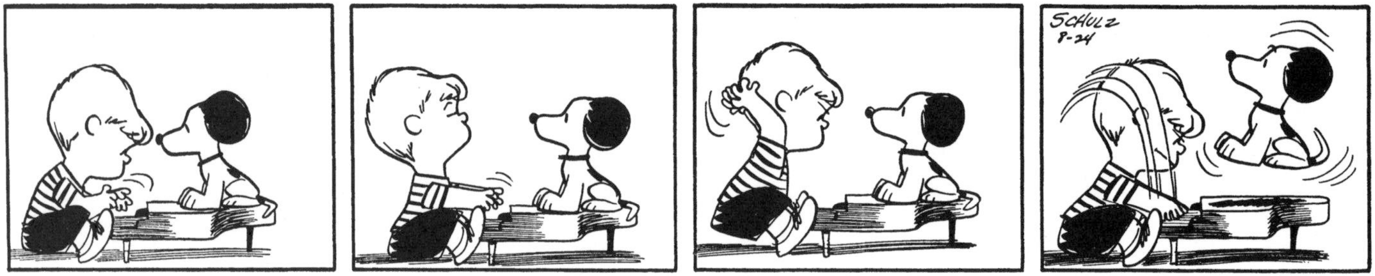
SCHULZ
8-24

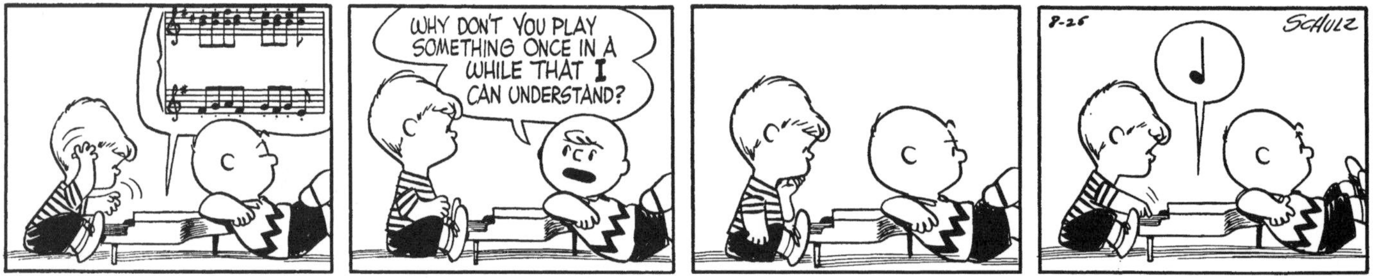
WHY DON'T YOU PLAY SOMETHING ONCE IN A WHILE THAT **I** CAN UNDERSTAND?
8-25
SCHULZ

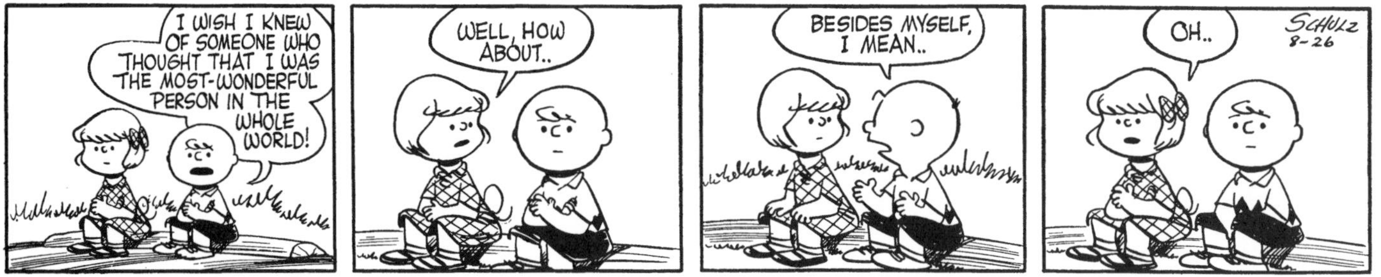
I WISH I KNEW OF SOMEONE WHO THOUGHT THAT I WAS THE MOST-WONDERFUL PERSON IN THE WHOLE WORLD!
WELL, HOW ABOUT..
BESIDES MYSELF, I MEAN..
OH..
SCHULZ 8-26

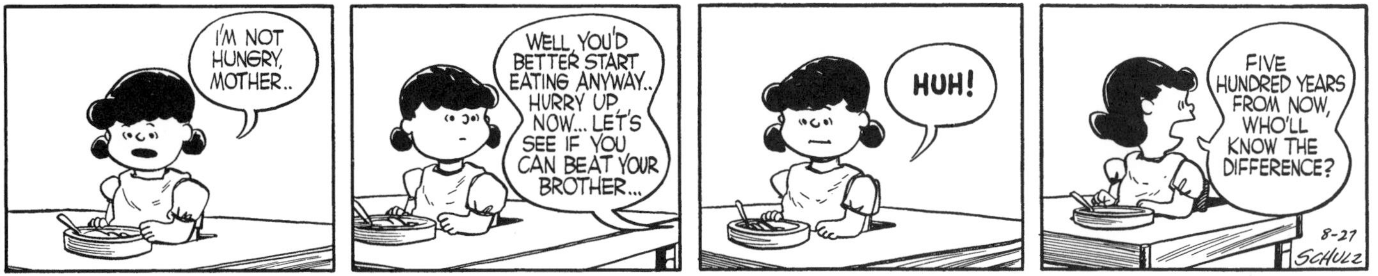
I'M NOT HUNGRY, MOTHER..
WELL, YOU'D BETTER START EATING ANYWAY.. HURRY UP, NOW... LET'S SEE IF YOU CAN BEAT YOUR BROTHER...
HUH!
FIVE HUNDRED YEARS FROM NOW, WHO'LL KNOW THE DIFFERENCE?
8-27 SCHULZ

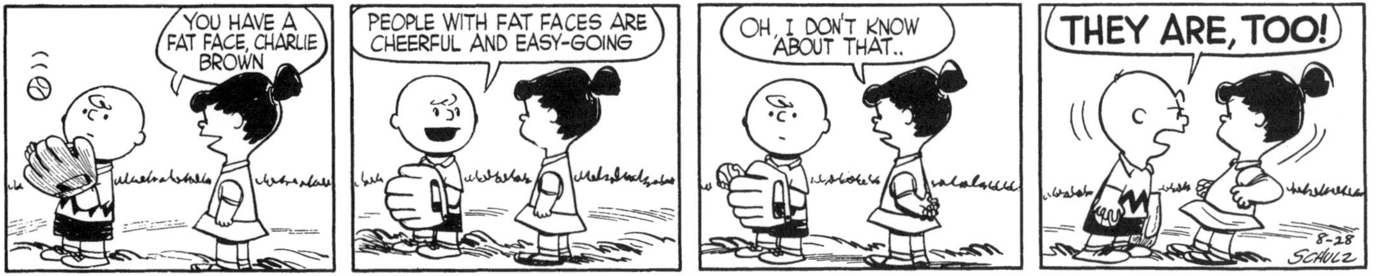
YOU HAVE A FAT FACE, CHARLIE BROWN
PEOPLE WITH FAT FACES ARE CHEERFUL AND EASY-GOING
OH, I DON'T KNOW ABOUT THAT..
THEY ARE, TOO!
8-28 SCHULZ

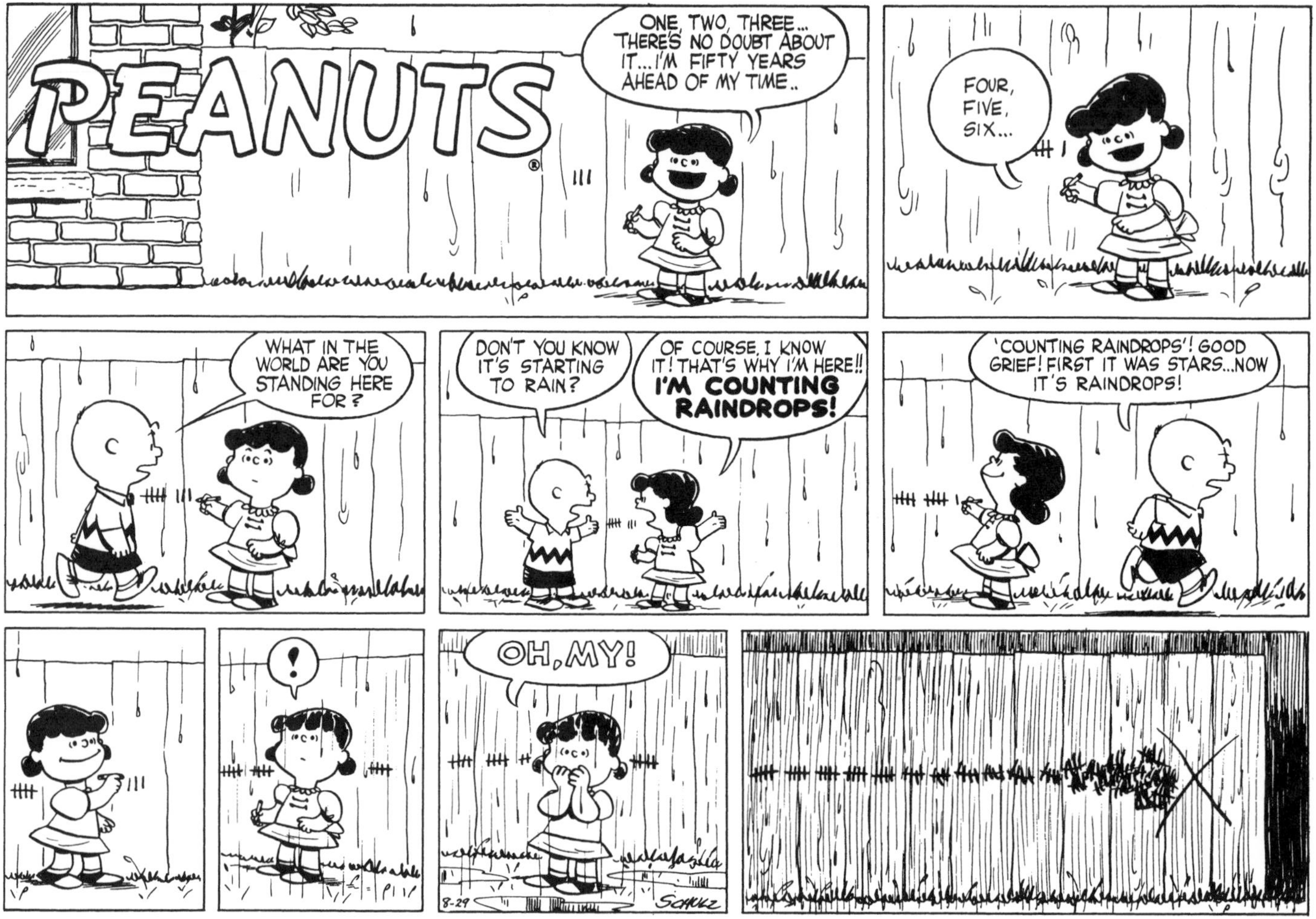
PEANUTS
ONE, TWO, THREE... THERE'S NO DOUBT ABOUT IT...I'M FIFTY YEARS AHEAD OF MY TIME..
FOUR, FIVE, SIX...
WHAT IN THE WORLD ARE YOU STANDING HERE FOR?
DON'T YOU KNOW IT'S STARTING TO RAIN?
OF COURSE, I KNOW IT! THAT'S WHY I'M HERE!! I'M COUNTING RAINDROPS!
'COUNTING RAINDROPS'! GOOD GRIEF! FIRST IT WAS STARS...NOW IT'S RAINDROPS!
!
OH, MY!
8-29
SCHULZ

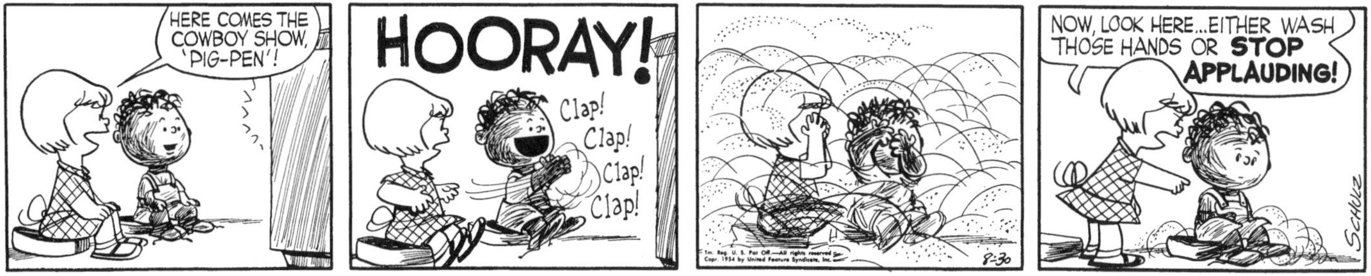
HERE COMES THE COWBOY SHOW, 'PIG-PEN'!
HOORAY!
Clap! Clap! Clap! Clap!
Tm. Reg. U. S. Pat. Off.—All rights reserved Copr. 1954 by United Feature Syndicate, Inc.
8-30
NOW, LOOK HERE...EITHER WASH THOSE HANDS OR STOP APPLAUDING!
SCHULZ

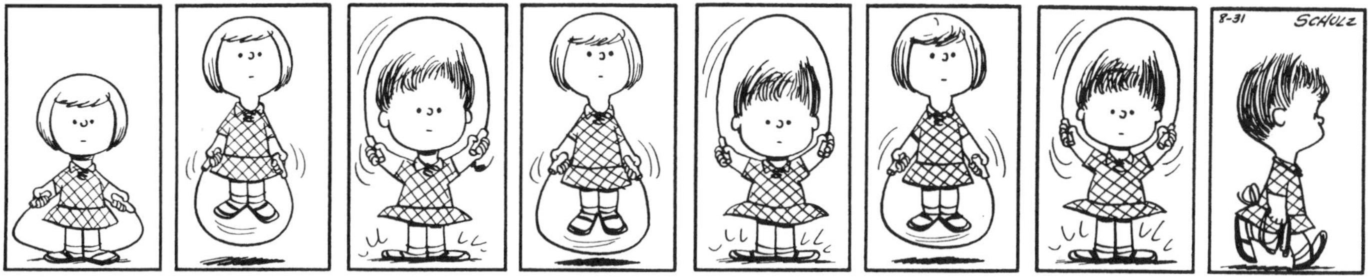
8-31
SCHULZ

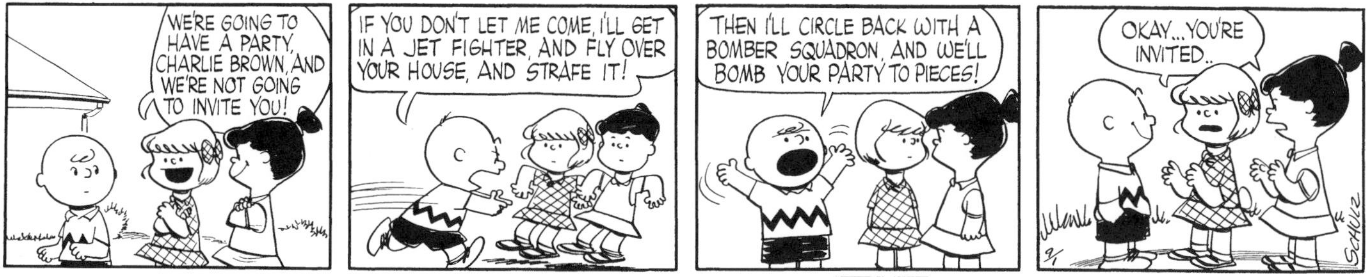
WE'RE GOING TO HAVE A PARTY, CHARLIE BROWN, AND WE'RE NOT GOING TO INVITE YOU!
IF YOU DON'T LET ME COME, I'LL GET IN A JET FIGHTER, AND FLY OVER YOUR HOUSE, AND STRAFE IT!
THEN I'LL CIRCLE BACK WITH A BOMBER SQUADRON, AND WE'LL BOMB YOUR PARTY TO PIECES!
OKAY... YOU'RE INVITED..
9/1
SCHULZ

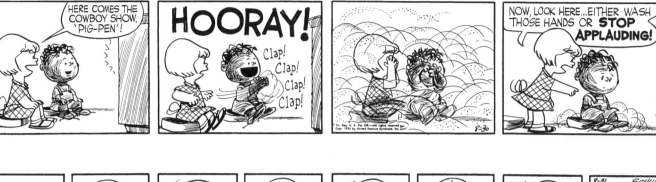

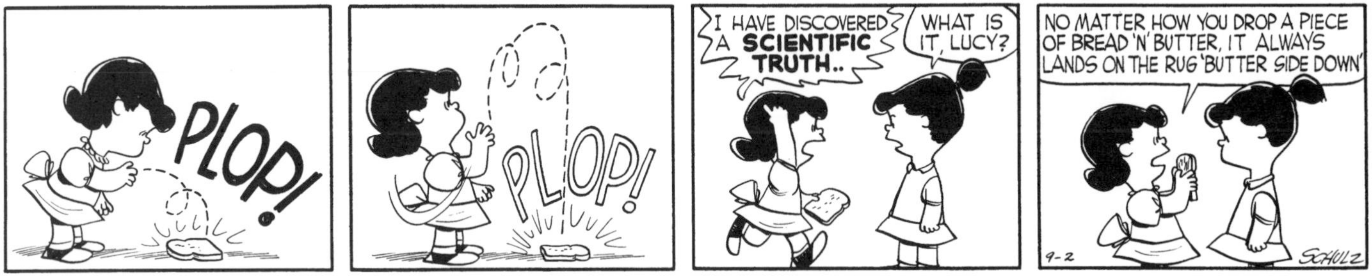
PLOP!
PLOP!
I HAVE DISCOVERED A **SCIENTIFIC TRUTH**..
WHAT IS IT, LUCY?
NO MATTER HOW YOU DROP A PIECE OF BREAD 'N' BUTTER, IT ALWAYS LANDS ON THE RUG 'BUTTER SIDE DOWN'
9-2
SCHULZ

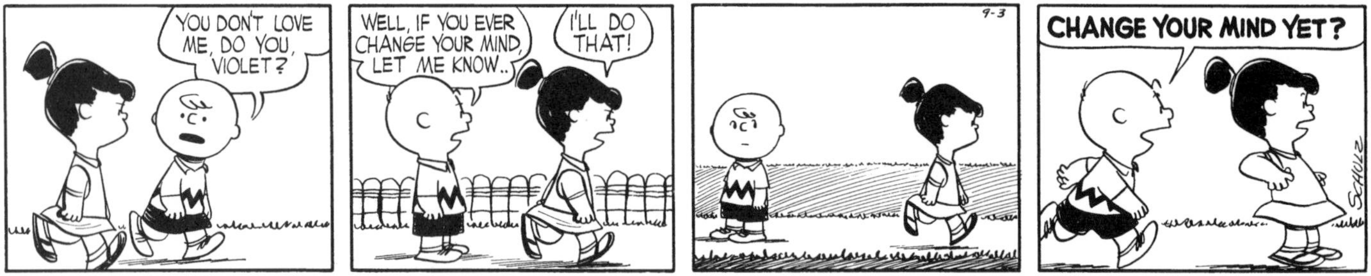
YOU DON'T LOVE ME, DO YOU, VIOLET?
WELL, IF YOU EVER CHANGE YOUR MIND, LET ME KNOW..
I'LL DO THAT!
9-3
CHANGE YOUR MIND YET?
SCHULZ

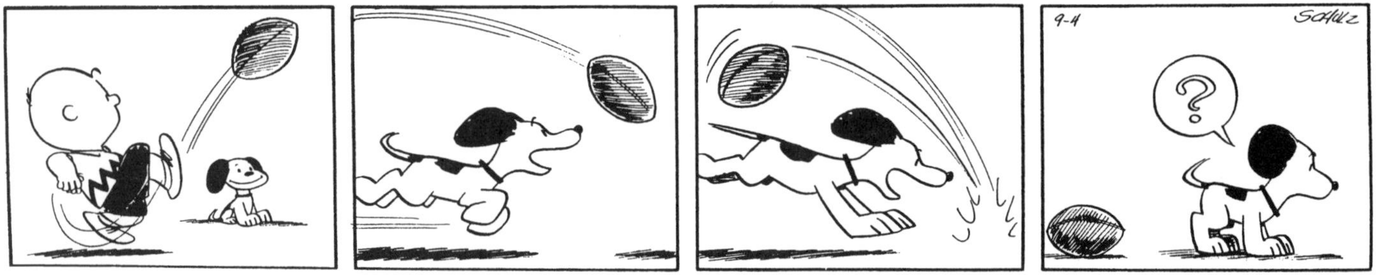
9-4
SCHULZ
?

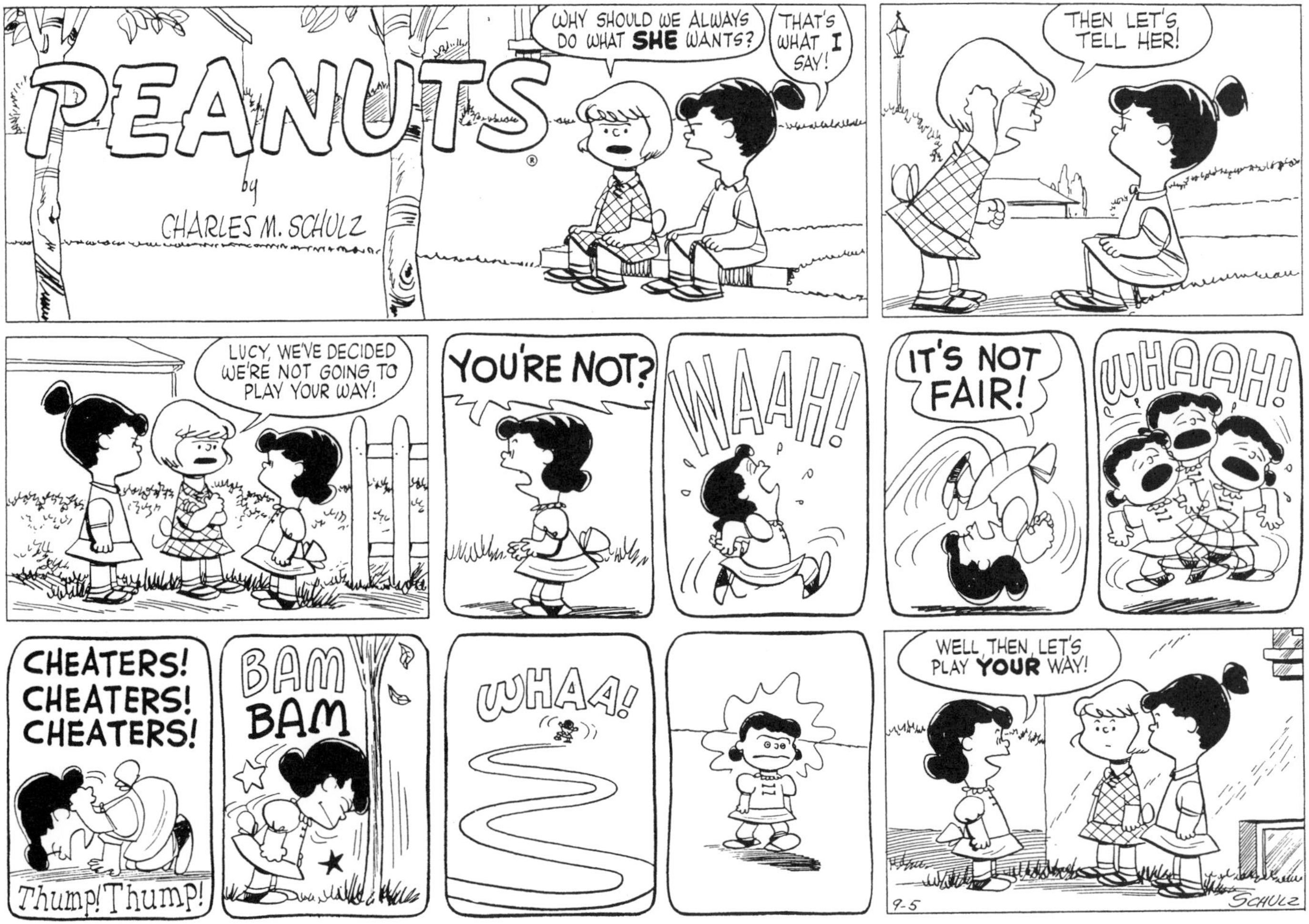
PEANUTS
by
CHARLES M. SCHULZ
WHY SHOULD WE ALWAYS DO WHAT SHE WANTS?
THAT'S WHAT I SAY!
THEN LET'S TELL HER!
LUCY, WE'VE DECIDED WE'RE NOT GOING TO PLAY YOUR WAY!
YOU'RE NOT?
WAAH!
IT'S NOT FAIR!
WHAAAH!
CHEATERS! CHEATERS! CHEATERS!
Thump! Thump!
BAM
BAM
WHAA!
WELL, THEN, LET'S PLAY YOUR WAY!
9-5
SCHULZ

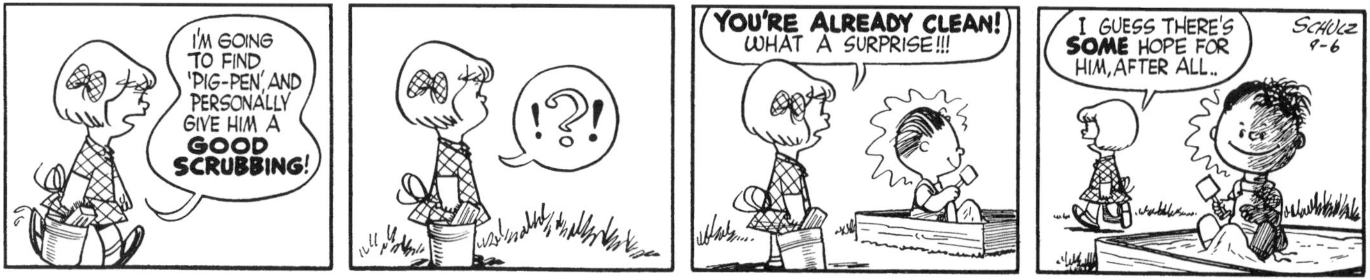
I'M GOING TO FIND 'PIG-PEN', AND PERSONALLY GIVE HIM A GOOD SCRUBBING!
!?!
YOU'RE ALREADY CLEAN! WHAT A SURPRISE!!!
I GUESS THERE'S SOME HOPE FOR HIM, AFTER ALL..
SCHULZ 9-6

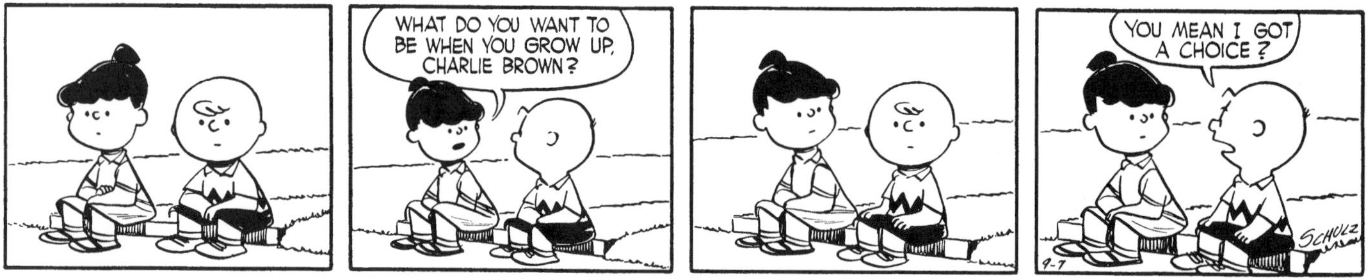
WHAT DO YOU WANT TO BE WHEN YOU GROW UP, CHARLIE BROWN?
9-7
YOU MEAN I GOT A CHOICE?
SCHULZ

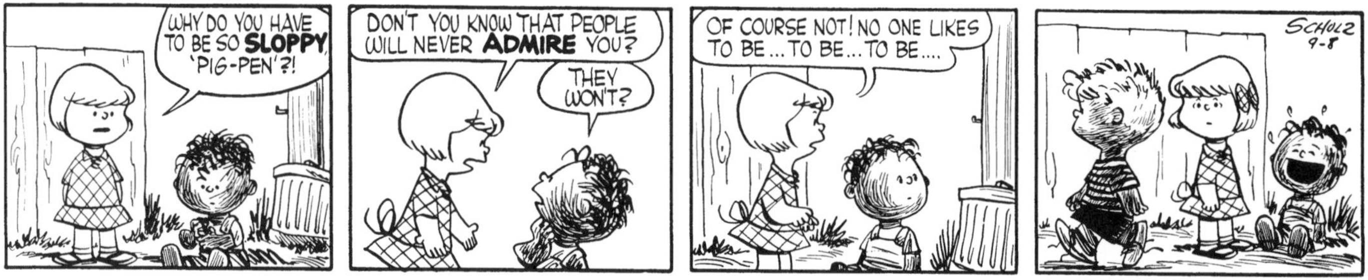
WHY DO YOU HAVE TO BE SO SLOPPY, 'PIG-PEN'?!
DON'T YOU KNOW THAT PEOPLE WILL NEVER ADMIRE YOU?
THEY WON'T?
OF COURSE NOT! NO ONE LIKES TO BE... TO BE... TO BE....
SCHULZ 9-8

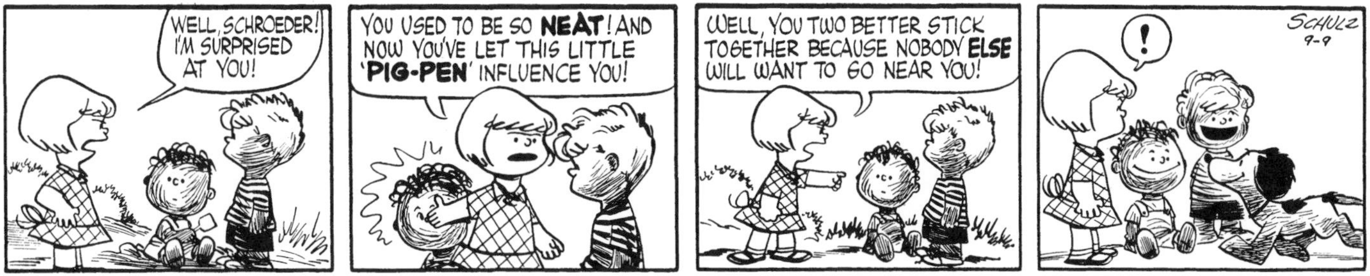
WELL, SCHROEDER! I'M SURPRISED AT YOU!
YOU USED TO BE SO NEAT! AND NOW YOU'VE LET THIS LITTLE 'PIG-PEN' INFLUENCE YOU!
WELL, YOU TWO BETTER STICK TOGETHER BECAUSE NOBODY ELSE WILL WANT TO GO NEAR YOU!
!
SCHULZ 9-9

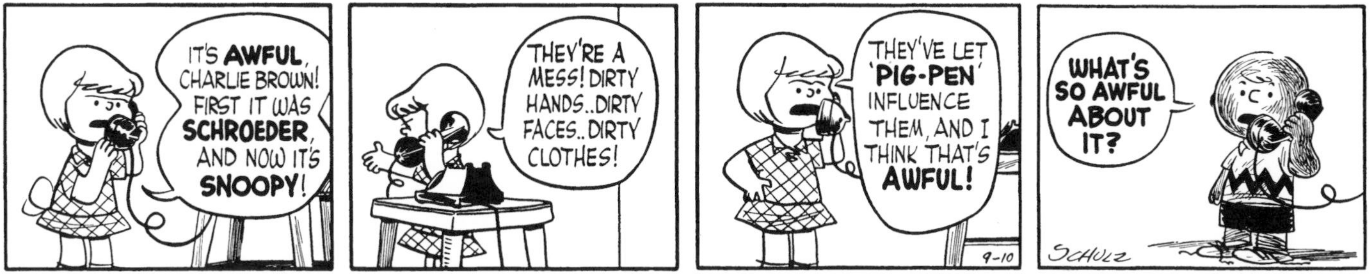
IT'S AWFUL, CHARLIE BROWN! FIRST IT WAS SCHROEDER, AND NOW IT'S SNOOPY!
THEY'RE A MESS! DIRTY HANDS..DIRTY FACES..DIRTY CLOTHES!
THEY'VE LET 'PIG-PEN' INFLUENCE THEM, AND I THINK THAT'S AWFUL!
9-10
WHAT'S SO AWFUL ABOUT IT?
SCHULZ

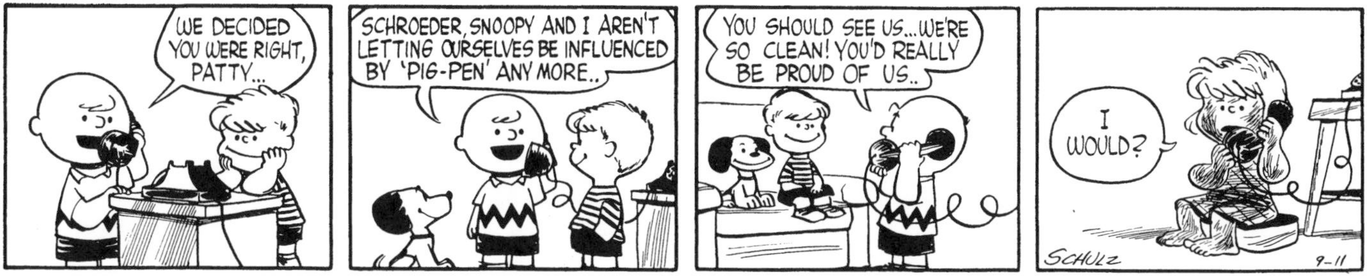
WE DECIDED YOU WERE RIGHT, PATTY...
SCHROEDER, SNOOPY AND I AREN'T LETTING OURSELVES BE INFLUENCED BY 'PIG-PEN' ANY MORE..
YOU SHOULD SEE US...WE'RE SO CLEAN! YOU'D REALLY BE PROUD OF US..
I WOULD?
SCHULZ
9-11

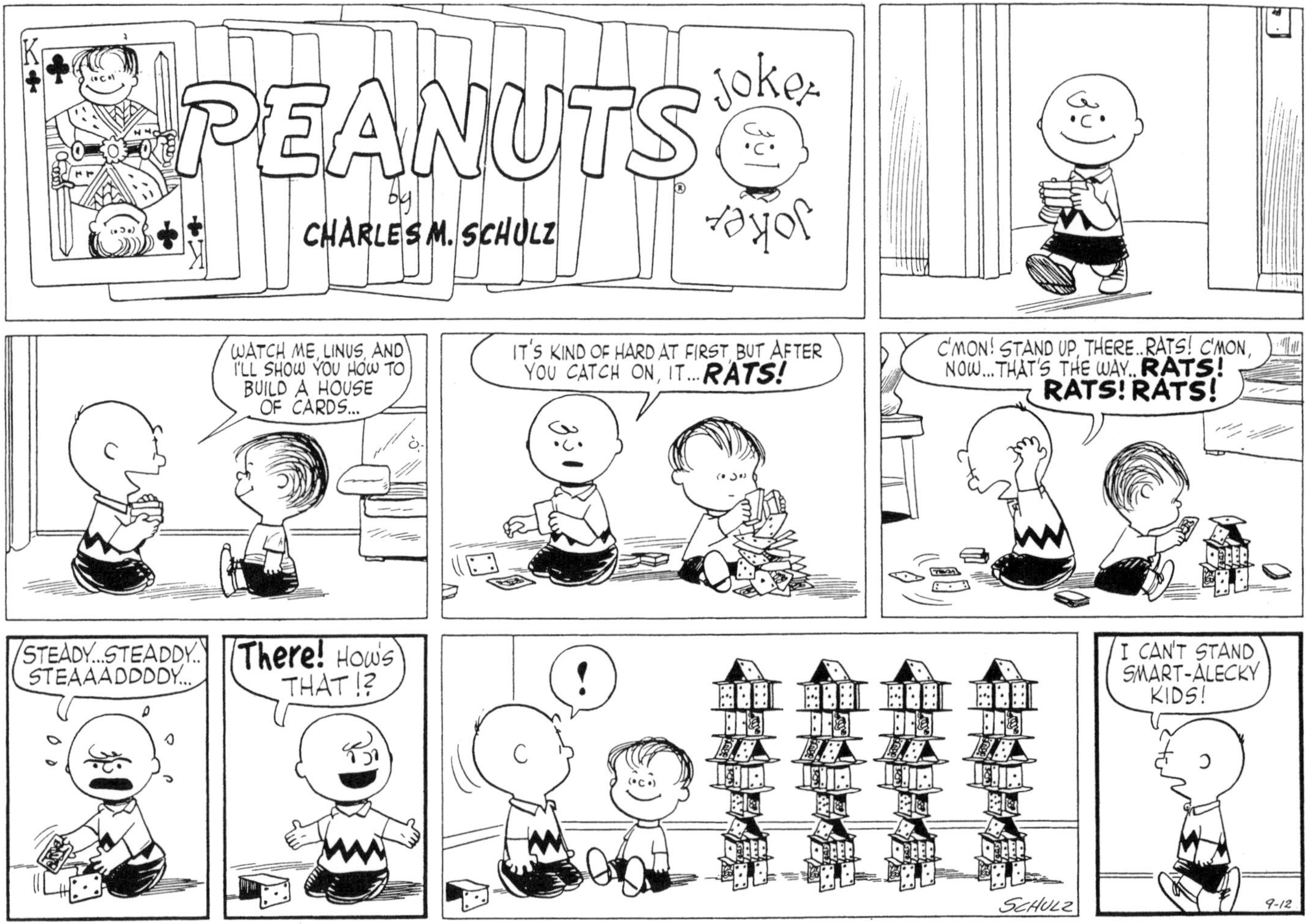
PEANUTS
by
CHARLES M. SCHULZ
K
K
Joker
Joker
WATCH ME, LINUS, AND I'LL SHOW YOU HOW TO BUILD A HOUSE OF CARDS...
IT'S KIND OF HARD AT FIRST, BUT AFTER YOU CATCH ON, IT... RATS!
C'MON! STAND UP, THERE.. RATS! C'MON, NOW... THAT'S THE WAY.. RATS! RATS! RATS!
STEADY...STEADDY.. STEAAADDDDY...
There! HOW'S THAT!?
!
SCHULZ
I CAN'T STAND SMART-ALECKY KIDS!
9-12

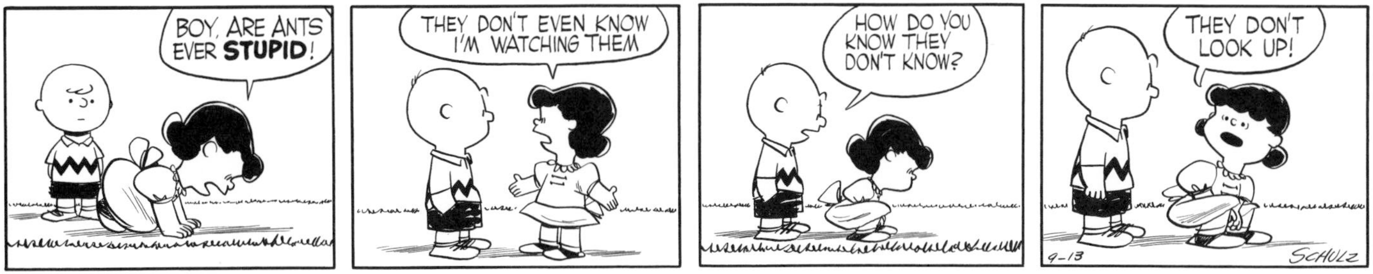
BOY, ARE ANTS EVER **STUPID**!
THEY DON'T EVEN KNOW I'M WATCHING THEM
HOW DO YOU KNOW THEY DON'T KNOW?
THEY DON'T LOOK UP!
9-13
SCHULZ

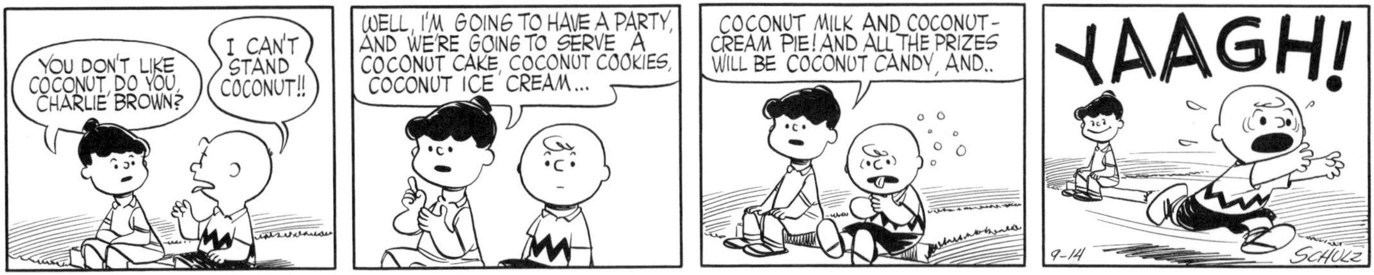
YOU DON'T LIKE COCONUT, DO YOU, CHARLIE BROWN?
I CAN'T STAND COCONUT!!
WELL, I'M GOING TO HAVE A PARTY, AND WE'RE GOING TO SERVE A COCONUT CAKE, COCONUT COOKIES, COCONUT ICE CREAM...
COCONUT MILK AND COCONUT-CREAM PIE! AND ALL THE PRIZES WILL BE COCONUT CANDY, AND..
YAAGH!
9-14
SCHULZ

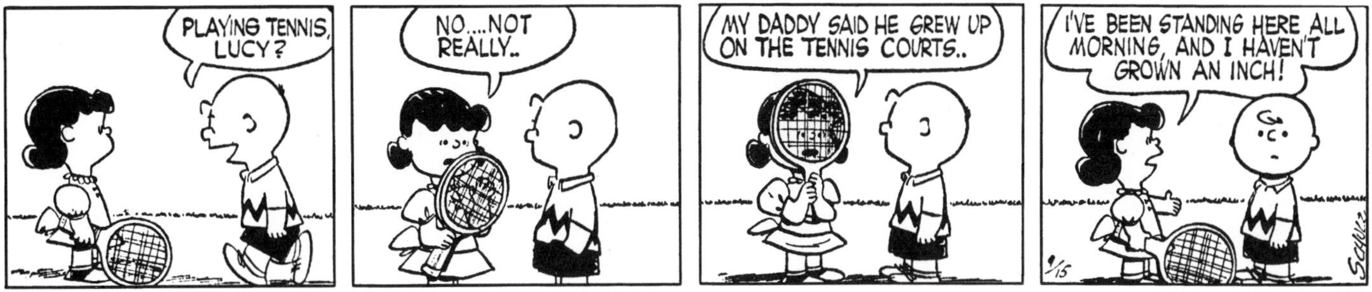
PLAYING TENNIS, LUCY?
NO....NOT REALLY..
MY DADDY SAID HE GREW UP ON THE TENNIS COURTS..
I'VE BEEN STANDING HERE ALL MORNING, AND I HAVEN'T GROWN AN INCH!
9/15
SCHULZ

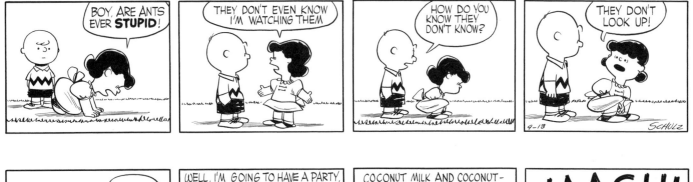

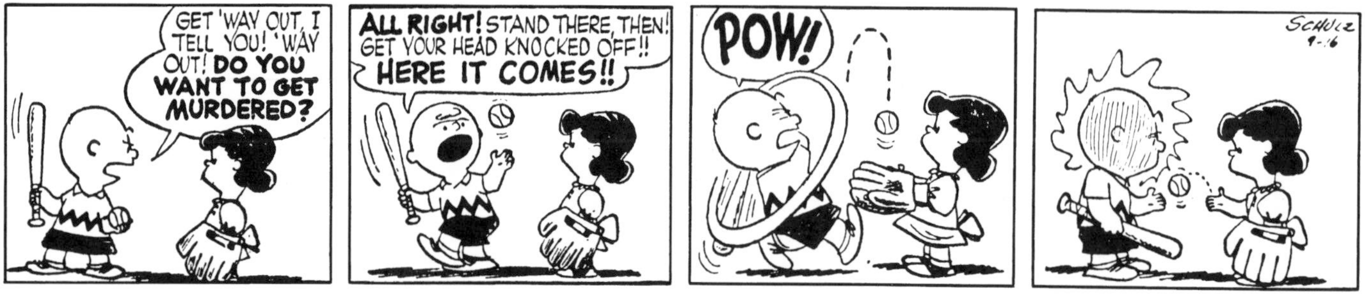
GET 'WAY OUT, I TELL YOU! 'WAY OUT! DO YOU WANT TO GET MURDERED?
ALL RIGHT! STAND THERE, THEN! GET YOUR HEAD KNOCKED OFF!! HERE IT COMES!!
POW!
SCHULZ 9-16

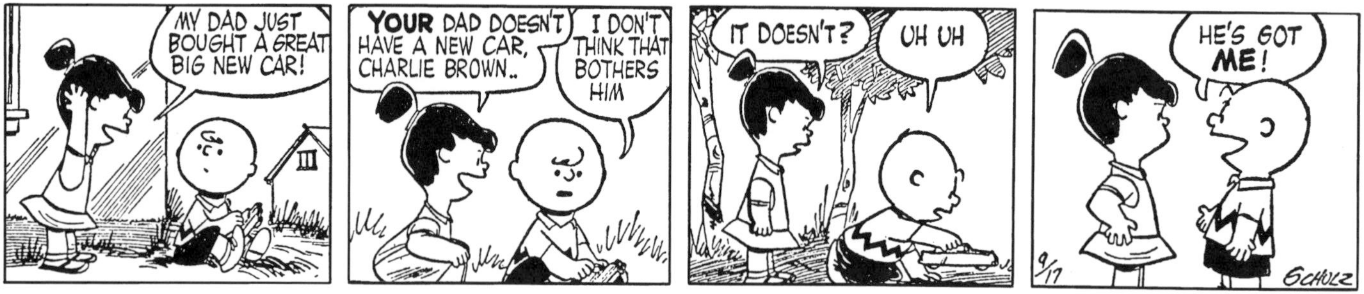
MY DAD JUST BOUGHT A GREAT BIG NEW CAR!
YOUR DAD DOESN'T HAVE A NEW CAR, CHARLIE BROWN..
I DON'T THINK THAT BOTHERS HIM
IT DOESN'T?
UH UH
HE'S GOT ME!
9/17
SCHULZ

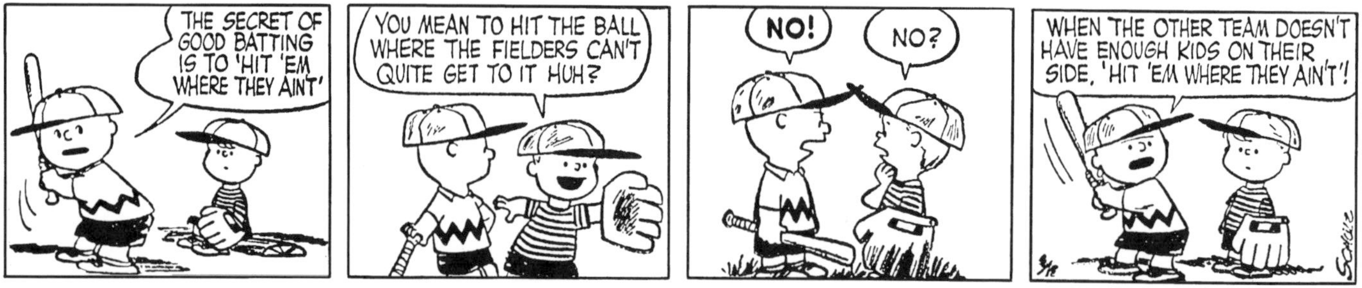
THE SECRET OF GOOD BATTING IS TO 'HIT 'EM WHERE THEY AIN'T'
YOU MEAN TO HIT THE BALL WHERE THE FIELDERS CAN'T QUITE GET TO IT HUH?
NO!
NO?
WHEN THE OTHER TEAM DOESN'T HAVE ENOUGH KIDS ON THEIR SIDE, 'HIT 'EM WHERE THEY AIN'T'!
SCHULZ

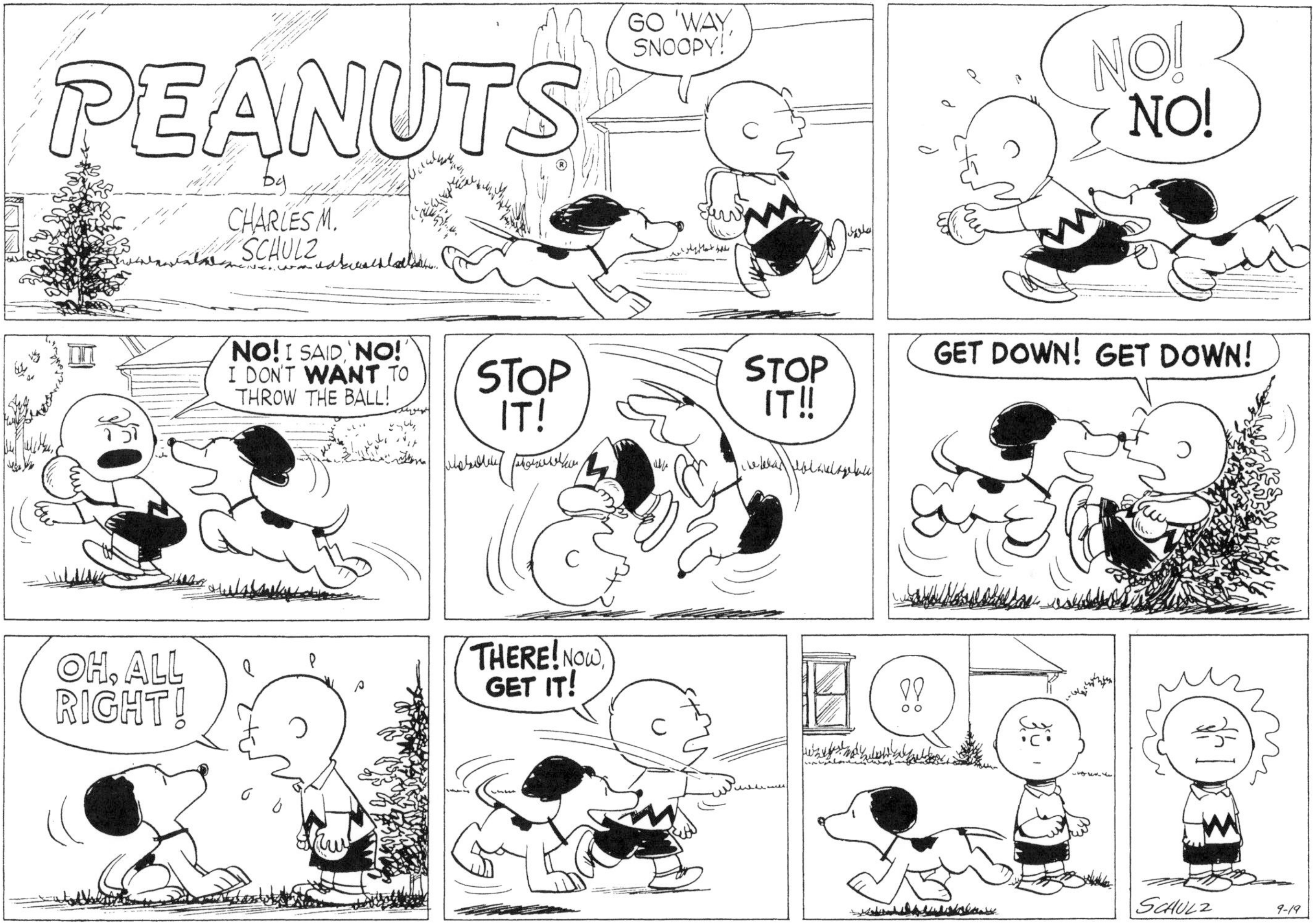
PEANUTS
by CHARLES M. SCHULZ
GO 'WAY, SNOOPY!
NO! NO!
NO! I SAID 'NO!' I DON'T WANT TO THROW THE BALL!
STOP IT!
STOP IT!!
GET DOWN! GET DOWN!
OH, ALL RIGHT!
THERE! NOW, GET IT!
!!
SCHULZ
9-19

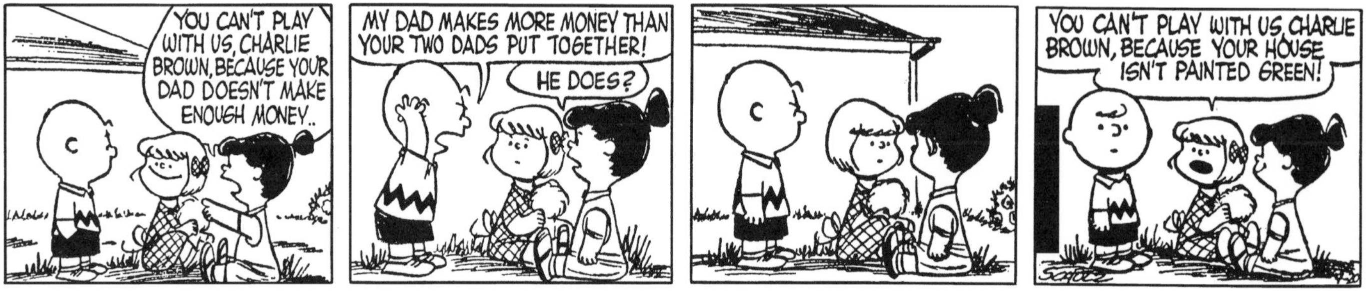
YOU CAN'T PLAY WITH US, CHARLIE BROWN, BECAUSE YOUR DAD DOESN'T MAKE ENOUGH MONEY..
MY DAD MAKES MORE MONEY THAN YOUR TWO DADS PUT TOGETHER!
HE DOES?
YOU CAN'T PLAY WITH US, CHARLIE BROWN, BECAUSE YOUR HOUSE ISN'T PAINTED GREEN!

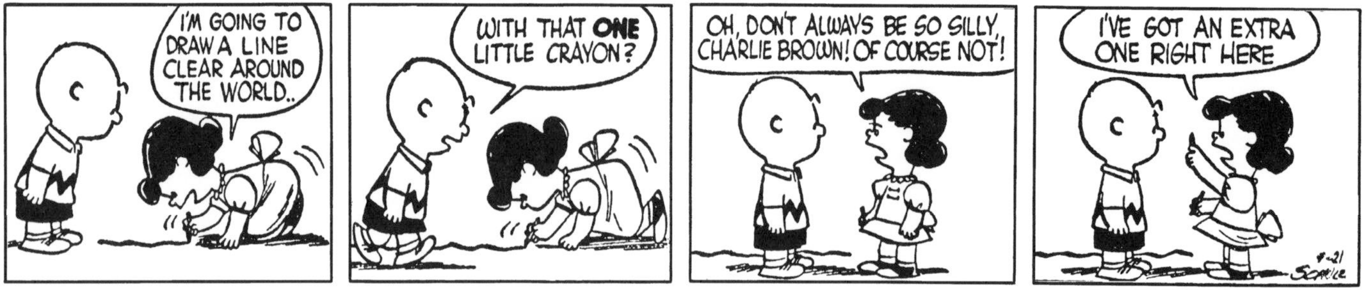
I'M GOING TO DRAW A LINE CLEAR AROUND THE WORLD..
WITH THAT **ONE** LITTLE CRAYON?
OH, DON'T ALWAYS BE SO SILLY, CHARLIE BROWN! OF COURSE NOT!
I'VE GOT AN EXTRA ONE RIGHT HERE

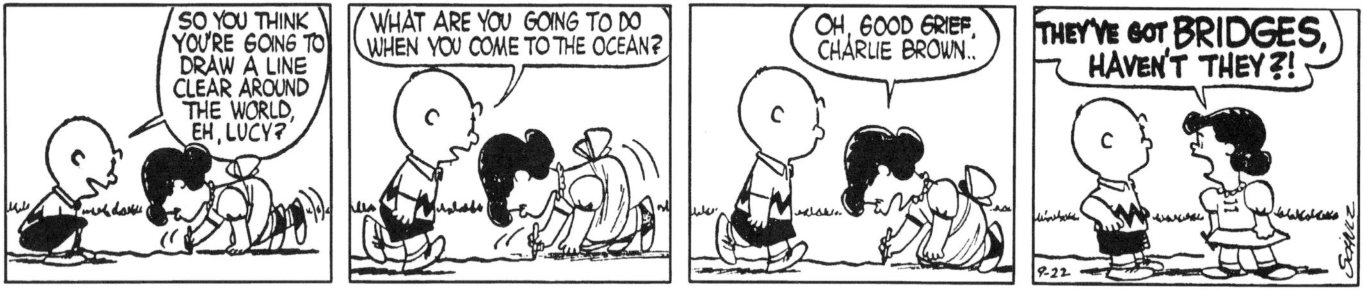
SO YOU THINK YOU'RE GOING TO DRAW A LINE CLEAR AROUND THE WORLD, EH, LUCY?
WHAT ARE YOU GOING TO DO WHEN YOU COME TO THE OCEAN?
OH, GOOD GRIEF, CHARLIE BROWN..
THEY'VE GOT BRIDGES, HAVEN'T THEY?!

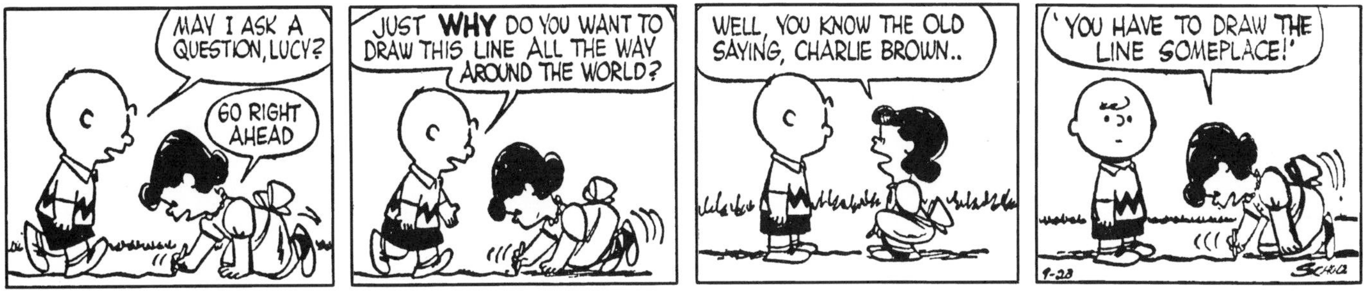
MAY I ASK A QUESTION, LUCY?
GO RIGHT AHEAD
JUST WHY DO YOU WANT TO DRAW THIS LINE ALL THE WAY AROUND THE WORLD?
WELL, YOU KNOW THE OLD SAYING, CHARLIE BROWN..
'YOU HAVE TO DRAW THE LINE SOMEPLACE!'
9-28

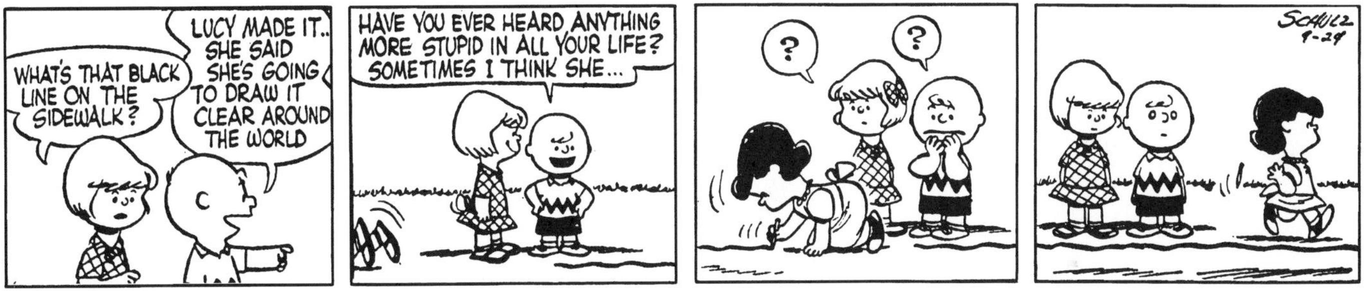
WHAT'S THAT BLACK LINE ON THE SIDEWALK?
LUCY MADE IT.. SHE SAID SHE'S GOING TO DRAW IT CLEAR AROUND THE WORLD
HAVE YOU EVER HEARD ANYTHING MORE STUPID IN ALL YOUR LIFE? SOMETIMES I THINK SHE...
?
?

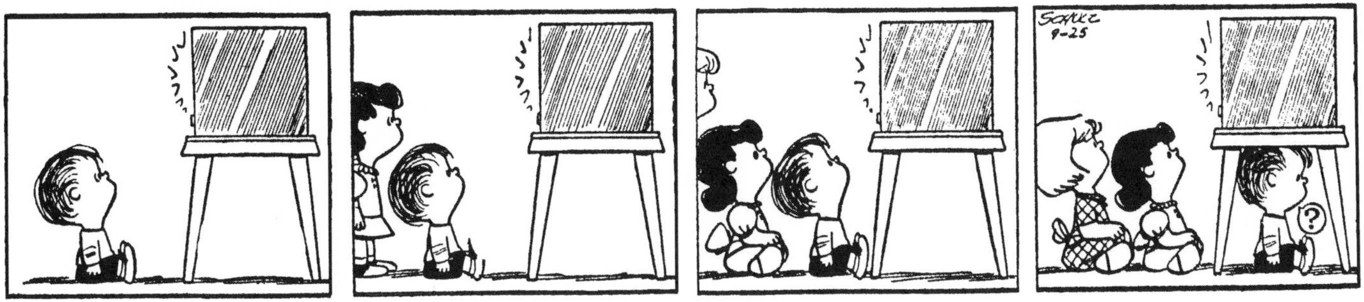
?

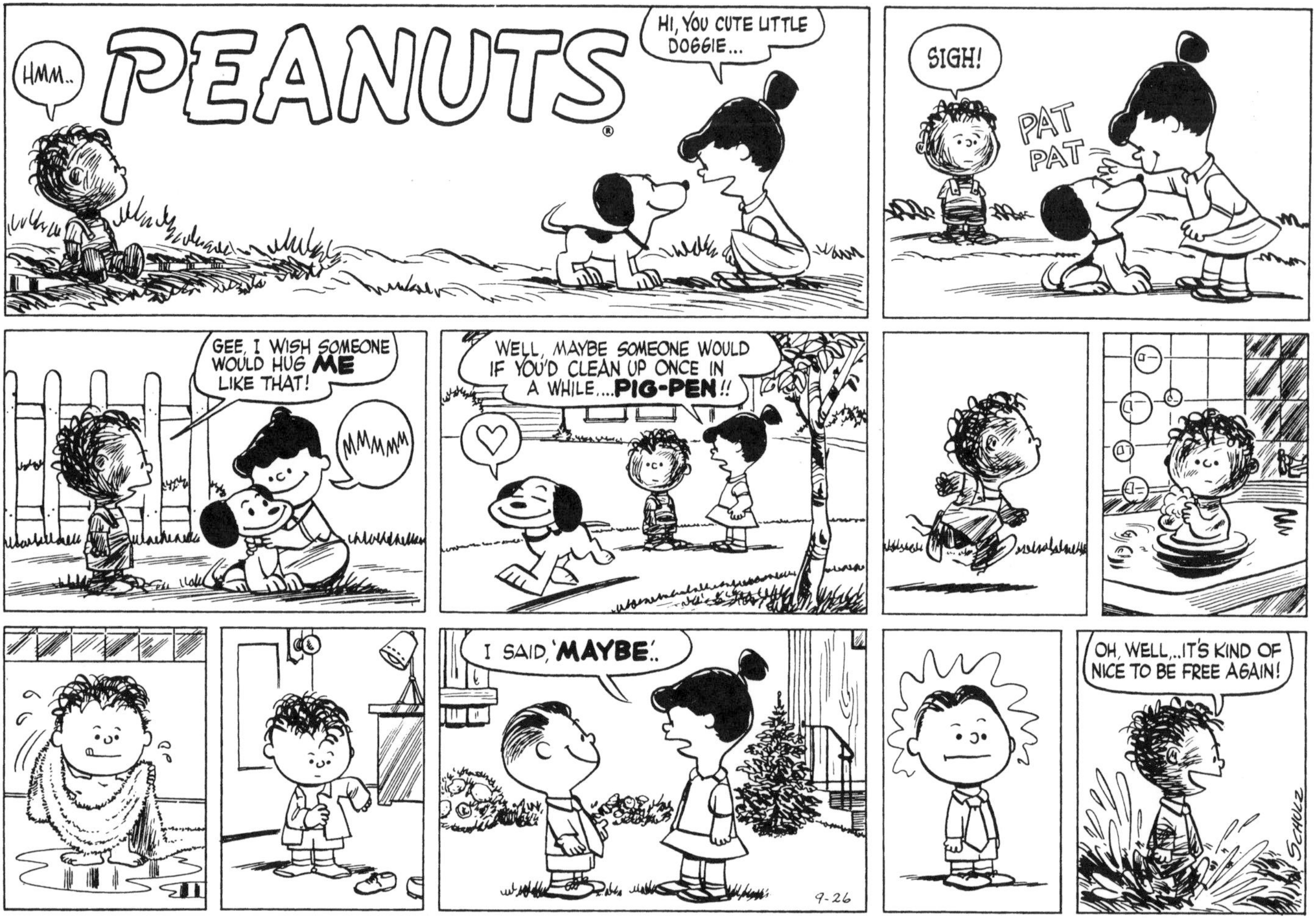
HMM..
PEANUTS
HI, YOU CUTE LITTLE DOGGIE...
SIGH!
PAT PAT
GEE, I WISH SOMEONE WOULD HUG **ME** LIKE THAT!
MMMMM
WELL, MAYBE SOMEONE WOULD IF YOU'D CLEAN UP ONCE IN A WHILE....**PIG-PEN**!!
I SAID, '**MAYBE**'..
9-26
OH, WELL,..IT'S KIND OF NICE TO BE FREE AGAIN!
SCHULZ

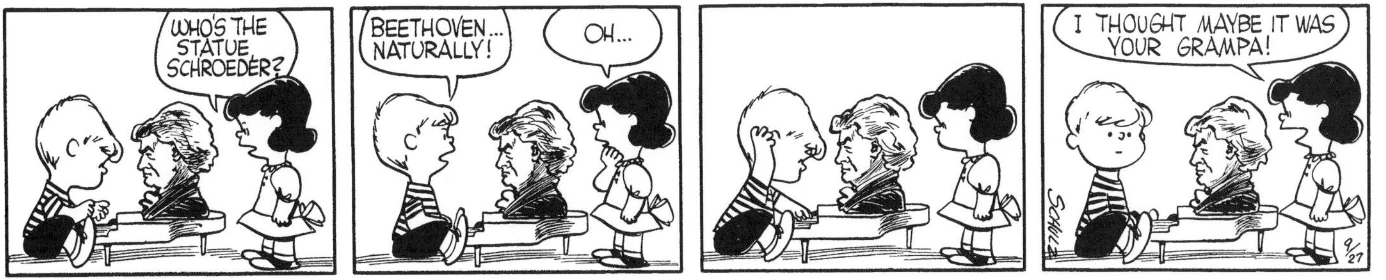
WHO'S THE STATUE SCHROEDER?
BEETHOVEN... NATURALLY!
OH...
I THOUGHT MAYBE IT WAS YOUR GRAMPA!
SCHULZ
9/27

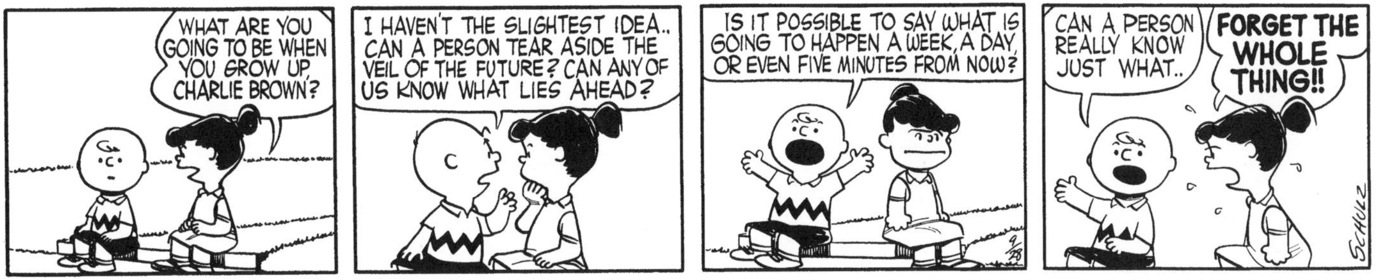
WHAT ARE YOU GOING TO BE WHEN YOU GROW UP, CHARLIE BROWN?
I HAVEN'T THE SLIGHTEST IDEA.. CAN A PERSON TEAR ASIDE THE VEIL OF THE FUTURE? CAN ANY OF US KNOW WHAT LIES AHEAD?
IS IT POSSIBLE TO SAY WHAT IS GOING TO HAPPEN A WEEK, A DAY, OR EVEN FIVE MINUTES FROM NOW?
9/28
CAN A PERSON REALLY KNOW JUST WHAT..
FORGET THE WHOLE THING!!
SCHULZ

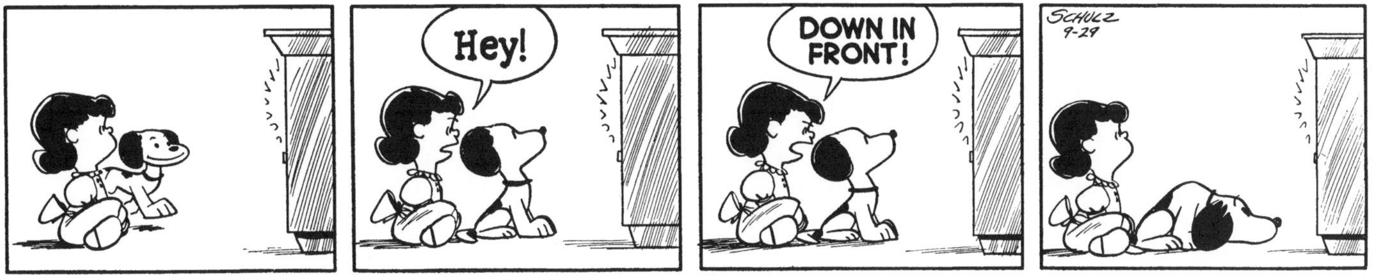
Hey!
DOWN IN FRONT!
SCHULZ
9-29

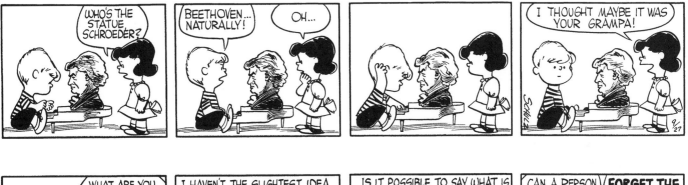

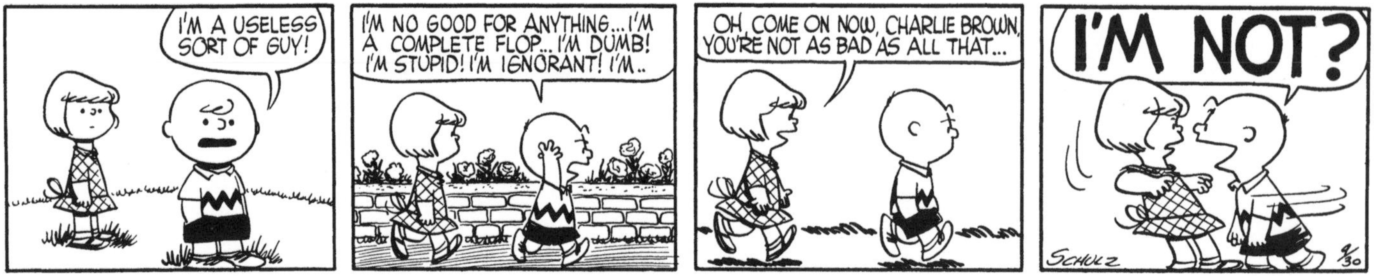
I'M A USELESS SORT OF GUY!
I'M NO GOOD FOR ANYTHING... I'M A COMPLETE FLOP... I'M DUMB! I'M STUPID! I'M IGNORANT! I'M..
OH, COME ON NOW, CHARLIE BROWN, YOU'RE NOT AS BAD AS ALL THAT...
I'M NOT?
SCHULZ
9/30

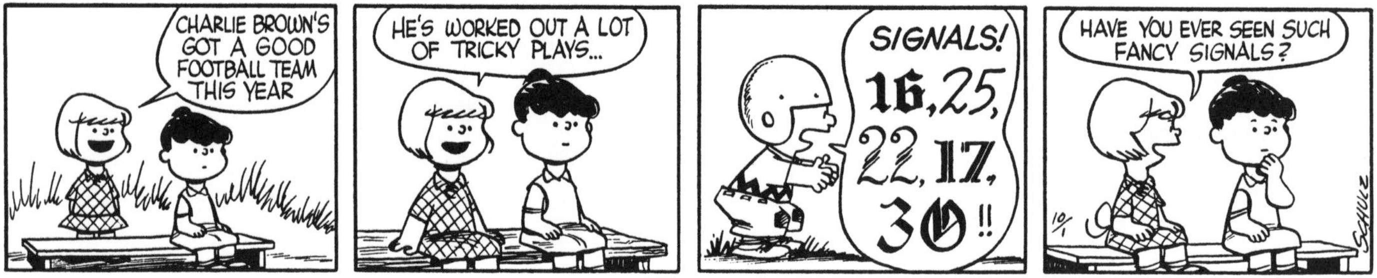
CHARLIE BROWN'S GOT A GOOD FOOTBALL TEAM THIS YEAR
HE'S WORKED OUT A LOT OF TRICKY PLAYS...
SIGNALS! 16, 25, 22, 17, 30!!
HAVE YOU EVER SEEN SUCH FANCY SIGNALS?
10/1
SCHULZ

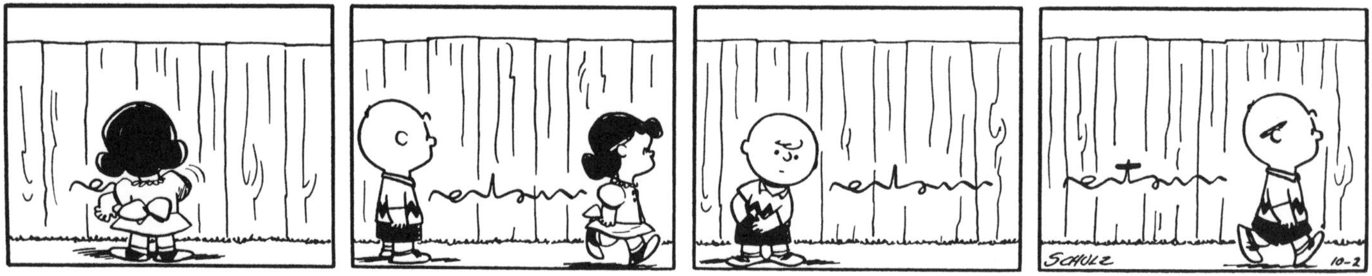
SCHULZ
10-2

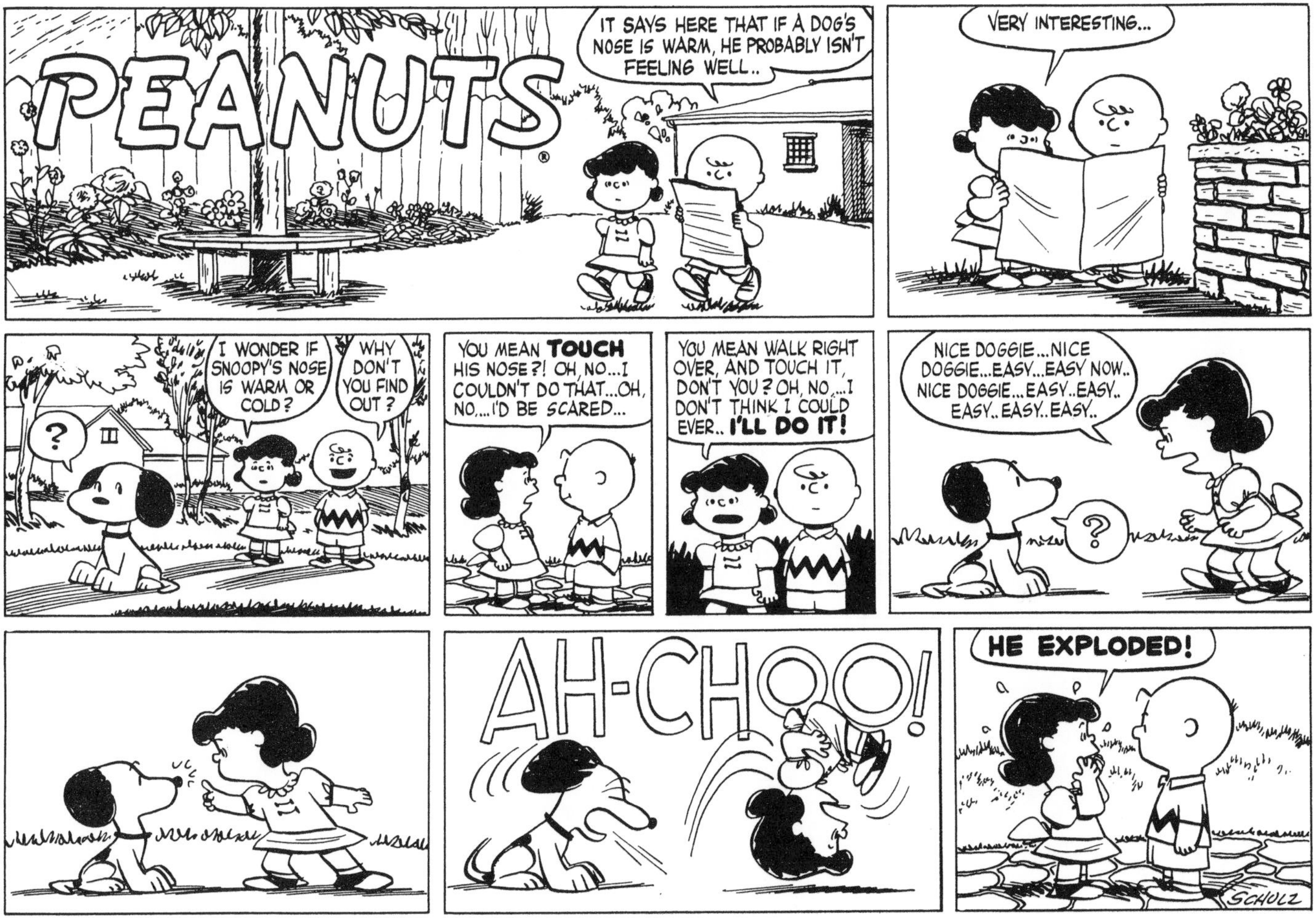
PEANUTS®
IT SAYS HERE THAT IF A DOG'S NOSE IS WARM, HE PROBABLY ISN'T FEELING WELL..
VERY INTERESTING...
?
I WONDER IF SNOOPY'S NOSE IS WARM OR COLD?
WHY DON'T YOU FIND OUT?
YOU MEAN **TOUCH** HIS NOSE?! OH, NO...I COULDN'T DO THAT...OH, NO,...I'D BE SCARED...
YOU MEAN WALK RIGHT OVER, AND TOUCH IT, DON'T YOU? OH, NO,...I DON'T THINK I COULD EVER.. **I'LL DO IT!**
NICE DOGGIE...NICE DOGGIE...EASY...EASY NOW.. NICE DOGGIE...EASY..EASY.. EASY..EASY..EASY..
?
AH-CHOO!
HE EXPLODED!
SCHULZ

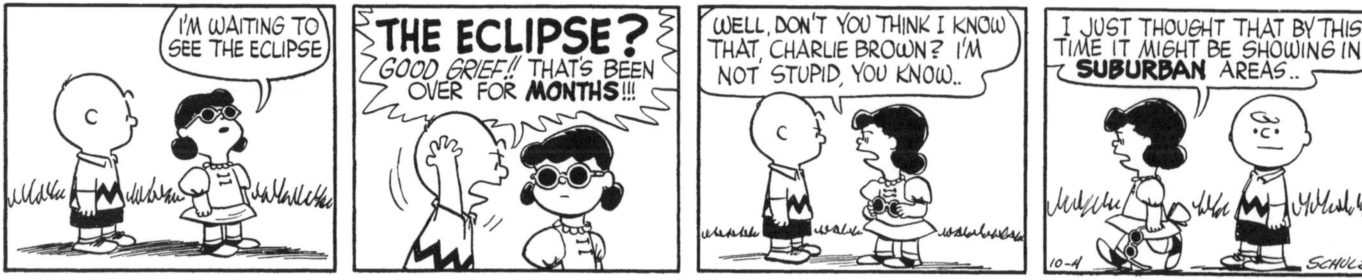
I'M WAITING TO SEE THE ECLIPSE
THE ECLIPSE? GOOD GRIEF!! THAT'S BEEN OVER FOR MONTHS!!!
WELL, DON'T YOU THINK I KNOW THAT, CHARLIE BROWN? I'M NOT STUPID, YOU KNOW..
I JUST THOUGHT THAT BY THIS TIME IT MIGHT BE SHOWING IN SUBURBAN AREAS..
10-4
SCHULZ

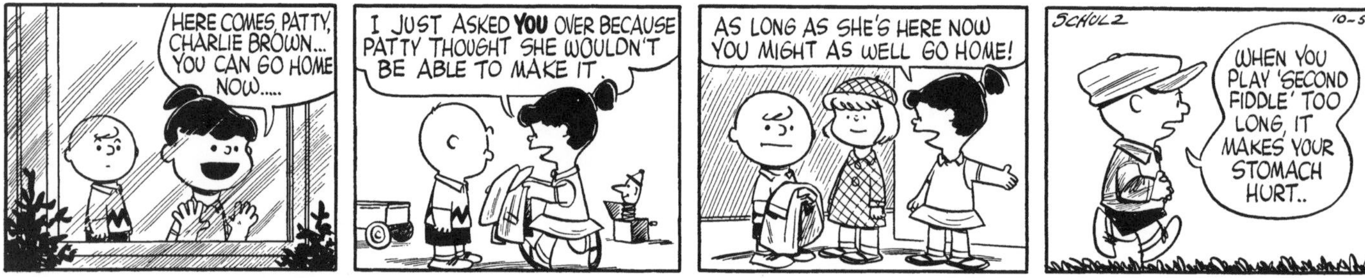
HERE COMES PATTY, CHARLIE BROWN... YOU CAN GO HOME NOW.....
I JUST ASKED YOU OVER BECAUSE PATTY THOUGHT SHE WOULDN'T BE ABLE TO MAKE IT.
AS LONG AS SHE'S HERE NOW YOU MIGHT AS WELL GO HOME!
SCHULZ
10-5
WHEN YOU PLAY 'SECOND FIDDLE' TOO LONG, IT MAKES YOUR STOMACH HURT..

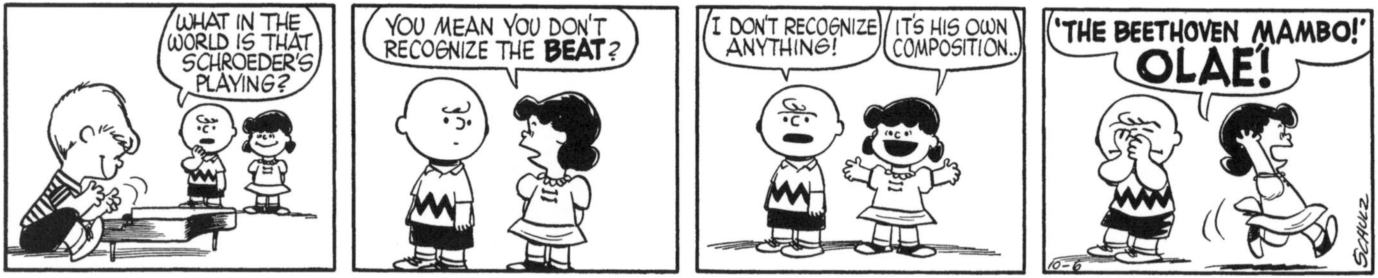
WHAT IN THE WORLD IS THAT SCHROEDER'S PLAYING?
YOU MEAN YOU DON'T RECOGNIZE THE BEAT?
I DON'T RECOGNIZE ANYTHING!
IT'S HIS OWN COMPOSITION..
'THE BEETHOVEN MAMBO!' OLAE!
10-6
SCHULZ

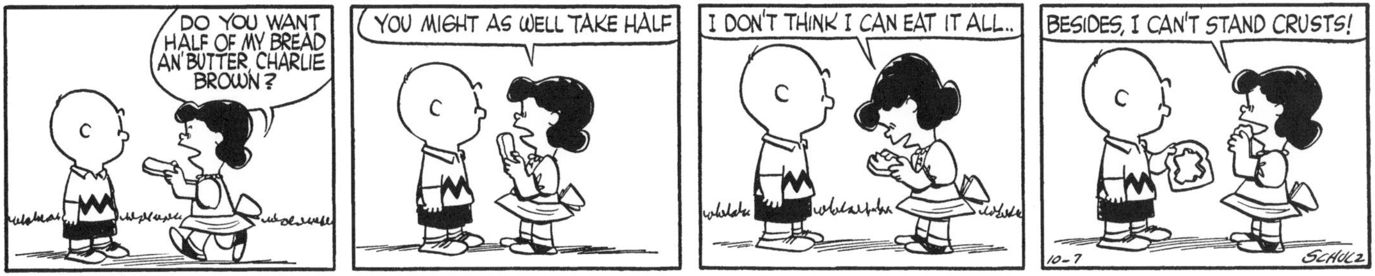
DO YOU WANT HALF OF MY BREAD AN' BUTTER CHARLIE BROWN?
YOU MIGHT AS WELL TAKE HALF
I DON'T THINK I CAN EAT IT ALL..
BESIDES, I CAN'T STAND CRUSTS!
10-7
SCHULZ

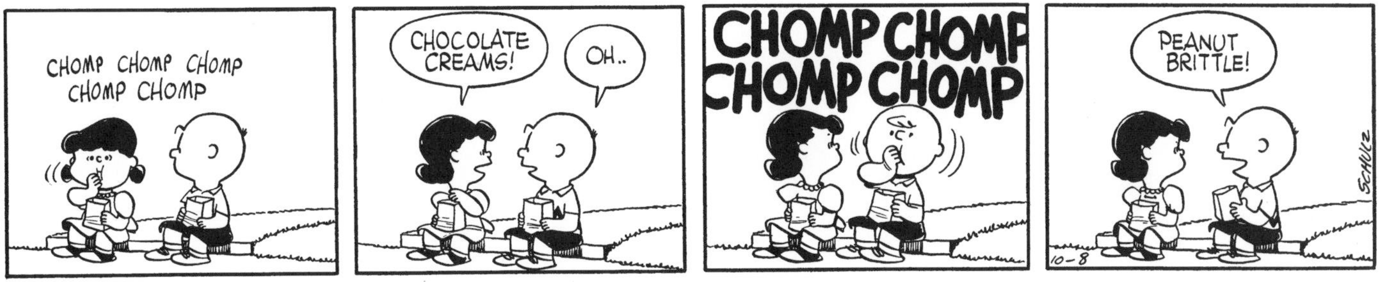
CHOMP CHOMP CHOMP CHOMP CHOMP
CHOCOLATE CREAMS!
OH..
CHOMP CHOMP CHOMP CHOMP
PEANUT BRITTLE!
SCHULZ
10-8

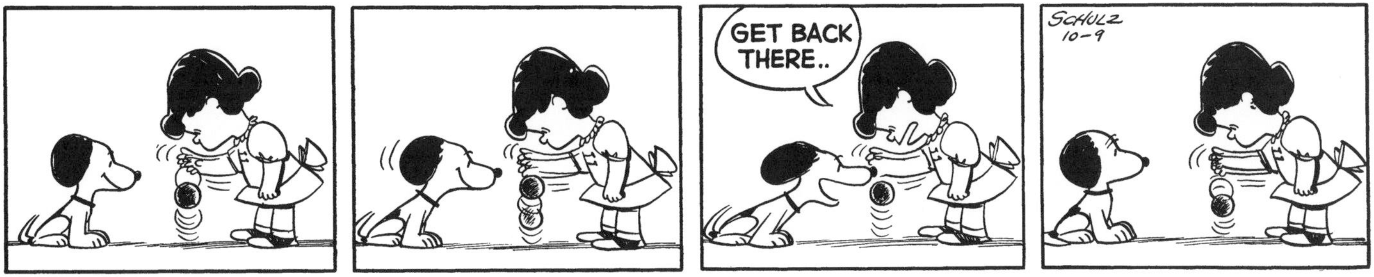
GET BACK THERE..
SCHULZ 10-9

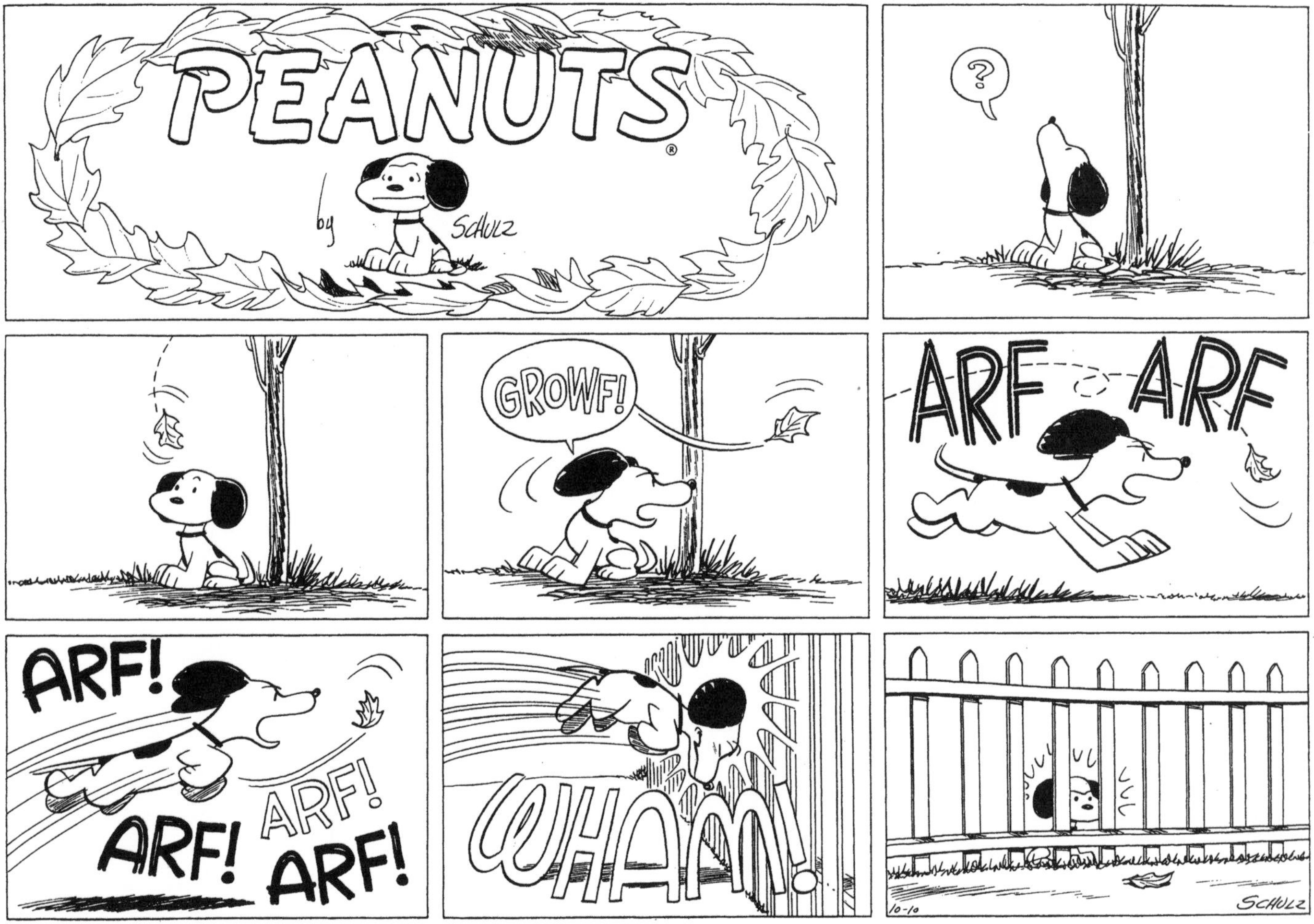
PEANUTS
by SCHULZ
?
GROWF!
ARF ARF
ARF!
ARF!
ARF!
ARF!
WHAM!
10-10
SCHULZ

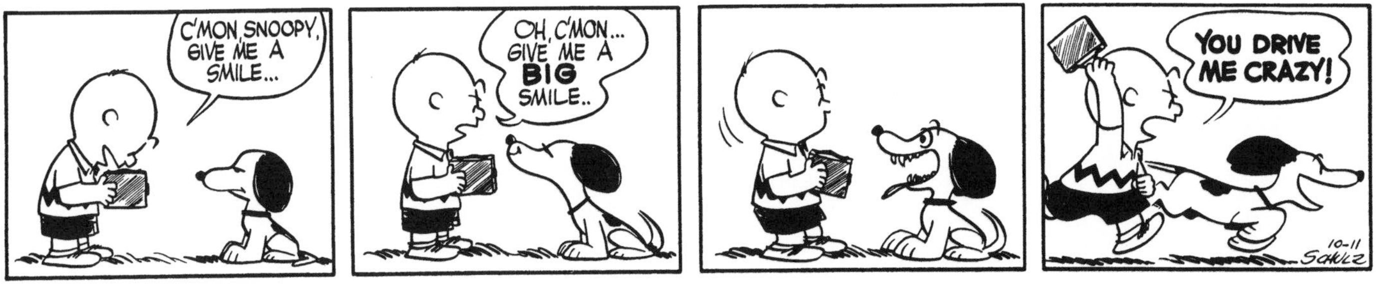
C'MON, SNOOPY, GIVE ME A SMILE...
OH, C'MON... GIVE ME A **BIG** SMILE..
YOU DRIVE ME CRAZY!
10-11
SCHULZ

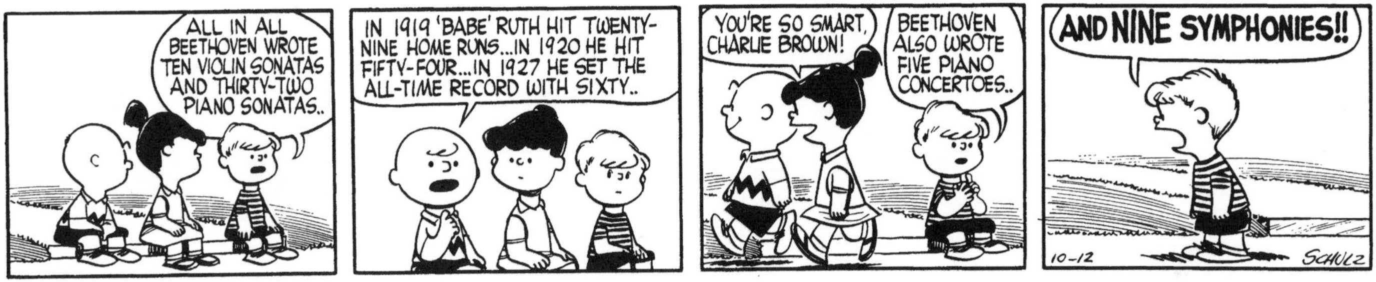
ALL IN ALL BEETHOVEN WROTE TEN VIOLIN SONATAS AND THIRTY-TWO PIANO SONATAS..
IN 1919 'BABE' RUTH HIT TWENTY-NINE HOME RUNS...IN 1920 HE HIT FIFTY-FOUR...IN 1927 HE SET THE ALL-TIME RECORD WITH SIXTY..
YOU'RE SO SMART, CHARLIE BROWN!
BEETHOVEN ALSO WROTE FIVE PIANO CONCERTOES..
AND NINE SYMPHONIES!!
10-12
SCHULZ

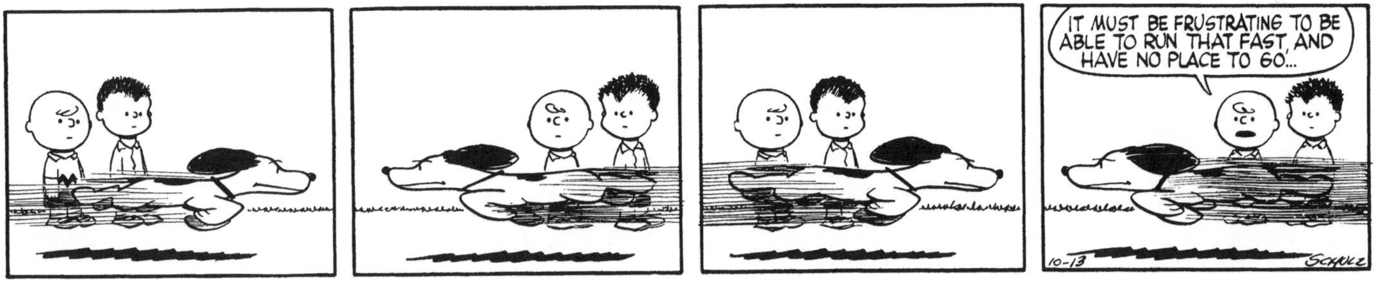
IT MUST BE FRUSTRATING TO BE ABLE TO RUN THAT FAST, AND HAVE NO PLACE TO GO...
10-13
SCHULZ

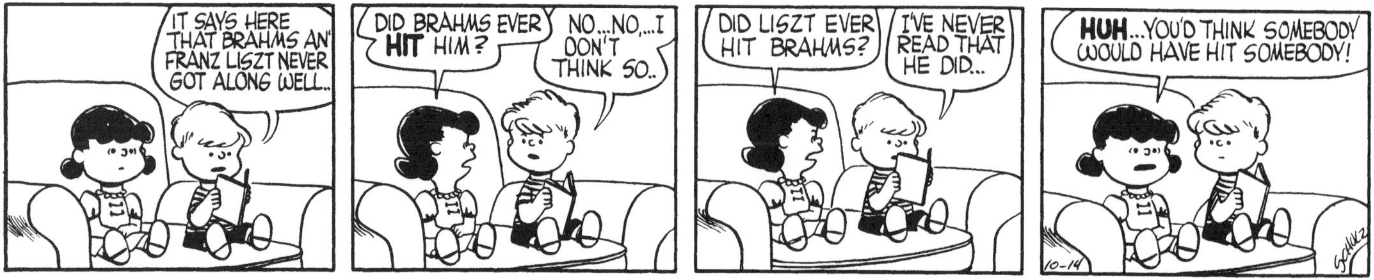
IT SAYS HERE THAT BRAHMS AN' FRANZ LISZT NEVER GOT ALONG WELL..
DID BRAHMS EVER **HIT** HIM?
NO...NO,...I DON'T THINK SO..
DID LISZT EVER HIT BRAHMS?
I'VE NEVER READ THAT HE DID...
HUH...YOU'D THINK SOMEBODY WOULD HAVE HIT SOMEBODY!
10-14
SCHULZ

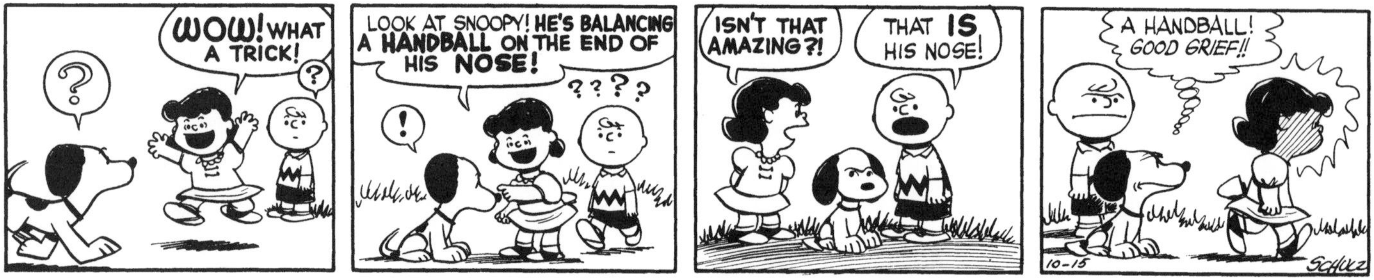
?
WOW! WHAT A TRICK!
?
LOOK AT SNOOPY! **HE'S BALANCING A HANDBALL ON THE END OF HIS NOSE!**
!
? ? ? ?
ISN'T THAT AMAZING?!
THAT **IS** HIS NOSE!
A HANDBALL! *GOOD GRIEF!!*
10-15
SCHULZ

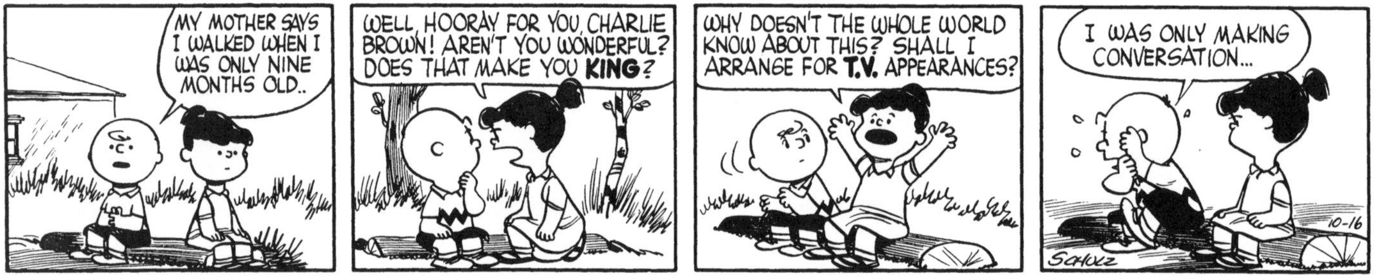
MY MOTHER SAYS I WALKED WHEN I WAS ONLY NINE MONTHS OLD..
WELL, HOORAY FOR YOU, CHARLIE BROWN! AREN'T YOU WONDERFUL? DOES THAT MAKE YOU **KING**?
WHY DOESN'T THE WHOLE WORLD KNOW ABOUT THIS? SHALL I ARRANGE FOR **T.V.** APPEARANCES?
I WAS ONLY MAKING CONVERSATION...
10-16
SCHULZ

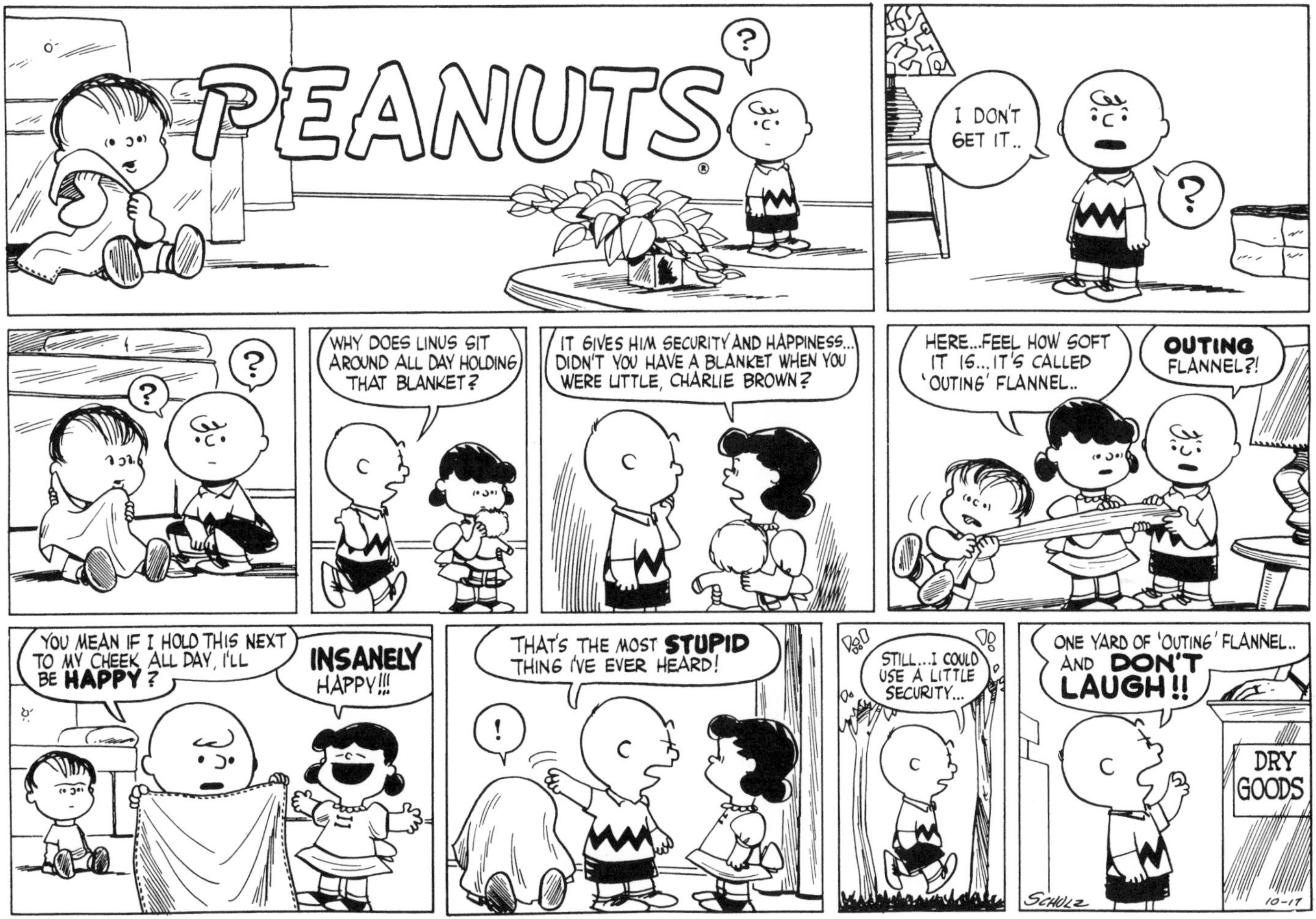
PEANUTS
?
I DON'T GET IT..
?
?
?
WHY DOES LINUS SIT AROUND ALL DAY HOLDING THAT BLANKET?
IT GIVES HIM SECURITY AND HAPPINESS... DIDN'T YOU HAVE A BLANKET WHEN YOU WERE LITTLE, CHARLIE BROWN?
HERE...FEEL HOW SOFT IT IS...IT'S CALLED 'OUTING' FLANNEL..
OUTING FLANNEL?!
YOU MEAN IF I HOLD THIS NEXT TO MY CHEEK ALL DAY, I'LL BE HAPPY?
INSANELY HAPPY!!!
THAT'S THE MOST STUPID THING I'VE EVER HEARD!
!
STILL...I COULD USE A LITTLE SECURITY...
ONE YARD OF 'OUTING' FLANNEL.. AND DON'T LAUGH!!
DRY GOODS
SCHULZ
10-17

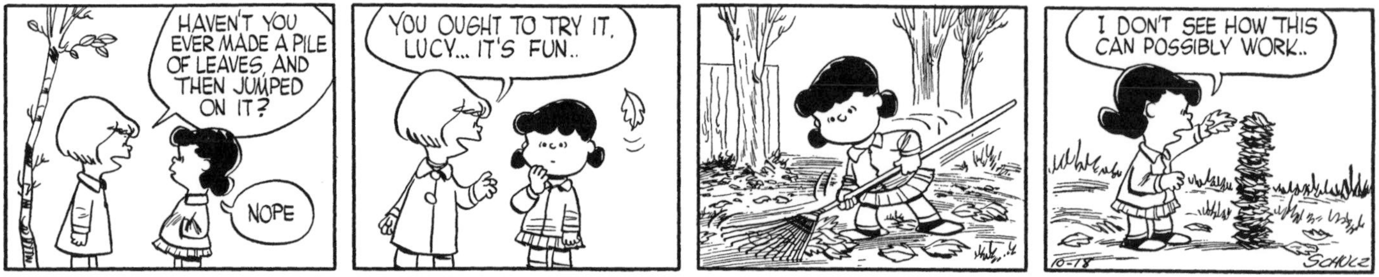
HAVEN'T YOU EVER MADE A PILE OF LEAVES, AND THEN JUMPED ON IT?
NOPE
YOU OUGHT TO TRY IT, LUCY... IT'S FUN..
I DON'T SEE HOW THIS CAN POSSIBLY WORK..
10-18
SCHULZ

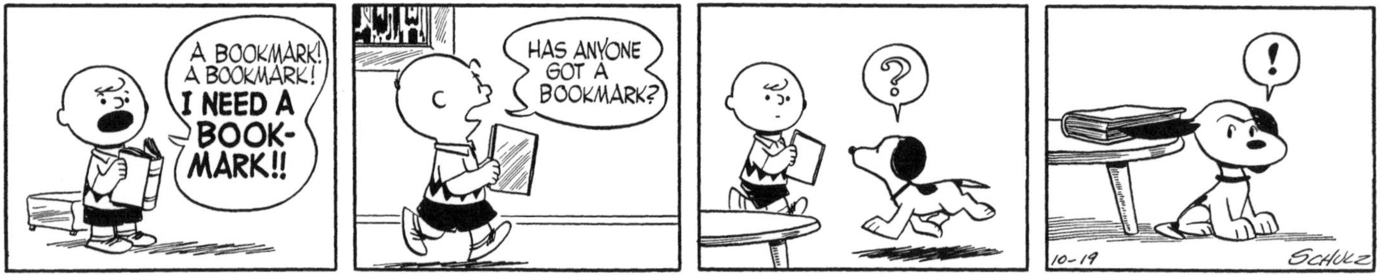
A BOOKMARK! A BOOKMARK! I NEED A BOOK-MARK!!
HAS ANYONE GOT A BOOKMARK?
?
!
10-19
SCHULZ

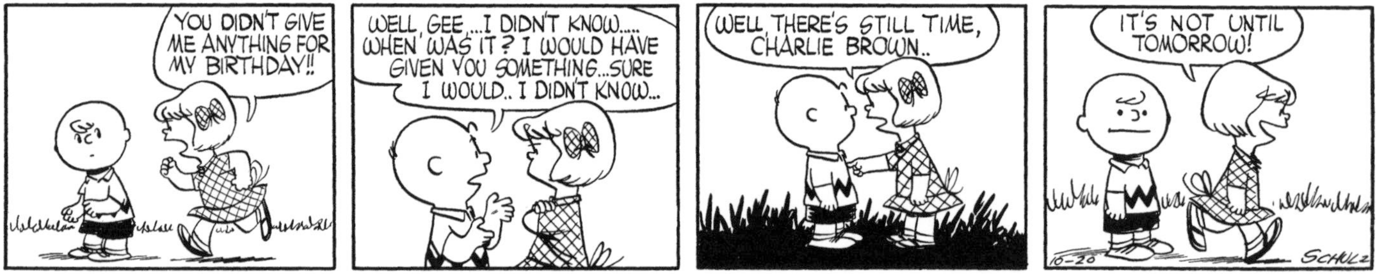
YOU DIDN'T GIVE ME ANYTHING FOR MY BIRTHDAY!!
WELL, GEE,...I DIDN'T KNOW..... WHEN WAS IT? I WOULD HAVE GIVEN YOU SOMETHING...SURE I WOULD.. I DIDN'T KNOW...
WELL, THERE'S STILL TIME, CHARLIE BROWN..
IT'S NOT UNTIL TOMORROW!
10-20
SCHULZ

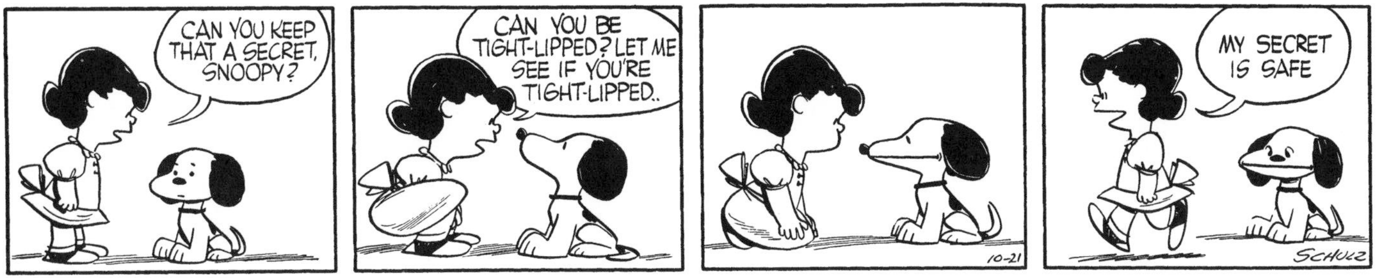
CAN YOU KEEP THAT A SECRET, SNOOPY?
CAN YOU BE TIGHT-LIPPED? LET ME SEE IF YOU'RE TIGHT-LIPPED..
10-21
MY SECRET IS SAFE
SCHULZ

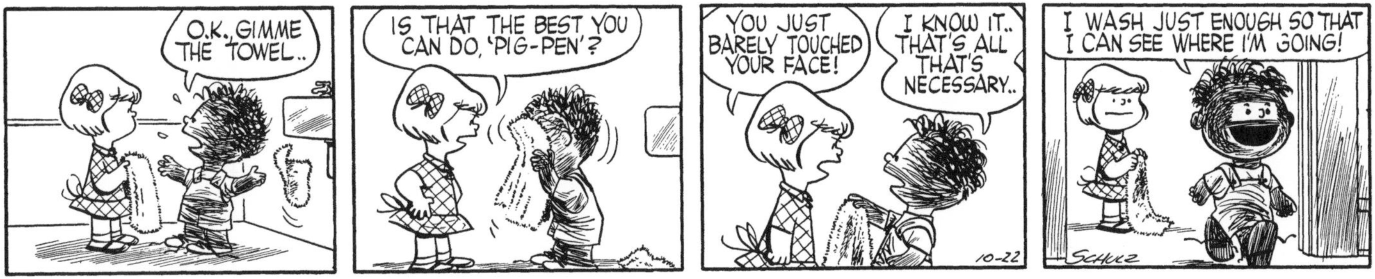
O.K., GIMME THE TOWEL..
IS THAT THE BEST YOU CAN DO, 'PIG-PEN'?
YOU JUST BARELY TOUCHED YOUR FACE!
I KNOW IT.. THAT'S ALL THAT'S NECESSARY..
10-22
I WASH JUST ENOUGH SO THAT I CAN SEE WHERE I'M GOING!
SCHULZ

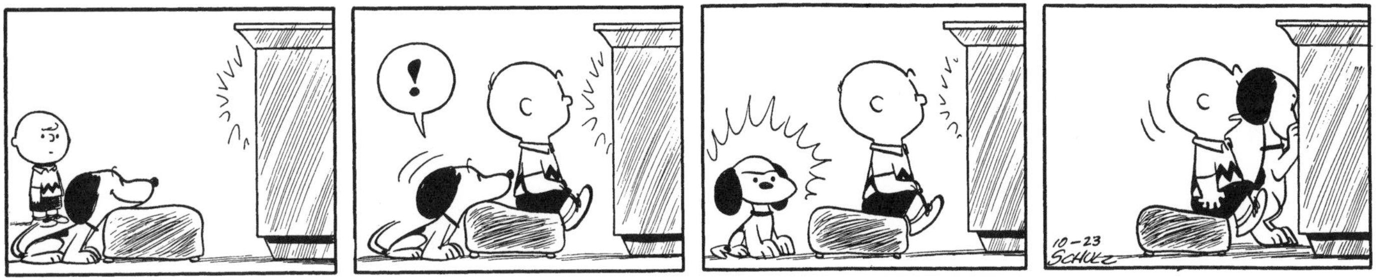
!
10-23
SCHULZ

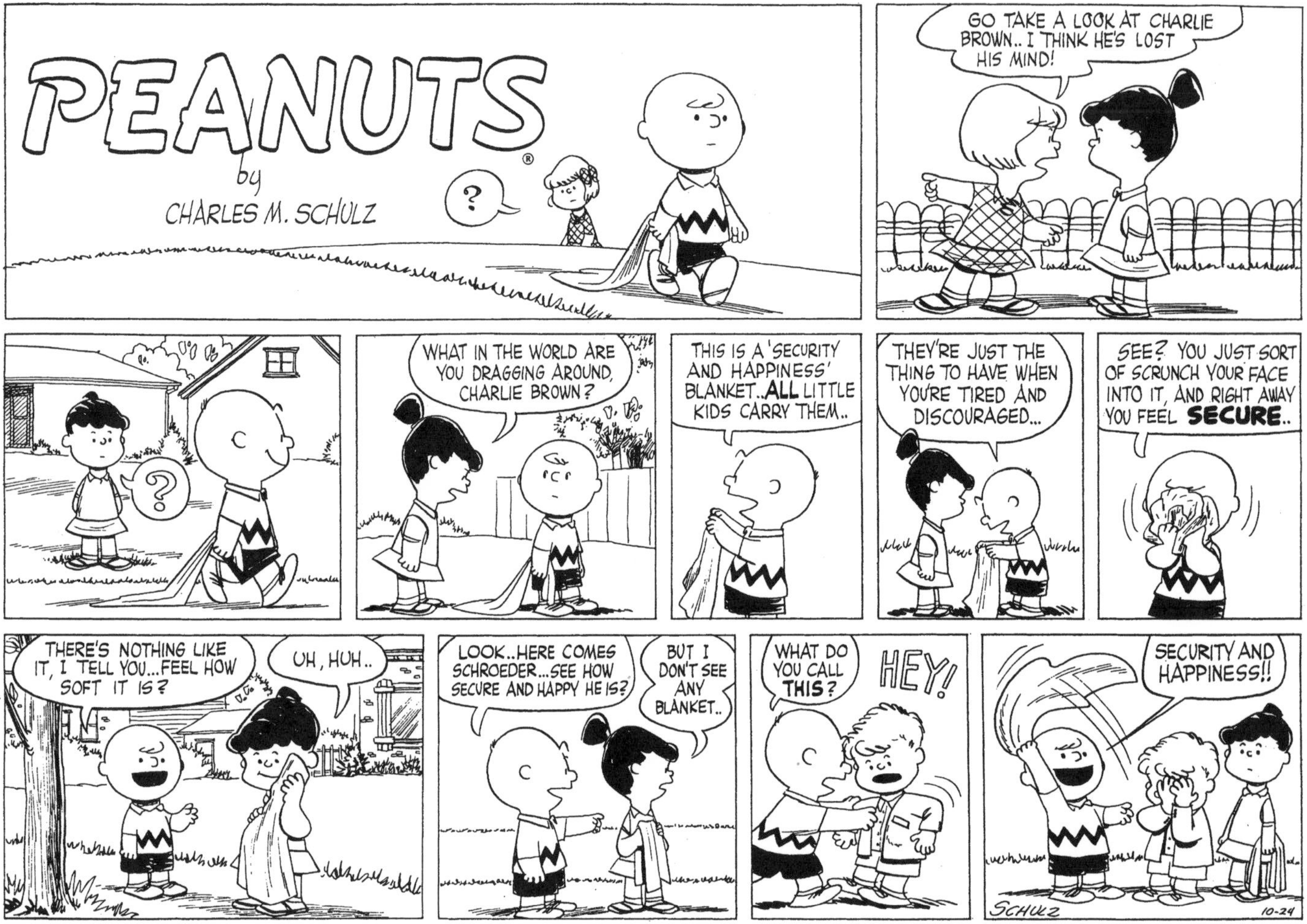
PEANUTS
by
CHARLES M. SCHULZ
?
GO TAKE A LOOK AT CHARLIE BROWN.. I THINK HE'S LOST HIS MIND!
?
WHAT IN THE WORLD ARE YOU DRAGGING AROUND, CHARLIE BROWN?
THIS IS A 'SECURITY AND HAPPINESS' BLANKET..ALL LITTLE KIDS CARRY THEM..
THEY'RE JUST THE THING TO HAVE WHEN YOU'RE TIRED AND DISCOURAGED...
SEE? YOU JUST SORT OF SCRUNCH YOUR FACE INTO IT, AND RIGHT AWAY YOU FEEL SECURE..
THERE'S NOTHING LIKE IT, I TELL YOU...FEEL HOW SOFT IT IS?
UH, HUH..
LOOK..HERE COMES SCHROEDER...SEE HOW SECURE AND HAPPY HE IS?
BUT I DON'T SEE ANY BLANKET..
WHAT DO YOU CALL THIS?
HEY!
SECURITY AND HAPPINESS!!
SCHULZ
10-24

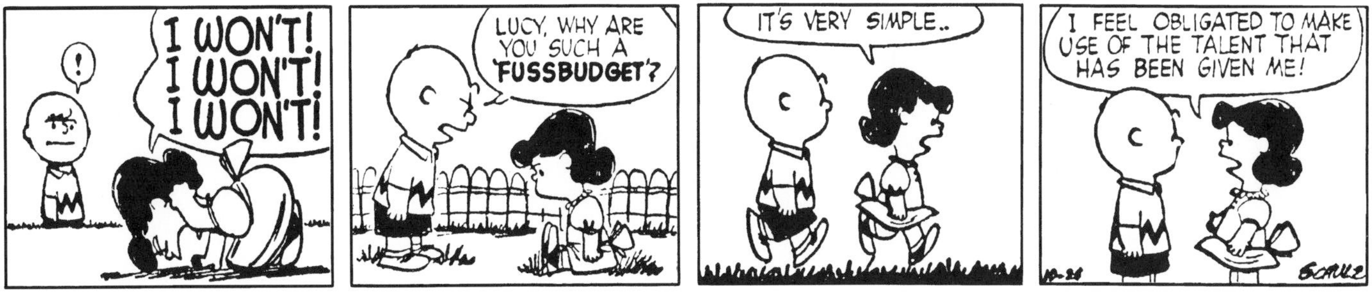
!
I WON'T! I WON'T! I WON'T!
LUCY, WHY ARE YOU SUCH A 'FUSSBUDGET'?
IT'S VERY SIMPLE..
I FEEL OBLIGATED TO MAKE USE OF THE TALENT THAT HAS BEEN GIVEN ME!
SCHULZ

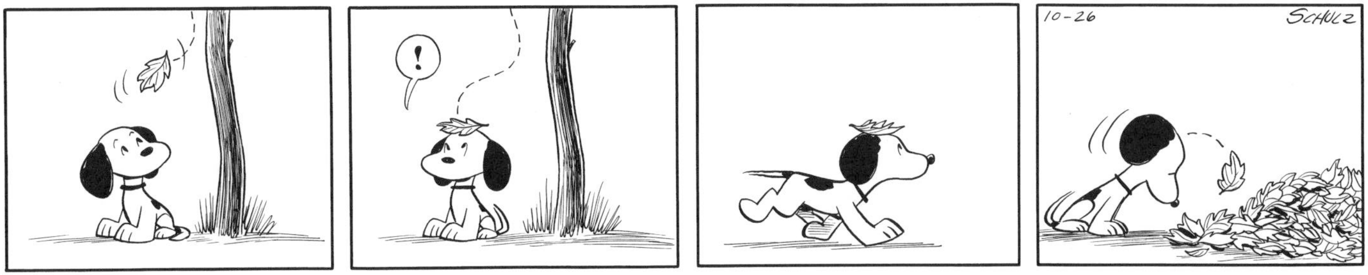
!
10-26
SCHULZ

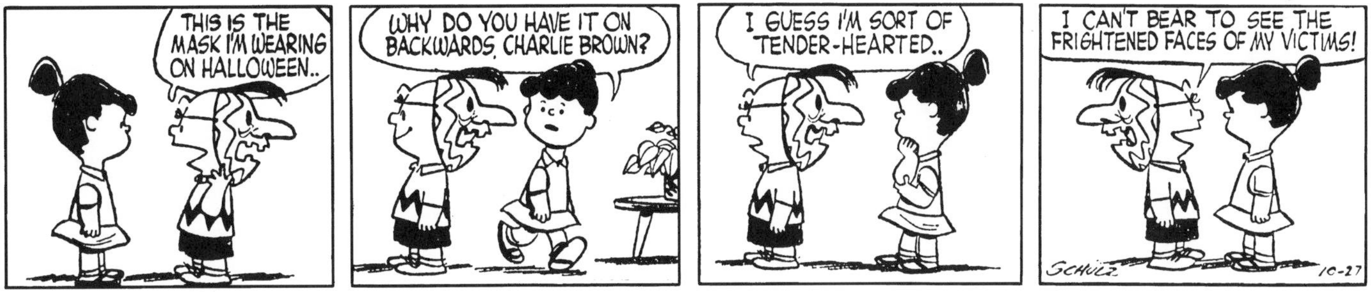
THIS IS THE MASK I'M WEARING ON HALLOWEEN..
WHY DO YOU HAVE IT ON BACKWARDS, CHARLIE BROWN?
I GUESS I'M SORT OF TENDER-HEARTED..
I CAN'T BEAR TO SEE THE FRIGHTENED FACES OF MY VICTIMS!
SCHULZ
10-27

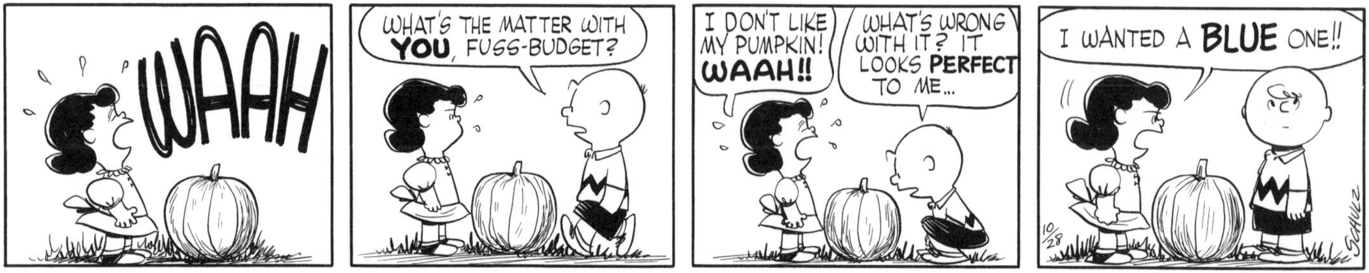
WAAH
WHAT'S THE MATTER WITH YOU, FUSS-BUDGET?
I DON'T LIKE MY PUMPKIN! WAAH!!
WHAT'S WRONG WITH IT? IT LOOKS PERFECT TO ME...
I WANTED A BLUE ONE!!
10/28
SCHULZ

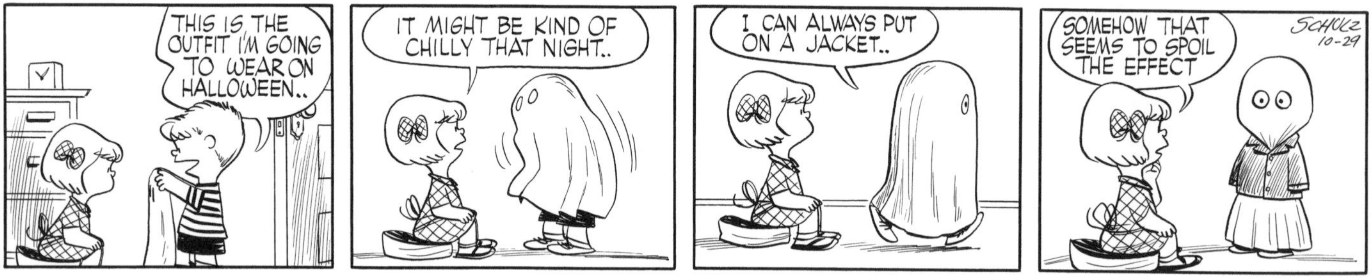
THIS IS THE OUTFIT I'M GOING TO WEAR ON HALLOWEEN..
IT MIGHT BE KIND OF CHILLY THAT NIGHT..
I CAN ALWAYS PUT ON A JACKET..
SOMEHOW THAT SEEMS TO SPOIL THE EFFECT
SCHULZ 10-29

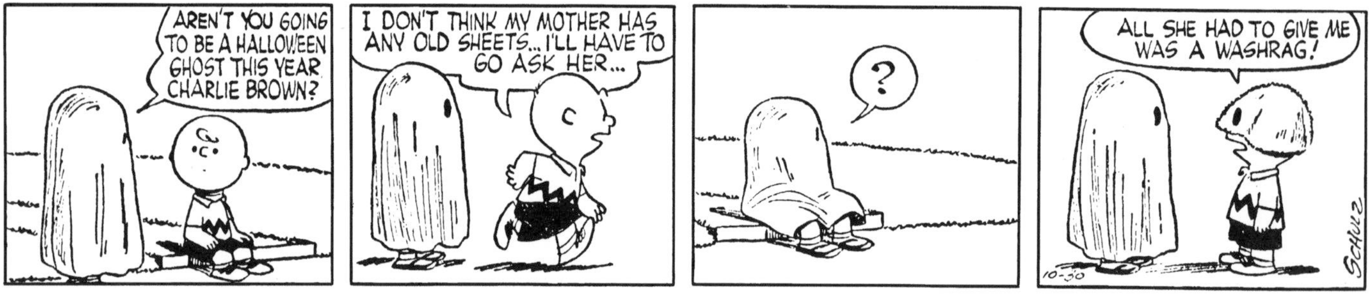
AREN'T YOU GOING TO BE A HALLOWEEN GHOST THIS YEAR CHARLIE BROWN?
I DON'T THINK MY MOTHER HAS ANY OLD SHEETS... I'LL HAVE TO GO ASK HER...
?
ALL SHE HAD TO GIVE ME WAS A WASHRAG!
10-30
SCHULZ

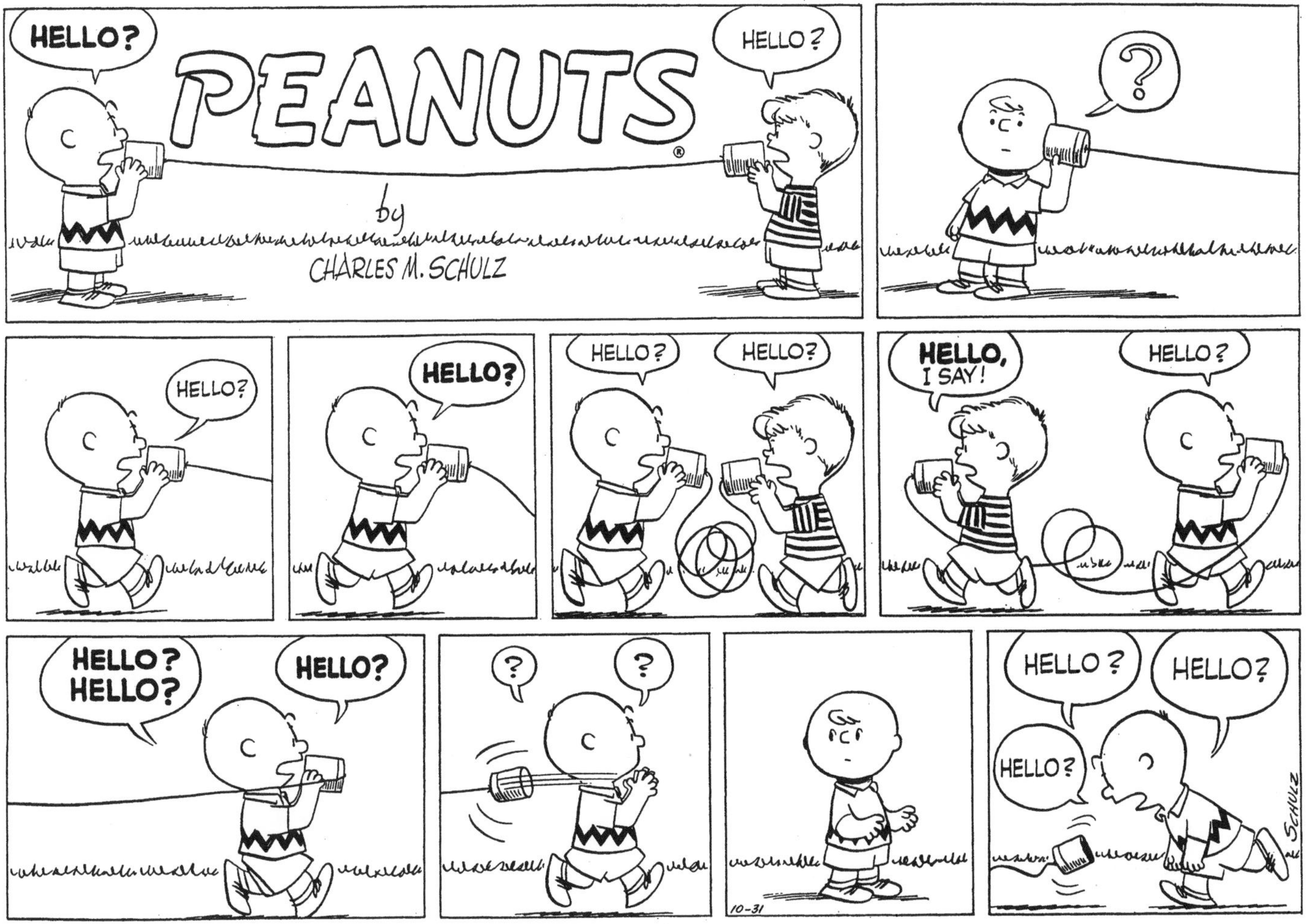
HELLO?
PEANUTS
by
CHARLES M. SCHULZ
HELLO?
?
HELLO?
HELLO?
HELLO?
HELLO?
HELLO, I SAY!
HELLO?
HELLO? HELLO?
HELLO?
?
?
10-31
HELLO?
HELLO?
HELLO?
SCHULZ

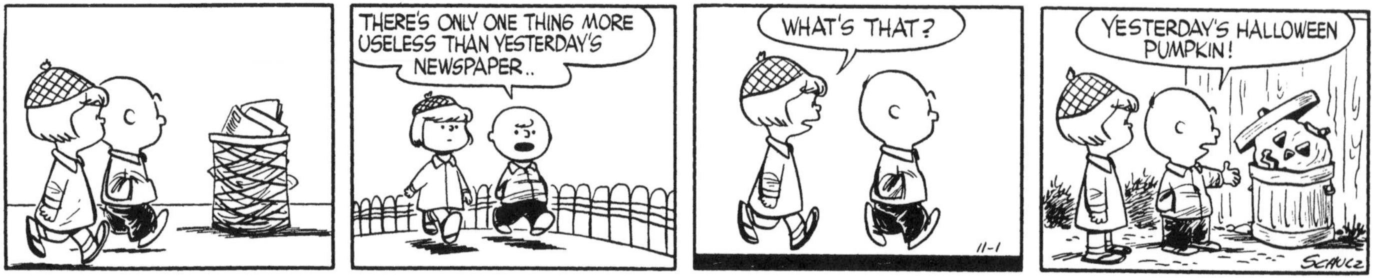
THERE'S ONLY ONE THING MORE USELESS THAN YESTERDAY'S NEWSPAPER..
WHAT'S THAT?
11-1
YESTERDAY'S HALLOWEEN PUMPKIN!
SCHULZ

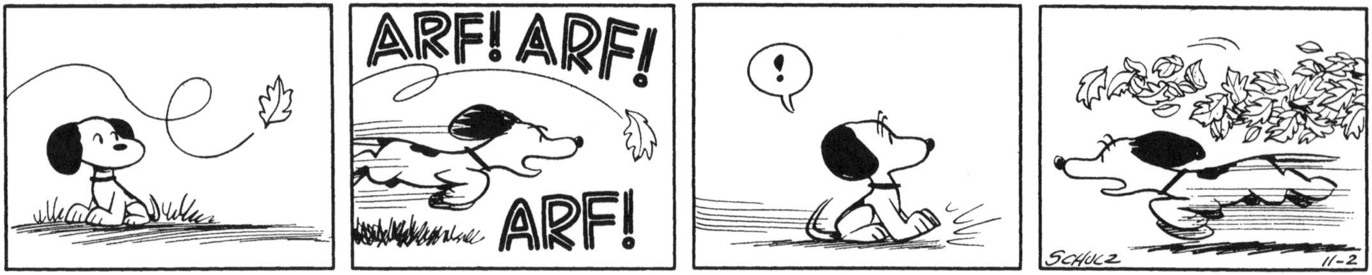
ARF! ARF!
ARF!
!
SCHULZ
11-2

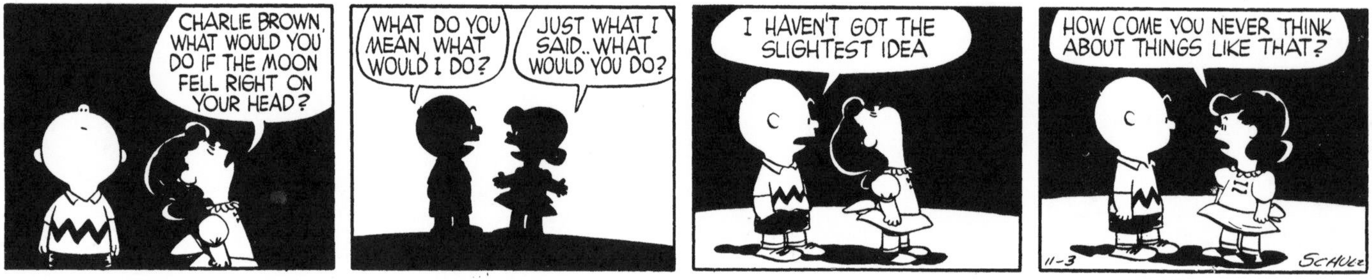
CHARLIE BROWN, WHAT WOULD YOU DO IF THE MOON FELL RIGHT ON YOUR HEAD?
WHAT DO YOU MEAN, WHAT WOULD I DO?
JUST WHAT I SAID.. WHAT WOULD YOU DO?
I HAVEN'T GOT THE SLIGHTEST IDEA
11-3
HOW COME YOU NEVER THINK ABOUT THINGS LIKE THAT?
SCHULZ

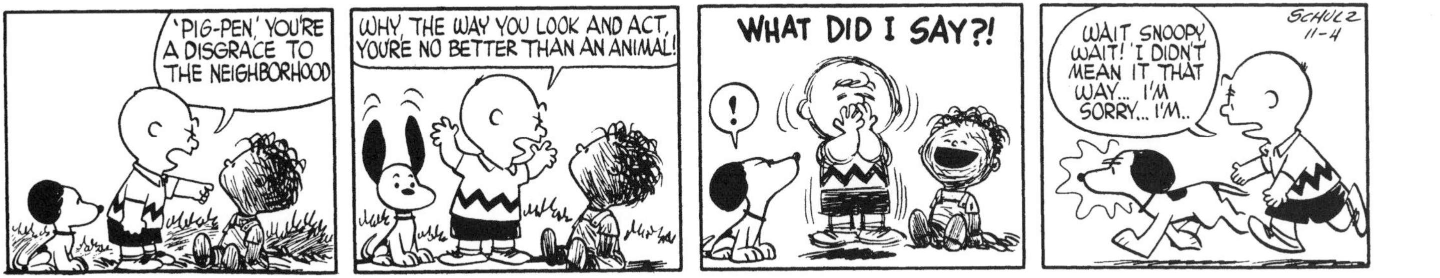
'PIG-PEN,' YOU'RE A DISGRACE TO THE NEIGHBORHOOD
WHY, THE WAY YOU LOOK AND ACT, YOU'RE NO BETTER THAN AN ANIMAL!
WHAT DID I SAY?!
!
SCHULZ 11-4
WAIT SNOOPY, WAIT! 'I DIDN'T MEAN IT THAT WAY... I'M SORRY... I'M..

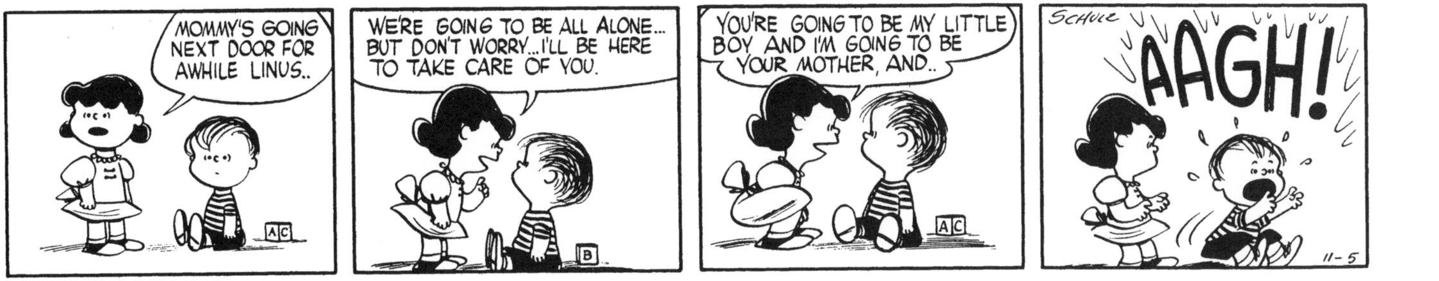
MOMMY'S GOING NEXT DOOR FOR AWHILE LINUS..
WE'RE GOING TO BE ALL ALONE... BUT DON'T WORRY... I'LL BE HERE TO TAKE CARE OF YOU.
YOU'RE GOING TO BE MY LITTLE BOY AND I'M GOING TO BE YOUR MOTHER, AND..
SCHULZ
AAGH!
11-5

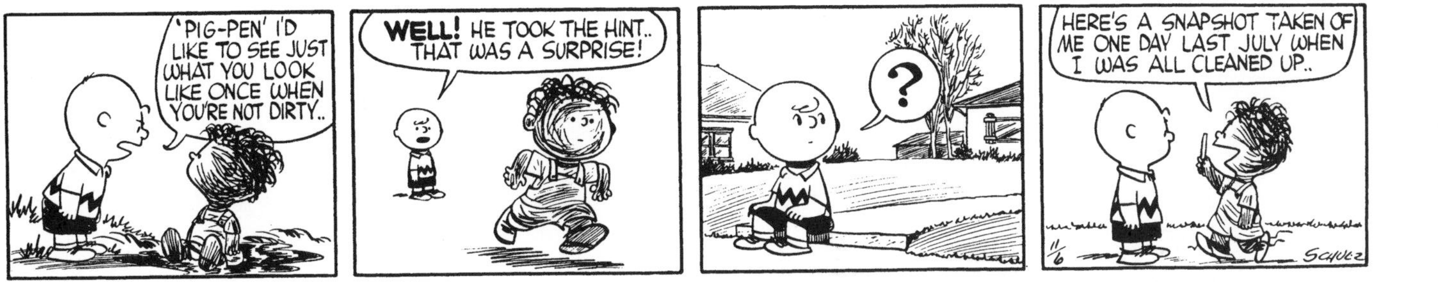
'PIG-PEN' I'D LIKE TO SEE JUST WHAT YOU LOOK LIKE ONCE WHEN YOU'RE NOT DIRTY..
WELL! HE TOOK THE HINT.. THAT WAS A SURPRISE!
?
11/6
HERE'S A SNAPSHOT TAKEN OF ME ONE DAY LAST JULY WHEN I WAS ALL CLEANED UP..
SCHULZ

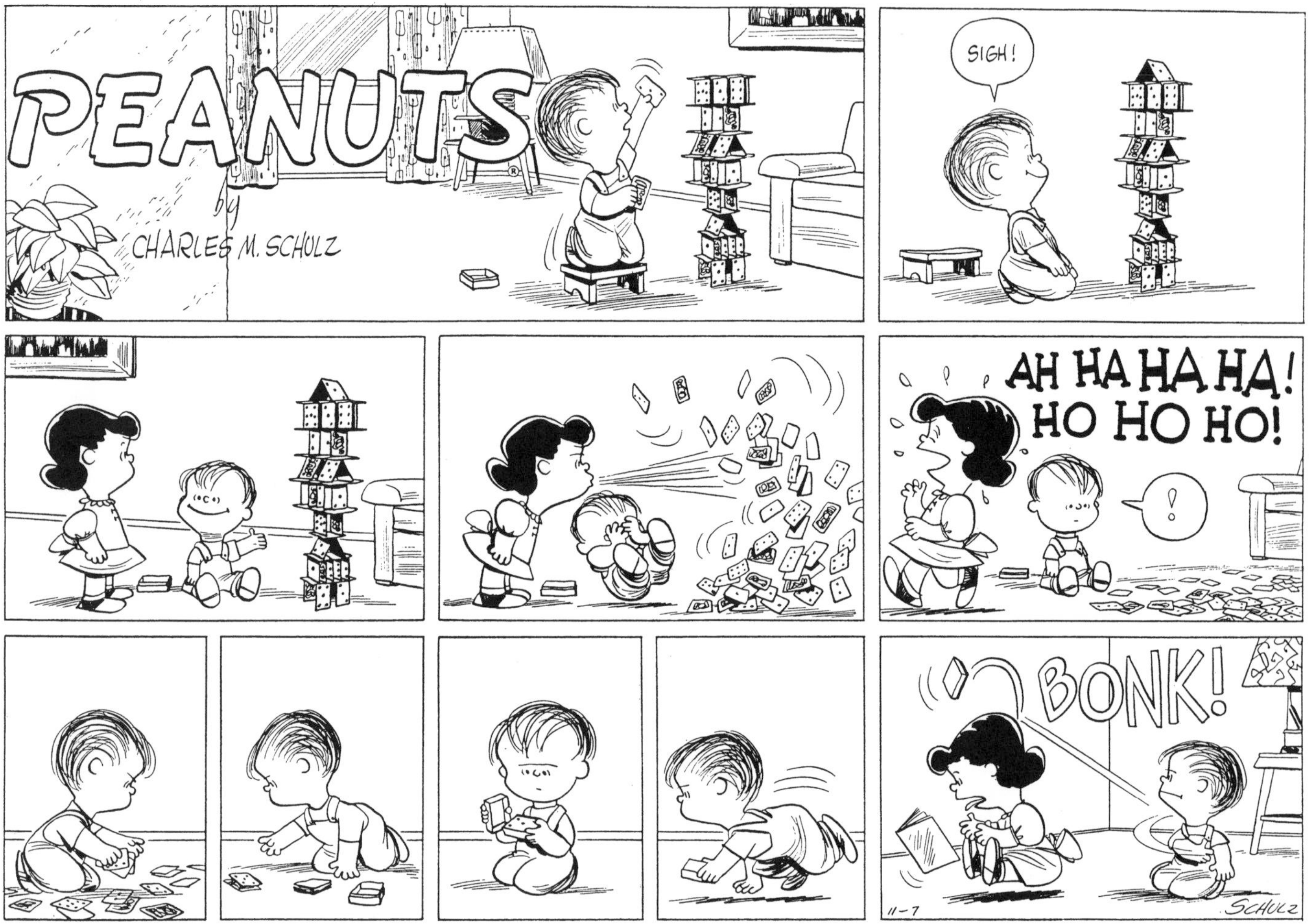
PEANUTS
by
CHARLES M. SCHULZ
SIGH!
AH HA HA HA!
HO HO HO!
!
BONK!
11-7
SCHULZ

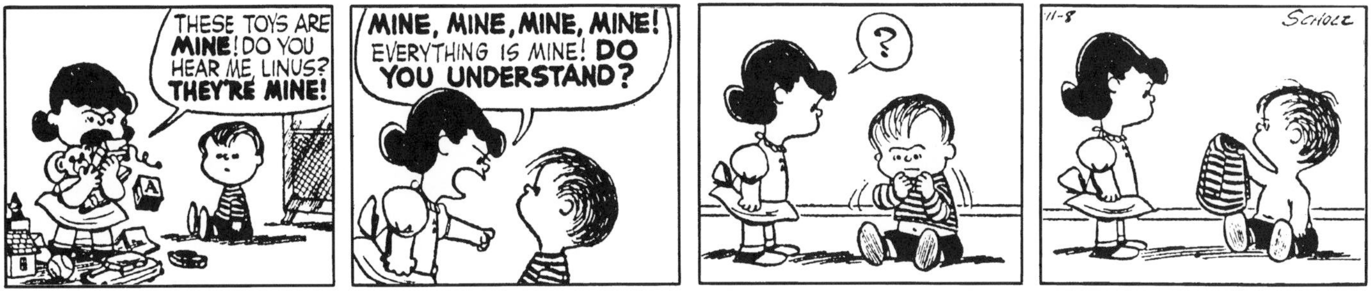
THESE TOYS ARE **MINE**! DO YOU HEAR ME, LINUS? **THEY'RE MINE!**
MINE, MINE, MINE, MINE! EVERYTHING IS MINE! **DO YOU UNDERSTAND?**
?

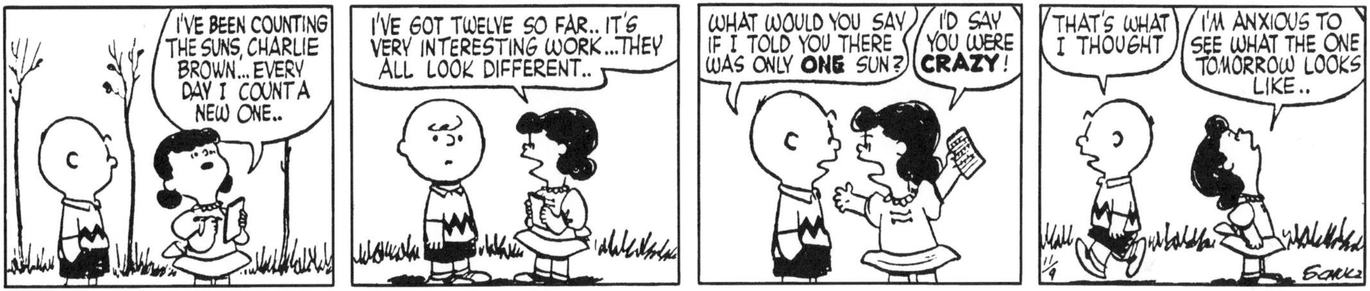
I'VE BEEN COUNTING THE SUNS, CHARLIE BROWN... EVERY DAY I COUNT A NEW ONE..
I'VE GOT TWELVE SO FAR.. IT'S VERY INTERESTING WORK...THEY ALL LOOK DIFFERENT..
WHAT WOULD YOU SAY IF I TOLD YOU THERE WAS ONLY **ONE** SUN?
I'D SAY YOU WERE **CRAZY**!
THAT'S WHAT I THOUGHT
I'M ANXIOUS TO SEE WHAT THE ONE TOMORROW LOOKS LIKE..

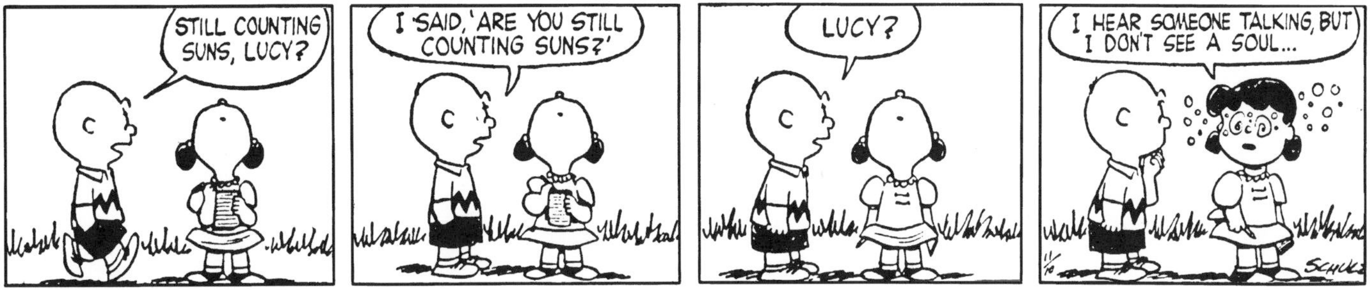
STILL COUNTING SUNS, LUCY?
I SAID, 'ARE YOU STILL COUNTING SUNS?'
LUCY?
I HEAR SOMEONE TALKING, BUT I DON'T SEE A SOUL...

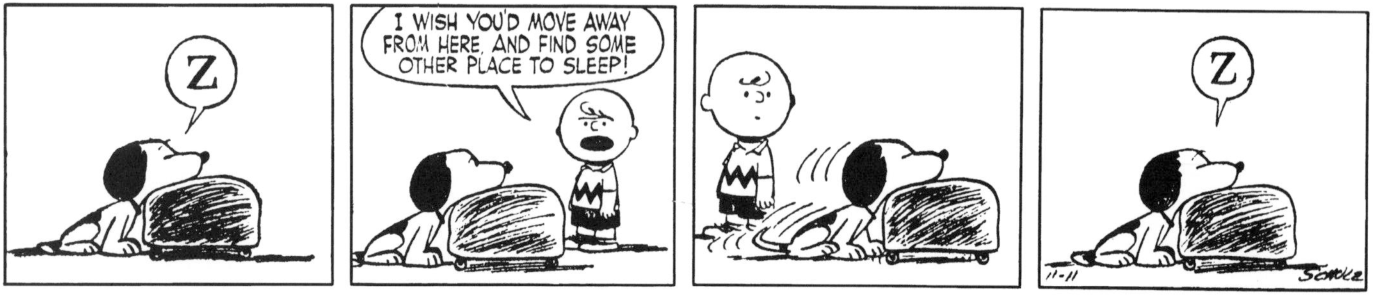
Z
I WISH YOU'D MOVE AWAY FROM HERE, AND FIND SOME OTHER PLACE TO SLEEP!
Z
11-11

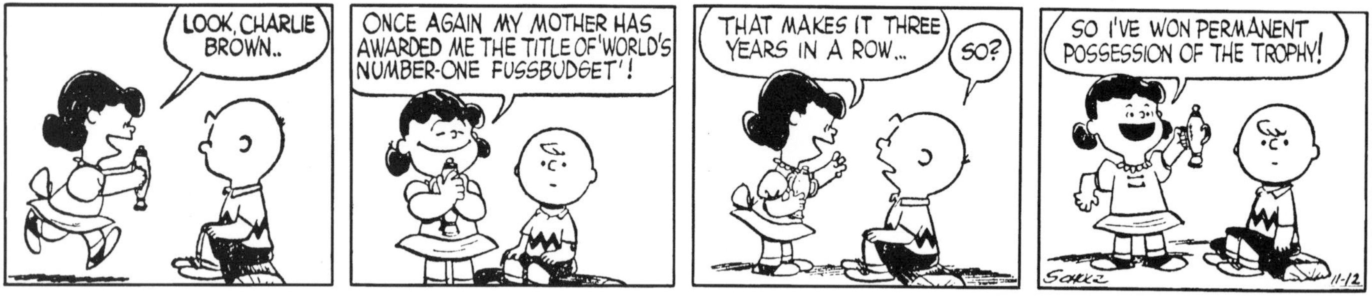
LOOK, CHARLIE BROWN..
ONCE AGAIN MY MOTHER HAS AWARDED ME THE TITLE OF 'WORLD'S NUMBER-ONE FUSSBUDGET'!
THAT MAKES IT THREE YEARS IN A ROW...
SO?
SO I'VE WON PERMANENT POSSESSION OF THE TROPHY!
11-12

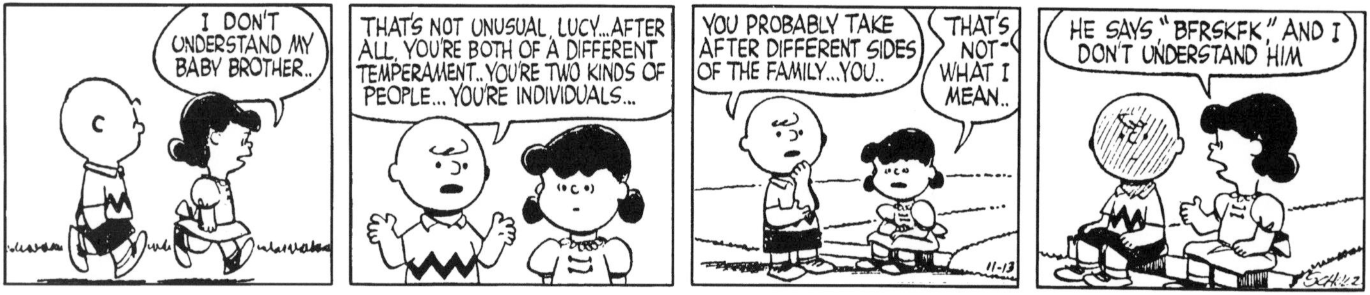
I DON'T UNDERSTAND MY BABY BROTHER..
THAT'S NOT UNUSUAL, LUCY...AFTER ALL, YOU'RE BOTH OF A DIFFERENT TEMPERAMENT..YOU'RE TWO KINDS OF PEOPLE... YOU'RE INDIVIDUALS...
YOU PROBABLY TAKE AFTER DIFFERENT SIDES OF THE FAMILY...YOU..
THAT'S NOT-WHAT I MEAN..
11-13
HE SAYS, "BFRSKFK," AND I DON'T UNDERSTAND HIM

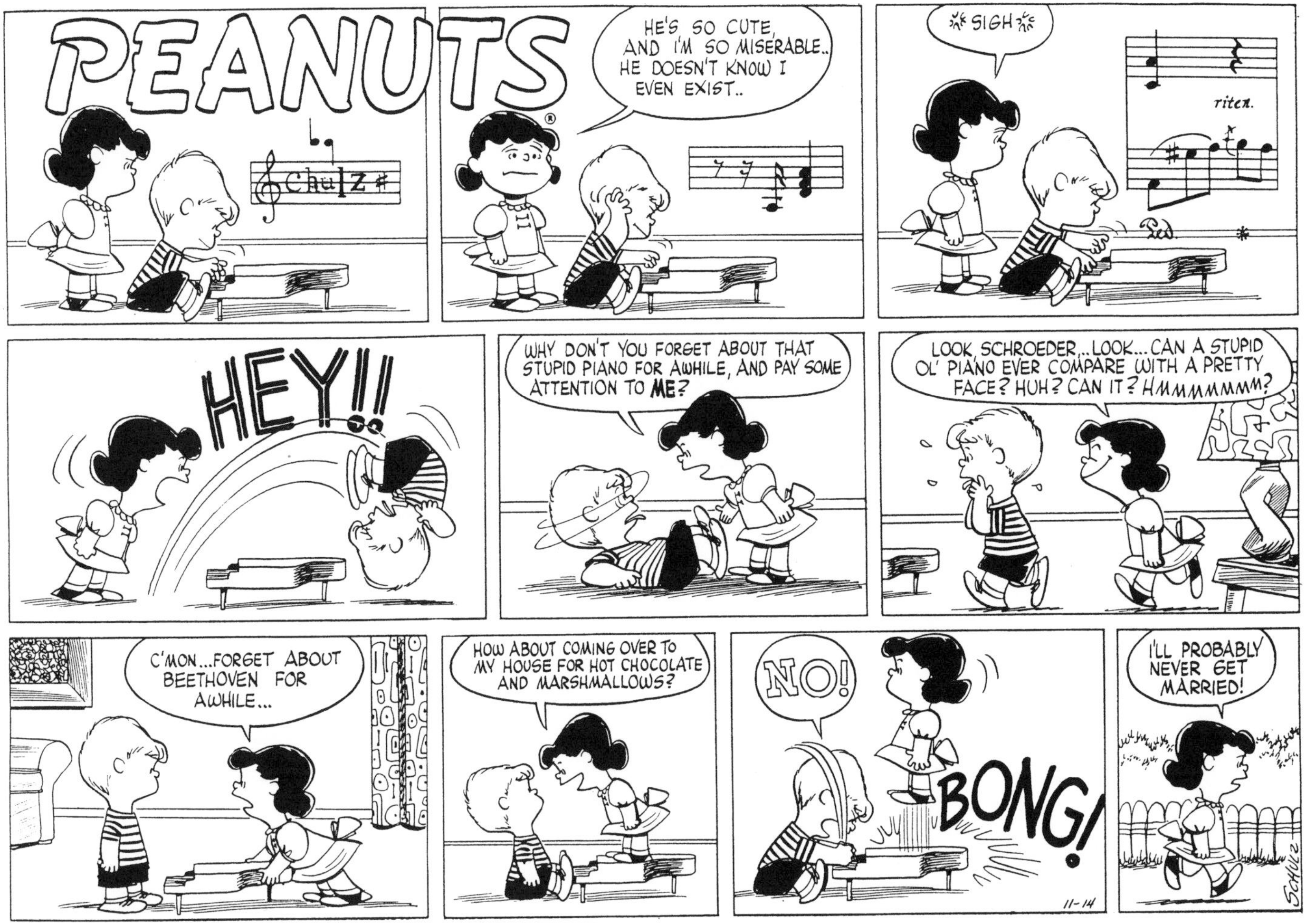
PEANUTS
by Schulz
HE'S SO CUTE, AND I'M SO MISERABLE.. HE DOESN'T KNOW I EVEN EXIST..
SIGH
riten.
HEY!!
WHY DON'T YOU FORGET ABOUT THAT STUPID PIANO FOR AWHILE, AND PAY SOME ATTENTION TO ME?
LOOK, SCHROEDER...LOOK...CAN A STUPID OL' PIANO EVER COMPARE WITH A PRETTY FACE? HUH? CAN IT? HMMMMMMM?
C'MON...FORGET ABOUT BEETHOVEN FOR AWHILE...
HOW ABOUT COMING OVER TO MY HOUSE FOR HOT CHOCOLATE AND MARSHMALLOWS?
NO!
BONG!
11-14
I'LL PROBABLY NEVER GET MARRIED!
SCHULZ

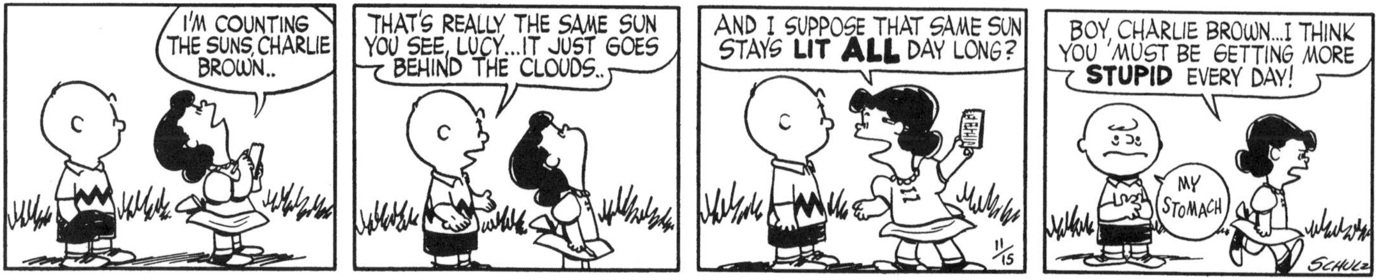
I'M COUNTING THE SUNS, CHARLIE BROWN..
THAT'S REALLY THE SAME SUN YOU SEE, LUCY...IT JUST GOES BEHIND THE CLOUDS..
AND I SUPPOSE THAT SAME SUN STAYS **LIT ALL** DAY LONG?
11/15
BOY, CHARLIE BROWN...I THINK YOU MUST BE GETTING MORE **STUPID** EVERY DAY!
MY STOMACH
SCHULZ

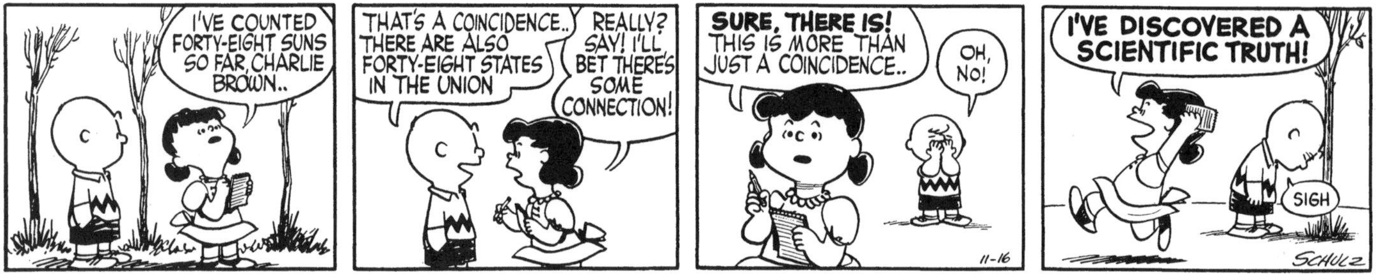
I'VE COUNTED FORTY-EIGHT SUNS SO FAR, CHARLIE BROWN..
THAT'S A COINCIDENCE.. THERE ARE ALSO FORTY-EIGHT STATES IN THE UNION
REALLY? SAY! I'LL BET THERE'S SOME CONNECTION!
SURE, THERE IS! THIS IS MORE THAN JUST A COINCIDENCE..
OH, NO!
11-16
I'VE DISCOVERED A SCIENTIFIC TRUTH!
SIGH
SCHULZ

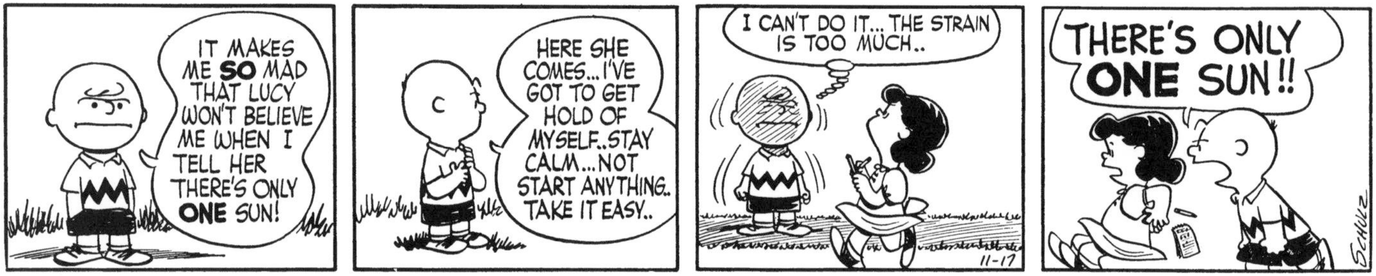
IT MAKES ME **SO** MAD THAT LUCY WON'T BELIEVE ME WHEN I TELL HER THERE'S ONLY **ONE** SUN!
HERE SHE COMES...I'VE GOT TO GET HOLD OF MYSELF..STAY CALM...NOT START ANYTHING.. TAKE IT EASY..
I CAN'T DO IT... THE STRAIN IS TOO MUCH..
11-17
THERE'S ONLY **ONE** SUN!!
SCHULZ

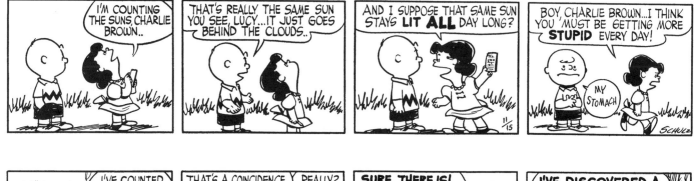

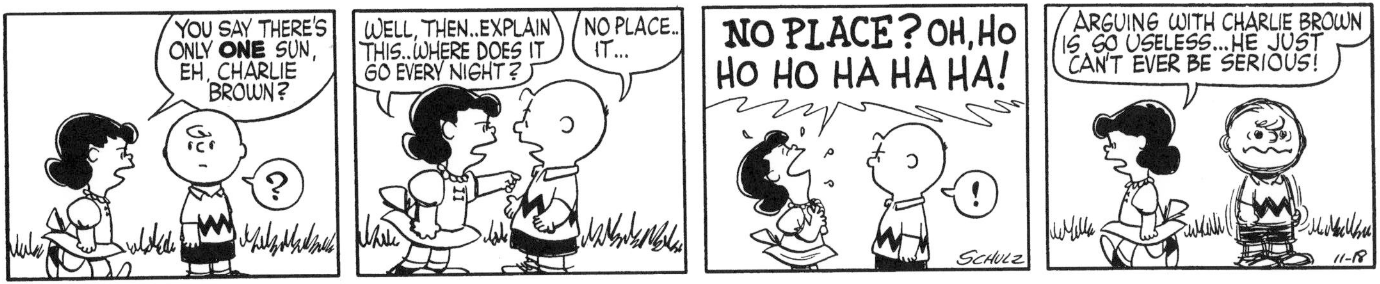
YOU SAY THERE'S ONLY **ONE** SUN, EH, CHARLIE BROWN?
?
WELL, THEN..EXPLAIN THIS..WHERE DOES IT GO EVERY NIGHT?
NO PLACE.. IT...
NO PLACE? OH, HO HO HO HA HA HA!
!
SCHULZ
ARGUING WITH CHARLIE BROWN IS SO USELESS...HE JUST CAN'T EVER BE SERIOUS!
11-18

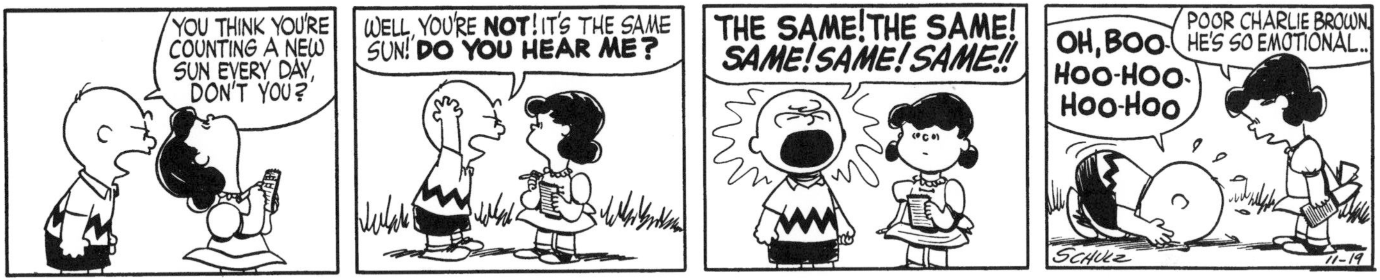
YOU THINK YOU'RE COUNTING A NEW SUN EVERY DAY, DON'T YOU?
WELL, YOU'RE **NOT**! IT'S THE SAME SUN! **DO YOU HEAR ME?**
THE SAME! THE SAME! SAME! SAME! SAME!!
OH, BOO-HOO-HOO-HOO-HOO
POOR CHARLIE BROWN. HE'S SO EMOTIONAL..
SCHULZ
11-19

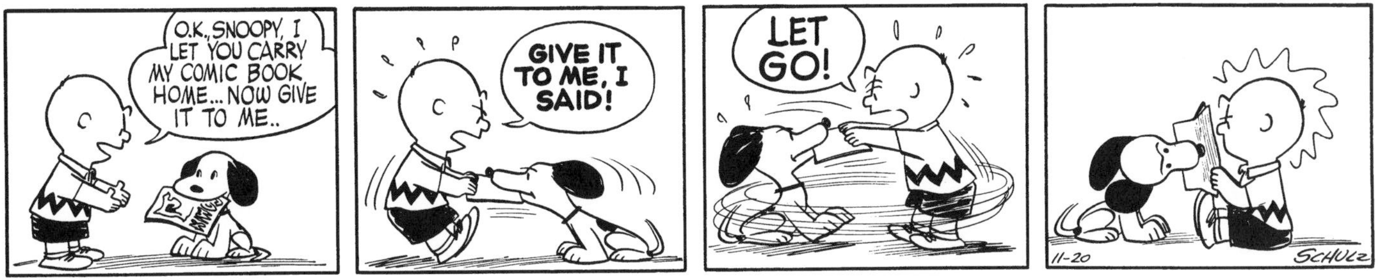
O.K., SNOOPY, I LET YOU CARRY MY COMIC BOOK HOME... NOW GIVE IT TO ME..
GIVE IT TO ME, I SAID!
LET GO!
11-20
SCHULZ

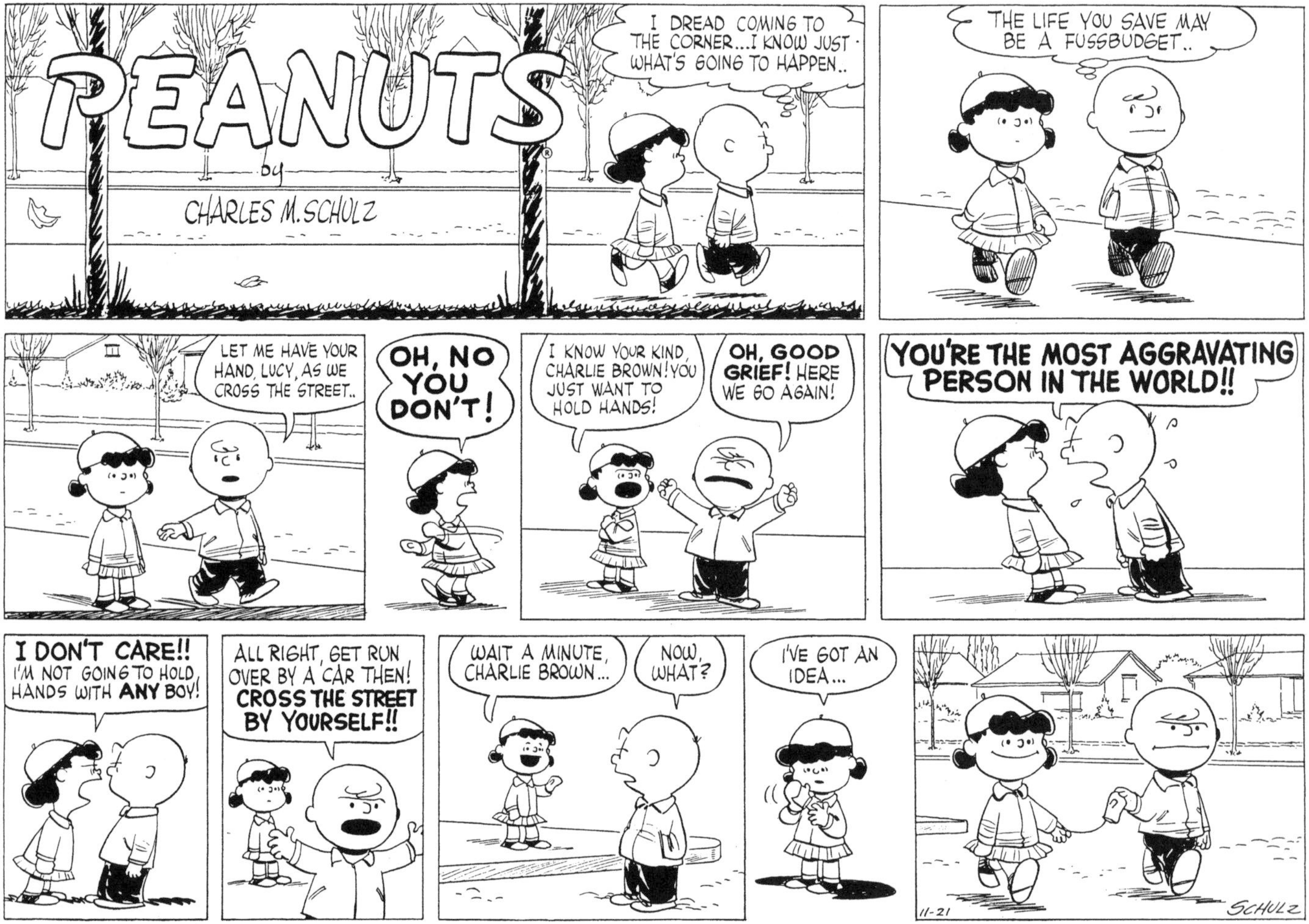
PEANUTS
by
CHARLES M. SCHULZ
I DREAD COMING TO THE CORNER...I KNOW JUST WHAT'S GOING TO HAPPEN..
THE LIFE YOU SAVE MAY BE A FUSSBUDGET..
LET ME HAVE YOUR HAND, LUCY, AS WE CROSS THE STREET..
OH, NO YOU DON'T!
I KNOW YOUR KIND, CHARLIE BROWN! YOU JUST WANT TO HOLD HANDS!
OH, GOOD GRIEF! HERE WE GO AGAIN!
YOU'RE THE MOST AGGRAVATING PERSON IN THE WORLD!!
I DON'T CARE!! I'M NOT GOING TO HOLD HANDS WITH ANY BOY!
ALL RIGHT, GET RUN OVER BY A CAR THEN! CROSS THE STREET BY YOURSELF!!
WAIT A MINUTE, CHARLIE BROWN...
NOW, WHAT?
I'VE GOT AN IDEA...
11-21
SCHULZ

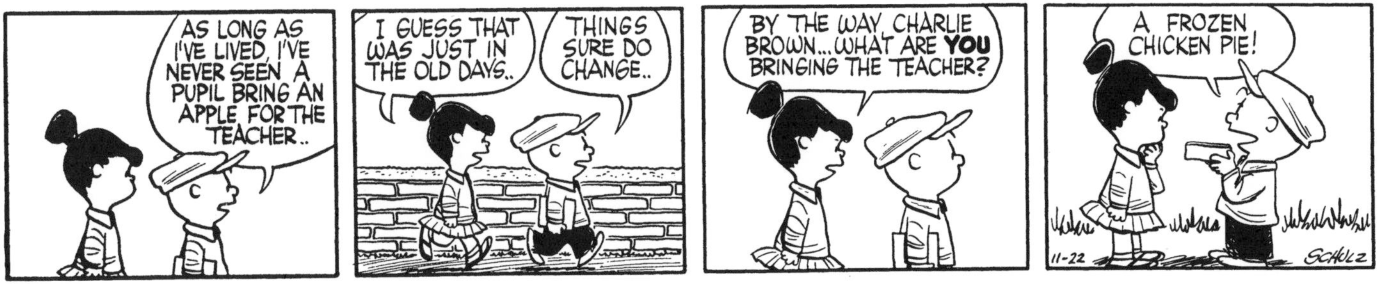
AS LONG AS I'VE LIVED, I'VE NEVER SEEN A PUPIL BRING AN APPLE FOR THE TEACHER..
I GUESS THAT WAS JUST IN THE OLD DAYS..
THINGS SURE DO CHANGE..
BY THE WAY, CHARLIE BROWN... WHAT ARE **YOU** BRINGING THE TEACHER?
A FROZEN CHICKEN PIE!
11-22
SCHULZ

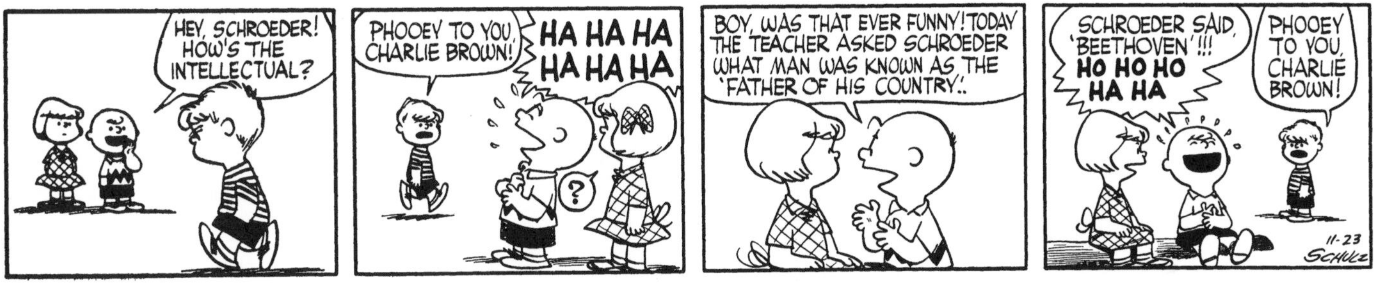
HEY, SCHROEDER! HOW'S THE INTELLECTUAL?
PHOOEY TO YOU, CHARLIE BROWN!
HA HA HA HA HA HA
?
BOY, WAS THAT EVER FUNNY! TODAY THE TEACHER ASKED SCHROEDER WHAT MAN WAS KNOWN AS THE 'FATHER OF HIS COUNTRY'..
SCHROEDER SAID, 'BEETHOVEN'!!! **HO HO HO HA HA**
PHOOEY TO YOU, CHARLIE BROWN!
11-23
SCHULZ

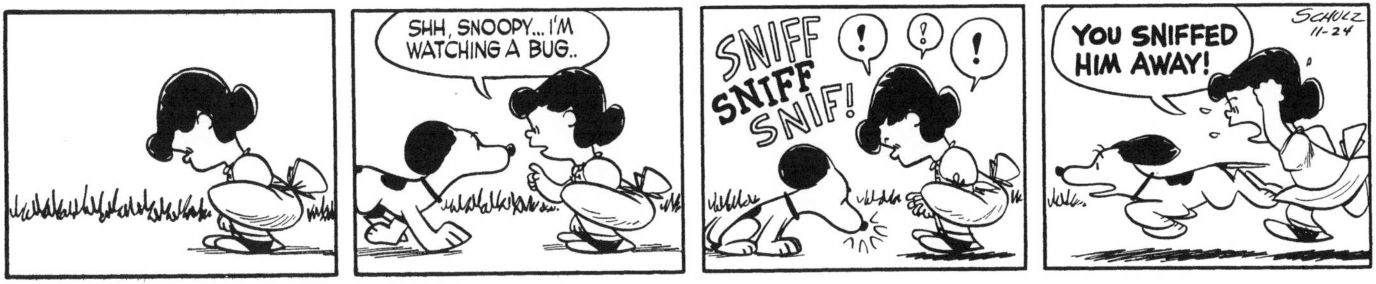
SHH, SNOOPY... I'M WATCHING A BUG..
SNIFF
SNIFF
SNIF!
!
!
!
SCHULZ 11-24
YOU SNIFFED HIM AWAY!

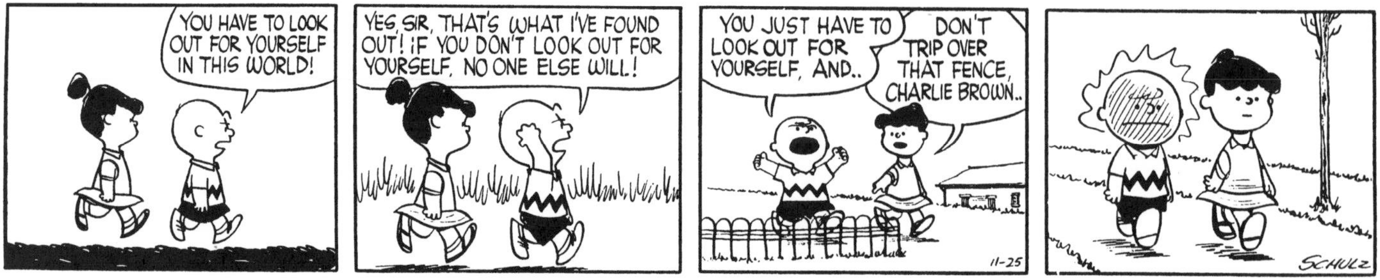
YOU HAVE TO LOOK OUT FOR YOURSELF IN THIS WORLD!
YES, SIR, THAT'S WHAT I'VE FOUND OUT! IF YOU DON'T LOOK OUT FOR YOURSELF, NO ONE ELSE WILL!
YOU JUST HAVE TO LOOK OUT FOR YOURSELF, AND..
DON'T TRIP OVER THAT FENCE, CHARLIE BROWN..
11-25
SCHULZ

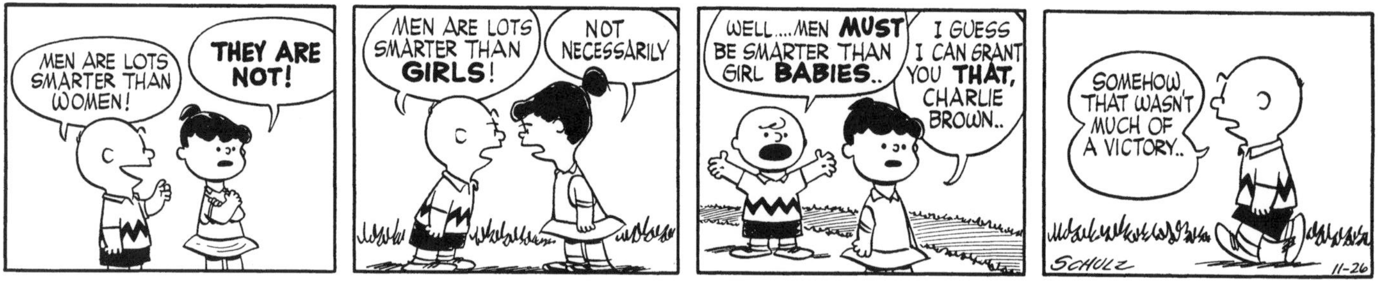
MEN ARE LOTS SMARTER THAN WOMEN!
THEY ARE NOT!
MEN ARE LOTS SMARTER THAN GIRLS!
NOT NECESSARILY
WELL....MEN MUST BE SMARTER THAN GIRL BABIES..
I GUESS I CAN GRANT YOU THAT, CHARLIE BROWN..
SOMEHOW THAT WASN'T MUCH OF A VICTORY..
SCHULZ
11-26

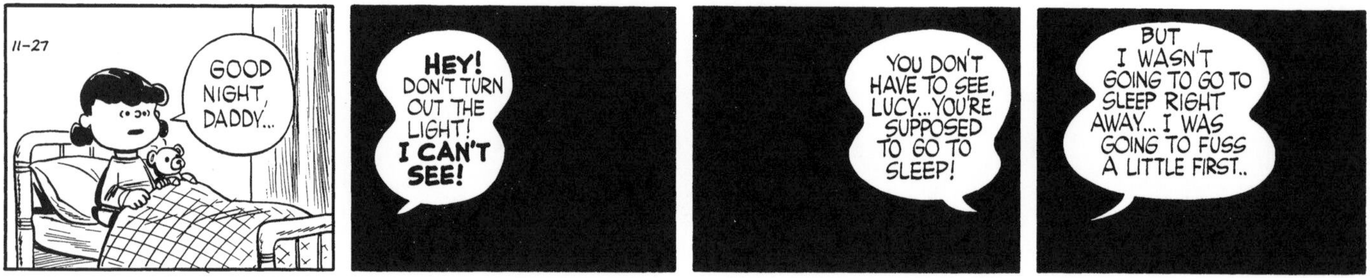
11-27
GOOD NIGHT, DADDY...
HEY! DON'T TURN OUT THE LIGHT! I CAN'T SEE!
YOU DON'T HAVE TO SEE, LUCY...YOU'RE SUPPOSED TO GO TO SLEEP!
BUT I WASN'T GOING TO GO TO SLEEP RIGHT AWAY... I WAS GOING TO FUSS A LITTLE FIRST..

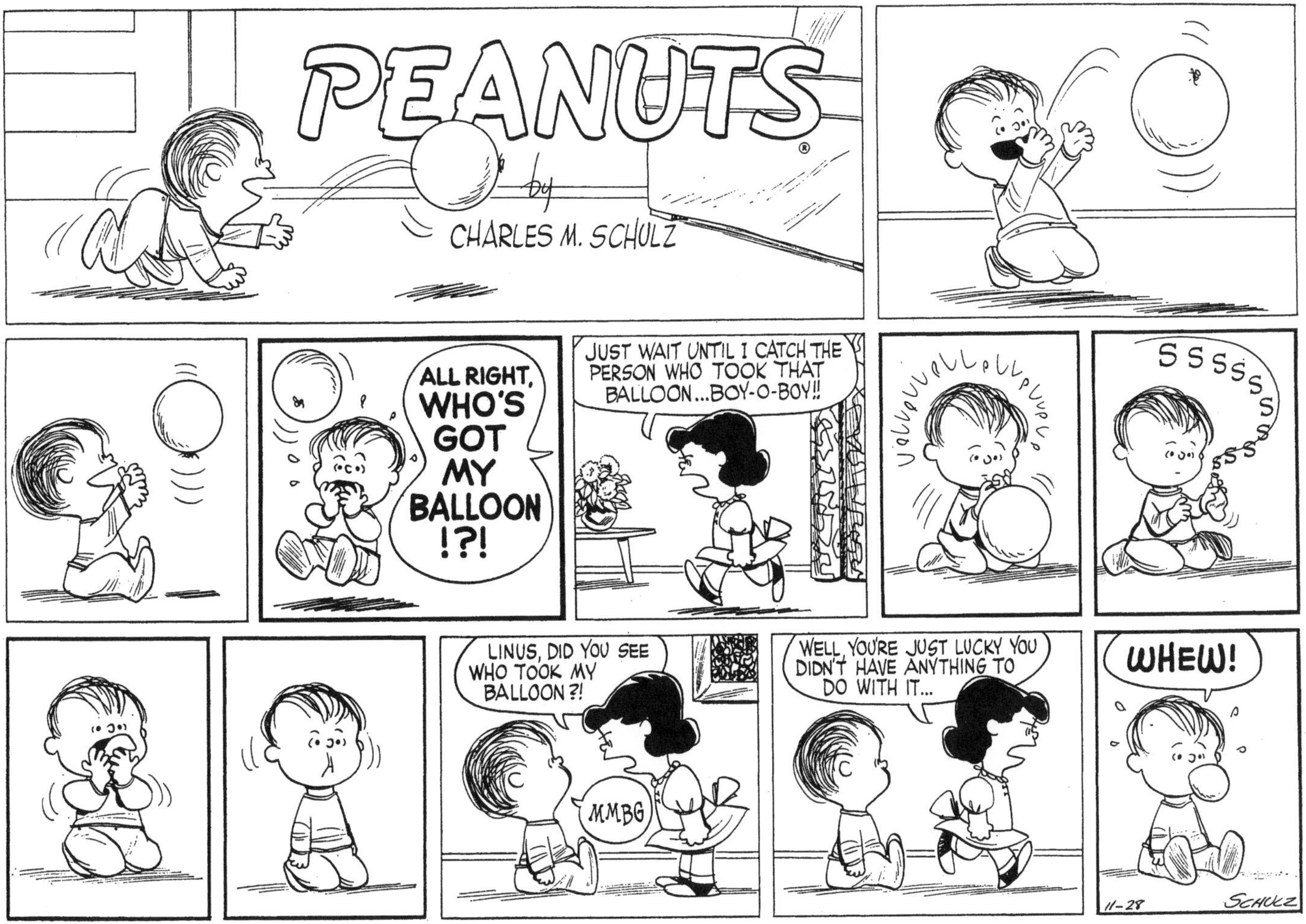
PEANUTS®
by CHARLES M. SCHULZ
ALL RIGHT, WHO'S GOT MY BALLOON !?!
JUST WAIT UNTIL I CATCH THE PERSON WHO TOOK THAT BALLOON...BOY-O-BOY!!
SSSSSSSSS
LINUS, DID YOU SEE WHO TOOK MY BALLOON?!
MMBG
WELL, YOU'RE JUST LUCKY YOU DIDN'T HAVE ANYTHING TO DO WITH IT...
WHEW!
11-28
SCHULZ

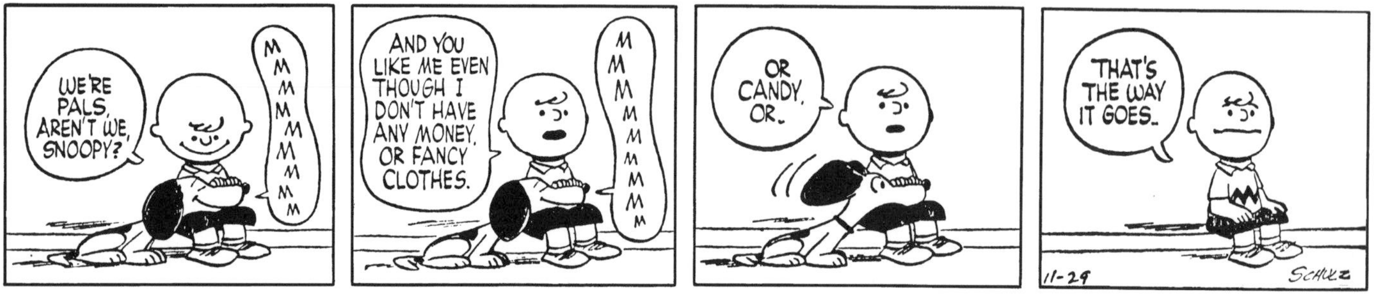
WE'RE PALS, AREN'T WE, SNOOPY?
MMMMMMMMMM
AND YOU LIKE ME EVEN THOUGH I DON'T HAVE ANY MONEY, OR FANCY CLOTHES.
MMMMMMMMMMM
OR CANDY, OR..
THAT'S THE WAY IT GOES..
11-29
SCHULZ

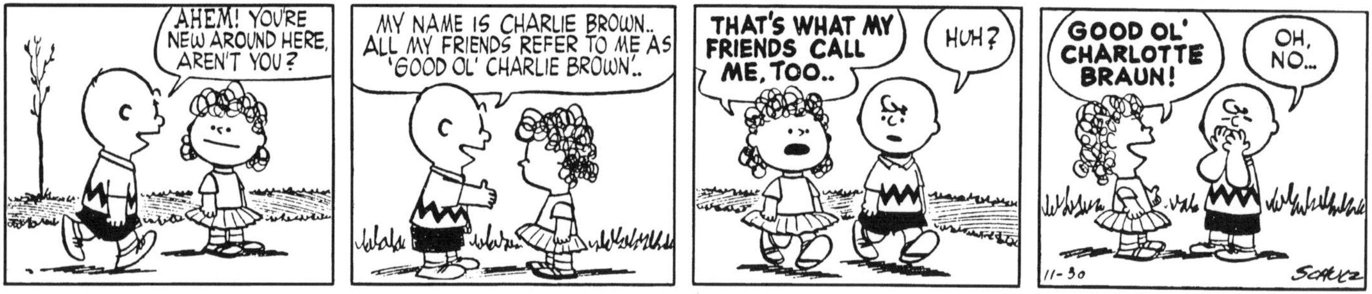
AHEM! YOU'RE NEW AROUND HERE, AREN'T YOU?
MY NAME IS CHARLIE BROWN.. ALL MY FRIENDS REFER TO ME AS 'GOOD OL' CHARLIE BROWN'..
THAT'S WHAT MY FRIENDS CALL ME, TOO..
HUH?
GOOD OL' CHARLOTTE BRAUN!
OH, NO...
11-30
SCHULZ

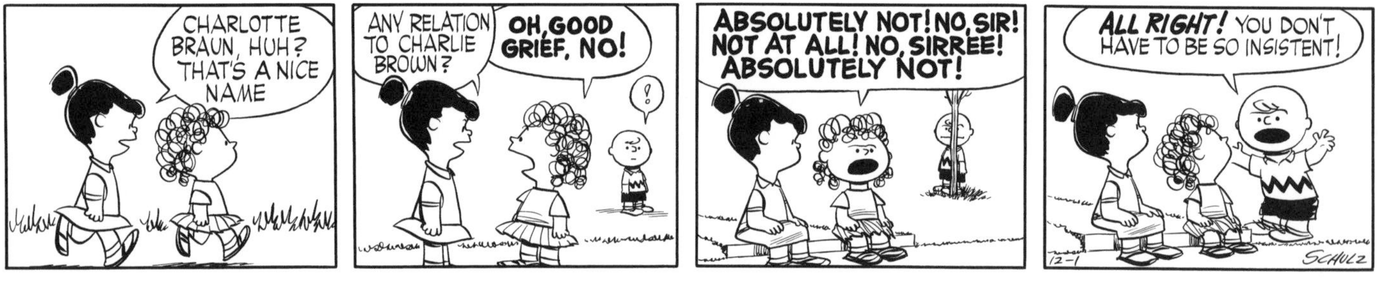
CHARLOTTE BRAUN, HUH? THAT'S A NICE NAME
ANY RELATION TO CHARLIE BROWN?
OH, GOOD GRIEF, NO!
!
ABSOLUTELY NOT! NO, SIR! NOT AT ALL! NO, SIRREE! ABSOLUTELY NOT!
ALL RIGHT! YOU DON'T HAVE TO BE SO INSISTENT!
12-1
SCHULZ

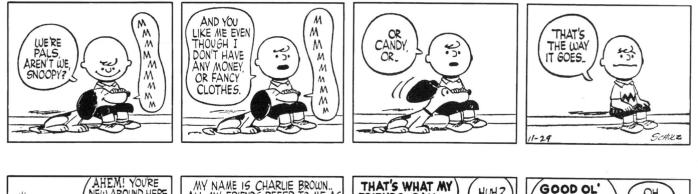

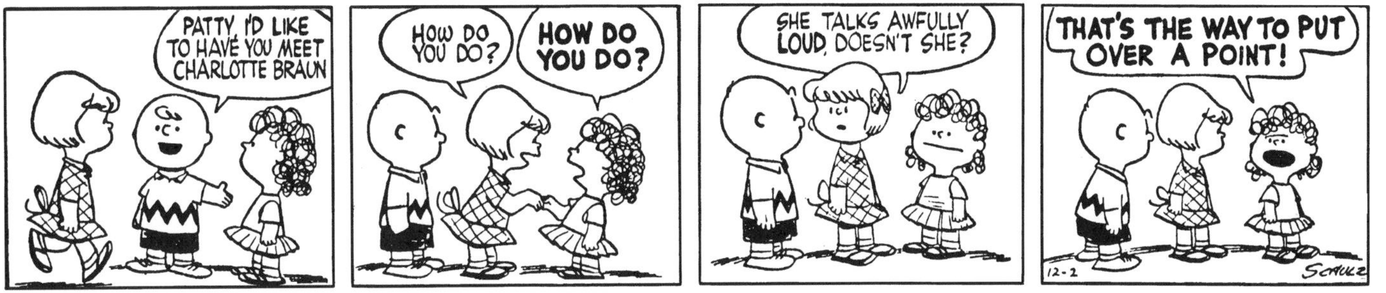
PATTY, I'D LIKE TO HAVE YOU MEET CHARLOTTE BRAUN
HOW DO YOU DO?
HOW DO YOU DO?
SHE TALKS AWFULLY LOUD, DOESN'T SHE?
THAT'S THE WAY TO PUT OVER A POINT!

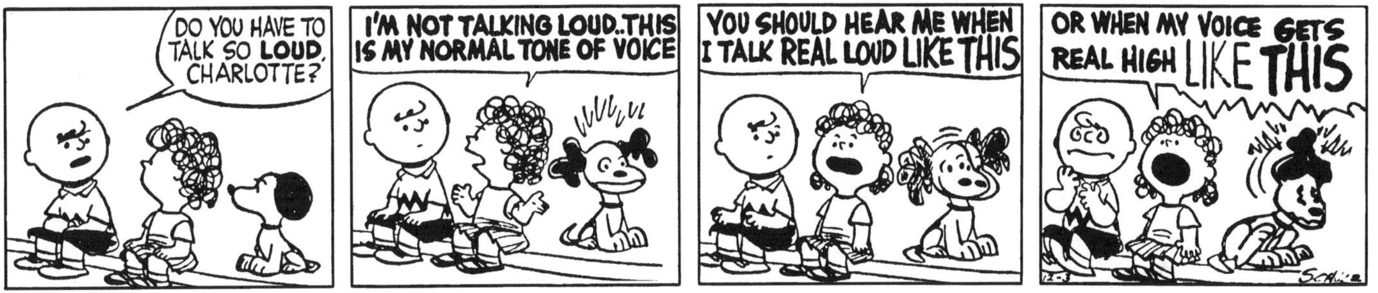
DO YOU HAVE TO TALK SO LOUD, CHARLOTTE?
I'M NOT TALKING LOUD..THIS IS MY NORMAL TONE OF VOICE
YOU SHOULD HEAR ME WHEN I TALK REAL LOUD LIKE THIS
OR WHEN MY VOICE GETS REAL HIGH LIKE THIS

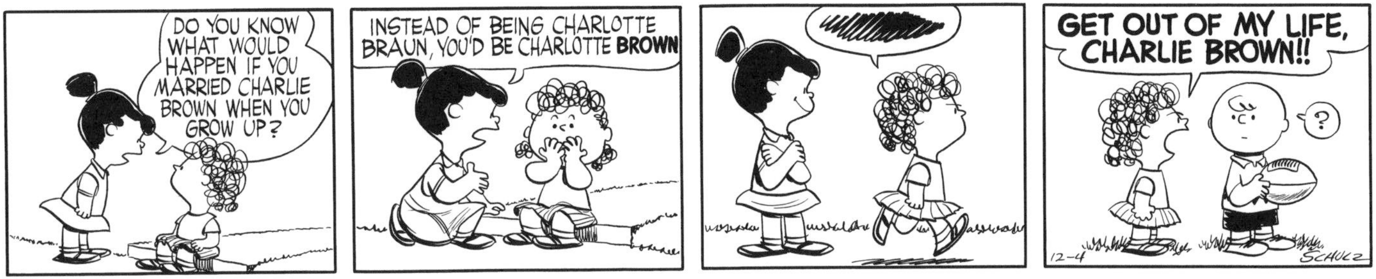
DO YOU KNOW WHAT WOULD HAPPEN IF YOU MARRIED CHARLIE BROWN WHEN YOU GROW UP?
INSTEAD OF BEING CHARLOTTE BRAUN, YOU'D BE CHARLOTTE BROWN
GET OUT OF MY LIFE, CHARLIE BROWN!!
?

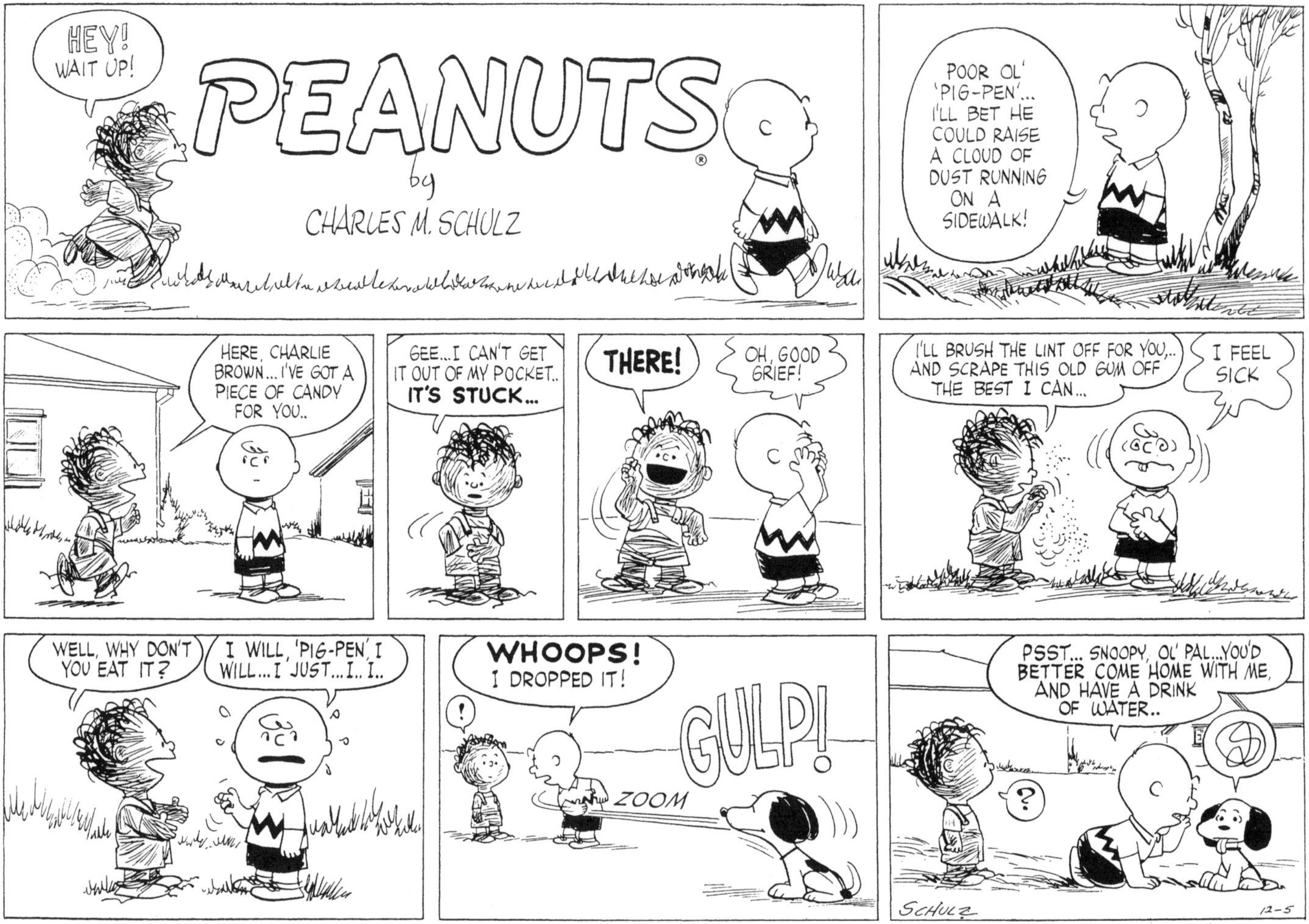
HEY! WAIT UP!
PEANUTS
by CHARLES M. SCHULZ
POOR OL' 'PIG-PEN'... I'LL BET HE COULD RAISE A CLOUD OF DUST RUNNING ON A SIDEWALK!
HERE, CHARLIE BROWN... I'VE GOT A PIECE OF CANDY FOR YOU..
GEE...I CAN'T GET IT OUT OF MY POCKET.. IT'S STUCK...
THERE!
OH, GOOD GRIEF!
I'LL BRUSH THE LINT OFF FOR YOU,.. AND SCRAPE THIS OLD GUM OFF THE BEST I CAN...
I FEEL SICK
WELL, WHY DON'T YOU EAT IT?
I WILL, 'PIG-PEN', I WILL... I JUST... I.. I..
WHOOPS! I DROPPED IT!
!
GULP!
ZOOM
PSST... SNOOPY, OL' PAL...YOU'D BETTER COME HOME WITH ME, AND HAVE A DRINK OF WATER..
?
SCHULZ
12-5

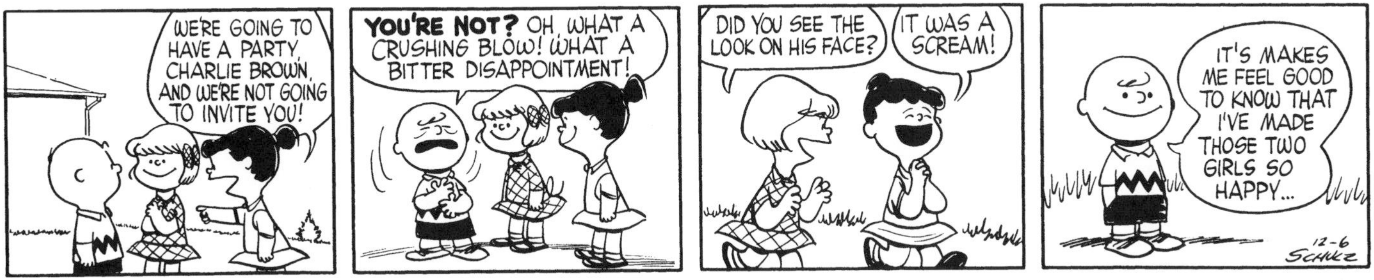
WE'RE GOING TO HAVE A PARTY, CHARLIE BROWN, AND WE'RE NOT GOING TO INVITE YOU!
YOU'RE NOT? OH, WHAT A CRUSHING BLOW! WHAT A BITTER DISAPPOINTMENT!
DID YOU SEE THE LOOK ON HIS FACE?
IT WAS A SCREAM!
IT'S MAKES ME FEEL GOOD TO KNOW THAT I'VE MADE THOSE TWO GIRLS SO HAPPY...
12-6
SCHULZ

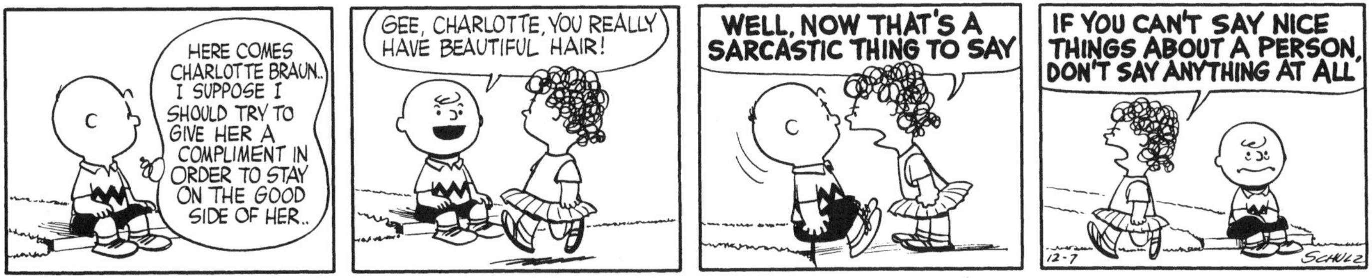
HERE COMES CHARLOTTE BRAUN.. I SUPPOSE I SHOULD TRY TO GIVE HER A COMPLIMENT IN ORDER TO STAY ON THE GOOD SIDE OF HER..
GEE, CHARLOTTE, YOU REALLY HAVE BEAUTIFUL HAIR!
WELL, NOW THAT'S A SARCASTIC THING TO SAY
IF YOU CAN'T SAY NICE THINGS ABOUT A PERSON, DON'T SAY ANYTHING AT ALL
12-7
SCHULZ

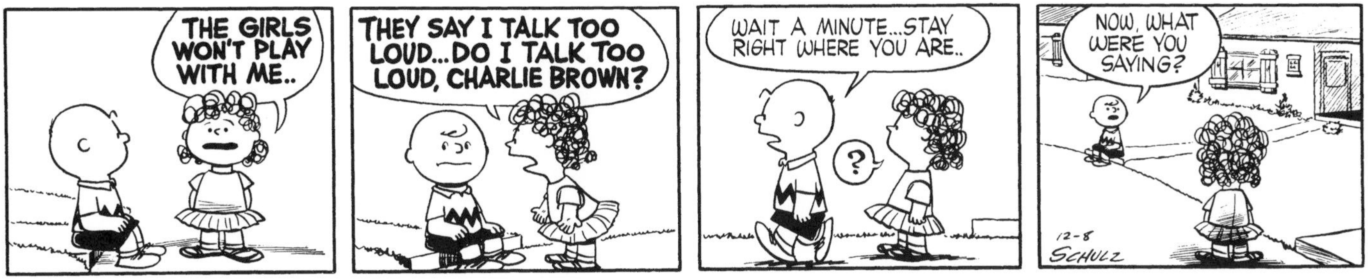
THE GIRLS WON'T PLAY WITH ME..
THEY SAY I TALK TOO LOUD...DO I TALK TOO LOUD, CHARLIE BROWN?
WAIT A MINUTE...STAY RIGHT WHERE YOU ARE..
?
NOW, WHAT WERE YOU SAYING?
12-8
SCHULZ

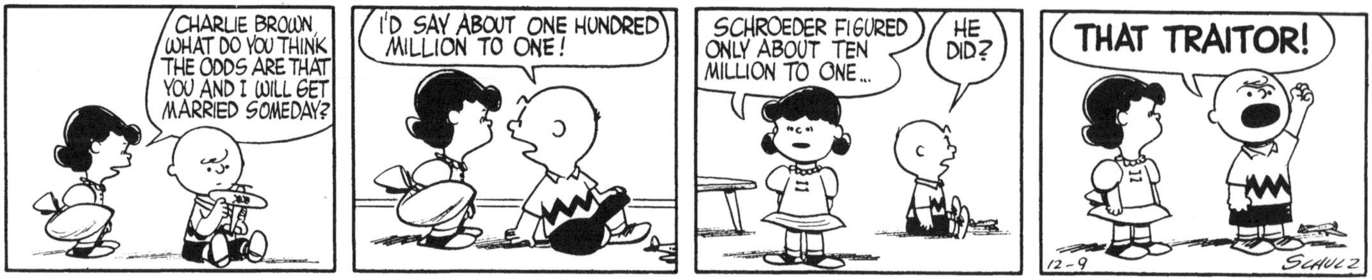
CHARLIE BROWN, WHAT DO YOU THINK THE ODDS ARE THAT YOU AND I WILL GET MARRIED SOMEDAY?
I'D SAY ABOUT ONE HUNDRED MILLION TO ONE!
SCHROEDER FIGURED ONLY ABOUT TEN MILLION TO ONE...
HE DID?
THAT TRAITOR!
12-9
SCHULZ

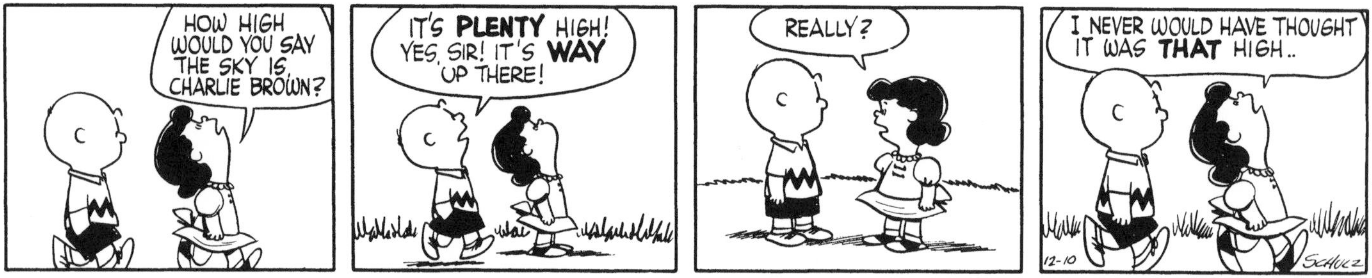
HOW HIGH WOULD YOU SAY THE SKY IS, CHARLIE BROWN?
IT'S PLENTY HIGH! YES, SIR! IT'S WAY UP THERE!
REALLY?
I NEVER WOULD HAVE THOUGHT IT WAS THAT HIGH..
12-10
SCHULZ

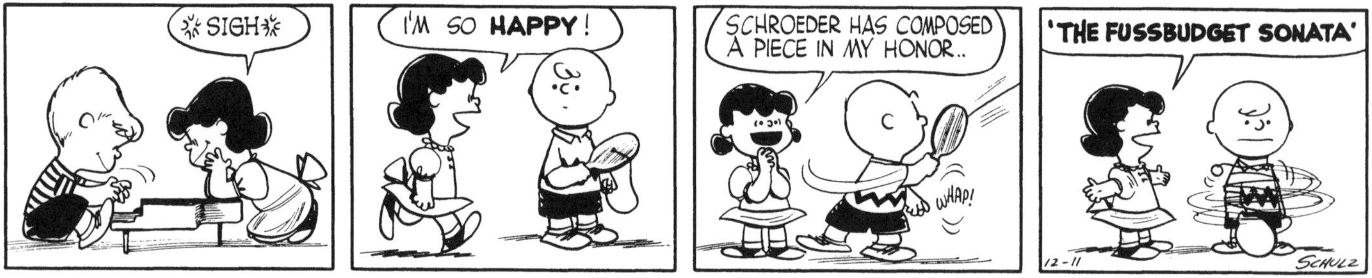
SIGH
I'M SO HAPPY!
SCHROEDER HAS COMPOSED A PIECE IN MY HONOR..
WHAP!
'THE FUSSBUDGET SONATA'
12-11
SCHULZ

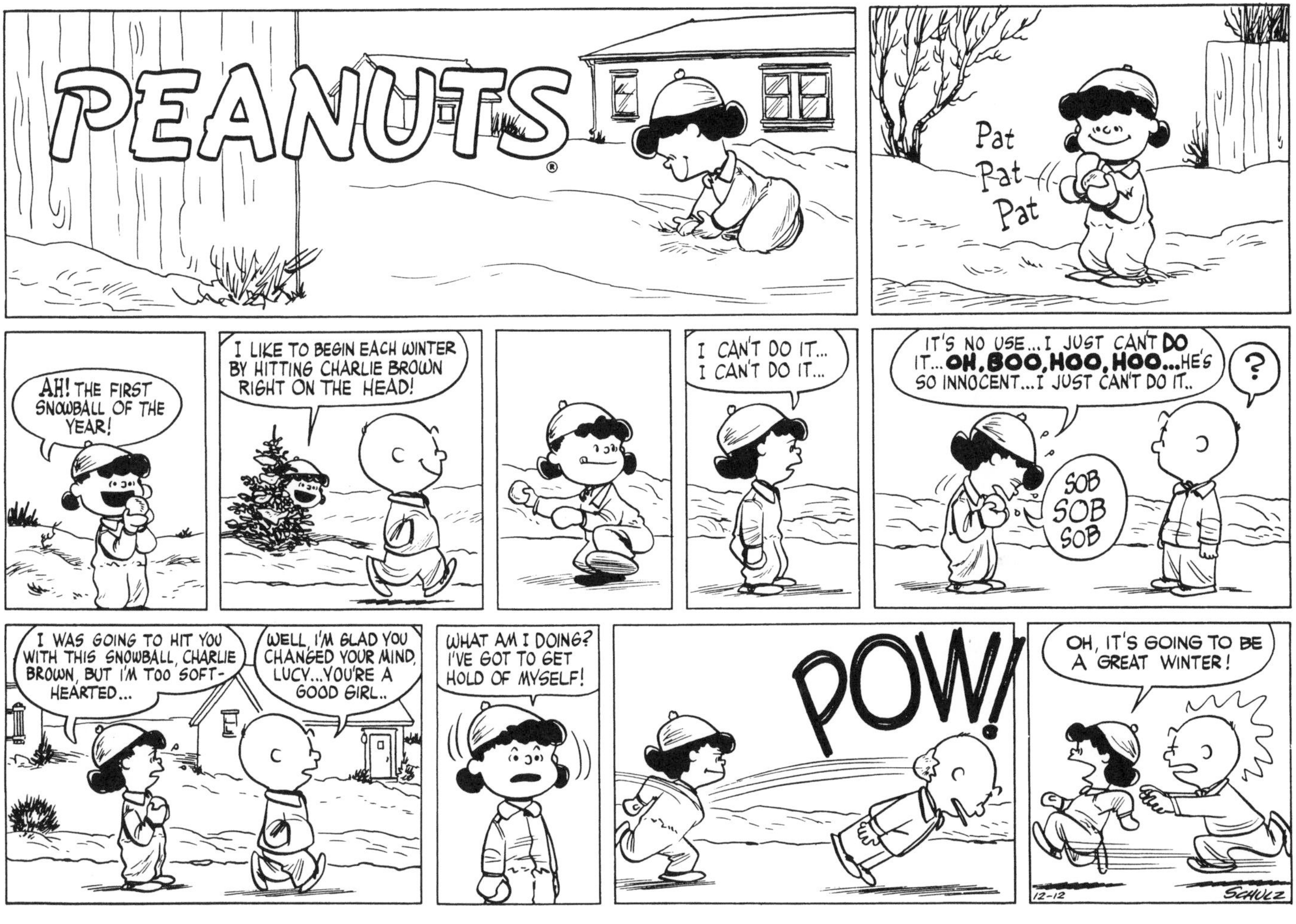
PEANUTS
Pat Pat Pat
AH! THE FIRST SNOWBALL OF THE YEAR!
I LIKE TO BEGIN EACH WINTER BY HITTING CHARLIE BROWN RIGHT ON THE HEAD!
I CAN'T DO IT... I CAN'T DO IT...
IT'S NO USE...I JUST CAN'T DO IT...OH, BOO, HOO, HOO...HE'S SO INNOCENT...I JUST CAN'T DO IT..
?
SOB SOB SOB
I WAS GOING TO HIT YOU WITH THIS SNOWBALL, CHARLIE BROWN, BUT I'M TOO SOFT-HEARTED...
WELL, I'M GLAD YOU CHANGED YOUR MIND, LUCY...YOU'RE A GOOD GIRL..
WHAT AM I DOING? I'VE GOT TO GET HOLD OF MYSELF!
POW!
OH, IT'S GOING TO BE A GREAT WINTER!
12-12
SCHULZ

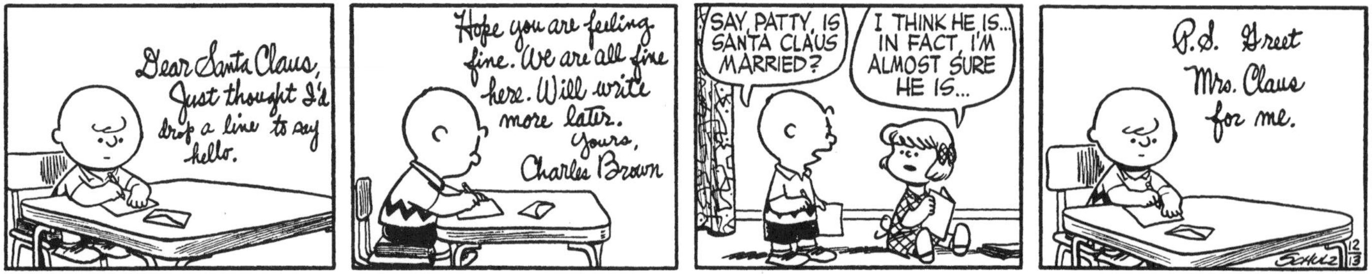
Dear Santa Claus, Just thought I'd drop a line to say hello.
Hope you are feeling fine. We are all fine here. Will write more later. Yours, Charles Brown
SAY, PATTY, IS SANTA CLAUS MARRIED?
I THINK HE IS... IN FACT, I'M ALMOST SURE HE IS...
P.S. Greet Mrs. Claus for me.
SCHULZ
12/13

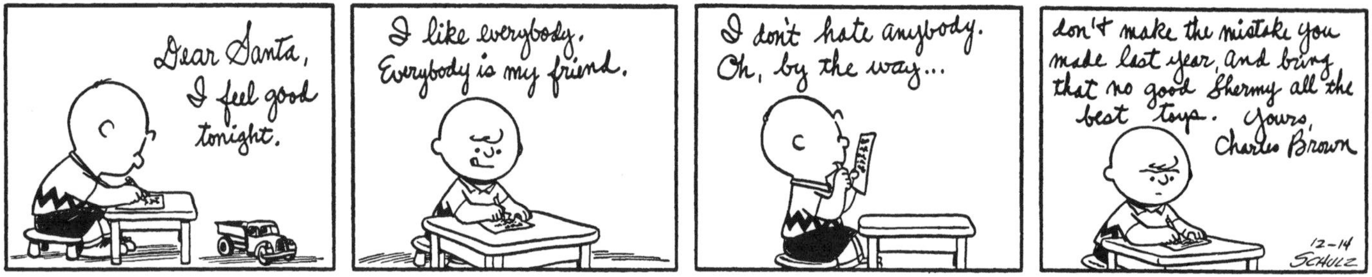
Dear Santa, I feel good tonight.
I like everybody. Everybody is my friend.
I don't hate anybody. Oh, by the way...
don't make the mistake you made last year, and bring that no good Shermy all the best toys. Yours, Charles Brown
12-14
SCHULZ

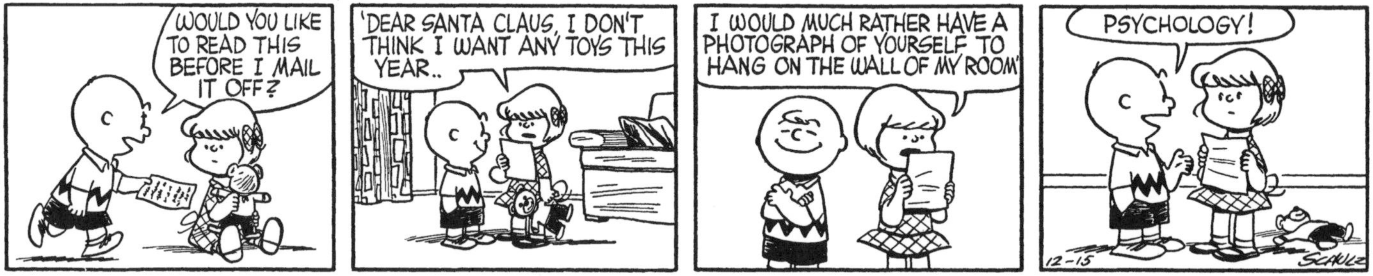
WOULD YOU LIKE TO READ THIS BEFORE I MAIL IT OFF?
'DEAR SANTA CLAUS, I DON'T THINK I WANT ANY TOYS THIS YEAR..
I WOULD MUCH RATHER HAVE A PHOTOGRAPH OF YOURSELF TO HANG ON THE WALL OF MY ROOM'
PSYCHOLOGY!
12-15
SCHULZ

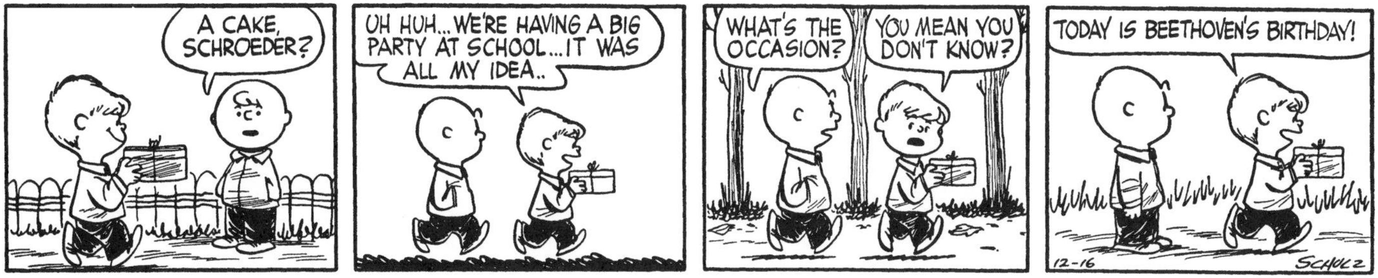
A CAKE, SCHROEDER?
UH HUH...WE'RE HAVING A BIG PARTY AT SCHOOL...IT WAS ALL MY IDEA..
WHAT'S THE OCCASION?
YOU MEAN YOU DON'T KNOW?
TODAY IS BEETHOVEN'S BIRTHDAY!
12-16
SCHULZ

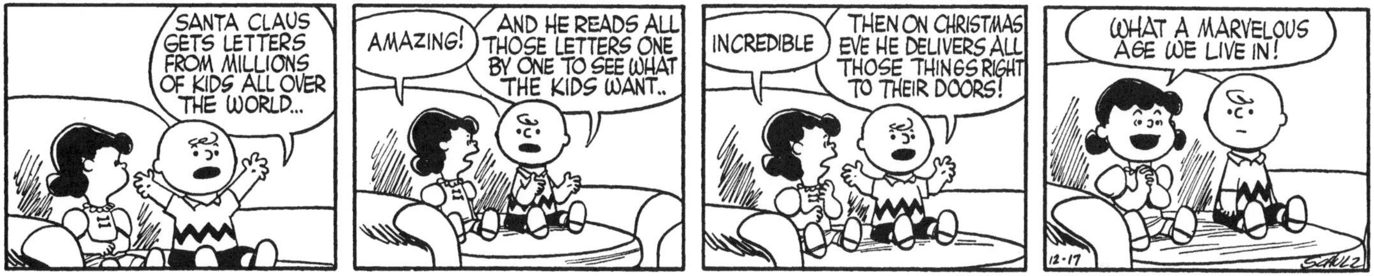
SANTA CLAUS GETS LETTERS FROM MILLIONS OF KIDS ALL OVER THE WORLD...
AMAZING!
AND HE READS ALL THOSE LETTERS ONE BY ONE TO SEE WHAT THE KIDS WANT..
INCREDIBLE
THEN ON CHRISTMAS EVE HE DELIVERS ALL THOSE THINGS RIGHT TO THEIR DOORS!
WHAT A MARVELOUS AGE WE LIVE IN!
12-17
SCHULZ

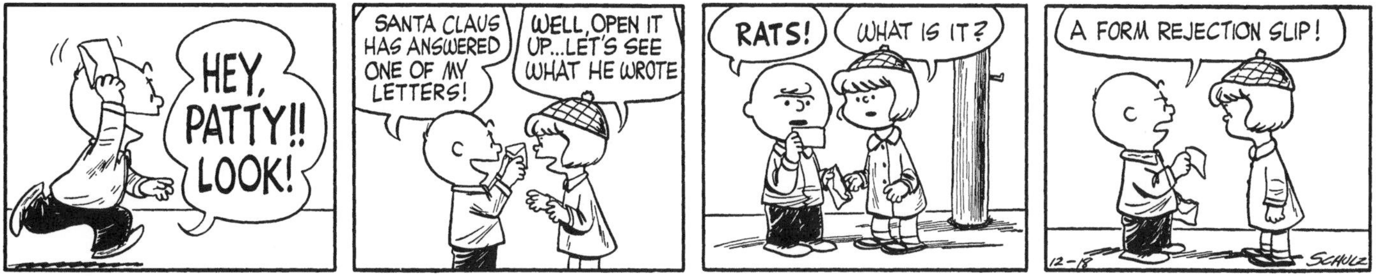
HEY, PATTY!! LOOK!
SANTA CLAUS HAS ANSWERED ONE OF MY LETTERS!
WELL, OPEN IT UP...LET'S SEE WHAT HE WROTE
RATS!
WHAT IS IT?
A FORM REJECTION SLIP!
12-18
SCHULZ

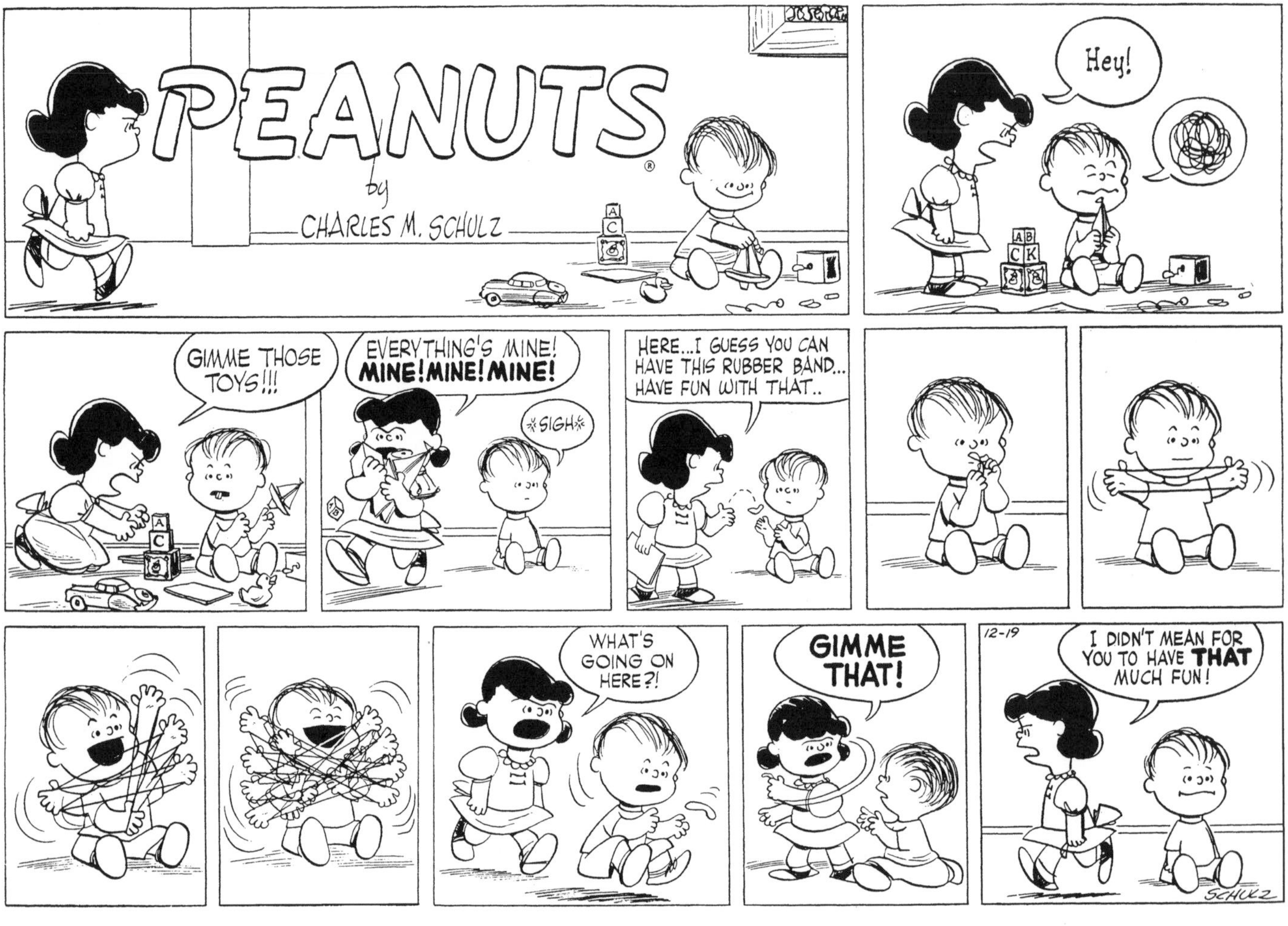
PEANUTS
by
CHARLES M. SCHULZ
Hey!
GIMME THOSE TOYS!!!
EVERYTHING'S MINE! MINE! MINE! MINE!
SIGH
HERE...I GUESS YOU CAN HAVE THIS RUBBER BAND... HAVE FUN WITH THAT..
WHAT'S GOING ON HERE?!
GIMME THAT!
12-19
I DIDN'T MEAN FOR YOU TO HAVE THAT MUCH FUN!
SCHULZ

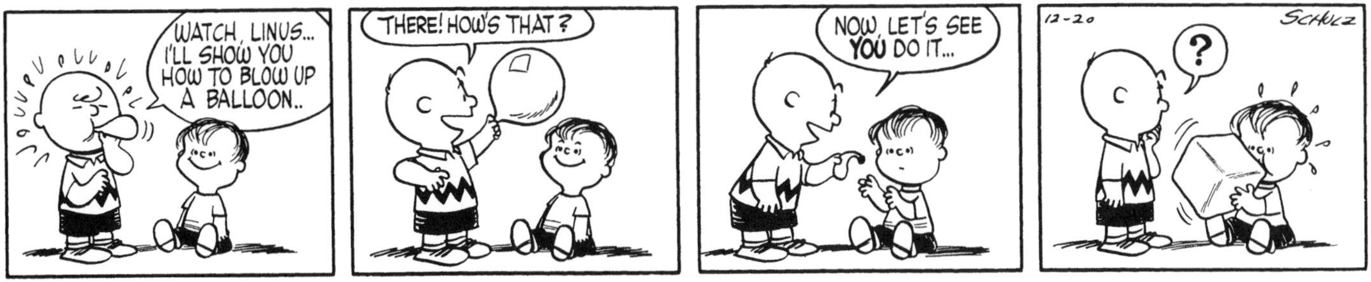
WATCH, LINUS... I'LL SHOW YOU HOW TO BLOW UP A BALLOON..
THERE! HOW'S THAT?
NOW, LET'S SEE **YOU** DO IT...
12-20
SCHULZ
?

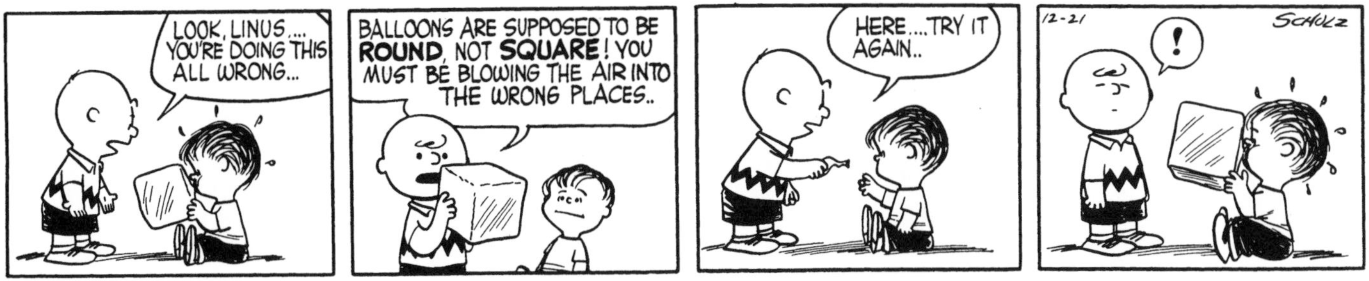
LOOK, LINUS.... YOU'RE DOING THIS ALL WRONG...
BALLOONS ARE SUPPOSED TO BE **ROUND**, NOT **SQUARE**! YOU MUST BE BLOWING THE AIR INTO THE WRONG PLACES..
HERE....TRY IT AGAIN..
12-21
SCHULZ
!

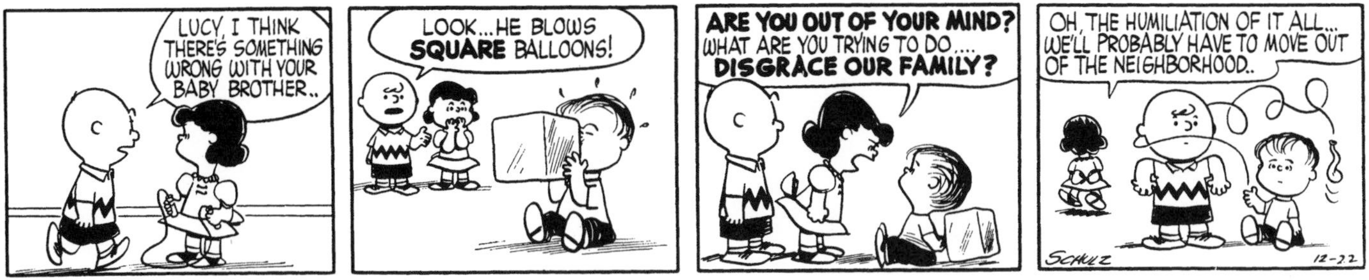
LUCY, I THINK THERE'S SOMETHING WRONG WITH YOUR BABY BROTHER..
LOOK...HE BLOWS **SQUARE** BALLOONS!
ARE YOU OUT OF YOUR MIND? WHAT ARE YOU TRYING TO DO.... **DISGRACE OUR FAMILY?**
OH, THE HUMILIATION OF IT ALL... WE'LL PROBABLY HAVE TO MOVE OUT OF THE NEIGHBORHOOD..
SCHULZ
12-22

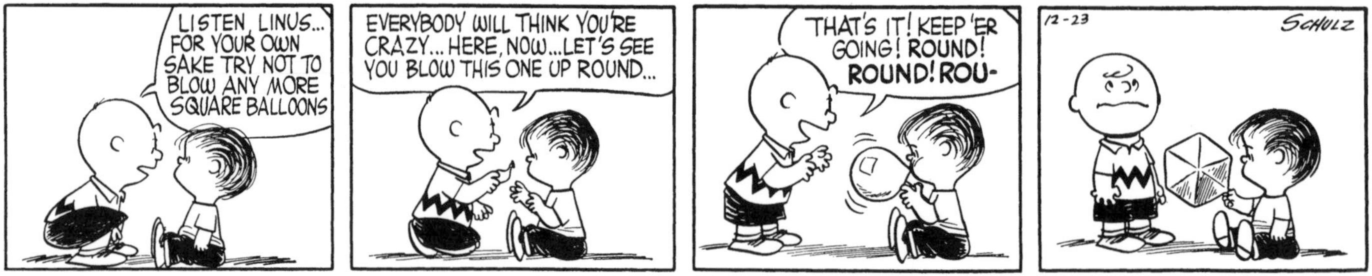
LISTEN, LINUS... FOR YOUR OWN SAKE TRY NOT TO BLOW ANY MORE SQUARE BALLOONS
EVERYBODY WILL THINK YOU'RE CRAZY... HERE, NOW...LET'S SEE YOU BLOW THIS ONE UP ROUND...
THAT'S IT! KEEP 'ER GOING! ROUND! ROUND! ROU-
12-23
SCHULZ

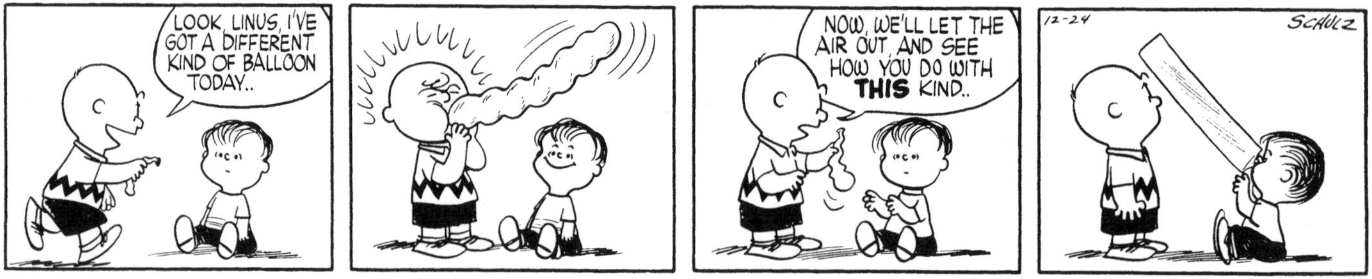
LOOK, LINUS, I'VE GOT A DIFFERENT KIND OF BALLOON TODAY..
NOW, WE'LL LET THE AIR OUT, AND SEE HOW YOU DO WITH THIS KIND..
12-24
SCHULZ

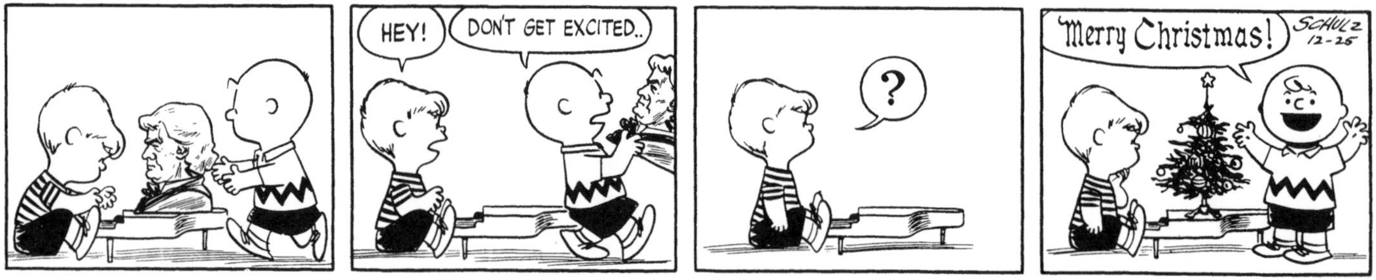
HEY!
DON'T GET EXCITED..
?
Merry Christmas!
SCHULZ
12-25

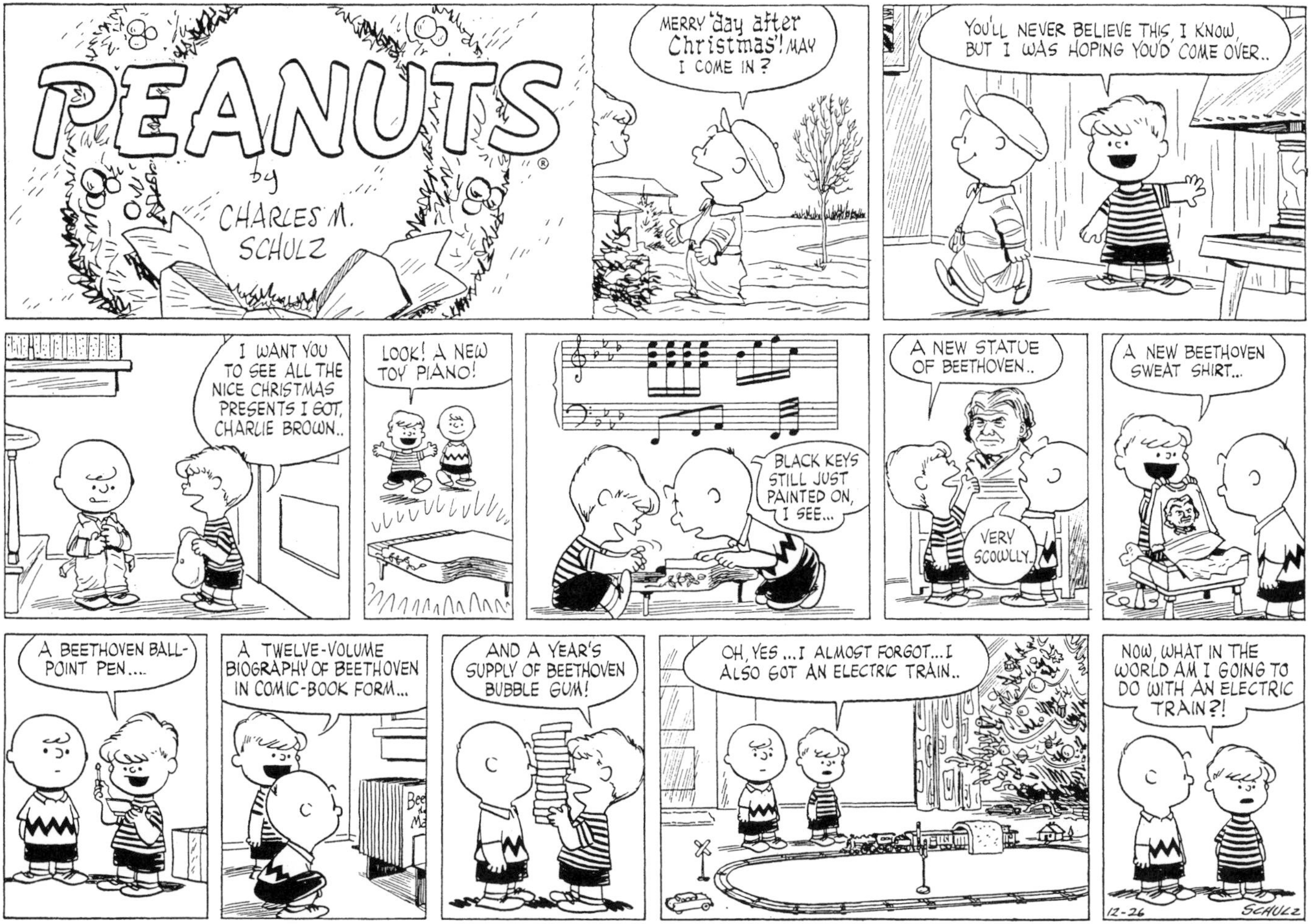
PEANUTS
by CHARLES M. SCHULZ
MERRY 'day after Christmas'! MAY I COME IN?
YOU'LL NEVER BELIEVE THIS, I KNOW, BUT I WAS HOPING YOU'D COME OVER..
I WANT YOU TO SEE ALL THE NICE CHRISTMAS PRESENTS I GOT, CHARLIE BROWN..
LOOK! A NEW TOY PIANO!
BLACK KEYS STILL JUST PAINTED ON, I SEE...
A NEW STATUE OF BEETHOVEN..
VERY SCOWLLY..
A NEW BEETHOVEN SWEAT SHIRT...
A BEETHOVEN BALL-POINT PEN....
A TWELVE-VOLUME BIOGRAPHY OF BEETHOVEN IN COMIC-BOOK FORM...
AND A YEAR'S SUPPLY OF BEETHOVEN BUBBLE GUM!
OH, YES ...I ALMOST FORGOT... I ALSO GOT AN ELECTRIC TRAIN..
NOW, WHAT IN THE WORLD AM I GOING TO DO WITH AN ELECTRIC TRAIN?!
12-26
SCHULZ

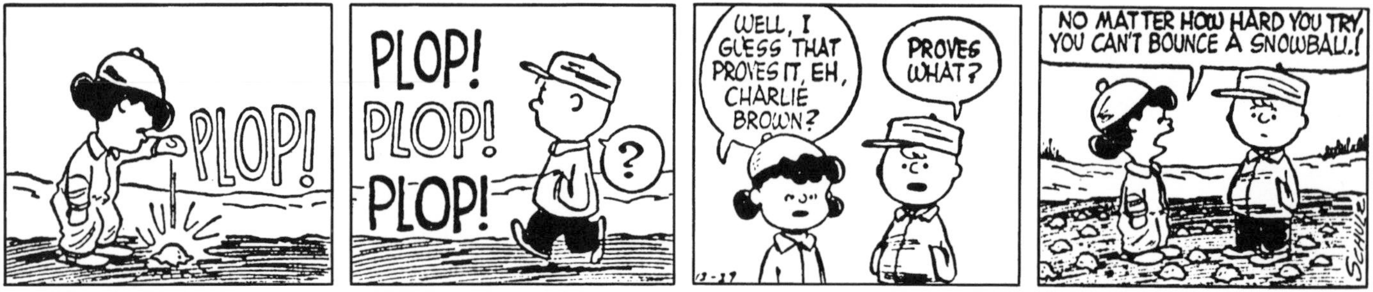
PLOP!
PLOP!
PLOP!
PLOP!
?
WELL, I GUESS THAT PROVES IT, EH, CHARLIE BROWN?
PROVES WHAT?
NO MATTER HOW HARD YOU TRY, YOU CAN'T BOUNCE A SNOWBALL!

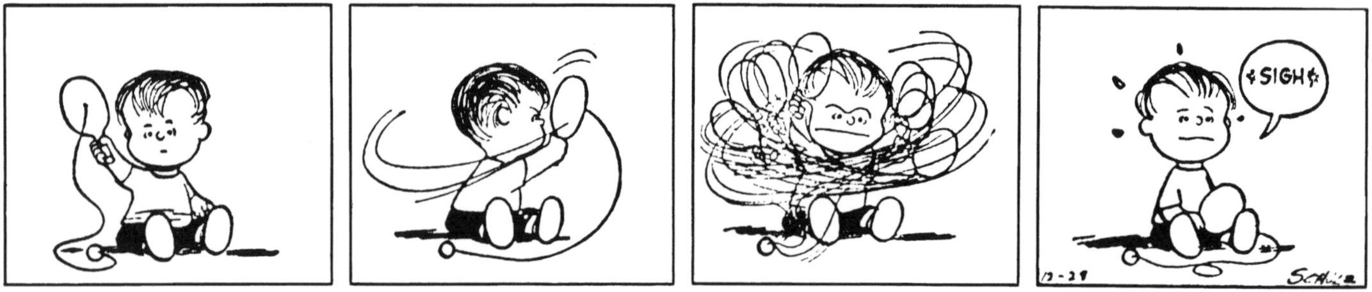
SIGH

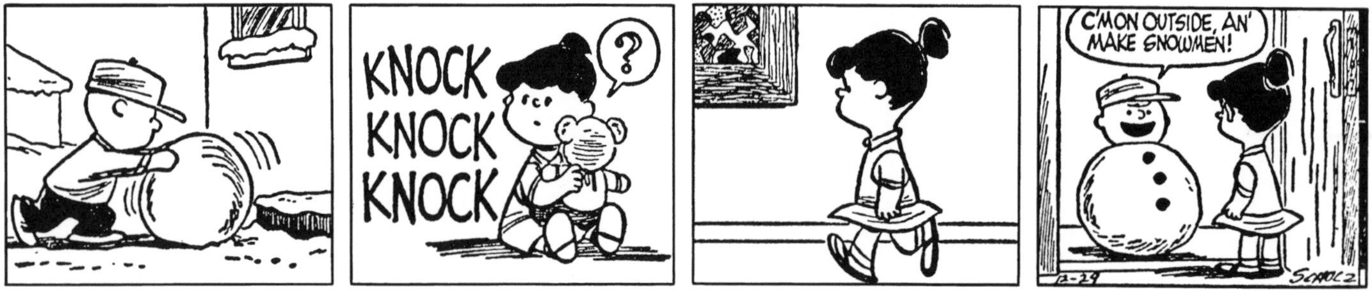
KNOCK
KNOCK
KNOCK
?
C'MON OUTSIDE, AN' MAKE SNOWMEN!

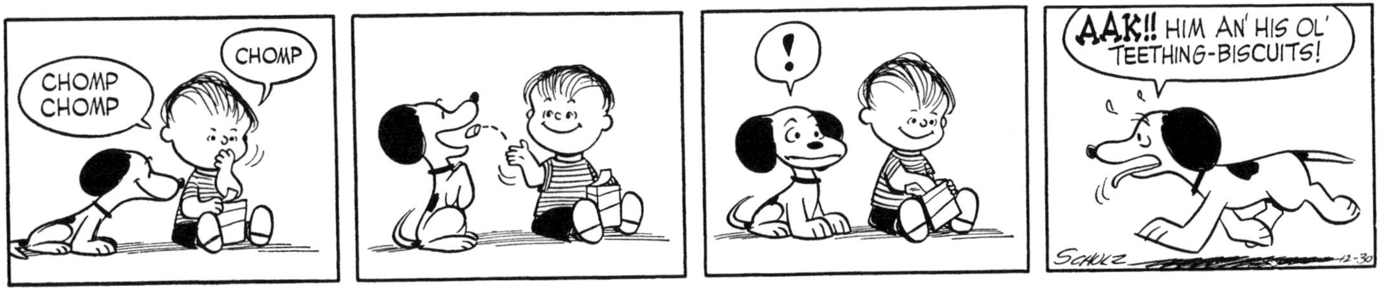
CHOMP
CHOMP
CHOMP
!
AAK!! HIM AN' HIS OL' TEETHING-BISCUITS!
SCHULZ
12-30

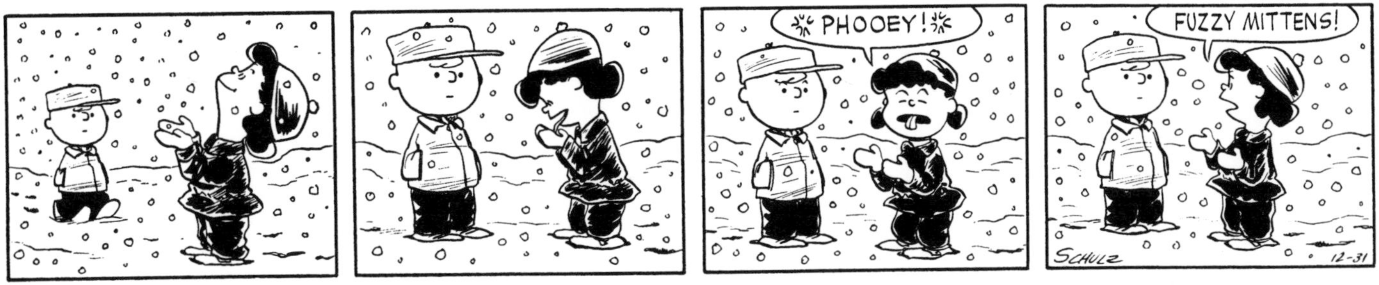
PHOOEY!
FUZZY MITTENS!
SCHULZ
12-31

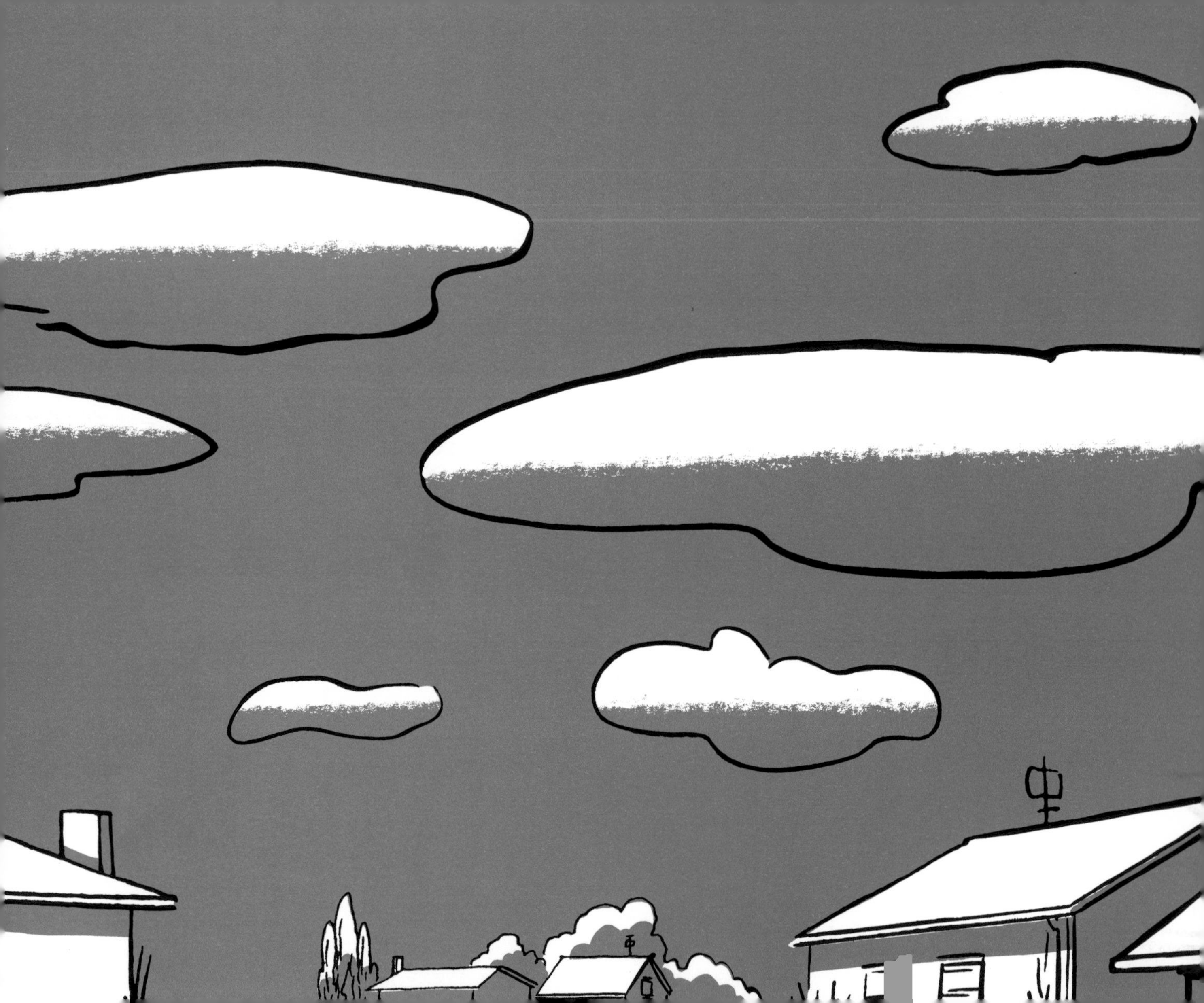

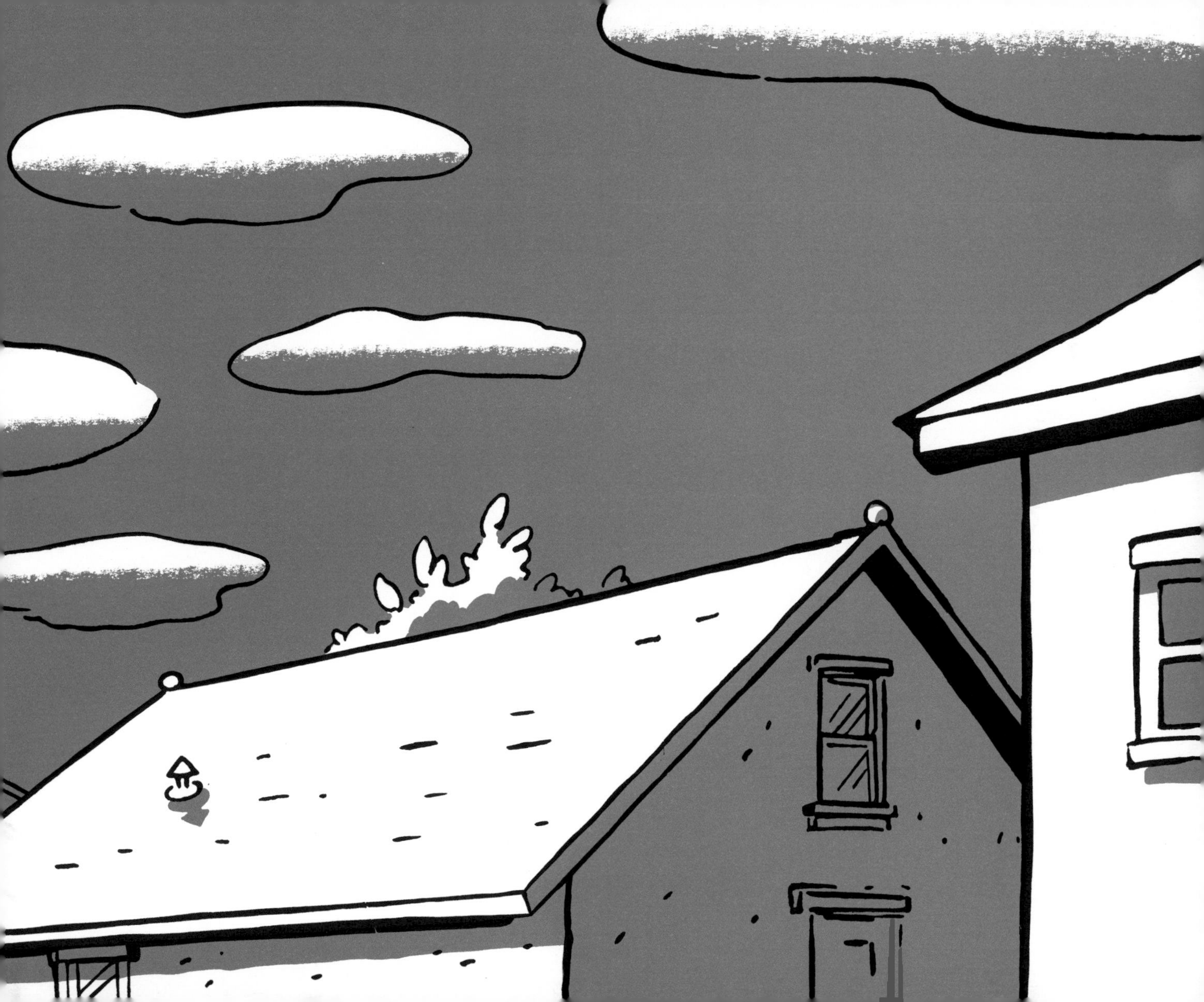

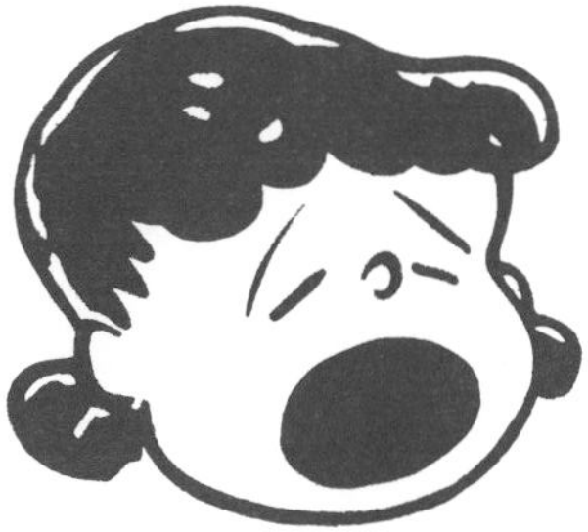

INDEX

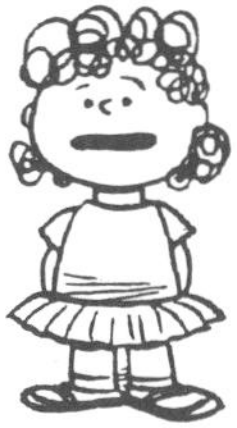

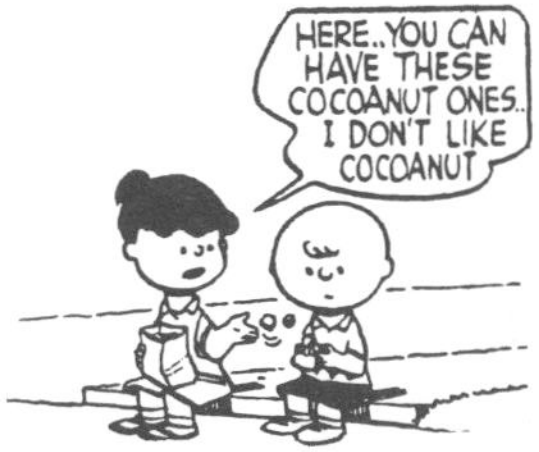

HERE..YOU CAN HAVE THESE COCOANUT ONES.. I DON'T LIKE COCOANUT

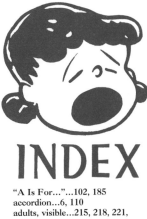

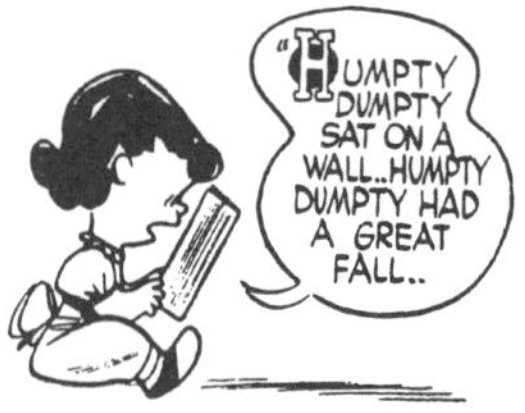
"HUMPTY DUMPTY SAT ON A WALL..HUMPTY DUMPTY HAD A GREAT FALL..

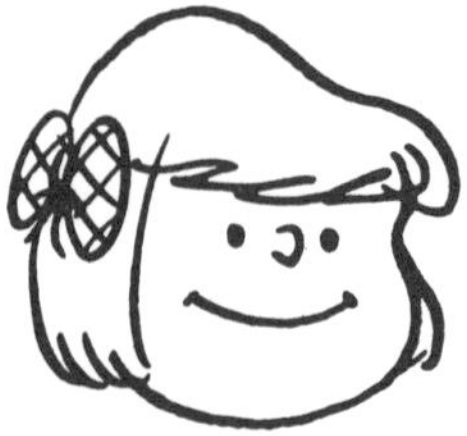

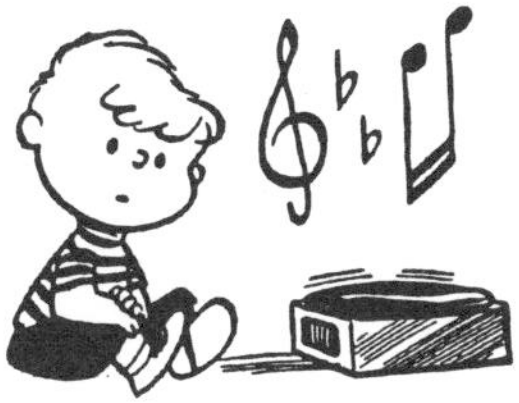

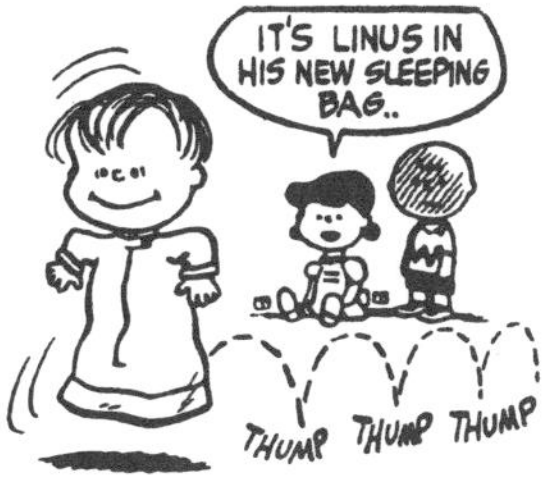
IT'S LINUS IN HIS NEW SLEEPING BAG..
THUMP THUMP THUMP

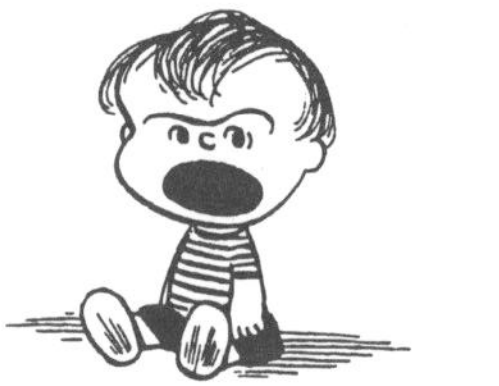

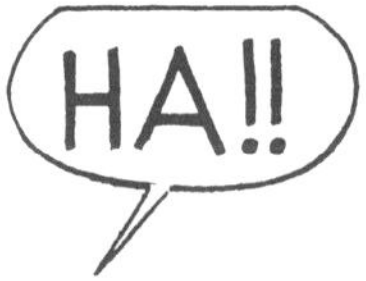
HA!!

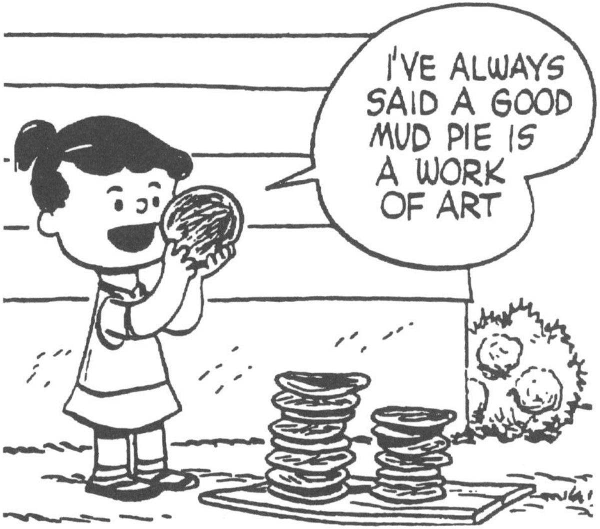
I'VE ALWAYS SAID A GOOD MUD PIE IS A WORK OF ART

A NOTE ABOUT REPRODUCTION QUALITY

Although the great majority of the 17,897 *Peanuts* strips Schulz wrote and drew have been carefully archived by Charles M. Schulz Creative Associates, a number of strips, particularly from the earliest years, were not saved, and have never been reprinted since their original appearance in newspapers around the country.

To complicate matters further, *Peanuts* appeared in only a handful of newspapers in its early days, and most major newspapers have, tragically, divested themselves of their precious archival copies in favor of microfilm versions (which, while fine for researching old articles, are next to useless for reproducing graphics).

Great effort has been made to track down the very best copies of these elusive strips, and to restore them. Special kudos is due to Nicholson Baker, who through his American Newspaper Repository saved a vintage set of *Peanuts*-carrying *Chicago Tribunes*; to Duke University, now the custodian of this priceless resource and whose newsprint elves have been diligently scanning otherwise unavailable strips for us; and to *Peanuts* expert Nat Gertler, who has located a number of otherwise "missing" strips in obscure *Peanuts* collections of yore.

Nevertheless, some of the strips presented here (particularly in the last four months of 1954) ultimately do bear some evidence of the limitations of our sources, and on these we ask the reader's forbearance. Should we locate better copies as the series progresses, new editions will incorporate these improvements.

Finally, one strip has proven at least partly "lost": the May 3, 1953 Sunday page (page 53). We have found only two copies of it, neither of which includes the top tier (the title panel and panel following it). The version reproduced in this volume is a composite of a trimmed but relatively clean copy from the *Chicago Tribune* extensively retouched and re-inked to incorporate material visible in a very blurry but more complete microfilm copy; the top tier has been created from scratch by the book's designer, Seth. If there is a Holy Grail so far as *Peanuts* strips is concerned, May 3, 1953 is it, and we hope future editions of *The Complete Peanuts* 1953-1954 will be able to present it. Should we find one, we promise to publish it in the next available *Complete Peanuts* volume, so that loyal readers won't have to buy a second copy of this volume just to complete their collection.

—The Publishers

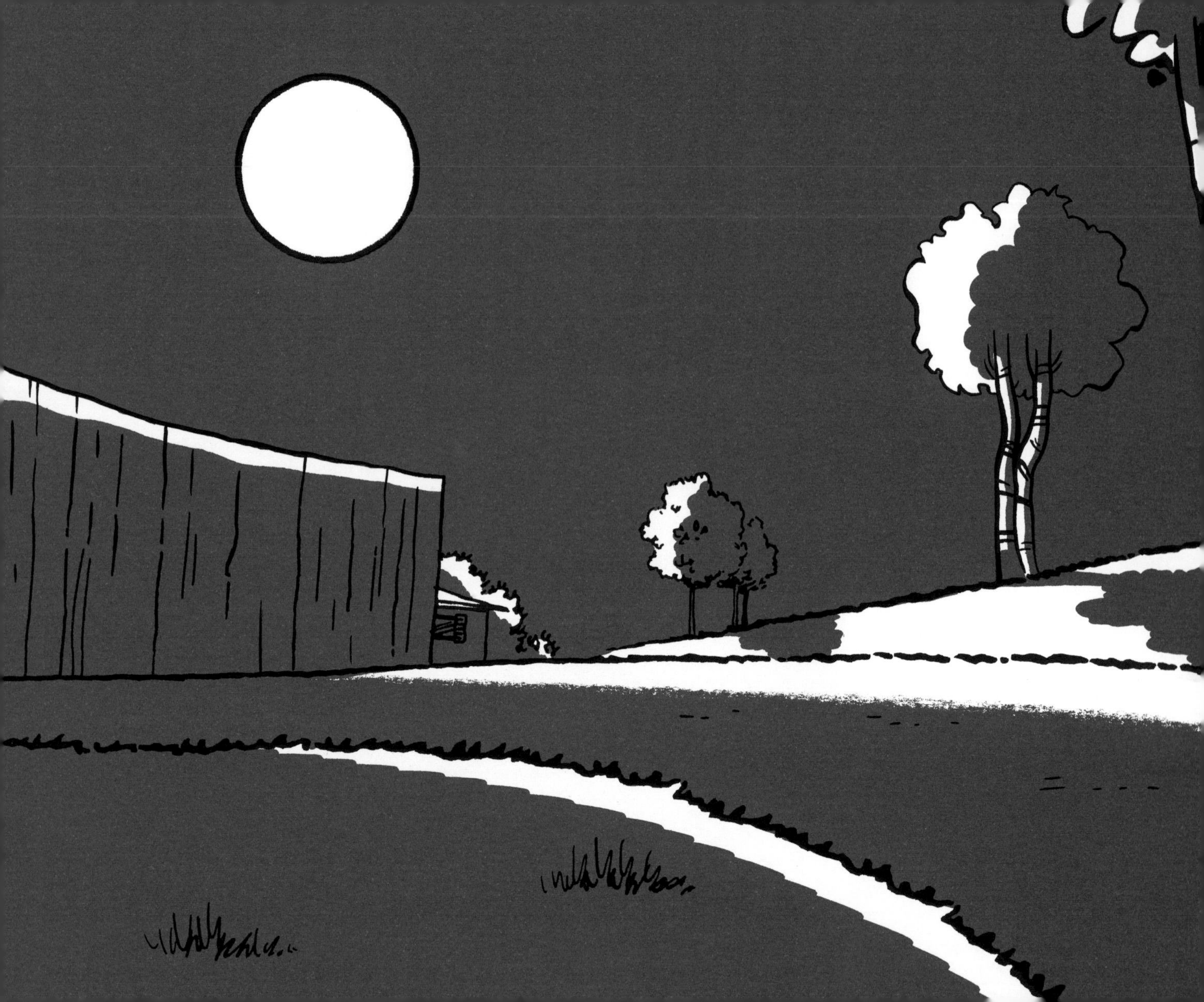

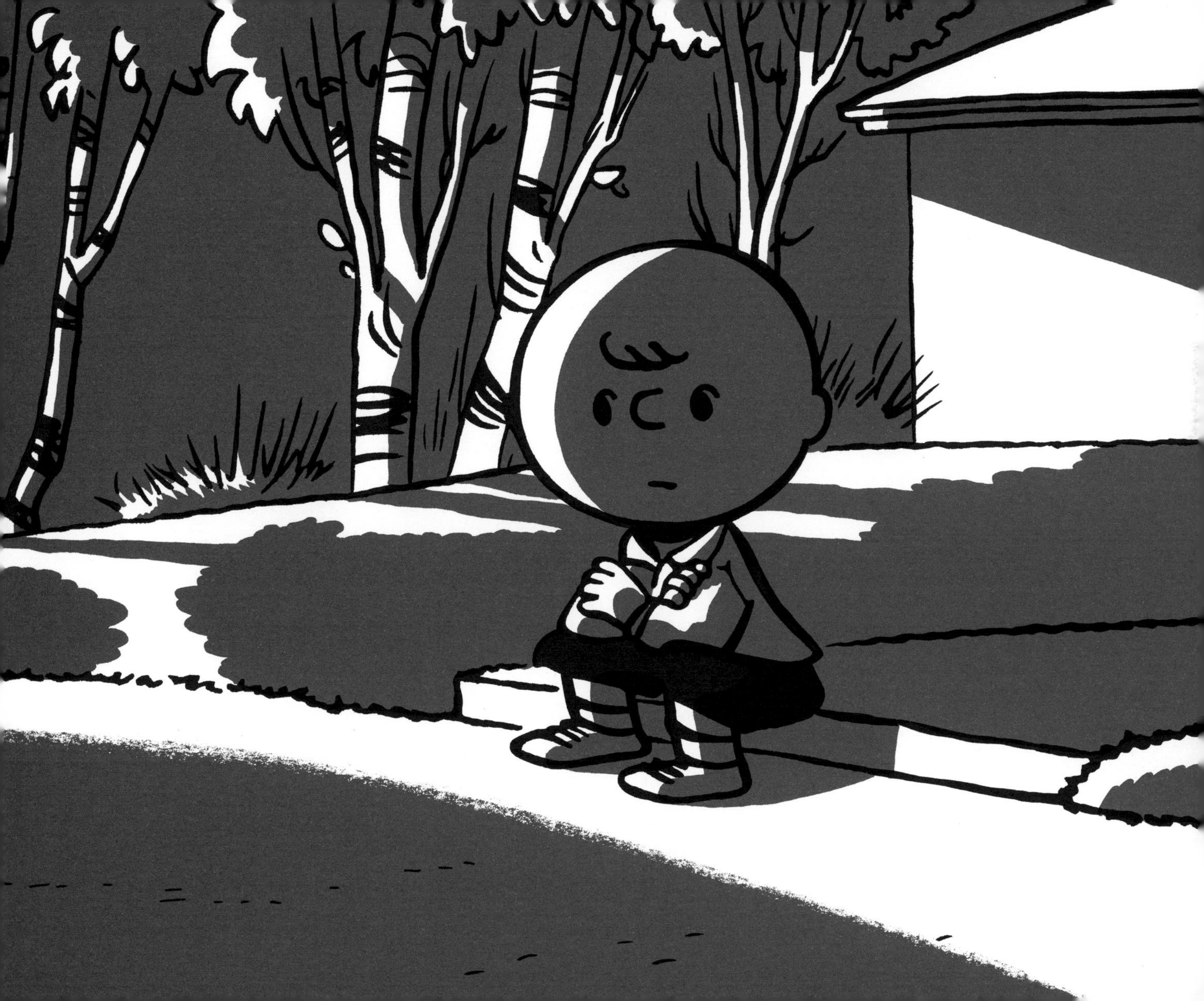

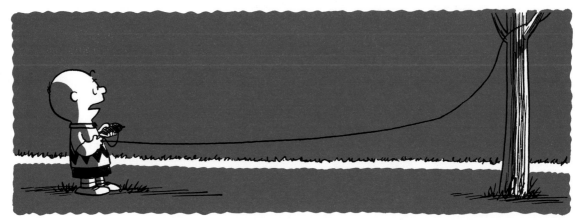

CHARLES M. SCHULZ · 1922 To 2000

Charles M. Schulz was born November 25, 1922 in Minneapolis. His destiny was foreshadowed when an uncle gave him, at the age of two days, the nickname Sparky (after the racehorse Spark Plug in the newspaper strip *Barney Google*).

Schulz grew up in St. Paul. By all accounts, he led an unremarkable, albeit sheltered, childhood. He was an only child, close to both parents, his eventual career path nurtured by his father, who bought four Sunday papers every week — just for the comics.

An outstanding student, he skipped two grades early on, but began to flounder in high school — perhaps not so coincidentally at the same time kids are going through their cruelest, most status-conscious period of socialization. The pain, bitterness, insecurity, and failures chronicled in *Peanuts* appear to have originated from this period of Schulz's life.

Although Schulz enjoyed sports, he also found refuge in solitary activities: reading, drawing, and watching movies. He bought comic books and Big Little Books, pored over the newspaper strips, and copied his favorites — *Buck Rogers*, the Walt Disney characters, *Popeye, Tim Tyler's Luck*. He quickly became a connoisseur; his heroes were Milton Caniff, Roy Crane, Hal Foster, and Alex Raymond.

In his senior year in high school, his mother noticed an ad in a local newspaper for a correspondence school, Federal Schools (later called Art

Instruction Schools). Schulz passed the talent test, completed the course and began trying, unsuccessfully, to sell gag cartoons to magazines. (His first published drawing was of his dog, Spike, and appeared in a 1937 *Ripley's Believe It Or Not!* installment.)

After World War II had ended and Schulz was discharged from the army, he started submitting gag cartoons to the various magazines of the time; his first breakthrough, however, came when an editor at *Timeless Topix* hired him to letter adventure comics. Soon after that, he was hired by his alma mater, Art Instruction, to correct student lessons returned by mail.

Between 1948 and 1950, he succeeded in selling 17 cartoons to the *Saturday Evening Post* — as well as, to the local *St. Paul Pioneer Press*, a weekly comic feature called *Li'l Folks*. It was run in the women's section and paid $10 a week. After writing and drawing the feature for two years, Schulz asked for a better location in the paper or for daily exposure, as well as a raise. When he was turned down on all three counts, he quit.

He started submitting strips to the newspaper syndicates. In the Spring of 1950, he received a letter from the United Feature Syndicate, announcing their interest in his submission, *Li'l Folks*. Schulz boarded a train in June for New York City; more interested in doing a strip than a panel, he also brought along the first installments of what would become *Peanuts* — and that was what sold. (The title, which Schulz loathed to his dying day, was imposed by the syndicate). The first *Peanuts* daily appeared October 2, 1950; the first Sunday, January 6, 1952.

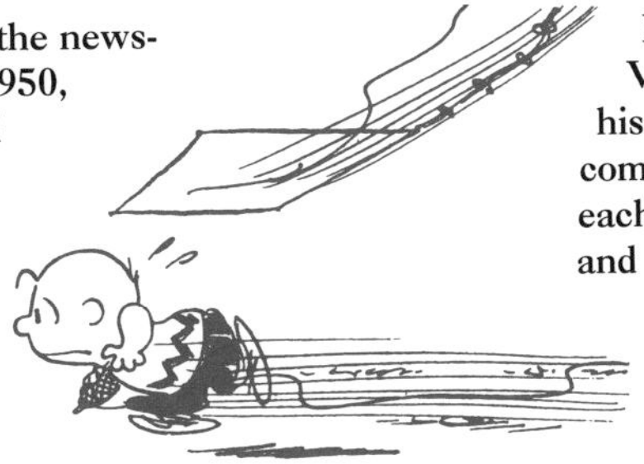

Prior to *Peanuts*, the province of the comics page had been that of gags, social and political observation, domestic comedy, soap opera, and various adventure genres. Although *Peanuts* changed, or evolved, during the 50 years Schulz wrote and drew it, it remained, as it began, an anomaly on the comics page — a comic strip about the interior crises of the cartoonist himself. After a painful divorce in 1973 from which he had not yet recovered, Schulz told a reporter, "Strangely, I've drawn better cartoons in the last six months — or as good as I've ever drawn. I don't know how the human mind works." Surely, it was this kind of humility in the face of profoundly irreducible human question that makes *Peanuts* as universally moving as it is.

Diagnosed with cancer, Schulz retired from *Peanuts* at the end of 1999. He died on February 13th 2000, the day before Valentine's day — and the day before his last strip was published — having completed 17,897 daily and Sunday strips, each and every one fully written, drawn, and lettered entirely by his own hand — an unmatched achievement in comics. *—Gary Groth*

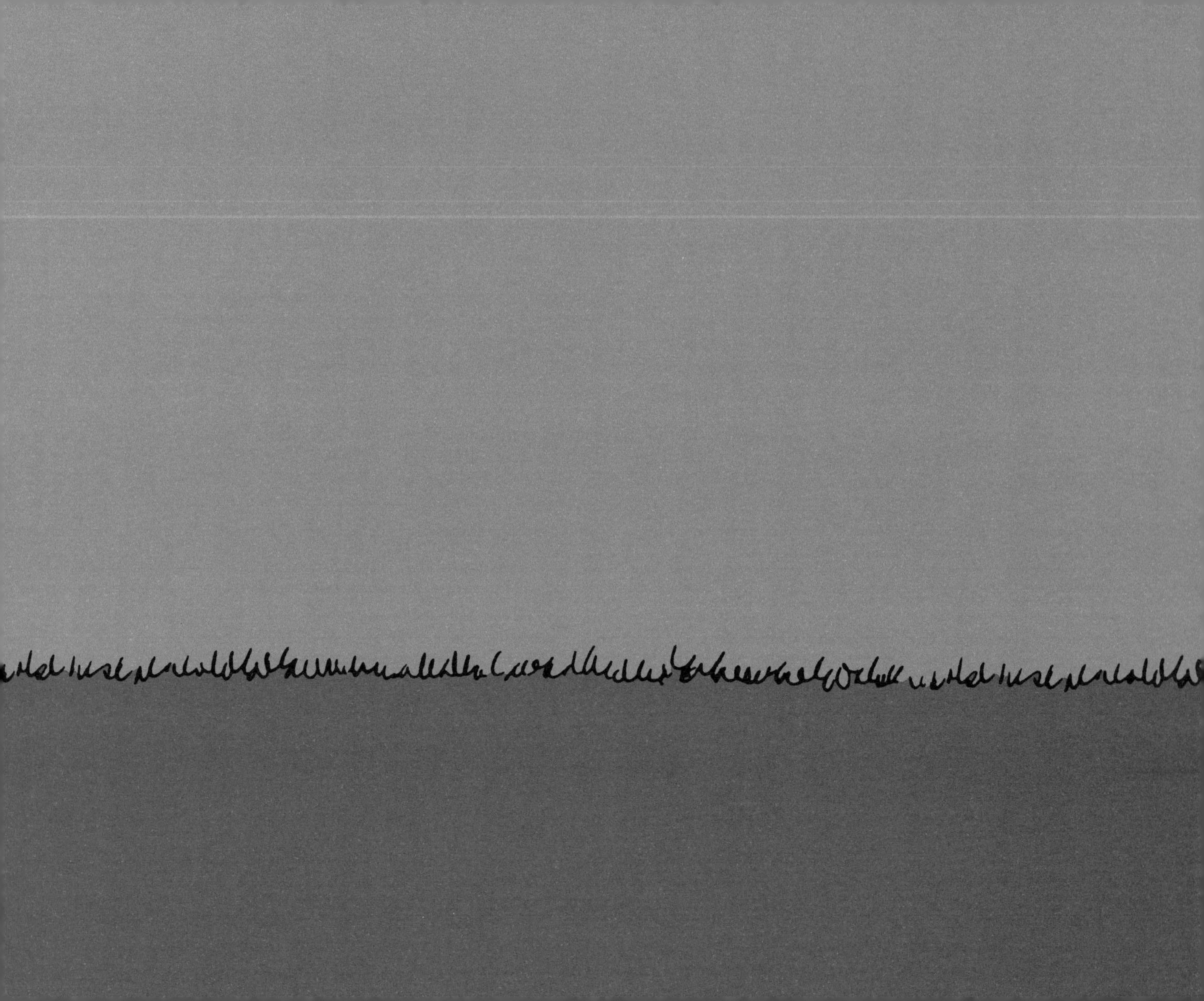

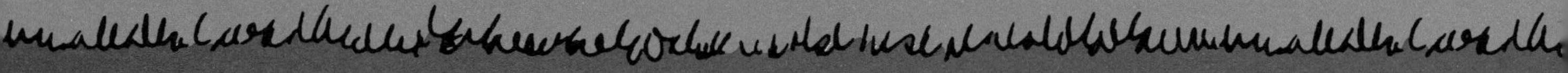

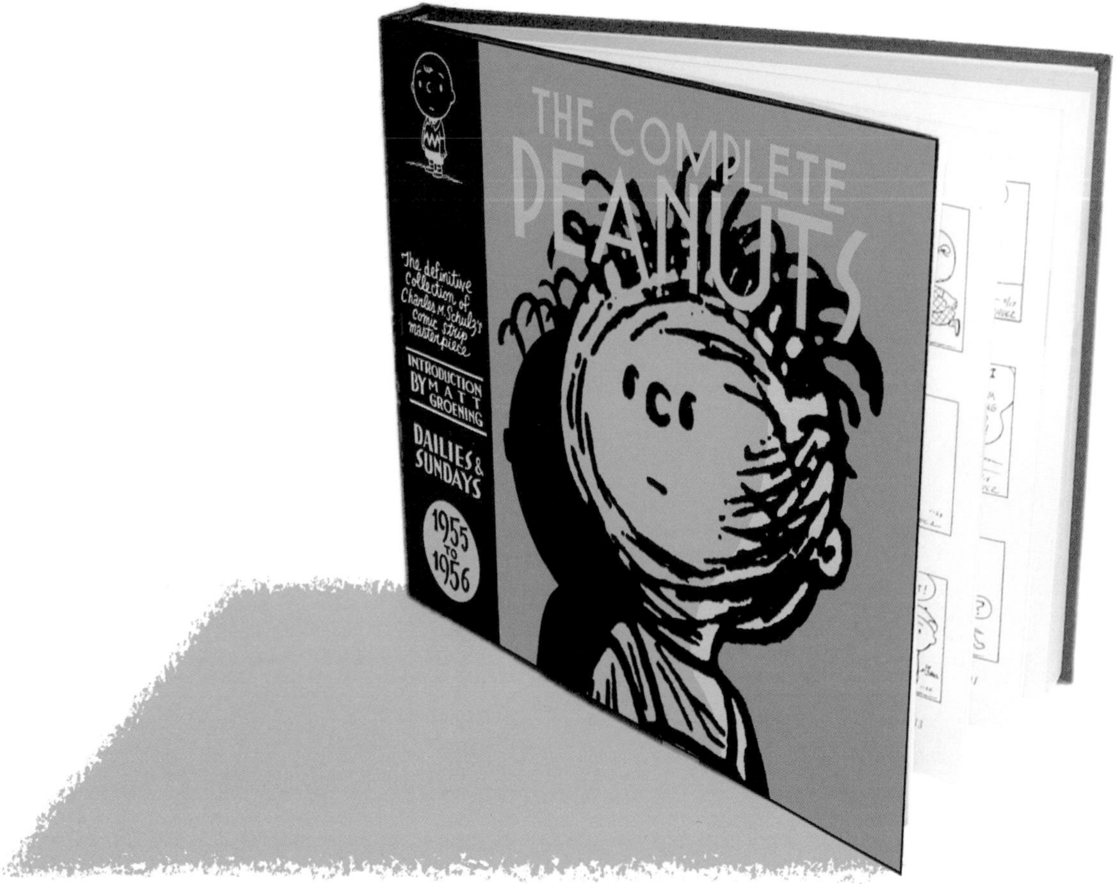
THE COMPLETE PEANUTS
The definitive collection of Charles M. Schulz's comic strip masterpiece
INTRODUCTION BY MATT GROENING
DAILIES & SUNDAYS
1955 TO 1956

COMING IN *THE COMPLETE PEANUTS: 1955-1956*

Pig-Pen settles in for the long haul... Charlie Brown's first sad Valentine's day... Baby Linus finally speaks (and develops an obsession with firearms)... Snoopy begins his career as an impressionist (rhinoceros, pelican, moose, kangaroo, alligator, Beethoven)... Charlie Brown's battle with kites heats up ("Burn, you monster!")... and an introduction by Matt Groening.

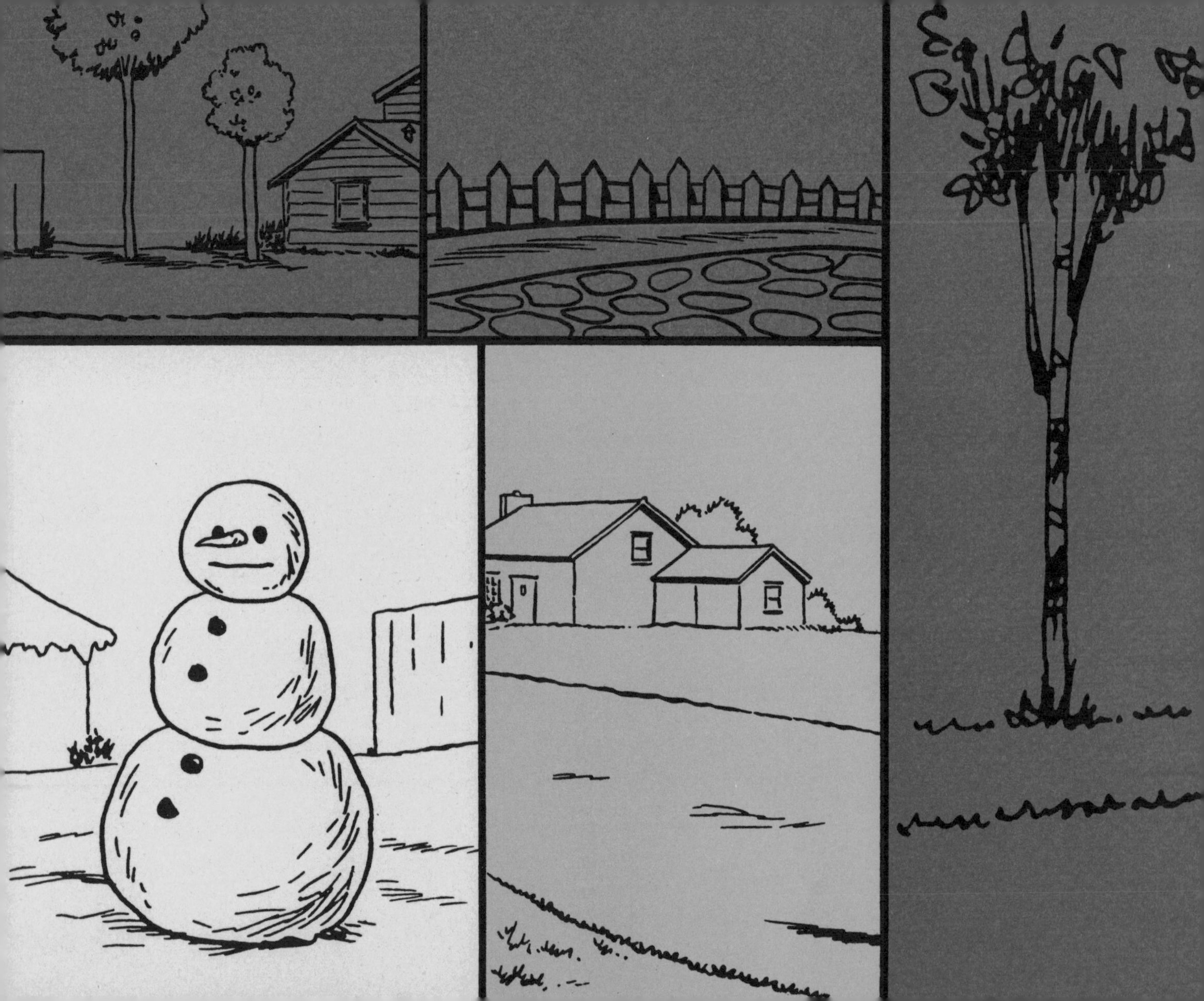